SOCIAL PSYCHOLOGY FOR SOCIAL WORK AND THE MENTAL HEALTH PROFESSIONS

SHEILA FELD & NORMA RADIN

1982
COLUMBIA UNIVERSITY PRESS
NEW YORK

PREFACE AND ACKNOWLEDGMENTS

The major impetus for writing this book was our observation of the needs of the students we taught in a Master's degree course, Social Role and the Small Group, at the University of Michigan School of Social Work. Because the readings for the class were located in diverse sources, and usually did not link the reported theory and research to social work practice, we collaborated on a set of handouts for students that provided a brief integration and linkage to practice for each of the major concepts covered. Year after year we added sections to the handouts, and finally we conceived the idea of using these documents as the basis for a text. Thus our first debt is to those early students whose appreciation of the handouts encouraged us to contemplate a wider audience.

As we began to consider this idea seriously, however, we realized that the two major social psychological topics covered in the course, role and small group theory, restricted the scope of the areas of social psychology applicable to social work. Discussions with our colleagues further expanded our view of the social psychological concepts that were relevant to social work practice. In particular, Martin Gold and Harvey Bertcher provided helpful suggestions at this point, and a doctoral seminar jointly taught by Sheila Feld and Edwin Thomas helped to illuminate the potential links between certain social psychological topics and innovations in interpersonal practice.

During the ensuing years, as we pursued this by now burgeoning project, many more people and institutions provided assistance. Each of us, while on sabbatical, finished the initial stages of our bibliographic searches. Norma Radin was graciously granted the use of the library facilities at Stanford University in Palo Alto. The provision of office space and library access to Sheila Feld at the National Institute for Social Welfare in London, through the kind efforts of David Jones, its principal, was similarly helpful. During that period the interchanges with the entire staff at the National Institute, and especially with Nano

McCaughan, also advanced the project, as did access to the Tavistock Institute Library and the assistance of its staff.

As we continued our writing and rewriting after resuming our responsibilities at the University of Michigan, many of our Michigan colleagues, in particular Brett Seabury, Charles Garvin, and Philip Fellin, dean of the School of Social Work, once again provided stimulation and encouragement. The comments of several groups of students who participated in seminars and courses in which previous drafts of the book were used were also significant and we thank them all for their patience in reading the manuscript in its rough form and for their thoughtful reactions. The participants in one seminar who provided detailed written critiques of substance and style of the first public draft of the book deserve special thanks. They included students from the doctoral program in social work and social science—Audry Begun, Rami Benbenishty, Eli Fresquez, Greg Hilliker, and Kathy Pottick—and Herbert Bisno, at that time a visiting professor at the University of Michigan School of Social Work. We are indebted to them all for their honest criticisms and helpful suggestions for improvements.

We are also indebted to those people who helped us prepare the manuscript itself. Netta Berlin provided invaluable assistance with the preparation of our reference list, and several excellent secretaries—Jean Blair, Kristen Driscoll, Diane Katz, Betty McClean, Jacqueline Moore, and Bonnie Wilde—cheerfully struggled to decipher our handwriting and to provide us clear copy, which we then promptly revised.

Finally, we must mention the patience and encouragement of a number of people who suffered from the long period of time and the many hours we spent completing this task. Our families, particularly Norma's husband Norman and both our mothers, saw less of us than we or they desired, yet complained little. Our editor, John Moore, saw deadline after deadline pass and yet kept encouraging us to continue. We hope your patience and confidence in us has been rewarded by the product, but in any event you deserve our thanks and we accept responsibility for any inadequacies in the results. We shared equally in the task of preparing this text over the past five years and wish it were unnecessary to list one name before the other in citing authorship. Since some order was clearly needed, we followed the alphabet and listed Sheila Feld before Norma Radin on the title page.

SOCIAL PSYCHOLOGY FOR SOCIAL WORK AND THE MENTAL HEALTH PROFESSIONS

INTRODUCTION

Although social work evolved with the growth of wisdom concerning meeting human needs gained in practice, there is also a long-standing interest in the profession in using social science knowledge to enhance theory development and service delivery. The utility of social science knowledge for social work became a topic of increased concern in the social work literature during the 1950s. The Council on Social Work Education sponsored the publication of two important pamphlets on the topic in 1958: *Social Science in the Professional Education of Social Workers* by Grace Coyle (1958) and *Social Processes in the Community and the Group* by Grace Coyle and Margaret Hartford (1958). Numerous articles and conference papers that specify the use of social science knowledge by social workers have been presented (see Hartford 1971:6). Specific illustrations of this linkage between social science and social work are plentiful. Psychological theories of child development provided one of the influences on the development of child welfare services (Kadushin 1967). Psychoanalytic theories provided a large part of the knowledge base for social casework (Germain 1970). Social psychological concepts of group dynamics and role theory were used widely in social group work (Coyle and Hartford 1958; Hartford 1971; Vinter 1960), and social casework also made use of role concepts (H. H. Perlman 1960). More recently, learning theory has provided the framework and principles underlying behaviorally oriented social casework and social group work (Fischer 1978; Thomas 1967), and theory and research from sociology have been applied to community practice (Rothman 1974; R. L. Warren 1979).

It has become increasingly difficult, however, for social workers to employ the knowledge and theory developed in another domain. Some relevant knowledge that might help clients cope with difficulties may be overlooked entirely, or there may be problems in articulating knowledge with relevant practice situations. These difficulties stem from several sources, only some of which we will note. (For a more extensive discussion of some of the difficulties in the application of social science

Social psychology is the scientific study of the experience and behavior of individuals in relation to social stimulus situations. (Sherif and Sherif 1969:8)

Behind the selection of topics in this book is the conceptions of social psychology as the study of interpersonal behavior. (Schellenberg 1970:v)

[Social casework uses] processes which develop personality through adjustments consciously affected, individual by individual, between men and their social environment. (Richmond 1922:98)

The social work method is the responsible, conscious, disciplined use of the self in a relationship with an individual or group. Through this relationship the practioner facilitates interaction between the individual and his social environment with a continuing awareness of the reciprocal effects of one upon the other. (Working Definition, *Social Work*, April 1958:6)

The focus of social work practice is on the interactions between people and systems in the social environment. (Pincus and Minahan 1973:3)

Every instance of social work involves an intervention into the relationship between people and their social environment in order to improve the quality of that relationship. (Middleman and Goldberg 1974:32)

These quotations are selective, but they are not atypical of many similar definitions of the two fields. Both social workers and social psychologists have the same object of analysis and concern: The individual in relation to his or her social environment. The social psychologist's interest in this phenomenon is primarily a scientific one: to understand and predict; the social worker's interest is primarily a practical one: to sustain, improve, or change the relationship. The thesis of this book is that knowledge gained from the scientific study of individuals in relation to their social environment can be put to practical use by social workers concerned with assisting individuals to sustain, improve, or change their relationships with their social environment.

The time seems propitious for engaging in this systematic effort to connect social work and social psychology. There is a burgeoning of interest within social work in linking innovations in social work methods to empirical grounding (Fischer 1978; Thomas 1978a). Clinical psychologists have begun to try to apply the knowledge of social psychology to their mode of helping troubled individuals (S. Brehm 1976; Fairweather 1964a; Sheras and Worchel 1979; Varela 1978). And contemporary social psychologists, like some of their earlier colleagues (D. Katz and Schanck 1938; Lewin 1948; Moreno 1934), seem to be once again interested in the application of their theories to practical problems (Argyris 1975; M. Deutsch and Hornstein 1975; Frieze, Bar-Tal, and Carroll 1979; Saks 1978). Thus we approach the task of interfacing social work and social psychology in a context that seems highly favorable for that endeavor.

To accomplish this task we have systematically surveyed the writings of contemporary social psychologists and compiled information based on the two admittedly subjective criteria of direct applicability to social work and empirical validity or generalizability. We have not attempted to present a comprehensive summary of contemporary social psychology. Instead, only those aspects of social psychological theory and research that appear to us to have the most direct relevance for social work problems are presented. The empirical validity was determined by our judgment of the soundness of the evidence for the social psychological phenomena. As testing in social work contexts has been minimal, we did not limit our consideration to instances where there was also evidence for the validity of the phenomena in social work situations. Instead, the tested limits of extrapolations were noted and some needed future research highlighted, particularly in the afterword. In this way, we hope to begin to answer the question of which social psychological theories of human behavior are most important to social work practice, and under what conditions and with what types of people are they most applicable. Some general gaps can be noted immediately. One is the relative shortage of recent experimental social psychological research conducted with subjects other than college students. Without further research we cannot be sure about the appropriateness of generalizations to persons whose age, social class, racial or ethnic heritage, or education are different. And young middle-class college students are not the persons typically of concern to social workers. Another and related omission in recent experimental work is the relative lack of studies of interpersonal relationships in which the actors or individuals are of unequal power rather than peers.

One further point should be made about the nature of social psychology generally, and as it is presented here. Modern social psychology is a diverse field. There are few grand theories to explain the totality of human beings' interactions with their social environment, although there are several major orientations to the field (Shaw and Constanzo 1970). Most research is oriented toward increasing the understanding of a given class of social phenomena—group dynamics, helping behavior, interpersonal attraction, leadership—or testing the limits of a particular theoretical concept—causal attribution processes, cognitive dissonance. This means that no single perspective can be used to explore social psychology. It is not possible to present a theory of social psychology and then trace its implications for social work practice, as one might do for psychoanalytical theory, for example. Various theories, perspectives, and sets of research findings that do not always mesh neatly need to be understood and considered. This complicates the task for the authors as well as the readers, but it cannot be avoided.

A SOCIAL WORK FRAMEWORK

Social work, like social psychology, is a broad and diverse field, and it is important to make clear what boundaries we have placed on it in this endeavor. The type of social work to which we have attempted to link social psychology is what might be referred to as direct practice—intervention with or on behalf of individuals, families, small groups, and neighborhood or community groups. Some reference will be made to social work practice that focuses on institutional change, modifications of social policy, and administation of social services, but the emphasis is on practice at the interpersonal level because it is here that we see the greatest potential application of social psychological knowledge.

Yet even within this restricted area of practice there are many methods used—casework, group work, social treatment, community practice—as well as various conceptual models and techniques of practice—social systems, social learning, task-centered, ego-psychological, behavioral. Our goal of presenting relevant social psychological knowledge in a social work framework required finding the commonalities among these diverse approaches. A review of current textbooks on social work practice, primarily in the direct practice area (Compton and Galaway 1975; Cox et al. 1979; Fischer 1978; H. Goldstein 1973; Meyer 1970; Middleman and Goldberg 1974; Morales and Sheafor 1977; R. Perlman and Gurin 1972; Pincus and Minahan 1973; Reid and Epstein 1972; Roberts and Nee 1970; A. Schwartz and Goldiamond 1975; Siporin 1975; Timms 1964; Whittaker 1975) led us to conclude that there is a general consensus about the overall sequence of activities in social work intervention, although terminology may differ. The first phase involves making contact with the client or significant other individuals in the client's life. This involves the client or worker reaching out to make contact and begin the establishment of a client-worker relationship, or a collaborative relationship between a relevant other person and the social worker on behalf of the client. The second phase is that of assessing the problem. This involves collecting and interpreting data. The third phase is that of formulating goals with the client or significant others, and agreeing on the obligations and expectations of worker and client, or significant other, to achieve these goals. The fourth phase is implementing the intervention plan. This includes maintaining the intervention plan and making modifications when necessary. It also requires maintaining the relationship and continually monitoring the effectiveness of the plan in relation to the goals set for the intervention. The final or fifth phase consists of making a final evaluation as to whether the goals have been attained, and terminating the relationship. When appropriate, some type of followup plan is also incorporated into phase five.

This five-phased view of the helping process is the social work framework adopted for the present book except that phase three, formulating goals and contracting, will not be discussed, so that the length of this book may be kept within the bounds of a single semester text. It should be noted that the book is not linked to any particular theoretical orientation or change strategy. On the contrary, it is meant to be broad enough to be consistent with a variety of practice models, and to define activities that any model of practice would need to deal with in some way. Nor is the listing of phases meant to imply a single line sequence always occurs. We recognize, for example, that data collection occurs throughout the sequence and that the client may terminate contact at any phase. But we assume that the overall trend in a planned change effort is in the sequence delineated.

THE PLAN OF THE BOOK

The four phases of the helping sequence to be dicussed can also be described in more social psychological terminology. The phase of making initial contacts may be seen as "beginning social relationships." Problem assessement may be viewed as "understanding social functioning." The intervention phase is "changing or stabilizing behaviors and attitudes," and termination may be called "ending social relationships." Although the social psychological labels are not inclusive, it is felt they capture the essence of stages in the helping process.

The major parts will each focus on one of the four phases in the helping sequence. Each chapter will present major social psychological theories, concepts, and research related to that phase of planned social change, and indicate how they might be used in direct practice.

Part One, Beginning Social Relationships, focuses on the social psychological concepts of interpersonal attraction, including the bases of attraction, such as similarity, empathy, physical attractiveness, and personal space. Part Two, Understanding Social Functioning, includes chapters on role theories, attribution theories, and frames of reference for self-evaluation processes. Part Three, Changing Behaviors and Attitudes, is divided into four sections. Section I, Implementing Dyadic Intervention Plans with Clients, has a chapter on theories of attitude and attitude change, including those on self-perception and cognitive dissonance, and another on social influence theories. Section II, Implementing Dyadic Intervention Plans with Significant Others, includes a chapter on helping behavior and altruism and one on the social learning theory topics of observational learning, self-regulatory processes, and locus of control beliefs. The chapters in Section III, Implementing Group Intervention Plans with Significant Others, cover the topics of group problem solving, decision making, and performance, and of leadership in groups. The chapters in Section IV, Implementing Group Intervention Plans with Clients, focus upon group cohesiveness, group composition, norm enforcement in groups, group development, and role playing as a group activity. Part Four, Ending Social Relationships, highlights knowledge about social comparison level, exchange theory, problems in role leaving and role shifts, and group cohesiveness in a chapter on unplanned termination, and about psychological inoculation and ritualistic behavior in a chapter on planned terminations.

The book concludes with an afterword offering exemplary research questions that emerged from each of the parts. The authors hope that it will stimulate the readers of this volume to undertake investigations of their own in the field. Only when a large number of practitioners engage in such endeavors will the potential of social psychological knowledge be fully realized by the social work profession. We further hope that the statement of these research questions will provoke some social psychologists to test the limits of their research endeavors in more socially relevant contexts.

PART ONE

BEGINNING SOCIAL RELATIONSHIPS

INTRODUCTION

The initial contact between a social worker and a client, or group of clients, or between a social worker and a member of a client's social network, is in some ways like any encounter between strangers. The participants probably arrive with some preconceived notions about the other person, form impressions of one another upon meeting, feel more or less attracted to one another, and convey to one another some aspects of their impressions and feelings. But the initial social work encounter is not simply like a casual meeting between strangers. The initial social work contact comes about because one or both parties have recognized the existence of some problem whose solution may require joint or interdependent action.

Recent social work theorists have specified the objectives of the initial encounter in quite different terms, but all seem to agree upon the need for the development of a relationship satisfactory enough to facilitate communications about the nature of the problem and the possible relevance of the social worker's actions and transactions to the solution of the problem. H. Goldstein (1973) describes the initial phase of social work practice as one of role induction, in which he includes the first three phases in our framework. Among the characteristics of this role induction phase is the initiation and development of bonds of affinity and interdependence as well as development and clarification of roles, norms, and objectives. Whittaker (1974) labels the first part of the direct helping social treatment sequence as "intake," and sees its primary objective as the determination of whether help is needed and if so, whether the particular agency is the appropriate one to offer the help. This involves decisions by both worker and client. It is during this period that the worker helps clients to specify the problems or potential problems that cause them to seek help. According to Whittaker, from the first moment of contact the social worker should be concerned about offering help and support, building the relationship, and conveying the message that the worker respects the client and is concerned about the client's problem.

For Reid and Epstein (1972), who also focus on direct client-worker interactions, the goal of the initial interview is definition of the primary target of intervention and formulation and selection of the task of the client. To accomplish this goal social workers must be concerned about the quality of their communication. The worker's communication should be related systematically to the particular step in the casework process, initially task formulation, and should be responsive. Responsive communication conveys interest, acceptance, empathic understanding, and builds upon the client's communications, according to Reid and Epstein.

Social work theorists concerned with intervention in larger target systems as well as in work with individual clients also recognize the importance of the initial contact. Middleman and Goldberg (1974) propose "stage setting" as one of the basic social work skills, by which they mean the worker's behaviors aimed at enhancing the beginning of the interaction process. The objectives of these behaviors are to provide the physical environment and socioemotional climate conducive to an interaction based on rapport. Pincus and Minahan (1973) discuss the actual beginning of a social relationship as part of the practice skill area called "negotiating contracts," in which the basic strategies include establishing an initial relationship and identifying the purposes of the contract. They point out that in any initial contact, whether between social worker and client, social worker and other professionals, or social worker and persons significantly related to a client, each individual expects the other to act in certain ways and revises these expectations based on data presented during the encounter.

Interpersonal attraction is also of major concern to group workers, for cohesiveness has been defined as the group's overall level of member-to-member attraction (A. P. Goldstein 1971). For a group to remain intact and effective, cohesiveness is essential. It has been shown to influence attendance at meetings and to result in greater behavior change as members alter their behavior to conform to group norms and to win the approval of group members (Cartwright and Zander 1968; A. P. Goldstein 1971). Thus, so long as clients are free to participate or not participate in a group, some attraction must be felt by most clients toward the other members and/or the leader, or there will not be a second session; there will be no group.

R. Perlman and Gurin (1972) apply a problem-solving approach to community organization. They propose that the first two phases involve defining the problem and building structure. These phases include the interactional tasks of obtaining information about the problem from those experiencing it and from other sources, building communication lines, and obtaining some commitment from relevant persons to address the problem.

Various social psychological concepts and findings are relevant to the processes involved in effecting satisfactory initial contacts with clients, other targets of change, or other individuals who can facilitate change in clients, and in clarifying the possible goals for further action and interaction. They can all be subsumed under the major topic of interpersonal attraction, in which we include studies on empathy and personal space. Although the social psychological research on these topics is more directly relevant to the relationship than to the goal setting aspects of the initial social work contact, there are some implications for the latter as well.

CHAPTER ONE

INTERPERSONAL ATTRACTION

The study of interpersonal attraction is concerned with two major questions: why persons like or dislike other individuals and what consequences such like or dislike has on interaction. A review of some of the outcomes of interpersonal attraction makes clear why this area of social psychologicaal research and theory is important to social work in general and to the objectives of the initial social work encounter in particular. (See Huston and Levinger 1978; Lott and Lott 1972, for detailed reviews of this area of research.)

CONSEQUENCES OF INTERPERSONAL ATTRACTION

QUALITY AND QUANITY OF APPROACHES

Interpersonal attraction has been shown to affect the quality and quantity of approaches people make to one another. Liking for others was found in several studies to be related to the degree of looking at others. For example, the amount of time an undergraduate interviewee spent gazing at an interviewer's eyes was related to liking for the interviewer, but not to evaluations of the task-related competence of the interviewer (G. N. Goldberg, Kiesler, and Collins 1969). The physical distance between persons is closer when liking occurs, both in laboratory studies and in a wide variety of natural situations. One study measured the distance between college students who had just returned from a computer-arranged date as they stood in front of the experimenter's desk. The couples whose ratings of interpersonal attraction were high stood closer together (Byrne, Ervin, and Lamberth 1970).

This relationship between liking and approach behavior has also been demonstrated in one of the early empirical studies of social work clients. Polansky and Kounin (1956), in a study to which we will refer again, interviewed 150 clients who had just completed their first contact with a helping person in one of six agencies. The clients' reports on the likability of the interviewer were significantly associated with their replies to a question concerning how they would feel about seeing this person again to discuss their problem. And replies to the latter question were significantly associated with whether or not the subset of clients who had some choice about returning to the agency did actually do so. Thus, clients who liked the helping person were more willing to indicate they would return again, and when they had the choice, actually were more likely to return.

COMMUNICATION FREQUENCY AND QUALITY

Communication frequency and quality are affected by liking, both in dyadic and group interactions. The amount of communication has been shown to be linked to degree of liking both in natural groups of college students engaged in discussions (Lott and Lott 1961) and in industrial training groups (Moran 1966). In a laboratory study undergraduates were asked to role-play meeting a person to whom they were very attracted or not very attracted and were then observed interacting with a naive fellow student (Rosenfeld 1966). Those who role-played under the attractiveness instructions talked more, smiled more often, were more attentive to the other person and less often shook their heads. Thus, the quality as well as the quantity of communication was affected. This was also shown in a seminaturalistic study with naval personnel who were told they were participating with a fellow sailor who might be their partner in a long sea mission. They were to get acquainted with one another to see how they would work together in the future mission. The partner was actually a confederate who varied his behavior in ways designed to enhance or detract from his attractiveness to the subject. The sailors who participated under conditions designed to enhance the attraction of the confederate talked about more aspects concerning themselves, with greater depth, and for longer periods, than did those who participated under conditions designed to detract from their attraction to the confederate (Taylor, Altman, and Sorrentino 1969). Similarly, students who met one another in a laboratory situation disclosed more about themselves to a partner they liked than to one they disliked (Kohen 1975).

DEGREE OF INFLUENCE

Liking for someone affects the degree of influence the other person has. Undergraduates' judgments about an optical illusion were more influenced by the stated judgments of another person when that other individual was well-liked (Sampson and Insko 1964). Information about the purported beliefs of fellow group members had a greater effect on opinions in natural groups of college students when there was greater liking among group members (Lott and Lott 1961). A similar effect has been found in an important study of a smoking clinic (Janis and Hoffman 1970). Adults who voluntarily went to the clinic were paired off in one of three ways for their five weekly visits with a staff member at the clinic: 1) the same partners always met together and they were instructed to talk daily by phone to one another; 2) the same partners always met together, but they were instructed not to contact one another between clinic vistis; 3) partners varied from week to week. The highest contact group reported greater liking for one another at the end of the treatment. And while all three groups reduced their smoking by the end of the clinic sessions, only the highest contact group maintained this reduced level of smoking in followups six months and one year later. The highest contact group's interpersonal attraction was also reflected in greater eye contact observed during the clinic sessions. They also interacted in different ways during the clinic contact period, as reflected in the greater number of statements they made to partners during the clinic sessions expressing commitment to not smoking; more evaluative statements were also made in response to partners' reported adherence or nonadherence to this norm between clinic sessions. This social support was not maintained later; that is, these partners did not remain in contact significantly more than did the other groups after the clinic sessions ended. The authors concluded that the most plausible mediating factor in the behavioral change was an "increase in interpersonal attraction produced by daily contact with a fellow member, which makes for an increased valuation of the group and the internalization of its norms" (Janis and Hoffman 1970:35).

HELP GIVEN AND HELP EXPECTED

People are more likely to help and to expect help from someone they like than from someone they dislike or to whom they feel neutral. Children were more likely to "help" a doll who had fallen down on the way to a movie when the doll was presented as representing a liked peer than a disliked peer (Lott and Lott 1972). Male college students were placed in a simulated job situation where supervisors were dependent upon the performance level of their supervisees; by improving their own performance the workers "helped" supervisors who were liked more than supervisors who were disliked (Daniels and Berkowitz 1963). In another laboratory study, under conditions designed to enhance or reduce interpersonal attraction, white undergraduates anticipated interacting with white or black fellow students who were to be future task partners. Those students in the enhancement condition anticipated significantly more cooperation from their partners, regardless of race (S. Johnson and Johnson 1972b).

THE EXPERIENCE OF STRESS

The presence of a liked person reduces the experience of stress. College students who were exposed to stress by working on unsolvable problems displayed less physiological arousal when they experienced failure in the presence of a friend than when alone or with a stranger (Kissel 1965).

SUMMARY AND CONCLUSIONS

The relevance of these effects of interpersonal attraction to the initial social work encounter is unambiguous. Clients or significant others who like the social worker are likely to be more apt to engage in the kinds of behaviors that would facilitate communication about problems and problem-solving interactions. At a minimum, so long as clients are free to accept or reject the service of a social worker, they must have some positive feeling toward the practitioner in order to continue the interaction. Even if a client has very little choice, as when seeking financial aid or conversing with a probation officer, negative feelings toward the worker, over and above those attributable to role factors, will probably reduce the likelihood that the conversation will be profitable. This conclusion, primarily based on social psychological research, is in accordance with that reached in two recent reviews of quantitative research on psychotherapeutic outcomes. According to the authors, the client's feeling of attraction to the counselor is one of the major factors fostering favorable therapy outcome (Gomes-Schwartz, Hadley, and Strupp 1978; Luborsky et al. 1971).

Sometimes overlooked is the fact that the worker also experiences more attraction to some clients than toward others, and that this will affect behavior toward these other persons. Although one of the goals of professional training is to reduce such differential behaviors, it is doubtful that they are entirely eliminated (Kadushin 1972). Feelings of differential attraction may influence the behavior and decisions of social workers in much the same way that social class, racial, ethnic, or religious stereotypes may intrude inappropriately in the client-social worker relationship (Hollingshead and Redlich 1956). The impact of social workers' initial feelings toward the client has been demonstrated indirectly in two studies in which social workers, psychiatrists, and clinical psychologists viewed films of clients being interviewed during an initial contact (Strupp 1973). At various points during the interview, the film was stopped and the professionals were asked to indicate what they would have said or done at that point. At the end of each film, the professionals completed a questionnaire indicating their felt attraction toward the client as well as various diagnostic and prognostic evaluations of the client. The scores on the various questionnaires were significantly associated: Therapists who liked the clients were more likely than those who did not like the clients to evaluate them in other positive ways, for example as better adjusted and more mature, and what is perhaps more important, to recommend certain types of treatment techniques. Further, analyses of what the professionals would have said to the clients at various points in the film indicated that therapists who liked the clients would have talked more to them. Independent ratings of the content of their remarks were also judged to be more warm and empathic. Similar results have been found with advanced clinical psychology graduate students (A. P. Goldstein 1971: ch. 4) suggesting that the findings may have validity for numerous professional groups.

DETERMINANTS OF INTERPERSONAL ATTRACTION

Having demonstrated the power of liking, what can we say about the determinants of liking, especially those that may be amenable to the control of the social worker? Most social psychological research and theory dealing with initial social encounters has developed from the general assumption that we like those persons who tend to provide us with satisfactions. Several major conditions that are likely to enhance the interpersonal attraction of one person for another have been studied: similarity of attitudes, beliefs or values; similarity in status characteristics; positive reinforcement, evaluation, or liking; empathy; similarity or complementarity in personality characteristics; facilitation of goal accomplishment; physical attractiveness; and appropriate use of personal space.

ATTITUDINAL SIMILARITY

Attitudinal similarity has been shown to be related to interpersonal attraction in a variety of social contexts. One systematic line of research by Byrne and his colleagues (Byrne 1971; Clore and Byrne 1974) has shown that there is a linear relationship between the proportion of similar attitudes held by an unfamiliar member of a peer group and the attraction felt toward that stranger; the greater the proportion of similar attitudes, the greater the attraction. In the typical investigations supporting this proposition, the subjects fill out an attitude questionnaire, examine a similar questionnaire filled out by another subject, and then indicate the attraction felt for the other individual. The experimenter manipulates the information in the questionnaire from the stranger so as to vary the proportion of items with same replies as the subject. Most of these experiments were carried out with college students, but there is also evidence that a similar linear relationship between initial attraction and information on proportion of similar attitudes is found for children in grades four through twelve (Byrne and Griffith 1966), surgical hospital patients, hospitalized alcoholics and schizophrenics, and job corps trainees (Bryne et al. 1969).

Other research in natural situations suggests that the impact of attitudinal similarity on attraction is dependent on the importance of the attitude to the particular relationship. Fraternity men's liking for one another was significantly related to similarity on one key political attitude but not to similarity-dissimilarity on a wide range of other attitudes (Banikotes, Russell, and Linden 1972). Comparable results were found when passersby in a New York City neighborhood were given a four-question questionnaire said to have been completed by a local resident and asked to say whether they would like or dislike the person. Only attitudinal similarity on these questions that had been selected because of their salience to local issues in a prior study in that neighborhood produced attraction; similarity or dissimilarity on issues irrelevant to that environmental context, on the other hand, was irrelevant to interpersonal attraction (Sole, Morton, and Hornstein 1975).

Other researchers interested in the general relationship between attitudinal similarity and interpersonal attraction have approached the problem in different ways. Newcomb (1961) observed the formation of friendships among two groups of college men living in an experimental residence during their first semester on campus. Repeated data were collected from these men on their own attitudes, beliefs, and values, those they believed held by their fellow residents, and their liking for one another. One of the major findings was that actual agreement on attitudes and values at the onset of acquaintance predicts pair attraction at the end of the semester of joint living, but not during the early stages of acquaintance. During this early period, perceived similarity was associated with interpersonal attraction among pairs of the college men. The author concluded that when the attitudes in question are quite stable or firmly held, and people have the opportunity to interact and discover one another's attitudes, high-attraction preferences move toward those persons with whom one is more closely in agreement. When individuals first meet in natural situations, they probably cannot accurately assess one another's attitudes. Thus, actual attitudinal similarity, as could be determined by independently querying each person, is not related to interpersonal attraction. Rather, at that stage of acquaintanceship, people who are attractive to others are perceived by those individuals to have similar attitudes to their own. An alternate explanation is that people like those whom they perceive as holding similar attitudes, but at the early stage of the acquaintanceship, these perceptions are typically inaccurate.

Various interpretations have been proposed for the link between attitudinal similarity and interpersonal attraction. The explanation given to the finding about the linear relationship is that we are attracted to those who provide reinforcements, and attitude similarity is one basis for inferring reinforcement potential. It is reinforcing to be in the company of individuals who hold the same attitudes as yourself because they provide consensual validation of one's views. On the other hand, disagreements imply one's views may be incorrect. Thus, interactions with those who hold other views would not be reinforcing and might possibly be punishing. This equation of attitudinal similarity with consensual validation of one's beliefs is in keeping with the social comparison theory of Festinger (1954b), who postulated that there is a desire to know what is correct and true in the social sphere. He referred to this "correct" social information as social reality. Since there is no way of knowing what is true when there are no physical dimensions to be measured with a ruler or scale, the judgments of others whom we consider to be like ourselves provide the measurement function. It indicates to us what is socially "real." Perhaps finding that peers agree with our attitudes establishes the fact that our view of social reality is true. This conclusion tends to be reinforcing and hence we like members of our peer group with similar attitudes to our own.

Theories of cognitive balance also have been used to interpret the attitudinal similarity-attraction relation (Heider 1958; Newcomb 1961). These approaches assume that there is a desire to engage in balanced or consistent relationships with other persons. Two persons who hold similar attitudes toward some object would be in a balanced relationship if they held positive attitudes toward one another, and conversely, persons who held dissimilar attitudes toward an object would be in a balanced relationship if they held negative attitudes toward one another. According to this interpretation, we like those persons whose attitudes are similar to our own because then our attitudes toward the person and other objects are consistent or in balance. Such a state of balance is believed to be pleasurable.

Regardless of interpretation, these lines of research suggest that it would be desirable for social workers and their clients to hold similar attitudes, or to perceive that they do, so that attraction will be enhanced and an effective relationship begun. The same principle would apply to members of a group which a worker may be forming. The direct evidence testing the application of this principle to a client-professional helping situation does not, however, support such a straightforward idea, and instead has yeilded conflicting results (Gomes-Schwartz, Hadley, and Strupp 1978). Although this research has been restricted to psychotherapeutic encounters, it should also apply to a social work context. For example, as part of a large research program that attempted to apply findings from psychological research to psychotherapy training and procedures, A. P. Goldstein (1971: ch. 9) conducted three studies in which clients were given information about their therapists' attitudes on various topics prior to their first contact at a university vocational counseling center or at a treatment program for incarcerated alcoholics. Goldstein failed to find the hypothesized relationship of attitude similarity between client and therapist and positive feelings toward the therapist after their first interview. To explain this lack of agreement with earlier research it was suggested that clients may not wish to find their therapists holding the same attitudes as they do; if clients wish to change their own behaviors and therefore are seeking to develop new attitudes, at least in some areas, similarity may even reduce the credibility of the therapist. Similarity in attitude may be sought in peers but not in therapists. A possible rationale for this proposition can be offered on the basis of Festinger's social comparison theory. Individuals seek to know whether their view of social reality is correct by seeing how those like themselves perceive the world. Such individuals form a social comparison group for them and are seen as attractive. On the othe hand, individuals who are different cannot help establish social reality. Thus, there is neither confirmation nor disconfirmation for one's views when someone who is clearly in a different class, status, position, etc., holds different views. The conclusion to be drawn is that similarity to clients may not increase a therapist's attractiveness, but neither will dissimilarity. Goldstein's research supported this hypothesis.

This points to the need to define the conditions under which social comparison will be sought and hence when similarity in attitudes will be satisfying. For example, in self-help groups is similarity between old members and new members facilitative of change? Should indigenous aides working with social workers be hired on the basis of their similarity to potential clients? In either case, is there an optimum amount of dissimilarity, particularly in the ability to cope with experienced problems?

Another explanation for Goldstein's failure to find a direct effect of similarity on attraction may be that the conversational interchange between the clients and therapists during the first interview changed the clients' views about their dissimilarity to the therapist. Two laboratory experiments have shown that allowing undergraduates to reply in their own words to information indicating attitudinal disagreement from a stranger results in increased attraction to the stranger (Brink 1977). The mediating mechanism in this shift was the subjects' belief that they had influenced the stranger's opinion towards similarity to their own position. In real-life situations, such as an initial meeting between client and social worker, the typical experimental relationship between similarity and attraction may thus be modified by conversation. The effect of conversation on attraction may depend on how effective individuals believe their persuasive statements are in changing the other's opinion toward similarity.

Certain personality characteristics may affect the relationship between attitudinal similarity and interpersonal attraction. Self-esteem seemed to have such an effect in one study, in which undergraduates interviewed a fellow student of the same sex who was presented as an applicant for a job (Leonard 1975). The information applicants revealed to the subjects about their attitudes and demographic characteristics was varied on the basis of prior knowledge about the subjects. It was found that only students with positive self-concepts evidenced greater liking, and more favorable job ratings, for applicants more similar than dissimilar to themselves. Subjects with poor self-concepts showed the reverse effect; they evaluated dissimilar job applicants as more attractive and as better job prospects. The results were interpreted as suggesting that self-esteem is a boundary condition to the similarity-attraction relationship: persons with poor evaluations of themselves probably have a history of past failures to achieve goals; such persons may associate similar others with these unpleasant outcomes and be less attracted to them. This study is consistent with Goldstein's hypothesis that attractiveness of a therapist to a client may not be associated with attitude similarity between client and worker since it is likely that many clients applying to a social agency have self-concepts with significant negative components. Such clients may well feel a negative attraction to others whom they perceive as similar, including social workers. Attempts to highlight similarity between such clients and social workers may well be a mistake inasmuch as attraction to worker has been described as one of the factors that sustains a relationship through crises that would otherwise result in the client's abrupt departure (Carson 1969). The question remains unanswered as to the optimum amount of similarity between clients with very low self-images and indigenous aides or peer counselors assigned to work with them.

Finally we return to the findings cited earlier (Banikotes, Russell, and Linden 1972; Sole, Marton, and Hornstein 1975) and others (Kandel 1978; Santee 1976) that indicate the differential impact of attitudinal similarity on attraction as a function of the centrality of the attitude to the particular relationship. This suggests that client-worker similarity may be important only in certain areas. Studies showing that patients who felt that their therapist did not understand their problems were likely to drop out of treatment (Kline, Adrian, and Spivak 1974; Saltzman et al. 1976) or that shared initial beliefs about how therapy should be conducted led to positive therapeutic outcomes (P. J. Martin, Sterne, and Hunter 1976) suggest that congruence of belief between client and worker about the nature of the client's problems and their future interactions may be critical. This is an area which clearly calls for further research.

STATUS SIMILARITY

Before dismissing the importance of attitudinal similarity on interpersonal attraction between worker and client, however, the specific case of major status dissimilarity between worker and client must be examined. By status we refer to those characteristics of individuals that define their social position in society, such as sex, race, ethnicity, social class, occupation, etc. There is no need to belabor the point that persons in certain statuses are often reacted to negatively; evidence of institutionalized hostility and discrimination against persons with particular social statuses is clear. There is also the phenomenon of reverse racism, or hostility by oppressed minorities toward outside groups. In any given social encounter, as between a social worker and a client or significant other, it is also important to understand the interpersonal behaviors of the individuals toward one another. Kadushin (1972: ch. 7) reviewed the literature on the effects of typical status dissimilarities encountered in social work on the ability of social worker and client to form a positive relationship. Race and social class differences between worker and client have each been shown to have deleterious effects on communications during interviews and on client reactions, although there is contrary evidence as well. In any event, it is clear that some clients prefer a worker of similar race, ethnicity, religion, social class background, or sex and also that the current demographic composition of the social work profession often precludes such matching even if client preferences were sought and taken into account. This means that any research evidence pointing to conditions that facilitate interpersonal attraction despite status dissimilarity is relevant.

Quite a few studies have dealt with the relationships among attitudinal similarity, racial or ethnic similarity, and interpersonal attraction. They all suggest that under certain circumstances or for certain types of persons, belief congruency can have a stronger effect on interpersonal attraction than racial dissimilarity. Several important implications for social work can be drawn from these studies.

Rejection of persons of different racial or ethnic groups is associated with assumptions about dissimilarity in beliefs between self and the rejected other. This conclusion was drawn in three separate studies with white subjects. In one, Mexican-American and white ninth-grade children were asked to rate pictures of unknown Mexican-American and white children in terms of how friendly and similar the pictured child was likely to be (Goebel and Cole 1975). A measure of desired social distance between self and both ethnic groups was also obtained from all children. White children who had indicated unwillingness for close associations with Mexican Americans perceived the white youngsters as more similar and more friendly to themselves than the Mexican-American children. The other children did not differ in the similarity or friendliness ratings given to pictures of whites and Mexican Americans. White undergraduates reacted similarly when asked to guess the attitudes of pictured same-sex black and white college students (Byrne and Wong 1962). Unknown black students' attitudes were guessed to be more unlike the subjects' attitudes than those of the depicted white students. Similar results were obtained when white teenagers were asked to provide information on desired social distance from whites and blacks and their own feelings of friendship towards unknown white and black teenagers (Stein, Hardyk, and Smith 1965). In the absence of any information about the beliefs of other teenagers, race was found to have a significant effect on ratings of social distance and friendliness, and the black teenager was reacted to as if he had beliefs dissimilar to those of the white subjects. But when given information on the unknown teenagers' beliefs on a questionnaire the subjects had completed themselves some months previously, similarity in beliefs was a stronger predictor of social distance and friendliness ratings than was race.

Although the evidence on assumed belief dissimilarity is unfortunately only from white subjects, it does not seem unreasonable to propose that social workers proceed on the assumption that clients from different racial or ethnic groups from their own arrive at the initial encounter with expectations of dissimilarity in beliefs and lack of friendliness. Furthermore, other studies with both white and black children (Insko and Robinson 1967) and college students (Mezei 1971; Rokeach and Mezei 1966; C. R. Smith, Williams, and Willis 1967) as well as with certain ethnic groups (Anderson and Cote 1966; Rokeach, Smith, and Evans 1960) do support the view that when knowledge about similarity of beliefs is available about a stranger, feelings of friendliness are often more strongly related to belief similarity than to racial or ethnic similarity. This suggests that a social worker meeting a client of a different racial or ethnic group might attempt to seek out and emphasize areas of belief congruency in an effort to overcome potentially disruptive expectancies about belief incongruity.

To do this requires that social work education provide knowledge about the culture of ethnic or racial groups likely to be encountered in practice so that areas of real client-practitioner similarity can be recognized (A. Jones and Seagull 1977). Increasing the social worker's understanding about the oppression, discrimination and lack of equal opportunity suffered by certain racial and ethnic groups should also be an important part of social work education. Such understanding would be valuable for social workers not only because it would promote a better understanding about the source of a client's difficulties, but also because it could enhance belief congruency between client and worker about a vitally important issue.

This extrapolation from laboratory studies to the social work encounter requires direct testing, but some indirect support is available. Aguilar (1972) alludes to a similar situation in his discussion of initial contacts with Mexican-American families. According to Aquilar, social workers must recognize the importance of a leisurely opening of discussion and of understanding the attitude of the Mexican American toward religion, the role of the male, and the significance of the extended family. Mizio (1972) makes a similar suggestion in pointing to the need for white workers with minority clients to recognize and develop means to overcome the clients' potentially negative initial expectations. Thus, it appears that when there is the possibility of grossly dissimilar views between client and worker, attitutudinal congruence becomes increasingly significant. This may be particularly important for members of oppressed groups who may be unwilling to trust those belonging to groups that are responsible for the oppression.

One recent approach to improving cross-cultural interactions through enhancing knowledge about other cultures uses a technique known as the cultural assimilator. This might be valuable to social workers, although its application to helping relationships has not yet been made (Fiedler, Mitchell, and Triandis 1971; Landis et al. 1976). This technique involves the development of a programmed learning experience based on critical incidents in social interactions between persons of two cultures, sets of interpretations of the interactions, and feedback about the correctness of the interpretations and the reasons for their correctness. For example, one item consists of the following:

> The white CO of a racially integrated unit tried to recommend promotions on the basis of his men's work and proficiency scores. After the list of promotions was posted, a black Spec 4 entered his office and asked why he had not been promoted. The Spec 4 claimed that he had fairly good scores and asked the CO to review his decision. The CO was surprised at this behavior, but promised to give some attention to the complaint. Upon reflection, the CO noted that promotion reviews were requested much more frequently by blacks in his unit than by whites. The CO was puzzled and surprised by this realization. (Landis et al. 1976: 174–75)

The question is then asked, "Why did more blacks than whites request reviews of promotion decisions?" Four options with rationales are listed, for example,

> Option 1. Blacks feel they won't be given a promotion unless they ask for one.
>
> Rationale: Many blacks feel that a good mark record alone is not sufficient for a promotion. They feel that unless they call attention to their case, it will not be acted upon. This action is not to be taken as disrespectful, but rather as an action which is assumed to be necessary for promotion. (Landis et al. 1976: 175)

The respondent is asked to state which option is correct. Feedback is given immediately on whether the choice selected is the right one and, to help the respondent understand the other culture, an explanation is provided of the underlying principle of the correct response (Landis et al. 1976). Essentially, this technique is designed to increase shared beliefs about appropriate responses in cross-cultural social interactions. There is some evidence that white Americans can improve their relations with persons of Thai, Arab, Greek, and Honduran cultures (Fiedler et al. 1971) and with black Americans (Landis et al. 1976; Weldon et al. 1975) using this technique.

A series of studies on counseling and job interviews presents a useful conceptualization of another means by which similarity, here in terms of comembership, can be established for pairs who do not share ethnic or racial identity (F. Erikson 1973, 1975; Shultz 1975). Comemberships are particularistic categories of shared social identity and can be based on a wide variety of similarities. Some categories are compehensive—based on social position such as race, ethnicity, or sex, or on broad life experiences, such as childhood in a large urban city. Others are narrow—intense interest in wrestling, or fondness for a particular type of music. The important thing is that the individuals realize they share this identity, and thus have a bond between them even if they are not members of the same racial or ethnic group.

One study attempted to test the hypothesis that the more alike counselor and counselees were in social identity categories, the more smoothly the counseling interactions would proceed, and the more special help the counselors were likely to give the counselees—male students in a junior college (F. Erikson 1975). The hypothesis was confirmed in general, but it was found that differences in race or ethnicity could be overcome by comembership, or nonracial and nonethnic factors that the helper and person being helped discovered they shared. For example, independent judges' ratings of the emotional tone or friendliness of the videotaped interviews were significantly associated with similarity of race or ethnicity between counselor and counselee as well as with degree of comembership established during the interview. The conclusion drawn was that counselors do not treat all counselees universalistically, or by the same set of rules. Rather, particularistic factors leak in; that is, factors related to personal status, beliefs, interests, or characteristics of the counselor. The study concluded that people do not establish their social identity by use of only one variable, such as class, or race, ethnicity, or pan-ethnicity (i.e., a hyphenated American), but rather use a combination of factors, some of which are only accidentally discovered.

Erickson suggests that counselors either can be trained out of these particularistic responses or that social identity categories can be made salient and counselees allowed to select a counselor on that basis. These suggestions and findings apply equally to social workers. We would further suggest that social workers who know they differ in class, race, or ethnicity from their clients might seek to establish comembership with these clients; that is, find some interest or experience they share and make the sharing salient during the initial encounter. This invariably involves some self-disclosure by the workers but should facilitate the helping process.

This suggestion is consistent with Kadushin's (1972) recommendation that the social work interview begin with a brief general conversation to help make the transition from the way individuals typically relate to one another in an ordinary social relationship to that required in a professional interview situation. He further indicates that the conversation may be about "any event or situation which is widely shared . . . the weather, parking problems, cooking, baseball, or the high cost of living. . . . Small talk establishes the interviewer's interest in the interviewee as a person and reinforces a sense of human mutuality as they discuss matters of common interest and concern" (131). It is in such preliminary chit-chat that areas of similarity in beliefs or attitudes or comembership categories may be uncovered.

POSITIVE EVALUATION

A number of other factors besides attitudinal or status similarity have been found to be associated with interpersonal attraction. One of the most potent of these has been shown to be the receipt of positive evaluations. Many studies support this proposition—we will mention only a few. (See Berscheid and Walster 1969: ch. 5 for a review.) A research study with college women on the effect of being evaluated (Landy and Aronson 1968) showed that the liking for an evaluator was greater when he praised than when he criticized the individual. It made no difference if the evaluator was qualified to make judgments or how discerning he was. The conclusion drawn was that expression of liking or disliking from others may indeed be a powerful determinant of interpersonal attraction. A similar effect was obtained in a study with white college students who rated their attraction toward pictures of black students of their own sex about whom they were given information relating to their attitudinal similarity to the subjects and expected evaluation of the subjects (Byrne and Ervin 1969). Both attitudinal similarity and positive evaluations by the strangers were associated with more liking for the stranger than were attitudinal dissimilarity or negative evaluations, but the weight attached to the stranger's personal evaluations was greater than that for attitudinal similarity. These effects are in keeping with the proposed "reinforcement rule" governing attraction (Clore and Byrne 1974), which states that evaluation of a person is influenced by the reinforcements and punishments associated with that person, and with the "exchange theory" of social attraction (Homans 1961; Thibaut and Kelley 1959), which proposes that attraction is dependent upon a person's evaluation of the potential benefits and costs in the relationship. Because a negative evaluation by a judge tends to be punishing or costly to one's self-esteem, one would expect that such a judge would not be evaluated positively and would not be seen as attractive.

These studies imply that it would be desirable for social workers to convey their positive regard for clients to enhance their attractiveness to the client and thus foster effective communication. Direct evidence on this is available from a number of studies. For example, in a university counseling center judges' ratings of counselors' liking of clients differentiated significantly between cases judged successful or unsuccessful on separate criteria. In another study, clients' perceptions of counselors' level of regard for them was significantly related to the counselors' ratings of degree of change at completion of treatment (Rogers 1961). The reciprocal nature of the attraction between client and social worker was further emphasized in a study in which graduate students in clinical psychology interviewed four persons they believed were being seen for an initial interview at a university counseling center (Heller, Myers and Kline 1963). The clients were actually student actors who varied their behaviors in predetermined ways. Independent ratings of observations of the interview revealed that counselors displayed significantly more encouragement, kindness, and friendliness toward the clients who behaved in a friendly than in a hostile way toward them.

We conclude that every appropriate opportunity should be taken by the social worker and agency to indicate to the clients that their behaviors are approved and their opinions respected. Encouraging them to participate in decisions is one such technique; using behavioral techniques in which the social worker provides reinforcement is another. The latter strategy should enhance the attractiveness of the worker to the client as well as modify the client behavior upon which reinforcement is contingent.

Other methods of communicating approval and liking focus on nonverbal behavior. Research findings suggest that there may be differences in the way males and females communicate approval nonverbally (Duncan 1969). One study revealed that male undergraduates tended to engage in more head nods when asked to indicate approval to an individual of the same sex with whom he was conversing; females tended to gesticulate more and look more at their female partners (Rosenfeld 1966).Both men and women engaged in more smiling behavior and showed greater responsiveness verbally and nonverbally when indicating approval. A strong association was found between the frequency of head nodding and the recipient's rating of his or her partner's attractiveness. Thus, the link between nonverbal reinforcement and perceived attractiveness of the reinforcer was confirmed. When verbal and nonverbal messages of approval-dissapproval are in conflict it has been suggested that the recipient believes the true attitude of the sender is reflected in the nonverbal signal (Argyle 1975). Although there is some research support for this suggestion (Argyle, Alkema, and Gilmore 1974), other findings suggest that negative messages prevail under these circumstances, regardless of whether they are verbal or nonverbal (Bugenthal, Kaswan, and Love 1970). Although it is not appropriate here to describe the vast literature that is concerned with the subtleties of nonverbal communication (see, for example, Argyle 1975; Exline 1971; Mehrabian 1972), social workers attempting to foster perceptions of positive evaluations by clients cannot neglect to monitor their own nonverbal behaviors; they should also try to be aware of their own feelings of attraction toward clients that might be reactions to clients' nonverbal communication of positive or negative evaluations of worker. We are not advocating that social workers convey false positive evaluations or expressions of liking for clients. This would not only be unethical, but also ineffective. A series of studies on ingratiation has shown that when a positive evaluation is perceived by the recipient as given with the purpose of obtaining some benefit, it is unlikely to lead to attraction to the source of the positive evaluation (E. E. Jones 1964). Various theorists recognize this point and include both positive regard for a client and genuineness in the relationship with the client among the requirements for a change-producing environment (Truax and Carkhuff 1967; Kadushin, 1972; Rogers 1961). The implication appears to be that workers who become aware of a negative feeling toward a client should directly address the issue of whether it is appropriate to work with that client, and if so, how the negative feelings should be handled. In some instances, it may be necessary to request a change in assignment.

EMPATHY

The communication of positive feelings is not the only type of communication that has been shown to induce interpersonal attraction in the recipient. In the study cited earlier of nonverbal communication patterns in men and women (Rosenfeld 1966), high attractiveness ratings were given a partner when there were frequent recognitions and referencess by the partner to the other individual. In contrast, high levels of partner self-manipulations and self-references were associated with low attractiveness ratings. These findings suggest that the communication of interest in or an attempt to understand another person's point of view enhances interpersonal attraction. A similar interpretation can be made from a study of girls attending a nursery school (F. Deutsch, 1974).The girls who were able to take the listener's viewpoint into account in describing a drawing to a child who could not see the picture were observed to be more popular with their peers than those who were egocentric in their descriptions. Thus, it appears that even at an early age, the awareness of the other person's perspectives and interests facilitates being liked and approached in a positive manner.

Most social psychologists have used the concept of empathy to indicate the ability to take the perspective of another person, although the concept includes more than that. Perhaps their focus on taking the role of another person is related to the assumption that this is basic to effective social interaction. Working in this tradition, social psychologists have defined empathy as the process of sensing or responding to other people's thoughts and feelings (e.g., Bronfenbrenner, Harding, and Gallwey 1958). There has been general agreement that both cognitive and emotional aspects are relevant to what is meant by empathy; both the thoughts and feelings of another person need to be understood, and the understanding must occur both cognitively and emotionally. Some researchers have, however, stressed the understanding of emotions. Stotland (1969),for example, has focused his research on the ability to react emotionally to cues transmitting the emotional experiences of another or to match the emotions of another.

D. W. Johnson (1975) has stressed that empathy involves the ability to take the perceptual or physical perspective of another. He found that in ten-year-old children the ability to take the emotional perspective of another is independent from the ability to take the physical perspective; that is, to look at the environment from the position occupied by someone else, or tell them how to create a design they cannot see. Kurdek (1975) also found that perceptual, cognitive, and affective perspective-taking were not correlated in children five through eight years of age. There are indications that for adults these three abilities or tendencies are more closely related. In one investigation college females were instructed to empathize with a target individual; that is, to see the situation as she sees it, to imagine how she feels, to be her at this moment (Regan and Totten 1975). These students were later asked to rate the influence of situational factors and dispositional factors (characteristics of the target individual) on the target person's behavior. It was found that merely being instructed to empathize with another affected the causality attributed to her behavior. The empathizers interpreted the cause of the target person's behavior much as that individual herself explained it: as largely due to the contingencies in the environment. The situation itself was seen as the major determinant of the behavior. Those students observing the same scene and not instructed to empathize with the target individual attributed her behavior to her personal characteristics.

These findings suggest that trying to respond emotionally as another individual is closely related to seeing and interpreting the immediate situation as she does. Thus, emotional, perceptual, and cognitive perspective-taking are not independent in adults.

Unlike social psychologists, theorists and researchers concerned with interpersonal helping have typically used the term empathy to include not only the decoding process of understanding other people's thoughts and feelings but also the encoding process of conveying this understanding to the other person. Truax and Carkhuff (1967) define a therapist's accurate empathy as "sensitivity to current feelings and his verbal facility to communicate this understanding in a language attuned to the client's current feelings" (46). Kadushin (1972) also stresses the communication aspect of empathy:

> In empathic understanding the worker is demonstrating . . . she understands, sensitively and accurately, the nature of the client's experience and the meaning this has for him. . . . It is not enough simply to be empathically understanding; one needs to communicate to the client the fact that one accurately perceives and feels his situation. (52)

Whether the emphasis in communicating understanding is on the emotional or cognitive aspects of the client's meaning will vary with the social work method: a community worker meeting with a residents' committee to discuss housing inadequacies may need to convey an understanding of their analysis of the housing defects, whereas for a worker in a family agency the communication of an understanding of a client's emotional reaction to a family crisis might be more appropriate (Keefe 1976). Both practitioners need to reflect cognitive and emotional empathy; it is only the emphasis that differs.

As for nonverbal communication, there is evidence that skill at decoding the emotional meaning of messages received is not necessarily associated with skill at encoding or sending emotional messages (Argyle 1975). Rogers (1961) suggested that the critical aspect of empathy in the interpersonal helping context is the communication from the helper to the client of an attitude of desiring to understand. In support of this view he cites a study in which different raters judged degree of counselor understanding of client (i.e., empathy) either while listening to tapes of entire sequences of client-counselor interactions or of only the counselor's responses. The judges ratings under these two conditions showed high agreement, and both sets were related to successful outcome of the counseling.

The link between the communication of accurate empathy and successful interpersonal helping has been supported by a number of researchers (Bergin 1966; Carkhuff 1971; Rogers 1961; Truax and Carkhuff 1967) who studied clinical psychologists, psychiatrists, university dormitory counselors, and counselor aides in rehabilitation centers. There has been less emphasis on empathy per se as a social work skill; however, Middleman and Goldberg (1972) indicated that the structured experience technique used in human relations training groups would be excellent for teaching generic social work skills to students, and most of these exercises include activities designed to foster an understanding of how others feel. Similarly, Gifford (1968) and Papell (1972) urged the use of sensitivity training for learning group work skills. A recent dissertation on the applicability of sensitivity groups to social work education (Balgopal 1971) advised employing interpersonal growth methods for social work education because sensitivity training given early in the program was likely to develop empathy, sensitivity, and intervention skills. Anderson (1975) urged that fostering of empathy in clients be considered by social group workers as a treatment goal but did not stress the importance of enhancing practitioners' empathy. It appears that there have been no studies directly correlating social work outcomes with the worker's level of empathy.

Most of the studies by Rogers, Carkhuff, and their colleagues were based on the theory that accurate empathy, genuineness (the ability to be nondefensive and authentic), and nonpossessive warmth (the ability to provide a safe atmosphere by showing positive regard and acceptance) are the three common elements in effective human interaction. Unfortunately, there are relatively few studies that examine separately the effects of these three elements or pinpoint the specific mechanism by which they influence helping outcomes. There is some evidence from studies in both the United States and Germany that counselors' accurate empathy and warmth, as measured by the Truax and Carkhuff (1967) rating scales, are directly linked to self-exploration by clients (Truax and Mitchell 1971). In those studies therapists deliberately attempted to increase, decrease, then increase again their levels of warmth and empathy with the same patients over several interviews. Independent judges' ratings confirmed these variations in therapist behavior, and other judges' ratings of patients' self-exploratory statements showed concomitant shifts. Another study (D. W. Johnson 1971a) investigated Carl Rogers' proposal that clients' perceptions that they have been heard and clearly understood facilitates successful treatment because such perceptions lead to reduced defensive adherence to one's own position, reduced feelings of threat, and greater willingness to engage in cooperative problem solving with the other person. In that study four college students were trained to express either warmth or coldness through nonverbal techniques such as smiling and leaning toward the other person, and to make either complete and accurate or incomplete and inaccurate restatements of another person's positions and feeling about an issue under discussion. They then engaged in conversation with other undergraduates. When the trained students communicated accurate rather than inaccurate understanding, their partners were significantly more likely to indicate they felt the other was trying to understand them and did understand them. There was also greater agreement at the end of the discussion on a joint decision. The conveying of warmth was also associated with partners' feeling that they were understood. But unlike the accurate restatement condition, warmth was not linked to reaching agreement. It was, however, associated with liking for the other person; accurate restatements were not. This suggests that communicating empathy may not be directly linked to interpersonal attraction, although the rather intellectual impersonal nature of this interaction situation may account for the results.

Carkhuff and Pierce (1967) suggested that empathy, warmth, respect, and concreteness are particularly essential in the first interview when the therapist and client are of different races or classes. Perhaps empathy serves as a bridge between individuals who under ordinary circumstances are unlikely to be involved in a trusting or close relationship. Frank (1962) made a similar point in discussing the social context of treatment for mental or physical disorders. He suggested that the personal qualities of socially designated helpers, such as their capacity to form empathic relationships with particular clients, is important only when the client has reason to doubt the legitimacy of the role of helper or when the client enters the relationship with mistrust. Thus, the qualities of empathy and warmth are seen as facilitative; that is, they may foster the development of change in a helping relationship.

There is evidence of individual differences among professional helping personnel in their level of accurate empathy (Truax and Carkhuff 1967), and there is also evidence of the efficacy of training to increase it. Truax and Carkhuff (1967) and Carkhuff (1971) found that intensive training can improve the ratings of empathy in helping personnel. Other studies (Stotland 1969; Regan and Totten 1975) suggested that even simple instructions to imagine that one is in someone else's place and feeling what he or she is feeling can enhance the empathic response of college students in controlled interaction situations. Relatively brief training in attending to critical cues in voice quality (Davitz 1964) or children's facial expressions (Jecker, Maccoby, and Breitrose 1965) also seems able to foster understanding of these nonverbal communications. A programmed text developed at the University of Michigan for social work students (Milnes and Bertcher 1980) appears to enhance the communication of verbal empathy. A comparable instructional tool is clearly needed for the nonverbal area.

PERSONALITY MATCHING

Thus far we have discussed the evidence that matching for similarity of attitudes and of various status characteristics may enhance interpersonal attraction. There are, however, other ways workers and clients can be matched to increase interpersonal attractiveness and to establish a helping relationship; that is, on the basis of personality traits or psychological needs. The social psychological research on interpersonal attraction in a variety of life situations, as well as direct research on the determinants of attraction in helping relationships, all suggest that similarity, dissimilarity, or complementarity of personality can each be associated with interpersonal attraction (Duck and Spencer 1972; Gardner 1964) with both the situational context and type of personality characteristic determining which type of matching is important.

Studies of college women's actual friendship choices (Duck and Spencer 1972), college students' reactions to their instructors (Menges 1969; Runkel 1956), and industrial subordinates' likings for their supervisors (Triandis 1959) support the view that similarity in cognitive structuring of the world enhances interpersonal attraction, although individual beliefs may differ. These studies have been interpreted as suggesting either that similar cognitive structuring facilitates understanding among persons or that similarity in the ways people organize the world about them can be a basis for providing consensual validation about social reality. Thus, the relationship between cognitive structuring and attraction is analogous to the relationship between attitudes and attraction.

But dissimilarity between college teacher and student in other characteristics has also been shown to be associated with teacher attractiveness (Grush, Clore, and Costin 1975). In that study students rated themselves and their instructors on variety of personality traits, and also rated their teachers' classroom skills and their attraction to the teacher. For those personality traits of teachers that were significantly related to teaching competence, dissimilarity between teacher and student personality was associated with liking for the teacher when the dissimilarity was due to the teacher being rated as having more of the trait than the student. For those personality traits of teachers that were unrelated to competence, neither similarity nor dissimilarity was associated with student liking for teacher.

The authors concluded that dissimilarity on personality dimensions relevant to teaching competence was predictive of liking because teacher and students were not peers but rather were in a role relationship in which the status of one was higher than the status of the other. Further, the students were not attempting to obtain consensual validation of their views, that is, evidence of the truth of their views, through the agreement of similar others. Rather their purpose was to evaluate their teachers. Thus, similarity with the teacher was not reinforcing or associated with instructor attractiveness. The authors postulated that the students' thinking went as follows: "If teachers are to direct me in the learning process, they ought to possess more of those traits important for effective teaching than I do; if they only possess the same amount as I do, how can I learn anything from them?" (Grush, Clore and Costin 1975: 787).

The relevance to social worker attractiveness to client is evident; the client and worker are in an unequal status role relationship and clients may perceive that certain personality characteristics are needed for the worker to carry out the helping role. Thus, clients may wonder how they can be helped by someone like themselves. What are not evident, however, are the specific characteristics in which client and social worker should differ to achieve maximum effectiveness. Perhaps warmth, genuineness, concreteness, and empathy are the most relevant in view of their association with interpersonal helping.

There have been several systmatic efforts to study the effect of personality matching between helper and client in non-social work settings, based on a scale designed to tap characteristics relevant to effective interaction between two individuals; it is referred to as Fundamental Interpersonal Relations Orientation Scale or FIRO (Schutz 1957).The scale is based on the assumption that there are three needs central to interpersonal exchange: inclusion, control, and affection. The first refers to being part of a group, the second to determining outcomes, and the third to expressing warmth. The more two people are similar in the importance these needs have for them, the more compatible they are assumed to be. But compatibility also requires complementarity between each individual's wish to receive or originate the behavior respresenting the need. Thus, compatibility on FIRO reflects both similarity and complementarity on the three need dimensions. The instrument provides a Total Compatibility Index and three subscales: 1) Reciprocal Compatibility or the similarity of the behavior and the other individual's wish for the behavior; 2) Originator Compatibility or the matching of the desire to originate with the desire to receive behavior in each of the three need areas; and 3) Interchange Compatibility or agreement on the amount each individual wants to become involved in each need area. One investigation of the instrument found a highly significant relationship between female hospitalized patients' improvement in therapy and the total compatibility score on the FIRO of the patient and psychiatrist (Sapolsky 1965). The patients' feeling of being understood by the doctor at the time of discharge was also significantly associated with compatibility. Another study (A. P. Goldstein 1971) found that when hospitalized mental patients and ministerial counselors had high FIRO total compatibility scores, the patients evaluated the therapeutic relationship significantly more favorably than did patient-counselor pairs with low FIRO total compatibility scores. In addition, both the Reciprocal Compatibility scores and Interchange Compatibility scores correlated significantly with relationship scores. Originator Compatibility scores did not. In a comprehensive review of psychological literature relevant to psychotherapeutic attraction (A. P. Goldstein 1971: ch. 9), it was concluded that compatibility matching on an instrument such as the FIRO can increase patient attraction to therapist.

These findings suggest another basis for assigning workers to clients even in initial interviews, and that is the compatibility of their personal needs. The scores for the workers can be kept on file. Perhaps some brief questionnaire administered to the client might provide data which would maximize the benefits obtained from the service rendered by the agency.

GOAL FACILITATION

Up to this point, the factors discussed as determinants of interpersonal attraction might be characterized as primarily relevant to the relationship-development rather than to the problem-definition function of the initial social work encounter. There is evidence, however, that those who facilitate one's goal accomplishment are perceived as more attractive (D. W. Johnson and Johnson 1972a) and that those who frustrate one's goal attainment are disliked (Zajonc and Marin 1967). Similarly, when southern white men in the military service worked on an interdependent task with a black serviceman who was actually a confederate of the experimenter, the white men expressed greater liking for their coworker when they were led to believe they had succeeded at the task than when joint failure was induced (Blanchard, Adelman, and Cook 1975). These findings support M. Deutsch's (1962) proposition that cooperative interaction, or the expectation of it, leads to increased interpersonal attraction. This suggests that a belief by clients and workers that they are working together on a goal which both are attempting to achieve, e.g., the reduction of a child's delinquency, should enhance both the workers' and the clients' attractiveness. This conclusion is consistent with the stress placed by various social work theorists on early mutual problem or goal definition.

It is important to note, however, that we do not always like those who facilitate our goal attainment. Some theorists have called attention to two separate aspects of interpersonal preference: liking or admiration for someone's competence, and liking or friendliness toward someone's socioemotional qualities (Bales 1970; Rubin 1973). Evidence for this differentiation has been found in decision-making groups in which the person who is judged by group members as best liked is not typically also judged to have the best ideas (Bales and Slater 1955). Dyadic attraction may also be distinguished in this way, although the evidence is not entirely clear.

One review of ten studies in which subjects were given information about strangers and then asked to indicate their probable liking for and enjoyment in working with them, found the replies to these two questions highly correlated (Byrne and Nelson 1965). This would imply that respect and liking are assumed to coexist in initial social encounters. But a factor analysis of college students' judgments about acquaintances yielded one factor having to do with task-related attraction and another independent dimension concerned with socially based attraction (McCroskey and McCain 1974).

The latter finding is supported by a study of clients' reactions to an initial helping encounter in social work and other settings, which distinguished problem-centered tension changes and relationship-centered tension changes (Polansky and Kounin 1956). The problem-centered tension changes were associated with clients' judgments of problem clarification and of progress toward problem solution, and with independent judges' assessments of interviewer competence, ability to integrate facts, and skill in diagnosing and focusing. The relationship-centered tension changes were generally found to be associated with a different set of variables including whether the client saw the interviewer as a likable person who wished to continue seeing the client, and whether judges described the interviewer as listening attentively, being easy to communicate with, and seeming unhurried. Some client perceptions as well as judges' assessments were, however, associated with both types of tension shifts.

Two studies of laboratory analogs to helping relationships also found that a distinction between relationship-centered and problem-centered satisfactions in an initial interview was useful (Kounin et al. 1956; Tessler 1975). Tessler asked college students to participate in a study to train counselors by role playing an initial counseling interview. The students were given varying information about the experience of the counselor and the value similarity between themselves and the counselors. After an actual interview, the students' ratings of satisfactions with the interview were found to be related to value similarity and to the degree of counselor informality during the interview. Problem-centered satisfactions were related only to prior information about the counselor's experience.

These studies indicate the need to enhance both goal attainment and personal acceptance during the initial contact. There is some evidence that the relative importance of these two aspects of interpersonal attraction may vary for different clients depending on their personality predispositions and past experiences. In a study of army enlisted men's attraction to their squad leader, perceived similarity between self and supervisor was significantly related to attraction to the supervisor, and the army in general, only for those men who had high scores on a measure of motivation for close interpersonal relations (Hansson and Fiedler 1973). Men who did not show high levels of such motivation did not indicate greater attraction toward more similar squad leaders. Their attraction toward their squad leaders and army life in general was assumed to be based on other criteria, perhaps related to achievement-oriented goals. Mayer and Timms (1970), in a study of the reactions of working-class clients to an initial interview in London family welfare agencies, suggested that clients' needs for social satisfactions within the interview varied. Some clients did not have informal confidants with whom they had shared their problems; these clients were especially pleased to have the social worker available to talk with them and this was sufficient as a basis of positive attraction. Other clients indicated they had talked their problems over with informal sources, and that solace and comfort but not problem solution was obtained in such interactions; for these clients just having the social worker available to talk with them was not sufficient to produce feelings of satisfaction with the initial contact. A sense of progress toward problem solution was required.

Our conclusion from these studies is that it is important not only for agencies to consider the appropriateness of matching of social workers and clients on relevant characteristics and for social workers to seek to communicate to new clients in ways designed to enhance attraction. Initial contacts should also be task-focused vehicles for beginning joint problem solving. If they are not, clients may not return for a second session.

PHYSICAL ATTRACTIVENESS

Thus far the emphasis has been upon the client's attitude and liking of the social worker. Equally important are factors affecting the worker's liking for the client. Social work training has recognized this in certain respects, and its emphasis on self-awareness and respect for client views is directed toward counteracting the consequences of differential worker attraction to clients based on attitudinal or status similarity, personality matching, positive responses toward the worker, and/or progress toward problem solution. It is possible that some characteristics of the clients not usually discussed may also affect workers' attraction to them. One characteristic is their physical attractiveness, the second is their use of personal space.

The importance of physical attractiveness has in the past been neglected by social psychologists. It has been suggested that social psychologists preferred to focus on variables that could be modified and may have put physical beauty in a class with genetics: "These factors influence behavior but since we cannot do anything about it, let's ignore the topic." Even more important, social psychologists may have felt, at some level of awareness, that it was inequitable to judge people on their physical characteristics; surely what is under the skin is more important (Berscheid and Walster 1974). The general public has also shown an unwillingness to acknowledge the relevance of physical attractiveness to social relations. Studies of young adults in the United States and Western European countries have indicated that both men and women report that physical attractiveness is relatively unimportant in their liking for others even though their behavior has been shown to be significantly affected by good looks (Berscheid and Walster 1974; Rommetveit 1960).

What research has been undertaken in this area has indicated that physical attractiveness does mediate interpersonal relationships not only in the area of dating and marital choices, but in other domains as well. Popularity of men and women college students with their same-sexed dormmates was related to independent judges' ratings of their physical attractiveness; the students who were most isolated from their peers, receiving few choices or rejections, were those judged least physically attractive (Krebs and Adinolfi 1975).

Even six-year-old children react to the physical attractiveness of their peers and report greater liking for their more physically attractive classmates (Berscheid and Walster 1974). And in a study of kindergarten and fourth-grade children's ratings of color photographs of black, Mexican-American, and Anglo children, the physical attractiveness of the children in the photographs was the most important predictor of ratings of liking, smartness, friendliness, and aggression. This was more important than the ethnicity of the child raters or of the children in the photographs (Langlois and Stephan 1977).

Because differential treatment between beautiful and ugly individuals thus seems to start very early in the life of the child, it is likely that this differential treatment will elicit divergent behaviors from children varying in physical attractiveness. The development of these differential behaviors is supported by the work of Langlois and Downs (1977). Those investigators observed children playing together in prearranged pairs at ages three and five. There were no differences in the play behaviors of the three-year-olds related to their physical attractiveness. But the five-year-old unattractive children were more active and hit their playmates more than the attractive children did.

By the time adulthood is reached it is therefore difficult to know to what extent the beautiful and unattractive are treated differently because they actually behave differently as a result of their divergent socialization experiences and to what extent they are treated differently solely on the basis of their appearance and the assumptions others make on that basis.

Two explanations have been offered for the more positive response frequently given to physically attractive individuals. One is based on the reinforcement-affect model of attraction, which suggests that beauty has reinforcement value and so leads to a positive affect or liking toward beautiful individuals. The second explanation is a cognitive one: that people believe attractive individuals possess socially desirable qualities and have greater potential, and are therefore attracted to them. There is a wide variety of evidence supporting the cognitive explanation. Physically attractive people are predicted to have rosier futures (Dion, Berscheid, and Walster 1972). Unattractive children are perceived by adults as less virtuous and more likely to commit a further transgression after an initial one was observed (Dion 1972).

One important investigation tending to support the cognitive hypothesis involved college students in a jurylike setting (Sigall and Ostrobe 1975). Undergraduates were asked to sentence defendants after they had read their cases and seen their photographs. The students gave more lenient sentences to attractive defendants when the crime was not related to attractiveness (burglary, for example), but gave more severe sentences to attractive defendants when the offense was attractiveness-related (swindle, for example). The results were interpreted as suggesting that the attractive defendants were perceived as generally having greater potential and more virtue; hence they were more likely to be rehabilitated and were given a lighter sentence. The exception was the attractive individual who used his or her "God-given gifts" to cheat others—these received a harsher sentence than did nonattractive defendants. If the reinforcement-affect model alone were at work, attractive defendants would have been given lighter sentences regardless of type of offense. The study also revealed that the sentences given to the unattractive defendants did not differ from those given the control group, in which physical appearance was unknown. It was the attractive defendants who were treated differentially.

This finding has implications for social work practice. In examining their own responses to new clients, workers should be particularly sensitive to their reactions to beautiful females and handsome males. The literature suggests that views are less likely to be distorted with unattractive clients.

The potential boomerang effect for physically attractive individuals has been shown in other studies as well. Both male and female college students judged photos of females on a variety of characteristics. The more physically attractive women had more generally desirable characteristics and outcomes attributed to them, but they were also seen as vain, egotistical, and divorce-prone (Dermer and Thiel 1975). And in the previously described study of popularity of same-sexed dormmates, the very popular and the most actively rejected students were among the most physically attractive (Krebs and Adinolfi 1975). Other research of Berscheid and Walster (1974) indicated that attractive college women tend to feel less happy in their marital lives after twenty years than did their unattractive peers. One reason given for these results was that the women compared their current states to more rewarding experiences they had had in the past. The concept of a comparison level will be discussed more fully in the following part, but it is highly relevant to the behaviors of physically attractive and unattractive individuals. It appears that they may evaluate current male-female relations differently because their past experiences were highly divergent. Thus, very favorable past experiences may make current outcomes more disappointing.

In general, however, physical attractiveness is associated with positive outcomes. Adolescent girls' physical appearance was found to be significantly related to upward mobility via marriage, especially for girls from working-class backgrounds (Elder 1969). Another study revealed that non-heroin-involved prisoners with some physical disfigurement who were given plastic surgery showed a lower recidivism rate than did equally disfigured prisoners who were given counseling or no treatment (Furzberg, Safar, and Cavior, as cited in Berscheid and Walster 1974). The conclusion drawn was that to achieve social adjustment, sometimes money is better spent on surgery than on therapy.

There has been very little research on the topic in relation to professional helpers, but what evidence there is is consistent with the research cited above. Berscheid and Walster (1974:209) report that several investigators knowledgeable about mental hospitals have suggested that physically unattractive patients receive less help from the professional staff. One commentator on the criminal justice system has observed that "Even social workers accustomed to dealing with all types often find it difficult to think of a normal, pretty girl as being guilty of a crime" (Monahan 1941:103). We were able to find just one study that deals directly with this important issue—that of Barocas and Vance (1974). In a university counseling center, the judgments of trained masters' or doctoral level male and female counselors of the personal adjustment and prognosis of clients they had seen correlated significantly with clients' physical attractiveness. Of course, this covariation may have been valid if others also reacted differentially to these clients, but counselor bias may have also been involved.

It is possible that social workers, tending to sympathize with the less fortunate, show more warmth toward the unattractive individual and find the physically beautiful more "unlikable." Or perhaps, being aware of their negative reaction to the unattractive, social workers might attempt to compensate and express exaggerated warmth. Junior-high-school pupils who interacted with other pupils made up to appear to be physically handicapped displayed more stereotyped and unnatural motoric behaviors toward the "handicapped" but also reported more favorable impressions of them than of the "normals" (Kleck 1968). The complex reactions of the nonhandicapped to the physically stigmatized, including the tactic of acting as if there is no defect, have been described vividly by E. Goffman (1963), who also points to the deleterious effects of such a tactic. There is some evidence that compensatory reactions to negative feelings occur with those in the helping professions. A. P. Goldstein (1971) reported that patients rated their counselors as unattractive when the counselors and patients had a low total compatibility score on the FIRO. However, the counselors, who were ministers in a pastoral counselor training program, did not rate their incompatible patients as unattractive. Subsequent conversations with the therapists revealed some type of "overcompensatory process" was operating, according to Goldstein. Several of the therapists reported becoming aware of negative feelings toward such patients and experiencing guilt in response to those feelings. They then reevaluated their feelings, found more attractive features in these patients, and redoubled their therapeutic effort since they felt that if they did not help such "unlikable" patients, no one would. The fact that the patients found the incompatible counselors unattractive in spite of those redoubled efforts suggests that the overcompensation did not produce the desired effect. It is possible that a similar process is at work when social workers find their clients physically "unlikable." At this point, all that can be concluded is that physical attractiveness has been found to affect responses in a number of areas. It would be wise for social workers to monitor their own behavior carefully, especially during initial encounters, to determine if their feelings, either negative or positive, are having a deleterious effect on the interaction.

PERSONAL SPACE

A second factor often neglected in social work training that may affect practitioners' behaviors and attraction to clients during initial contacts is that of clients' physical proximity and orientation, although Middleman and Goldberg (1974: ch. 7) have discussed the importance of the social worker being aware of the impact of positioning on the client's comfort. Two anthropologists, E. T. Hall (1966) and R. Sommer (1969), have made major conceptual contributions to the study of humans' use of space, by calling attention to cultural differences in such aspects as the distances persons maintain for various types of social interaction and the implications of such differences for cross-cultural communication.

Sommer (1969) has been concerned with what he and others (e.g., Evans and Howard 1973) call "personal space," which is defined as an area with invisible boundaries surrounding a person's body into which intruders may not come. This portable territory is proposed to differ in major ways between cultures. Hall (1966) gave the name proxemics to the observations and theories of man's use of space as a specialized elaboration of culture. Based on his observations of proxemic patterns in several cultures (i.e., German, English, Arabic, French), he also concluded that there were strong cultural differences in proximity of interaction, touching behavior, and type of orientation; that is, in how directly or obliquely people face one another. For middle-class American adults on the East Coast he proposed four distances or zones of human interaction: intimate, personal, social, and public. These zones are culturally defined as appropriate for various types of social relations.

The *intimate zone*, which includes distances up to one and one-half feet, is used when close friends, lovers, family members interact. In this zone the presence of the other person is unmistakable. The persons can easily touch one another. Sight, often distorted, olfaction, heat from the other person's body, sound, smell, and feel of the breath all combine to signal involvement with another body. There is a feeling that one's body boundaries extend to the intimate sphere and discomfort, if not anger, is felt by Americans when this zone is entered inappropriately. The use of intimate distance is governed not only by the relationship between the individuals concerned, but by the general social event as well. According to Hall, intrusion into the intimate zone is not considered proper in public places by adult, middle-class Americans. Crowded subways or elevators bring strangers into intimate spatial relations, and Americans handle this violation of expected behavior by being as immobile as possible and by withdrawing, if at all possible, if their trunks touch another person. The hands are kept at the side and the eyes fixed on infinity; fellow riders are treated as objects rather than as persons (Sommer 1969). It is taboo for strangers to enter this zone, as is the enjoyment of bodily contact with strangers.

Other cultures have different proxemic patterns for intimate distance, both in terms of the types of relationships and location considered appropriate. For example, Hall noticed that Middle Eastern residents do not express outraged reaction at being touched by strangers, and find it acceptable to bathe the partner in a conversation in one's breath. It is even seen as offering the other individual a pleasing olfactory experience. These differences from American middle-class patterns have also been found when Arab and United States students were observed under standardized conditions (D. M. Watson and Graves 1966).

Personal distance is the term used by Hall to designate the distance separating individuals who are not in an intimate relationship. It might be thought of as a protective bubble that an organism maintains between itself and others. It extends to the point where two people can touch fingers if they both extend arms. It is the limit of physical domination. Subjects of personal interest can be discussed at this distance, which is between one and one-half and four feet. The voice level is moderate, and details of the other person's features are clear. No body heat is perceptible and olfaction is not normally present for Americans, although it may be for people from other cultures. The difference is particularly notable for men, since in many other cultures men wear cologne as freely as do women.

Social distance is the area beyond touching (about four feet) but below twelve feet. Impersonal business occurs at this distance. People who work together or those attending a casual social gathering tend to use social distance. At the far end of social distance, it is important to maintain eye contact for conversations of any significant length. To fail to hold the other person's eye is to shut him out. Hall observed differences across cultures in the volume of the voice at this distance. The American voice was less loud than that of the Arab, the Spaniard, and the Russian, but louder than that of the upper-class Englishman or Japanese.

Public distance is defined by Hall as that distance beyond the circle of involvement. For middle-class Americans it extends from twelve feet to over twenty-five feet. Thirty feet is the distance automatically set around important public figures, such as presidents. It is the distance typically used on public occasions. Nonverbal communication must be expressed by rather bold body stance and gestures. The voice is amplified and the tempo drops. Shades of meaning conveyed by normal voice and facial expressions are lost.

The significance of the above descriptions of various zones is twofold: violation of these zones can lead to rejection, embarrassment, or subsequent avoidance of the violator; the zones are culturally defined and learned in early childhood, often without awareness. Thus, cross-cultural or subcultural interactions based on differing proxemic assumptions can lead to irritation and miscommunication.

The relatively early learning of the links between proximity and type of social relationship is evident in one study where American children in kindergarten through the third grade were shown photographs of pairs of adults at varying distances (Scott 1974). They were asked to identify which photos showed people talking about a secret, dinner, directions to a store, etc. Kindergarten children did not associate particular distances with types of interaction, but thereafter there was a gradual differentiation with age. Public distance was learned first, intimate next, and personal and social last. Similarly, white sixth-grade boys and girls from a middle-class American school saw silhouetted pairs of figures presented at varying distances from each other and then ranked them as friends, acquaintances, and strangers (Guardo 1969). The rankings were highly correlated with the distance between the figures.

The deleterious effects of violating personal space has also been experimentally demonstrated in a number of studies. When a stranger sat alongside and at a very close distance to male mental patients seated alone, or to female university students reading at a library table, the amount of time the subjects remained seated was significantly less than for control groups of patients or students who had not been approached (Felipe and Sommer 1966). This effort to get away from a stranger who violates one's personal space was also shown in several studies in which a stranger stood at varying distances from male and female pedestrians waiting alone at a traffic light (Konecni et al. 1975). The pedestrians approached at one or two feet subsequently crossed the street faster than those approached at five or ten feet; they also were less likely to pick up and return a pencil the stranger dropped while crossing the street. The authors interpreted this finding as reflecting the pedestrians' imputation of motives to the violators that were not conducive to initiating further interactions.

When individuals from cultures with differing proxemics meet, they may inadvertently insult one another. Hall (1966) points out some examples of this. Arabs more freely touch casual acquaintances, stand closer together when talking, and face one another more directly than do western Europeans. He also observed more pushing in public and feeling and pinching of women in public conveyances, and explained that this was not considered impolite since Arabs tend to believe the "person" exists somewhere down inside the body and the boundaries of the self do not extend to the periphery. In northern Europe, the skin and the clothes of the person are synonymous with the individual and permission to touch either is needed if one is a stranger. Englishmen indicate attentiveness to someone else's speech by maintaining eye contact rather than by head nods or "uh-huhs"; they feel that if you break eye contact with them, you are not listening. Germans consider looking at strangers an intrusion on their privacy; the English consider phoning someone an intrusion on privacy.

It is unfortunate that Hall did not analyze the proxemic patterns of groups with whom social workers frequently come in contact. He suggested that subcultural groups in America such as Spanish-speaking residents and blacks have proxemic patterns different than those described above, but did not elaborate. Some subsequent research has tended to support this contention, although the evidence is not entirely clear. This lack of clarity is at least partly because proxemic behaviors of persons from only loosely defined subcultural groups observed in various social relationships and social settings have been indiscriminately compared.

One experimenter systematically observed the distance between hundreds of pairs of adults, of the same sex and ethnicity, viewing various exhibits at the Houston Zoo, and found significant differences among ethnic groups (Baxter 1970). Mexican-American pairs stood closest together, white pairs next, and black pairs furthest apart. A greater distance between conversing pairs of blacks than of whites was also found in a study where social greeting distances among college students in several natural settings were observed (Willis 1966), but oppostie results were found in another study in which college students were asked to approach another student, who was of their same sex and race, as closely as they felt they comfortably could (Bauer 1973). Under these conditions black college students approached closer than white ones. In contrast, there were no significant ethnic differences in distance or directness of orientation among same-sexed adults talking to one another on streets in neighborhoods in New York City that were predominantly Puerto Rican, black, Italian, or Chinese (S. E. Jones 1971).

The ethnic differences observed among adults at the Houston Zoo were also found for young children (ages about five to ten) and adolescents (ages about ten to twenty) in that same study (Baxter 1970). Supporting the Baxter findings were the results of a study of judgments of a comfortable interpersonal distance on a paper-and-pencil measure; white high school and college students reported smaller distances for pairs of same-sex whites than black students did for pairs of same-sex blacks (Duke and Nowicki 1972). On the other hand, no significant differences were observed in the distance between talking pairs of black and pairs of white children (of the same sex) in three school playgrounds in Toronto, Canada, including integrated schools in two lower socioeconomic areas and one middle-class area (Scherer 1974). The only significant difference in that study of first through fourth graders was that white pairs in the middle-class school talked to one another at a greater distance than did white children at the lower-class schools.

Social class variations in proximity behavior among interacting children may also be the critical variable in another study of school playground behaviors, although ethnic variations might also be at work (Aiello and Jones 1971). Pairs of first and second graders of the same sex were observed in predominantly black or Puerto Rican lower socioeconomic areas of New York City and in predominantly white middle-class suburban areas near New York City. The middle-class white children stood further apart from each other than did the lower-class black or Puerto Rican children, while the latter two groups did not differ from each other. Thus, it appears that in the United States black children converse in closer proximity to one another than do white children, but black adults stand farther apart than do white adults in their discussions.

There are also indications that child-adult proxemic behaviors may differ across ethnic groups. Native Americans consider it rude for children to have direct eye contact with adults when engaged in conversation; lowered eyes and head signify respect (D. L. Davis 1979; Wax and Thomas 1971). According to Lewis and Ho (1975), for Native Americans, looking someone in the eyes is not merely rude, it implies intimidation. There are some indications that a similar belief is held by Puerto Rican parents. In contrast, for the typical classroom teacher in the United States, the failure of child to look an adult in the eye when being addressed connotes guilt, shame or, at the minimum, inattention.

Despite the lack of fully consistent findings concerning ethnic differences in Americans' proxemic behaviors, there is sufficient credibility to this line of research for social workers to be sensitive to the different proxemic patterns among their clients. It is clear that offense can easily be given or taken by the distance kept between individuals, the directness with which they face another, the visual or tactile contact made, any olfactory stimulation, etc. Social workers would do well to be aware of the possibly different subcultural patterns and not react negatively to clients who violate their intimate space, or who orient themselves more directly than seems appropriate.

On the other hand, the social worker should also be aware that their own nonverbal communication and use of space may give offense. There is a tendency to stay farther away from disabled individuals (Sommer 1969). The social worker who backs away from a disabled client may communicate distaste. As extroverts have been found to stay closer together and introverts and anxious individuals to stay farther apart (Sommer 1969), an outgoing social worker may unknowingly threaten the new client. In sum, not only is what you say and how you say it important, but also where you are situated when you are saying it.

The sex of the client and worker may also contribute to the proxemic communication difficulties. A number of studies indicate that the preferred orientation of men and women differs, with women more likely to position themselves alongside a liked other and men opposite a liked other (Sommer 1967). Intrusion into these preferred positions by strangers has been shown to elicit different reactions by male and female college students (Fisher and Byrne 1975). All students were seated alone at a table in the university library when a stranger of the same sex or of the opposite sex sat down near them for five minutes. Shortly after the stranger left the students were interviewed. The results showed that women expressed less interpersonal attraction to a stranger who had been sitting in the chair alongside them than opposite them; exactly the reverse pattern was found for the men. These differences were found regardless of the sex of the stranger. The same researchers observed the behavior of another group of college students in the library and found that women placed barriers, such as clothing and books, in such a way as to protect the empty chair alongside them from access by someone else, while men defended the seat opposite them from intrusion. Thus, the clients' or workers' choice of seating positions during an initial interview may inadvertently affect interpersonal attraction.

One study of staff and clients at a counseling center attempted to study this positioning effect directly, although unfortunately the data were not analyzed by sex (Haase and DiMattia 1970). Photographs of same-sexed persons described as client and counselor were shown seated in two chairs in four positions: side by side at a 45° angle, directly opposite, at the corners of a table, on opposite sides of a table. The clients preferred the corners of the table position, while the counselors preferred either of the positions without an intervening table. The authors concluded that since professionals often control the physical arrangements, they may be offending or raising the anxiety of their clients by assuming similarity in proxemic preferences. This research, as well as that described earlier about possible ethnic or sex differences in position or distance preferences, leads us to several suggestions. First, greater flexibility in the physical arrangements in offices may be desirable so that the furniture can be rearranged to suit the preferences of the clients. Additionally or alternatively a variety of seating arrangements could be made available so that clients can select the spot they prefer; this suggestion is consistent with Seabury's (1971) conclusion based on observations of variations in waiting room and interview room furniture arrangements in a variety of social work practice settings. Finally, it might be wise to arrange the client-worker seats at 90° angles from one another, e.g., at the corners of a table or desk, to avoid many undesirable seating arrangements.

CONCLUSIONS AND UNRESOLVED ISSUES

A. P. Goldstein (1971) summarized other research performed in the laboratory which suggested additional variables that might be related to the attractiveness of the therapist. These were: belief by the client that the therapist was someone the client would like; the belief that the therapist possessed a central attribute such as warmth which was generally seen as desirable; the belief that the therapist had high status; the need by the client to make some effort to obtain the treatment; the observation by the client of client models who approved of the therapist; group pressure in the form of hearing peers evaluate the therapist very highly; and role playing the part of a client prior to initial contact with the therapist. Goldstein also examined a variable that would lead the therapist to find the client attractive; that is, the belief that the client possessed a central attribute such as warmth. Experiments were conducted to test whether procedures could be developed to heighten each of these variables in such a way that they enhanced the attraction the client felt for the therapist. The results indicated that the manipulations did sometimes enhance therapist attractiveness for students coming to university counseling offices, who Goldstein described as young, attractive, verbal, intelligent, and successful clients (YAVIS). However, the experiments did not result in increased therapist attractiveness for psychiatric patients at a veterans hospital or for incarcerated alcoholics—non-YAVIS clients, as Goldstein described them. In a few cases where the manipulation was effective with a subgroup of non-YAVIS clients, they seemed to form a homogenous subgroup who resembled the college YAVIS clients. Goldstein concluded that there is a need for research on social influence variables affecting nonyoung, nonattractive, nonverbal, nonintelligent, nonsuccessful clients. We would concur.

One conclusion to be drawn from the above is that anything that can be done to enhance clients' expectations about worker likability or status, within ethical boundaries, should be considered by a social work agency. Information from former or current clients who express confidence in the worker might also facilitate the formation of a positive relationship in the early stages. This emphasizes the importance of the agency's as well as individual worker's reputation in the community to be served. There seems little need to add to the effort required for clients to reach a potential source of help. The existence of waiting lists in many public and private agencies, transportation difficulties, restricted hours of opening, etc., should provide sufficient obstacles to obtaining social work services so that in most cases clients already perceive themselves as making an effort to obtain service. However, if Goldstein's findings are correct, these activities are likely to have little effect on lower-class, or less capable, or less attractive, or deviant clients. We return to some of the research cited earlier for some conclusions about attraction enhancement conditions for these clients, as well as for others.

In situations where client and worker do not share the same social status, perhaps during the initial encounter greater emphasis should be placed upon seeking out areas of shared interests and beliefs to establish other bases for comembership. The public image of the agency personnel may also be relevant here, in terms of stands they have taken on issues relevant to the clients. This may influence clients' expectations of shared beliefs. For example, individual workers' prior participation in community committees may serve to convey their beliefs and attitudes to potential clients. Community workers should be particularly alert to this.

Matching clients and workers on central interpersonal needs or allowing client selection to operate should also be considered. The worker should also be alert to opportunities for clearly conveying to the client sincere approval, liking, and respect, both verbally and nonverbally. Workers who do not have some positive feelings toward their clients should not be working with them.

Worker statements indicating an understanding of the client's emotional and cognitive perspective on the issues under discussion are also essential. Agency policies and practices can also convey these attitudes prior to the initial encounter between worker and client, in such areas as appropriate forms of address, consideration in the handling of telephone inquiries, and scheduling of appointments. For example, appointments should be made at the client's convenience, not the worker's.

The importance of focusing on establishment of shared goals between worker and client, interdependence in the achievement of these goals, and expectations of actual progress toward problem solving is also indicated. Some type of time line of anticipated goal attainments may be efficacious in selected situations. A flexible office that would allow clients a choice of comfortable personal space arrangements would not only reduce anxiety and enhance attraction in itself, but would also convey respect for client opinions. Coupled with self-monitoring of workers' reactions to clients, including reactions to physical characteristics and proxemic behaviors, the approaches described above, e.g., comembership enhancement, delineation of shared goals, should serve to enhance the worker's attraction to the client.

Finally, if there is reason for clients to assume that they and their workers have highly divergent beliefs, efforts might be made to find workers who more closely share the views of such clients, or to give clients an opportunity to select workers whom they feel would be more similar to themselves in orientation and lifestyle. While worker choice of client might also be indicated under certain circumstances, the danger of certain clients not being served makes this approach questionable. It should be explored within limits, however, and evaluated to determine if effective service is thereby enhanced.

A number of issues remain unresolved in the social psychological literature on the determinants of interpersonal attraction that are important to efforts to apply these findings to social work practice. Although some research has been conducted with subjects other than college students, and we have attempted to highlight such studies, the vast bulk of research is still based on work with college students. The generality of relationships obtained must be tested in other populations not only because of concern with misapplication of the findings to practical situations, but because of concern for the adequacy of conclusions. This admonition is particularly relevant to the area of interpersonal attraction. The use of college students or other young persons may have also contributed to the focusing of research on attraction in terms of friendship among peers.

Although the sphere of liking for peers is important, such a focus does leave unanswered many questions of interest to social psychologists as well as social workers, for example, the basis of interpersonal attraction in dyadic role relationships with unequal power, or with reciprocal role partners who are likely to be in conflict, such as the probation officer and the delinquent. Expansion of research on interpersonal attraction to include a variety of role relationships is essential for more effective social work practice, particularly in the stage of initiating a relationship with clients.

PART TWO

UNDERSTANDING SOCIAL FUNCTIONING

INTRODUCTION

The goal of the assessment phase in social work is to specify the nature of the problem or potential problem encountered by the client in ways that lead to the delineation of possible intervention approaches to problem reduction or resolution. To achieve this assessment goal the social worker must collect relevant information concerning the physical and social environment in which the client functions and also about personal factors that might contribute to the difficulty. In addition, the practitioner must judge the possible meaning of such data. As most social work models presume that the client's definition of the problem is critical to the agreement about intervention goals, the client is not seen only as provider of information, but also as an active participant in the evaluation of such data.

Various social work theorists analyze the assessment aspect of the social work intervention process as involving somewhat different tasks, but virtually all imply that there are both information-gathering and information-processing aspects in making an assessment. They further generally agree that information to be collected and assessed must include data on the interface between the individual and the social environment in which the individual functions.

Middleman and Goldberg (1974) refer to reaching for information, connecting discrete events, and recasting problems. Siporin (1975) discusses assessing the clients' personality, analyzing the situation, and evaluating the ecological gestalt of the case. Whittaker (1974) describes the worker's activities in the assessment and social diagnosis phase as collecting and assessing relevant information concerning the physical, psychological, and social functioning of the client, as well as collecting and assessing information about the environmental context. Pincus and Minahan's (1973) list of the major practice skill areas of the social worker includes assessing problems and collecting data by questions, observational techniques, and use of written material. Sundel, Radin, and Churchill (1974) describe the diagnostic procedure in group work as including worker and client activities aimed at collecting and synthesizing information that will enable them to set specifiable intervention goals.

Writers describing community organizing also identify an assessment phase. Spergel (1974) indicates the importance of facilitating the flow of information about community problems to the community group and of examining the nature of the problem as a prelude to community action. Cox and colleagues (1979) devised a schema for community problem solving that includes problem analysis based on a definition of the problem from perceptions by worker, client groups, and significant others and an understanding of the social context of the problem. R. Perlman and Gurin (1972) note that defining the problem includes eliciting and receiving information, grievances, and preferences from those experiencing the problem and from relevant others as well as analyzing, describing, and conceptualizing the problematic situation.

Several social psychological concepts are highly relevant to the goals of assessment in social work practice. The role theory framework can help the social worker determine the critical information to be collected and how to conceptualize the impact of the social context on personal functioning. Attribution theories, with their focus on factors that affect persons' perceptions of the causes of their own and others' behavior, can be a useful way to conceptualize problems clients may face in social functioning and to understand the process of assessment itself. Frames of reference for self-evaluation is the overarching label used to describe several social psychological concepts concerned with individuals' reference standards, such as social comparison and reference groups, relative deprivation, equity, and status consistency. These frameworks can be useful to the practitioner in understanding clients' sources of discontent. Each of the theoretical approaches will be summarized in one of the following chapters, and their utility to the assessment process will then be explicated.

CHAPTER TWO

A FRAMEWORK OF ROLE THEORY

The application of role concepts to social work practice is not a novel idea (H. H. Perlman 1957, 1968). Indeed, Strean has stated that " . . . the concept of social role has become part of the very web of social work thinking and literature" (1967:77). This is not surprising in view of the characterization of the role concept as linking the individual to the social structure (Linton 1936; Thomas and Biddle 1966); as we have seen, this linkage is a key orientation of social workers.

The basic assumption of role theorists is that the behavior of individuals in social situations can largely be understood in terms of society's expectations concerning what is appropriate behavior for specific position holders in specific situations. This perspective does not deny the influence of other factors on a person's response to a social stimulus, but the emphasis is on knowing an individual's place in the social structure in order to understand that person's behavior.

BASIC CONCEPTS

Although there are important differences in the ideas and terminology used by various theorists in explicating the general role perspective (see Biddle 1979; Thomas and Biddle 1966), we will not focus on those differences except to note the two basic points of view that exist. The interactionist orientation, as in the early work of G. H. Mead (1935) and more recently in the writings of R. H. Turner (1962) and Robert Bales (1966), emphasizes consistencies observed in the behavior of regularly interacting types of individuals and the process of change in these consistencies of behavior in informal groups and situations. Such roles include family scapegoat, harmonizer, and task specialist in small groups. The structural orientation to roles, exemplified by Linton's (1936) seminal work, focuses on the recognized social positions or social statuses in formal organizations and societies and the cultural perscriptions and proscriptions attached to them. Examples of such positions or statuses are client, employer, student, father, and social worker. While certain roles viewed from an interactionist perspective may refer to occupants of positions in social structures, this would not be the defining characteristic. Virtually anyone can play the role of scapegoat or harmonizer.

In discussing the role theory framework in this chapter we have adopted the structural approach because it more clearly links the individual to the larger environment. We will return to some of the interactionists' contributions later in the book, when discussing small group processes and group intervention strategies. The basic role concepts from the structural perspective are described below.

Individuals in society occupy certain *positions* for various lengths of time. A position is a unit that can be located in the social structure; for example, wife, client, teacher. This definition implies that positions exist only in relation to other positions. To define the unit labeled wife, one needs to recognize the complementary position of husband; students are linked to teachers; social workers to clients. This definition, by its focus on the social structure, implies that a position denotes a category of persons who are in some way recognized, and that the position exists regardless of the particular individual who occupies it at any given time.

Associated with each position, regardless of the occupant of the position, is a set of expectations concerning how the position-holder should behave, think, and feel. These expectations are called *role demands*. The term "demands" implies that other members of the system exert influence upon position-holders to meet these expectations, and will reward when role demands are met and punish when they are not.

Role demands are conceived of as external pressures upon individuals occupying any given position and are one source of influence on their behavior. In addition, each person occupying a position has a personal set of expectations about how someone in that position should behave, think, and feel. These expectations are called *role conceptions* and also influence the behavior of a person in a given position. Role demands and role conceptions must be differentiated from *role performance* or role enactment, which is the behavior of an occupant of a position. Role enactment may be a close approximation of the occupant's role demands, or a compromise between the two if there are differences.

Thus, a role analysis involves consideration of both the individual and the social system. Role theory attempts to explain how ideas that are part of the culture get "inside" the individual, that is, how external role demands become internalized as role condeptions, and how behavior is influenced by these external and internal factors. Figure 2.1 may clarify this point.

It should be noted that other more sociological theories explain how societal expectations get attached to particular positions and how the structures of social systems evolve, that is, how new positions get created, and how existing ones change or disappear. Such processes are not directly relevant to role theory. It is important, however, for anyone using role theory to recognize that neither the set of positions nor their associated role demands are unalterable. Position occupants can influence the role demands for that position, and social movements often have this as one of their goals. While the study of social movements per se is a sociological rather than social psychological matter, some issues relevant to them will be mentioned under the topic of the social system of role relationships later in this chapter.

Social positions, sometimes called statuses (Linton 1936) or offices (K. Davis 1966), can be differentiated into two main types in terms of how individuals acquire the right to occupy them. *Ascribed positions* are those occupied by virtue of some attribute individuals acquire simply by birth, such as sex, age, race, nationality, kinship. A person is not usually thought to have a choice about occupying such positions, but an individual may attempt to reject societal role demands associated with them or try to mask occupancy. *Achieved positions* are those entered by virtue of a particular person's accomplishments or efforts that are recognized by others; examples are president of an organization, college student, or social work client. It is possible to leave such positions: clients may cease coming to a social agency,

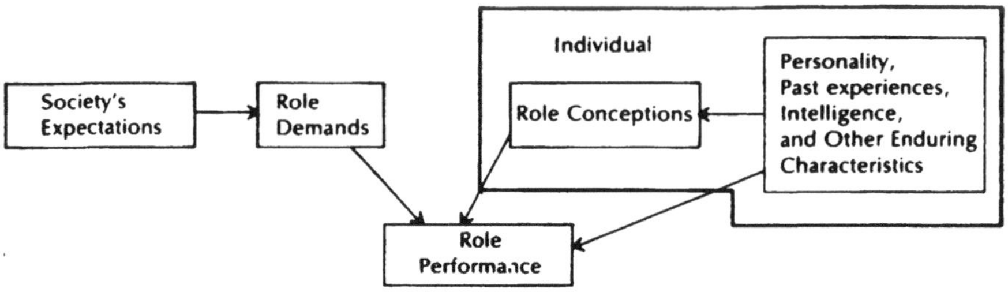

Figure 2.1. Basic Assumptions for a Framework of Role Theory

students may drop out of school. Some theorists (Spiegel 1960) have also delineated *adopted positions*, those in which individuals place themselves without having met the socially recognized criteria for occupancy. A member of a jury who calls the group to order and tries to set the rules for discussion without having been designated chairperson would fit this category. In adopting a role, the individual automatically assigns the complementary or reciprocal role to someone else (Spiegel 1960). For example, the person who adopts the role of leader assigns to others the role of follower. Here the critical issue is whether others will assume the positions which have been unofficially delegated to them in this fashion.

ROLE DEMANDS

Role demands may be communicated either formally or informally, but they share one attribute: they can be described independently of the person occupying the relevant position. Examples of formal communication of role demands are job descriptions in large organizations or written constitutions that specify the duties of officers. Even when such statements exist, they rarely, if ever, totally define the role demands. Further sources of expectations are the ideas held by persons in related positions (such as supervisors, group members) or persons in parallel positions (such as fellow employees or officers). Societal positions such as grandmother, bachelor, and retired person do not have formal statements describing acceptable and unacceptable attitudes, feelings, and behaviors for persons in such positions, but the mass media communicate such demands, as do persons in related and parallel positions.

Research investigators have succeeded in clarifying some of these informal role demands at any given period of time by questioning a great many people and soliciting their views. For example, adult expectations held about males and females were studied in this manner in the United States (Broverman et al. 1972) as were children's expectations in the United States and Britain (Best et al. 1977). Specific behaviors and attributes were associated with each sex, e.g., women were seen to be less competent and less logical than men; men were perceived as lacking interpersonal sensitivity and warmth in comparison with women. To obtain these sex-role stereotypes, as the authors labeled the list, the opinions of many groups differing in sex, age, marital status, and education were obtained. As societal expectations can change, sometimes rather rapidly as in the case of women's sex-role attitudes during the last twenty years (Iglehart 1979; Thornton and Freedman 1978), it is important to use such information from the appropriate historical period. Accurate knowledge of stereotypes is important because they can act as societal role demands that affect the role conceptions and role performance of persons occupying the positions to which stereotypes are attached. This has been shown in an experiment with female undergraduates (Zanna and Pack 1975) who were led to believe they would be meeting a male undergraduate as part of their participation in a study of impression formation. The information they received about the man was designed to portray him as either a highly or not at all desirable friend and as one whose views of the female role in society were either traditional or unconventional. The women then filled out questionnaires about themselves and took anagrams tests purported to measure intelligence, the results of which were to be given to the partner before they met. The findings showed quite clearly that when the man was desired as a friend, the woman presented herself as holding sex-role attitudes similar to that of the man and her performance on the anagrams task differed accordingly: women who expected to meet a man with unconventional female sex-role attitudes performed significantly better on this purported test of intelligence than did those who expected to meet a man with a traditional view of the female sex role. Women whose future partners were not desirable did not vary in their self-presentation or task behavior as a function of partners' sex-role attitudes. The authors concluded that sex differences in attitudes and behaviors can be accounted for in part by the expectations important others hold; in other words, role demands can affect role conceptions and role performance.

Knowledge of stereotypes held by social workers is also important because they can affect assessment, as Bronson (1977) has shown in a study in which half the members of the graduate faculty of a school of social work were given a female case and the other half a male case. In both cases all the symptoms were identical, yet the female was generally viewed as healthier.

Before proceeding further, a clarification of the term stereotype is necessary. A stereotype is a set of beliefs or disbeliefs about a group of people. These can include beliefs about behaviors, personality traits, achievements, skills, etc. These beliefs can be thought of as expectations about how members of the group in question should behave, think, or feel; thus thay can function as informal role demands, and communicate to members of the group in question how others expect them to behave. There has been a great deal of research showing that racial and ethnic stereotypes are common in American society (e.g.,

D. Katz and Braly 1933; H. J. Ehrlich and Van Tubergen 1971). Stereotypes associated with sex, race, and ethnicity can be identified both in individuals' judgments and in the mass media. A number of studies of contemporary books, for example, have shown that depictions of blacks and whites follow stereotypic traits (e.g., Waite 1968), as do characterizations of men and women (e.g., W. Martin 1971).

The existence of societal stereotypes associated with ascribed and achieved positions can be a source of social conflict and social change. Contemporary movements for racial, ethnic, and sexual equality, and for rights of the handicapped, involve, in part, a rejection by the occupants of particular positions of the role expectations attached to that status and insistence on changes in traditional role demands. Such concerted action has clearly brought about changes at larger societal levels, for example, on role performance of blacks and women as depicted in films and on television.

It is also important for social workers to recognize subcultural variations in role demands associated with major societal positions such as parent or spouse in order to understand the kinds of pressures faced by clients. Cross-cultural research can be especially helpful to social workers seeking to understand the role demands encountered by clients from different backgrounds. For example, Martinez (1977) provides valuable information concerning Chicanos' and Anglos' views of mothers and fathers, and Beckett (1976) reports the differing expectations placed on working wives among blacks and whites.

Structural properties of the system also influence the expectations associated with organizational and societal positions. The number of levels of supervision in a business, the social agency's operating hours, the size of a family, or the age distribution in a community all can affect the types of behavior expected of position occupants. Although not immutable, these variables are difficult to change and may create serious problems, for they may exert conflicting pressures about the same behavior. In some places and times the role demands attributed to structural factors are congruent, clear, and unambiguous, for example, in such centrally controlled societies as the People's Republic of China.

ROLE CONCEPTIONS

Although role demands do affect behavior, the power of these pressures has sometimes been exaggerated. The person occupying a position should not be assumed to know or accept all these demands. Faulty communication from persons in related positions can prevent knowledge of the expectations associated with a position. A faculty member may fail to mention some expectations for students. A husband may assume his wife knows that he expects her to quit work as soon as his earnings are sufficient to support them both, but he may not actually say so. The person occupying a position may be the source of difficulty in faulty communication rather than persons holding reciprocal roles. The student might not have been listening when the faculty member explained the course requirements. The wife's own interest in her career may be so strong that she failed to take seriously her husband's disparging remarks about men who could not support their families without their wives' salaries. Even then a position occupant knows what the role demands are, the actor's role conception may not directly mirror these demands. Other positions the person holds, or has previously held, may influence the role conception; personal characteristics, skills, and goals also are influential, as figure 2.1 indicates. For example, not all masters of social work or even graduates of the same school of social work have the same conception of the social worker role. The MSW whose mother was once a welfare recipient in Alabama is likely to have a very different conception from that of the MSW who is the daughter of a Boston psychiatrist.

ROLE PERFORMANCE

Role performance is similarly the joint result of social system pressures, or the role demands, and the specific actor's own contribution in the form of role conception and skills and personality. Past experiences may also exert an influence on a role behavior, for example, the client may not be on time for an appointment because of having been kept waiting in prior agency contacts. Much role performance is subject to some external surveillance that is aimed at fostering congruence between role demands and role performance by the use of sanctions of one type or another. Some writers claim that there is no such thing as personality predisposition and that our behavior reflects nothing more than an accumulation of behaviors associated with our past and present positions (Levinson 1959). This view is called the "sponge" perspective of role theory. Others, such as some psychoanalysts, believe that our current role performance is no more than a reflection of our personality. This is called the "mirage" perspective of role theory (Levinson 1959). Our own view is that both past and present positions and personality factors affect behavior. Thus, both social system variables and individual variables must be considered in trying to understand a client's behavior.

The classic study used to illustrate the impact of changes in positions upon attitudes was carried out in a home appliance factory, where workers' attitudes toward management and union were assessed at several points in time (S. Lieberman 1950). Although workers who later were promoted to foremen and those who later were elected shop stewards initially exhibited similar attitudes, after occupying these new positions their attitudes diverged and became more congruent with the differential role demands for their positions. Workers who became foremen changed toward more favorable management attitudes, and those who became shop stewards changed toward more favorable union attitudes. These differences became greater the longer the workers remained in these new positions. Furthermore, those foremen who later were demoted reverted to their initial attitude positions. Stewards who were not reelected did not, however, reduce their pro-union attitudes. The author concluded that by virtue of their position shifts from worker to foreman or shop steward the individuals took on the shared expectations about how foremen or stewards should think and feel and received sanctions for conformity to these expectations.

A more recent study has provided a rather dramatic demonstration of the power of the social system to affect behavior following position shifts that were only contrived and temporary (Zimbardo 1975). Paid volunteer male college students who were all strangers to one another, judged to be physically and mentally stable, and uninvolved in antisocial behavior, were randomly assigned to the position of prison guard or prisoner in a simulated prison situation. A temporary prison was designed with three cells to hold the eleven "prisoners" for twenty-four hours a day. The eleven "guards" worked three-man, eight-hour shifts at the prison and returned to their ordinary life activities at other times. The experimenters assumed the positions of prison superintendent and warden. There was minimal orientation to the role demands prior to the start of the experiment, but once it began, many aspects of real prison rules and regulations as well as physical arrangements were used. "Prisoners" were picked up at their homes by city policemen and booked, fingerprinted, etc., at the police station before being brought to the mock prison where they were incarcerated.

The experiment lasted only six days rather than the planned two weeks because the experimenters realized that the situation had become too real; the behavior of experimenters, guards, and prisoners had changed drastically and very disturbingly. Filmed records showed these behavior differences: "guards" issued commands, insulted prisoners, and verbally and physically abused them; "prisoners" generally emitted fewer behaviors than guards and those behaviors mainly involved asking questions and answering questions. These differences became stronger as the experiment continued. Each guard was observed to behave in an abusive and dehumanizing way toward the prisoners. All prisoners reported mental anguish; some became so anxious or depressed that they were released. Note that these dramatic differences occurred despite the random assignment of subjects to the positions of guard or prisoner, and despite the total lack of differences between guards and prisoners on various personality measures administered prior to the experiment.

There are many lessons to be learned from this experiment, but at present we cite only one of the experimenter's conclusions:

> Individuals carefully selected for their normality, sanity, and homogeneous personality traits were, in a matter of days, acting in ways that *out of this context* would be judged abnormal, insane, neurotic, psychopathic, and sadistic. Their behavior was role-dependent and not attributable to pre-existing traits. (Zimbardo 1975:47)

We are not, however, suggesting that research supports only the view that behavior is totally determined by role demands associated with positions. Even in the Zimbardo (1975) prison-simulation experiment, differences in the behavior of "prisoners" was in one instance related to personality: those prisoners with higher scores on a measure of authoritarianism were less likely to suffer severe psychological distress than were prisoners whose own personality was less authoritarian. Other experiments also show the dual impact of personality characteristics and position. Smelser (1961) had male undergraduates work together on a cooperative task in which one was assigned a dominant position and the other a submissive one. Men who were extremely high or low on a personality scale of dominance were assigned as partners. Those pairs in which the assigned positions agreed with the personality tendency of the persons involved performed better than did pairs in which personality and position were in conflict.

In sum, it is important to understand the differences among these role concepts—role demands, role conceptions, and role performance—even though they are interdependent. Each is a potential source of problems, and identification of the primary loci of role problems should be one goal of assessment. In attempting to assess the source of clients' problems so that appropriate interventions can be proposed, practitioners should determine the major positions held by the client, and the impact of such positions upon the problems under consideration. This point has been emphasized by H. H. Perlman (1968), who argues that problems associated with central or major life roles, such as those related to occupational positions, are the most likely reasons help is sought from social workers. Her recommendation is that the first diagnostic questions workers pose should concern what vital life roles are at the center of the problems confronting clients and what about these roles or their enactment are causing the problems. We concur in this recommendation.

THE SOCIAL SYSTEM OF ROLE RELATIONSHIPS

Having identified the basic role concepts from the point of view of a particular individual, we will now turn to the description of the social system of role relationships. It has previously been noted that positions exist in relation to other positions within a social structure. This has important implications for role analysis and its application to social work practice. It suggests the need to study the relationships among persons occupying different positions and further, that such an analysis can focus on any position within the system. The relational perspective indicates the dynamic aspect of role theory. Role demands, conceptions, and performance are not static; they are modified as a result of interaction. This is critical for designing social work interventions. The recognition that a role analysis can focus on any position in the relevant social system is also important to social workers. It suggests, for example, that when a child is brought to an agency by a parent because the child is disobedient, the worker might attempt to assess not only the role demands received by the child, the child's role conception, and the child's role performance, but also the role demands received by the parents and their role conceptions and performances. Similarly, a community worker seeking to assist community members who are experiencing problems in housing maintenance would want to analyze the situation from the perspective of both the tenants and the house manager.

The role episode. To describe the relationships among various positions in a social system a number of further concepts are useful. The person occupying any given position that is the focus of analysis or assessment at a given time is called the *focal person*. It is important to note that this term can be applied to any position in the system; it simply indicates the person who happens to be the focus of the analyst's attention. This person can experience role demands from occupants of all positions that are affected by the focal person's role performance. These related positions make up the *role set* for the focal person. For example, a husband's role set might consist of his wife, parents, in-laws, children, and friends. Each member of the role set be considered to be a *role sender* and the focal person can be considered to be a *role receiver*. The role senders hold role expectations for the focal person, communicate these expectations in some fashion, and attempt to influence the focal person's role behavior or performance. These communications and influence attempts are called the *sent role* and comprise part of the role demands. The focal person receives and interprets the sent role, and the resulting perception is called the *received role*.

The focal person's role performance is affected by the received role as well as by other factors to be discussed shortly. This role performance in turn affects future role expectations of the role senders, as they evaluate the similarity of the focal person's performance to their own role expectations for that person. Subsequently sent roles reflect the new expectations. Thus, cyclical relationships exist between role senders and role receivers: the expectations and behaviors of each influence the expectations and behaviors of the other, and the system is dynamic and changing. This interplay has been labeled a *role episode* by D. Katz and Kahn (1966) and is represented in figure 2.2 by the two boxes and by the solid arrows labeled 1 and 2.

Such role episodes occur in specific contexts. The context includes: 1) the social structure or organization within which the role set exists; 2) the personal attributes and personality of the role senders and the focal person; and 3) the interpersonal relationship that already exists between the actors (role senders and focal person) in the role episode. These are relatively stable characteristics of the context and influence all interactions between role senders and focal persons. The three relatively unchanging variables will be discussed in detail for they are often the root cause of role problems.

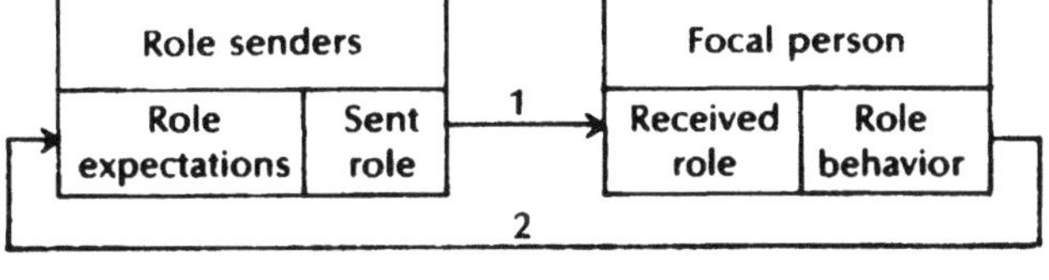

Figure 2.2. The Role Episode
A theoretical model of factors in the taking of organizational roles. (Adapted from D. Katz and Kahn 1966)

Organizational and social structural factors. These include any variables that describe the social system in which the role set occurs. For role sets in formal organizations, for example, such factors include the number of echelons in the institution and whether wages are received on an hourly rate or piece rate. For role sets linked to general societal positions, such as mother or father, social structural factors are also relevant. Some of these are comparable to the organizational factors noted above, such as the number and kinship relations of individuals residing in the household, or the age distribution of children. Others concern the broader social context within which the family exists; American spouses are likely to be living in dwellings designed to accomodate only the nuclear family—spouses and their children. Families of workers from certain industries such as the automobile industry, have to deal with night shifts and layoffs. The sent and received roles of black parents or of those from other groups facing discrimination are influenced by their limited access to adequate housing.

Other examples of social-structural factors associated with specific social classes or racial and ethnic groupings that influence role relationships can be cited. Of great importance to practitioners is the fact that the definition of the role set for family roles appears to differ for blacks and whites in American society. Billingsley (1968) has suggested that the household composition of family units is quite varied for American blacks, and that in addition to nuclear family households where one or both parents reside with their children, there are extended families, that is, nuclear families plus other relatives such as grandparents or siblings of parents, and augmented families, which include individuals unrelated by marriage or kinship. In a study of matched midwestern black and white families who had preschoolaged children, William and Mindel (1973) found that the black families not only were more likely to have other relatives residing with them, but more frequently visited relatives other than their own parents and were more likely to indicate that such relatives' advice was respected and important to them. Both these studies suggest that the role set for blacks' family or parental roles may be larger than that for whites. Similar extended family networks are found in Mexican-American families (Sotomayor 1971) and in those of American Indians (Red Horse 1980).

A major factor determining social class, the occupation of the father, has been found to influence role expectations. Pearlin and Kohn (1966) showed that in both the United States and Italy working-class fathers were more likely to value their children's conformity to external prescriptions than were middle-class fathers, who instead value their children's self-direction. Such differences in paternal values are undoubtedly reflected in the sent role of father to children.

We cannot review all the research on subcultural variations in values or behavioral patterns that may be linked to vital life roles, but we emphasize that social workers should be alert to the possible relevance of such variations to their assessment of client problems. In particular, they must be cautious about assuming that their own role conceptions are shared by clients from other subcultural groups, be they geographical, religious, racial, ethnic, or class-related. Instead, assessments of whether role problems exist must be founded on the clients' own role conceptions and on the role messages sent by members of their own role sets.

It should be noted that organizational and social structural factors are designated as stable because no single role episode can influence them. However, over a period of time, if many focal persons refuse to perform their roles in accordance with traditional role demands, such structural factors may be modified. For example, as more and more teachers go on strike, the power structure of the public school may change. The teachers union may become one of the legitimate authorities that defines role responsibilities that previously were solely within the jurisdiction of the school administration.

Assessment of structural and organizational factors' influence on role problems of clients is therefore important not only as a way to achieve better understanding of the clients' situation, but as a guide to the nature of relevant intervention. Support for concerted social action, rather than direct interpersonal intervention, may be the "treatment" of choice in some instances.

Personal attributes. Personality characteristics (motives, values, preferred defense mechanisms), skills, abilities, and any other variables (such as reinforcement hierarchy) that describe a given individual's tendency to behave in certain ways are included here. Various personal attributes of the focal person can evoke different expectations of the person by the role sender. The personal attributes of the focal person also affect both the way the sent role is experienced and the way the role is performed. For example, a hardworking physically handicapped student (the focal person) may not be expected by the teacher (the role sender) to get outdoor clothes on for recess as quickly as other classmates. But this role message may be experienced as discriminatory by the child who may strive hard to be no different from any other student in the class. His role performance may be one of defiance of the teacher's sent role—he may attempt to get his coat on before other students. This role behavior will undoubtedly influence future expectations of the teacher (arrow 2 on figure 2.2).

It should be noted that the personality of the role sender exerts as much influence on the role episode as does that of the focal person, for the personalities of role senders affect their expectations and their influence attempts (sent roles). For example, to return to the case of the teacher and the handicapped student, the teacher may be relatively rigid and insensitive. She may therefore miss the messages sent to her by the mildly disabled student about his desire to be treated like everyone else and hence repeatedly communicate reduced expectations for this youngster. The focal person, in this instance the boy with the handicap, is also influenced by the role sender's personality. If the youngster perceives his teacher to be unwilling to alter her sent role in response to his role behavior, it is unlikely that he will try to speed up his dressing. Instead, he is likely to withdraw.

Although the impact of the personal characteristics of the focal person and the role sender on their role behavior are important to recognize, it is equally true that persistent role behavior can affect the personality of the focal person. For example, consider a woman who starts to engage in assertive behavior in her new position as business executive. It is likely that she would be rewarded for this behavior on the job by achieving more success as a manager. According to learning theory, she would be expected to show an increase in assertive behavior, especially if she has a group of friends who also reinforce her new behavior. Cognitive social psychologists would also predict such a shift in future behavior based on changed self-perception (e.g., D. J. Bem 1967). Such tendencies to behave in certain ways are what we mean by personality characteristics, and, as the above example illustrates, these tendencies can be influenced by alterations or new role behavior over an extended period of time.

One personal characteristic that is frequently related to role performance is self-confidence. Recent research indicates that performance in certain roles may have differential impact on individuals' self-conceptions depending on their stage of life. In a national sample study of young men followed from the time they were in the tenth grade until they were approximately twenty-three years old, successful academic performance was associated with high self-esteem while the boys were in high school, when the student role was a central aspect of life (Bachman and O'Malley 1977). However, during early adulthood, when the job role was presumably central, a high-status job was associated with high self-esteem. These results suggest that one focus of assessment should be on performance in central life roles; intervention aimed at enhancing such performance can be an effective strategy for reducing the self-doubts that may bring clients to social work agencies.

Interpersonal factors. These factors may influence the interaction between role senders and receivers. They include such things as the degree of prior positive feelings that have been experienced or expressed between a role sender and the focal person, how much prior support, trust, suspicion, etc. The effects of these factors are similar to those of the personal attributes. They affect the role sender's expectations for the focal person and the kinds of messages sent to the focal person, and the focal person's interpretations of the sent role and role behaviors. Both the sent role of the role sender and the role behavior of the focal person in turn affect the characteristics of the interpersonal relations; e.g., a sudden shift in a person's tendency to comply with a given role sender's requests could change the sender's liking for the focal person. Thus, when the interpersonal context of a role relationship is determined to be a contributor to a client's role problems, one goal of intervention may be to modify those factors.

A number of issues raised by this type of analysis lead naturally into discussions of role problems. For example, the concept of a role set, all of whose members send role messages to the focal person, leads to questions about the agreement among role senders and the effects of varying degrees of agreement on the focal person. The entire conceptualization of the role episode leads to questions about the effects of varying degrees of congruence between personal attributes of the focal person and the sent role. For example, what ensues when the focal person gets great satisfaction from being domineering and the sent role indicates that compliance with the role sender is expected?

ROLE CONFLICTS

Various terms have been used to describe role problems. Thomas (1967a) refers to lack of role synchronization; Merton (1966) discusses lack of articulation among members of role sets; Spiegel (1960) employs the phrase of disequilibrium and lack of complementarity in roles. All of these phrases imply that there is imperfect meshing of reciprocal roles, that is, between role senders and role recipients or role senders and focal persons. These role problems can be called *role sender/focal person conflict*. Not all role problems involve two individuals, however. A person may hold mutually incompatible role conceptions for a given position or an individual's role conceptions for two or more mutually held positions may be in conflict. A person's role conceptions may not mesh with personal attributes, a situation that has been described as a lack of person-role congruence (Veroff and Feld 1970). Using the terminology of Yinger (1965), we shall refer to such conflicts as *internal role conflicts.*

A third type of role problem was labeled by Yinger as *external role conflict.* In this situation, the focal person is confronted with incompatible expectations from two or more role senders. We shall also include in this category incompatible role demands from a single role sender. Thus, we can describe three types of role conflicts, or situations in which an individual is faced with incompatible role expectations: 1) role sender/focal person conflicts; 2) internal role conflicts; 3) external role conflicts.

It is also important to note that not all role problems involve contradictory expectations; role problems may also stem from deficiencies, for example, of knowledge, funds, or ability. Role deficiencies refer to the absence of personal or social system resources or attributes that are necessary for adequate role performance or position attainment. Either source of role problems, conflict or deficiency, can lead to role strain, which refers to felt or experienced discomfort in filling a role. Role strain may also be reflected in physiological symptoms such as increased blood pressure (French and Caplan 1973). The social worker who is faced with a client experiencing role strain is more likely to be able to suggest an effective intervention if the type of role problems that may be causing the strain are determined. Before discussing the three types of role conflict in detail, it is necessary to consider whether role problems are related primarily to a single position that an individual holds or to difficulties in the relationships between simultaneously occupied positions. Everyone occupies several major life positions and these positions can be mutually compatible or conflictual, for example, parental and occupational roles of women. Because the issue of whether one or more positions of the focal person are involved in role problems is so important in analyzing the root of role conflict, number of positions involved is used in defining the dimension of "Type of Conflict" in both table 2.1 and in the discussion to follow.

CONFLICTS INTERNAL TO THE FOCAL PERSON

This type of conflict refers to mutually incompatible role demands or role concepts held by one person for himself or herself. It is one type of intrasender conflict. (There is another type which will be discussed at a later point.) Internal role conflicts may take various forms. One common source of intrasender conflict is the focal person's own role conceptions. Modern society typically segments the job and family role conceptions of men, but unusual events may cause incompatibility to arise (table 2.1: B1). This is dramatically illustrated by the research of Killian (1965), who interviewed residents of towns struck

Table 2.1.
Sources of Role Conflict

SOURCE OF CONFLICT	*TYPE OF CONFLICT*	
	Intraposition	*Interposition*
Internal to Focal Person	A1. Among components of role conceptions	B1. Role conceptions for one position vs. role conceptions in another position
	A2. Role conceptions vs. role performance	B2. Role conceptions for one position vs. role performance in another position
	A3. Personal attributes vs. role conceptions or role performance (alienation)	B3. Personal attribute required for one position vs. role conceptions or role performance for another position
External to Focal Person	C1. Among several role demands of one role sender	D1. Among several demands of one role sender who occupies two positions that are reciprocal to two positions occupied by focal person
	C2. Role demands of one role sender vs. role demands of another role sender	D2. Role demands of one role sender occupying position reciprocal to focal person vs. role demands of another role sender occupying a different reciprocal position to focal person

Continued

Table 2.1. *(Continued)*

SOURCE OF CONFLICT	TYPE OF CONFLICT	
	Intraposition	*Interposition*
Role Sender/Focal Person	E1. Role sender does not acknowledge focal person's right to occupy position	F1. Role sender does not acknowledge focal person's right to occupy two positions simultaneously
	E2. Role demands from role sender vs. role conceptions of focal person	
	E3. Role demands from role sender vs. personal attributes of focal person	
	E4. Role demands from role sender vs. role performance of focal person	
	E5. Role sender's criteria for evaluating performance of focal person vs. focal person's criteria	

by physical disasters (e.g., explosive fires, floods). Men whose jobs would ordinarily have oriented them to community responsibilities, such as policemen and firemen, reported feeling severe conflict between these job role conceptions and family obligations during the disaster. Conflict of this type can be associated with poor performance in one or more of the positions involved. This was shown in a study of 200 air-force officers who were also faculty members at staff schools (Getzels and Guba 1954). The variations in the extent to which these men perceived their positions as officers and as teachers to be in conflict was associated with ratings by others of how effective they were as teachers in the classroom.

An individual's role conceptions concerning a single position may also be the source of internal role conflict (table 2.1:A1). Role conceptions for major life positions are complex and involve several components that may be incompatible. An elementary schoolteacher's conception of her role may include both warmth and acceptance of children and the maintenance of firm classroom discipline, and these components may sometimes clash.

Person-role conflict is a term that has been used to refer to internal role conflicts that stem from a clash between personal attributes of the focal person and that individual's role conceptions or role performance (A3). Personal attributes include those characteristics of individuals that are relatively stable, or hard to change. Such areas as intellectual level, motives, personality traits, preferred defense mechanisms, basic values, are all covered by this term.

Personal attributes can conflict with one's own role conceptions. College-educated persons hold marital role conceptions that are likely to include the recognition of the legitimacy of joint decision making and mutual influence of husband and wife. In a national study of Americans (Veroff and Feld 1970), college-educated men with strong motivation to avoid feelings of powerlessness expressed greater marital discontent than those for whom this type of motivation was not particularly relevant. This suggests that the personal motivational orientation of some of these men was in conflict with their marital role conceptions (table 2.1:A3). A similar conclusion was drawn from a study of male undergraduates at a prestigious liberal arts college (Komarovsky 1973). Men who scored low on personality scales of self-confidence and dominance and whose conception of the male role involved being domineering and decisive evidenced role strain.

Role behaviors may also conflict with personal attributes (A3). When individuals' own views of how they are behaving contradict their personal values, the situation is labeled alienation—the feeling that one's own behavior is not really part of oneself. Personal attributes essential in one position may conflict with an individual's conception of a second role (B3). Such conflicts may present themselves to a woman executive whose job requires that she behave in hard and driving ways. These traits are likely to be perceived as incompatible with demands for the maternal role and may lead to self-doubts about maternal role performance (Darley 1976). It is also possible for an individual's role performance in one role to be incompatible with his or her role conception of a second role (B2). For example, the highly competitive businessman who is harsh on those who owe him money may find his performance in his occupational role conflicting with that in his religious role, which calls for sympathetic helping of the weak and the needy.

Assessment of person-role conflict can direct practitioners to several types of intervention strategies. Personal attributes, although relatively enduring, may be modified to be congruent with role demands or conception: assertiveness training may be useful. Role demands or conceptions may be revised: a client might be encouraged to discuss job requirements with a supervisor. Where neither person nor role demands or conceptions appear amenable to change, position shifts may be indicated: a client might be aided in finding a new job more congruent with personal motives or skills.

CONFLICTS EXTERNAL TO THE FOCAL PERSON

Some conflicts external to the focal person are intrasender, or within one person. The father who expects his son to be both assertive and compliant is an instance of intrasender conflict associated with a single position (C1). As certain individuals are members of overlapping role sets for a given focal person, there can be intrasender conflict concerning two or more positions (D1). A father and son who work in the same business enterprise may confront this problem if, for example, the father's view of his son's obligations to be loving and respectful of his father conflicts with his role demands to his staff to present their own views forcefully and without regard for agreement with his own views.

Conflict external to the focal person can also be intersender, or located between two individuals. Such intersender conflict refers to mutually incompatible expectations from two or more role senders. This may involve just one position of the focal person (C2), that of wife for example, in which the husband may make demands for housewifely tasks at home, whereas friends may expect participation in local civic affairs as part of one's wifely duties. There are a variety of reasons for expecting that women's family roles (as spouse and mother) may be common sources of such problems. For example, young, college-educated American men and women differ in their conceptions of the proper role for women, with a higher proportion of women than men undergraduates in 1973 expressing modern views of the female role (Orcutt 1975). This suggests that young women are likely to experience intersender conflict, between female friends and spouse, concerning their marital and parental roles.

Certain job roles may also be more likely to elicit intersender conflict. W. F. Whyte's (1948) classic study of waitresses pointed to the role strains they typically experience because they are required to relate to a large variety of complementary positions, including other waitresses, supervisors, pantry workers, bartenders, and customers. The key aspect relevant to identifying the kinds of positions likely to elicit external intersender role conflicts appears to be the diversity of positions included in the role set. This was demonstrated in a national study of male and female employees (Snoek 1966), in which the greater the number of different types of positions a person's job required contact with, the greater was the reported job role strain. This was true even when other job and person characteristics typically associated with job role strain were controlled (e.g., size of organization, whether the person had supervisory responsibility, sex, education level).

External intersender conflict may also involve multiple positions of the focal person (D2); for example a man's wife may make demands for her husband's participation in family leisure activities that clash with his mother's demands for financial support from her son. One critical implication of the identification of the source of an important role problem as external to the focal person is that intervention goals may need to be focused on someone besides the client. Such interventions may involve the social worker directly with the significant other or with the client in order to enhance the client's ability to influence the significant other's sent-role demands.

CONFLICTS BETWEEN ROLE SENDERS AND FOCAL PERSON

The most basic role conflict between a focal person and role sender concerns a person's right to occupy a given position (E1). This is termed allocative discrepancy by Spiegel (1960). There is rarely any conflict about ascribed positions, those that are the result of one's physical characteristics, blood relationships, or factors related to "the accident of birth" such as illegitimacy or family size. But, when conflicts do exist about the occupancy of such positions, they are considered serious, and society typically requires formal legal action to resolve them. Courts decide on matters of parental rights, paternity, or inheritance.

Allocative discrepancy conflicts are more common in achieved positions. These can stem from two sources: questions about legitimacy of entrance into the position or about adequacy of role performance to maintain the position. A tenant's organization may refuse to deal with a community organizer who does not have the right credentials for working in that community, by virtue of lack of past association with the neighborhood, lack of support from key community leaders, etc. A social worker in protective services may be confronted by a mother who still desires to care for her child although the child was made a ward of the court because the mother was adjudged unfit. In these instances the legitimacy of occupying a given position and carrying out the obligations and receiving the privileges associated with it can be identified as key aspects of the problem by the social worker.

Allocative discrepancy conflicts concerning occupancy of two positions by one individual, that is, about the right to occupy a position when another one is already occupied, are also common. (F1) When these concern a clash between ascribed and achieved positions, we speak of discrimination, as when sex, race, age, ethnicity, etc., are used to prevent entry into certain jobs. The same college application sent to various universities resulted in more admissions when the applicant's name was that of a male rather than a female (Clifford and Walster 1972). In this instance persons monitoring entrance into achieved positions acted as if the holding of such positions was more compatible with the ascribed position of male rather than female. The female applicants saw no conflict. Some individuals occupying low-prestige ascribed positions may themselves view the attainment of certain achieved positions as incompatible with their sex, race, or ethnic status, and limit their aspirations, whereas others see no conflict in the situation. In an important study of students at ten traditionally black colleges in the South during the period from 1964 to 1970 (P. Gurin and Epps 1975), the several colleges were shown to vary in the degree to which attendance at them encouraged students to revise their occupational aspirations in the direction of jobs not traditionally held by blacks in the United States. The unfortunate frequency in our society of conflict concerning the right to occupy some achieved positions while occupying other ascribed positions should alert social workers to consider this source of role problems with clients whose ascribed status is likely to lead to such problems. Even our Constitution creates such an obstacle—no one can become president of the United States who was not born in this country.

There can also be allocative conflict concerning the right to occupy some achieved positions while simultaneously holding other achieved positions (F1). Such discrepancies are often termed conflicts of interest. Social work practitioners may encounter such conflicts when memberships in advisory borads are considered or reviewed. Many feel that the individual who can gain finacially by some decisions of the board should not be a member. For example, in the view of some (but not all) officials, the owner of a parcel of land being considered for park development should not be appointed to a city recreation board.

Identification of allocative discrepancy problems is valuable because it can alert social workers to the need to clarify the entry requirements for the position in question as well as the criteria of adequate performance to retain the position. Intervention can then focus on changes in definition of these entry or performance criteria or on modification of the skills, knowledge, etc., to meet criteria.

If we consider that focal persons are their own role senders, we can see that one form of intersender conflict can occur when a person's own role conception or role performance contradicts the demands of other role senders. A woman's conception of her wifely role may not agree with that of her husband (E2). The president of a neighborhood action group may speak out publicly about the organization's view without specific authority from the group and thereby come into conflict with the group's demands for the president's role (E4).

Personal attributes may conflict with demands from role senders (E3) because the role prevents the person from using capacities or satisfying goals. In a national study of Americans (Veroff and Feld 1970), young men who were strongly motivated to avoid feelings of powerlessness and who held jobs where they were closely supervised expressed greater job dissatisfaction than did those in jobs with less supervision. Role demands may also exceed personal attributes and thereby cause strain, as was shown in a national study of American high-school-aged boys (French, Rodgers, and Cobb 1974). When the required intellectual level as reported by teachers in particular schools exceeded the boys measured intelligence, the boys reported lower self-esteem and a higher subjective probability of dropping out of school than when the teachers' demands and boys' achievements were congruent.

The criteria the focal person and the role sender use for evaluating the focal person's role performance can also be in conflict (E5). A father may view his use of corporal punishment as appropriate to the disciplinary and socialization aspects of his role, whereas his wife may reject this type of role performance and consider him an inadequate father (Nye 1976).

The identification of role conflict between the focal person and one or more role senders as central to the reason a client seeks help, like the identification of conflict external to the focal person, raises the issue of whether the social worker's intervention plan should involve someone besides or in addition to the initial client. Further, the nature of the role sender/focal person conflict identified can guide the focus of the intervention, along the lines of clarifying criteria for position occupancy for example, or of emphasizing increasing congruence between role conceptions and role demands.

To conclude the discussion of role conflict, we propose that by identifying the specific nature of the role conflicts that may be confronting clients the worker can be aided enormously in reaching agreements with the clients about appropriate intervention goals and strategies, as Atherton, Mitchell, and Schein (1971) and Chescheir (1979) have recently suggested. For this type of assessment can reveal whether a role conflict is enmeshed in the client's problem, and if so, can delineate the specific nature of the conflict, that is the type of conflict, and the positions and role senders relevant to the problem.

ROLE DEFICIENCIES

Role problems can also occur when there are no contradictions among expectations, but where personal or systemic deficiencies are the source. The deficiency may be of several types. There may be a deficiency in knowledge about a position held, a deficiency in clarity of role demands, a deficiency in skill, resources, time, or energy required by a role, or a general deficiency in commitment to a position. Finally, there may be a deficiency in the number of roles one has to enact.

ABSENCE OR LOSS OF A POSITION

To start with the last term mentioned, the absence or loss of a position can be the source of role problems. This state can be labeled role underload (Harrison 1976). Persons who retire from their jobs lose not only the obligations that were part of job demands, but the satisfactions that resulted from the social contact linked to the job role and the positive evaluations accorded jobholders in our society (Cavan 1962). The meaning of work and the deleterious effects of its absence is similar in the unemployed (Kaplan and Tausky 1974). Loss of a valued position can result in self-doubts about one's own adequacy, as well as similar judgments from others. In addition, the loss of one position may have a mushrooming effect and remove access to other positions. This often happens in cases of divorce, where friendship ties that were linked to the marital couple disappear. Widowhood can have the same result (Abrahams 1972; Lopata 1971), as can dropping out of school. The sight of dropouts "hanging around" the school they left is a familiar one to secondary-school educators.

Failure to enter certain positions can be as troublesome for the individual as loss of a position. Young men and women who have never married are less satisfied with most aspects of their lives, including their jobs, than are married persons of the same age (A. Campbell, Converse, and Rodgers 1976). The person who occupies few of the major life positions—worker, spouse, parent, friend—is likely to have relatively few sources of satisfaction. Assessment of a deficiency in positions should lead the social worker to other questions: What are the reasons for a client's being in such situations? Are these conditions amenable to change? Can other kinds of positions provide the satisfactions of those lost or absent?

Role underload can also be found when the full capacities of the individual are untapped in the major roles he or she plays. The aeronautical engineer who can find a job only as a clerk would experience role underload, as would the woman who majored in English literature in college but is working as a typist. These are examples of qualitative underload. Quantitative underload would be found when the role player has ample time and few demands made upon that time; e.g., the mother in the empty nest, the salesperson in the empty store.

In all instances of role underload the focal person is most likely suffering from an inadequate number of role demands, a state which Durkheim (1951) referred to as anomie, or normlessness. As Durkheim well illustrated, such a condition can lead to severe depression and even to suicide.

LACK OF KNOWLEDGE

Lack of knowledge about what position(s) a person occupies will interfere with interpersonal relations, as will casting a person into an inappropriate position (Steiner 1967). Social relations proceed more smoothly if persons locate themselves and others appropriately in the social system (Sarbin and Allen 1968). Various social devices are used to identify relevant positions. Uniforms, badges of offices, the use of formal titles in introductions are the most obvious devices used to label a person's relevant position. More subtle symbols are also used: style of dress, manner of speech, posture, gestures can all identify positions. Part of our socialization into a given society or subgroup involves the learning of cues that identify position holders, and one of the common problems in entering cultures or subcultures other than one's own is the recognition of these more subtle identifiers of positions. Social workers should be alert to this potential problem when working with clients who themselves need to deal with more than one set of subcultures—minority-group members—or clients from a different ethnic or racial group from their own. In both these circumstances increased knowledge about the signs needed to identify the positions of members of other subcultural groups could enhance effective functioning.

Lack of knowledge about what positions are in the role set may result in an individual ignoring role demands from a relevant other. This is probably a more common problem for new occupants of a position. Part of the socialization into a position involves learning who the relevant role senders are, as well as the nature of their role demands, and social workers assisting clients to enter new positions especially need to be alert to this potential source of role problems. For example, those becoming foster parents for the first time may not know that the child's natural parents, siblings, teacher, and school friends may all be affected by the way the foster parent carries out that role and therefore may attempt to influence that role performance either directly or via the foster child. Clearly the worker needs to be concerned about the implications of a lack of positional awareness (Hunt 1967) and plan an intervention to overcome this knowledge deficiency.

Lack of knowledge about role demands is another important type of deficiency. Such deficiencies can often be a result of dissimilarity between the role demands for consecutive positions that a person holds. This condition has been labeled role discontinuity. More generally lack of knowledge about role demands is due to a lack of adequate socialization into the role. A child from a foreign land who enters a U.S. school for the first time would be expected to encounter such problems. New workers are often formally oriented to their jobs to alleviate this problem, but such orientations may be inadequate. This is another area in which subcultural differences can lead to role problems.

New immigrants to Israel from other Middle Eastern areas, for example, have been found to write letters appealing customs decisions that include personalistic rationales that bureaucratically oriented customs officers consider irrelevant to the letter-writer's role (Danet and Gurevitch 1977). Similarly, lower-class clients of bureaucracies in the United States may be less aware of the rules governing bureaucratic encounters and hence more likely to have their behavior judged inappropriate (Sjoberg, Brymer, and Farris 1966). In such situations the social worker's intervention plan may be largely educational, for example, foreign or minority children can be assisted to learn the role demands for pupils in suburban schools and school personnel can be made aware of the children's lack of knowledge of what is expected in this context.

At times the worker may attempt to have some school procedures modified if they conflict with the value system of the children's culture. For example, until recently it was public school practice in the Southwest to punish children for speaking Spanish in school. Such a rule clearly violated the values of Mexican-American families. In that instance, social workers involved in the school system could have made efforts to modify the educational system's practices rather than to educate the Mexican-American child never to speak Spanish when on school property.

LACK OF CLARITY

Lack of clarity about the expectations of role senders or role ambiguity has been identified as another significant source of role strain. The problem in such circumstances is not that expectations are contradictory, but rather that they are too vague to permit the focal person to feel adequate in role performance. Ambiguity can occur either with respect to role demands or to the criteria for evaluation of role performance. Rossi (1968) has characterized the parental role in contemporary American society as lacking guidelines for determining successful performance.

A number of studies have shown that workers who perceive high degrees of role ambiguity in their jobs' demands show evidence of role strain. An intensive interview study of over fifty supervisory personnel in seven different business and industrial settings found that low evaluations of job clarity and uncertainty about expectations from others were significantly associated with tension and job dissatisfaction (Kahn et al. 1964). Nurses in community hospitals (Lyons 1971), nurses' aides in a university hospital (Brief and Aldag 1976), and military and civilian employees at military bases (T. W. Johnson and Graen 1973) were found to be more likely to leave their jobs voluntarily when job role ambiguity was at high levels.

On the other hand, there is some evidence that role ambiguity can facilitate adequate role performance. This seems to occur when ambiguity in role demands can be used to adapt the demands to one's own role conceptions or personal attributes; role ambiguity can then provide flexibility (Preiss and Ehrlich 1966). An example of such flexibility is seen in the role of the school social worker (Radin 1975). Thus, role ambiguity does not always cause problems; certain interventions may focus on helping clients use their role ambiguity to meet their own desires.

Our illustrations of role ambiguity have so far concerned only a single position. It is also possible for role problems to result from a lack of clarity about the priority of the role demands when multiple positions are held by a single person. Fortunately there are often metarules, or rules about rules, that govern the relationships among multiple positions held by one individual. The traditional view of women's marital and job roles is clear about the priorities between these positions: in cases of conflicting expectations, marital role demands are to take precedence. With contemporary shifts in views about the centrality of jobs and marriage to women, such situations may now lack clear societal guidelines. Is a married woman expected to leave a good job to move to another city so that her husband can take a new job there? Or is the husband expected to refuse the new job unless his wife can also get a good job in the new location? It has been suggested that ambiguity about how to articulate women's job and family roles helps explain both women's avoidance of occupations that require high degrees of commitment, and selective discrimination against women's entry into such positions (Coser and Rokoff 1973). In a similar vein, it has been proposed that the lack of clear prescriptions about priorities when family and job roles are held is one of the critical dilemmas for both husbands and wives in dual career families (R. Rapoport and Rapoport 1969). But this problem may not be as widespread as observers of professional and college-educated women suggest. In a recent representative national sample of Americans most young married women (ages eighteen through twenty-nine) employed outside the home reported that their job was of less importance to them than their housework (A. Campbell, Converse, and Rodgers 1976). Thus, although social workers should be aware of this potential source of role ambiguity in modern American society, they should be cautious in inferring its occurrence without objective evidence.

When organizational or societal role demands are ambiguous, there is often a greater need for negotiations among members of a role set to define role expectations. The facilitation of this negotiation process may be the focus of social work intervention when an assessment establishes role ambiguity as a role problem. Aldous (1974) has identified this activity as important for family practitioners because of contemporary shifts in age and gender roles. She described the process as facilitating role making, by which she means clarifying role demands in newly emerging positions.

LACK OF SKILLS

Lack of skills for adequate role performance may stem from similar socialization deficiencies or role transition problems, as lack of knowledge about role demands. For example, with decreasing family size fewer people have the experience of caring for younger brothers or sisters or of observing others do so. Thus, there is likely to be insufficient anticipatory socialization for parental role performance. Anticipatory socialization refers to the acquisition of behaviors, ideas, and feelings appropriate to positions in which persons are not currently occupants but to which they aspire or are about to move (Merton 1966). This requires contact either directly or symbolically with persons already in those new positions, and an opportunity to practice relevant behaviors. Because many youngsters are unable to observe parents caring for young infants in their own families or those of relatives or friends and there are few formal courses in this area, they are likely to have a deficit in child care skills.

It is sometimes difficult to distinguish between role problems due to a deficiency in skills to carry out role demands and a lack of fit between personal attributes or capacities and role demands. Some conceptualizations of human behavior, for example, would consider the tendency to behave in authoritative ways as characterizing a personality trait of dominance. Others would describe these behaviors as learned skills. We are not attempting to propose a particular view of personality traits but suggest that regardless of the particular theoretical bias of the social worker, some characteristics of individuals are more easily learned than others. When an assessment results in the identification of a deficiency in an easily modified area, such as knowledge of infant care, the implication is that intervention be directed to training. When an assessment results in the identification of a deficiency in a more stable aspect of human functioning, intellectual capacity, for example, training may not be the most appropriate intervention; instead, modification of role demands or a shift in position may be more appropriate.

LACK OF FACILITIES OR RESOURCES

Lack of facilities or resources for adequate role performance refers to deficiency in material resources, including money, goods, or tools. This is obviously a frequent source of role problems for social work clients; a child who goes to school hungry will probably not perform adequately as a student; a single mother whose apartment doesn't have adequate heat can't care properly for her child. Sometimes the absence of resources is not such an obvious source of role problems. The fact that there is no room large enough for cooperative child care may discourage neighbors from dealing with their concerns about neighborhood safety. People may also be considered resources necessary for role performance, and insufficient access to certain people can result in role problems. The scarcity of physicians in certain areas is an illustration; parents in such areas cannot meet role requirements for seeing to the health of their children. An asymmetrical sex ratio on college campuses makes it more difficult for the overrepresented sex to engage in role-appropriate heterosexual activities (Komarovsky 1973). In all these instances intervention efforts should be aimed at increasing resource availability.

LACK OF TIME OR ENERGY

Lack of time or energy to fill all the role demands one faces is the familiar situation known as quantitative role overload. A wide variety of signs of strain, both psychological (job dissatisfaction, low self-esteem) and physiological (high cholesterol or heart rate, increased smoking), have been shown to be associated with quantitative role overload on the job (French and Caplan 1973). Time demands for one position can also interfere with adequate role performance in another position. In a British study (Willmott 1971), men reported major time conflicts between job and family demands. Factory workers complained that long hours and extra shifts left them with insufficient time to carry out family responsibilities. Senior managers indicated that their energies were still directed to job pressures and worries at home and that this interfered with their interpersonal attentiveness to their families. Problems may also involve the scheduling of time. In a study of men employed in two large manufacturing plants with both fixed and rotating shifts, workers on the fixed daytime shift experienced few problems performing nonjob roles. Men on the afternoon shift reported difficulties in their paternal roles because they rarely saw their children; those on the night shift described problems in the sexual aspect of their marital roles. Men on rotating shifts had fewer friends than did those on any shift (Mott et al. 1965).

The role overload concept may be particularly important for social workers whose clients are impoverished. A. Smith (1972), in reviewing the Work Incentive (WIN) program designed to assist mothers receiving aid to families of dependent children to find and keep employment, concluded that one of the key areas for future research was the analysis of overload experienced and how it could be reduced. As she pointed out, WIN participants hold multiple positions—mother, housekeeper, welfare client—and participation in the WIN program adds a further one, that of trainee or employee. The lack of money available to these women meant that they often must spend a great deal of time carrying out their roles: using health clinics can involve waiting for service, public transportation can be very slow, hours can be spent in waiting rooms at a department of social services. This analysis applies to many social work clients, not just those involved in the WIN program.

Deficiencies in energy to carry out role demands may stem from the state of the actor rather than from the nature of demands. Illness or depression, for example, may make it difficult for a mother to carry out her maternal role as she had done without problems at other points in her life.

In all these instances an assessment that role overload is an important aspect of client's problems would suggest a number of interventions to reduce time requirements. For example, the worker could try to improve the client's efficiency in fulfilling the role demands, reduce role demands by shifting some obligations to other members of the role set, or improve the client's resources to carry out role demands.

LACK OF COMMITMENT

A number of theorists (Fried 1978; Haavio-Mannila 1971; Hunt 1967; Merton 1966; Nye 1976; H. H. Perlman 1968) have discussed the fact that people identify differentially with the various roles they enact. Nye focused on the intrinsic gratification obtained from performance of certain roles. Fried emphasized the impact of macro-level forces on defining priorities attached to various roles; others discussed the emotional involvement displayed in regard to some roles. It is clear that some positions are more central to our lives than others. Problems arise, however, when one partner in a reciprocal relationship is highly committed to the role while the other individual is not. Thibaut and Kelley (1959) discuss this phenomenon in relation to the power held by the partner who is least committed to a relationship since that individual is free to leave at any time.

Although a low level of identification with a single position may not be a problem to the person involved, it can be a source of difficulty to members of the role set. Thus, many secondary school teachers are deeply concerned about the lack of commitment of a student to the role of learner. Officers in the Armed Forces are very sensitive to low morale in soldiers; managers spend much time maintaining the commitment of their salespersons to the product involved. Thus from the point of view of the role senders, if not that of the focal persons themselves, a deficiency in commitment to a role is indeed a problem that must be handled.

RESPONSES TO ROLE PROBLEMS

As has been suggested above, the existence of role conflicts or deficiencies tends to produce role strain, that is, felt difficulty in fulfilling role obligations (Goode 1960). The concept of role strain is the psychological aspect of a role perspective; it refers to the individual's reaction to role problems. Although role problems do not always elicit role strain, it is likely that either the client or some member of the client's role set has experienced role strain, and that this is one reason the social worker and client are in contact. A man may visit a vocational rehabilitation agency because he experiences anxiety on his job. A child may be referred to a mental health clinic because the teacher is frustrated in trying to get the child to carry out school assignments. A group of neighbors may be willing to meet with a community organizer because they feel distressed by their lack of success at having a traffic light installed on a busy intersection.

The degree of role strain experienced is affected by a number of factors. Probably most important is the salience of the position or positions in which role conflicts or deficiencies exist (Fried 1978; Haavio-Mannila 1971). By salience is meant the prominence or importance of the position in the person's life situation, or the amount of emotional involvement in the position (Hunt 1967). Conflicts or deficiencies in family roles, for example, would be expected to produce more role strain than those in leisure roles. Intersender role conflict with members of the role set who are in frequent face-to-face contact with the focal person tend to cause more strain than conflict with role set members who rarely see the focal person (Merton 1957b; Walsh 1975). The degree to which conflicting role demands or role conceptions concern obligatory rather than discretionary aspects of a role also affects role strain (Getzels and Guba 1954; Komarovsky 1973).

Spiegel (1960) has suggested that responses to role problems can generally be placed in one of two categories: unilateral efforts undertaken by one person to reduce conflict or deficiencies; bilateral efforts made jointly by two or more members of the role set. Another important dimension for differentiating among efforts to reduce role problems is whether their goal is to remove the source of the role problem or alleviate the strain. Efforts to change role demands so that those from different role set members are not in conflict illustrate attempts to remove the source of role problems, as would efforts to seek additional resources to meet role demands. Keeping role performance difficulties a secret or ignoring role demands from a less powerful member of one's role set could reduce role strain without effecting a change in the nature of the role problems.

We will first describe types of unilateral efforts to reduce role problems, focusing initially on those directed at eliminating the source of the problem, and then on those designed to reduce role strain. In each instance some of the difficulties clients may face in using the approach will be indicated.

UNILATERAL EFFORTS TO REDUCE ROLE PROBLEMS

Rewarding or punishing can be used to change the role demands a focal person receives. An adolescent who has a temper tantrum when a parent seeks to enforce a bedtime rule may succeed in inducing the parent to avoid making such demands. This can, however, produce other problems such as refusal to grant additional privileges to the child who appears too immature to handle them. Threats of future punishment or of withdrawal of rewards can be used to coerce changes in role demands or role performance. But defiance by the other party can neutralize such efforts unless threats are actually carried out. Promises of future rewards can be a means to coax changes in role demands or role performance of others. Unless rewards actually follow, such efforts may not have the desired effect of changing received role demands.

Persuading through rational arguments can be attempted in similar situations to those where rewards and punishments can be manipulated, as an effort to induce changes in role demands or role performance. The wife who lists the many benefits and few costs of her obtaining a job in an effort to gain her husband's agreement to shift his marital role demands would be an illustration. Such arguments may not be convincing, or the role partner may refuse to listen to them, or may respond with an even longer list of counter arguments.

Making conflicts public can modify the communication system in a way designed to make members of the role set holding conflicting demands aware of their conflict. A woman whose husband and mother expect her to care for her child in quite different ways could attempt to induce them to argue it out with each other and resolve their differences or recognize the difficulties their differences are causing her. A similar strategy can be used when intrasender conflict occurs, as when employees make their supervisors aware that they cannot simultaneously demand an increase in output and in quality of work performed. Although the focal person can make sure that such inconsistencies reach the attention of others, awareness of contradictions is not a guarantee that revisions in role demands will occur.

Trying to increase knowledge, skill, facilities, and access to positions can reduce or remove deficiencies. Enrolling in job-training programs, applying for food stamps, reading about child rearing—all illustrate such unilateral efforts to remove the source of certain role deficiencies. Becoming a foster parent or asking a friend to arrange a blind date are efforts to remove positional deficiencies. Most such efforts require cooperation from other members of the role set.

Abridging the role set can eliminate certain intersender role conflicts. A newly married man may stop seeing some of his friends when their role demands conflict with those of his wife. A teacher whose school social worker suggests unappealing classroom management techniques can stop consulting with the worker. This device can, of course, only be used to a limited extent. Some members of the role set for a given position are in essential relationships with the focal person and cannot be dropped. For example, it would be difficult for teachers to remove principals from their role sets as readily as school social workers.

Leaving a position removes a person from an entire role set, thereby eleminating role conflicts and deficiencies linked to that position. Obtaining a divorce, moving out of a shared apartment, and leaving a job are all examples of this. Unless other positions can provide the gratifications previously obtained, new problems may result. Furthermore, not all positions can be left. There are legal limitations to rejecting one's military status, for example, and others may refuse to accept one's rejection of ascribed statuses, denigrating such behavior as attempts to "pass."

A variety of unilateral efforts can be conceived as attempts to reduce role strain without removing the source of underlying role problems.

Limiting communication can reduce the recognition of conflicts between role demands. Masking, withholding correct information, lying, or deceiving can prevent a role sender from being informed about malperformance or becoming aware of conflicting role demands. When employed in socially sanctioned ways this can be described as being tactful, as when a teacher does not disagree with a parent's praise of a child's musical performance. All such efforts are subject to detection.

Partially meeting demands may reduce strain due to role conflict or role overload. This mechanism is less likely to be useful in reducing role conflict when the persons sending conflicting demands have frequent contact with the focal person, or when demands that are in conflict are essential rather than discretionary to the position. One way to partially meet demands is to postpone or stall role performance. This may be done in hopes that the role sender will forget the demand, or change it in the interval; this may not occur. Working wives have been shown to spend appreciably less time on housework than do nonworking wives, presumably as a solution to role overload problems (Walker 1970).

Segregating positions or scheduling the meeting of role demands may reduce the experience of role conflict. The meeting of filial role obligations on certain days of the week may avoid repeated discussion about the choice between filial and marital role demands. If friends made at college do not meet one's parents when parental and friendship role demands are in conflict, the focal person may not be required to choose between obligations to parents and friends. Role demands for positions with overlapping role set members, for example, situations where many of the individuals with whom one works also are relatives, are less easily scheduled or segmented. Small towns or cohesive neighborhoods may provide more difficult environments for this approach to reducing role strain.

Resisting, ignoring, or repudiating one set of role demands is another means of avoiding conflict between two sets of demands. Children who resist parental demands for frequent church attendance may prevent rejection by their friends who are not churchgoers. The choice of which set of demands to ignore or resist will be limited by such factors as the relative value of various positions, the persistence with which role senders communicate demands, and the legitimacy of the demands.

Following metarules is another device for handling role conflicts or role overloads. A metarule is a rule that governs other rules, in this case rules about relationships among positions or role demands. Use of a moral code to decide which of conflicting role obligations should be met is an example (Gross, McEachern, and Mason 1966). Societal values that grant more legitimacy to role obligations to family members than to conflicting demands of peers would be another. The adoption of an expedient view or deference to the role demands of the person with the most power would be a third type of metarule. Metarules may reduce role strain because they aid the individual in deciding which conflicting demands to meet even though they do not eliminate the conflict. They may also facilitate support for the particular decision if the metarule used is one accepted by the role set members. Someone whose job performance had fallen off because his energies were directed toward caring for an acutely ill wife would be less likely to be criticized by his boss than another worker whose performance decrement was related to his interest in football. If other role set members do not accept the validity of the particular metarule invoked, negative feedback may result.

Evading observation is another way of avoiding conflicts or recognition of deficiencies in role performance. The secret drinker may avoid sanctions. To the extent that role performance can be insulated from observation by role senders, this approach to reducing role strain is possible. Limiting contact with certain role set members is one way of accomplishing this. It is rare that all troublesome aspects of role performance can be shielded from others.

BILATERAL EFFORTS TO REDUCE ROLE PROBLEMS

Bilateral efforts, in which more than one member of a role set join together to try and reduce role difficulties, are generally aimed at problem elimination rather than mere amelioration of strain. According to Spiegel (1960) they are more enduring than unilateral solutions. Bilateral efforts require acknowledgement rather than avoidance of the conflict or deficiency; this in itself is a major step in the direction of finding long-term solutions. The interaction between social worker and client around client's role problems are usually variants of the following approaches.

Exploring one another's ideas and willingness to change is often the first step in bilateral problem solving. New types of role demands may be uncovered through this process and variations in existing relationships considered. Ways to increase resources, knowledge, and skills may be discovered. In itself, the availability of new ideas doesn't guarantee their acceptance, but such a possibility is more likely after exploratory efforts.

Compromising or revising role demands may eliminate some conflicts or deficiencies. Role modification has then occurred, in Spiegel's (1960) terms. Since role demands are often linked to gratifications for role senders, modification is often difficult and new sources of gratification must be built into the revised role demands.

Arbitrating or allowing a third party to resolve conflicts can be used when compromise hasn't been achieved. The third party must retain a neutral stance to keep the respect and gain the agreement of the parties in conflict. Coalition between the arbitrator and one of the original parties can interfere with the effectiveness of this approach. If arbitration is successful, compromise and revision of role demands will modify the role.

SUMMARY: IMPLICATIONS OF ROLE THEORY FOR SOCIAL WORK

Role theory suggests that social dysfunction is attributable to the situation in which individuals find themselves; that problems are often not intrapsychic. It is incumbent upon social work practitioners to explore the possibility that the positions their clients are currently occupying in their daily lives are largely responsible for the pain and problems they are experiencing. If this proves to be the case, the solution lies in aiding clients to modify their contemporary role relationships through changing their own role conceptions and role performance, the role demands they receive from others, the positions they hold, or through combinations of these approaches. Further, if practitioners wish to prevent problems from occurring in high-risk populations, an effective strategy is to analyze the role demands of positions the clients will occupy in the near future and help them to acquire the skills, knowledge, and resources to perform the roles competently. This process, known as anticipatory socialization, will be discussed at greater length in a subsequent chapter.

CHAPTER THREE

THEORIES OF ATTRIBUTION

One of the difficulties in assessment, as was mentioned earlier, is determining if observed role performance is more reflective of the individual's personal characteristics or of the role demands of the system. This question is central to the work of attribution theorists, who are concerned with the causality that people attribute to the behavior they observe in others and in themselves (Heider 1958; E. E. Jones 1979; E. E. Jones and Davis 1965; E. E. Jones and Nisbett 1971; Kelley 1967, 1971, 1972, 1973). The question investigated by attribution theorists is not whether the behavior is actually determined by factors in the environment or the person, but the conditions under which it is interpreted as such by someone observing the behavior (called the observer) or by the person engaged in the behavior (called the actor). A causal attribution made to the environment means that the attributor believes that the individual actor's own personality, ability, or momentary motivational state is not primarily responsible for the behavior. If, on the other hand, it is believed that the behavior is the result of personal qualities of the individual, the interpretation is that the "true" individual preferences and tendencies are reflected in the observed behavior and that environmental pressures or constraints are not the primary causes.

Attribution theorists assume that many types of social interaction include efforts by the participants to understand and draw causal inferences about the behavior of the other persons in the interaction. Such understanding is seen as useful in achieving one's goals when engaging in social interaction. It is further assumed that people try to understand the causes of their own behavior and make inferences or judgments about their own competence, attractiveness, freedom of choice, etc. Thus, attribution theorists alert us to the fact that assessment of what is happening, and why, is not only an activity of professionals, but is part of everyday life. Two potential uses of attribution theories for social workers are immediately apparent: 1) they may aid the worker in understanding clients' views of the causes of their own behavior and the views about clients held by significant others, both of which may be contributing to the presenting problems or may need to be dealt with in developing an intervention plan; and 2) they may alert workers to their own inferential processes by pointing out potential biases in workers' judgments.

THE LOGIC OF ATTRIBUTIONS

Both Heider (1958), whose work in attribution theory was seminal, and Kelley (1967), one of the most important extenders of that work, seek to explain how persons use information available to them in a systematic and logical way to disentangle the various possible factors that might cause a particular behavior. In effect they posit that people's inferences are based on rules of covariation of cause and effect that are analogous to the rules used by scientists to infer effects based on experimental methods. Kelley (1967) has delineated three types of covariations that influence any individual's tendency to attribute causality to external or personal sources: consistency across time; distinctiveness across objects; and consensus (or agreement in behavior) across individuals. According to Kelley, when an individual's behavior is consistent across time, is not distinctive across all objects—that is, various people or things are all reacted to in the same ways—and lacks consensus in that others do not behave in the same way, then the behavior is attributed to the person's dispositional factors. Stated more simply, when the individual reacts the same way to different objects and people time and time again, and others do not act the same way, causal attribution is made to the individual who performs the behavior, not to the situation. On the other hand, the more the individual regularly reacts differentially to specific objects at specific times, and the more others react in the same way in those circumstances, the more likely the behaviors are to be attributed to the situation. This hypothesis suggests therefore that the attribution process is influenced by knowledge of an individual's past behavior at different times and toward different objects and people, and of how other individuals behave toward those same objects and people on various occasions.

The worker may find it useful to keep Kelley's three factors in mind when attempting to assess the factors influencing problematic behavior in clients and to collect adequate data to test each factor. If others in the same position as the client behave in the same way over and over again in the same situation, and the client's behavior is not the same in response to all people or objects, then the worker may form a tentative hypothesis that there are strong positive and negative contingencies in the situation eliciting the behavior. For example, suppose a school social worker is seeing a junior-high-school child who has been referred because of disruptive classroom behavior. If the worker knows that most children in that child's room are frequently disruptive when one teacher is there, but not when another teacher is in charge of the class, the tentative conclusion that can be drawn is that the first teacher is eliciting the behavior; it is not concluded that the referred child and his or her classmates are aggressive and disruptive students. When, however, only the referred child is always disruptive, regardless of who teaches the class, and the other children are concentrating on their work, the tentative conclusion to be drawn is that major dispositional factors within the child are responsible for the behavior. It is also possible that the child is responding to situational factors that occurred at home in the morning or on the bus coming to school, or that the teacher is behaving differently toward this particular child. These possibilities must be explored. The critical aspect of these varying assessment inferences is that quite different intervention strategies would follow from them—in the first illustration, consultation with the teacher concerning classroom management techniques and in the latter, work directly with the child, or with the teacher on motivating this child to learn.

Kelley's attributional model may also be relevant to a hypothesis that a client's problems are rooted in attributional differences between the client and significant others, especially when the client's attributional process does not seem to follow the logical covariation priciples. For example, a foreman's social relations may be disrupted by his attributing others' hostility toward him as due to the nature of the tasks he has to perform. He might be helped to observe systematically the behavior of others. If he observes that the same persons he believes are hostile behave in friendly ways toward other foremen performing the same tasks, the client might be helped in recognizing the ways in which his own behavior elicits the hostile behavior from others.

SOURCES OF ATTRIBUTIONAL BIASES

The above illustration points out that not all attributions follow the logical covariation rules posited by Kelley. Two main sources of deviations from these rules have been studied: the perspective of the person making the judgment and the role congruency of the behavior.

PERSPECTIVES OF ACTORS AND OBSERVERS

It has been postulated by E. E. Jones and Nisbett (1971) that actors and observers of those actors are likely to have divergent perceptions of the cause of the actor's behaviors. They hypothesize that observers tend to attribute behavior to the disposition of the actors, whereas actors tend to attribute their behavior to the situation. To put it another way, they propose that self-perceptions of causality focus on external or situational factors; in constrast, perceptions of others' behaviors emphasize the actors' own contributions. This hypothesis has received considerable support in studies with undergraduates (Arkin and Duval 1975; Gurwitz and Panciera 1971; E. E. Jones and Nisbett 1971; McArthur 1972; Nisbett et al. 1973; Ruble 1973; Snyder and Jones 1974). In one typical study (Nisbett et al. 1973) male undergraduates were asked to explain their own choice of a girlfriend or a college major and that of their friends. Self-perception (of the actors) focused on qualities of the girl or the major, that is, on situational factors affecting the choice. In contrast, these same subjects were more likely to attribute their friends' choices to personal dispositions such as ability, interests, personality, etc.

Two explanations have been offered for this divergence in attribution between actor and observer: that of information deficit and that of information processing. The former focuses on the fact that there is more information available to the actors than to the observers. The actors know how they behaved in past situations that were similar, for example, that they behaved differently. Actors also have more specific information about the situation per se. Observers can therefore suffer from an information deficit: full information about the actors' history and their reactions to other similar conditions is lacking. The information-processing explanation stresses the fact that there is a difference in the way actors and observers process the same information available to both. Because of their divergent physical perspectives, individuals see different components of the situation as the most salient. Actors' visual receptors are poorly located for them to monitor their own behavior, but the visual cues coming from the surrounding situation are salient. Also the actors' attention is often necessarily focused outside themselves as a way to try and respond sensitively to the situation or to adapt to the changing environmental contingencies. On the other hand, for observers the action itself is salient, often involving movement by an active figure against a relatively stable background. Heider (1958) described an observer's perspective as influenced by the fact that the actor's behavior "has such salient properties that it tends to engulf the total field" (54). Thus the information-processing explanation for the divergence in actors' and observers' attributions is that an observer's perspective leads to a bias toward attributing the behavior to the dispositional condition of the actor, and the actor's perspective results in a bias toward attributing the cause of the same behavior to the situation.

Support for the E. E. Jones and Nisbett (1971) informational processing hypothesis concerning the actor's viewpoint was found in two ingenious studies (Duval and Wicklund 1973). In one, a group of undergraduates responded to questions while seated in front of a large mirror; a control group did not face the mirror. The other study involved one group who responded to questions while performing a motoric task that directed their attention away from themselves; the control group simply answered the same questions. The questions involved hypothetical situations in which the subjects were asked to provide attributional outcomes involving themselves. As predicted by E. E. Jones and Nisbett, the subjects who were seated before the mirror gave more dispositional attributions (located causes within themselves) whereas the subjects whose attention was directed away from themselves gave relatively more situational attributions (located causes outside of themselves).

Further support for the E. E. Jones and Nisbett informational processing hypothesis, with its focus on differential perspectives, was found in a study in which college women observed a videotape of two girls getting acquainted (Regan and Totten 1975). One group was asked to imagine that they were one of the girls in the tape and to try to experience what she was feeling all through the discussion. The control group was given no special instructions other than to watch the videotape. Both groups were then asked to indicate on a rating scale the degree to which the target individual's friendliness, talkativeness, nervousness, and dominance were influenced by personal characteristics and how much by characteristics of the situation. The results indicated that the observers who received instructions to empathize with the actor provided significantly more situational and fewer dispositional attributions than did those who were told merely to observe the tape. As both groups were provided with the same videotaped information, it appeared that the information-processing explanation was more powerful than the information deficit explanation for it was the manipulation of the observer's perspective that accounted for the differences in attributions obtained.

Finally, we cite a study that successfully attempted to change both the actors' and observers' visual perspectives (Storms 1973). Dyadic interactions were videotaped from different camera angles and then shown to participants in the interactions (actors) and nonparticipants (observers). The typical differences between actors and observers were found when actors viewed the tape shot from the actor's perspective, i.e., when looking at the person with whom they were interacting, and when observers viewed the tape looking at the actor. But when the viewpoints were reversed, with actors viewing a tape where the camera focused on them and observers seeing the tape focused on the other person, the attributions were also reversed. Actors made more dispositional attributions to themselves than observers did.

It is clear then that divergent perceptions by actors and observers may well precipitate conflict between persons in reciprocal role relationships, e.g., mother and child, practitioners and supervisor, welfare applicant and assistance worker. Thus social workers who are attempting to gather information about problematic situations will be able to perform the assessment more competently with an understanding of this type of attributional bias. Such an understanding can alert the worker to the potential for attributional differences that result in communication problems and conflict over proper courses of action. It can also help the worker understand how different members of a role set can have quite different interpretations of one another's behaviors and suggest ways to alleviate the discrepancy.

The evidence on actor-observer attributional differences should also alert workers to divergent interpretations that they and the clients may have about clients' behavior and workers' behavior. For example, if the client loses three different jobs or comes late for three appointments, the worker may well assume that such behavior reflects a lack of motivation to earn a livelihood or engage in treatment. The client, on the other hand, may feel there were specific conditions in the situation which brought about these behaviors and that they are not reflective of the kind of person "I really am" at all. On the other hand, from the client's perspective, if the worker seems rushed or has misplaced information about the background of the problem, the client may well attribute the worker's behavior to a lack of interest in clients; in contrast, the worker, being very aware of having just been involved in handling a crisis situation, may attribute the hasty behavior to the situation because this is atypical behavior for the experienced professional.

Perhaps the most common type of discrepancy between worker and client, however, occurs when clients seek help for what they perceive to be situational problems and are offered help by a practitioner for personal problems. For example, client-worker discrepancies were found in a major study of family agency services in which 4000 active clients from 266 agencies and the counselors they saw were studied (Beck and Jones 1973). Workers were less aware than clients of the clients' environmental problems and more aware of their personality problems. Similar results were found in a controlled experiment using male theology graduate students being trained as counselors (Batson 1975). They and a control group of male undergraduates listened to nine tapes of referral interviews in which a male client sought help in getting a situation changed. Various types of information about the client were presented. In some tapes a preliminary diagnosis of a personal or mental problem was given, in others a social problem was tentatively diagnosed, and in some no diagnostic information was provided. In other tapes information about the credibility of the client was varied by presenting high and low test scores concerning the client's self-awareness and interpersonal manipulativeness. Both the persons in professional training and unselected undergraduates tended to reject the clients' definition of the problems as requiring situational changes, attributed problems to personal qualities of the clients, and would have made referrals to agencies oriented to changing the individual rather than the social situation. Situational attributions were made more often by nonprofessionals, when there was no prior diagnostic information, and for clients with high credibility. But even when all three conditions were present, at least 37 percent of the observers rejected the client's own definition of the problem as attributable to situational causes. The implications of these studies are clear even in circumstances in which the professional's judgment that a client's problems are primarily caused by the client's disposition is more accurate than the client's attribution of these problems to situational causes. It is important for the worker to be alert for differences in client-worker judgments because attributional conflict may cause difficulties in worker-client communication.

A bias toward attributions of actors' behavior to personal causes rather than situational ones also can have a profound impact on social policy relevant to social work. For example, individualistic reasons for being poor or wealthy appear to predominate in public opinion over structural ones (Feagin 1972; Huber and Form 1973). Based on this attributional assumption social programs are designed to enhance work motivation or better money management whereas it may be more appropriate to increase job availability and wages. Direct practitioners may not often be involved in social program design, but they do frequently use available social programs in helping clients. It is important that their own attributional biases do not lead to inappropriate assessments and referrals that further compound biases among social planners. Thus for a number of reasons the worker should be alert to the possibility that an observer bias has influenced the professional assessment. Fortunately, the research cited above provides clues about methods to reduce observer-actor differences in perspective.

Conscious attempts to empathize with the other person, to try and feel what the other person is feeling, can be useful (Regan and Totten 1975; Wegner and Finstuen 1977). In role terminology, this involves placing oneself in the position of the other person and trying to experience the role demands that impinge on that position. Social work training is usually designed to promote this skill in taking the clients' perspective. Clients too can be encouraged to imagine themselves to be in the position of significant other persons in their lives to enhance their understanding of those persons' attributions about the client. Similarly, mechanical devices such as mirrors or audio- or videotapes can be useful in shifting either an actor's or an observer's focus (Carver and Scheier 1978; Duval and Wicklund 1973; Storms 1973). These techniques are often used in the training of social workers, and could, we feel, enhance clients' understanding of how others perceive their behavior. It has also been shown (E. E. Jones 1979) that specific instructions to subjects to estimate how likely it is that subtle environmental cues influence an actor's behavior shift attributions of observers to more situational factors. We would suggest, therefore, that social workers specifically include in assessment summaries a section on what situational factors may be involved in clients' problems as a way of ensuring adequate attention is given to these factors and as a possible way to reduce client-worker discrepancies in perspective. Therefore, when an attributional conflict has been assessed as contributing to a client's problems, or when a worker is trying to ensure that an assessment includes the client's perspective, we would suggest the use of these techniques for shifting informational perspectives of actors and observers. The important point is that the worker must be aware that attributions of causes of behavior are continuously being made, and there is not always concordance about these attributions.

IN-ROLE AND OUT-ROLE BEHAVIORS

Other variables than the divergent perspectives of actor and observer have been found to affect the attribution process. Behavior that is contrary to social norms is likely to be interpreted as caused by dispositional factors or by the true attitudes of the actor (E. E. Jones and Davis 1965; Wrightsman and Brigham 1973). Thus behavior that is inappropriate to the role being performed is more likely to be interpreted as reflecting the individual's true feelings, whereas the causal inferences drawn from behavior congruent with role demands may be ambiguous.

This proposition was supported in a study in which subjects heard a tape of someone playing the role of a man applying for a job (E. E. Jones, Davis, and Gergen 1961). The subjects were asked to judge the kind of person the applicant really was. Each subject heard someone being interviewed either to be an astronaut or a submariner. These jobs were described as requiring quite different personality characteristics, for example inner-directedness for the astronaut and outgoing friendliness for the submariner. Half the subjects listening to the astronaut interview heard someone present himself as possessing the inner-directed qualities desired in the job and the others heard a gregarious self-presentation. Similarly, subjects hearing the submariner interview heard either an in-role (friendly) or out-role (self-reliant) presentation. For both job types, the job applicant who displayed role incongruent behaviors was rated by the listeners as clearly displaying those characteristics, i.e., the astronaut applicant was seen as extremely friendly and gregarious whereas the submariner was viewed as extremely independent and self-directed. But listeners were less sure of their judgments of job applicants who exhibited role congruent behaviors, and the interviewees were seen as only moderately independent (the astronaut) or moderately outgoing (the submariner).

The implication for the social worker is that in assessing the client's behavior, one should not overemphasize the contingencies in the situation when the client is performing socially acceptable role functions. The client may well have internalized the role demands sufficiently so that the rewards and punishments in the immediate situation no longer control the behavior. Similarly, it is important not to underemphasize the reinforcements that may be operative in a context when inappropriate out-of-role behavior is observed. Thus a mother who neglects her infant may not be essentially unloving, but rather she may find the crying of the fretful child too aversive to tolerate. Furthermore, according to Wrightsman and Brigham (1973), since socially desirable pressures are usually toward mature, rational, positive behaviors, irrational, negativistic behaviors will be the ones from which people will draw the most inferences regarding underlying attributes. Clients also may be too quick to interpret the behavior of others as due to the person's being "crazy" (a dispositional attribution), or to assume that "in-role" behavior is not sincere (a situational attribution). Such assumptions may well generate conflict among family members and in work groups (Horai 1977); social workers need to be alert to such conflicts as they assess clients' problems.

SELF-ATTRIBUTIONS

Most of our discussion of attribution theories thus far has concentrated on social interactions where two or more individuals seek to understand the causes of their own and the other person's behavior as part of the interactive process. It is useful now to direct our attention to the self-attribution process, that is, to how actors interpret their own behavior.

DETERMINANTS OF SELF-ATTRIBUTIONS

D. J. Bem (1972) has argued that to the extent that internal cues are weak or ambiguous, individuals come to understand themselves—including their attitudes and emotions—by observing their own overt behavior and the circumstances under which it occurs. Actors are thus also observers of themselves and use similar external cues to infer inner states. For example, Bem postulated that if individuals observe that they have emitted behaviors in the absence of sufficient external cause or external pressure—i.e., there were no promises of rewards or threats of punishment—they attribute the behaviors to their own dispositions. This self-attribution, according to Bem, must be incorporated in some way into one's self-perception or self-concept, and the individuals will now see themselves as the kinds of persons who do such things and will expect to display similar behaviors in the future. This expectation about stability in one's own future behavior is directly comparable to any observer's expectation of future consistency in an actor's behavior after a dispositional attribution has been made. And just as external observers' attributions can affect their behavior toward the actors, the actors' perception that their own behaviors are internally caused can mediate their subsequent behavior. Thus individuals who steal when there appears to be no external reason to steal may see themselves as thieves and then engage in subsequent stealing—this behavior is congruent with the self-perception. Similarly, a person who helps someone in distress when there is no apparent pressure to do so, or no clear gain for the helper, may develop a self-perception that "I'm a helpful person" and become self-sacrificing. The social worker who is knowledgeable about Bem's self-perception concepts may have a better understanding of clients who seem to be enacting a self-fulfilling prophecy and therefore may be able to make a more perceptive assessment and to develop a more appropriate intervention. Such clients may need help in recognizing potential external pressures that may be causing their dysfunctional behavior. Such an awareness may lead to a shift in self-perception, and subsequently to a change in behavior.

Attributions of causality may be self-serving or designed to protect or enhance one's self-esteem (Bradley 1978; Sicoly and Ross 1977). It is often difficult, however, to distinguish biases in causal perception which are unconscious from distortions in causal descriptions which are conscious efforts at impression management (D. T. Miller 1978). Thus, while it is important to recognize that national surveys of Americans have shown both men and women attributing most of their marriage problems to situational or interpersonal circumstances rather than assuming responsibility themselves (Veroff and Melnick 1977), it is difficult to know whether these, or client reports, are veridical assessments of causality, defensive self-deceiving perceptions, or descriptions designed to influence others' views. Yet, such distinctions are an important aspect of the assessment process, since differing interventions are suggested by these several interpretations.

ACHIEVEMENT ATTRIBUTIONS

One particular type of self-attribution has generated considerable research, namely, causal attributions related to one's own achievement-related behaviors or accomplishments. B. Weiner (1974) has summarized the theory and research evidence and concluded that there are typically two types of internal descriptions of causes for success or failure: ability and effort. Similarly, external attributions can be based on the difficulty of the task or on luck. Thus, stable and unstable causes are possible for both internal and external attributions. Effort is an unstable internal cause; ability is a stable internal cause. Attributions to luck recognize an unstable external cause; task difficulty is a stable external cause. The implication of Weiner's conceptualization for the practitioner is that in working with clients whose problems relate to failures in achievement arenas, for example, school work for students or job performance for adults, it would be important to determine the clients' views of the possible reasons for failure. Intervention strategies would vary depending on the clients', as well as the worker's, attributions. Children who think that they are "dumb" are not likely to increase their efforts to improve school performance. Interventions may first need to be aimed at changing self-perceptions of ability. An auto mechanic who sees his poor performance evaluations and job loss as due to his foreman expecting too much, rather than to his own lack of skill, is not a good candidate for job retraining programs aimed at improving skills.

It is also important to understand client attributions concerning their successes and failures because such attributions have been shown to affect expectancy of future success. They also have an impact upon the emotional consequences of success and failure (B. Weiner and Kun 1976). Attributions to ability, a stable characteristic of the person, or to task difficulty, a stable characteristic of the environment, lead to increased expectations of future success after success, and increased expectations of future failure after failure. Attributions to the person (ability and effort) lead to stronger feelings of pride or shame after success or failure than do attributions to the environment (task difficulty or luck), which often lead to emotions directed at the environment, such as frustration or anger. Further, persons with rather low expectations for themselves, e.g., some women, tend to attribute their successes to luck and their failures to dispositions (J. Parsons et al. 1976). Thus the worker's awareness of the links between attributions and emotions can lead to more meaningful assessments of clients' feelings and consequently, to more effective intervention strategies.

SUMMARY

Attribution theory may be of relatively limited utility to some behavioral therapists who believe that only the contingencies present in the current situation determine behavior, and to some dynamically oriented practitioners who believe that current behavior is totally reflective of unresolved past conflicts. These workers are likely to have few personal doubts concerning the causality of behavior. However, for the larger number of social workers who tend to be more eclectic in approach, attribution theory will not only be important in understanding how their clients view the world and how these views may be in conflict with those of certain members of their role set, but also how they may be biased in their own efforts to determine causality.

CHAPTER FOUR

FRAMES OF REFERENCE FOR SELF-EVALUATION

Our discussion of attribution theories has been directed at the causality that is attributed to clients' behaviors by themselves and others. In this section we continue our focus on clients' self-views, but here the emphasis shifts from assigning causes to behavior to evaluating the appropriateness or adequacy of one's opinions, behaviors, rewards, or abilities, and hence to self-satisfaction and dissatisfaction.

In the past twenty years, a number of concepts and theories have emerged from sociology and psychology that address the issue of the social context for self-evaluation. Pettigrew (1967), who performed a masterful job of integrating these conceptualizations of self-evaluation, starts his analysis by pointing out that two tenets lay at the core of all of these concepts: human beings learn about themselves by comparing themselves to others; and the process of social evaluation leads to self-ratings that are relative to the standards set by those who are used for comparison. The proposition that self-evaluations are relative to some standard that is influenced by the behaviors of others is a critical one for social workers engaged in the assessment process. Clients who are dissatisfied with themselves, or with the conditions of their lives, can probably be helped most easily if some understanding is gained of the basis for their critical evaluations. Because clients are often unable to articulate these standards themselves, theories elucidating the anchors employed in any social evaluation are highly relevant to social work practice.

The self-evaluation theories and concepts to be discussed below include social comparison and reference group theories, the concept of comparison level, the principle of relative deprivation, the concept of distributive justice and equity theory, and finally theories of status equilibration and status crystallization. There is much overlap among these conceptualizations, but there are also important differences concerning such aspects as the focus of the evaluation, the relevant decision to be made as a result of the evaluation, or the size of the social system taken into consideration.

ASSESSMENTS OF APPROPRIATENESS OF BEHAVIOR

SOCIAL COMPARISON THEORY

Festinger (1954a, 1954b) posits the existence of a drive to evaluate one's opinions and abilities. Because there are no objective standards for evaluating opinions, and such standards are often lacking for abilities as well, the only available source of evaluation lies in comparison with others. A key question, then, for Festinger's theory of social comparison, is the choice of the individual or group used as a point of comparison. The answer proposed is the central proposition of this theory: people compare themselves with someone similar to themselves rather than with someone divergent in opinion and ability because sharply divergent comparisons make a subjectively precise evaluation impossible. This proposition implies that self-evaluations based on comparisons with similar others will be more stable than those based on dissimilar others because similar others provide better information. A further derivation from the major proposition is that when comparisons are made with referent individuals who are very similar, but not identical with the evaluator, there will be a tendency to change one's opinions, and even abilities at times, to make them more similar to those of the comparison person or group. Additional derivations are that people will be more attracted to situations in which others are similar to themselves than those in which they are divergent, and that the existence of a deviant opinion or ability in a group will lead to action to reduce the discrepancy. Thus, individuals who belong to groups of similar individuals, or know of groups of similar individuals, will use those groups to assess the correctness of their opinions, and will alter their views if they appear to be very different from those of other group members. The opinion can be about any object or situation that cannot be assessed objectively; for example, adequacy of working conditions (Patchen 1961), or the appropriateness of one's marital arrangement.

These basic tenets of social comparison theory have received some empirical support, although the theory has also been criticized (M. Deutsch and Krauss 1965; Singer 1966). Several investigations support the theory's contention that similar referent individuals are selected when individuals are given a range of possible referents by which they may assess their positive attributes (e.g., S. C. Jones and Regan 1974;

Wheeler 1966). But when negatively valued characteristics are being evaluated, such as hostility toward one's parents, there seems to be a choice of referent individuals who are dissimilar in possessing the negative attribute to a strong degree (Friend and Gilbert 1973; Hakmiller 1966). The assumption that the absence of similar referent individuals leads to inaccurate and unstable self-evaluations has also received experimental support in a study with Navy men who were led to believe that their performance on a test of eye-hand coordination was average, clearly superior, or clearly inferior (Radloff 1966). The latter two groups of men were considerably less accurate in judging their own performance than was the average group, presumably because most persons' performance would be so different from theirs that comparison would not provide useful information. Only when the unaverage performers were given information about a large number of other men with similar task scores to their own was there an increase in their accuracy.

Schachter (1959) extended the theory from opinions and abilities to emotions and proposed that people use similar individuals to evaluate their own emotions when confused. In an experimental study with female undergraduates, he found that as anxiety increased, there was an increasing tendency to want to be with others who were facing a similar anxiety-evoking situation. It was presumed that this preference was based on a desire to compare one's own emotional reactions to the situation to those of others.

Although the basic propositions of social comparison theory dealing with the drive for self-appraisal and the choice of similar others as referents cover evaluations of both opinions and abilities, the theory also recognizes differences in these two areas. Festinger (1954a) suggests there is a motive only to improve abilities and thus comparisons may be more likely to be made with persons whose ability is somewhat superior to one's own than to someone similar. Pettigrew (1967) suggests abilities are adjusted both upward and downward to match the modal level of the social comparison group, and cites the underachiever as an example. Both points of view have received some support.

College males and females were given a test described either as reflecting a typical masculine or feminine ability, and then asked to choose among a long list of male and female groups of different types to get comparative information (Zanna, Goethals, and Hill 1975). Nearly all of the subjects (97 percent) chose to get comparison information from a group of the same sex as themselves, and typically the group had a college major or occupation similar to their own, thus supporting Festinger's general similarity proposition of social comparison. But when the test was described as one typically excelled in by the opposite sex, the subjects' second group choice was likely to be of an opposite-sex group, thus supporting the relevance of information about standard setters in evaluating one's own ability.

Ability comparisons have also been described as possibly more oriented to self-enhancement than to accurate self-appraisal. This was shown in a study of college students who took a test purported to measure environmental problem solving, and then received initial feedback that suggested that their own performance was superior, average, or inferior to that of other undergraduates (Samuel 1973). The students' desires to get further information about the test protocols of other undergraduates were dependent upon the preliminary information they had about their own performance, and most importantly, the students who thought their test scores might be quite poor did not show any stronger desire to get further information about someone from their own college than about someone from a distant dissimilar school. Thus these students did not seem to be seeking accurate self-appraisal of a potentially negative characteristic. A comparable phenomenon may operate whenever self-appraisal involves an opinion or attribute that is negatively valued, as in the Hakmiller (1966) study of hostile attitudes, cited above.

The more general point to be made about the implications of these and other studies is that accurate information about oneself can either enhance self-esteem or threaten it. Knowing that others have similar opinions or abilities can legitimate behavior and enhance self-esteem; encountering persons differing in opinions or abilities can initiate self-questioning and doubt (S. Morse and Gergen 1970). Illustrative of the latter point is the finding that encountering someone who had similar training but who has achieved greater success may threaten the individual's self-esteem more than meeting a person with both greater training and greater success (Mettee and Riskind 1974). The explanation lies in the implications about differential abilities. The social worker seeking to assess the impact of the availability or absence of similar referents on clients needs to evaluate the effect on both accurate self-appraisal and on self-esteem. It is also important to keep in mind that when self-esteem is threatened, the information available from similar others may not be sought out—it may even be avoided.

Social comparison theory has been particularly powerful in predicting how people establish views concerning larger societal issues. E Katz and Lazarsfeld (1955) discovered that opinion leaders are referent individuals for their circle of friends in particular areas of interests, and their opinions determine the views of many others. Similarly, it was found that friends and coworkers are used in evaluating one's status (Runciman 1961), and that residents of rigidly stratified countries, such as England (Runciman 1961, 1966) and France (Stern and Keller 1953), rarely use those in a superior social stratum as a standard for self-evaluation. In both countries, the highly divergent countrymen stand apart and are not relevant in assessing one's own situation.

Social comparison theory offers several clues to the social worker assessing a client, groups of clients, residents of a particular neighborhood, or members of a community organization. If either evaluations of a condition that cannot be measured objectively or self-evaluations appear unstable or confused, the individuals may not have an available social comparison group to provide guidelines for their assessment. This situation may be found when individuals have recently moved into a new geographic area or into a new social position. It may also apply when individuals are suddenly confronted with a new anxiety-producing situation such as widowhood at a young age, unexpected illness of a child, desertion by a lover, unemployment, or the opening of an adult bookstore in their residential area. The implication of this type of assessment for intervention is clear: efforts to assist the client or community residents to locate or become aware of similar others who can provide a framework for self-evaluation would be appropriate.

If self-evaluations or evaluations of social situations are highly stable but unrealistic, it would suggest that the worker investigate if the clients' views have been adjusted to be in conformity with the individuals or groups used as a basis of social comparison. This situation might occur when a physically handicapped child who is being mainstreamed in a regular classroom aspires to the physical prowess of classmates and consequently is very dissatisfied with his own abilities in this area, for example. This assessment has complex intervention implications—the worker would need to determine why the particular reference person or group was being used for social comparison and whether other comparisons would be available and acceptable. In any event, it is important to recognize that these referents are truly invisible participants in any social worker-client encounter, and may be exerting as powerful an influence as if they were physically present.

Clients are not the only individuals who carry an invisible audience with them. Practitioners should be aware of their own social comparison groups, for members of the helping professions also use referents in establishing views of themselves and interpreting ambiguous situations. Thus the worker may hesitate to ask for consultant help in assessing a client or a community problem if it is felt that former classmates would not approve of such behavior. Or the new worker may tend to distrust the information provided by certain clients when disbelief is the accepted behavior of the worker's social comparison group of the long-time agency employees. No external pressure whatsoever need be involved here; the pressure can be entirely internal to the new worker.

COMPARATIVE REFERENCE GROUPS

The concept of comparative reference groups is similar to that of social comparison groups although there are some differences. No evaluative drive is implied in the former, for example. A comparative reference group has been defined as a group that a person uses as a reference point or standard in making self-evaluations and evaluations of others (Kelley 1952). The behaviors, attitudes, or other characteristics of its members represent comparison points used in making judgments and evaluations. A comparative reference group may be a group to which an individual belongs or a group in which membership is desired. It should be noted that the term "aggregate" may be more appropriate to use than "group" when discussing both comparative reference groups and social comparison groups. A group suggests that individuals interact, define themselves as group members, and are so defined by others; these conditions may not always apply in the comparison process. The basic concept underlying both social comparison and comparative reference groups is the same, however: that there is a category of individuals used as a standard for self-evaluation. The fundamental issue is also the same: identification of the conditions under which an aggregate or group comes to be used as a standard by the individual.

Festinger stresses similarity to the individual in discussing the selection of social comparison groups. Other factors have been emphasized in regard to comparative reference groups. Comparative reference group theorists have pointed out that face-to-face contacts tend to have predominant influence, but when there is lack of consensus among these face-to-face pressures, respondents often use other aggregates for guidance. Merton (1957a) cited several conditions under which individuals are likely to refer their evaluations and behavior to groups and aggregates to which they do not belong: if a nonmembership group has a greater ability to bestow prestige upon individuals;

if individuals are not centrally situated in the membership groups, that is, if they are marginal persons; and if individuals are in a social system with a high rate of social mobility. In the latter instance, the individual is likely to adopt nonmembership group referents as part of the "anticipatory socialization" process of upward striving (Parker and Kleiner 1970). Personality factors can also be important factors in the selecting of reference groups. For example, those who accept responsibility for their conditions will compare themselves with others who appear to have determined their own fate rather than with those who attribute most things to impersonal external factors.

Among the behaviors and attitudes affected by comparative reference groups are levels of aspirations and norms of acceptable behaviors. The impact of comparative reference groups on occupational aspirations has been used to interpret a classic study by J. A. Davis (1966) of a large probability sample of college students receiving their bachelor's degree in 1961. One of the major findings was that students' grade point averages were more predictive of their choice of high performance career fields than was the quality of the school they attended. Thus, it appeared that college classmates were an important comparative reference group, and that a student's grades relative to those on his or her own campus affected career choices. This meant that students who received high grades were encouraged to choose difficult careers even when they attended colleges with relatively unselective admissions policies, as reflected in the average performance of freshmen on the National Merit Scholarship exam. Furthermore, feelings of future success appeared more problematic for individuals attending highly selective schools even though there may be a great deal of value attached to success at such schools. Thus, one's comparative reference group can both enhance mobility aspirations and motivation for challenging job choices or dampen them. In either case, the impact may be problematic and hence relevant to social workers' efforts at problem assessment.

The impact of the larger social system on the choice of comparative reference groups has been noted by Merton (1957a). In nations where a rigid system of stratification is generally accepted as legitimate, individuals within each stratum are likely to use only those within their stratum as comparison points. But as legitimation for rigid stratification is reduced, as occurred in the United States during the rise of the civil rights movement, comparative referent groups may shift as well. The choice of cross-ethnic comparative reference groups has been shown to have complex implications for aspirations and self-satisfaction in recent studies of Chicano children (Aboud 1976) and black children and college students (Aboud 1976; I. Katz 1970). For example, majority group individuals are used as comparative referents by some minority individuals to evaluate their own achievements and aspirations but given the continued economic and social advantages of the majority populations in America, such comparisons can be both motivating and discouraging. In spite of the complexities, social workers could strengthen their assessments considerably if they identified the comparative reference groups their clients or community organization members and leaders use for various aspects of their definitions and self-evaluations.

Other important aspects of behavior have also been shown to be affected by information about comparative reference groups. The pain tolerance of male undergraduates in an experimental situation was shown to be influenced by information about tolerance levels of groups with which they reported close identification (Buss and Portnoy 1967). Participation in political activity such as signing petitions was affected by whether or not the petitioner was identified as a member of the solicited individual's comparative reference group (Garrett and Wallace 1975; Suedfield, Bochner, and Matas 1971). Thus knowledge of an individual's comparative reference groups can help in the assessment of behaviors viewed as acceptable in a wide variety of situations.

In sum, identifying comparative reference groups can be important for direct practioners' and community organizers' understanding of the mobility expectations and standards of those with whom they work. The file clerk who holds the behavior of the top secretary as a standard to be used in assessing self-performance probably hopes to move into that position someday; similarly, undergraduates who emulate the behavior of lawyers working for reform-oriented, nonprofit organizations provide information about their aspirations for the future. By learning the composition of the comparative reference groups of clients or other relevant actors, the worker learns a good deal about the hopes and aspirations of the individuals, regardless of what the current life situations may be. The information obtained may not always be to the practitioner's liking. The adolescent may admire drug pushers or pimps whose high style of living is envied, or recording stars who appear to move in a thrill-packed world. At this point, clarification of the worker's own values is needed. The issue of whether the worker's own value system is being imposed on others needs to be examined carefully by the practitioner, and possibly by the supervisor involved as well.

NORMATIVE REFERENCE GROUPS

According to Kelley's (1952) analysis of the literature, normative reference groups illustrate the second function of reference groups. The normative function involves setting and enforcing attitudinal and behavioral standards; the comparison function involves setting evaluative standards for self-appraisal. Thus there are normative reference groups and comparative reference groups, each fulfilling a distinct function. The same group may serve both functions for an individual, but this does not always occur. Normative reference groups typically pertain to membership groups with which an individual desires continued association or with which apprenticeship is being served. In these instances individuals will conform to norms established by the group so that no sanctions will be meted out, and membership, or future membership, will not be endangered. The question here is not "Am I measuring up to standards?" Rather the issue is, "Am I acting in a way they will approve?" or "Am I acting the way a group member is supposed to act?" One critical difference between comparative and normative reference groups is that only the latter directly reward or punish conformity to standards of the group. Thus normative group members observe and evaluate an individual's behavior. In role theory terms such groups may be seen as defining the permissible variability in role performance, whereas comparative reference groups are used to learn how to enact the role and to evaluate one's own role performance (Kemper 1968).

Many different types of behaviors have been demonstrated to be influenced by individuals' views about the norms of groups to which the individuals belong or desire to belong. The adoption and later rejection or continuation of tobacco smoking by a random sample of adults was found to be related to interacting with others who supported or rejected smoking (L. G. Erickson and Cramer 1976). Similarly, a longitudinal study of marijuana smoking among high-school and college youth demonstrated the importance of peer group influence on this behavior (Jessor, Jessor, and Finney 1973). The sexual behavior of students became more similar to that of close friends during the college years (Mirande 1968). Studies of high-school-age students in both Britain (Sugarman 1968) and the United States (Sewell and Shah 1968) indicated that over and above the influence of IQ and socioeconomic status on school performance was the support or rejection of school achievement by close friends and parents.

Politically relevant behaviors are also subject to normative reference group influences. White undergraduates' attendance at NAACP meetings on campus (Fendrich 1967) and their commitment to participate in civil rights actions in their home towns (Ewens and Ehrlich 1972), or white residents' signing of petitions for or against open housing (DeFriese and Ford 1969) could be understood best by knowing both the individuals' own attitudes and their perceptions of the attitudes of significant others. Two classic studies of women undergraduates show there were changes over time in political attitudes as a consequence of residence in dormitories holding certain views (Siegel and Siegel 1965) and of identification with the liberal political attitudes of the college community regardless of family conservatism (Newcomb 1965).

Thus, another variable predictive of clients' behaviors is the norms of the groups to which they belong and care about. Students who ridicule teachers or young adults who refuse to conform to parents' demands concerning sexual behavior may well be displaying behavior and attitudes that are rewarded in their normative reference groups. There are invisible guests in the community meeting hall and in the interview room, guests who reward and punish clients for conformity or nonconformity with the groups' rules about acceptable behavior. Understanding the client's performance is impossible without knowing something of the unseen referents. Such knowledge is not readily acquired, however, for in modern society individuals may belong to many groups, each of which can serve normative referent functions, and normative and comparative reference groups may not overlap. Further, as culture is not uniform across populations in the United States, the various normative reference groups can exert conflicting influences, or their influence may be compartmentalized (Shibutani 1967). Thus to make a full assessment of problematic behavior the worker needs to learn which groups serve a normative function for the client, and for which life arenas. Clearly the task of understanding clients is complex but an understanding of reference group theory reduces the complexity considerably. In the words of Pettigrew (1967), "Modern society brings a clash of overlapping but conflicting standards and perspectives; and this characteristic makes the concept of reference group particularly useful, especially in predicting sharp changes in behavior from one social context to another" (254).

ASSESSMENTS OF ADEQUACY OF REWARDS

COMPARISON LEVEL (CL)

The concept of comparison level (CL) adds another dimension to self-evaluation: that of the individual's own past experiences. Thibaut and Kelley (1959) define comparison level as some type of average value of all outcomes known to a person, by virtue of personal or vicarious experience, with each outcome weighed by its salience. For personal experiences, only those for which responsibility is assumed are relevant. CL is a neutral point on a scale of satisfaction—dissatisfaction with one's rewards in life. The proposition put forth is that each new outcome of an experience is measured against an individual's past gratifications that are salient, and an assessment is then made concerning the current satisfaction state associated with the new experience. Individuals who had many gratifications in the past, or vicariously experienced gratification through the pleasures of their reference groups, are likely to be disappointed in situations that offer only modest satisfactions. In contrast, deprived individuals who have known hardship usually will see the same current situation as pleasing.

The CL concept was referred to previously in relation to physical attractiveness; women who were physically very attractive as college students tended to be less happy twenty years later than women who had not been as attractive as young adults (Berscheid and Walster 1974). CL was also found by Sears and McConalay (1970) to be one of the factors affecting the likelihood that young adults participated in the 1965 Watts riot in Los Angeles. In interviews conducted by black residents of the affected area, the consensus in the black community was that blacks in Los Angeles were generally better off than those in the south. This suggests that the CL of blacks native to Los Angeles would be higher than that for those who had been raised in the South and then moved to Los Angeles. Support for this assumption was reflected in such phenomena as the greater optimism among young Los Angeles natives than southern migrants about attaining desired levels of education. But high comparison levels were coupled with dissatisfaction with current situation among native Angelenos, and this combination was predictive of active participation in the uprising, especially when accompanied by feelings of powerlessness. These subjective factors rather than objective differences in socioeconomic status were the keys to participation among young adults.

The conclusion is that the objective facts of an individual's current life do not guarantee satisfaction or dissatisfaction. The present must be put into the context of the past. Social workers must be continuously aware of this fact in conducting assessments for inferences cannot be drawn about clients' concerns and frustrations from a knowledge only of their current experiences. The clients' CL levels, or neutral points of satisfaction, are equally important.

A concept related to CL is that of comparison level for alternatives

(CL_{alt}) which is defined as the lowest level of outcomes an individual will accept in light of available alternative opportunities (Thibaut and Kelley 1959; 21). This concept is important because knowing an individual's CL would not enable one to predict continuance or disruption in an ongoing relationship. Many who are below their CL do continue to engage in the same activity because the options open to them are even less desirable. The gratifications to be expected from alternatives must therefore also be taken into consideration. If clients are in unsatisfactory arrangements, for example, if they are abused married women with small children, they may continue this pattern because the options they perceive to be available appear to be even less satisfactory, for example, that of having no home and no source of income. Thus, part of the assessment process must include a discussion of the alternatives the clients perceive to be available, and the gratifications they believe will be available from each one.

RELATIVE DEPRIVATION

The concept of relative deprivation shares many of the postulates undergirding the concepts of CL, comparative reference group, and social comparison group. It is similar to CL in that it refers to a satisfaction-dissatisfaction dimension; it is similar to comparative reference groups and social comparison groups in that individuals are looking to some other aggregate to assess their own conditions. Relative deprivation occurs when an individual or class of individuals feels deprived in comparison to relevant reference groups or individuals. One can also speak of relative gratification when an individual or class of individuals feels gratified in comparison to others, but this is a more unusual use of the concept. The principle of relative deprivation was developed by Stouffer and his associates (Stouffer et al., 1949) who studied Army morale in World War II. It was found that in units where promotions were slow, such as the military police, there was less dissatisfaction than in the air corps where promotions were rapid. The air corps' wide-open system of promotions led airmen to expect such swift elevation that even the routine promotions left them relatively dissatisfied; this was not true in the military police where the few advances were unexpected and appreciated. It was concluded that it is not the absolute level of attainment that makes for poor morale so much as the discrepancy between what one anticipates and one receives. Comparing oneself with a nondeprived referent leads to high expectations, that, if unfulfilled, lead to feelings of deprivation and unfairness.

More recently, relative deprivation and gratification have been shown to influence the negative aftereffects of aversive noise levels (Singer and Glass 1975). When people in experimental situations believed that others were experiencing less noise, they showed greater detrimental aftereffects, such as decreased performance on further tasks after noise cessation, than when they believed others were experiencing more noise than they were. Thus even physical aspects of environmental conditions seem to be evaluated in relative terms, a conclusion the social workers need to recall in discussing housing and job situations with individual clients and community residents during the assessment process.

J. A. Davis (1959) extended Stouffer's theory and considered the consequences of comparing oneself with those outside and inside one's own group. He started with the assumption that on any aspect of life conditions the entire population can be partitioned into the deprived and the nondeprived, with the latter state being universally preferred to the former. If individuals compare themselves to other persons differing in deprivation within their own group, they will experience a feeling opposite in direction to the evaluation of the other's condition. Thus if another member of one's group is seen as more deprived, the individual will feel relative gratification. If the other person is seen as less deprived, the individual will feel relative deprivation. In either case, the individual will also have questions of fairness concerning the similarity of his or her state to that of peers.

If individuals compare themselves to persons who are not members of their own group, similar processes occur. A sense of relative subordination results when deprived persons compare themselves with nondeprived out-group members; an attitude of relative superiority results when nondeprived individuals compare themselves with deprived out-group members. Many self-evaluations include both in-group and out-group comparisons, and the joint impact of these two has been described by J. A. Davis (1959) as follows. When a social categorization, such as occupation, that defines group membership is combined with objective deprivation, such as in income, feelings of relative deprivation will be found most frequently among individuals who are in relatively deprived situations within the *non*deprived group, e.g., low paid white-collar workers. Relative gratification will be found more frequently in the more favored individuals within the more deprived category, e.g., higher paid blue-collar workers. To clarify this point, Runciman (1961) suggested using different terms for the relative deprivation felt when the comparison is to one's own group, and that felt when outside groups are involved. Runciman calls the relative deprivation felt when comparing oneself to others in the same group "egoist deprivation" since its focus is on the ego or self, and the deprivation felt about one's entire group when comparing it with outside groups "fraternalist deprivation" for here the focus is on the associated group.

In social work an example of an egoistically deprived individual from a nondeprived group would be a child of a middle-class intact family who experiences less attention or receives fewer gifts and privileges than siblings. An example of the relatively gratified individual in the fraternalistically deprived group would be the low-income father who wins $500 in the state lottery. The major point is that a system perspective is needed in considering the satisfactions of these individuals. The individual is part of a small group, but also part of a much larger group. Rivalry can be experienced in the smaller system and in the larger system simultaneously. Falling behind one's sibs in the smaller system is frustrating even though one has more privileges than children in the larger system. Thus, in the assessment process the social worker must determine the systems to which clients feel they belong, and how they rate their condition in relation to their peers in each system. The family of origin, the conjugal family, and the local group are likely to be involved in these comparisons as the smaller systems. However, the other systems that are relevant to the clients' self-evaluations and feelings of dissatisfaction are often not obvious, and this information must be gathered through careful interviewing. For example, are members of their own or different religious organizations the relevant groups? Members of their own or different ethnic groups? Members of their own or different occupations and professions? Answers to these questions are necessary to assess the sources of discontent and satisfaction, and hence to pinpoint intervention goals.

A method for operationalizing the degree of relative deprivation experienced by an individual, developed by Cantril (1965) for cross-national survey research, has applicability to social work. The method operationalizes aspiration level as well. Cantril presented a diagram of a ten-step ladder and asked the subject to imagine "that the top of the ladder represents the best possible life for you and bottom represents the worst possible life for you." The respondent was asked to describe the qualities that would define the best possible life, and the worst. Thus, the respondents' own assumptions, perceptions, goals, and values defined the endpoints of the scale represented in the ladder. In doing this, Cantril was recognizing that subjective standards govern aspirations and fears. What is described as the best possible life for one person may be far short of that end state for someone else. Having defined the anchors of the scale, the respondent was asked: "Where on the ladder do you feel you personally stand at the *present* time? Where on the ladder would you say you stood *five years ago*?And where do you think you will be on the ladder *five years from* now?"

By using this type of systematic inquiry social workers can tap clients' hopes and fears, and also obtain a clear picture of clients' comparison levels (CL) and feelings of relative deprivation. This information can be obtained from the responses concerning the past, present, and future. One further aspect of Cantril's technique can be useful in assessment. After asking respondents about their own personal standards and evaluations, a similar set of questions was asked by Cantril about the respondents' own country. The worker applying this strategy can ask about clients' social comparison groups rather than country to obtain important information. If clients see themselves currently at a lower point on the ladder than they were five years ago, especially if that point is also below the location of their referent figures five years ago, the worker could assume that the clients are functioning below their CL and are dissatisfied. If clients are at a higher point on the ladder than they were five years ago, but still much below the present level of comparative reference groups, one can assume some degree of relative deprivation is being experienced. An exception might be the client in a student or apprentice role who anticipates moving up to the level of his comparative reference figures within a relatively short time.

Questions pertaining to the future provide information about the aspirations of clients. If there is an anticipation of downward mobility, or of no further mobility for someone who has moved upward in the past five years and whose comparison figures continue to rise, the worker can infer some degree of dissatisfaction. The syndrome is common in middle-aged men who have steadily risen in the occupational world but have now reached their peak and can anticipate only a downward motion or stagnation at the current level. The situation is particularly frustrating if referent figures move on to become vice-presidents, managers, etc. Although this middle-age syndrome has been observed most frequently in men in the past, one can anticipate a replication in women with the growth of the women's movement and increased female labor force participation. So long as women considered wife and mother roles central to their identity, their rise in the occupational world held less importance. However, with the emergence of the work role as central for many women, the cessation of mobility at the midpoint of a career is likely to carry with it the same seeds of frustration men have known.

The advantage of Cantril's ladder for the practitioner is that it does not require literacy and is self-anchoring, that is, it compares the individual's feelings about the past and future with his or her feelings about the present. Thus there is no intrusion of societal values by use of class, job, or financial labels. Further, there is no intrusion of worker values concerning educational level, marital status, etc. Whether the ladder can be used with children remains to be determined.

DISTRIBUTIVE INJUSTICE

The concept of distributive injustice, as discussed by Homans (1961), is essentially a recasting of the theory of relative deprivation. Distributive justice, however, is not equivalent to relative gratification; rather it is analogous to the neutral comparison level. According to Homans, distributive justice prevails in exchange relationships with other individuals when the rewards each person receives are proportional to his or her costs in the relationship:

$$\frac{\text{Rewards}}{\text{Costs}} \text{ of A} = \frac{\text{Rewards}}{\text{Costs}} \text{ of B}$$

The greater the costs, the greater should be the rewards. In addition, distributive justice can be described in terms of profits and investments. Profits refer to rewards (positive outcomes) − costs (negative outcome); investments are such things as effort, training, education, status. Distributive justice prevails when the ratio of A's profits to A's investments equals B's profit/investment ratio:

$$\frac{\text{Profits}}{\text{Investments}} \text{ of A} = \frac{\text{Profits}}{\text{Investments}} \text{ of B}$$

This formula permits an analysis of whether justice prevails when individuals or groups receive unequal profits. If their investments are similarly unequal, distributive justice prevails; if the investments are the same, it does not. The persons who are disadvantaged in the latter situations can be expected to strive for distributive justice through efforts to increase their rewards, decrease their costs, or diminish their investments.

The notion of investments is an important addition to relative deprivation theory, for it helps to formulate a theory about how reference groups and individuals are selected. According to Pettigrew (1967), the chief weakness of reference group theory is its failure to explain the basis for selecting reference figures. This issue is particularly important to social workers attempting to understand their clients' self-evaluations. Reference groups and individuals may be those whose investments are known, and whose investments are used as the basis of comparisons. If the group's investments are the equivalent of the evaluator's, the profits are checked to see if they are similar. If the investment of the referent is smaller, the evaluator's own profits should be superior; if the referent's investment is larger, the evaluator's profits should be inferior.

EQUITY THEORY

Equity theory is a similar attempt to conceptualize the feelings of distress and dissatisfaction associated with perceived unequal exchanges or returns on investments. Adams (1963), who presented a theory of equity in cognitive dissonance terminology, stated that there are norms or expectations that the ratio of an individual's inputs (effort, training, personal attributes, skill, and status) to outcomes (benefits received) should equal the comparable ratio of one's reference person or group. Thus equity exists if the following equation describes a relationship:

$$\frac{\text{Input}}{\text{Outcome}} \text{ of A} = \frac{\text{Input}}{\text{Outcome}} \text{ of B}$$

If this equality does not exist, dissonance is established and the individual is distressed and will try to reduce the dissonance by a variety of means. The two ratios can be made more equal by increasing or decreasing one's inputs (e.g., by working more or less hard) or outcomes (e.g., by increasing or decreasing pay received), by trying to change the comparison person's inputs or outcomes, or by distorting evaluations of inputs or outcomes. The referent other used could also be changed as when an adolescent no longer seeks out a very popular neighbor as a companion. If none of these efforts to restore a sense of equity succeeds, the individual can try to escape the situation entirely, for example, by quitting the job or becoming an isolate.

Recent theoretical and empirical work in equity theory has been summarized and reconceptualized by Leventhal (1976b) and by Walster, Berscheid, and Walster (1976), who emphasize several points of relevance to social workers. Walster, Berscheid, and Walster focus on one-to-one interpersonal relationships and propose that participants in such relationships scrutinize the relative outcomes and inputs of themselves and the other party. Thus judgments of equity or inequity are assumed to pervade most social relationships, be they those of worker-boss, husband-wife, client-social worker, and at times, even parent-child. Social workers encountering distress associated with any interpersonal relationship should consider whether the distress is linked to a judgment of inequity. The consequences of such judgments can be severe, indeed. It is believed that one of the causes of child abuse is a belief by the abuser that the infant is deliberately withholding gratifications from its hardworking parent (Parke and Collmer 1975).

The second way that the Walster, Berscheid, and Walster (1976) position may help in the social worker's job of assessment concerns the proposition that all types of inequity are distressing: both persons who feel they are in an inequitable relationship because their outcomes are relatively low and those who feel their outcomes are inequitably high experience distress, and attempt to reduce that distress. The mechanisms that are proposed to reduce distress for the advantaged person, who might be considered as doing harm in the inequitable relationship, are similar to those described above as available to the disadvantaged person, or victim. They can be grouped roughly into those involving rectification of the inequity through revising inputs and outcomes for oneself or the partner, and those involving justification of the inequity through distorting of the inputs or outcomes. It is in the latter category that the advantaged and disadvantaged members in an inequitable relationship use somewhat different approaches. Disadvantaged persons may distort their perception of the outcomes they receive or the contributions they make by denying neglect or abuse from their partners, or by downplaying their affection for the other person, for example. The advantaged person can distort the inputs or outcomes of the disadvantaged persons by derogating their contributions as sloppy or lazy, or by minimizing their distress; they can also deny their responsibility for the outcomes of their partner, as in the case of a husband who has been unfaithful to his wife blaming his actions on his wife's lack of sexual responsiveness.

The social worker thus needs to be aware of and seek to assess any distortions in clients or caregivers' reports about their own and relevant other persons' contributions to problematic relationships. A foster mother may describe the child's defiance of her requests as more frequent than an independent observer, thereby reducing the child's inputs, if she feels her outcomes in that relationship are disproportionately high considering her inputs; an adult son who feels he is not contributing much to his elderly mother's support but who is well cared for in her home may exaggerate the time he spends with her to increase his inputs and restore psychological equity. Social workers also need to be aware of their own tendency to maintain equity in client-practitioner relationships. For example, it is possible that when positive outcomes cannot be achieved with delinquent adolescents in spite of considerable worker effort, there may be a tendency to minimize the youths' inputs and to suggest that they lacked motivation to improve.

It is important for the social worker to recognize that equity, like relative deprivation and distributive justice, is in the eye of the beholder. Individuals evaluate their own inputs and outcomes and those they attribute to others, and experience varying degrees of social justice based on their own assessments of the various inputs and outcomes. Thus, the initial assessment issue for the social worker is not whether an objective observer would describe a client's situation as inequitable, but whether the client so views it. Also critical in the assessment process is determination of the degree of congruence between clients' views of inequity and those of significant others involved in the relationships. Where congruence is high, interventions would focus on changing either or both partners' actual inputs or outcomes; where congruence is low, attention must be paid to identifying sources of disagreements about either party's contributions and/or either party's rewards.

That inequity is in the eye of the beholder also is relevant to larger units of social conflict, as Adams and Freeman (1976) have noted: "[A] vast array of social conflicts are perceived fundamentally as problems of inequity. . . . Women and ethnic minorities voice unjust discriminatory treatment, while other portions of the public claim that remedies for discrimination force them to bear inequitable costs" (55). Thus, whether the problem being assessed is at the interpersonal, the community, or the societal level, issues of perceived inequity may be fundamental to the difficulty.

It is also important to recognize, as Adams (1963) did, that the principle of equity is a norm, a socially agreed-upon basis for defining justice. As such, there may be situations, as Leventhal (1976a) and Sampson (1969) argue, where the equity norm does not operate. Instead the norm of *equality* defines justice. In certain social groups participants may agree that benefits to each should be the same, regardless of their particular contributions. All persons are entitled to one vote in government elections, regardless of their contributions to society. Parents are expected to provide affection and care to all their children equally rather than in proportion to the assets of each child.

Leventhal (1976a) summarizes research showing that equality as the basis for judging fairness is likely to be emphasized either when the maintenance of harmony and solidarity or the avoidance of conflict among participants is important or when the basis for judging contributions or investments is very complex or difficult to ascertain.

A third basis for judging whether benefits are distributed fairly, according to Leventhal (1976a), is the needs rule. This rule dictates that fairness exists when an individual's legitimate needs and desires have been satisfied and suffering prevented. Thus, parents may feel that their handicapped child needs more help than their other child who is not handicapped, and therefore may not see any injustice in spending much more time with the handicapped child. The needs rule is likely to be judged as appropriate to evaluate fairness in situations where close, friendly relationships exist, where the individual feels directly responsible for the other person's welfare, or when the individual feels personally contented or successful.

The above analysis, and other research (Messe 1971), suggest that some social conflicts may arise out of disagreements about the applicability of the norm of equity, the norm of equality, or the norm of needs. One extended family member may feel that all family resources should be shared equally; another may feel that the individuals who contribute less of the resources should reap fewer benefits; for others the legitimate needs of the individuals may be most vital. Some community members believe that the state should equalize the funds available to support each child in school so that the wealthy districts would help to support the poor ones. Others believe that school districts that raise more taxes from their residents are entitled to better educational resources for their children. Still others believe that schools in which the pupils have the most difficulty, such as those with a large proportion of pupils who are visually or physically handicapped, should receive the most funds. Each group feels distressed when tax moneys are distributed in a manner contrary to its view of fair conduct.

There is considerable empirical support for both distributive justice and equity theories. Investigation of the satisfaction with earnings among oil refinery workers found that respondents were satisfied in their comparisons of themselves with professionals who earned more; the professionals' earnings were viewed as commensurate with their larger investments in their jobs (Patchen 1961). However, in comparisons with blue-collar workers who were earning more, oil workers experienced dissatisfactions, for the other blue-collar workers had equivalent investments yet were reaping greater rewards.

Additional support comes from a study which concluded that under conditions of extreme inequity, when one receives a far smaller share of available rewards than other individuals who have similar investments, some people will actually reduce their own payoffs, that is, engage in self-depriving behavior, to induce feelings of guilt in others (Leventhal and Bergman 1969). Thus, they may take on the role of martyr to bring about a change in the situation, thereby signaling the other party that an injustice has been done. This interaction is captured when a hardworking waitress returns a dime tip given to her by a diner, stating she does not need the ten cents. The social worker assessing a client who works far harder than other family members would do well to explore the possibility that this individual is experiencing severe inequity or distributive injustice and is attempting to elicit shame or guilt in spouse, children, or parents.

Studies have also shown that one response to inequity is exiting from the inequitable relationship. Male and female undergraduates who described their current dating relationships as inequitable in terms of their own and their partner's ratios of contributions and outcomes to the relationship expected the relationship to be less permanent and were in fact less likely to still be dating three-and-one-half months later than were students whose relationships were equitable (Walster, Walster, and Traupmann 1978). Both managers (Dansereau, Cashman, and Graen 1973) and hourly workers (Telly, French, and Scott 1971) were found to be more likely to quit their jobs when they viewed pay as inequitable in relation to inputs. Thus, when the ratio of inputs to outcomes cannot be adjusted to what seems to the individual to be a just level, the problematic social situation may be rejected entirely even when that alternative is also costly. Suffering deprivation when unemployed may be preferable to being deprived while working hard at a low-paying job; the costs of being without a sexual partner may pale in comparison to continuing to give more and get less from a relationship than one's partner does. There is also evidence that persons who "illegally" receive relatively high outcomes in a social relationship, either through allocating unfairly high outcomes to themselves or through causing poor outcomes for others, tend to justify their advantages. Laboratory studies show that harmdoers derogate their victims (K. E. Davis and Jones 1960), and minimize their victims' suffering and deny their own responsibility for the harmful act (Brock and Buss 1962). Similar efforts at self-justification were found in interviews with juvenile delinquents (Sykes and Matza 1957), who often argued that their victims deserved punishment or were not harmed very much.

ASSESSMENTS OF CONSISTENCY OF STATUS COMPONENTS

The concepts of status congruence, status consistency, and status crystallization are also relevant to self-evaluations. By status is meant the relative power, wealth, or prestige associated with one's social position in a hierarchy of social positions or one's rankings on those dimensions. It is generally assumed that any individual holds several positions that are associated with a status or ranking on different vertical hierarchies. Status is not a single rank on one dimension.

Once this assumption is granted, the question of inconsistency in ranks associated with various positions arises. The three achieved characteristics of income, occupation, and education are commonly used in research to study the consequences of consistency among dimensions of socioeconomic status. The ascribed statuses of sex, age, race, ethnicity, and religion have also been investigated. The terms status congruence (Sampson 1969), status crystallization (Lenski 1954), and status consistency (I. W. Goffman 1957) have been used to describe the situation of those whose status components are at the same rank.

A number of theorists (e.g., Benoit-Smullyan, 1944) have proposed that there is a strain toward consistency in status ranks, as well as an attempt to maximize status by raising lower attributes to the level of the highest. A number of interesting hypotheses have been developed about the behavioral and attitudinal consequences of status inconsistency. For example, if inconsistency persists, the individual may be directed toward supporting societal changes that might reduce it. This proposition has been supported in studies that show those with status inconsistency to be politically liberal in the general American population and in other Western societies (I. W. Goffman 1957; Lenski 1954, 1956, 1967) and among professional social workers as well (Kolach 1965).

The preference for social change among status inconsistents need not always imply liberalism. An investigation in Oregon revealed a positive association between status inconsistency and right-wing extremist attitudes (Rush 1967).

Because status inconsistency can imply conflicting cross-pressures from different reference groups or from interpositional role conflicts, its relationship to social participation has been studied. Status inconsistents tend to be socially withdrawn, that is, they are less likely to interact with their relatives, neighbors, coworkers, and friends and are less likely to be active in volunteer organizations (Lenski 1954, 1956; D. I. Warren 1970). Black residents of a compact heterogeneous ghetto who were status inconsistent in regard to occupation, income, and education, experienced more anomie or social isolation than similar residents whose status was crystallized (D. I. Warren and Easto 1972). The findings were related to the existence of different reference groups or subcultures existing side by side. Presumably the status inconsistents were unclear about their own identity and about those with whom it was safe to associate.

Reduced social participation and enhanced desire for social change do not exhaust the predictions emerging from status inconsistency theory. It has also been found in a national sample survey that adults who had a high ascribed status as measured by race, but low achieved status as measured by education or occupation, tended to report far more psychosomatic symptoms than did other respondents (E. F. Jackson 1962). The conjunction of these findings with those obtained by Lenski (1954), who found greater political liberalism in status inconsistents with low ascribed status and high achieved positions, led Jackson to suggest that political action and psychosomatic symptoms may be alternative functional equivalents for handling the tensions created by status inconsistency. He further suggested that persons with high ascribed and low achieved statuses may believe they have only themselves to blame, and may punish themselves psychosomatically; they may also be seeking an acceptable reason for their low achievement. In contrast, someone with low ascribed and high achieved statuses can more readily blame society and wish to change conditions as they are not accorded the full status privileges that normally accrue from significant achievement. The civil rights and women's movements may well obtain some of their drive from the discontent felt by high achieving minority members or women who have a low ascribed status by virtue of having been born brown or black or female. The Chicano physician who is treated as an orderly by visitors to a hospital is understandably indignant and likely to seek redress of such grievances.

The tension accompanying status inconsistency has been attributed to two sources by Pettigrew (1967). First, membership in more than one class can generate stressful situations of cross-pressures and conflicting expectations. Second, the presentation to others of inconsistent status cues may cause others to behave toward the individual in an unpredictable manner. The lack of certainty concerning how people will react is assumed to be stressful to the status inconsistent. Other theorists (Adams 1963; Benoit-Smullyan 1944) noted that disconfirmation of an individual's own expectations that status rankings should be congruent can in itself be a source of tension and feelings of injustice.

The concept of status congruency has also been applied to relations between individuals. Here the focus is on discrepancies in status rankings between individuals and the effect this has on social relations. Marital relations were the focus in one large-scale study of urban residents which showed that status inconsistency between spouses was associated with marital stress only under certain conditions (Pearlin 1975). If a man or woman placed high value on social status and married someone whose background was of a lower social status than his or her own, marital stress was common. But with this same type of status discrepancy and less status consciousness, there was no evidence of unusual marital stress. Similarly, when the status discrepancy was of the opposite type—where the spouse's status background was higher—marital stress was not inordinate. These findings suggest that cultural conflict between spouses with different social rankings is not inherently a source of stress; people whose spouse's status was higher than their own did not report value conflicts, lack of reciprocity, or other signs of stress. Thus, as with status inconsistency within single individuals, different kinds of inconsistency have different consequences.

The above analysis suggests that the consistency in an individual's status components should be examined by the social worker as a part of the assessment process, for lack of consistency may be a source of tension. Similarly, discrepancies in status between client and significant others should be investigated as a possible source of strain. The Jackson analysis suggests that strain can be expected in any individual with a low ascribed status, including members of all minority groups in this country, and a relatively high achieved status in occupation, income, or education. The practitioner should be alert to this possibility. Perhaps the greatest contribution of the status inconsistency concept to social work practice lies in its emphasis on structural factors that affect human behavior and feelings. Thus it may not be necessary to seek reasons for discontent in clients' unique social histories. The reasons may be found in their ambiguous location in the social structure. How clients respond to the strain will depend on their own backgrounds and personality predispositions. Strain can be suggested, however, merely by the data that appear on the face sheet of a case record or in the demographic profile of a neighborhood.

PART THREE

CHANGING BEHAVIORS AND ATTITUDES

INTRODUCTION

Part Three will focus on efforts by social workers to bring about change. The primary emphasis of section I is on dyadic interactions in which a social worker is involved with a client directly, that is with an individual whose problems or potential problems are the primary target of change. The next section also centers on work with a single individual, someone who is a significant person in the life of others and who can act as a facilitator of change in others; the focal problematic behavior to be prevented or alleviated by these interventions does not primarily involve the individual with whom the practitioner is working. Small group interactions in which one or more social workers are engaged in working with several other persons—clients or persons relevant to clients—are the topics of the following sections. How intervention approaches and social psychological topics are divided is introduced here.

Various strategies can be employed by social workers to bring about change. For example, Garvin and Glasser (1971) analyzed the means of influence used by workers with social groups as *direct means*—workers attempt to bring about change in group members by personally influencing those individuals; *indirect means*—workers attempt to help members achieve their goals by modifying group conditions including group composition, group structures such as the communication network, or group processes such as problem-solving approaches; and *extra group means*—efforts are made to change the behavior or attitudes of persons in the clients' environment or in large social systems within which both clients and other individuals function, e.g., to modify the attitudes of classroom teachers of clients or the suspension policy of a school system.

G. Goldberg (1974) provided a different perspective for analyzing social work intervention, a framework that encompasses work with individuals and with groups but does not deal with the context of the worker-client interaction referred to above in the indirect means of influence. Goldberg suggested examining workers' activities in terms of two dimensions. One is the locus of concern—the number of persons for whom help is sought, which can vary from a single individual to all individuals with similar problems. The other is the type of person(s) engaged—which can vary from the one(s) for whom help is sought (sufferers) to those who do not themselves need help (nonsufferers); thus the number of persons engaged does not define this dimension. By placing the two dimensions perpendicular to each other such that they intersect at the midpoints, four cells are created (figure 3.1).

Cell A represents strictly microlevel intervention; it involves all activities in which the practitioner engages John G. out of concern for his plight. As you move to the midpoint of the locus of concern dimension Cell A also includes a practitioner's interaction with a specific group of sufferers who are trying to help one another, such as self-help groups organized for the sole benefit of the people in that group. Cell C is strictly a macrolevel interaction; it encompasses the social worker engaging others, nonsufferers, seeking to alleviate the problems of a category of persons suffering some common social problem or distress: the universe of John G's. Examples of such activities include a social worker lobbying a state legislator for support of a bill designed to improve mental hospital conditions or working with a citizen's group planning improved service delivery systems for the elderly. Cells B and D contain both micro and macro elements. Cell B represents efforts of the worker to engage one or more John Gs in efforts to reduce the

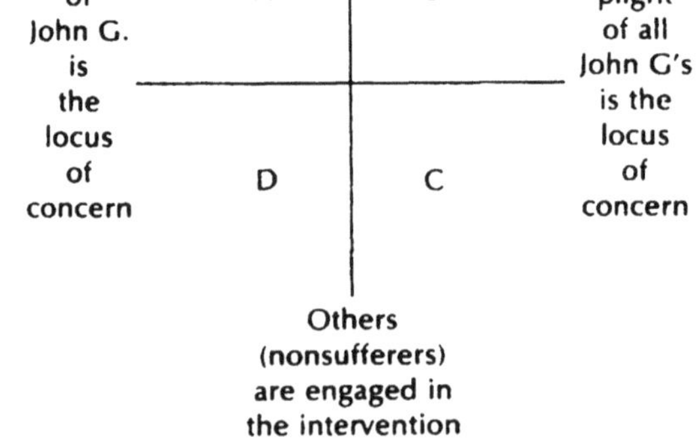

Figure 3.1. A Model of Social Work Intervention. (Adapted from G. Goldberg 1974.)

suffering of all fellow sufferers, for example, engaging one or more abused wives in efforts to establish a network of shelters for battered wives. It thus encompasses actions to alleviate social problems by persons suffering from that problem. Cell D includes the activities of a social worker with one or more nonsufferers on behalf of a single individual or several specific sufferers. A case conference with a coordinated effort to help the client would fall into this cell. So would the activities of a social worker who organized a group of citizens to take patients from a nearby mental hospital on trips to the community to prepare for their imminent discharge.

Radin (1976a) suggested a modification of the Goldberg paradigm for school social work practice. The horizontal dimension (locus of concern) remains the same in the Radin paradigm, but the vertical dimension (persons engaged) has at the top One Social Worker, and at the bottom Members of the Helping Professions in a School Building, e.g., psychologists, counselors, nurses, teacher consultants, plus interested teachers and administrators: number of helpers engaged. Thus cell A would subsume casework and groupwork interventions; cell B would contain efforts by the single worker to engage in social action programs or system intervention on behalf of many children in the school. Cell D would include activities by the mental health team working to help a single student, and cell C would encompass the mental health team working together to optimize the development of many or all children in the school. The Radin modification is applicable to any host setting in which social workers function, such as medical or correctional settings.

From an ecological perspective, Hartman (1974) described the generic approach to interpersonal practice and arrived at a conceptualization similar to that of Goldberg. According to Hartman, practitioners should take one of two stances: the extended action system stance or the extended client system stance. In the former, the worker starts with the need of an individual case and follows the problem wherever it leads, utilizing a variety of interventive methods and mobilizing whatever action system appears to be appropriate. According to Hartman, the idea is hardly a new one. "It has been called the extended model of casework because attention remains focused on the individual case or instance, and it has led creative caseworkers and agencies into conjoint family intervention, . . . into intervention aimed at the various service systems impinging on the well-being of the client . . . and into advocacy" (203). The second stance, the extended client system stance, differs from the first in that the initial point of entry is through a more extended potential client system—through a group of people sharing a common problem, status, or limited geographical locale (e.g., an entire fifth-grade class, the total ward of a hospital, a ghetto area of a suburban county). The guide for action is the same as in the extended action system stance: to follow the problems wherever they lead and to utilize whatever action system, roles, or strategies appear useful and appropriate.

From a behavioral perspective, Stuart (1972) cited several skills needed for direct human service, including skill in interpersonal management relevant to processes of inducing, maintaining, and terminating client participation in treatment, e.g., persuasion and techniques of interpersonal influence. Also cited were the skills of analyzing and changing organizational variables which facilitate or impede service delivery. Other behaviorists discuss work with mediators of reinforcers, such as teachers and parents of clients, in addition to direct work with individual clients (e.g., Lovaas et al. 1973). Although Fischer (1978) focuses on the clinical/behavior change role, he recognizes other social casework roles, including those of consultant, educator, broker, and advocate.

In sum, in spite of their differences, all of the above models refer to influence techniques used with clients directly and those used with others who influence the client's life. All include the situation where the plight of a single person is the target of change; some explicitly refer to work with small groups whereas others imply such activities. All allude to intervention in larger systems. As a way of organizing the social psychological theory and research relevant to efforts by social workers to effect change, we have summarized the similarities in these strategies along two dimensions, each of which is dichotomized for purposes of clarity. The first describes the *Position in the Intervention Process* of the person(s) with whom the worker interacts. The persons may be those whose plight is the primary target of change in the intervention process, the client, or those significant others who can facilitate change in another individual whose problematic condition is the primary target of change. This distinction is similar to Goldberg's between sufferer and nonsufferer. The second dimension is *Level of Intervention,* where two categories will be used: the dyad, consisting of the social worker and a single client or significant other, and the small group, consisting of one or more social workers and several clients, or one or more social workers and several significant others. Combining the two parameters results in the fourfold table 3.1. The social psychological concepts that we perceive as most relevant to the

Table 3.1
Types of Social Work Intervention and Relevant Social Psychological Concepts

Level of Intervention	*Position in the Intervention Process*	
	Clients[a]	*Significant Others*[b]
Dyad	Quadrant A (Section I) Attitudes Social influence	Quadrant B (Section II) Altruism and helping Social learning
Small Group	Quadrant D (Section IV) Group cohesiveness Group composition Norm enforcement Group development Role playing	Quadrant C (Section III) Group decision making and performance Leadership in groups

[a] Those whose problems or future problems are the targets for change.
[b] Those who can facilitate changes in problems of others.

quadrant appear in each box. As in the case of the overall organization of this book, the concepts will have relevance in other areas as well. For the most part however, they will have maximum utility in specific situations typical of one quadrant.

Quadrant A, discussed in section I, is the traditional casework situation in which a social worker attempts to help a single person cope more effectively with his or her problem or prepare to cope with a future problem. The focus of the intervention in this quadrant is on direct interaction of the client with the social worker. The goal of the intervention is the reduction or alleviation of the client's problem through changes in the client or in the client's environment. Two main categories of social psychological theories and research are particularly applicable to this quadrant. One set relates to attitudes and their influence on behavior. These include theories based on means-end considerations such as Fishbein's behavioral intention theory, and those pertaining to attitude change that results from efforts to restore cognitive consistency such as Festinger's cognitive dissonance, Rokeach's human value, and Bem's self-perception theories. The other set of theories and research relevant to work with clients on a one-to-one basis are those dealing with social influence. Included here are concepts relating to the bases of social influence, Jones' ingratiation theory, and reactance theory, especially as investigated by Brehm.

Quadrant B, discussed in section II, is also a common form of social work intervention, for despite theoretical differences, social workers recognize that the environment in which individuals currently function affects their social functioning. It is therefore often appropriate for social workers to develop intervention strategies for working with a person who has significant impact on a client's environment. Thus one strategy social work practitioners can use is to work with a significant other in a client's environment to facilitate change in the client's behavior or to maintain client gains.

The person with whom the practitioner is interacting in such situations may be linked to the client as a family member, teacher, foster parent, aide in school, attendant in hospital, nurse, or day care mother. Labeling these individuals as facilitators of change in others does not rule out change in these individuals in the course of the work with the practitioner. What differentiates these persons from those worked with in quadrant A (or D) is the fact that the major focus of the contact with the social worker will not be on their difficulties in social functioning or their social environment but rather on the difficulties of someone else with whom they are in close contact. Most of these individuals will not perceive of themselves as "clients" of the worker, yet the word "colleague" would not be entirely appropriate since that implies some type of professional similarity which is not always the case. Unfortunately, there is no simple word that encompasses the cluster of caregivers/teachers/significant others of someone experiencing difficulty in coping with societal demands. To simplify our own discussion we will refer to them as Significant Others.

Two major social psychological areas of theory and research will be discussed which are potentially extremely useful to social work practitioners interacting in dyadic relationships with significant others—those who are in a position to facilitate and maintain the improved social situation or functioning of clients: theory and research on altruism and helping behavior and on social learning. In the latter category will be included observational learning, self-regulatory processes, and locus of control beliefs.

Quadrants C and D will be discussed in sections III and IV, and we will indicate here only that the same general distinction applies to quadrant C versus D as to quadrant A versus B. In quadrant D is located group work with persons defined as having problems needing alleviation or persons whose life conditions have created or may lead to problems in social functioning, e.g., preretirement groups. Quadrant C encompasses such activities as in-service training for attendants at a home for disturbed children, or group work with parents of handicapped children.

We now turn to a discussion of the social psychological theory and research most relevant to quadrant A.

SECTION ONE

IMPLEMENTING DYADIC INTERVENTION PLANS WITH CLIENTS: QUADRANT A

INTRODUCTION

Efforts by social workers to bring about change in the problems of an individual with whom they are interacting on a one-to-one basis is the heart of social casework. Although some casework practitioners would state that their goal is to bring about changes in the behavior of clients and that they are unconcerned about the clients' thoughts and feelings, most caseworkers would add to the objective of behavioral change that of changing clients' views of themselves and the environment about them. Other caseworkers would recognize that the alleviation of some clients' problems would be greatly facilitated by the practitioners or the clients being able to influence the significant other persons in the clients' environment.

To accomplish these objectives, two factors must be taken into consideration—the client's attitudes toward persons and objects, and the potential power of the worker to modify the attitudes and behaviors of clients. Hence, the two chapters in this section will focus on those two dimensions and the social psychological theories and research findings most applicable to them. Chapter 5 deals with attitude formation and attitude change theories that are relevant to social workers understanding and influencing the determinants of clients' attitudes and the conditions that lead to changes in attitudes. Chapter 6 presents theory and research on social influence, especially those dealing with the characteristics of influencers that facilitate the success of their efforts, and the conditions under which their influence attempts are resisted.

CHAPTER FIVE

ATTITUDES

Although social psychology has been concerned about attitudes since its beginning, there is an unfortunate lack of consistency in use of the term. One of the major sources of confusion has been between the use of the term attitude to mean a global evaluative response toward an object (or class of objects) that includes emotional, cognitive, and behavioral components, and the use of the term to refer only to the emotional responses to objects (or classes of objects). To avoid confusion in our discussion we have adopted the latter usage; attitude will refer to variations in favorable or unfavorable *feelings* toward things, people, or behaviors. Verbs such as like/dislike, love/hate, attract/repel, favor/oppose, convey the affective reactions included in the concept of attitude. The term belief will refer to cognitive judgments about things, people or behaviors. Beliefs are ". . . perceptions that an object or person [or behavior] has certain characteristics, qualities, or attributes or is related to some other concept, object, or person [or behavior]" (Fishbein and Ajzen 1972:494). The statements that former mental patients are dangerous, teenagers are rebellious, or eating lead-based paint will make you ill are all statements of beliefs. Finally, the behavioral aspect of evaluative responses will be considered as a separate concept. Here the focus can be either on people's overt behaviors in relation to objects or people, or on their intentions to behave in certain ways in relation to an object or thing—going to the movies or planning to do so, keeping an appointment with a dentist or expressing a willingness to do so, renting a room to a former mental patient or telling a canvasser you would be willing to do so.

As can be seen even with the few examples given above, some beliefs seem to imply certain kinds of behaviors while others do not. A landlord who believes mental patients are dangerous may refuse to rent to a former patient, but a person who believes teenagers are rebellious may not avoid all teenagers. And even when behavior is implied by a belief, it may not occur—the landlord who is desperate for funds may rent a room to a recently discharged inmate of a state hospital. Similarly, although some feelings may appear to be consistent with certain beliefs or behaviors, this apparent consistency may be absent for certain people or under certain circumstances. A woman may love her husband even though she believes he is unfaithful. A landlord may fear mental patients but rent them an apartment anyway if local renting ordinances make such discrimination a crime. However, to the extent that attitudes or beliefs are stable over time and predispose one to behave in favorable or unfavorable ways to a person, they are of interest to social workers. Thus intervention efforts may well focus on changing attitudes or beliefs.

It is also important to note that although our emphasis here is on the relevance of theory and research on attitudes to dyadic intervention situations with clients, attitudes of significant others toward the client may be the critical point of other interventions. This point has been highlighted by Segal (1978) in his review of research evidence on limited changes in the public's attitudes toward the mentally ill in the last twenty years. In view of the recent deinstitutionalization movement shifting the care of the mentally ill from hospitals to community, such public attitudes may become increasingly problematic to ex-patients and mental health workers may need to engage in efforts to change public attitude.

Most social workers would agree that even when the primary intervention emphasis is on changing attitudes or beliefs, this is done with the assumption that behavioral change will also occur. But often research evidence documenting this link is absent (Segal 1978), or mixed. Unfortunately, attitudes and beliefs are not always precise guides or predictors of behavior. Years of research have been devoted to determining the mediating variables between expressed attitudes and relevant overt behavior, without total success. This knowledge is critical for with it one could predict behavior and also develop more effective techniques for helping clients achieve desired behavior change through changing attitudes or beliefs. However, progress in unraveling the important factors is being made, as can be seen in the following review of current research and theory in the field.

MEANS–END THEORIES OF ATTITUDE FORMATION

One major type of attitude theory has been described as based on means-end or instrumentality-value analyses (McGuire 1969): ". . . attitude toward an object is defined as a composite of the perceived instrumentality of that object to the person's goals, weighted by his evaluation of those goals" (McGuire 1969:153). These theories are essentially based on a model of rational human behavior. People are assumed to like those things, people, or behaviors that are means to achieving satisfactions and conversely, to dislike things, people, or behaviors that lead them to dissatisfactions.

ROSENBERG'S AFFECTIVE-COGNITIVE CONSISTENCY THEORY

Rosenberg's theory of attitudes is one important such conceptualization (1956, 1960). His major premise is that attitudes (feelings) toward an object or event are a function of the totality of an individual's beliefs about the consequences of the object or event, weighted by his or her evaluation of these consequences. The belief about what will follow the event has been referred to as the expectancy, and the evaluation of these consequences has been referred to as the value. According to Rosenberg's affective-cognitive consistency theory, an attitude (the affective component) is a summation of the product of all the beliefs about what consequences will ensue, expectancies, and of all the values placed on those consequences (the cognitive components). Thus behaviors believed to have consequences that are valued highly by the individual in a favorable or unfavorable sense are predicted to weigh heavily in attitude formation, and Rosenberg expects consistency between affect and cognitions:

> . . . strong and stable positive affect toward a given object should be associated with beliefs to the effect that the attitude object tends to facilitate the attainment of values, while strong negative affect should be associated with beliefs to the effect that the attitude object tends to block the attainment of important values. Similarly, moderate positive or negative affects should be associated with beliefs that relate the attitude object to less important values, or if to important values, then with less confidence as to the existence of a clear-cut instrumental relationship between the attitude object and the values in question. (Rosenberg 1956:367)

This model enabled Rosenberg to predict the attitude of college students toward whether members of the Communist Party should be allowed to address the public, a controversial issue during the McCarthy era when this research was carried out. This prediction was based on information obtained by having the students review a list of thirty-five values (e.g., that people should be well educated, that others should be allowed to make their own decisions) and indicate how much each was a source of satisfaction to them (value importance) and whether and to what extent the value in question would tend to be blocked or facilitated by the policy of allowing Communist Party members to address the public (perceived instrumentality). In addition, it was found that the expectancies that certain values would follow the event predicted the attitude when the importance of the values was held constant, and the importance of the values predicted the attitude when the expectancies were held constant. Thus Rosenberg concluded that there are two separate cognitive dimensions, "value importance" and "perceived instrumentality," which influence attitudes. Furthermore, other research has shown that the instrumentality and value dimensions can be manipulated independently to achieve attitude change (Carlson 1956).

Other research on whites' attitudes toward blacks (Fishbein 1963) and attitudes of white and black low-income women toward the use of birth control (Insko et al. 1970) also supported the view that attitudes could be predicted from beliefs about perceived instrumentality and values. In the latter study it was also found that attitudes of the black and white women toward birth control were correlated with their self-reported frequency of use of birth control devices. Thus there is some evidence for a clear attitude-behavior link from research within the affective-cognitive consistency framework. Unfortunately, not all research found such associations and consequently various theorists have attempted to identify further variables that would need to be considered to predict when attitudes and behavior would be congruent.

FISHBEIN'S BEHAVIORAL INTENTION THEORY

Among the most influential revisions of Rosenberg's theory has been the work of Fishbein and his colleagues (Ajzen and Fishbein 1970, 1973, 1977; Fishbein 1967). They proposed that behavior is typically preceded by an intention to behave in a particular way and that this behavioral intention is a dual function of personal attitudes and social influences. e.g. peer pressures. So to Rosenberg's focus on perceived instrumentalities and value importance as determinants of personal attitudes, Fishbein added a focus on normative influences. He conceived of these as a multiplicative function of a person's beliefs about what significant others expect him or her to do or feel and the person's motivation to comply with these expectations. Parallel to Rosenberg's conception of cognitive influences on attitudes, Fishbein predicts that behaviors believed to be expected by highly valued significant others will have strong impact on behavioral intentions. (The concept of normative influences on behaviors is similar to the concept of role demands discussed in chapter 2.) Finally, Fishbein suggested concen

All the beliefs of the client about the probability that an act will lead to certain consequences	×	Client's evaluation of the relevant consequences	→	Client's Attitude toward the Behavior
				+
All the beliefs of the client about the expectations of significant others that the client should or should not perform the act	×	Client's motivation to comply with the expectations of significant others	→	Normative Influences on the Client's Behavior
				↓
				Specific Behavior Intention of Client
				↓
				Specific Behavior of Client

Figure 3.2. Fishbein's Behavioral Intention Theory
A schematic presentation of the components relevant to the behavior of a client individual whose problem is the target of change.

trating on measuring attitudes toward, and normative influences upon, actions rather than objects, e.g., skipping school versus school per se, as a way of improving predictions of actions. In sum then, as figure 3.2 shows, behavior is proposed by Fishbein to be predicted from behavioral intentions to engage in that particular behavior, which in turn results from the sum of personal attitudes toward the behavior and normative influences on the behavior. Thus, according to the Fishbein's behavioral intention model, to predict a specific behavior, one should seek out the individual's intention to engage in that behavior. This should be a summation of all beliefs about the consequences of that behavior weighted by the value of the consequences to the individual, and of the perceived expectations of all significant others concerning that behavior weighted by the motivation to comply with the expectations of those particular others.

Several independent studies relating to family planning supported the Fishbein behavioral intention model, as have studies about intentions to donate blood (Pomazal and Jaccard 1976), attendance at discussion sessions about poverty programs (Rosen and Komorita 1971), and game behavior (Ajzen 1971; Ajzen and Fishbein 1972). The consistency in the results of the family planning studies make them worth describing in some detail.

One investigation (Kothandapani 1971) was based on interviews conducted in the homes of over 400 low-income married black women by trained black female interviewers. Questions concerned behavioral intentions (e.g., "I would walk a mile to get my birth control supplies"), feelings (e.g., "The very thought of birth control disgusts me"), beliefs (e.g., "I believe that birth control causes many birth defects"), and the current use of birth control. The latter self-reports about usage were verified through reliable peer reports and information about receipt of free birth control supplies. Two findings were particularly important. Factor analysis of the interview data showed that questions about behavioral intentions, beliefs, and feelings about birth control were distinguished into three independent factors. Thus these were separate, not necessarily consistent, components of the women's total views about birth control. And the index of behavioral intentions toward birth control discriminated much better between women currently using and not using birth control than did either feelings or beliefs about contraception.

Another study (Werner, Middlestadt-Carter, and Crawford 1975) questioned a small group of women with two children concerning their intention to have a third child in the next three years. This variable was then predicted from the two sets of factors the Fishbein theory identifies: 1) beliefs about the probability that different consequences would ensue from having a third child and the value placed on those consequences, and 2) beliefs about what significant others would think about their having a third child and their motivation to comply with the beliefs of these significant others. When the components of these two factors were used to predict the women's intention to have a third child, a highly significant multiple correlation was obtained, indicating that 64 percent of the variance in intention to have a third youngster had been explained. The correlation obtained was much higher than any obtained from scores on personality tests, measures assessing deep-seated motives, or scales reflecting general attitudes toward contraception. In one of the few studies of family planning in which both husbands and wives were interviewed, Kaplan-Vinokur (1975) found similarly good predictions to intention to have another child from a combination of variables measuring beliefs, values, normative beliefs, and motivation to comply concerning having or not having another child. Although these studies did not provide any information about whether or not the women did indeed have another child during the ensuing years, other longitudinal research, conducted in Taiwan, has shown good correlation between behavioral intention to have another child and later birth of a child (Freedman, Hermalin, and Change 1975).

The methods used in these several studies give clues to those who might want to influence a couple's intentions to have an additional child. For example, one might try to alter the woman's belief that another child would foster her self-development. If one knew that the woman valued her own development and that she believed her husband would support a decision to have another child, the intervention focus could be on the husband's beliefs about the consequences of having another child, such as influence on the family's ability to maintain an acceptable standard of living.

The above discussion suggests that overt behavior can be predicted from a knowledge of the relevant attitudinal and normative components involved. One further piece of information is relevant, however, to increase the precision of the prediction. The proponents of the behavioral intention model (Ajzen and Fishbein 1973) indicated that the relative importance of the personal and normative components may vary from one behavior to another for a given individual or from one individual to another in the same behavioral situation. Family planning behaviors, for example, seemed to be more influenced by normative beliefs, especially those of a spouse, than by personal attitudes (Kaplan-Vinokur 1975). The behavior of college students playing a two-person game in a laboratory setting was more influenced by their personal attitudes toward the game behavior than their beliefs about their partner's expectation of them if the game was played under competitive instructions, but the predictive weight of normative beliefs of the partner was greater under cooperative instructions (Ajzen 1971). The behavior of authoritarian subjects was predicted by an equation in which the normative component had greater weight than the personal attitude one (Fishbein 1972).

It is not assumed that social work practitioners will attempt to compute complex formulas in deciding when attitude modification is appropriate. But the worker should be aware that at least five factors have to be considered in such an effort: 1) the perceived instrumentality of the action contemplated to various goals; 2) the value of the consequence of the action; 3) the role demands of significant others in the client's life; 4) his or her motivation to meet those expectations, and 5) the importance of the significant other in this particular situation or to this particular individual.

Applying these theories of attitude change to interventions of workers interacting with a client, we suggest that efforts might be directed at each of these factors: 1) to modify the client's beliefs that specific objects or events will lead to outcomes that are desired; 2) to modify the value placed by the client upon those outcomes; 3) to help the client modify the expectations of significant other people in the environment; 4) to modify the client's desire to maintain the approval of particular significant others; or 5) to learn the relative importance of personal factors versus normative factors for the client and to modify the balance between the two clusters when necessary. Each of these approaches will be discussed below.

Exemplifying the first strategy are the activities of family planning advocates directed at modifying beliefs about the consequences of having large or small families. Drug education often has a similar conceptual focus. At a more individual level, the modification of instrumental beliefs would include attempts to help a client understand the likely outcome of a new behavior pattern such as expressing true feelings toward a spouse, or going for a job interview. One intriguing set of findings relevant to this area concerns the apparent usefulness of simply asking individuals to spell out their reasons for being willing to engage in a particular behavior. Such activity seems to result in an attitude shift in the direction of strengthening or intensifying the person's original attitude (Clary, Tesser, and Downing 1978; Tesser 1978). Thus, encouraging someone to spend a few minutes thinking, writing, or talking about his or her own view of the perceived consequences of an action should result in a consolidation of attitude toward the act, which may be desirable, as when a young man feels mildly positive about seeking out a new job, and the worker wishes to increase these positive feelings. All such influence attempts should effect behavior only to the extent that the consequences are important to the individual and that normative factors do not conflict with the personal attitude.

Insofar as the second approach is concerned, explicit value modification is not the focus of social work interventions—the client's values and not the social worker's should determine the goals of intervention. But programs such as values clarification in school settings may highlight the importance of some values to the students and increase the likelihood that future behaviors will be congruent with those values.

Should the worker decide that the variable most problematic is the value associated with consequences of an event, it is important to be aware of Rokeach's (1968a, 1973) conception of the organization of values. According to this analysis, values are conceived of as enduring beliefs that a specific mode of conduct or end state is personally or socially more satisfying than the opposite mode or state. Beliefs about desirable modes of conduct, concern about how one ought to behave, e.g. be honest, are called instrumental values. Beliefs about desirable end states of existence that are worth attaining are called terminal values; illustrations are a comfortable life, a sense of accomplishment, true friendship. Rokeach's position is that terminal values are generally more central than instrumental values, but that both instrumental and terminal values are organized into value systems that are hierarchical, that is, certain values within the system are of greater importance or centrality to the individual than others. The more central or important the value, the more difficult it is assumed to be to change. When more central values do change, the implications are greater, for the greater the centrality of a value, the greater the number of other values and beliefs that are connected to it.

The implications of Rokeach's theory are twofold. Social work practitioners are likely to be least successful if they attempt to alter highly central values and most successful if they focus on less central instrumental values. But the more centrality a value has to a person, the greater effect its revision will have; more actions will be linked to central than peripheral values; more behavioral intentions will be affected by a shift in a central value. Rokeach has elaborated further on his conception of value change and this theory will be discussed later in this chapter, along with other cognitive consistency theories.

The third strategy, client modification of the expectations of significant others, can be approached in three major ways: by helping the client change the beliefs of current referent others, by modifying the client's beliefs about the current expectations of significant others, or by increasing the salience of different referent persons. Probably the first approach should be to clarify and verify the client's beliefs about the expectations of significant others. As was discussed in chapter 2, faulty communication between role partners is not uncommon and misperception about norms for behavior can occur. For example, when a client believes her husband would disapprove of a behavior that she would find gratifying, such as finding employment, the client may need assistance in checking out this perception. Such verification could occur either through the client's describing the behavior of her husband that led to the perception to determine if the worker concurs with the interpretation, or through the client's discussing the behavior openly with her spouse. If the perception appears accurate, the worker might assist the client in changing her husband's beliefs about the consequences for him of her going to work. Here the educational effort is directed at the spouse's belief system rather than the client's.

An expectancy that an individual should behave in a specific way is a role demand or norm that is applied either because the individual is occupying a specific position, or because the individual is a member of a group in which such norms are applied. The functioning of such groups will be discussed in the next chapter, but relevant to the dyadic situation is the fact that if the expectations of others cannot be modified, the client can be encouraged to join other groups whose norms are congruent with the behavioral intention being fostered. The social worker might inform the client about the existence of such groups and pave the way for entry through contacts with other members whom the worker knows. If no such group exists, the worker might try to start one so that the client could participate. Examples of such formed groups would be those of retirees seeking new activities to replace occupational endeavors, or adolescents attempting to resist peer pressure to become involved in drugs.

If norms constraining clients' development of desired behavioral intentions are associated with specific positions they occupy, for example that of invalid, and the expectations of role senders are rigid, efforts may be made to help clients take on new positions, such as that of volunteer aide. An alternate strategy would be attempts by the worker to modify the expectations of role senders who are making dysfunctional role demands—for example, demands by the invalid's family that the disabled client stay home all day and be cared for by others. Techniques of altering such role expectations were discussed in chapter 2, and other factors important to working with significant others will be discussed in the next chapter, under the topic of intervening with significant others.

Insofar as modification of the motivation to comply with the expectations of others (the fourth strategy) is concerned, the worker will have to acquire information about the significant other's source of influence on the client, and how strongly the client wishes to remain in the group or in the specific position, assuming there is some choice involved. One way to collect the latter information is to determine what the client's comparison level (CL) is and what gratifications are available from alternate groups or roles, the comparison level for alternatives (CL_{alt}). (These concepts were discussed in chapter 4.) The motivation to comply will be weak if the client is currently below his or her CL (e.g., past rewards were more gratifying) or in a situation where the CL_{alt} is high (e.g., other cliques are available to the adolescent). If neither case is true, it may be more productive to help the client try a different strategy of coping with the role expectations, one that does not simply involve compliance with the demands of salient role senders. For example, the client could establish metarules about which role demands are met first and under what conditions. Perhaps the clients can determine when their own role conceptions and attendant role demands take top priority. (See chapter 2 for a full discussion of resolution of role conflicts.) Another approach would be to change the type of power the referent other is perceived to have in relation to the client. We will return to this approach at a later point when we discuss theories of social influence.

The fifth strategy is based upon the assumption that the choice of which element among the four affecting behavioral intentions to focus upon should be determined in part by the relative importance of personal and normative factors on the behavior in question. For example, it is of little use to change people's views of the consequences of an action, if the relevant behavioral intention is primarily determined by their views of others' expectation of them. This was well demonstrated in the laboratory study of college men and women playing a two-person game, mentioned earlier (Ajzen 1971). The experimenter was able to revise the subjects' attitude toward the game behavior through persuasive messages about the strategy most likely to facilitate winning, or for other subjects, to revise normative beliefs about what the other player expected them to do. But the impact of these changes on the subsequent game behavior of the players varied with whether they were playing under competitive instructions or cooperative ones. It was changes in personal attitude under competitive conditions and changes in normative beliefs under cooperative conditions that primarily affected subsequent behavior. This suggests that social workers need to try and assess the relative weights of personal and social factors on behavior, and try and work on the aspect that is more powerful in the particular instance. Alternatively, if the more potent factor is not amenable to change it might be possible to change its importance. Some of the techniques suggested above could have such an effect: engaging clients in a full discussion of their own views about means-end relations may increase the salience of these views; a shift in reference groups may increase the importance of normative beliefs.

Another important contribution of the work of Fishbein and his colleagues to the concern about the conditions under which attitudes are predictive of behavior has been their emphasis on appropriately defining the elements of the behavior of interest (Ajzen and Fishbein 1977; Fishbein and Ajzen 1974). If the focus is on increasing or maintaining the occurrence of a particular behavior toward a given person in a particular situation over time, such as getting to work on time, the relevant attitudinal and normative factors to be assessed and possibly influenced would be those relating to that particular action. But often the behavior of concern is broader in scope, in the sense that a category of different acts may be the concern, such as friendly behavior toward strangers, which can include not only greeting behavior but positive responses to their questions, interest in their ideas, sharing of one's own ideas, or inviting them to one's home, etc. In the latter case Fishbein and Ajzen suggest that the unit of concern in assessing attitudes and normative influences should be the class of behaviors and that in checking predictions to behaviors one should compile and measure various exemplars of that class of behaviors. For unless the attitudinal, normative, and behavioral measurements are made at comparable levels of specificity or generality, one would not expect them to be interrelated in the manner outlined in figure 3.2.

The importance of measuring the appropriate cluster of behaviors is illustrated in a field study of attitudes toward the environment (Weigel and Newman 1976). Town residents took part in a survey that included a scale measuring attitudes toward environmental concerns. Beginning three months later and for several subsequent months some residents had the opportunity to participate in several organized ecology projects. Each project was presented by a different person and there was no indication that it was related to the earlier survey. The behaviors observed included signing petitions and circulating them, participating in a citywide roadside litter pickup program and recruiting a friend to participate, or putting out bottles and cans for recycling pickups over an eight week period. The attitude scale predicted a composite measure of environmentally relevant behaviors much better than it did any single behavior (signing a given petition) or even frequency of particular behaviors (number of petitions signed). The implications for a community organizer working with an ecology organization are clear—interventions should be directed at influencing attitudes toward clusters of related behaviors, and effectiveness should be evaluated by a multiple-behavior criterion. The implications are similar, however, for a caseworker; for here too a set of behaviors may be congruent with a desired goal, for example, establishment of independence from a parent, and if so, that set should be specified. An intervention strategy focused on that cluster should then be selected and multiple behaviors be examined in assessing the effectiveness of the intervention. A similar point has been made by Radin (1979) in a model for evaluating the effectiveness of school social work: there may be multiple desired outcomes and each of these must be defined and measured.

A somewhat different approach than that taken by Fishbein was adopted by Rokeach and his colleagues to deal with the conditions under which correspondence should be expected between verbally expressed general attitudes and overt behavior. Rokeach and Kliejunas (1972) criticized the tendency of social psychologists to study the attitudes towards persons and objects in isolation. They point to the need also to consider the individual's attitude toward the context within which different people or objects are found, that is, the attitude toward the situation across persons or objects within the context. According to these researchers, whenever an attitude toward a person or object is activated, an attitude toward the situation per se is also activated. To predict behavior from attitudes, it is essential to consider both categories of attitudes. Further, to improve the prediction, one must know the importance of the two attitudes with respect to one another. In some cases the attitude toward the situation, for example, a public welfare office, may be more important than the client's attitude toward a particular worker. In other instances, the attitude toward the specific person or object, an alcoholic husband for example, may be more salient to an individual than any context in which she interacts with the spouse.

To operationalize the predictions derived from the above theory the researchers asked individuals to offer their own estimates of the percentage of their behavior in specific situations determined by their attitudes toward the specific persons involved, and the percentage determined by the situations in which they interact with the persons. Using this approach they were able to account for 25 to 50 percent of the variance in behavior of undergraduates in regards to attending a psychology course. In addition, as Rokeach and Kliejunas (1972) predicted, the attitude toward the situation (a psychology class) was a better predictor of cutting class than the attitude toward the specific instructor when each attitude was considered alone. Thus, a social worker attempting to alter the behavior of a client, a boy who gets into fights in school, for example, should focus on his attitude toward the situation in which the relevant behaviors will occur (e.g., a schoolroom) as well as his attitude toward the significant individuals involved. Further, knowledge of the relative importance of the two attitudes provides important clues concerning the specific attitude on which to focus the most effort. An alternate treatment approach would be to attempt to modify the relative weights given to the two attitudes so that the more positive attitude will gain importance for the client. For example, with the aggressive student mentioned above, if the youngster finds being in school aversive and this colors his feelings about everyone encountered in that situation, the social worker might attempt to change that attitude. If, on the other hand, his feelings about his school situation are generally positive but he dislikes or fears certain classmates, the worker might attempt to engage the boy in new types of group activities with these youngsters so that his contacts with them would become more reinforcing.

When confronted with the task of how to go about altering an attitude toward a situation or an object, the practitioner might well return to the behavioral intention paradigm. It therefore appears that a combination of the Rosenberg-Fishbein and the Rokeach-Kliejunas models would provide the social worker with the fullest list of critical factors to influence in order to bring about behavior change through attitude change. The list of determinants of the behavioral intentions, and subsequent behaviors, includes 1) the expectations concerning the consequences of an intended act; 2) the value placed on the consequences; 3) the views of referent figures toward the behavior in question; 4) the motivation to comply with the expectations of referent figures; 5) the importance of the referent figures in the given situation; 6) the attitude toward the situation in which the behavior will occur; 7) the attitude toward the relevant object or person; and 8) the relative importance placed on the latter two attitudes.

FUNCTIONAL THEORIES

In concluding our discussion of means-end theories of attitude formation it is useful to point out that the instrumental function of attitudes is not the only function that they serve; they also fulfill three additional functions. These four major functions of attitudes have been delineated by social psychologists (D. Katz 1960; McGuire 1969; M. B. Smith, Bruner, and White 1956). The *instrumental function* of attitudes focuses on the utility of attitudes in aiding a person to reach goals, satisfy values, obtain social rewards, or avoid social rejection. This focus on the adaptive aspect of attitudes is common to the means-end theorists discussed above as well as to reinforcement views of attitude formation (Staats 1967) or to the view that attitudes can be held because they bring gratification. A positive attitude towards one's own intelligence which is based on reality would be an example of the latter. Attitudes can also have an *ego-defensive function* which protects individuals from acknowledging uncomplimentary truths about themselves or the harsh realities of their external world. This attitude function is stressed by Freud and other theorists (Adorno et al. 1950) concerned with the influence of unconscious conflicts on attitudes and behavior. The *value-expressive function* of attitudes refers to the pleasure experienced from expressing an attitude appropriate to personal values or self-conception. Both ego psychology (e.g., R. W. White 1959), with its stress on self-expression and development of competence, and Freud's view of the cathartic value of expression of emotion exemplify this function. The *knowledge function* of attitudes is based on an individual's need to understand and give structure to the world. Such attitudes can serve to simplify a complex situation.

These four major functions are not mutually exclusive. One attitude may serve an instrumental function for a person while another attitude of that individual may be primarily ego-defensive. And the same attitude may have multiple functions. An attitude of hostility toward members of other ethnic groups, for example, may be ego-defensive in avoiding recognition of one's own inadequacies and also utilitarian in facilitating the exclusion of out-group members from access to jobs desired by one's reference group.

As the function of an attitude is related to the approaches that might lead to its change, social workers should consider this issue in planning strategies of attitude change. To change instrumental attitudes one would focus on changing either goals or perceived links between established goals and the object of the attitude (Rosenberg 1956). Shifts in ego-defensive attitudes may require client insight into internal conflicts and their link to the attitude in question (D. Katz, Sarnoff and McClintock 1956). Changes in expressive attitude may require the provision of alternate means to assert one's values or the linking of another value to the attitude object (Di Vesta and Bossart 1958). Modifications in attitudes that serve a knowledge function may be effected by providing new information about the relevant person or object, but the information must indeed be relevant to the knowledge needed by the individual (N. Maccoby et al. 1962).

CONSISTENCY THEORIES OF ATTITUDE CHANGE

Up to this point we have been presenting research and theory in which the focus is the determinants or predictors of attitudes and the conditions under which attitudes predict behavioral intentions or behavior, although in our discussion attitude and behavior change implications have been noted. Now we turn our attention to theories and research in which the focus is directly on how attitudes can be changed. The prediction of an individual's current attitudes is not of particular concern, but the conditions under which change in that attitude can be induced to occur is of concern. Quite a few cognitive consistency theories exist in social psychology and they all share the key assumption that consistency among various attitudes, beliefs and behaviors is a satisfactory psychological state and that inconsistency is dissatisfying or arousing. They further assume that attempts by individuals to reduce inconsistencies can lead to changes in attitudes, beliefs, and behaviors. Three types of attitude change theory will be described, along with their implications for social work intervention: 1) cognitive dissonance, as exemplified in the work of Festinger (1957) and J. W. Brehm (Brehm and Cohen 1962; Wicklund and Brehm 1976); 2) the self-confrontation approach based on the theory of human values of Rokeach (1968b, 1973); and 3) D. J. Bem's (1967, 1972) self-perception theory, previously introduced in chapter 3. Although these theories do disagree in several respects, for example, Bem's theory does not assume that inconsistency is arousing as does Festinger's, one key difference is that they focus on different aspects of the entire matrix of possible relationships among attitudes, beliefs, and behaviors in trying to explain attitude change. Cognitive dissonance theory has generated a great deal of research about the consequences of inconsistency between one's behavior and an attitude or belief relevant to that behavior. Rokeach's efforts to change values and behaviors through a self-confrontation technique focuses on inconsistencies between certain types of attitudes and beliefs, namely values and self-concept. Bem's focus is on the implications of observing one's own behaviors on one's attitude toward and beliefs about the self.

COGNITIVE DISSONANCE THEORY

According to Festinger (1957), who originated the theory, cognitive dissonance exists when two cognitions held by an individual are related to one another but are obverse, that is there is an inconsistent relation between them; they do not fit together, or do not follow one from the other. The lack of fit may be due to logical inconsistencies (for example praying by someone who does not believe in God), to cultural norms (a woman opening a door for a man), to disconfirmed expectancies (a person working very hard to move to New York City and then finding it is unpleasant), or a variety of other situations where one element psychologically contradicts another. The cognitions that may be dissonant are defined quite broadly to include information, beliefs, or attitudes about other persons or things, or about one's own behavior or oneself. Whenever cognitions about two beliefs, two attitudes, two behaviors, or an attitude and a behavior, etc., are psychologically inconsistent, dissonance is experienced as discomfort and motivates the individuals to change one of the elements so that it is no longer inconsistent with the second. Most research done within the cognitive dissonance framework has concerned inconsistencies between cognitions about one's own behavior on the one hand, and an attitude, or belief. In such situations, since behaviors cannot be undone, the more likely element to change is the attitude or belief. When attitudes or beliefs are in conflict however, it is difficult to predict which one will be modified to reduce the dissonance.

Two major situations in which attitude change occurs have been studied by cognitive dissonance researchers. One type is the attitude change that occurs following a free choice between alternatives each of which had been attractive prior to the decision. This is known as postdecision dissonance. Many laboratory and field studies have shown that following such a decision, the liking for the selected item increases and that for the rejected one decreases. According to cognitive dissonance theory, the closer the original attractiveness of the alternatives, the greater the dissonance; it is not harmonious to consider two objects as equally attractive yet to select one and reject the other. Two types of behavior-belief-attitude dissonance can exist in such situations. A choice between two attractive alternatives is usually based on multiple characteristics of each and the ratio of desirable to undesirable characteristics is assumed to be higher in the chosen than rejected alternative. Thus the chosen alternative involves some negative features, and this is dissonant, and the rejected alternative is likely to have some positive qualities, also a condition of dissonance. These two dissonances can be reduced by emphasizing the positive qualities of the chosen item and the negative characteristics of the rejected one after the choice is made, thus changing attitudes or beliefs about one, or the other, or both alternatives. This phenomenon was observed after automobile purchases (D. Ehrlich et al. 1957), after children selected one toy from among many (J. W. Brehm and Cohen 1959), at the voting booth (Frenkel and Doob 1976), after a bet was placed at a racetrack (Knox and Inkster 1968), after simulated hiring decisions (Davidson and Kiesler 1964), and even after the decision to become formally engaged (A. R. Cohen 1962b).

The other major situation cognitive dissonance researchers have studied is usually called a forced compliance situation, though we will see shortly that this label may be misleading. Essentially this situation occurs when an individual performs an act that is contrary to an attitude or belief and that person cannot explain the action by virtue of a large reward or threat of severe punishment. This is referred to as dissonance following attitude-discrepant behavior with insufficient justification; there is dissonance between behavior and one's prior beliefs or attitudes related to that behavior and this dissonance can be reduced by attitude or belief modification. For example, in one of the earliest studies (Festinger and Carlsmith 1959) it was found that when students had participated in an extremely dull experiment (peg turning and stool sorting) and then were asked to tell the next subject (a confederate) that the task was interesting and exciting, they were more likely to rate the experimental task favorably later than were controls who did not engage in the counterattitudinal behavior of telling someone the task was fun. Further, among the experimental subjects, those who were paid twenty dollars showed much less attitude change than did those paid only one dollar. A similar effect was found when college men were induced to write an essay in favor of police handling of students, a view they personally opposed (A. R. Cohen 1962a). Those paid ten dollars did not change their negative attitude toward the police after writing the essay, but those who wrote the essay and received only one dollar or fifty cents became more favorable toward the police. The researchers interpreted these findings as indicating that dissonance had been established in the individuals who believed one thing and yet behaved differently without sufficient justification, i.e. those who received low monetary reward. The act could not be undone, but the attitude or belief could be changed to reduce the dissonance, and hence a change was obtained.

Later modifications of Festinger's theory (Aronson 1973; J. W. Brehm and Cohen 1962; Festinger 1964; Wicklund and Brehm 1976) have tried to specify further those conditions that must exist in the two types of situations described above for dissonance to occur. The major specification is that the individual must feel personal responsibility for the relevant behavior, either the decisional choice or the counterattitudinal behavior. Unless some personal responsibility for the behavior is felt, dissonance will not occur, and the greater the perceived responsibility the greater the dissonance. This perception can come about in a number of ways—through the individual feeling that a choice existed to engage in the behavior or not or to choose one alternative or another, through the individual foreseeing the consequences of the action, or through attribution of responsibility for the action to the actor by some other significant person. A number of studies have shown that when individuals do not feel responsible for their own behavior the attitude change predicted to follow dissonance does not occur (e.g., Collins and Hoyt 1972; Reiss and Schlenker 1977). This point is crucial for social work applications and will be discussed further below.

Another quality also seems essential for dissonance to occur: at least one of the cognitive elements that is in a dissonant relationship must be somewhat resistant to change. In other words, the person must have some commitment to the behavior or attitude, or the behavior or attitude must have some importance to the individual for dissonance to occur, and the greater the resistance the greater the dissonance. To ensure such commitment in research, the decisional choice or counterattitudinal behavior is often made overt and public rather than covert and private (Kiesler, Pallak, and Kanouse 1968). Importance has been manipulated by indicating the behavior is relevant to personal ability (Glass, Canavan, and Schiavo 1968) or to future interactions (Kiesler and Corbin 1965).

A final further condition that is widely accepted as necessary for dissonance to occur is that counterattitudinal behavior must have unwanted or aversive consequences for oneself or someone else. For example, the Festinger and Carlsmith study was replicated (Cooper and Worchel 1970), with the variation of the confederate indicating whether or not he was convinced by the subject's description of the experiment as interesting—in this case the attitude change occurred only for subjects who believed they had falsely convinced the confederate.

There are other conditions that seem to enhance the occurrence of dissonance, although they do not appear to be essential to its occurrence. Effort is one such factor that is especially relevant to social workers. Counterattitudinal behavior that requires a great deal of effort or discomfort to carry out appears especially likely to arouse dissonance (Aronson and Mills 1968; Gerard and Mathewson 1966; Zimbardo and Ebbesen 1970). Another dissonance-enhancing factor is the self-esteem of the person. Aronson (1973) has argued that counterattitudinal behavior will be more dissonant for persons who view themselves as capable and logical than for those who feel inadequate. Capable persons who see themselves acting in ways that do not follow from their feelings would be made uncomfortable by this inconsistency and by that between a self-image of thoughtfulness and engagement in counterattitudinal behavior. Aronson carries the argument one step further and states that if individuals see themselves as "shnooks," then acting logically would create dissonance and acting illogically or foolishly would be consonant with this self-image. Such a person would not be disconcerted by feeling one way and acting another. A similar factor seems relevant to postdecisional dissonance effects (Gerard, Blevans, and Malcom 1964). After choosing between alternatives a person with high self-esteem may be more motivated to justify the decision through derogating the rejected alternative and emphasizing the virtues of the chosen one than would a person with low self-esteem. For example, a man with very low self-esteem who has a hard time deciding between two cars, but buys one, is likely to dislike the chosen car more rather than less—the purchase of a "lemon" would be consonant with this self-image of "being a shnook." Aronson also hypothesizes that if the dissonance has utility, the individual will not try to remove it but will relish it. For example, the car purchaser who made a hasty decision and bought a lemon may openly dislike the car he purchased to teach himself a lesson not to buy an expensive item without sufficient comparison shopping. Finally Aronson and others (e.g., D. J. Bem 1970) acknowledge that different people can tolerate different amounts of dissonance, and we cannot predict at this time who can tolerate dissonance and who cannot, although some research has been done on this topic (Glass, Canavan, and Schiavo 1968).

Let us now consider when a social worker might make use of the knowledge that attitude change may occur when people engage in behavior discrepant with their own attitudes or beliefs. Suppose a client in a family agency is concerned about her husband's ensuing release and return home from a psychiatric hospital. She fears that he will disrupt the family's current satisfactory mode of adjustment. The worker and client may believe that a change in the area of the wife's attitude toward her husband's return would be desirable. The issue is not that the wife does not know how to welcome her spouse home, but rather that she will not because her attitudes do not support such behavior. If the wife agreed to prepare a festive meal for her husband for his first evening at home, this behavior would be dissonant with her opinion that he is likely to upset the family. Dissonance could then be reduced by the wife's changing her opinion. This change in opinion would then further support the continuance of such behavior with little worker involvement, for it would be consonant with the revised opinion. The dissonant behavior is also likely to elicit positive responses from the discharged patient, and hence be reinforced. Such reinforcement would also serve to perpetuate the behavior.

It is the contention of theorists who have advocated the utility of cognitive dissonance ideas to helping professionals (S. Brehm 1976; Cooper 1974; Wicklund and Brehm 1976) that similar situations to the one described above are common occurrences; one goal of intervention is often to get clients to engage in behavior that they are capable of, but are not performing because of nonsupportive beliefs or attitudes. Belief or opinion change is thus desirable. What is different about the cognitive dissonance approach to this situation from that of the means-end attitude theorist is the assumption by the former that attitude change is brought about through behavior change. In this respect the approach has some similarity to that of the behaviorist where the intervention focus is directly upon behavior. But the cognitive dissonance perspective suggests somewhat different conditions under which behavior change is most likely to lead to attitude change and hence persistence of the behavior. The conditions are those that enhance dissonance under insufficient justification, namely clients are induced to perform the behavior under minimal external justification, with perceived personal responsibility for the decision to try the behavior, a commitment to carry out the behavior in a fashion that prevents its reversal, and a recognition that negative consequences may follow. In laboratory experiments these conditions have often been created through deception: for example subjects are made to believe they have a choice when they do not. This would clearly be unethical for the social worker. There are, however, a number of honest and appropriate means by which the conditions that facilitate dissonance arousal can be enhanced by the social worker. Personal responsibility can be maximized by low external incentives, free choice, and verbal support for the clients' responsibilities for their own actions. The social worker should thus use only as many external inducements, such as rewards, as are needed to obtain the behavior. Workers should also encourage clients to discuss and decide whether they are willing to try the novel behavior in these cases and later remind clients that they have made the choice themselves. To be avoided, according to the cognitive dissonance approach, would be efforts by the social worker to promise extremely rewarding outcomes, to ask clients to do something without giving them a choice, or to tell clients that the worker recognizes that they engaged in the action because the worker desired it. These conditions would reduce clients' responsibility for their own actions and hence reduce dissonance arousal.

Not only should client responsibility be maximized if dissonance arousal is desirable, so should client commitment to the behavior. Overt, public, repeated behaviors would thus be preferable. The woman described above whose husband is about to be discharged could be encouraged to tell her husband how happy she is to have him home when others are around to hear her being appreciative of her spouse, and to agree to find opportunities to repeat those statements each day. The behavior thus becomes more salient and arouses greater dissonance with a continued belief that the husband is likely to disrupt the family and is unwanted.

Dissonance would be further enhanced if clients foresaw possible negative consequences from commitment to engage in a freely chosen counterattitudinal behavior without strong external justification. Since many novel behaviors are likely to have some aversive consequences the social workers would be well advised to point these out in advance. Cooper (1974) has emphasized this in his discussion of appropriate means to encourage population planning. A recognition by couples of certain negative consequences of small families accompanied by their choice to use birth control should lead to changes in attitudes that can then buttress family planning behavior. The wife in our example above may feel embarrassed at welcoming her husband in front of his friends if she has previously expressed her fears of him. The discharged patient's surprise at his wife's warmth may initially evoke a rejection rather than an appreciative reply. Such consequences should be pointed out in advance.

To cite another example of a social worker's application of cognitive dissonance theory, a father may be antagonistic to the young man of a different religious or ethnic group whom his daughter is going to marry. Asking the father to discuss some of the assets of the boyfriend, for example, how he would describe the fellow to some distant relatives or business acquaintances he was trying to impress, may help arouse the dissonance process so that the father's attitudes will change in a more favorable direction. Should he be willing to taperecord the statements for replaying at a later point, his commitment to these counterattitudinal comments may increase, particularly if the tape is played for other family members. It would be important to forewarn the father that his relatives may criticize his defense of the future son-in-law. Before moving to use this somewhat contrived strategy, the worker should be alert to any spontaneous comments by the client which appear to be counterattitudinal. For example, if the father mentions having discussed his future son-in-law with his supervisor on the job, and if it appears that the description was more favorable than would be expected, the worker might ask for details about the conversation so that the client will openly quote himself uttering counterattitudinal statements. If these statement are made spontaneously, or induced by the worker, the opportunity should not be lost to point up the discrepancies from previous statements, assuming that a change in attitude is perceived as beneficial.

We need to recognize, however, as others have done (S. Brehm 1976; Cooper 1974; Darley and Cooper 1972; Kiesler 1971), some potential problems in using dissonance principles. There is good research support for the idea that inducements to engage in counterattitudinal behaviors that are just barely sufficient to obtain the behavior are more dissonance producing than very large inducements, but it is not always clear what is sufficient. And research has also shown that when some positive inducements exist but they are insufficient to elicit the behavior, the situation may have the opposite effect to the one desired. For example, one study asked students to write a counterattitudinal essay (advocating a strict school dress code) under conditions where it was likely that the request would be refused (Darley and Cooper 1972). Subjects were offered either fifty cents or one dollar-fifty to write the essay; the room in which they were to work was extremely hot and uncomfortable. All subjects refused the experimenter's request. The subjects who had hardly any inducement to engage in the behavior (fifty cents and hot room) did not change their attitudes any more than did a control group who were not requested to write the essay. But the subjects who turned down the larger but still insufficient reward (one dollar-fifty) became more extreme and more confident in their anti-dress code attitudes than did the control group. For these students their behavior of refusing to write the essay was dissonant with their desire for the dollar-fifty, and this dissonance was reduced by enhancing their original attitude which was contrary to the content requested in the essay. Thus a social worker should be fairly confident that a client will agree to perform a counterattitudinal act to avoid a boomerang effect, in which the client chooses not to do so and consequently becomes more entrenched in an undesirable attitude or belief.

Insofar as postdecision dissonance is concerned, the most relevant situation for the social worker is that in which the client is in a quandry trying to decide between two similarly desirable, or undesirable, choices. Cognitive dissonance theory and research include two important principles for social workers in this type of situation: 1) once the decision is made, the individual will find the chosen alternative the more desirable one and a reduction of discomfort will ensue; and 2) dissonance arousal will be stronger the greater the perceived similarity among the alternatives prior to the choice. This suggests that during the exploration of alternatives the worker should seek to facilitate the client's awareness of similarities to foster dissonance arousal after the decision is made. But unnecessarily prolonging the debate between fairly equal choices is likely to be nonproductive. For example, postponing a decision about which job to take or which college to attend is likely to result in prolonged discomfort that is dysfunctioal. One of the choices may even disappear due to inaction, in which case postdecision dissonance will not be operative as no free choice decision was made. The client may possibly even feel contempt for his or her own inability to make a choice when a choice was available. Thus if after all the alternatives have been thoroughly explored and the client still seems reluctant to come to a decision, the worker might well encourage the individual to reach some conclusion. In doing so the worker should keep in mind certain conditions fostering dissonance: free choice, or personal responsibility for the decision, and commitment to it. If the client feels responsible for the decision and acts on it, strong postdecisional dissonance and dissonance reduction mechanisms are likely. The client will recall the attractive aspects of the chosen alternative and the unattractive elements of the rejected one. At this point in the decisional process the worker can reinforce this dissonance reducing behavior.

Because personal responsibility enhances dissonance, however, the clients may be reluctant to act on their own in arriving at a choice. Although it may be tempting for the worker to step in and take some responsibility in order to get some action, this can have negative consequences; there could be less postdecisional dissonance and hence less dissonance reduction leading to solidification of the attractiveness of the chosen alternative. It might be more beneficial in situations in which clients are reluctant to assume responsibility for making a decision for the worker to support the client's capacity for good decision making. One could point to past choices that were beneficial, or if these are not available, build in opportunities for easier decisions by the client in other areas.

One important decision in any helping situation involves the client's choice to come for help in the first place and to continue coming. To enhance a positive attitude toward the encounter and continued contact, dissonance theory suggests that the client should be made aware that this decision is his or hers to make, that each appointment kept involves at least some level of free choice and a commitment to carry out contracted-for behaviors, and finally that certain negative consequences are likely. There is usually a loss of free time, transportation costs, embarrassment at discussing private matters, and other difficulties inherent in continuing in a social work relationship. So long as these negative consequences do not become stronger than the positive ones, dissonance theory suggests the worker should encourage their anticipation.

Also relevant to the engagement of the client in the social work relationship is the finding that expending increased effort while carrying out counterattitudinal behaviors increases dissonance and attitude or belief change in the direction of consistency with behavior. The fact that the client often has to wait for a considerable period of time before getting an appointment with the worker, or has to complete complex procedures beforehand, should result in an enhanced view of the value of treatment, according to cognitive dissonance theory. The proviso, of course, is that the effort not be so great as to exceed the client's initial opinion about the value of the services sought. It is also possible for the worker to use the concept during interviews in order to facilitate goal attainment by the client. For example, if the worker wishes to employ an intriguing approach, such as videotaping the clients so that they may revise their views of how they appear to others, the worker should not try to make the taping session seem effortless. If the clients must help carry the heavy video equipment, or if the taping session is very lengthy, it may create more dissonance than if the worker sets up the machine and a short comfortable session is held immediately after the idea is broached. Similarly, it has been suggested (S. Brehm 1976) that role-playing techniques used to practice new behaviors should be made effortful—through their length, complexity of the situation being role played, or even the presence of distracting environmental conditions such as noise. Similar approaches are relevant when the worker is about to try other new strategies. If the worker is attempting to organize a group for the clients to join, an explanation of the difficulties entailed in such an arrangement would not only be truthful but also beneficial. Once again however, the worker may have to decide whether creating delays and obstacles where none are necessary is ethical. Certainly however, if the realities of the situation require effort to take the next step, the worker should not hesitate to let the clients know about the difficulties involved.

In concluding our discussion of cognitive dissonance theory, two other potential areas of application can be mentioned in addition to the one described (increasing dissonance as a means of achieving attitude change). Cognitive dissonance may be a useful concept to consider as a source of client discomfort during assessment, and the reduction of such dissonance may be one goal of intervention. When an assessment is made that conditions in a client's life are disturbing because they arouse dissonance, the worker could focus on helping the client remove the source of the dissonance through changing behaviors or changing attitudes to increase their congruence. Alternatively, if this is not possible the intervention focus could be on reduction of those conditions that enhance the experience of dissonance. Here the worker could help the client to identify the external justifications that control the client's behavior, or the lack of free choice the client has about engaging in the dissonant actions, or to reduce the negative consequences of carrying out certain actions. In short, the approaches described above as useful to increase dissonance can be reversed to reduce undesirable dissonance.

SELF-PERCEPTION THEORY

As developed by D. J. Bem (1967, 1972), self-perception theory seeks to explain many of the same phenomena of concern to cognitive dissonance theories. The key difference is in the reason proposed for why a person might change an attitude or belief after behaving in some way relevant to it. Bem proposes that the change stems simply from the individuals' observation of their own behaviors and the circumstances in which they occur. According to Bem, such observations cause self-attributions based on the individuals, in effect, asking themselves the question, "What must my attitude be if I am willing to behave in this fashion in this situation?" Unlike the cognitive dissonance theorists, Bem does not postulate that dissonance is aroused in the counterattitudinal behavior or free choice situations, or that the individual is motivated to reduce dissonance.

We are not particularly concerned here with comparing systematically the dissonance and self-perception approaches or evaluating whether the research evidence favors one or the other—these are complex issues as yet unresolved by social psychologists. But we do want to point out certain similarities and differences because they are germaine to social work. Both types of theories focus on the effects of behavior on subsequent attitude change, and thus direct us to consider behavior change as one way to change attitudes in practice settings. Further, the key attitude (or belief) changes that Bem considers are feelings or opinions about oneself. Am I angry? Am I the kind of person who actively supports political causes? Although Bem's behaviorist view of how self-perceptions are formed does not clearly specify how self-perception shifts can then influence subsequent behavior shifts, a number of other researchers have suggested such links, and these links are of interest to social work practitioners.

For example, in a number of field studies it was found that compliance with a second moderate request will increase if there was prior compliance with an initial small request for aid (Cann, Sherman, and Elkes 1975; Freedman and Fraser 1966; Pliner et al., 1974; Snyder and Cunningham 1975). The explanation offered was that of changing self-perceptions. Although the details of these studies differ, all include a number of similar features: 1. Adult residents are contacted at their homes or in other natural settings by a stranger who asks them to agree to do some small action that is socially useful (wear a pin symbolizing a charity, put a small sign in their home window in support of a safety campaign, answer a short telephone survey conducted by a public service organization). 2. Nearly all persons comply with the initial request. 3. Another larger, more time-consuming, or more difficult request is received from the same or a different person (contribute money to a local charity, place a very large poorly lettered sign on their front lawn, answer a very long telephone survey). 4. Compared to control subjects who only received the larger request, the experimental subjects are more likely to comply with the second request.

The phenomenon has been labeled as the "foot-in-the-door" effect. According to Bem's self-perception theory, if individuals observe themselves doing something out of free choice, the behaviors are attributed to their disposition, not to external forces, and the conclusion reached is that "I am that sort of a person." Some theorists further assume that individuals will act accordingly in future similar situations. In this case, individuals who complied with the initial small requests are presumed to have arrived at the conclusion that "I am the type of individual who agrees to socially desirable requests." Hence, when asked for aid on a second occasion, the individual acts in accord with this self-perception. This proposed shift in self-perception seems supported by the generality of the effect, which occurs regardless of whether the second request is made by the same or a different person, concerns the same social cause or a different one, or is made in close time juxtaposition or up to two weeks apart.

Cognitive dissonance interpretations of the effect are also possible (S. Brehm 1976; Wicklund and Brehm 1976). According to this explanation, individuals who agree to a request for help experience dissonance between their behavior and their prior opinion of the causes' worthiness and/or their view of themselves as supporters of the cause. Dissonance is then reduced by redefining the value of the cause or by viewing oneself as the sort of person who helps socially desirable causes. In either case, a subsequent request for aid is met so as to avoid uncomfortable dissonance between the individuals' new beliefs and behavior. Though the two views are similar, cognitive dissonance theory focuses on motivation to end or avoid discomfort; Bem's theory focuses on a perceptual/cognitive process: "This is what I am like."

Both explanations enter into a social psychological interpretation of the processes involved in the decision to donate organs or tissue for transplant surgery (Saks 1978). In the typical situation a family member is the potential donor and the decision is usually delayed until the end of an extended selection process. The process involves the individual taking tests and providing information that are used to determine if the transplant is feasible. Each step in the process can yield a foot-in-the-door effect of small agreements and commitments that lead the potential donor to view himself or herself as having the unique potential to help. Furthermore, the tests and other procedures make the initiation into the position of donor difficult, thereby increasing the cognitive dissonance between engaging in those behaviors and not agreeing to donate the organ or tissue. Thus the typical process seems to enhance the likelihood of a decision to donate.

There are important implications for social work practice of the foot-in-the-door phenomenon, and for both explanations of it. Following cognitive dissonance ideas discussed earlier, one clinician suggests a successive approximations or "dissonance shaping" procedure to facilitate clients' carrying out prosocial behavior (S. Brehm 1976). If such a goal is appropriate, the social worker could encourage the client to perform some relatively easy behavior of the desired type under conditions likely to arouse dissonance, thereby getting a foot in the door. For example, the worker could suggest that an isolated elderly widow phone a lonely child in a hospital. Then gradually increasingly difficult behaviors could be encouraged under low justification, voluntary commitment conditions. The goal here is to increase the clients' willingness to carry out behaviors already in their repertoire, such as being helpful to someone else. The self-perception view would suggest a slightly different but not contradictory focus in such situations—that if a worker can help individuals to change their perceptions about themselves (in the above case, by getting the reclusive widow to see herself a helper to sick children), it is likely there will be an alteration in subsequent relevant behaviors. One way to bring about altered self-perceptions is through eliciting counterattitudinal behaviors, as just described. A self-perception focus would further suggest that in such dissonance-arousing situations, the worker should highlight the relevant self-attributions, e.g., should point out that an action indicates that the client is a supportive person.

An alternative self-perception strategy would focus more directly on the self-attributions, by having the worker make attributions about the client that are congruent with desired but not currently accepted self-perceptions. This technique was effective in fostering young children's continued sharing of prizes with classmates or with unknown needy children (Grusec et al., 1978). In that study children were encouraged to be altruistic by a variety of techniques, and then they were told either that they had shared because they liked helping people (the self-attribution groups), or because the adult expected them to, or were given no reason. In a generalization test with different prizes, children in the self-attribution groups shared more with another child than did either those who had received no attribution feedback or children who had been given an external attribution.

In a situation more closely linked to client problems typically encountered by school social workers, a similar intervention aimed at revising children's self-perceptions was also successful. The retraining was used in special individual sessions with youngsters identified by teachers, school psychologists, and the principal as displaying both high expectations of failure and performance decrements in situations where they encountered failure (Dweck 1975). A combination of repeated successes interposed with occasional failures that were explained to the children as due to their own lack of effort was more effective than simply a series of success experiences. In a generalization test, the children who received the attributional retraining showed both a decrease in performance disruption and an increase in self-attribution to effort after failure.

A similar technique was also effective with children in a more natural classroom setting (R. L. Miller, Brickman, and Bolen 1975). It was found that when teachers repeatedly told children that they were the kinds of youngsters who behave, feel, or think a certain way (e.g., are good at or like math, are neat), this was sufficient to bring about a change in self-attributions (e.g., about their math competency or neatness) and subsequent desired behavior (e.g., math performance or littering). Whether this technique would work with adults has not been tested, although the damage done by labeling delinquents and retardates as such is well known. The self-fulfilling prophecy is a phenomenon that has been observed for decades although the connotation has been negative rather than positive. Miller and his colleagues indicated that the "labeling" process worked, and that, like modeling, it elicited desirable behavior. There is an ethical problem in this research, since it involved lying by those who told the client that they were certain types of individuals (e.g., neat), when they were not. This process has been referred to as the use of misattributions to bring about desired behaviors (Shaver 1975).

Another example of obtaining beneficial results from misattributions was found in a study by Storms and Nisbitt (1970). Insomnia sufferers were given placebo pills and were told either that the pill would produce an accelerated heart rate and wakefulness or that it would relax them. Those given the pills under arousal instructions reported falling asleep earlier on nights they took the pills than on nights they did not, and earlier than those given pills to "relax" them. The interpretation was that the "arousing" pills permitted the insomniacs to attribute their unease at bedtime to the pills, to worry less about internal symptoms, and hence to sleep. In this case, a nonveridical attribution was therapeutic. It is possible that in a number of situations characterized by the occurrence of symptoms, worry about the symptoms, and further exacerbation of the symptoms, a misattribution that would externalize the cause of the symptom would be beneficial (Shaver 1975). But it must be pointed out that such a procedure involves lying to someone who trusts you. Even if the social work practitioner could overcome the moral objections to violating a trust and explicitly lying, such deception is likely to be discovered and the worker would lose virtually all credibility in future interactions.

All things considered, it is probably more judicious to try to elicit behavior from clients that will alter their own perceptions of themselves and to support such self-perceptions verbally rather than to manipulate labels independent of the clients' behaviors. This approach was used to reduce stress in patients about to undergo surgery (Langer, Janis, and Wolfer 1975). In an intervention that stressed the patients' control over their own thoughts, the patients were trained to think about the positive aspects of their hospitalization and to maintain an optimistic view whenever an unpleasant aspect occurred. Compared to patients who received information about the pre- and postsurgery procedures or to a nontreatment control group, those who received instruction in the self-coping device displayed fewer signs of stress both before and after surgery—they expressed less concern to their nurses and asked for fewer pain pills or sedatives. Parallel to this are the several different intervention approaches that involve asking clients to try out new roles in protected environments (Kanfer and Phillips 1969; Kelly 1955; Reid 1975; Reid and Epstein 1972; Rose 1974a; Thomas and Carter 1971; Zimbardo 1977). This strategy is sometimes referred to as a behavioral assignment (Rose and Sundel 1974) or instigative influence (R. L. Levy and Carter 1976). A low-key behavior that can be elicited without too much difficulty from shy young adults is that of attending social gatherings, perhaps after coaching, where they are unknown—in this case nothing is lost if the evening is a failure. Once the clients find they can perform the new role successfully, their self-perceptions, and perhaps their performance in future situations, may be altered.

It might be equally effective to highlight for the clients some behavior they had described performing in the past that is indicative of a characteristic the clients had not acknowledged about themselves. For example, if a mother who fears her uncontrolled anger toward a child describes some occasions when she had been able to control temper outbursts without external pressure, these occasions can be pointed out as indicative of self-control in the face of provocation. Or an inept, helpless divorced man who had described a period prior to marriage when he coped independently with housework may see himself in a new way if these activities are highlighted as reflective of his strength and adaptive ability. Here the goal is to correct misattributions held by clients. Such focusing of attention on instances in past behavior that are not congruent with current self-perceptions may bring about desirable shifts in attributions.

An alternative to inducing clients to try new behaviors or to use their own past histories to alter self-perceptions is to provide them with information about how other people respond in similar situations. If clients can be shown that their responses are similar to those of many others, they may arrive at the conclusion that the behavior they are exhibiting is attributable to the situation and not to their own dispositions. Information about other peoples' successes and failures have a particularly potent influence on perceptions about one's abilities (Nisbett et al. 1976). It has been shown that such information may be used to evaluate certain achievement tasks as easy or hard and to make decisions about one's own willingness to engage in the tasks among adults (B. Weiner and Kukla 1970) and among grade-school children (Feld, Ruhland, and Gold 1979; Veroff 1969). This suggests a potentially useful way to alter those self-perceptions about ability that may be interfering with the competent functioning of some clients. For example, if a woman doubts her ability to do graduate work because of low grades in a statistics course, offering the student information about the number of other individuals, especially women, who did equally poorly and still managed to obtain a graduate degree is likely to modify her view of herself. She may come to feel that the cause of her poor performance relates to qualities of the quantitative tasks and to her socialization as a female in our society rather than to her general ability. The grade is not an indication that she is unable to do graduate work. According to attribution theory, discussed in chapter 3, the situation is seen as causing a behavior to the extent that the response is widely shared and to the extent that the actor does not respond in that manner to all situations. Thus, the woman in graduate school who knows that she does not receive low grades in all subjects and who comes to understand that many women do poorly in statistics, is likely to attribute the cause of her difficulty to the situation and not to her own disposition. A change in attribution here does not necessarily suggest that grades will improve, but merely that the receipt of low grades will result in less self-denigration.

Unfortunately, providing individuals with data about how large groups perform, sometimes referred to as consensus or base-rate information, appears primarily to alter attributions about ability (B. Weiner et al. 1971), probably because since early childhood ratings of abilities are made in terms of the performance of others. Additional attempts to modify behavior with this approach have failed, for example, to reduce feelings of depression by indicating that many other people are responding similarly in these situations (Nisbett et al. 1976). Nisbett and his colleagues hypothesized that when consensus data conflict with direct, firsthand reports from a few individuals personally encountered, or from vivid exceptions to the general trend, the base-rate data will be ignored because concrete, emotionally interesting information has greater power to generate inferences than does abstract, mathematical information. Thus, for example, when undergraduates were asked to predict how much shock individuals would be likely to accept in an experimental situation, they were likely to use videotaped interviews with a few past subjects to predict those responses rather than numerical data about how a large number of past subjects responded to the same experiment. Concrete details outweigh contradictory abstract information about faceless individuals aggregated into tables, lists, or averages.

As further evidence of the power of a few vivid examples to influence when dry numbers fail, Nisbett and colleagues cite the fact that waiting lists at cancer detection clinics increased enormously shortly after the mastectomies performed on Mrs. Gerald Ford and Mrs. Nelson Rockefeller were reported in the press. The issuance of new statistics by the Surgeon General, American Medical Association, or any other organization never produced the same effect. Nisbett and colleagues suggest that the power of the emotional example stems from its ability to call up mental schemas or scripts involving similar information known to the individuals, e.g., a sister-in-law who had the same experience. The inference about what caused the problem, or what is likely to occur in the future, then proceeds along well-worn lines of the old scripts very familiar to the actor. This explanation has not been proven but it does appear reasonable.

In view of the above discussion, social work practitioners might keep in mind that information about groups of other persons is probably useful in altering self-perceptions when abilities are concerned, as may commonly occur for children with problems in school or adults with job difficulties, but not in other areas. In other areas, some vivid, concrete examples are likely to be more effective in influencing the self-attributions of clients as to the causes of their behaviors. Such emotionally arresting examples may be detailed descriptions of popular figures who responded in the same ways as the client when confronted with the same problem, for example, the suicide of a spouse. Experiences shared in groups composed of individuals who became aware that it was not their own dispositions but factors in the situation that were causing some problematic behaviors can also result in altered self-perceptions. For example, in recent years, the consciousness of a number of oppressed groups, such as blacks, Hispanics, women, gays, the aged, and most recently, the physically handicapped, has been raised as the members of these groups have come to realize that their inability to obtain jobs comensurate with their education, or an education comensurate with their abilities, was not due to their personal failings but to the discrimination to which they were subject.

On the other hand, a social worker may be confronted with clients who unrealistically attribute their difficulties to factors beyond their control when these individuals may be at least partially responsible for the problem because of their own skill deficits, lack of effort, or poor physical condition. In these situations, the worker might do well to employ the vivid, concrete example to help these individuals recognize some of their own contributions to the situation. For example, the worker could provide a detailed, vivid account of or arrange a meeting with a similar individual who enrolled at a community college or in adult education programs and managed to get a promotion or find an initial job, to prompt the clients to alter their self-perceptions. Participation in a group composed of similar individuals who were attempting to learn to type, or to stop drinking, may offer clients a wide variety of emotionally arousing examples of individuals who are changing themselves rather than attributing blame for all of their difficulties on external factors. Some self-help groups, such as Alcoholics Anonymous, have as one of their major goals changing the attributions members make about the cause of their difficulties from external forces to internal factors.

It is clear that the worker must be cautious when attempting to alter the self-perception of clients in the direction of self-attribution of difficulties. There must be ample evidence that the clients can modify their own abilities or efforts to perform once becoming convinced that this step is needed. If clients internalize blame or guilt for a difficult situation and then are unable to change, the net effect may be an exacerbation of the difficulty rather than its reduction.

Regardless of the particular method selected to redirect self-perceptions, or the particular self-perception that was targeted, the research and theory cited above suggest that social workers should be alert to the importance of assessing whether a shift in self-perceptions could facilitate attainment of the client's goals. A number of writers on behavior therapy have already suggested that the procedures for behavior modification be reviewed to enhance their likelihood for affecting shifts in self-perceptions. Bandura (1977) has proposed that behavioral changes induced by interventions related to a wide variety of perspectives are mediated by shifts in cognitions about self-efficacy expectations, expectations that one can successfully execute the behavior required to produce a desired outcome. He has shown, for example, that for adults with chronic snake phobias, the outcomes of treatments by passive modeling, participant modeling, or systematic desensitization techniques were predicted by the self-efficacy expectations of the clients at the completion of the interventions (Bandura, Adams, and Beyer 1977). His conclusion is that when using techniques to enhance the skills or incentives for performance, the practitioner should also be concerned about fostering the clients' sense that self-directed mastery, rather than some external factor, is responsible for behavioral change. A similar point is made by Meichenbaum (1975), and by Kopel and Arkowitz (1975) in their review of the implications of attribution and self-perception theory and research for behavior therapy. They conclude that it is likely that self-attributed behavior changes are generalized or maintained to a greater degree than are behavior changes attributed to external agents because attribution to one's own abilities or motivation has implications for future action in a variety of situations whereas external attributions apply only if conditions are stable. Further, they suggest a number of ways in which the salience of self-responsibility for successful intervention outcomes can be enhanced, such as emphasis on self-monitoring of behaviors via counting procedures, the use of focused self-observations of video- or audiotapes, and active involvement of clients in deciding what can be done to enhance self-attributions for subsequent behavior. Social workers of nonbehavioral persuasions would also be well advised to consider carefully the impact of their techniques upon the self-perceptions of their clients.

HUMAN VALUE THEORY AND SELF-CONFRONTATION

In the theory of human values developed by Rokeach (1971, 1973, 1975), self-confrontation is seen as an approach to changing attitudes, values, and behaviors. The strategy is premised upon the assumption that making individuals aware of inconsistencies between their self-conceptions and values will arouse self-dissatisfaction, which in turn will lead to attitude, value, and behavior changes. A number of ingenious studies using this approach have shown behavior changes relating to participation in civil rights organizations (Rokeach 1971), interracial behavior (Penner 1971), teaching performance (Greenstein 1976), and cessation of smoking (Conroy, Katkin, and Barnette 1972). It is useful to describe in some detail one of the first studies of this type (Rokeach 1971).

The goal of this intervention was to increase college students' concern for and participation in civil rights activities. Preintervention measures of attitudes toward equal rights were obtained in various classes. A week later students completed Rokeach's instrument designed to measure the relative importance of major terminal values, that is, beliefs about end states that are personally desirable, and they received immediate feedback about the average rankings of students at their college. They were directed to consider specifically their peers' rankings of the values of equality (brotherhood, equal opportunity for all) and freedom (independence, free choice). It was pointed out that most of their peers ranked freedom for oneself ahead of equality for others. Next they were asked to compare their own value rankings to those of their peers. After this the experimenter asked them to note on a form whether they were sympathetic with the aims of civil rights demonstrations or had participated in such demonstrations. Finally he gave them information about how other students who were for and against civil rights ranked the values of freedom and equality and interpreted that information in a way designed to arouse self-dissatisfaction among participants whose self-conceptions and values were inconsistent. The data provided, based on actual research, showed that students who were more sympathetic to civil rights were more likely to rank equality ahead of freedom than were those opposed to civil rights demonstrations. The experimenter interpreted this as suggesting that ". . . those who are against civil rights are really saying they care a great deal about *their own* freedom but are indifferent to other people's freedom. Those who are *for* civil rights are perhaps really saying they not only want freedom for themselves, but for other people too" (Rokeach 1973:238). For participants who considered themselves as morally committed to civil rights and had just ranked freedom ahead of equality, this information was expected to arouse self-dissatisfaction. About 25 percent of the subjects fit this condition. The experimenter closed the session with the comment that it was up to each student to think seriously about his or her own values and to use the facts about themselves and others as they saw fit.

In thinking about the likely impact of this intervention, the reader will notice that at least two of the conditions cognitive dissonance theorists have emphasized as enhancing dissonance arousal were present: (1) personal responsibility, for the value statements and any future actions, and (2) commitment, to their stated values and civil rights attitudes, which were inconsistent. This commitment was fostered by having the students keep their questionnaire replies before them and consult them during the discussion. It is not surprising that significant effects were found for this intervention on value rankings and relevant behaviors for a period of almost two years. In replies to mailed questionnaires received three weeks, three to five months, and fifteen to seventeen months later, the experimental group (described above) showed more value shifts on the targeted values of equality and freedom than did a control group who had simply completed an initial value ranking. Even more impressive were the responses of the two groups to mail solicitations to join the NAACP sent three to five months and fifteen to seventeen months later. These solicitations, which came directly from the local chapter and were not in any obvious way connected to the experiment, elicited significantly more favorable responses from the experimental than from the control subjects. Furthermore, among a subgroup of subjects who had the opportunity as a regular part of their curriculum to enroll in a course on ethnic and religious intergroup relations twenty-one months after the intervention, significantly more experimental than control subjects actually did so.

This study, and others cited above, demonstrate that when individuals are made aware of existing inconsistencies between their self-conceptions and values by receiving information about the values of relevant reference groups and having certain key aspects highlighted, it is possible for wide-ranging value and attitude shifts to occur. Notice that this approach does not require that the client be persuaded to try new behaviors. Nor is any misinformation involved. It does require the intervenor to recognize inconsistencies that the client has not acknowledged or has tried to gloss over, and to provide information to the client that arouses self-dissatisfaction with the state of inconsistency. These requirements can be met in a variety of social work contexts. A well-educated newcomer to a small town who suffers from social isolation may see herself as a friendly and available person, for example, yet may act toward her acquaintances in ways that suggest she values privacy and competence much more than she does close companionship. In situations such as this it would be appropriate for the social worker to share this assessment with the client to try and determine the client's own views. The newcomer who seems to the worker not to recognize her preference for achievement and privacy over companionship might be told about the basis for this inference—an incident where the woman turned down an invitation to join a local civic club because she was too busy keeping up with her professional literature. She might further be asked to think about how an admired, popular woman would react to a similar situation. Rokeach's theory would suggest that since the clients' self-conceptions are the most central part of their belief systems, inconsistencies would be resolved in ways that maintain or enhance self-conceptions—through shifts in other more peripheral values and attendant behaviors.

It is worth pointing out some of the similarities and differences between this approach and that of cognitive dissonance and self-perception theorists. Like the former, this is a cognitive consistency theory of attitude change; inconsistency is seen as discomforting and the motivation for change. But a particular type of inconsistency—between cognitions about the self and about one's values—is assumed to be most likely to lead to major and persistent changes in attitudes and behaviors because these cognitions are viewed as central to a hierarchically organized system of cognitions. Rokeach's focus on self-cognitions as mediating long-term changes is quite similar to that of self-perception theorists, but he views self-conceptions as extremely resistant to change. Instead of trying to change them, he seeks to assist people in bringing their values and behaviors into alignment with their self-views.

With any given client, the worker will need to assess with that individual whether the intervention goals require fairly specific behavior and attitude shifts, whether these would be facilitated or inhibited by changes in self-perceptions, or whether increased integration among selfviews, values, and behaviors is central. The theory and research most congruent with the goals for that particular client should then be brought to bear upon these goals. If specific behavior and attitude shifts are most important, then cognitive dissonance theory would be most useful. If shifts in self-perception are critical to achieving the intervention goal, then self-perception theory is most relevant. Finally, if the integration of self-percepts, values, and behavior is of major importance, then Rokeach's theory of human values would be the theory of choice.

CHAPTER SIX

SOCIAL INFLUENCE

In our discussion so far of social psychological concepts relevant to dyadic situations of a social worker in direct interaction with a client, we have pointed to circumstances when changing beliefs, values, behaviors, or the impact of normative factors, or arousing dissonance could be useful means of achieving intervention goals. The reader may have been aware that in so doing we did not always specify how these changes could be brought about—under what conditions a client is likely to agree to engage in a novel, dissonant behavior suggested by the worker. When will the social worker's information about the likely instrumental value of a belief be accepted as valid? When will a worker's attribution of social competence to a client's behavior be believed? To put the issue more generally, what are the conditions under which the social worker is likely to be able to influence the beliefs, attitudes, or behaviors of clients?

Many writers have recognized the importance of social workers' influence on clients. For Pincus and Minahan (1973), exercising influence is one of the eight major skill areas in social work practice. Middleman and Goldberg (1974) developed a set of propositions regarding the types of social influence, the conditions under which each is likely to succeed, and the probable consequences for the social work relationship of the use of each type. Frank (1973), in discussing psychotherapy in modern as well as primitive societies, concludes that the professional designated by society as a helper or healer must influence the attitudes or behaviors of the help-seeker to be effective. In short, the exercise of influence is recognized as intrinsic to social work practice.

POWER AND INFLUENCE THEORIES

What does social psychological theory and research tell us about the conditions under which influence attempts are likely to be effective? This question has been addressed by many writers in quite a broad fashion. We cannot deal with the full array of research here, but it is useful to point out the major categories of variables that have been studied. These are basically of three types: those related to the source of the influence attempt, those related to the target of change, and those concerning the message sent from the source to the target (Triandis 1971). Variables such as whether the message is written or oral, arouses fear, presents one or both sides of an argument, have all been studied (see Hovland, Janis, and Kelley 1953; Eagly and Himmelfarb 1978), but will not be reviewed here. Instead, we will concentrate our attention on the characteristics of the source of the influence attempt and the target's evaluation of these characteristics as most relevant to social work practice.

Several recent reviews have pointed to the credibility of the source as the most potent predictor of successful influence (Eagly and Himmelfarb 1978; Ronis et al. 1977; Simons, Berkowitz, and Moyer 1970). A credible source is one who is viewed by the recipient of a message as believable. Thus credibility is a characteristic of a potential source of influence as judged by the target. Various bases have been specified for making such an attribution, but the three main conditions are the expertise or knowledge of the source compared to that of the target, the trustworthiness or sincerity of the source, and the attractiveness of the source to the target.

In addition to these several aspects of credibility, two other major characteristics of communicators have been identified as important to influence: the target's acceptance of the legitimacy of the particular source seeking to exercise influence and the extent to which the source exercises control over resources to reward or punish the target. These several types of influence not only have different roots, they can also have different effects. The important theorists discussing these issues are Kelman, and French and Raven.

KELMAN'S VIEW OF SOCIAL INFLUENCE

The relationship of the bases of influence to attitude change was analyzed in considerable depth by Kelman (1965), who hypothesized that there were three different influence processes by which attitudes could be changed: compliance, which occurs when individuals accept influence because they hope to achieve a reward or approval from another person; identification, which occurs when individuals accept influence because they want to establish or maintain a satisfying, self-defining relationship to another person either by taking over that individual's role or taking a reciprocal role; and internalization, which occurs when individuals accept influence because of the content of the induced behavior, belief, or attitude. In the case of compliance, attitude change takes place because of the satisfaction derived from the results of accepting influence; here the influencer must possess the power to reward or punish for conformity to take place. In the case of identification, attitude change occurs because of the satisfaction derived from the association with the influencer in the desirable relationship, from the act of conforming per se. The source of the influencer's power in this case is his or her attractiveness to the recipient of influence, for this induces the desire for a self-defining relationship with the influencer. Finally, in the case of internalization, attitude change is achieved because the content of the new attitude is intrinsically rewarding and congruent with the value system of the recipient of influence. The source of the influencer's power in this instance is his or her knowledge, or perceived expertise in the area, which Kelman calls credibility. (Most writers use the term credibility more broadly, to refer to any basis for believing a message.)

Kelman also delineated the conditions under which the induced behavior is enacted or attitude expressed. In the case of compliance, the recipient of influence will perform appropriately only under conditions of surveillance or expected surveillance by the influencing agent. In the case of identification, the recipient tends to perform the induced behavior so long as the desired relationship remains salient. In the case of internalization, the induced behavior tends to be performed under conditions of relevance of the issue, regardless of surveillance by the influencer or salience of the relationship. Because internalization, in Kelman's terms, is not dependent upon monitoring or visibility of the relationship, the behavior or attitude induced in this way is most enduring. It has become an integral part of the recipient's cognitive schema. Thus Kelman's theory predicts both the occurrence and persistence of attitude change (T. D. Cook and Flay 1978).

Kelman conducted a series of studies to test some of these ideas in 1954, shortly before the U.S. Supreme Court was expected to hand down its decision on public school desegregation. In these studies black undergraduates attending segregated colleges in border states heard various taped radio interviews in which the "guest" advocated that some private black colleges should be maintained if the Supreme Court ruled segregation unconstitutional. This was a position with which most of these students disagreed at that time. Different students heard the guest introduced in various ways designed to make him seem either attractive, knowledgeable and trustworthy, possessing high reward and punishment power over budgets of black colleges, or lacking in these sources of influence. Also manipulated were whether the students believed that the radio interviewee would learn about their responses (surveillance) and the amount of time between hearing the interview and the students' being asked to give their own views (the salience of the communicator). The findings generally supported Kelman's theory about conditions affecting attitude change (T. D. Cook and Flay 1978). For example, the students became more favorable to the maintenance of some private black colleges when the communicator was said to be (a) the president of a foundation that supported black schools and was to receive the questionnaire results, thus evoking compliance; (b) a leading well-respected university expert on minority groups in the United States, who elicited internalization; or (c) the president of the student council at a leading black college, the source of identification. But change did not occur when he was a white southern citizen with segregationist views. Thus, means control, expertise, and attractiveness all served as bases of influence.

Attractiveness of the source to the target does not, however, always seem relevant to attitude change. Simons, Berkowitz, and Moyer (1970) have reviewed the research in this area, and we now can identify more precisely the situations that do conform to Kelman's theory. The major way that attraction has been varied in social psychological research is by providing information about similarity between the individuals; therefore they reviewed studies linking attitude change with similarity between the source of influence and the receiver of influence. Among the type of similarities investigated were similarity in attitudes and in membership groups. Although they found that attitude similarity and attraction are positively correlated in many studies, as was discussed in chapter 1, attitude similarity was found to relate to attitude change only when the similarity between source and target of influence was relevant or instrumental to goal attainment by the target. On the other hand, some types of dissimilarity, for example, the greater expertise of the source, can enhance attitude change if they are instrumental to the target's goal attainment. Thus, only when similarity or dissimilarity is pertinent to the goal of the influence attempt, can it enhance the target's perception of the knowledge or trustworthiness of the source. For example, in a study of the influence of paint salesmen on the kind of paint customers purchased (Brock 1965), to establish similarity with the patron the salesmen described personal experiences they had with the paint they recommended. However, they varied whether or not the experience was relevant to the job for which the customer was purchasing the paint. Only when experience with the same paint was relevant was the actual purchase decision affected. Shared membership groups, such as sex, race, church, occupation, function in a parallel fashion, according to these authors. In the absence of a belief by the targets that their own group is less knowledgeable or trustworthy, membership similarity should enhance attitude change. But when one's own group is perceived to be lacking in information, joint membership will not facilitate influence, as, for example, when city dwellers turn to suburbanites or farmers for advice on how to grow vegetables. Thus the effective influencers of attitudes may resemble the political opinion leader (Lazarsfeld, Berelson, and Gaudet 1948) or the influential physician (E. Katz 1967). They are similar to their followers in many ways—they belong to the same primary groups and share many key attitudes and values, but are also different in that they are more informed and have wider contacts with the outside world. (This issue was also referred to in chapter 1 when the relationship between similarity and attraction to a change agent was discussed.)

The practice implications of the association between similarity, liking, expertise, and attitude change is that workers should be perceived as having greater expertise than clients in areas relevant to the intervention goal, and be similar to clients in other relevant areas. The question of which areas are relevant will have to be determined by the worker in each individual situation. In general, prudence would suggest highlighting all the areas of similarity that do exist, for example, widowhood, age, city of birth, or ethnicity. This may enhance the practitioner's ability to influence the client in ways that have been legitimated by prior joint goal setting. The key attitudinal area of similarity, the desire of both the social worker and client to improve the life situation of the client and their agreed-upon intervention goal, should of course also be made salient. In these ways, according to the Kelman theory, change based on identification and internalization should be fostered.

The potency of attributions of expertise by the client to the worker has been further supported in several other studies (Aronson, Turner, and Carlsmith 1963; Bergin 1962; Koslin, Stoops, and Loh 1967). When the source of the influence had high expertise, greater attitude change was obtained as the opinion of the source was increasingly discrepant from the initial views of the recipient of influence. When the source had only moderate expertise, increasing the discrepancy was accompanied by opinion change in the recipient only up to a point;

if the discrepancy became extreme, the opinion change ceased. Thus, it appears that workers who can establish high skill levels or knowledge with clients have the potential of obtaining considerable attitude and behavior change on relevant topics. Among the areas where this latent power might be exerted effectively would be in a discussion of the consequences likely to ensue from a given act, for example, taking an elderly parent into the home, or of the value placed on the outcome of that act.

FRENCH AND RAVEN'S CONCEPTION OF THE BASES OF SOCIAL POWER

The legitimacy of an influencer was added to the three sources of power discussed by Kelman, i.e., means control, attractiveness, and expertise, by French and Raven (1968) in an important conceptualization of social influence. According to these authors, legitimate power exists when recipients of influence attempts perceive that the source of the attempt has the legitimate right to prescribe behaviors or attitudes for them in the domain of the influence attempt. This view can be based on the position held by the source in a role system, by general moral or cultural imperatives such as to respect one's elders, or by designation from another legitimate authority as when a teacher puts one child in charge of a group. Like influence based on attraction and expertise, that based on legitimacy does not require surveillance because it rests on the client's belief in the authority. According to this view, even if the influencer does not have means control or expertise, and is not personally attractive (or a referent figure to use the terminology of French and Raven), influence can be exerted if the influencer is seen as legitimately possessing power. The well-known work of Milgrim (1965) substantiated the latent power of someone who is seen as "in authority." In a number of studies, Milgrim demonstrated that seemingly ordinary people would inflict pain on innocent subjects during an experiment because the inflicters were told to do so by the experimenter who appeared to be legitimately in charge of the situation. However, there were conditions under which individuals were not likely to conform with unreasonable demands of those in authority. This was seen in Milgram's work when the experimental subject heard or saw other people refuse to carry out the experimenter's instructions. Under these circumstances, there was a dramatic decrease in the percentage of conformity—from 60 percent in the solo condition to 10 percent when two other persons refused.

Another difference between Kelman's and French and Raven's analysis of influence concerns means control. The latter writers stress the differences between reward power and coercion power. Like other writers (Byrne 1971; Thibaut and Kelley 1959) they point out that induced behaviors or attitudes that are consistently rewarded by the influencer result in the influencer becoming more attractive to the recipient; thus compliance can become transformed into identification and the need for surveillance reduced. Furthermore, surveillance is less difficult when reward power is used: the target for influence desires the dispenser of rewards to know about behavior linked to rewards (Raven and Kruglanski 1970). In contrast, coercive power based on the influencer's control over punishments should decrease the attractiveness of the source, though this impact might be modulated by the perception that the source has the legitimate power to punish, and concealment efforts could increase surveillance requirements. These ideas modify somewhat the implication of Kelman's views of means control as only a temporary source of influence that requires surveillance. Influence that starts from control over positive reinforcements can become more general if the source of the rewards becomes attractive. This may be the case in social work contexts such as behaviorally based school programs based on positive reinforcement.

Both reward and coercive power can be linked to the target's view of the source's attractiveness in another way as well. As was pointed out in chapter 1, attraction is often assumed to be mutual—you perceive that people you like also like you. This perception can affect your belief that an influencer will use available rewards and punishments, as has been shown in a study in which threats from a disliked source elicited greater compliance than did threats from a liked source (Tedeschi, Bonoma, and Schlenker 1972). Although the research evidence is not clear, it has also been suggested that assumed high mutual attraction can interfere with the exercise of influence based on reward power. As reward power is based on linking compliance to reward, if the individual being influenced assumes the person controlling the rewards will dispense them out of a sense of friendship regardless of compliance, reward power could be diminished. This suggests that in situations in which social workers try to use rewards personally to influence clients' behaviors and there is a warm relationship between worker and clients, the strategy may be unsuccessful in achieving the desired goals.

The specification of the sources of expert power in French and Raven's conception is also relevant to social work practice. Two conditions are necessary for expert power: the recipient must view the influencer as possessing relevant knowledge and as honestly sharing that knowledge. Experts must be trustworthy to have influence. They must be seen as using their knowledge for the welfare of the target rather than for self-interest, as a number of studies have shown (Powell and Miller 1967; Walster, Aronson, and Abraham 1966). Deceptive strategies, as was pointed out earlier, can interfere with trust and thus vitiate potential influence based on expert knowledge and skills of the social worker. It is therefore important to demonstrate early in contacts with a client that the worker not only possesses the skills and knowledge to help, but will share these and use them on the client's behalf.

Informational power has also been distinguished by French and Raven (Collins and Raven 1969; French and Raven 1959; Raven 1965; Raven and Kruglanski 1970). Here the content of the communication is the source of influence rather than the expertness of the influencing agent or the nature of the social relationship between the source and recipient of the influence. When children gain understanding of a new mathematical concept after it is explained by the teacher, or members of a political audience are convinced by the logic of the candidate's argument to change their opinions, we have instances of influence based on information. The importance of this distinction for social work practice is that once the new information becomes part of the cognitive structure of the client any attitudinal or behavioral change it induces is likely to persist without reminders or surveillance; the change thus becomes independent of the agent of change. Thus, informational influence, or the provision of new ideas, knowledge, or skills to clients, is particularly congruent with the social work intervention goal of enabling clients to improve the management of their lives. In order for information provided to be accepted and used in this way, however, it must tie the changed attitudes or behaviors into existing cognitive structures, including values. Providing information to parents about how to encourage curiosity in children will not produce changed parental behavior unless the parents value curiosity. Giving unemployed youths information about the location, office hours, or procedures of the local state employment services office is not likely to affect their job seeking if they believe that employers will not hire them because of their age or their race.

SOCIAL WORKERS AS SOURCES OF INFLUENCE

Several studies of social workers have shown the direct relevance of ideas on the multiple bases of power. One investigation demonstrated that public assistance workers' judgments of their supervisors' influence over them and their own influence over their coworkers were clustered along four of the five power dimensions defined by French and Raven: expertness, positive sanctions, negative sanctions, and legitimacy (Galinsky, Rosen, and Thomas, 1973). Only attraction as a source of influence failed to be identified, and the researchers suggested that the questions they asked in that area may not have been appropriate. Two other studies directly linked clients' perceptions about social workers' characteristics relevant to power to the clients' behavior. In a study by Polansky and Kounin (1956), clients' reports of their willingness to follow the advice of the worker were significantly related to their evaluation of the competence of the worker as displayed during the initial interview. And as mentioned in chapter 1, clients' satisfaction with the interpersonal aspects of the initial interview was related to their liking for the worker and their willingness to see the interviewer again, a precondition for further influence. Similarly, Levinger (1960) found that casework clients' commitment to continuation in treatment was linked to their perceptions of the worker as an expert, competent person who was committed to helping them.

In sum, there are several major implications of these influence theories for social workers who are in a dyadic situation with clients. Fundamentally, the theorists suggest that if influence is to be exerted, the persuader must have some source of power. All agree that the power to reward or punish results in the least enduring attitude change unless reward power is used for a sufficient length of time to result in the rewarder's becoming an attractive individual to the recipient of influence.

Yet it is important to recognize that many social workers do have, and are perceived by their clients as having, means control power—to gain access to financial benefits, better housing, or food, or to deny parents access to their children. These writers suggest that sole reliance on these sources of influence would be unwise. The more potent bases of influence are expertise, legitimacy, and to a lesser extent personal attractiveness. Thus, practitioners must be certain they communicate to clients that: 1) they are knowledgeable about the topic under consideration and will use that knowledge for the client's benefit; 2) they have been granted the authority by some legitimate organization or licensing body to offer services, and will live up to the limits on their legitimate areas of influence included in the client-worker contract for intervention goals; and 3) they are warm and caring individuals who respect the client. These theorists also suggest that any single base may be sufficient to influence other individuals, but relying on only a single base incurs too much risk for a social worker. One cannot be certain that all clients will wish to establish a self-defining relationship with the worker, and the contact may be very short in duration; thus relying on personal attractiveness alone may be unwise. Expertise is always an asset but unless one's knowledge is congruent with the value system of the recipient of influence, the influence may not be accepted. Lack of information or skills may not be particularly relevant to a client's problem, and even acceptance of information is tied to value congruence. Since a worker cannot be certain of the value systems of all clients prior to considerable contact, it is risking a good deal to assume that credibility or new information alone will be sufficient to bring about attitude change in clients. Finally, legitimacy may be unambiguous but Milgrim's studies have indicated that some individuals will not accept influence from those in authority if the content of the influence is contrary to their belief system. Thus, one cannot rely on legitimacy alone.

In short, workers would do well to maximize the base of their influence by displaying in the interview room the legitimacy of their position, clearly indicating their respect and liking for the client, and exhibiting expertise in areas in which they hope to exert influence, be it political action, job training, alcoholism, drugs, child abuse, senescence, child rearing, or communication between spouses. In addition, since the bases for the social workers' influence in large measure stem from their positions as social workers and their own and the clients' views about the appropriate role behaviors associated with this position, it is important that these mutual role expectations be clarified in the early phases of the contact.

The worker should also be sensitive to possible individual differences in susceptibility to various bases for influence, as Triandis (1971) has suggested. Authoritarian individuals may tend to conform more when the base of power of the influencing agent is means control; those who are high in need for affiliation, that is, who obtain great gratification from feeling that they are liked, may be influenced most by attractiveness to the source of influence; and individuals who are abstract in their thinking and have a well reasoned view of the world tend to be influenced by the knowledge revealed in the nature of the argument per se. This suggests that social workers who know clients well enough to describe them in terms of their authoritarianism, need for affiliation, and cognitive structure should consider highlighting the base of power to which these individuals are most responsive. For example, workers might quickly demonstrate that they have the power to supply reinforcements to the more authoritarian clients, express liking in unambiguous terms to those high in need affiliation, and offer logical and thoughtful explanations to clients who think in more abstract terms.

Cautions on the social worker's use of influence. These deliberate efforts by the worker to enhance the likelihood that planned influence attempts are successful are, however, not the only ways in which workers influence clients. In many subtle, and often unplanned ways, the behavior of social workers and other helping professionals has been shown to influence clients. For example, in one study twelve therapists in a child guidance clinic were rated by their colleagues on their ability to express hostility, and independent judges rated their interviews with parent clients on the extent to which they made an encouraging response after the client expressed low or high hostility (Bandura, Lipscher, and Miller 1960). Not only were therapists who were themselves more open in expressing hostility more likely to make an encouraging remark when their clients expressed hostility, but nearly all the time (92 percent) such remarks were followed by another hostile statement by the client while only rarely (43 percent of the time) was a discouraging remark by a therapist followed by another hostile client statement. Thus, the therapists' own attitudes toward hostility had an influence on the extent to which their clients displayed hostile behavior. Similar demonstrations of the conditioning of verbal behavior through subtle interpersonal cues has been shown in other practice settings (e.g., Krasner 1958; Truax and Carkhuff 1967). Both deliberate and unintentional social approval can have reinforcment value. And the potency of this reinforcement value is likely to be a function of the characteristics of the source of the approval discussed above, including attraction, expertise, and means control (Nord 1969). It is important, therefore, for workers to be sensitive to the subtle ways they may be molding the clients' words in an interview situation.

Although we have emphasized the importance of social workers attempting to maximize their sources of power in order to assist clients in reaching agreed-upon goals, it is also important to recognize the danger in having too much power over the client. In many ways the context of worker-client relations in our society can place the worker in a powerful relationship to the client. The worker is often in a higher status position in society than the client, thereby gaining expertise. The interaction typically takes place in the worker's home base, so that the client is less familiar with the territory, less knowledgeable about what is expected and what will transpire. Some workers function in organizational contexts where they control important resources, such as food stamps, visiting rights to children, and entry to job training programs. Also, the worker's position has legitimacy in the larger society and in the particular organizational setting. It is therefore critical that this power not be abused, that the limits of legitimate influence be maintained (Kelman 1972). These limits are defined both by the general value system of professional social work—including the requirements of confidentiality, facilitation of clients' access to needed services, and respect for the dignity and individual values of clients—and by the specific agreements reached by a client and worker about those areas of the client's life that are to be the focus of the intervention and the techniques to be used to achieve intervention goals.

That social workers often have greater power in the intervention situation than clients can also have ramifications for their views about their clients' capabilities, and their selection of appropriate means for influence. For example, in one laboratory study subjects believed they were participating in a simulation of a work setting where they held a supervisory position over others, and some of them also controlled resources, such as the pay received by their workers and job transfers, while others simply had the title of manager (Kipnis 1972). Subjects with means control made more influence attempts and in these attempts relied more on the use of resources to reward or punish worker performance and less on persuasive communications than those with only legitimacy as a power base. Further, the supervisors with means control were less positive than were the other supervisors about the workers' ability and performance, and were less likely to attribute the workers' effort to their own motivation and more likely to attribute it to monetary incentives. Kipnis (1972) entitled the article in which he reported this research "Does Power Corrupt?" His answer was yes, under certain circumstances it does. The parallel to certain social work settings is frighteningly clear. Poor clients who are dependent upon social workers for needed material resources are unfortunately sometimes viewed as unreliable, in need of close supervision, not really trying to help themselves. We must be alert to the possibility that these evaluations stem more from the worker's powerful position than from the client's behavior.

We do not mean to suggest that the client is a passive recipient of the social worker's influence attempts. As Kadushin has indicated, the social work interview ". . .is a system in which each participant is seeking, accepting, or resisting the other's efforts to influence him" (1972:67). Two areas of social psychological research are especially relevant to the ways in which clients might resist influence attempts—ingratiation and reactance theory.

INGRATIATION THEORY

According to E. E. Jones (1964), who introduced the concept to the social psychological research scene, ingratiation is a strategy used by the low-power member in a relationship of unequal power. It is designed to increase the attractiveness of low-power persons to high-power ones, thereby enhancing the power of the "underdog." For as dependent persons become more attractive to the powerful ones, the value of their sanctions increases and the powerful persons cannot punish them without inflicting cost on themselves. Three tactics of ingratiation have been identified: conformity with the attitudes, beliefs, and behaviors of the powerful person; favorable self-presentation, that is, a selective overemphasis on one's valued behaviors or attributes, and other-enhancement or flattery. Laboratory research has supported the prediction that these tactics of ingratiation are used in situations where one person is dependent upon the other for important outcomes and where the more powerful person has some discretionary power to provide or withhold these outcomes (E. E. Jones et al. 1965; Kaufman and Steiner 1968; Stires and Jones 1969). Another unequal power condition that fosters ingratiation is one in which the more powerful person is known to care about cooperation, understanding and cohesion with the other person (E. E. Jones et al. 1965). Thus, many social worker-client relationships seem typical of situations likely to foster ingratiation by the client: workers can control access to valuable resources and services, they often must make decisions on access based on general or vague criteria, and they typically desire the esteem of their clients. Under those circumstances we can expect clients to feign agreement with workers' ideas and suggestions, or at least avoid mentioning disagreement, and to describe their behavior in a way that they believe the worker would approve. It is important to recognize that successful ingratiation tactics can be very subtle and that especially when the more powerful person is self-confident the sincerity of the communication is often not doubted (Kipnis and Vanderveer 1971). Thus, when the conditions for ingratiation are ripe, the social worker may need to be more careful about accepting all information received without further corroboration. Even more useful would be efforts to reduce clients' perceptions of the relationship as unequal in power, and to give the clients as much power as possible in determining their own fates. At the very minimum, practitioners should avoid suggesting to clients in any way that only through conformity, flattery, and deception will they receive the attention and help that they need.

REACTANCE THEORY

As developed by J. Brehm (1966; 1972), reactance theory is more relevant than ingratiation theory to a broad spectrum of social work situations. Reactance is defined as arousal in response to a reduction, or a threat of reduction, in an individual's potential for action. According to reactance theory, such threats to potential freedom for action can occur whenever persons perceive someone is making strong efforts to influence their attitudes or behaviors; these efforts threaten their freedom to hold any possible attitude toward a given behavior or action, or to engage in any given behavior previously available to them. Since we, and others, have pointed to influence as an essential ingredient in social work, the pertinence of reactance theory to practice is clear. The consequences of the arousal of reactance in response to social influence can be hostility toward the source (Mazis 1975; Worchel 1974), which is typically problematic for continued work together. An alternative consequence of reactance is a demonstration of freedom of choice by reasserting an attitude or engaging in a behavior counter to that advocated by the other person (J. Brehm and Sensing 1966), which clearly reduces the practitioner's influence.

A survey of laboratory research findings suggests a number of ways to avoid arousing reactance in work with clients (S. Brehm 1976). Strong pressures should be avoided. Such pressures include using language of command (J. Brehm 1966), e.g., "You should be more considerate of your husband's feelings," or drawing firm conclusions that impinge on the client's freedom of choice, e.g., "Obviously the only choice you have is to take the job offered to you," or making compliance very important to the requestor, e.g., "It would really make me feel I had done a good job if you remained in your seat all during your math class tomorrow." Notice that all these tactics reduce perceived choice, and thereby both increase reactance arousal and reduce likely compliance. Furthermore, cognitive dissonance principles would suggest that even if these tactics gained compliance, behavioral enactment would not increase commitment to that behavior because dissonance is minimized where there is lack of free choice. Instead, the opening up of alternatives and emphasizing decision freedom would be preferable. In the prior examples, reactance arousal would probably be less with questions or statements like, "Do you know how your husband feels when you act that way?" "Let us go over the advantages and disadvantages of taking the job offered to you," or "Would you like to try to remain in your seat during your math class tomorrow?"

Another way to reduce reactance in response to social influence, applicable in most situations if not all (e.g., with child abusers or parolees), is to emphasize the client's continuing freedom to engage in old behaviors. In encouraging a client to try out a new behavior such as visiting a spouse's family which has been a source of prior marital friction, it would be well to point out that options still remain: if the visit does not work out, it can be cut short, or the client need not go again. Or, newly discharged mental patients can be told of job openings and asked if they feel ready to apply for one, on a trial basis.

Finally, reactance appears to be minimized when social relations between source of influence and target of change are emphasized (Grabitz-Gniech 1971; Pallak and Heller 1971). This suggests that a continuing relationship between social worker and client, especially when the client finds the relationship satisfying, could minimize the client's arousal of reactance to social influence. Since both studies that showed this effect involved situations in which subjects believed they were jointly working on a task, the joint decision making that underlies social work practice should be emphasized.

Efforts to reduce reactance arousal may be particularly important with certain clients for whom threats to potential freedom are salient. Although this must be assessed on an individual basis, certain categories of clients are more likely to fit this description. Adolescents who are engaged in autonomy struggles with their parents, and others whose role partners are perceived to limit freedom of choice to an excessive level, for example, workers in closely supervised positions, should be especially sensitive to threats to freedom from the social worker. Institutional clients whose freedoms are already severely limited would be expected to exhibit stronger reactance, e.g., hostility, to a new limitation than would clients whose behavioral choices are broader. This is not to suggest that persons with limited choices are invariably more hostile. The critical issue is the proportion of freedom threatened. For example, reactance theory predicts that individuals whose residential possibilities are limited to three choices would find their freedom threatened much more if one is eliminated than would others who initially perceive the possibility for ten different residences and then find one eliminated; in the former case there has been a 33 percent reduction in freedom, while in the latter only 10 percent. The proposition that reactance is related to the proportion of freedoms threatened (J. Brehm 1966; Wicklund, Slattum, and Solomon 1970) is relevant to any client whose life situation has resulted in limited choices being available. The very poor, the chronically ill, persons with restricted skills, and those with very few support groups would all be expected to show strong reactance to any further limitations on their freedoms. What may appear to be a minor loss of freedom to the worker, like the suggestion that a child from an impoverished family not carry an old, smelly stuffed bear to the family day care home, may be a very significant loss of freedom to the child and family.

In sum, reactance theory and research suggest that two sets of forces probably operate in most social influence situations. One set of forces acts to move the client toward the position encouraged by the source of influence. These forces, discussed earlier in this chapter, include the sources of power of the influencer, dissonance reduction, consistency forces, and shifts in instrumentalities and values. The other set of forces moves the clients away from the position of the influencer, and these are the conditions that enhance reactance, including the strength of the threat to freedom of choice, and the proportion of freedoms threatened. Workers thus need to be aware of both sets of forces and be sensitive to situations where their efforts to influence border on threats to clients' freedom.

SECTION TWO

IMPLEMENTING DYADIC INTERVENTION PLANS WITH SIGNIFICANT OTHERS: QUADRANT B

INTRODUCTION

There are many reasons why social workers decide that it is important to extend their activities on behalf of clients to include contacts with other individuals. Someone already significant in the environment may be contributing to the problem experienced by the client—a common example of this is the school social worker who seeks out a teacher whose pupil seems to be having particular difficulty. It may be useful to enlist the assistance of a close friend or family member in supporting new behaviors that the client is trying to achieve—a handicapped teenager who has been trying to improve her grooming to enhance her heterosexual attractiveness may be helped by an aunt in whom she confides. The stresses a client is experiencing due to a life crisis may be reduced and deleterious changes in the client's behavior avoided if key persons in the client's social environment are made more aware of these stresses and the ways in which they could be helpful—social workers in medical settings frequently need to work with family members of patients. In general, it is recognized that persons who have sustained or extensive contacts with the clients are powerful sources of influence, and can be useful in facilitating desired changes in the clients' problems or in maintaining positive aspects of the clients' behavior and environment.

Evidence that such friends and family members play a critical role in a person's mental health abounds in the literature, as recent reviews show (Cobb 1976; Silver and Wortman 1980). Although negative effects are possible (for example, depressed people can be trapped into a suffering role by the ambivalent messages of support and rejection often received from those close to them—Coates and Wortman 1980), close social ties often lessen stress. Blue-collar workers who lost their jobs due to a permanent factory closing showed an elevation of a variety of physiological symptoms of stress, but those who perceived their families and friends as giving them high levels of social support during this trying period were more likely to have these stress signs return to normal levels (Cobb 1974). White-collar workers who experienced role strain on their jobs due to such problems as role overload were likely to exhibit high levels of risk factors associated with coronary heart disease if they did not have supportive relationships with their fellow workers (Caplan 1972). Patients suffering from hypertension were more likely to stick to the prescribed medical regime involving diet control and medication if they felt their physician was helpful and supportive (Caplan et al. 1976). Men and women trying to stop smoking were more successful if they were paired up with someone in the same situation with whom they talked each week between clinic sessions (Janis and Hoffman 1970). A high level of social support was associated with a decreased level of mental hospitalization for women after the birth of their first child (Cohler et al. 1974). Self-help groups such as Alcoholics Anonymous recognize the key role of support and give members the name and phone number of a fellow member to call in moments of crisis, when they fear returning to their problematic behavior.

The use of social services is also affected by availability of informal social supports. For example, among older men and women of higher socioeconomic status informal social supports can reduce the need for or utilization of public agencies or enhance the quality of service delivery received in hospitals or nursing homes (Z. Blau 1978; Dobrof and Litwak 1977). As patterns of social support may vary in different ethnic groups and social class (Billingsley 1968; Z. Blau 1978; Bott 1971; Leichter and Mitchell 1978; Sotomayor 1971; Sussman 1974; William and Mindel 1973), it is important to recognize the impact of these differences in developing services and in seeking to enlist help from facilitators of change.

The very maintenance of the client-worker contact itself has been shown to be influenced by supportive social relationships. One recent review of the research literature on why clients drop out of various forms of psychological treatment concluded that an important way to reduce discontinuances was to maintain contact with significant other persons in the client's environment and to engage the help of such persons (Baekeland and Lundwall 1975).

Thus, a large component of the practitioner's role is to seek out and engage significant others in the helping process. The importance of involving caregivers such as teacher, parents, peers, etc., in change efforts has been emphasized by many investigators (Becker 1971; Buckley and Hill 1970; Patterson 1969; Patterson and Guillon 1968; Radin 1972b; Radin and Wittes 1974; Rose 1974a; J. M. Smith and Smith 1966). It should be pointed out that it is often the caregivers, facilitators of change in others, or significant others, as they are referred to here, who initiate the contact with social workers. For example, it is not unusual for foster parents to seek help in handling aggressive or defiant children in their care, or for the spouse of an alcoholic to contact a family agency. Regardless of who initiates the interaction, contacts between practitioners and significant others comprise a major component of social work practice and warrant serious attention.

In working with a significant other as a facilitator of change in the problems of clients many of the same social psychological theories and research findings discussed under Quadrant A are relevant, especially when the client's problem might be alleviated by changes in the behaviors of the facilitator.

But in addition there are two major social psychological areas that are especially pertinent to this Quadrant. In situations where social workers seek out the facilitators, research and theory concerning altruism and helping behavior are initially quite important, and the next chapter will review that work and discuss its implications for social work. Once facilitators have agreed to act in that capacity, the principles of social learning theory become very relevant, including theory and research dealing with modeling, self-regulation, and beliefs about control over one's life; these topics will be presented in chapter 8.

All of these concepts will be discussed in detail along with their relevance to work with nonclients, that is, with people whose own problems are not perceived to be the primary focus of the intervention. At least insofar as these interactions are concerned, the focus is on the behavior, attitudes, skills, development and life circumstances of another individual, the client, whose problems the nonclient can help to solve.

CHAPTER SEVEN

ALTRUISM AND HELPING

Social psychological theories and research on helping behaviors are relevant to work with facilitators of change in problems of others in three ways. First, if it is important for significant others to participate in treatment plans or to modify their behavior toward clients, the social worker will need to know how best to gain their cooperation to these ends. This requires knowledge of the conditions that facilitate or hinder one individual helping another one. In some cases, help can be obtained because it is clear that significant others and clients will mutually benefit from the intervention, but that does not always occur, and when it does, the benefits are not always apparent simultaneously or immediately, nor are they always equal. Thus, for a period of time, workers may be engaged in efforts to win the cooperation of family members, coworkers, peers, teachers of clients, or other professionals with access to resources for clients under circumstances where there is no clear benefit to them from the helping behaviors. These efforts would fall in Quadrant C of table 3.1 if the joint help efforts of multiple colleagues, other professionals, or other nonsufferers was sought. If help was solicited for a single client or small group of clients from a single family member, teacher, friend or other professional, such efforts would fall in Quadrant B.

G. Goldberg (1974) alludes to a second situation in which helping theory is relevant to the intervention phase of social work practice and to work with significant others: that in which clients seek the help of another person like themselves to alleviate the problems confronted by similar sufferers. The client, in enlisting the interest of these other persons, like the social worker in the first example, needs to understand when and how concern about the welfare of others is a basis for action. Both these situations essentially concern recruitment of individuals into the position of facilitator of change in another person's problems.

The third application of the social psychology of helping to work with facilitators is relevant to Quadrant A as well as to Quadrant B. It is important for the social worker and other facilitators of change to understand the reactions of clients to help offered or received. What are the conditions under which help will be accepted and appreciated, and when will assistance be rejected, and hostility or withdrawal occur?

There is an additional situation in which concepts of helping are relevant to intervention efforts which should be noted although it does not pertain to facilitators of change. It concerns the need for workers to be aware of and sensitive to their own desire or lack of desire to help certain types of clients. Here the relevant question is, What characteristics of clients or the helping process will affect the social workers' desire to help the client and the kind and speed of help given?

In recent years there has been a burgeoning of research on prosocial behavior, behavior that benefits others. This research has taken two major directions. In one, the focus has been on identifying and understanding altruistic prosocial behavior, which has been defined as behavior motivated by a regard for the interests of others without concern for one's self-interest, or as self-sacrificial behavior, other-oriented behavior, or as helping behavior motivated by the other person being in need (Krebs and Wispé 1974). All definitions of altruism tend to focus on the other person in need, and on the intention of the benefactor to be helpful to that person. The other research thrust has been on the social conditions that foster helping, with the assumption that much behavior which has the consequence of benefiting others is undertaken because of the rewards to the benefactor of helping another, or the costs of not helping. In this research tradition, the focus is on the consequences for the benefactor of helping, or not helping, a person in need. This distinction has elicited much controversy among social psychologists, and some research has sought to distinguish clearly between altruistic (i.e., self-sacrificial) behavior and other prosocial helping behaviors.

It is important for social workers to be able to identify and enhance the conditions that foster helping and reduce those that inhibit it based both on concern for others and on benefits to the helper. Yet the distinction may often be irrelevant to the worker whose goal is to obtain assistance for a needy person. It may not matter, at least initially, whether the social worker gains a husband's agreement to help with child care because he has been helped to see it will give him pleasure to be with his children or because of concern about his wife's depression. Similarly, the critical fact for the practitioner in a hospital may be to get the ward nurse to agree to spend several minutes talking in a reassuring way with a fearful child en route to an operation, not whether the nurse's behavior has been fostered by the suggestion that this preparation may make the nurse's job of postoperative care easier. Therefore our focus in the review of research in this area will be an inclusive one. We will not limit ourselves to helping that is based solely on altruism, nor will we assume that all helping behavior is self-serving. It is clear from the theoretical and empirical literature that helping another person in need is a complex form of behavior with multiple determinants, and our task is to understand those determinants.

Much research has been conducted to determine the conditions under which helping behavior will be exhibited and the factors fostering its development, and a number of theorists have presented decision-making analyses of these phenomena (Latané and Darley 1970; C. J. Morgan 1978; I. M. Piliavin, Piliavin, and Rodin 1975; S. H. Schwartz 1977). Unfortunately, most of the experimental research has been conducted with individuals who are in only transitory relationships with one another. In contrast, the facilitators of change in others with whom social workers are concerned typically are already in role relationships with the client whose problems are the target of change. These role relationships may include role expectations for helping behavior. Even so these expectations may not be translated into appropriate role performance. Consequently, social workers may need to highlight role expectations or facilitate performance of helping behaviors on the part of significant others in the life of a client, facilitate a client's recruitment of other individuals in a helping relationship with him or her, or enhance their own or others' understanding of a client's response to the offer of help. Based on our review of the social psychological literature we believe the conclusions reached by this approach may be useful to social workers in these endeavors despite the limited social relationships in the situations upon which they are based.

We, and the above theorists, suggest that giving help to someone else is a decision that is based on three major conditions: 1) defining the situation as one in which another person is suffering and can benefit from help; 2) accepting personal responsibility for giving help in this situation; and 3) assessing the benefits of helping as exceeding the costs of helping. Table 3.2 summarizes our review of the variables that research has shown affect each of the phases of the decision process. Before turning to a detailed consideration of these factors, however, it is important to make clear that this approach does not assume that all aspects of the "decision" to help or not help are nec-

Table 3.2

Factors That Influence the Process of Helping

Major steps in the decisional processes in helping	*Variables Relevant to the Decisional Processes in Helping*	
	Characteristics of Potential Recipient[a]	*Characteristics of Potential Helper*[b]
1. Defining the situation as one in which someone is needy or in distress and can benefit from help	Degree and clarity of need Legitimacy of need Similarity to potential helper Attractiveness to potential helper	Empathy Egocentrism Self-concern Mood or affective state Just world beliefs Observational learning from model
2. Accepting personal responsibility for giving help	Occupancy of position defining dependency based on age, sex, family membership, friendship, infirmity Degree of prior help given to potential helper	Belief in social norm of giving; social responsibility; reciprocity, equity Diffusion of responsibility to other potential helpers Responsibility to help in given situation based on role obligations Competence to help in given situation Personal values or beliefs regarding reciprocity, social responsibility, equality; motivation to be altruistic Observational learning from a model

3. Assessing the positive consequences of giving help as outweighing the negative consequences	*Benefits of receiving help (and cost of not receiving it)* Reduced distress (sustained distress) Validation of self as worthy of help (denial of worthiness) *Costs of receiving help (benefits of not receiving help)* Indebtedness (freedom from debts) Reduction of self-regard and autonomy (maintenance of self-regard and autonomy)	*Benefits of helping (and costs of not helping)* Gratification in observing benefits to victim (absence of gratification) Reduction of empathic distress (maintenance of distress) Social reward, gratitude (criticism, hostility) Increased outcomes in cooperatively interdependent relationships (reduced outcomes) Enhanced self-regard (lowered regard) Maintenance of just world beliefs (threat to beliefs) *Costs of helping (and benefits of not helping)* Time, effort, use of resources (conservation resources) Exposure to danger (avoidance of danger) Reactance arousal (maintenance of decisional freedom)

[a] The clients in Quadrant A and D interventions or the social worker in Quadrant B and C situations of table 3.1

[b] The social worker in Quadrant A and D interventions or the Significant Others in Quadrant B and C situations of table 3.1.

essarily conscious, though they certainly can be, and it is likely that some components of any such decision process are always within cognitive awareness.

DEFINING THE SITUATION AS APPROPRIATE FOR HELP

It seems obvious that before someone offers to give help or agrees to a request for help the situation needs to be defined as one in which one or more persons is in need of help, but a moment's thought about such situations will make apparent the importance of recognizing this phase of the decision process. Consider the adult child of an elderly woman who does not recognize her failing health, or the middle-aged wife whose image of her husband as competent and self-reliant interferes with an appreciation of his fears about a diminution of his sexual prowess. These are instances of situations where needed help may not be forthcoming because the potentially helpful person does not define the other person as being in distress or in need of aid.

This aspect of the decision to help has been recognized by theorists concerned about several types of helping situations. Latané and Darley (1970) conducted a series of laboratory studies on bystander intervention with strangers in emergency situations. The Piliavins (I. M. Piliavin, Rodin, and Piliavin 1969; J. A. Piliavin and Piliavin 1972; I. M. Piliavin, Piliavin, and Rodin 1975) investigated bystander reactions to the staged collapse of a man on subway trains. S. H. Schwartz (1970a; 1974) studied both the willingness of Red Cross blood donors to volunteer as bone marrow donors, and of college students to pledge time to a bake sale to raise funds for Head Start. All these researchers concluded that variations in helping responses can in large measure be accounted for by the degree to which the situation is defined as an emergency, as arousing distress in the observer, or as one in which there is a lack of needed resources.

CHARACTERISTICS OF POTENTIAL RECIPIENT RELEVANT TO SITUATIONAL DEFINITION

Among the factors relevant to the potential recipient of help that have been shown to affect the situational definition, probably clearest is the severity of the need revealed by the sufferer. For example, when a victim needing a bone marrow transplant was described as a mother with young children, more persons volunteered as donors than when she was simply described as a young woman (S. H. Schwartz 1970a). A man who collapsed and was apparently suffering from a heart attack was helped more than one who seemed to have a bad knee (Staub 1974). Many kidney donors appear to base their decision primarily on the need of the donor with little consideration of the personal consequences of the organ donation (Fellner and Marshall 1970). Clarity of the need is also important. When undergraduates participating in a laboratory study heard loud noises from their partner in the next room, they were more likely to go to help if the partner shouted that some chairs had fallen on her than if only the loud noises of falling chairs were heard (Gaertner and Dovidio 1977).

The practice implications are clear: a social worker seeking to enlist help for a client from teachers, spouses, friends, professional colleagues, should highlight the needs of the client. The wide-ranging effects of expulsion from school on a youngster's feelings of self-worth, on his opportunities for further education, and on the likelihood of his becoming involved in criminal activity may all need to be stressed if help is to be obtained from his teacher in getting him returned to school. Clients may contribute to a potential helper's failure to recognize their state of need by their unwillingness to ask for help or to reveal how they feel. These tendencies may appear to protect self-esteem but can also cut off help from others. The social worker may be able to assist clients in being more open about their needs, or may have to provide some information directly to others who are in a position to help.

High need in itself, however, will not necessarily ensure that a potential helper will define the situation as one where help is needed. The legitimacy of the need is also relevant. Nonsufferers are less willing to help persons who appear to bring about their own difficulties than those where dependency, need, or distress seems to be caused by factors beyond the control of the victim (Heilman, Slochower, and Deutsch 1976; Langer and Abelson 1972; Schopler and Matthews 1965). An example of an externally caused dependency would be a physical disability stemming from a war injury. An internally caused dependency would be a physical disability resulting from a drug overdose or suicide attempt. The term "undeserving poor" used in *My Fair Lady* captures the feeling of the distinction. In reality, there is a continuum of internality or externality, not two dichotomous categories. Further, what appears to be due to internal factors may well be the result of external factors, and vice versa. In spite of these complexities, potential benefactors appear to make a judgment concerning the locus of the dependency, and this judgment affects their decision to give or not give help.

Other examples of problems that may appear to be self-induced are pregnancy, law breaking, truancy, child abuse, and sometimes alcoholism. Persons in need of help may blame themselves for their difficulties—indeed this may be a common response to even such traumatic events as rape (Wortman and Silver 1980)—and the sufferers own descriptions of their situation may thereby hinder them from receiving the help they need. The resistance to aiding clients in these and similar categories may be overcome if the practitioner anticipates such resistance and highlights, from the initial contact, the external factors that contributed to the problem, such as powerful peer pressure, academic deficiencies, societal norms that induce feelings of worthlessness, and alienation from societal norms after attempts to achieve success through legitimate means have failed. This approach was successfully used with volunteers working on a telephone hotline with abusive parents (Brickman and Holland 1979). Emphasis on the parents' excessive expectations for their children, their insufficient parenting skills, and lack of spouse and social support overcame the volunteers' traditional reluctance to help people performing deviant acts. Workers must also be sensitive to, and prepared to handle, their own resistance to helping clients with an internal locus of dependency, for workers are not immune from such negative feelings. Nor should it be assumed that the client's fellow sufferers do not differentiate the worthy from the unworthy. As one laboratory study with high-school boys showed, victims of unfair pay were biased against fellow victims who they believed were personally responsible for their own failures, and were even more attentive to locus of the responsibility for the injury to other victims than were nonvictims (Heilman, Slochower, and Deutsch 1976). The abusive parent who attributes his acts entirely to his own shortcomings may not be very helpful to another man whom he views as similarly at fault.

There is indirect evidence that role-playing techniques may be effective in reducing the distance between individuals who appear to have brought about their difficulties and potential helpers who are reluctant to give assistance. Role playing the experiences of a person in need has been found to elicit altruism in children if the situation is concrete and not hypothetical (Iannotti 1975; Staub 1971). Pearl and Reissman (1965) suggest role playing is an educational procedure especially compatible with the action-oriented, motoric style of learning of many low-income people. They describe its effectiveness in training low-income nonprofessional staff in various community action programs, where it was used to help this staff understand clients and to test worker-client relationship in a simulated setting under professional supervision. Role playing may well be effective more generally with facilitators of change to help foster empathy. For example, the angry mother of a pregnant teenager might be asked to enact what she would do if she were in her daughter's place.

Another strategy for recruiting significant others into the role of helper when the locus of dependency is seen as internal is to utilize the technique employed to foster situational attributions and reduce dispositional attributions. (In many ways, situational attributions, discussed in chapter 3, resemble dependency states that are seen as having an external locus, and dispositional attributions are analogous to dependency states with an internal locus.) Observers may be asked to imagine that they are the person whose behavior is to be examined and that they are engaging in the identical interactions as that individual. The goal is to feel what that person is feeling at the moment, and to look at others through his or her eyes. This procedure was found to increase the attributions made to situational variables, that is, to heighten sensitivity to the environmental factors affecting behavior. It is likely that the same procedure would tend to shift the perception of the potential facilitator of change with regard to locus of the client's dependency from internal to external factors, and thereby increase altruistic inclinations. The same procedure can be used by practitioners to bring to the surface their own temporarily submerged altruistic feelings, perhaps toward a particularly "self-destructive" client.

Based on our previous discussions in chapter 1 of the determinants and consequences of interpersonal attraction, the reader will not be surprised to learn that help has been shown to be more often given to someone who is attractive to, or liked by, the potential helper. For example, female undergraduates participated in an experimental questionnaire session either with a pleasant interviewer, one who thanked them for coming, made pleasant social conversation, offered coffee, etc., or with an unpleasant one, who said little, had a "Keep Off" sign near the coffee pot and was curt in ending the interview. Not only was the interviewer judged to be more likable in the former condition, but the subjects in that condition were more likely to agree to a request to complete another questionnaire for which they would receive no course credit (Gross, Wallston, and Piliavin 1975). Similarly, fellow pedestrians who had intruded upon the personal space of someone waiting to cross the street, and later dropped their keys while crossing the street, were less likely to be helped to retrieve the keys than if they had waited at a more appropriate distance (Konecni et al. 1975). The initial behavior presumably conveyed to the potential helper some information about whether this was the type of person with whom one might want to initiate interaction. In short, in an initial contact with a potential facilitator of change, as in any initial intervention, social workers need to be concerned about their attractiveness to the other person. Workers who are certain they are well liked can solicit aid fairly readily. However, practitioners who are unsure about how they are perceived had best be cautious in seeking assistance for a client. The more effective strategy in those instances would be to focus upon the qualities of the client that might be attractive to the potential facilitator.

As our earlier review indicated, individuals who are seen as similar to the judge are perceived as more attractive and are better liked. Individuals who share some interest, although they differ in ethnicity, race, or social class are likely to find one another attractive. Physically attractive individuals tend to be perceived as people who possess attractive inner qualities. Individuals who need one another to achieve their goals find their partners more attractive; those who are compatible or complementary in their needs for participation in a group, control, and affection tend to find one another attractive. All of these dimensions have also been shown to enhance willingness to help (Baron, Byrne, and Griffith 1974; F. Erikson 1975; Krebs 1970; Sole, Marton, and Hornstein 1975), and thus should be considered by practitioners attempting to enhance their own attractiveness or that of dependent clients. For example, in soliciting help from fellow sufferers for a client, the worker could highlight their shared problems, their similarities. Such a procedure might be effective in initial contacts with potential members of programs for single parents, siblings of retardates, or self-help groups for child abusers. Similarly, friends, peers, and family members of clients are more likely to offer assistance when they realize that their needs and preferences dovetail with those of the clients. For example, peers are more likely to include clients in their social group when the potential members enjoy the same type of music, sports, dancing, and films as the group members. Family members are likely to be responsive to requests for aid when the similarities in life experiences among family members are stressed, e.g., struggles to obtain a college degree or to overcome racism.

One particular way in which perceptions of similarity are expressed is by the placement of self and other into a category of "we." Often such a categorization is based upon shared common membership in a social category—female, black, ex-addict. Laboratory research has shown that when nothing is known about other experimental subjects besides whether or not they "belong to your group," which is undefined, resources and rewards are more often given to members of the in-group than to outsiders (Tajfel 1970). This feeling of "we" has been proposed as one of three conditions that enhance promotive social relations, that is relationships in which the goal attainment of another person is perceived as one's own goal (H. Hornstein 1972). The other two conditions are interdependence of the fate of the individuals, as when all team members win or lose, and the linkage of individuals by shared opinions. These are all conditions then that should promote helping.

Physical attractiveness is also relevant to the liking of a facilitator of change for either a social worker or client. The more physically attractive the clients, the more likely they are to receive assistance. It is therefore often in the clients' interest to help them look as attractive as possible. The same applies to the social worker's own physical appearance. Virtually all practitioners are dependent to some extent upon the good will of their colleagues and leaders in the community to function effectively. Thus the worker's appearance and behavior cannot be ignored. In some areas, wearing jeans and T-shirts may be encouraged; in others it is not. Workers may therefore have to decide before accepting employment whether they are willing to dress or behave in accordance with the norms of those whose support is needed. In a book entitled *Ribbin,' Jivin,' and Playing the Dozens* the author points out that elegant attire is very important to black urban male adolescents (Foster 1974). The social worker who dresses in work clothes may be ridiculed by these potential clients. Foster's book is directed at teachers but the advice applies equally well to community and outreach workers. In a rural area in the west, an attractive organizer who was attempting to work with the impoverished Indians was told by those who knew the region well that it would be impossible for her to function there if she engaged in sexual relations outside of marriage. The community would find out about it and would totally reject her. Thus the principle that dissimilarity engenders dislike appears to have wide applicability.

Application of that principle in educational contexts suggests that similarity between professionals whose help is being sought and the clients in need of assistance should be stressed if attempts to get critical extra effort are to succeed. As F. Erikson's (1975) study of junior-college counselors (discussed in chapter 1) showed, when the initial interview between counselor and student revealed particularistic co-membership, the counselor was more likely to offer help beyond that required by his minimal professional responsibility. It may be particularly important for the social worker to identify such similarities when seeking help on behalf of a client from someone who is of a different racial group or ethnicity from the client. There is some evidence of greater helping among both blacks and whites within racial lines than across them (Gaertner and Dovidio 1977; Penner, Dertke, and Achenbach 1973; I. M. Piliavin, Piliavin, and Rodin 1975; I. M. Piliavin, Rodin, and Piliavin 1969; West, Whitney, and Schnedler 1975), although this in-group bias is not always found (Dutton and Lennox 1974; Gaertner and Dovidio 1977; J. A. Piliavin and Piliavin 1972; Wispé and Freshley 1971).

In sum, to increase the probability that a facilitator of change will define the situation of a client as one requiring assistance it may be useful to ensure that the need of the client is clear; that it is perceived to be strong; that the source of the client's dependency is seen to be at least to some extent beyond his or her control; and that the facilitator of change has some basis for liking the client or the social worker.

CHARACTERISTICS OF POTENTIAL HELPER RELEVANT TO SITUATIONAL DEFINITION

The definition of the client's situation as one requiring help can also be affected by temporary states or relatively enduring traits of the facilitator of change. Several theorists (Berkowitz 1972; M. L. Hoffman 1975; I. M. Piliavin, Piliavin, and Rodin 1975; Staub 1974) have identified empathy of the potential helper—the process of experiencing the thoughts and feelings of another person—as enhancing the perception of the need for help. According to I. M. Piliavin and colleagues (1975), one reason people offer help in emergency situations, such as those involving physical danger, is that the observer vicariously experiences the distress of the victim and helps in order to reduce his or her own distress. It has been shown, for example, that heart rate changes occurred when undergraduates overheard noises in the next room indicating a possible injury to another student, and that the extent of this physiological arousal was correlated with the speed with which help efforts were initiated (Gaertner and Dovidio 1977). Thus any means of enhancing the empathy of a significant other with the feelings or emotional reactions of a client, through active or imaginal role taking, for example, should improve the likelihood of help being given (Aderman and Berkowitz 1970; Aderman, Brehm, and Katz 1974; Clore and Jeffery 1972; Staub 1971).

Related to the concept of empathy is that of the ability to take the perspective of a person in another social role, or the absence of social egocentrism (Piaget and Inhelder 1956). Egocentrism has been studied mainly from a developmental perspective and has been shown to interfere with young children's social judgments and to decrease with age (Looft 1972). Like empathy, social egocentrism can be thought of as a relatively enduring characteristic of an individual, but they both are also influenced by momentary situational conditions and by training. Boys known to the police for delinquent acts, for example, whose measured social egocentrism was considerably higher than that of members of a control group, benefited from a training program designed to help them see themselves from the perspective of others (Chandler 1973). This was accomplished by having small groups of boys and adults work on writing and making video films about teenagers of the boys' own age. Each boy played the parts of all characters in the stories, viewed each videotape, and participated in discussions of how to improve the film. While this study did not consider the consequences of reduced social egocentrism on helping behavior, we would expect that it would have at least increased the likelihood of concern about another's distress.

In contrast to empathy, aroused self-concern can reduce help, at least partially because it seems to interfere with empathy and recognition of others' needs (Berkowitz 1970). Self-concern that stems from a recent failure experience, from anticipated evaluation along a dimension important to the person (Berkowitz 1972), or from a recent experience of being unable to avoid distracting noise (Sherrod and Downs 1974) have all been shown to reduce help-giving when no external benefits accrued to the helper. This suggests, for example, that a widower who has recently lost his wife may not easily recognize his son's need for help with his school problems and that the school social worker must either first find help for the father's own distress, or attempt to arouse the father's dormant feelings of empathy with his son, if it is important to enlist the father as a facilitator of change. In contacts with a professional whose help is being sought on behalf of a client, it is important that workers avoid implying that they are making evaluative judgments about prior interactions between the client and the professional. It is possible, however, to utilize self-concern of a potential facilitator to heighten help-giving if social or self-worth benefits to the helper are highlighted, such as enhancement of their reputation in the organization, though this should affect perceptions of the consequences of helping more than the definition of the situation (Berkowitz 1972).

Feelings of the facilitator of change are relevant to the definition of another person as needing help in an additional sense as well. The mood of a potential helper has been shown to predict help-giving in quite a few studies (e.g., Berkowitz 1972; Levin and Isen 1975). It appears that individuals who are in a good mood (feel happy, content, satisfied) experience a "warm glow" that leads to greater helping, perhaps because their mood affects their empathic capacities (Berkowitz 1972) or their perception of the costs and rewards of helping (Levin and Isen 1975). In either case, certain social work implications are obvious. It is unwise to request aid from those who are feeling particularly depressed, frustrated, unappreciated or angry; it is preferable to wait until they are feeling more successful and self-confident. If a delay is not possible, efforts to enhance their positive feelings through appropriate compliments or unexpected offers of Coke or coffee may improve their mood, and hence the likelihood that they will help.

Certain cognitive characteristics of potential helpers can also influence their definition of the situation, most prominently the "just world belief." This concept refers to the phenomenon that people tend to believe that we live in a just world in which we get what we deserve and deserve what we get (Lerner 1971; Lerner and Miller 1978). Thus we tend to infer inputs from outcomes. Given the suffering of a victim, an outcome, there is a tendency for the observer to infer that the input of the sufferer must have been responsible in some way for what occurred or that the victim is an undesirable, lazy, untrustworthy person. The derogation of a victim helps the observer maintain a belief in a just world and avoid recognizing that misfortune can befall innocent people: "it could be my fate" (Lerner 1970). Lerner (1971) suggests that the just world belief may be an explanation for society's willingness to tolerate suffering of many disadvantaged individuals. Ryan (1972) has made a similar point about American attitudes and behaviors toward the black and poor. And Symonds (1975) proposed that there is a reluctance on the part of people to accept the idea that a rape victim is blameless because it may imply that they or their relatives and friends could be exposed to the offense at any time or place.

There is evidence, at least among American undergraduates, of wide variation in the degree to which individuals ascribe to such beliefs. Furthermore, these variations in beliefs have been shown to be related to evaluations of other persons who have suffered a loss or deficiency (D. T. Miller 1977; Rubin and Peplau 1973, 1975; Zuckerman, 1975). For example, in one study young men, whose beliefs in a just world had previously been assessed, listened in groups to the results of the 1971 draft lottery which decided who among them would have a high or low probability of being drafted (Rubin and Peplau 1973). The men with weak beliefs in a just world rated the losers as most likable and expressed strong sympathy with them; men with strong beliefs in the just world reacted as favorably to winners and losers and resented the losers more than winners. Another study suggested that sufferers will be derogated only when it is impossible for the observer of the suffering to help the victim (Lincoln and Levinger 1972). In that study white undergraduates who saw slides of white policemen attacking black civilians rated the black young men negatively when the ratings were given simply for the experimenter's benefit but not when they were part of data to be given to an investigative commission. Thus exposure to injustice or suffering appears more likely to elicit derogation of the victim when the observer cannot rectify the suffering, as in the draft lottery or the slide ratings with no consequence. This distinction is consistent with predictions from equity theory, previously discussed in chapter 4, that individuals will try to restore interpersonal equity, but when equity cannot be restored, defensive restructuring of the situation, including derogation of the victim or denial of the inequity, is likely (Walster, Berscheid, and Walster 1976).

All of the above suggests that significant others who are involved with victims of one misfortune or another, such as rape victims, battered wives, or unemployed fathers, may hold the just world belief to some extent and seek reasons to blame the victim. Workers who encounter any evidence of this tendency might want to discuss the phenomenon with the potential helper and highlight the societal, biological, or constitutional factors that might have contributed to the undesirable outcome in this particular case. Some examples of persons in need of aid who serve too often as "blamed victims" are members of minority groups who have been subjected to discrimination all of their lives and are not then as able to use sudden opportunities for advanced education as those with different life experiences; workers over sixty-five who are forced to retire and become depressed and unable to care for themselves because one of the central components of their identity has been taken from them; and middle-aged divorcées who suddenly find themselves with no salable skills, no job, and no family to nurture. By discussing the role of society in creating these problems the social worker may be able to affect the potential helper's definition of the person as worthy of receiving help. The practitioner should also be prepared to indicate how the facilitator can come to the aid of the sufferer to reduce his or her distress, for the arousal of sympathetic distress without a mechanism for reduction is likely to motivate the potential facilitator to restore equity by derogating the victim.

If some damaging act was performed by the client for which they are blamed by the facilitator, the worker might want to discuss some of the factors that should be taken into consideration in assigning responsibility: whether the act was intentional, whether the consequences were foreseeable, whether there was any justification for what occurred (Ross and DiTecco 1975). At the very minimum, the worker might want to help facilitators who are already in an on-going relationship with the client, for example, a family member, to become aware of their attributions of blame so that the biases will be visible and taken into consideration when interventions are planned.

One's definition of whether an emergency exists or someone is in need and worthy of help is also affected by the reactions of other persons to the same situation. This information may be the result of instruction or be more subtle, as when the behavior of another person is simply observed and provides information to the observer. Modeling effects on helping have been found in a wide variety of field and laboratory studies with adults and children. This vicarious learning by observing another person giving help or not giving help can affect all phases of the decisional process. Its likely impact on the definition of the situation was the explanation given in one study of bystanders' help when a man collapsed in a subway car (I. M. Piliavin, Piliavin, and Rodin 1975). The collapse occurred either in the presence of a man dressed as a medical intern or with no such person present, and the victim either had a clearly visible, and presumably offensive, large red birthmark on his face or did not. The least helping occurred for the disfigured victim with the intern present. The authors explained this as follows: "The inaction of the intern, who presumably was the most appropriate helper, allows them [the bystanders] to define inaction as appropriate, to redefine the situation as one not requiring their direct intervention" (p. 437). This may also explain why in two other studies there were some trials in which no one helped and some in which many bystanders helped (Latané and Dabbs 1975; J. A. Piliavin and Piliavin 1972). In these situations—where a bloody victim collapsed in a subway car or someone dropped a handful of coins in an elevator—the lack of helping from others seemed to be used as a cue that help was not necessary.

In another experiment in the natural environment involving navy enlisted men, it was found that a donating model increased the altruism of the observers but only when the cost of helping was low—a dollar a week donation to a charity for twenty weeks (Wagner and Wheeler 1969). In the high-cost situation, which involved giving a $20 donation in one week, the model had no effect. This finding suggests that in ambiguous situations, the model's behavior can tip the observer's behavior in the same direction. The researchers hypothesized that helping behavior may be strongly determined by the donor's perception of need, which is "validated" by a generous model and "invalidated" by a selfish one. The model provided a guide concerning the appropriate size of the donation, and to the extent of the valid need as well.

Thus it is possible that both a nonhelping and a helping model can affect an observer's definition of a situation, as well the acceptance of responsibility for personal action. We will return to these possible effects of modeling later in our discussion of this general topic. At this point it is sufficient to make two further points about the use of a model to foster altruism in those whose help is sought. It is desirable to provide models who are as much like the potential benefactor as possible. Thus, when help is needed from a peer of the client to implement an intervention strategy, the worker would increase the likelihood of receiving assistance if the assistance volunteered from another friend was made known to the facilitator of change. Similarly, when help is needed from a public assistance worker or public health nurse for a client, shared knowledge of past cooperation of other assistance workers or nurses in similar cases may be useful. Obviously, social workers should themselves serve as models of helpers. If live models similar to the potential helpers are not available, efforts should be made to highlight models from popular films, TV programs, and books. Such fictional characters often take on lifelike qualities to readers and members of the audience.

The findings of programs training young children to be more altruistic suggest that concern for others can be taught. Social workers employed in socialization agencies such as community centers or day care facilities may want to develop some programs on the theme of helping others. Important elements are instructors who are warm and nurturing, and who teach helping behaviors while practicing altruism themselves. School social workers and consultants to socialization agencies could themselves develop and conduct pilot training sessions on altruism for youngsters, or could help interested teachers and leaders to create their own programs. Such activities fit naturally into the area of affective education which focuses on interpersonal relationships and self-awareness.

Practitioners whose work falls more into the realm of parent and adult education may well find that altruism in children is a topic of interest to mothers, fathers, foster parents, and other child caregivers who have sought help for children in their charge. Again the importance of nurturance by the instructor, teaching through symbols (e.g., pictures, films, TV), and modeling helping behavior in concrete situations should be stressed. It is likely that parents and other caregivers could provide many illustrations of altruism modeled by children and suggest factors that impede altruism, such as contact with other youngsters whose parents value toughness and competition rather than helping. A stimulating discussion is likely to ensue. At the very minimum, such discussions should raise the consciousness of socializers about prosocial behavior and how it is fostered. In the past, far too much attention has been paid to negative child behaviors such as aggression, fighting, and rivalry; highlighting altruism should foster adult behaviors which enhance its development.

ACCEPTING PERSONAL RESPONSIBILITY FOR HELPING

The recognition that someone is suffering or in need of assistance does not automatically engage the observer in the process of help. Much theory and research has been directed toward identifying the conditions that facilitate and hinder the transition from perception that an individual is needy to the acceptance of personal responsibility for action.

CHARACTERISTICS OF POTENTIAL HELPER RELEVANT TO ACCEPTING RESPONSIBILITY

Both social and personal factors relevant to the potential helper have been proposed as influential. Compliance to societal norms concerning social responsibility toward others (Berkowitz and Daniels 1964), giving (Leeds 1963), reciprocity (Gouldner 1967), and equity (Walster, Berscheid, and Walster 1976) have all been said to foster accepting personal responsibility to help those who are needy or disadvantaged. By norm is meant a shared idea of appropriate behavior in a particular group (M. A. Lieberman 1975), in this case society as a whole. The norms of social responsibility and giving reflect essentially altruistic concerns; they prescribe helping another based on the dependency or neediness of the other person. The norms of reciprocity and equity, on the other hand, prescribe helping others because they have helped you and to avoid indebtedness, and thus are based on a concern about past favors received. Norms imply positive sanctions from other group members for the behaviors that are in conformity with the shared ideal and negative ones for nonconformity; therefore all of the above norms may be thought of as based on self-concern to some degree. One could help someone in need because of concern for potential criticism for not doing so, as well as because one believes in accepting responsibility for those unable to help themselves. Further, both types of norms may operate in the same situation with cues present eliciting both the norm of responsibility and the amount of obligation required for reciprocity (Wilke and Lanzetta 1970).

Societal norms can be used by social workers to encourage a facilitator of change to accept responsibility if the norm's salience in the particular situation can be increased. This was shown in a number of studies. For example, undergraduates who were members of a campus community service organization were more likely to come to the assistance of a confederate of the experimenter who appeared to have a seizure if their membership in this service group had been emphasized in earlier instructions about an experimental task (Horowitz 1971). Similarly, voting in a campus election was more likely among undergraduates who had received a letter reminding them of their responsibility in a democratic society to vote (Gross et al. 1974).

Thus in discussing with potential foster parents their willingness to accept a particularly difficult child into their home, it may be useful to bring the church membership of the couple into the conversation or to emphasize societal ideals of helping. The norm of social responsibility is likely to be particularly powerful with members of extended family groups and oppressed minorities when the potential recipient of aid is a member of that family or minority group. For example, there is a high probability that practitioners will be able to induce black college students to work with troubled Chicano adolescents if the needs of the younger individuals are pointed out. Cousins, aunts, grandparents, godparents, and uncles are all potential benefactors and should not be overlooked by practitioners seeking supervision for children whose mother has been hospitalized, or home care for a post-surgery patient. If offers of help are not immediately forthcoming, describing the plight of the dependent individuals should evoke the norm of social responsibility and increase donations of time, housing, and material assistance.

Lerner (1975) has suggested that individuals define the basis for justice according to several major criteria: need, equity, equality, and entitlement. The choice among these is based upon one's view of the person suffering an injustice. Someone who is viewed as a unique individual, rather than as a position occupant, and who is perceived as like oneself, he suggests, is most likely to be reacted to on the basis of need. According to this analysis, then, the arousal of the norm of social responsibility would be enhanced by encouraging the facilitators to consider the client as a unique individual with attitudes, beliefs, and needs similar to their own.

One dyadic relationship in which this view might obtain is that between children and parents. Often teenagers, or newly independent individuals of any age, will be rebellious and will attempt to defy those upon whom they were previously dependent emotionally, financially, or physically. Such defiance often engenders anger and rejection. The worker can foster the willingness of the parent, or the previous caregiver, to help the rebel by pointing out the areas in which those individuals are still in need of aid in spite of their resistance and defiance. In this way the norm of social responsibility is likely to be elicited, and as a result the "significant others" will be more willing to participate in a treatment plan. (This application of the norm of social responsibility to social work practice was suggested by Diane Dennedy, a student at the University of Michigan School of Social Work in May 1976.)

In other situations, past help from the current sufferer may need to be emphasized, as in the enlistment of an adult child in the care of an aging parent. Or the inequity in access to resources may be pointed out, as when a monetary contribution is being sought for a summer camp program for poor children. The choice of which societal norm may be relevant must be made in each situation based on the social worker's knowledge of the facilitators of change and their past relationships with the clients.

We do not mean to suggest, however, that making these norms salient will always directly affect behavior. For example, when husbands and wives fight, neighbors rarely intercede to help the weaker individual. Perhaps the core of the problem is that there are conflicting norms in society, and most individuals are unsure which to apply when both might be enacted. Thus the norm of not interfering in families' private concerns often conflicts with the norm of social responsibility. This dilemma is particularly strong in large urban areas where survival demands adaptations, such as "urban norms" of impersonality and aloofness (Korte and Kerr 1975; Milgrim 1973). Residents of giant cities such as New York and Chicago would find it impossible to fill any of their roles and also respond to the needs of everyone they encounter on a typical day. Hence aloofness may be adaptive in these settings. Furthermore, the costs of carrying out normative behavior may be so high that the norm is regularly violated. We will discuss ways that social workers may avoid such problems in efforts to gain help for their clients in the next section.

The presence of other people during an emergency is another social influence that has been much studied. In many studies the presence of other potential helpers seems to diminish the likelihood that any individual will offer help (Latané and Dabbs 1975; Latané and Darley 1970; C. J. Morgan 1978; Wegner and Schaefer 1978), but this is not found in all studies (C. J. Morgan 1978; I. M. Piliavin, Piliavin, and Rodin 1975; I. M. Piliavin, Rodin, and Piliavin 1969). The diminution in helping can be due to several factors when the reactions of other potential helpers can be observed: 1) there is a diffusion of responsibility with others available; 2) modeling of others is operative so that when one person withholds aid, others do likewise; and 3) pluralistic ignorance is functioning: each individual looks to the others and when they seem calm, the conclusion drawn is that no help is needed as no one else appears worried (Staub 1974). The last explanation is similar to our description of the effects of others' inaction on the definition of the situation, and both it and the imitative explanation require that the observer be aware of the behavior of the other persons. In a number of laboratory situations, however, the subjects knew that others were present and exposed to the distress of the victim, but were unaware of the response of the others (e.g., C. J. Morgan 1978). In such situations the only one of the three explanations above that would be possible is diffusion of responsibility—that each individual feels less responsible to help when others can also help (Latané and Dabbs 1975). Regardless of the explanation, the social worker who is trying to enlist the assistance of facilitators should be alert to the possibility that if they are aware that other persons might also help the client, the facilitators may be reluctant to accept personal responsibility for the client's welfare. Research suggests that this may be especially true when the costs of helping are high and an alternative helper appears especially qualified to assist (C. J. Morgan 1978; I. M. Piliavin, Piliavin, and Rodin 1975). Well-thought-out efforts may be needed to overcome this resistance to accepting responsibility for helping.

The presence of helpful others can foster the perception of personal responsibility in facilitators of change who are not, in this instance, acting in conformity with their self-concepts. If models are to be used in such situations, they should be selected because they engage in behaviors ordinarily typical of the observers, e.g., being a generous donor. Thus the potential benefactors are likely to become aware that they are not acting in congruence with their self-images and may commence doing so. For example, some husbands who are usually supportive of their wives do not help sufficiently with the housework when the wives obtain full-time jobs or return to school. Meeting with a husband in a similar position who indicates he does provide substantial help is likely to make the uncooperative husband aware that he is not behaving "in character." The consequence may well be more helpful activity at home. In some cases, the potential benefactors may not in reality be as responsive to the needs of others as they would like to believe. The same approach should be effective with these individuals, however, for the important element is not what actually occurs, but the perception of what occurs. For example, some teachers see themselves as instructors who regularly prepare individual work for children having difficulty with class assignments. They may in truth prepare such individualized work only occasionally, but if they are made aware of a teacher in their school who offers to tailor all assignments to the needs of Spanish-speaking students who have difficulty with reading they may offer similar help in order to preserve their self-images.

There are a number of conditions that enhance the acceptance of personal responsibility and these can be fostered by the social worker in situations where diffusion of responsibility is of concern or in any other problematic contacts with a facilitator of change. As our discussion of role theory in chapter 2 indicated, persons in complementary role relationships have obligations toward each other, and in certain positions these may involve assisting the role partner. For example, Nye's (1976) study of family role demands indicated that the majority of couples in his sample believed that it was their obligation to help each other with personal problems. Also common were felt obligations to kin outside the nuclear family concerning economic assistance in time of need and maintenance of communication; here the husbands were expected to carry out the economic role obligations and the wives to enact the communication responsibilities. Role obligations were implicated in a series of laboratory simulations of a job situation with supervisors and workers. The subjects cast in the role of workers were more productive when told that their supervisor's chance of winning a prize was highly dependent on them than when the supervisor's outcome was not dependent on their productivity (Berkowitz 1972). Professionals' roles often involve obligations to help the needy, though in any given instance these obligations may need to be made salient. Such enduring familial or professional role obligations may be a basis for social workers enlisting the assistance of a facilitator of change in the support of clients in need of aid.

Obligations must be linked to feasible behaviors, however, before they are translated into action. At minimum, the perception that one is able to carry out the behaviors needed to give assistance is required (Latané and Darley 1970; S. H. Schwartz 1977). This principle requires that the social worker be careful about what a particular facilitator is asked to do, especially when a nonprofessional's help is being sought. A working mother with a large family may be unable to spend an hour a night with a boy who needs help with his homework. An aging father may not be accepted into his daughter's home if she feels incapable of providing the daily injections he requires. In such instances the worker may need to work to improve the skills or available time of the facilitator before asking for a commitment to help.

A recognition by the facilitators of change that they possess unique skills, abilities, or access to information that may be helpful to the client can be the basis for their accepting personal responsibility for action (S. H. Schwartz 1970b). This was shown in a study of the willingness of former clients of a state vocational rehabilitation agency to be helpful to current agency clients (Cowan and Inskeep 1978). The former clients, who no longer needed help themselves from the agency, were asked to call or visit current clients who wanted information about what it was like to attend a particular training school. When they were uniquely qualified to provide the information—they had attended that school themselves and were told they were the last person who was able to be contacted—they were most likely to agree to help. Similarly, the unique potential of familial organ donors is a key aspect of such help (Saks 1978). This general approach can be applied to any situation in which a fellow-sufferer's help is being sought. Many other kinds of unique qualifications, including access to the clients in need of help, can also be invoked.

The personal values, beliefs, and motives of facilitators of change will also influence their response in some situation. For example, S. H. Schwartz (1977) has reported several studies in which the strength of self-reported personal or moral obligations to persons in need were correlated with helping behavior, especially when the individuals with strong personal helping norms also were high in the tendency to become aware of the consequences their own behavior had for others. For Schwartz, what distinguishes personal norms from social ones is that the sanctions relevant to personal norms are attached to the self-concept rather than to social feedback. These personal norms must be elicited by the particular situation; no individual will feel moral obligation to help all persons in all situations. When a social worker believes a potential facilitator has a strong personal norm to be helpful, it is still necessary to link this obligation to the particular current situation of the client. Schwartz's approach is similar to that of Rokeach (1968a, 1973), discussed earlier. One of the major values Rokeach identified is helpfulness, and the congruence between behavior and a person's values is seen as linked to maintenance of a positive self-concept. Further, maintenance of a positive self-concept is seen as motivating behavior.

M. L. Hoffman (1975) has also postulated a personal rather than a strictly social basis for helping behaviors, and has argued that the typical course of human development makes it likely that we are motivated to help others for altruistic reasons, namely the reduction of someone else's distress, rather than solely by selfish goals. Two conditions are proposed as necessary to the development of an altruistic motive: experiences of empathy or affective reactions to another's feelings, and the cognitive ability to recognize the distress of another person who is distinct from you and whose immediate situational distress may be linked to other life conditions. According to this view, if the above conditions obtain, both training in role taking and exposure to information regarding the life situations of others should be especially likely to foster helping if they direct the person's attention to the feelings of others.

Thus the Schwartz, Rokeach, and Hoffman views all suggest the usefulness of understanding the particular motives, values, beliefs that are important to individual facilitators of change if their help is to be elicited. Self-perception theory, as discussed previously in chapter 5 as useful in situations located in Quadrant A of table 3.1, can then be relevant. For example, contributors to one charity when solicited in a door-to-door campaign were either told that they were generous and charitable persons or were simply thanked (Kraut 1973). Several weeks later those labeled charitable gave more money to another solicitor. The theories cited above would suggest that these attributions by the solicitors would have had most impact among residents whose self-concept included value for giving, or who were motivated by others' needs.

Self-images and threats to these constructs were proposed to explain the differential behavior of white Canadian undergraduates toward blacks and whites seeking help (Dutton and Lennox 1974). In this study the subjects were selected to include only students whose self-reports indicated they viewed themselves as more egalitarian and less prejudiced than their peers. A considerable time after these self-reports were obtained, the subjects participated in an experiment designed to make them question these self-views: the experimenter indicated (falsely) that their autonomic feedback to pictures of blacks indicated prejudice. Immediately after the experiment, some subjects encountered either a black or white student in need of twenty-five cents. More subjects helped the black student than the white one. The authors suggest that the threat to the egalitarian self-image of the subjects induced by the experimental procedures was reduced by a contribution to the black student. This effect was only short-lived, however, for a request to all subjects a few days later to commit time to a campus group working on an interracial brotherhood campaign revealed that the subjects who had previously helped a black student committed less time to this endeavor than did those who had helped a white student or who had had their egalitarian self-images threatened but had not encountered a request for aid after the initial experiment. Only the latter groups apparently were still suffering from a threat to their self-images as egalitarian persons, and reduced this threat by commitment to an interracial activity. In short, while situationally induced questioning of self-images can affect subsequent helping behavior relevant to the threatened values, a rather minor retribution can restore the threatened self-view.

The social worker seeking to increase the likelihood that a facilitator of change will agree to help can consider doing so through making discrepancies between self-views and behavior salient, but this is probably a technique that has the danger of fostering only a temporary helping response. In the long run techniques designed to enhance self-attributions of altruistic ideals, such as the worker labeling certain behaviors as congruent with altruistic ideals of the facilitator, may be a better means of enhancing continuing acceptance of personal responsibility to help.

The fostering of personal beliefs, values, and motives congruent with altruism is another arena in which models may be influential.

Krebs (1970) specified several reasons models may influence the altruistic behavior of onlookers. Models can increase the salience of the norms of reciprocity and social responsibility, and give information about the consequences of helping behavior, particularly when helping could conceivably endanger the donor, e.g., stopping on a road to help someone with a flat tire. Models may also foster the internalization of altruistic dispositions. The latter would clearly require models who are in contact with the individual over prolonged periods. In keeping with this proposition, it has been found that altruistic parents are more likely to have altruistic children than are parents who stress competition and status needs. Further, in accordance with socialization theory, nurturant parents who are altruistic are emulated by their children more than parents who are not affectionate and loving (Rutherford and Mussen 1968). Similarly, in a naturalistic study of civil rights workers, it was found that the more dedicated workers reported having close ties with their parents who were themselves committed to altruistic causes (Rosenhan 1969). It was concluded that these workers grew up identifying with nurturant, altruistic models.

The Rosenhan findings were replicated in the laboratory when an altruism training program for preschool children was developed under two conditions: one with a nurturant adult caretaker and one with a nonnurturant caretaker. It was found that in realistic encounters with mild distress, the children working with nurturant models who had been modeling helping gave more aid, verbalized more sympathy, and were more consistently altruistic than were the youngsters with nonnurturant models (Yarrow, Scott, and Waxler 1973). The study was conducted with middle-class white children and lower-class black children and the same results obtained. It was concluded that the identification process was operative, inasmuch as the children's adultlike altruism was seen under conditions of no pressure and no cue from the model. Further, both the model's overt and covert behaviors were expressed by the youngsters. Another laboratory study with children seven to eleven years of age also concluded that modeling of altruism can result in internalization of these values—the behavior was demonstrated not only immediately but two months later as well (Rushton 1975). These studies with children suggest a strategy for working with mainstream classmates of handicapped children. School social workers could try to directly enhance the altruistic values of the peers of the target child, or could assist classroom teachers in setting up such training.

In contrast with these findings, Krebs (1970), after reviewing the literature of altruistic modeling with adults, decided that only temporary effects were produced. Perhaps, by the time individuals reach adulthood, they have already internalized values concerning altruism, and a brief encounter with a model is likely to influence behavior only in that particular situation. For a resocialization of adult values, both high affect and high control may be needed (Brim and Wheeler 1966). It is unlikely that such conditions could, or would, be produced in an experimental situation.

CHARACTERISTICS OF POTENTIAL RECIPIENT RELEVANT TO ACCEPTING RESPONSIBILITY

Certain qualities of the person in need of help are also particularly relevant to whether the facilitator of change is likely to accept personal responsibility to help. Sufferers who occupy certain positions in societal, organizational, or family systems are usually assumed to be in dependent role relationships. Children, the aged, the infirm, occupy societal positions which give responsibility to adults to help them. Family obligations were mentioned earlier. A friend in distress is more likely to be helped than a stranger (Sawyer 1966). Women experiencing physical emergencies are more likely to be helped by strangers than are men (Latané and Dabbs 1975; Penner, Dertke, and Achenbach 1973).

The norm of social responsibility, that those in need of help will be aided regardless of whether or not they assisted someone in the past, may be the key to understanding such assistance. The concept of Christian charity expresses the connotation of the social responsibility norm. Because there is no expectation of reciprocity, the norm of social responsibility is frequently applied to those who are not peers, for example, to the very young, the powerless, the impaired. In attempting to evoke the norm of social responsibility in powerful individuals, practitioners are likely to be most effective if the needs of powerless clients or client systems are made salient. For example, in seeking foster parents, social workers might describe the potential of the youngsters to be placed, along with the chances that the potential will never be realized if loving, stable homes are not located for the children. Similarly, efforts to find part-time jobs for out-of-school black youths may be enhanced if prospective employers and influential community leaders are given information about the unemployment rate of minority youths and the unsuccessful efforts they have made to find jobs. By evoking the norm of social responsibility through a focus on special status of the needy individual, the social worker may also be able to obtain citizen volunteers for an out-of-institution program preparing residents of mental hospitals to live in the community. Citing the needs of the patients and the ability of the potential benefactors to meet those needs should increase the probability of success in efforts to recruit homemakers and retired workers to participate. Whether general societal norms or specific role relationships define these special characteristics of the clients, the worker can use them to enhance helping behavior from facilitators of change.

One specific set of behaviors on the part of clients for whom assistance is now being sought can also be relevant—that of their prior helpfulness to the facilitator of change. The social norm of reciprocity is more likely to be invoked when the social worker can point to prior help received by the facilitator from the client or from the social worker. Practitioners who go out of their way to respond to requests for help from colleagues are likely to receive help when they are in need of assistance. It can be considered credit in the bank, especially if past help was freely and voluntarily given (Gross and Latané 1974). When employed in a host setting, such as a prison, school, hospital, social workers are likely to be bombarded with requests for help from various staff members. In the fabric of interacting roles in any large organization, there are many segments in which the occupant of a single position cannot function adequately without the cooperation of those in reciprocal positions. If the social worker helps to meet the needs of the occupational therapist, physical therapist, speech therapist, receptionist, intake worker, staff physician, psychologist, teacher, typist, and especially administrator, the likelihood is significantly increased that the norm of reciprocity will function in the social worker's and the client's behalf at a later time. The norm is operative outside of formal organizations as well as within. As components of larger systems, staff members of many organizations interact in a community. Thus assistance or consultation to juvenile police officers or public health nurses will likely be returned to social workers in schools, halfway houses, departments of social services, and community mental health centers.

The norm of reciprocity is also likely to function on behalf of the client, for example, an aged widower, if the worker makes salient to his family and friends the occasions on which he provided assistance to them. The general point is that past behavior of clients can sometimes appropriately be made relevant in ways that emphasize their current dependency status as a change in the calculus of equity and reciprocity.

Related to the concept that help should be returned is the expectation that a hurt will be rectified. Perhaps the inference is that if it is not, some form of hurt will be reciprocated. Thus atonement to alleviate guilt may be a technique of warding off vengeance. It has been found that individuals who feel they have harmed someone else want to expiate their guilt by helping the injured parties, but only if the individuals harmed do not have to be confronted (Freedman, Wallington, and Bliss 1967). Guilt, in addition, appears to enhance altruism to individuals who were not necessarily injured themselves (Carlsmith and Gross 1969). Thus, if workers are aware that members of clients' primary or secondary groups are experiencing guilt for some past behaviors, the feelings may be relieved if the workers can create opportunities for those individuals to perform acts of atonement. It is important, however, not to require that the injured party be confronted. For example, if a potential facilitator is experiencing severe guilt feelings because of vindictive acts toward an unemployed spouse or hyperactive child, the worker may develop a plan with the facilitator for expiating the guilt by performing some beneficial act for the injured person without necessarily linking the aid given to prior injury. In those instances, the worker can help two individuals by providing an opportunity to the significant other to relieve guilt and at the same time provide assistance to the client. For example, if attendants in a state hospital are made aware that they have been neglecting some unattractive patients, they may be more than willing to cooperate in a behavioral management program dispensing reinforcements for appropriate behavior to the neglected patients and others who are similar.

There are instances in which a worker might want to evoke guilt in order to achieve desirable goals but the ethics of such a procedure must be considered very carefully. Some variables that might be weighed are the amount of guilt elicited, the ability of the individual to handle the guilt, and the possibilities of obtaining cooperation from a nonsufferer through other means. For example, in a community where racial tensions are high, some adolescent leaders may be induced to participate in a biracial or multiethnic program when they are made aware of the hurt they have inflicted upon innocent youngsters. Similarly, children who have been teasing handicapped peers may be willing to include them in their games when an optimum amount of guilt is evoked. The power of guilt to influence behavior should not be underestimated. A recent humorous but insightful book included specific directions for controlling children through guilt; the title of the book is *How To Be a Jewish Mother*.

ASSESSING THE CONSEQUENCES OF HELPING

An extensive review of the literature is not necessary to convince the reader that a potential helper's actual behavior will be influenced by the anticipated positive and negative consequences of giving or not giving help in a given situation. Regardless of whether they assume an essentially egoistic basis for helping behaviors based primarily on rewards and costs to the helper directly (e.g., as in Latané and Darley 1970, or I. M. Piliavin, Piliavin, and Rodin 1975), or propose that at least some helping behaviors are primarily motivated by regard for the other person (e.g., M. L. Hoffman 1975; S. H. Schwartz 1977), all social psychological theorists assume that the actual and anticipated consequences of helping or not helping in a given situation affect current and future behavior. What is of interest then is the specification of the kinds of benefits and costs that may be relevant to the potential helper, and the ways in which the social worker could attempt to maximize benefits relative to costs in order to enhance the likelihood of enlisting assistance from facilitators of change.

BENEFITS TO POTENTIAL HELPER

Increasing the benefits of giving help for the potential helper can be accomplished in a number of ways. The degree of need or amount of distress of the client and the extent to which the potential help can clearly serve to reduce these states are key aspects of two types of benefits associated with helping (or costs associated with not helping). One type is the pleasure a helper can experience in observing the lessened pain of a sufferer; the second is the alleviation of the distress a potential helper may feel in the face of someone else's suffering. Both of these emotions would be expected to affect the rendering of help and have implications for those attempting to elicit aid on behalf of others. For example, to enhance helping, facilitators of change should be given opportunities to see the fruits of their assistance, perhaps an appreciative smiling child or bed-ridden patient. If face-to-face contact is not possible, the more vivid or concrete the presentation of a sufferer's plight, the more one would expect the arousal of empathic distress and the benefits of its reduction. In addition, when the assistance sought will not place facilitators in direct contact with the recipients of their help, it would be useful for the social worker to provide feedback to the helpers on the ways in which their gifts, access to resources, provision of information, etc., have reduced the distress of the social worker's clients. Similarly, if the facilitators appear motivated by their own empathic experience of distress elicited by the suffering of another, the condition of the sufferer, for example, prisoner or mental patient, should be kept salient to enhance the costs to the potential helper of not helping, and the relief of the sufferer must be evident to make the benefits of having given help obvious.

Direct social benefits can of course accrue from giving help and social costs from not doing so. The reward may be appreciation expressed by the worker, the benefactor's supervisors or colleagues, or by the recipient of help. The worker may not always be in a position to provide such reinforcements but should not overlook the opportunity to build in social gratifications whenever possible for those whose help is needed. Anticipated rewards from the recipient of help was cited as an explanatory variable in the finding that women were helped more than men, particularly in the south (Latané and Dabbs 1975). According to the researchers, one of the factors affecting helping may be the desire to earn the gratitude of others, and gratitude from women is especially rewarding since they know how to use the "soft" currency of smiles and "thank you". Southern women appear to be particularly adept in this area. But men also know how to reward others. Anticipated approval from colleagues appeared relevant to understanding the frequencies of helping behaviors in an emergency among members of a college community service club and a social fraternity (Horowitz 1971). When men who were members of the former group thought their peers were also present during the emergency, they were even more likely to help than when they were alone. In the latter group, however, where helping others was apparently not a group norm, the opposite result occurred.

Helping has also been shown to be more evident when the help to be given is clearly delineated, when the recipients will find out who extended aid, and when help is not automatically given because of high dependence (Berkowitz and Daniels 1963). The researchers speculated that those giving help may have experienced relative deprivation when they expended effort to assist someone and did not receive even gratitude in return. This hypothesis again emphasizes the fact that helping behavior at times is only partially altruistic, that is, based entirely on concern for another's welfare. Similarly, concrete acknowledgment to all who offered assistance can foster future helping. For example, a handmade certificate to a child who volunteers to help a handicapped classmate is often highly appreciated and remembered, often framed. Written notes expressing appreciation to colleagues for their efforts also foster good will, even in the most cynical professionals. As evidence, the chances are high that the reader of this volume recalls with pleasure the last written message received from a supervisor or colleague praising the way a job was performed.

There are many situations in which social benefits to the giver and recipient of help are interdependent. Interdependence refers to the fact that each member needs the other members in order to attain his or her own goals. When such interdependence exists it probably should be highlighted, and when it does not, it may be useful to create it. The former condition is found in many situations when the facilitators from whom assistance is requested are colleagues, administrators, or staff members of an organization in which a client is functioning. To illustrate, the staffs of most institutions would like to have their settings perceived as effective and efficient in delivering service. Thus a constructive recreation program for a hospitalized adolescent, visible to the community, would meet the youngster's needs and simultaneously enhance the prestige of the institution. Similarly, school principals tend to be concerned when their older students are seen idle on city streets. A work-study program in which an alienated youngster earns money painting city park equipment would therefore benefit both the administrator and the student. It would also bring credit to the recreation director who may have limited funds for maintaining equipment.

When the facilitator is closely related to the client, or a member of the same group as the client, the worker can enhance the likelihood of help being offered if stress is placed in their interdependence. In the case of a family or a natural friendship group, interdependence can be enhanced by citing past helping behavior by members in a time of the serious illness, a financial emergency, or trouble with the law. The enduring reassurance obtained from the knowledge that other members can be counted upon in a time of need can also be stressed. The interdependence may not always be obvious to the facilitator of change, and its recognition could enhance cooperation. For example, a mother who is being asked to carry out a behavioral reinforcement program with her child may clearly see the benefit to herself as well as her son if his tantrums are reduced in frequency, but the comparable mutual benefit when the targeted behavior is assertiveness may not be so obvious. It may be necessary to point out that a child who can ask his mother for what he wants in a reasonable way can be much pleasanter to have around than one who stores up his resentments only to have them burst out later in exaggerated forms. Parents do not always realize how dependent their peace of mind is upon the good humor of their young children.

When working with a group of children, it may be necessary to create some activities to give the youngsters a concrete example of what interdependence means; they may not always understand the concept in the abstract. For example, the group may decide to take a trip but need funds for transportation, food, and incidental expenses. A group fundraising effort will illustrate in very clear terms the nature of superordinate goals in which the entire group needs the efforts of all members in order to succeed. With this background of interdependence, the youngsters should more readily help a member to cope with a personal problem, such as temper tantrums or shoplifting.

The worker may want to create interdependence when very little appears to exist by developing a program in which all members may succeed or fail, and in which success requires that all members contribute to the effort. A rehabilitation program for delinquents called Positive Peer Culture (Vorrath and Brendtro 1974) is an extreme example of this approach. It is based on the hypothesis that young law violators can change only if their peers care about them and help them deal with their problems. Under the PPC program, the delinquent cannot be released unless the group members feel he or she is ready to handle freedom, and vote for the release. Evidence of such readiness is partially based on the youth's helping other members to face their own difficulties. Thus each individual's rehabilitation and discharge from incarceration is dependent upon the helping behavior of other members as well as on his or her own "altruism." Further, an entire group can be punished if one member runs away, for this indicates the group did not help the runaway.

Finally we should point out that competitive relationships between facilitators of change and clients increase the costs of helping. If such relationships exist, or are perceived to exist by the facilitator, help is unlikely unless the social worker can revise the relationship. It is for this reason that community organizers must often work to reduce the view that college students or low-income neighborhood residents of different racial or ethnic groups are competing with one another for scarce resources before joint efforts to gain greater total resources are possible.

A number of theorists have proposed that helping another person in need can often be motivated by seeing oneself as a good, kind, caring person rather than by explicit benefits (Bar-Tal, 1976; Berkowitz, 1970; S. H. Schwartz 1977). The reward for helping in such instances is enhanced self-regard and the cost of not helping is reduced self-regard. In view of our earlier discussion of compliance to influence based solely on external rewards and punishment, it is not surprising that total reliance on external sources can be problematic if continued helpfulness is needed. In one study, for example, women who helped a man in a shopping center by watching his bag of purchases for a minute were told that he needed help because he wanted to look for either a dollar bill he had lost or for his wallet (Uranowitz 1975). The women in the former condition, where there was minimal external justification for helping, more often subsequently helped another passerby than did those in the latter condition. The researcher concluded that helping under low external justification (low cost of not helping) was likely to increase the women's views of themselves as helpful persons, and hence to induce subsequent behavior in keeping with this self-image. This self-perception interpretation of the group differences was more directly tested in two other studies where undergraduates were asked to help someone under one of three conditions: payment for help was mentioned before the subject agreed to help; payment was not mentioned in advance but was given after help was received; or a no-payment control condition (Batson et al. 1978). After carrying out the agreed-upon actions all subjects also rated themselves on a variety of mood and trait characteristics, with the result that subjects who had been promised payment in advance saw themselves as less altruistic and less happy than the other two groups. It appears likely, according to the authors, that these subjects rewarded themselves less for their behavior and might be less helpful in the future. Self-perception also appears implicated in a study cited earlier (Kraut, 1973) in which subsequent charitable contributions were affected by labeling of earlier such actions as reflecting a generous, charitable person.

A similar effect occurs at the societal level. In the United States, for example, most blood donors are rewarded in some way for their contributions—through cash payments, the ability to designate its use for a particular relative or friend, or credits against which blood can be drawn for future needs. According to Titmuss (1971) only 7 percent of the blood donated in the United States during the 1965 to 1967 period was given with no strings attached, presumably for altruistic reasons, such as pleasure at others' reduced suffering or at being able to view oneself as charitable or kindly. Yet during that same period in Great Britain, where there are no external rewards for donations of blood, the total rate of blood donation per capita was the same as in the United States. Thus the availability of institutional arrangements that reward helpfulness can also act to inhibit self-reward for contributing to the greater social good. Titmuss argues that social policy should be set in ways to encourage altruistic rather than selfish giving. This recommendation applies equally well at the dyadic level.

The practice implications of attitude change theories of self-perception, cognitive dissonance, and self-confrontation, discussed under Quadrant A, are also applicable here. As much as possible, facilitators of change should be induced to help in ways that enhance their perception of themselves as helpful persons. In a related vein, Kanfer (1979) has recently argued that society should consciously train its members to obtain satisfaction from helping others as a means of increasing societal harmony. He proposes that altruism can be viewed as the self-control or the self-regulation of behaviors advantageous to an individual but detrimental to another individual or group. Viewed this way, altruism can be fostered by the same techniques used to enhance other types of self-regulation: by external reinforcements (social support for helping behaviors), self-reinforcements (self-statements of competence when one's own behavior has enhanced the well-being of others), and practice (the execution of prosocial behaviors followed by self-satisfaction). Relevant to our discussion of increasing the benefits of helping to potential facilitators of change are a number of situations he identifies as illustrations of contexts where it is possible to make clearer the benefits of reciprocal relationships based on contributing to the welfare of other; they include educational situations in which the success of the learner is reinforcing for the trainer, as when older pupils help younger ones, or when ex-mental patients help newly released patients cope with their community setting.

In addition to ways discussed earlier, the presence of models who act in helpful ways can be one means of arousing cognitive dissonance that can lead to helping behavior. In a study demonstrating that models who publicly donated money to the Salvation Army at Christmastime increased the donating of others, it was postulated that the model who contributed may have made the noncontributors aware of the fact that they were not acting in congruence with their image of themselves as benevolent and charitable individuals (Bryan and Test 1967). When made aware of this dissonance by the model the noncontributors changed their behavior so as to bring it into conformity with their self-perception.

Helping can also reduce dissonance in relation to one's belief in a just world or in maintaining equitable relationships with others. According to equity theory (Walster, Berscheid, and Walster 1976), if helping someone in distress can restore equity, restoration efforts will occur and be gratifying. But help that only partially restores equity will not reduce the helper's distress and thus alternate ways of restoring equity are likely, including derogating the victim or denying the victim's suffering; in such cases it is assumed that the benefits of not helping will outweigh those of helping. Just world beliefs are said to operate in a similar fashion (D. T. Miller 1977). Injustices that can be corrected through the helper's action do not seriously challenge an individual's belief in a just world existing in the long run since when one offers help, those who are in need do receive help and are restored to a positive state. If, however, suffering is only partially or temporarily relieved, one's belief in justice is threatened. Two experiments showed these effects among undergraduates with strong just world beliefs. They contributed more money to a needy family when the request was linked to needs existing at Christmastime than when the needs were presented as persistent, and more to a single needy family than to a group of needy families. The author hypothesized that in the situations of persistent or extensive need the potential contributors were unable to see their act of helping as verifying a just world, for their help did not remove that need. Thus, justice in those situations lay in seeing those in persistent need as probably deserving their plight. These ideas suggest that facilitators of change should be asked to help in ways that clearly have a beneficial impact. Arousing awareness in facilitators of overwhelming need which they are unable to alleviate may be a dangerous strategy.

COSTS TO POTENTIAL HELPER

Up to this point we have mainly been stressing ways of increasing the benefits of helping and costs of not helping as a way of enhancing the likelihood of enlisting a potential facilitator of change as a source of help. The alternate strategy is of course also pertinent—to reduce the benefits of not helping and the costs of helping. Some such techniques are simply the reverse of the benefit-enhancement ones. These have been alluded to in the preceding section, so will not be mentioned further here. Instead, we will describe briefly particular techniques for reducing the costs that may be involved in giving help or the benefits that may accrue from not giving help.

It is obvious that the practitioner should make the time, energy and resource costs of helping as low as possible, for professional colleagues, for members of larger systems within which the client or client system functions, and for friends and family members who could be helpful. One way to reduce such costs is to divide the work among a number of individuals so that no one person has to expend a large amount of time or effort. For example, if teachers, nurses, or aides are being asked to take time to encourage a client in academic work or rehabilitative efforts, it would be desirable to involve as many teachers, nurses, and aides as possible so the task will not be too physically or psychologically draining. Similarly, meetings with the worker should be at times and places convenient for the collaborators. If feasible, the worker should offer to provide secretarial assistance, transportation, and refreshments. Some cost is inevitable but it is important that they be kept to those essential to the well-being of the client. For a man who is being recruited to sponsor the release of a prisoner into a work program, the commitment of an offer of a job may necessarily involve risking having a poor employee, but it should not also be necessary for the sponsor to go to the probation worker's office to complete many forms. Similarly, any potential danger to the helper should be kept to a minimum. Recruitment of volunteers for a prisoner visiting program, for example, should stress the safeguards to the visitor's person built into the program. Antiseptic procedures used to protect hospital visitors may also require emphasis to reduce the potential costs considered by a person being recruited into this position.

Less obvious perhaps is the importance of avoiding both the arousal of threats to decisional freedom and the arousal of reactance. It appears, for example, to be especially important to stress the facilitator of change's freedom of choice in being helpful when the sufferer is highly dependent, or when continued rather than temporary help is needed (R. A. Jones, 1970), as in the cases of family members helping one another, or an aide in a psychiatric hospital being asked to assist in a treatment plan for a long-term patient, or staff working with highly dependent clients (Maslach 1978). The principle here is exactly the same as that in using reactance theory in relation to influencing a client (chapter 6); the worker should seek to minimize the threats to freedom of choice and the areas of freedom encroached upon when seeking the help of a facilitator of change.

BENEFITS AND COSTS TO POTENTIAL RECIPIENT

As the final set of variables to be considered in assessing the consequences of helping, the facilitator of change and the social worker need to be aware of the impact on the person being helped of receiving or not receiving aid. These extend beyond the apparent primary ones related directly to the maintenance or relief of the original distress which prompted the need for help.

Perhaps the most important secondary benefits and costs connected with the receipt of aid concern the impact on the recipient's self-regard. Depending upon how and what kind of help is received, it can affirm that one is worthy of it, that others recognize, for example, that external factors precipitated one's economic difficulties or exacerbated one's fears, or it can imply that one has caused one's own troubles. In Mayer and Timms' (1969) study of a family agency, previously described in chapter 1, for example, clients who broke off contact often expected that the social worker would help them pressure other family members to change their behaviors. Instead they encountered nondirective workers who sought to explore the clients' own feelings. Such clients saw the workers as rejecting and refused further help. Similarly, in a study of battered wives it was found that those who believed the battering was caused by their husbands' characteristics, and that these were stable in nature, left the relationship without seeking psychological help; in contrast, battered wives who believed that the cause of their problems were both internal to themselves and persistent sought long-term psychological help (Frieze 1979). Thus the meaning of seeking help, and presumably reactions to being offered help, would be quite different for these women depending on their causal attributions concerning the problem.

Even seeking help from an impersonal source, a set of written guidelines, has been shown to be influenced by its relevance to the individual's self-concept (Tessler and Schwartz 1972). In that study female undergraduates rated taped dialogue as neurotic or healthy under conditions that either made their own intelligence and mental health highly relevant or irrelevant to their skill at the task, and where they were told that most prior raters had needed help because of lack of information in the dialogues or that few had needed help because the dialogues were complete. These women were most likely to consult the written guidelines available to them when it was reasonable to attribute responsibility for failure to external causes—inadequate information in the tapes—or when central aspects of the self were not linked to task success. The latter was especially true for subjects with high self-esteem. The authors concluded that persuasive messages designed to overcome potential clients' reluctance to use social services are more likely to succeed if they offer external justifications for seeking help so that self-attributions of failure can be avoided.

One way to reduce the implication of failure associated with receiving help is by allowing the recipient to reciprocate. This also reduces indebtedness feelings aroused by the recipient's belief in a social norm of reciprocity. This seems to be particularly important when the helper and recipient are peers or in some significant way are similar to one another (Clark, Gotay, and Mills 1974; Fisher and Nadler 1974; Gergen et al. 1975; Nadler, Fisher, and Streufert, 1975). In such situations help is more readily accepted and the helper is liked more by the recipient, if reciprocation is possible. This implies that in situations such as peer counseling, neighborly assistance, or one child tutoring another, it would be important to build in opportunities for mutual aid. Students learning about peer counseling could also be made aware that they too can volunteer and be trained as counselors. A neighbor who has assisted in an emergency by caring for a young child whose mother is hospitalized should be encouraged to accept an offer of reciprocal child care even if she feels she could easily afford to hire a babysitter. The social worker who arranges for a child to be tutored in math by a classmate should try to find ways in which the tutored child can offer help—in sports activities, or repairing a bike. When the helper and recipient are not peers, however, as when for example the facilitator is a professional, reciprocity is not as relevant to acceptance of help or evaluation of the helper (Clark, Gotay, and Mills 1974; Fisher and Nadler 1974). Even here, however, the issue is not irrelevant, as will be shown in the chapter on termination.

Receiving help can also threaten the autonomy and decisional freedom of the recipient. So just as it is important for the social worker to provide freedom of choice to the facilitator to avoid reactance, it is important that facilitators be made aware of the need to allow the recipient to maintain autonomy.

Finally, one study has shown that subjects working on a very hard laboratory logic task were more likely to accept an offer of help than to ask for help even when informed they could do so (Broll, Gross, and Piliavin 1974). The recipients of help also liked the help more when it was offered rather than requested. Apparently asking for help was more suggestive of a self-attribution of failure than was help freely given. The authors suggested that a similar phenomenon may occur among clients of social service agencies and found support for this application in a field study of women receiving AFDC help (I. M. Piliavin and Gross 1977). All the women received income maintenance services, but some received social services under conditions where workers reached out to visit clients and offer such services, and others only if they initiated the request for social services. The latter group made fewer social service requests and were less satisfied with the help they received, especially when different workers provided the income maintenance and social services. Outreach programs may be effective not only because they provide new information about available help or because they reduce the physical costs of seeking help, but also because they reduce the psychic costs of receiving help. Potential help from friends, colleagues, or relatives is all too often not given because the potential recipient has not asked for it. Social workers may need to point out to such potential facilitators that an offer of help can be less threatening to the client than the clients' having to admit to themselves and others that help is needed. The offer, of course, should be given in such a way that attributions of failure are not implied nor autonomy threatened.

CHAPTER EIGHT

SOCIAL LEARNING THEORY

A detailed description of learning principles as applied to social work practice by theorists such as Thomas (1977), Gambrill (1977), A. Schwartz and Goldiamond (1975), or Krasner (1971) would be beyond the scope of a book on social psychology for social work. But there is a variation of learning theory that is highly relevant—social learning theory. Social learning has been described as the loosely organized body of literature dealing with changes in performance that occur as a function of contingencies which characterize social interaction (Patterson 1969). Many of the mechanisms that have been described for bringing about these changes have been linked to principles from social psychology, for example, those dealing with the processes of persuasion, modeling, and conformity. Another set of mechanisms has been based on principles of reinforcement as they apply to social interaction. While acknowledging the importance of external reinforcement, many social learning investigators such as Bandura and Walters (1963) have tended to emphasize that what has variously been called modeling, imitation, observational learning, or vicarious learning, occurs at least partially independent of extrinsic reinforcement. An emphasis on self-regulating processes also characterizes some social learning theorists (Bandura 1977; Kanfer 1979), as does a concern about cognitive influences on behavior as exemplified in the concept of locus of control beliefs (Bandura 1977; Rotter 1954, 1966). These three emphases of contemporary social learning theory on modeling, self-regulatory, and cognitive processes will form the bases for the organization of the remaining sections of this chapter. Although the theory and research on each of these topics overlap, for expository purposes we have attempted to treat the general topics and their implications for social work practice under separate headings: those of observational learning, self-regulation, and locus of control beliefs.

Social learning theory's focus on learning via the observation of a model is particularly relevant to social psychology, which has long sought to understand how imitation occurs, for imitation appears to account in large part for behavioral similarity among group members (S. M. Berger and Lambert 1968). The key questions are why one person will imitate another and what are the conditions that facilitate imitation.

The answers to these questions are critical to social workers in two major respects. First, in dyadic or group situations the social worker's behavior can be a model for the clients (Krasner 1971; McBroom 1970; A. Schwartz and Goldiamond 1975; Ullman 1968). The likelihood of the worker's behaviors being imitated will undoubtedly vary depending upon such conditions as the nature of the problem, the similarity in demographic characteristics between client and worker, and the worker's prestige, competence, and warmth. It is likely, however, that some modeling will take place in all worker-client relationships. Workers present the picture of caring individuals who are coping with their own problems and have at least a moderate amount of power and status. As such, the worker cannot help but be an object of emulation for a client who lacks some of these qualities. Second, in view of the limited number of hours any client spends with a practitioner, the more likely models of importance are individuals who have intensive and extensive contact with the client. These individuals are also in a far better position to provide many opportunities both for observation and for contingent reinforcements on an on-going basis. Hence the discussion of modeling appears here, in relation to work with facilitators of change in others, rather than with the discussion on work with clients.

Recent concern among social learning theorists with self-regulation of behavior, self-reinforcement, and intrinsic reinforcement is also important for social workers both in their own direct work with clients and in efforts to indirectly aid clients through contacts with individuals who can facilitate changes in clients' problems. Since neither social workers nor facilitators can continuously monitor and reinforce clients' behaviors or those of relevant actors in their clients' environment, persistent changes in behaviors would be enhanced by clients' self-regulation. Furthermore, the enhancement of self-regulation is in keeping with the ethics of social work practice that stresses the enhancement of individuals' autonomous control of their environments as an important goal. Hence the factors that facilitate or inhibit self-regulatory processes are often important to recognize. These factors are at least in part cognitive, and research on self-reinforcement and regulation is closely linked to that on the influence of expectancies on behavior, especially expectations about the relationship between one's actions and the outcomes that follow them. Research and theory on such expectancies is generally covered under the rubric of locus of control. These beliefs have been shown to exert important influences on behavior. Because facilitators are often in more extended and intensive contacts with clients, than are social workers, their interactions with clients are more likely to impinge upon these beliefs. This chapter will conclude with a discussion of the ways in which facilitators may need to conform to or influence clients' locus of control beliefs to improve client outcomes.

OBSERVATIONAL LEARNING

We will not attempt to review in detail all the social learning theory explanations for observational learning, but the major approaches will be noted in order to explicate the conditions that may enhance modeling and the uses of modeling in social work. The essential components of modeling situations are a social situation, a model who performs some act, and an observer of the model's actions. The model may or may not be observed to experience negative or positive consequences for the act, and the observer may or may not reproduce the action of the model; if he or she does, modeling or imitation is said to occur. Such modeling can then be reinforced by the model, or the modeled behavior can result in positive or negative consequences from other aspects of the environment.

THEORIES OF MODELING

According to Bandura (1969, 1971) when an observer sees someone else respond in a given way the model's responses act as cues that are linked to a perceptual response, that is, mental response, by the observer simply through contiguity. These perceptual responses of the observer are images or mental representations of the model's response. Such symbolic representations can be employed by the observer when the stimulus is not present to elicit the modeled response. Bandura and Walters (1963) distinguish between learning or acquisition of behaviors, which can occur from merely observing others, and the performance of behaviors, which may require reinforcements either of the model or the observer. Such observational learning is viewed as a major aspect of learning in children and adults because through it complex behaviors can be learned rapidly and in large chunks.

Other social learning theorists (Baer and Sherman 1964; Gewirtz 1969; Gewirtz and Stingle 1968) uphold a pure stimulus-response model and reject the need for any symbolic mediators or mental representations. According to Gewirtz, the process of generalized imitation can account for imitation in the absence of extrinsic reinforcement. If specific imitative behaviors, i.e., the matching of one's behavior to that of a model, have been extrinsically reinforced in the past, this will lead to a generalized tendency to imitate. What is critical to the development of generalized imitation is: 1) in various situations diverse responses that differ in specific content are reinforced; 2) reinforcements are based on the match of the responses to cues provided by the models' responses; and 3) the reinforced responses form a class linked by the reinforcement of matching. He further suggests that as specific instances of imitation are likely to be extrinsically reinforced only intermittently, once the generalized imitation response is learned it will be difficult to extinguish. Thus neither the model nor extrinsic reinforcement need be present for generalized imitation to take place. Such generalized imitation can also be focused upon particular individuals, if those persons are frequently observed and there is frequent reinforcement for imitating a variety of their behaviors. Thus through focused, generalized imitation, little girls typically have come to imitate their mothers and little boys their fathers.

Many natural examples no doubt come to mind, such as that of young children whose imitative babbling to match strange noises produced by a fond parent is greeted with parental glee, hugs, and other forms of social reinforcement. Gewirtz assumes that such examples are common occurrences for most children and thus their imitating becomes an instrumental response for gaining social reinforcements. In some situations, however, the generalized imitative response does not seem to have been acquired in the natural course of development, and several researchers have succeeded in teaching institutionalized children to be imitative as a means of improving their skills. Baer, Peterson, and Sherman (1967), for example, used this approach with retarded children who had previously been observed not to be imitative. Children were first physically assisted to make the desired imitative responses and were reinforced immediately for them; over time these children came to be able to imitate new behaviors without assistance.

Baer and his associates (Baer and Sherman 1964; Baer, Peterson, and Sherman 1967), however, account for this later imitation in the absence of extrinsic reinforcement in slightly different terms than does Gewirtz. They believe that after frequent reinforcement for matching behavior to that of a model, the mere similarity between the individual's and the model's behaviors acquires reinforcement value. Thus, further imitative responses that produce similarity will be strengthened and maintained in the absence of extrinsic reinforcement. Though Baer and Sherman discuss imitation that results from vicarious learning, they agree that the permanence of learning is enhanced by reinforcement techniques.

Patterson (1969) proposed a resolution of the dispute among social learning theorists regarding the need for symbolic representations. He suggested that modeling and persuasion can be considered to be eliciting procedures for producing behavior change. They are really catalytic mechanisms, which accelerate both the acquisition of social behavior and the alteration of these behaviors once they have been established. This statement applies to prosocial behavior and antisocial behavior. The behavior of a model increases the probability that a new behavior will be performed by the observer. However, for the behavior to become an important part of the individual's repertoire, its performance must be reinforced by the social environment. Patterson focused on children, but the principle is also applicable to adults. Thus modeling and persuasion accelerate the process of acquiring new behaviors under conditions where these behaviors are subsequently reinforced. The catalytic effects are particularly marked in modification of the behavior of highly deviant youngsters, such as autistic children, who display massive deficits in their repertoire of social behaviors.

Each of the essential aspects of the modeling paradigm—the situation in which a model performs some act in the presence of an observer—can be manipulated to increase the likelihood of the observation altering the behavior of the observer (Patterson 1969).

FACTORS INFLUENCING MODELING EFFECTS

Modeling influences behavior mainly through its infomative function: observation of others' behavior yields information about what is appropriate to do in certain situations and how to do it (Bandura 1977). To serve this function it is necessary for the observer to attend to and accurately perceive the behavior of the model. Thus conditions in the situation that make the model's behavior highly salient enhance imitation—for example, the sudden appearance in a quiet room of an exuberant, physically active person will capture attention. Retention of the information is also essential and this can be facilitated by availability of memory aids to the observer, including verbal or imaginal symbols with which to represent the behavior, and mental or active rehearsal of the observed behavior. To use the information in carrying out appropriate actions requires recall and enactment skills. The consequences in personal, social, or material rewards or punishments will also affect the use of information gained through observation.

Characteristics of the model have been found to be important, probably because they affect the attention given the model and the consequences the observer expects for enactment. The more prestigious, the more friendly, the more reinforcing the model, the more imitation ensues (Patterson 1969). Similarity to the observer in race and background has also been found to enhance modeling (Rose 1972; 1974b), as have as competence, knowledge, and power of the model (Krumboltz and Thoresen 1969). Differences in physical appearance that conveyed status or prestige affected the likelihood that pedestrians would imitate a model who violated a traffic signal (Lefkowitz, Blake, and Mouton 1955). The link between social influence and modeling is evident. There also appear to be differential effects of various personality characteristics of the model on observers of different ages. For example, it was found that the personality characteristics of the adult model was a more important predictor of imitative responses than the models sex for younger (six- and seven-year-old) boys, whereas for older (nine- to ten-year-old) ones the sex of the model was more important (Patterson, Littman, and Brown 1968). Although the effect of these characteristics varied from one age group of boys to another, a warm, motherly model appeared to be responded to positively by children of a large age range.

Although research has shown that a nurturing relationship between the model and observer is not essential for the occurrence of imitation, its presence can enhance it (Bandura and Walters 1963). Similarly, models who are observed to exert social power over a third party are more likely to be imitated, although such control of resources is not essential (Bandura 1967). In general, characteristics of the model are most influential when the response consequences to the observer of imitation are unclear (Bandura 1977).

An additional factor to be considered is the modality by which the model is presented. Possibilities include using a live model, or a model on film, videotape, or audiotape. There are advantages and disadvantages to each. Live models are vivid, salient, and are perceived by the observers as more realistic and therefore possibly more worthy of emulation. On the other hand, when teachers, parents, or peers are used as live models, the observer may be flooded with information and cues. As a result, there is confusion concerning the stimuli to which to attend (A. Schwartz and Goldiamond 1975). There is also the possibility that these untrained models might lose their tempers or exhibit other behaviors that should not be modeled. For these reasons, some investigators (e.g., A. Schwartz and Goldiamond 1975) prefer the use of film or tape when attempting to develop new behaviors. Filmed or taped models have additional advantages. They can be produced to highlight specific auditory or visual cues relevant to the behaviors which are of concern, and can be used again and again. Although audiotapes have limited utility—they omit nonverbal behaviors and are readily ignored—they have been found effective in helping underachievers to acquire better study habits (Beach 1969) and busy students to schedule their time more efficiently (J. E. Smith 1969). Audiotapes have an additional virtue: they are inexpensive.

Characteristics of the observer are also relevant. Younger children appear to be more responsive than older children to modeling (Patterson 1969). Further, boys whose behaviors are "socially adaptive" tend to be responsive to male models whereas those described as deviant tend to model female adults (Patterson 1969). Whether these findings will change as sex-role stereotypes diminish remains to be seen. For the present, the literature on sex-role development (Birns 1976; L. W. Hoffman 1976; Kohlberg 1966; E. E. Maccoby and Jacklin 1974) is in agreement that young boys more often model their fathers and young girls are likely to model their mothers. Maccoby and Jacklin point out that this differentiation occurs even when the parents do not wish it, because a self-socialization process takes place in children as young as three years of age in which the children, aware of their gender, seek models to imitate who fit their rough schemas of what males and females are like.

The past reinforcement history of the observer also influences the extent to which imitative behavior occurs, especially when information on the consequences of imitation is not available. Persons with histories of few prior rewards, including those with low self-esteem or with generally low levels of competence, or those who have been rewarded often for displaying matching behaviors have been shown to be especially prone to imitate successful models (Bandura and Walters 1963). Yet it is also important to recognize that many successful persons with high self-esteem model others' behaviors. These individuals are selective about modeling, however, and emulate those behaviors that can be functional for them (Bandura 1977). Perceived similarity on particular attributes between the observer and model also enhances the modeling of other response classes (Burnstein, Stotland, and Zander 1961). So too can emotional arousal of the observer (Bandura and Walters 1963).

Not often discussed is the possibility that an observer will develop a negative set toward the model. When this occurs, either no attention is paid to the model, or delayed imitation of an opposite behavior occurs. Essentially, negative modeling is taking place. Six-year-olds have been found to develop a negative set toward adults more readily than ten-year-olds. This phenomenon was attributed to the decrease in negativism found in children between two and twelve years of age (Patterson, Littman, and Brown 1968). Thus although younger children are more responsive to models, the danger of creating a negative set in these youngsters must be guarded against. Adolescents rebelling against authority may also tend to develop negative models, of parents and teachers for example.

MODELING AS A TOOL IN SOCIAL WORK

In general, the social learning theory view of modeling is most useful to practitioners when they are working with caregivers and socializers of children or of adults with large behavioral deficits such as the retarded (O'Brien and Azrin 1972), the deinstitutionalized mental hospital patient (A. P. Goldstein, Sprafkin, and Gershaw 1976), the unskilled and shy (Hosford and Sorenson 1969), and the autistic (Lovaas et al. 1973). To attempt to explain verbally how the appropriate behaviors should be performed would be virtually impossible with all of these individuals. It is also highly unlikely that waiting for the behavior to appear so that it can be reinforced would be fruitful. Needed is the repeated modeling in unambiguous terms of the desired behaviors, along with differential reinforcement for the observer's behavioral approximations to that model. For example, if parents want children to begin reading, or to increase the amount of time they spend reading, an effective approach is for the parents to read books, magazines, or newspapers on frequent occasions themselves (Wittes and Radin 1969). It is probably most profitable if the father engages in this behavior when young boys are involved (Radin 1972a, 1973, 1976b; Epstein and Radin 1975) and the mother when girls are the clients (Radin 1974a). Similarly, to induce any behavior, such as hanging up one's coat, the individual the child identifies with should demonstrate how the behavior should be performed and then demonstrate the behavior themselves. This may involve a combination of direct instruction and modeling. Such modeling is particularly effective when followed by praise and signs of approval immediately after the child emulates the caregiver. The child's first attempts at imitation may be fairly inaccurate and short-lived but reinforcing these efforts is very likely to increase the probability that they will be repeated. The criteria for approval can gradually be made more stringent as the imitation becomes more accurate and prolonged.

Behaviors that can be shaped in this manner by socializers of children include physical activities within the power of the child to perform, such as eating food appropriately, social interactions, such as asking for desired objects pleasantly rather than grabbing them, and cognitive processes, such as considering the consequences of an act before it is performed. Detailed procedures for teaching parents of young children how to instruct their youngsters in interpersonal problem-solving strategies have been developed (Spivack and Shure 1974; Shure and Spivack 1978). These guidelines focus on mentally considering the consequences of an undesirable behavior, such as tearing someone's picture, before doing it, and then selecting an alternative which will ultimately be more gratifying, for example, asking to share the other child's crayons. It was found (Shure and Spivack 1977) that teaching low-income black mothers interpersonal cognitive problem solving skills to solve their own childrearing problems resulted in improved interpersonal problem solving by their preschool-aged children. Although the authors attributed the findings to the mothers' improved ability to guide their children in solving real problems that arise, it is our view that modeling was also involved. Undoubtedly, the mothers learned to stop and think before reacting to their children's demands and may have even articulated the alternatives they were considering. From the results of several studies Shure and Spivack (1977) concluded that greater impact on the child occurs when both mother and child "are taught how to think." Thus the combination of direct instruction and modeling appears to be a powerful technique for changing children's problem-solving behavior. Perhaps the addition of contingent reinforcement for approximations would enhance the effectiveness of the procedures even further.

Shure and Spivack found the training program particularly effective with parents of impulsive and inhibited children who either lashed out when frustrated or withdrew from people and problems they could not solve (Spivack and Shure 1974; Spivack, Platt, and Shure 1976). It is likely to be equally effective with parents of any youngsters experiencing emotionally arousing problems, such as in newly integrated schools. Teachers and parents of educable mentally retarded children should also find the procedures highly productive. Practitioners might review the prepared materials and recommend them when appropriate to facilitators of change. Modifications can be designed by the worker or by the facilitators as needed.

Another approach the social worker can use in dyadic interaction with facilitators of change is to suggest they find peers of the clients who can be used as models. Once again, the principles delineated by Patterson (1969) would be applicable. The peer's modeling would be used to help elicit the desired behavior by the client and the performance of the behavior would then be differentially reinforced by the caregiver, and by the peer if possible. Peers who could be employed in this way could be older siblings, preferably of the same sex, friends of the clients who display the desired behavior, other students in the class if the facilitator is a teacher or teacher's aide, or other children on a hospital ward if the facilitator is a nurse or ward attendant. It has been shown that youngsters perceived as powerful or influential by their peers are imitated either to win the leader's approval or possibly to obtain the rewards that the leader receives (Lippitt et al. 1968). This suggests that caregivers may wish to highlight the desirable behaviors of peers with leadership qualities and then reinforce the clients for emulating these high-status friends. This technique could also be valuable in the attempt to reduce aversive aspects of the clients' environment, as when a handicapped child is being teased by classmates. If a popular child could be influenced to behave in a friendly manner to the client other classmates are likely to imitate this leader. It is essential in any such endeavor that the caregiver be clear about the behaviors they wish to see imitated. Merely observing a live model interacting with many people or in varied situations does not mean that the observer notes what the caregiver desires; observers need to be trained in what to observe (Nixon 1969).

Opportunities for observing peer models are increased if these individuals can be videotaped engaging in the appropriate behavior to be induced in others, such as resolving a dispute amicably. Teachers and staff members of hospitals, training schools, and similar institutions usually have access to video equipment. If so, it would be well for them to present the clients with tapes of peer models. Following this viewing with videotapes of the clients themselves engaging in the desired behaviors, such as applying for a job, would allow them to assess how closely their behavior matched that of the models. Audiotapes can be used in the same manner if video equipment is not available, particularly when some form of verbal behavior is the skill being taught.

Phobias and shyness have been found to be particularly amenable to the modeling approach to treatment. In the case of the former, there are indications that mildly handicapping phobias can be handled by facilitators of change. For example, it was found that young children who were afraid of dogs exhibited greater approach behaviors after observing a model in eight sessions interact fearlessly with a dog (Bandura, Grusec, and Monleve 1967). Phobias of snakes were also eliminated by a combination of desensitization procedures and modeling in a study which concluded that the combination was more effective than desensitization alone (Wolpe 1969). These findings strongly suggest that if teachers, attendants, foster parents, or child care workers who encounter youngsters with irrational fears expose them repeatedly to peer models interacting comfortably with the feared object, the problem is likely to be alleviated. Observing the model in the presence of a familiar and well-liked adult may provide some of the relaxation introduced in desensitization procedures.

Viewing a film in which a peer was seen talking comfortably with a school counselor appeared to provide shy children with skills and confidence to speak up more frequently in class (Hosford and Sorenson 1969). Fundamentally, the process involved is teaching a new social skill to an individual who has a deficiency. Providing a detailed picture of the desired behavior via a model, and then giving the clients opportunities to practice the new skills with feedback are the traditional and successful techniques for teaching any new behavior, from social dancing to responding empathetically. It should be noted that in these situations it is ususally assumed that the children or adults already exhibit the ability to learn through observation of others, or, in Gewirtz's terminology, already have acquired a generalized imitation response. The problem is identified as the absence of some particular category of responses or skills, and the solution largely focuses on making available appropriate models who exhibit these skills. Facilitators of change can often find such models and place them in appropriate contact with the client.

Other situations, however, may primarily involve inappropriate modeling—a child or adult may imitate the behavior of a model whose responses are viewed, at least by the facilitator of change, as antisocial or disruptive. The solution here is to be able both to provide alternative models and to make imitation of these new models more rewarding to the child than imitation of the undesirable ones.

Still another kind of situation may be encountered in which the problem seems to be the absence of the generalized imitative response, as in the Baer, Peterson, and Sherman (1967) work with retarded youngsters or Lovaas' (1966) treatment of nonverbal schizophrenic children. In such situations before specific social skills can be acquired through the provision of appropriate models, imitation itself may need to be elicited and then broadly reinforced. This is probably a much more difficult intervention strategy and may not be appropriate in the repetoire of techniques the social worker tries to teach to facilitators of change.

SELF-REGULATION

Although all social learning theorists recognize the importance of environmental influences in the form of social reinforcement of behavior, there is also growing recognition that social reinforcements are not the sole determinants of behavioral change. The focus of research has thus shifted to determining the conditions under which reinforcements offered in social interactions are least likely to be effective and those in which self-reinforcement is valuable.

UNDESIRED CONSEQUENCES OF EXTERNAL REINFORCEMENT

In situations that involve engaging in an activity because of the inherent pleasure received from the activity, when external reinforcements are then provided, they are either ignored or result in a reduction of that behavior in the absence of reinforcement. The phenomenon has been called "turning play into work" (Lepper, Greene, and Nisbett 1973). Lepper and colleagues concluded that children who get rewards for engaging in an intrinsically gratifying activity change their attribution of their behavior. They decide they were drawing, for example, because of the external situation rather than because of their own liking for drawing. As a result, when the external situation is changed, that is when the social rewards are removed, they no longer continue the activity. The social reward appears to have destroyed or diminished their intrinsic pleasure. The authors do not suggest that all external rewards are undesirable for children, but rather that they may be dysfunctional when children already engage in and enjoy the activity per se. This conclusion was disputed by more behaviorally oriented psychologists (Reiss and Sushinsky 1975) who showed that after multiple trials with rewards, the absence of rewards did not result in a decrease in the initial activity. Thus, it was reasoned, when rewards were offered in just one trial, as in the Lepper investigation, the children focused on receiving the reward, a distracting stimulus, and not on continuing the intrinsically gratifying behavior. Once the distraction lost its appeal because of repetition, the children resumed their previous activities. This was labeled the "competing response hypothesis."

Regardless of the reason offered for the phenomenon, it appears that providing occasional external reinforcement for activities readily engaged in without such reinforcement may be nonproductive, if not disruptive. The moral appears to be that contingent reinforcement should be used only to elicit and maintain behaviors that are not already high in the client's habit hierarchy. This suggests that the facilitator of change must create adequate opportunities to determine whether the client does indeed readily perform the desired behavior. It is possible to misperceive what is occurring because of biased observing or because merely one salient, atypical example is noticed. The findings of Nisbett and colleagues (1976) regarding the impact of a vivid, concrete example vs. that of consensus data may well apply here. The individual who usually eats appropriately, comes to work on time, or remains sober can be misjudged when there are a few flagrant exceptions to those patterns.

Other conditions in which the effects of external reinforcement appear to be limited are defined by the results of some research in the cognitive dissonance framework, discussed in chapter 5, which shows greater attitude change following small than large monetary rewards. Those results appear to conflict with the general findings from learning theory that the greater the contingent reinforcement, the greater the probability that subsequent behaviors will be affected. Instead they support the assumption that individuals behave in accordance with their cognitions about themselves and others.

An ingenious resolution of the conflict suggests that which theory is likely to account for behavior is determined by whether the situation involves free choice (Linder, Cooper, and Jones 1967). Cognitive theories, it is proposed, are useful in predicting behavior in situations perceived as involving free choice. In such situations, if a small reinforcement is offered individuals for behaving contrary to their own beliefs and they perform the behavior, they will alter their beliefs to be consonant with their behavior, according to cognitive dissonance theory; in terms of attribution theory, their self-perception will change and they will assume they must have held a different belief all the time since the small reward could not have accounted for their behavior. If the reward in a free-choice situation is high, however, little change in attitude will take place, for the individuals will attribute their behaviors to external factors. On the other hand, if the situation is not one of free choice but is compulsory, external attributions will be made regardless of the size of the reward and cognitive theories will not be relevant. Instead reinforcement principles will predict behavior. In such compulsory situations receiving a small reward after performing a counterattitudinal behavior may have little or no effect on the attitude. But performing a counterattitudinal behavior for a large reward will "condition" the behavior or associate it with a large reward, and thus the behavior will be seen more positively and the result will be a change of attitude relevant to that behavior.

According to this interpretation, then, self-cognitions are important in free-choice situations; external reinforcements are important where freedom of choice does not exist. Two experiments support these predictions. In both, college students wrote counterattitudinal essays under conditions that varied in whether the undergraduates had a choice about the decision to write the essay, and received small (fifty cents) or large (two dollars and fifty cents) monetary payments. When the conditions fostered the feeling that the subject was quite free not to comply with the essay writing task, the smaller reward resulted in more attitude change than the larger one. But when there was no choice given about participation, subjects receiving the larger reward changed their attitudes more than those receiving the smaller one.

A somewhat different integration of simple reinforcement learning and cognitive social psychological and social learning theories was offered by Gerard, Conolley, and Wilhemy (1974) who suggested that the amount of justification to act in counterattitudinal ways determines whether a conditioning process or cognitive process is operative in free-choice situations. When the justification for deciding to engage in a counterattitudinal behavior is just barely sufficient to gain compliance, there will be maximum attitude change in the direction of the behavior because of altered self-cognitions or the need to reduce dissonance. As the amount of justification increases, little attitude change will occur; the individuals will believe external factors were sufficient to justify the inconsistent behavior and no dissonance will be aroused. However, as the justification gets appreciably higher, the behavior will become associated with a very pleasant experience, and the attitude toward that behavior or situation will change in the direction of the behavior, through a secondary-reinforcementlike process. High justification is described as "sweetening" the behavior and thereby coloring the person's views of their attitudes toward that behavior.

This continuum of effects can be represented graphically by a U-shaped curve where the vertical axis (ordinate) is the amount of attitude change and the horizontal one (abscissa) is the amount of the reward. Such a figure would indicate a lot of attitude change when the incentive is quite low (based on dissonance reduction) or very high (based on incentive value of the reward) but not when it is in the moderate range. Gerard, Conolley, and Wilhemy postulate that the justification variable could be manipulated through varying the size of the monetary reward known to be available before a decision to engage in the counterattitudinal behavior is made, as has been done in much dissonance research. According to these theorists, however, the dissonance experiments were incomplete in that they only included two levels of rewards for writing an essay or delivering a speech that was contrary to one's own feelings, and limited the rewards to the low and moderate range. They predicted and found in a series of studies with high-school and college students that if the incentives range increased significantly, attitude change was obtained for both quite low and high levels, but not for moderate ones. In most of these studies subjects first tasted three bitter substances and rated their bitterness and then were asked to commit themselves to return a week later for further tastings, before completing the initial session of six tastings. The commitment was obtained either under a free-choice condition, in which the subjects were told they didn't have to participate if they didn't want to, or a no-choice situation, in which they were under high pressure to participate further. To vary amount of justification subjects were offered the same amount for the future tasting session as for the initial one, double that amount, or half the amount. Subjects then tasted the three remaining preparations and rated their bitterness. Changes in ratings of bitterness between the first three and last three solutions were the measurement of attitude change. The predicted U-shaped curve was found in these studies when the subjects knew of the value of the monetary incentives before making a choice to participate further. But when no choice about participation was given the subjects, the greater the relative value of the monetary incentive the more the attitude change; thus, as predicted by Linder and colleagues (1967), when free choice is absent, cognitive dissonance is not operative and the amount of reinforcement is directly associated with the amount of attitude change.

These conceptualizations concerning reward size suggest that to achieve attitude change in a noncompulsory situation, it is best for facilitators of change to offer either minimal rewards or very great rewards. Because huge reinforcements are often unrealistic for most caregivers and facilitators of change, the implication is that reinforcements should be kept at a low level; the clients should not feel that the desired behaviors are being "bought" by the incentive and therefore really not a part of their self-initiated behavioral repertoire. It appears possible to give an "overdose" of external reinforcement just as of medication. For example, when attempting to modify the behaviors of children in a day care home, childcare center, or school, both social learning theory and cognitive dissonance theory would suggest that teachers provide some reinforcements for performing the desired behavior. Dissonance theory would add, however, that the child's personal responsibility for the action should be emphasized and the reinforcement or incentive offered should be limited to a small preferred sweet or short period of play with a preferred toy rather than an entire meal at McDonald's or a week free of clean-up chores. The guiding principle would be to offer the smallest reinforcement needed to induce the clients to perform the new behavior.

The implication for situations perceived as lacking in free choice are different. Here the larger the rewards the more likely that behavioral compliance will lead to attitudinal change. Thus when social workers consult with personnel in prisons or in other involuntary settings, the importance of maximizing external reinforcements for those in their care should be stressed. Even here, however, one needs to be concerned that changes induced by reinforcement may not be maintained when the facilitator of change is no longer available to provide external reinforcements, for it is likely that little internalization has taken place. To avoid this, and for many other reasons discussed previously, we suggest attempting as often as possible to convert the social relation between the facilitator of change and client into one where the latter has some freedom of choice. Under these conditions, cognitive dissonance factors can become operational and foster attitude change in those who feel some responsibility for their decisions.

TECHNIQUES OF SELF-REINFORCEMENT

Another alternative to the use of very high rewards in constrained situations is the direct effort to place control over rewards under the control of the clients so that self-generated reinforcements rather than external ones regulate behavior. The importance to social workers of self-reinforcement is much broader than its application to total institutions. Bandura (1977) suggests that most activities are maintained through a process of self-reinforcement where ". . . people set certain standards of behaviors for themselves and respond to their own actions in self-awarding or self-punishing ways" (129). Social influences can be very important in such standard setting, as was discussed in chapters

2 and 4 in relation to such concepts as role demands, social comparison theory, comparison level, and reference groups, but the monitoring and reinforcement is done by the individual. A variety of research with children (Bandura and Perloff 1967; Drabman, Spitalnik, and O'Leary 1973) and adults (Jeffrey 1974; H. Weiner 1965) has shown that self-administered reinfocement can be as effective or more effective than externally determined reinforcement.

Understanding the value of self-reinforcement can be helpful to facilitators of change for a number of reasons. Even though some facilitators have more extensive contacts with clients than social workers might, there are limits on such contacts which do not exist if the client can reinforcement his or her own behavior. Further, self-reinforcement control should increase one's sense of personal causality, which is advantageous from a self-perception and expectancy viewpoint, as will be discussed further in the next section. In addition, practice with self-reinforcement can generalize—skills in self-regulation can carry over beyond the particular behavior relating to the target problem in a given interaction situation with the facilitator of change. Finally, an increase in self-reinforcement by clients would free up the time of such professional caregivers as teachers or nurses so that they could help other clients.

For these reasons there has been a burgeoning of interest in developing self-reinforcement techniques for people to change their own problematic behavior (Goldfried and Merbaum 1973; Homme 1969; Mahoney and Thoresen 1974). Some social learning theorists have stressed the importance of self-monitoring and the absence of the experimenter from desensitization procedures so that the individuals will attribute mastery to themselves and not to an external force (E. H. Cohen 1977; Hepner and Cauthen 1975; Kopel and Arkowitz 1975). For example, Bandura and his colleagues (Bandura, Jeffery, and Gajdos 1975) found that self-directed practice with snakes by phobic subjects who previously had handled the reptiles only under the guidance of the experimenter, resulted in more generalized approach behavior, less fear arousal, and more perceived competence.

Another example of such an intervention approach is the technique that has been developed to teach children to make contingency contracts with themselves (Homme 1969). "After I have done so much work, I can reward myself with so many goodies or time off for fun." This approach utilizes the Premack principle (Premack 1965) which states that a high-frequency behavior can be used as a reinforcer of low-frequency behavior. The Premack principle has been taught to adolescents and adults who want to modify some behavior such as daydreaming at work, smoking, or overeating.

In sum, it is wise for facilitators to think of clients as participants in the change process. The benefits of transforming as many "clients" as possible into "colleagues" in change efforts have been discussed in relation to group work (Radin 1974b), to work with adults (Oberman 1978), and for participants in weight-reduction programs (Rodin 1978). When social workers or other facilitators of change share their knowledge and skills with clients, clients are better able to make their own informed choices, their self-image and sense of competence rise, resistence to "being changed" is reduced, and many hard-to-reach adults, such as members of minority groups and highly educated professionals, become accessible.

LOCUS OF CONTROL BELIEFS

In addition to helping facilitators of change become aware of the role of extrinsic and intrinsic self-reinforcement in changing behaviors, it may be important for social workers to inform these individuals about how cognitions affect behavior. In particular, facilitators of change may sometimes find it useful in their working with, and caring for, clients to try to influence clients' views regarding their control over their life; at the very least they should be aware of how these beliefs influence behavior and be sensitive to how their own behavior may inadvertently affect such beliefs held by clients.

Two general traditions within social psychology have been reflected in studies of individuals' beliefs about their control over their own behaviors. In one, exemplified by the work of social learning theorist Julian Rotter and discussed below, the emphasis is on the relatively stable differences among individuals in these beliefs, how they develop, and how these variations affect behavior in different social contexts. The other approach emphasizes the general social conditions that foster or inhibit beliefs that one controls one's own destiny and the typical consequences of such beliefs. The attribution theories discussed in chapter 3 are of this type, as is the work of Glass, Seligman, and others on the effects of perceived control on the handling of difficult life situations, to be discussed below.

ANTECEDENTS OF LOCUS OF CONTROL BELIEFS

The concept of locus of control was developed by Rotter (1954, 1966), a cognitive social learning theorist. Locus of control refers to a person's general expectancy about the relationship between one's actions and outcomes that follow them. Persons with internal expectancies of control expect or believe that they are in control of their lives and that their own work and effort will result in reward or punishment. Persons with external expectancies believe that their lives are determined by chance, fate, or powerful people and that their own behaviors do not control the reinforcements they receive. They are pawns whose fate is in the hands of others. The result is an expectation of a lack of congruence between one's own actions and outcomes. The concept of internal locus of control is often associated with that of intrinsic reinforcement, although the two are not synonymous. The latter refers to pleasure obtained from engaging in an activity per se. The former refers to a belief that through one's own behavior one can control the rewards and punishments received. They are similar in some of their predicted consequences. When an activity is intrinsically rewarding to someone, that person would be expected to engage in it without external inducements. An individual with internal locus of control beliefs would also be expected to act independently of external inducements and perhaps be more likely to gain satisfaction from individual efforts—that is find things intrinsically rewarding—but this is not necessarily true. These people can control their own activities for other reasons, for example, in the expectation of long-term benefits. Internally oriented persons are not, however, unresponsive to extrinsic reinforcements. But unlike externally oriented individuals, they are more likely to see a causal link between their own behavior and the attainment of externally controlled reinforcements and, therefore, to modify their own behavior when needed to obtain desired external reinforcements.

Rotter (1966) suggests that consistency of parental discipline and treatment could be a critical antecedent to the development of internal-external control beliefs. Internal expectancies are probably based on a history of learning experiences where variations in one's own behavior were followed by predictable variations in reinforcement consequences and external expectancies are likely to reflect a history of a lack of congruence between actions and outcomes. Parents who consistently reward children for hard work, or for keeping their room clean, for example, and who consistently punish laziness or slovenliness probably contribute to the development of internal expectancies of control in their children. Such children probably come to believe that their own actions are sufficient to enable them to achieve outcomes they desire, whether they be social reinforcements, concrete reinforcements, or intrinsic ones such as those accompanying performance of skilled tasks like playing a musical instrument. The children of parents whose responses are unpredictable, sometimes punishing snatching a toy from a sibling and other times ignoring or encouraging such bullying, for example, are likely to develop external expectancies of control, in as much as the same behavior of the child is linked to different consequences. Similar effects on beliefs about one's control over reinforcements might be expected if there is inconsistency in response of different adults to the same behavior of the child. Further, children who experience few opportunities for making choices—about what clothes to wear or food to eat, for example—also are unlikely to develop an expectancy that they control their environment. In all these situations, the children's beliefs are likely to be that fate, chance, or powerful others rather than one's own behavior determines one's outcomes.

Rotter (1966) also suggests that cultural variations in these attitudes can exist. In support of this he cites a study of children in an isolated triethnic community where, as predicted from the adult community's religious world view, Ute Indians were more likely to hold external control beliefs than were either Spanish-Americans or Anglos.

Limited material resources and discrimination can also provide bases for direct teaching of external locus of control beliefs, according to Rotter. Black parents may themselves provide consistent contingent responses to their children's actions but also teach them that in many places in our society racism may defeat their individual efforts to gain desired outcomes. This potential disjunction between personal efforts and society's response has been emphasized by the Gurins (G. Gurin, 1970; P. Gurin et al. 1969; P. Gurin, Gurin, and Morrison 1978). They point out that Rotter's concept of internal control expectancies has two key beliefs linked together: a belief in one's own competence, which they term personal control beliefs; and a belief that the world is just, fair, and responsive to individual effort and competence, labeled societal control beliefs. For individuals who have found our social system to be unjust, whose political philosophy leads them to believe that social factors are more important than individual efforts, these two types of beliefs may not be linked. Consequently they may hold external expectancies about the way in which society operates not because they believe that they are not capable of attaining desired outcomes, or because they believe that luck determines one's fate, but because they believe the social environment in which they live does not permit rewards to accrue from efforts at achieving mastery. External societal control beliefs do not necessarily mean that the individual has external beliefs about his or her own ability to control personal outcomes in given situations.

CONSEQUENCES OF LOCUS OF CONTROL BELIEFS

For victims of gross discrimination and oppression, an external locus of control ideology may be realistic and adaptive, especially when these beliefs concern the general status of their group in society. Evidence for this conclusion exists in data collected from two types of youths: those with limited education and college students. Inner-city black youngsters in a job training and socialization program who blamed their own inadequacies rather than labor market discrimination when asked about the things that kept them from doing well in life had difficulty in getting placed on a job after completing the program (G. Gurin 1970). Those trainees who were immediately placed on jobs after completing the program had more often blamed racial discrimination for prior life difficulties. Similarly, southern black college students who blamed the low socioeconomic status of blacks on lack of skill, hard work, or ability (internal ideology) rather than on racial discrimination (external ideology), were less likely to aspire to nontraditional jobs at a time of expanding job opportunities (P. Gurin et al. 1969). In contrast, the students who blamed racial discrimination for the condition of American blacks not only had nontraditional job aspirations, but also favored collective group action rather than individual action to deal with discrimination. In that same study, however, it was shown that college grades were significantly correlated with internal *personal* control expectancies, presumably because in predominantly black colleges individual effort and ability was seen as linked to outcomes. The implications for social workers or facilitators of change who are attempting to help individuals who face real external obstacles to achieve control over their own outcomes are clear. The goal of intervention should include enhancing clients' understanding of the way the social system works and fostering their ability to distinguish situations where one's own skill and effort can effect change in outcome from those governed by external forces. In addition, it is incumbent upon practitioners to foster attempts to change the unjust system, as a member of a professional organization, as a private citizen, and when appropriate, as a practitioner.

For those who are not members of oppressed minorities, however, the distinction between societal locus of control ideology and personal control beliefs is probably not critical except for those who hold political beliefs comparable to those of oppressed individuals, e.g., left-wing radicals. For the former group, the typical measurement of internal locus of control has been found to predict mastery behavior in a variety of contexts, and to be functional. For example, children from grade-school through high-school ages who accepted personal responsibility for intellectual achievement successes and failure received better school grades (McGhee and Crandall 1968). Fifth-graders who experienced repeated failures with a particular adult were less likely to improve their performance when easier problems were posed if they held external locus of control expectancies for achievement than if they accepted personal responsibility (Dweck and Reppucci 1973). Patients in a tuberculosis hospital were more likely to ask doctors and nurses questions about their illness and be less satisfied with the information they had received if they had internal rather than external locus of control expectancies (Seeman and Evans 1962). Adults interviewed in their homes as part of a representative national sample survey reported more coping efforts and attempts at mastering life's difficulties when they held internal personal control expectancies, including taking part in parent or community school-improvement groups (P. Gurin, Gurin, and Morrison 1978). Smokers with internal control expectancies had greater success than those with external control beliefs at quitting smoking within a specified time after first hearing and believing the surgeon general's report on smoking (James, Woodruff, and Werner 1965).

Persons with internal locus of control expectancies have also been shown to respond differently to social reinforcements or influence attempts than those with external control beliefs. For example, black male fifth-graders were administered a form discrimination task and a measure tapping feelings of responsibility for intellectual achievement. Under reinforcement conditions in which the boys were able to determine for themselves whether they had answered correctly, internals learned faster than externals, but when only external reinforcement—positive or negative feedback from an adult—was available, the externals out-performed the internals (Baron and Gantz 1972). The authors concluded that self-discovery and unverifiable praise provide different incentives for the two types of children. The absence of an opportunity to evaluate their own performance interferes with the learning of internally oriented boys; the lack of external feedback is detrimental for boys with external achievement responsibility beliefs.

If we view external feedback about one's performance as a form of social influence, the conclusions from the above study of self-generated and extrinsic reinforcement are similar to those reached in a number of studies examining factors influencing persons with internal and external control expectancies. Rotter (1966:22–24) reviewed these investigations and concluded that individuals who perceive that they have control over their fate will resist suggestions from others, or manipulation attempts perceived as not to their benefit; they will also resist subtle attempts to influence them without their awareness. Suggestions from others may, however, induce conformity from internals if they are overt and are not perceived as interfering with personal choice. Baker (1979) reached a similar conclusion in reviewing the evidence on the utility of matching client control beliefs to the directiveness of psychotherapy approaches.

CHANGING OR ENHANCING LOCUS OF CONTROL BELIEFS

The above conclusions about the consequences of internal control beliefs may be especially useful to facilitators of change involved with children, such as day care workers, foster parents, and teachers. If these adults are concerned about a child's failure to display initiative or mastery efforts, it may be helpful to consider whether their own behaviors foster or inhibit the child's expectancies concerning personal control over outcomes, or whether the child's reinforcement history generally supports such beliefs. For example the social worker and foster parent may conclude that efforts would be appropriate to enhance internal locus of control expectancies by consistently rewarding mastery efforts, by labeling the child's efforts as the cause of desired results, or by providing opportunities for the child to choose a strategy for attaining a goal and then to observe the outcomes of the choice.

Such attempts to influence a child's locus of control beliefs may be appropriate for facilitators of change who have extensive contact with the child. In many situations, however, the facilitators may be in a more limited relationship, and a major impact on the child's belief system may be unlikely. Similarly, if a client is an adult, a more reasonable intervention goal for the facilitator may be to increase the congruence between the client's control beliefs and available learning conditions than to try to alter locus of control beliefs. In such circumstances the findings about extrinsic reinforcements and overt influence attempts would be most relevant. For example, a high-school teacher or one involved in adult education might conclude that the limited efforts permitted in the classroom would not be likely to be effective in modifying the expectancies of a student whose home environment supports external control beliefs. Thus, to increase the time the pupil spends on practicing arithmetic skills the instructor would focus on external reinforcements, for example, would stop by the student's desk frequently to check the arithmetic answers and provide praise for correct answers.

As facilitators of change cannot always assess the belief structures of clients, a wise general procedure might be to provide both self-generated and extrinsic reinforcements whenever possible to maximize the learning of individuals with varying locus of control orientations. Similarly, overt influence attempts that do not preclude the choice of whether or not to comply seem to be equally effective for persons with internal and external control beliefs, and they would seem generally preferable. For example, on occasions social workers may consult with nursing home aides who recognize the benefits to their aged patients of getting out of bed and interacting socially with others. Elderly patients with internal expectancies may see this as manipulation and resist—to avoid this, the aides could state their belief that such socializing would be of benefit and that they hope the patients will agree to carry out the suggestions, but that the choice is theirs. Such recognition by facilitators of change that variations in control beliefs are likely to affect responses of clients to influence attempts can assist the caregivers to tailor their helping efforts to the individuals with whom they interact, and thereby enhance the effectiveness of their interventions.

This increased awareness in facilitators of how their own behavior interacts with clients' expectancies of control is not, however, the only implication of the research and theory reviewed above. It is also important for significant others to recognize that clients' control expectancies are affected by social conditions outside the facilitators' control. Unless the social reality supports the change in causal attributions fostered by the facilitator, any modification achieved will not be maintained or generalized. This point is well illustrated in an analysis of the job training programs begun in the 1960s under the War on Poverty (G. Gurin 1970). These programs often emphasized the provision of controlled success experiences contingent upon the trainees' own performance because it was assumed that the fostering of internal personal control expectancies would enhance mastery efforts in the job market. Unfortunately this approach overlooked the other key belief linked to internal expectancies, the belief that the world is just and responsive to individual efforts, a belief that is often unrealistic among poor minority group members. Without interventions to increase the availability of jobs or to reduce discriminatory hiring practices these job training programs were not likely to be successful in modifying the control expectancies of the trainees for any length of time. Nor indeed would such a modification be desirable unless the social reality was also changed. Internal attributions for one's own outcomes in the face of continuing failure are likely to be dysfunctional, as has been discussed previously in this chapter.

As we have moved from discussing individual differences in control beliefs to dealing with the social conditions that determine such beliefs and their social consequences, we are recognizing, as did Rotter (1966) that an external locus of control was similar to a sense of powerlessness, as described by Seeman (1959). Individuals who have expectancies of powerlessness feel they are unable to control their own destinies. This is one element in alienation, in which the individual feels he or she is a small cog in a big machine and at the mercy of forces too strong or too vague to control. Recent research has shown that enhancing or impeding an individual's ability to predict events and to control both positive and negative consequences in particular circumstances can have profound effects.

Geriatric patients in a nursing home who were either given the power to control the frequency and duration of visits by undergraduates, or were told in advance when the visit would occur and how long it would be, showed significantly more physical and psychological improvement during the intervention than matched peers who received the same number of visits but were neither able to control nor predict them (Schulz 1976). It appeared that pleasant events had no beneficial effect for the aged when they were neither predictable nor controllable. The full implications of this intervention only become clear, however, when the patients' health status and zest for life were reassessed two or more years after the visiting program ended (Schulz and Hanusa 1978). The positive effects of patient control or foreknowledge of visits did not persist very long after the visits ended. It is important to recognize, as the authors suggest the patients did, that the cessation of the visits was not under the control of the patients and thus there was probably a shift in attribution of control to external sources. The investigators concluded that it is essential to help the aged to retain as much on-going autonomy over their lives as possible to inhibit or reverse a decline in their physical and psychological state, and that many of the negative consequences associated with aging may be mediated by the increased unpredictability and uncontrollability in the lives of the elderly.

An intervention strategy more appropriately designed to enhance continued control beliefs in geriatric patients was reported in another field experiment (Langer and Rodin 1976; Rodin and Langer 1977, 1978). One group of aged nursing home residents were encouraged to feel greater control and responsibility for day-to-day life events in two ways: 1) the home administrator spoke to the residents and emphasized their responsibility for taking care of themselves, and 2) each received a plant to tend. The control group heard a talk that emphasized the staff responsibility for taking care of the residents and were also given plants, but the staff watered them for the patients. Those in the self-responsibility group were initially more active, felt happier, showed increased alertness and participated more in home activities than did those in the staff responsibility group, and in a followup eighteen months later they were in better health, more active, showed less decline in mood and sociability, and had somewhat lower mortality than did the staff responsibility patients.

Similar results were obtained in a study of noninstitutionalized men and women over fifty (Kurtz and Kyle 1977). Individuals with more responsibilities in life, such as driving their own automobiles or being sought out for advice by family and friends, were significantly more satisfied with life, e.g., felt that these were the best years of their life. The authors concluded that those who continue to have responsibilities in their later years tend to find life more gratifying, and both institutional and noninstitutional programs for the elderly should therefore be designed to maximize their ability to manage their own affairs.

In contrast are the motivational, cognitive, and emotional deficits that have been found to result from prolonged experience with lack of contingency between individuals' behaviors and their outcomes (Seligman, 1975). For example, working on an important task with much exposure to noncontingent rewards produced helpless behavior in subsequent task situations (Schulz 1976). In addition, perceived control over aversive stimuli has been found to make a great difference. A review of many studies of the ways individuals adapt to noise and other stresses typically found in urban areas reached three main conclusions that are relevant to us (Singer and Glass 1975). First, most individuals adapted to noise stress and, after an initial period of disruption, continued working on tasks requiring concentration without performance decrements. Second, noise had quite deleterious effects on subsequent routine functioning on a variety of laboratory tasks and on the subjects' willingness to volunteer for other experiments. Third, and most important to our discussion, the deleterious aftereffects of noise stress could be reduced by any of three control-related factors: perceived *control*, or an individual's belief that the noise could be terminated by that individual even though the off switch was not used; the *predictability* of the noise; and whether or not the individual *chose* to undergo the noise as opposed to being *required* to do so. These cognitive factors were also shown to have similar effects on responses to other stressors, such as electric shock, arbitrary discrimination, or bureaucratic harassment. The authors concluded that physical and social analogues of urban stress in the laboratory have disruptive aftereffects that "are more a function of the cognitive circumstances in which they occur than of the sheer magnitude or intensity of the stressor" (Singer and Glass 1975:31).

Other workers have reached similar conclusions about the importance of cognitive factors in reactions to stress. Studies indicate that chosen endurance of an aversive stimulus produces less concurrent autonomic reaction and possibly less subjective distress than forced endurance (Bandler, Madaras, and Bem 1968; Corah and Boffa 1970). A recent reformulation of learned helplessness theory proposed that whether or not an individual becomes helpless in the face of continued frustration, failure, or noncontingent reinforcement depends on the person's attributions of the stability and cause of the stress, rather than simply upon the amount of stress (Abrahamson, Seligman, and Teasdale 1978). Prediction or control has been proposed to reduce stress in varied geriatric, clerical, and educational settings (Perlmutter and Monty 1977, 1979).

The implications of these investigations for facilitators of change in others are evident. When dealing with the aged, it is essential that they not be denied control over their lives, no matter how benevolently the control is removed, for example, concerning what to wear, which TV program to watch, or when to go to bed. The principle applies to other situations and age groups as well. For example, findings pertaining to cognitive control of stressors among patients undergoing painful medical treatment suggest that patients who can predict or control the onset of the pain should experience less discomfort than those who must simply wait for the pain to occur (Taylor 1979). Whether the facilitator of change is a teacher, an aide in a hospital, or a foster parent, the importance of maintaining the self-respect of the individual who is the focus of change cannot be overemphasized. They should be given choices about all aspects of the change efforts; they should know in advance what will happen, when and why; they should determine as many of these events as possible. Above all, the use of coercion should be used only where it is absolutely essential. As discussed above in relation to attitude change, controlling by coercion is the least effective way to achieve lasting change.

CONCLUDING COMMENTS ON SECTION II

It should be noted that the procedures described in section I on worker-client dyads apply to significant others as well. If the facilitator is particularly concerned about the attitudes expressed by rebellious adolescents, for example, some of the factors affecting attitude change can be discussed with the caregiver and techniques reviewed for modifying the normative component, the attitude toward the total situation, or the consequences the adolescent anticipates from a given act. The importance of associating overt behaviors with statements of specific intentions rather than statements of generalized attitudes should be stressed. Thus the teenager's sexual intentions in relation to one particular companion at a specific period of time are of much greater predictive value than her statements about intercourse or pregnancy in general. Expertise, attractiveness, power to reward and punish, and legitimacy are as relevant to the influence of significant others on clients as to social workers' power. In essence, we are suggesting that social workers share their knowledge of the social influence process with facilitators of change so that these caregivers can become effective change agents.

SECTION THREE

IMPLEMENTING GROUP INTERVENTION PLANS WITH SIGNIFICANT OTHERS: QUADRANT C

INTRODUCTION

This and the next section focus on aspects of social psychology relevant to efforts by social workers to bring about change or to stabilize desirable behaviors through planned on-going interactions among small groups of individuals. To carry out the scheme outlined in table 3.1 and parallel the distinction made in the last two sections, we have separated the presentation about work with groups into two parts: one dealing with client groups (Quadrant D) and the other with groups consisting of significant others who can facilitate change in problems of others (Quadrant C). The present section emphasizes the implications of social psychology for work with groups of individuals who have come together primarily either to acquire knowledge and skills or plan activities that could enable them to care for someone else more effectively. Some, but not all, of the groups Radin (1974b) describes as socioeducational groups fit this category, namely those in which the social worker functions as an educator-consultant with individuals who are socializers or caregivers of others to enhance the development of those for whom they have some responsibility. These individuals have or can have some significant impact upon the lives of other individuals whose problems are the primary target of change, thus we designate them facilitators of change in others. These groups are distinguished from groups in which the members' purpose in participating is primarily to alleviate or prevent personal problems through self-change or through changes they can effect in their own individual social environment; these groups, dealt with in the following section, are identified as groups composed of clients who are participating in treatment or growth groups.

The distinction between client and facilitator groups can easily be made for most groups with which social workers who primarily engage in direct practice interact. Social workers who help organize, lead, or participate in training groups for staff or volunteers in hospitals, nursing homes, institutions for the retarded, blind, handicapped, correctional facilities are working with facilitators of change groups (Konopka 1954); the group members' participation is designed primarily to improve the conditions of the residents though the means by which the improvement comes about may involve changes in the staff or volunteer group members. Similarly, it is clear that groups composed of individuals with relatives who have some significant problem—physical handicap, severe illness, alcoholism, job loss, etc.—are facilitators of change groups when the group's purpose is primarily to enhance the functioning of the family member who is not a group member. Meetings or case conferences in which several professionals review and plan future care for an individual client or categories of clients are also appropriately thought of as facilitators of change groups located in Quadrant C (e.g., Easton 1978). Included here would be individual educational planning meetings attended by teachers, school psychologists, and social workers, agency staff meetings focused on the development of a new service operation, team meetings of the ward staff in a psychiatric hospital, and many other types of staff committees at human service agencies (Trecker 1954; Tropman, Johnson, and Tropman 1979). Less obvious is how to categorize groups composed of individuals who come together to effect change in some social institution or social conditions that contribute to or can be problematic for them or for other individuals, for example, a group of working parents whose purpose is to arrange for the development of a better child care facility in their town, a neighborhood group that organizes to clean up the neglected vacant lots in the area. Because their focus is not primarily on self-change or changes in their individual social environments, for our purposes we view these groups as facilitator of change groups. These social-action-oriented groups can be thought of as facilitating change in the larger social system as a means of achieving change in the problematic conditions of other individuals.

The various examples of groups located in this Quadrant are alike in that the development of effective group decision-making strategies, problem solving, and the ability to achieve group goals and to act effectively on the social environment external to the group are critical for them all. These goals, in turn, are linked to several aspects of social psychological theory and research, namely that on group problem solving and decision making, the differences between individual and group decision making and performance, and the nature of leadership and other structures in groups.

These examples of facilitators of change groups can be contrasted with client groups, located in Quadrant D. The latter groups are composed of members whose own individual problems or potential problems are the primary focus of group concern. As the title of a popular book about social groups indicates, the purpose of such groups is to achieve *Individual Change Through Small Groups* (Glasser, Sarri, and Vinter 1974).

Included here is social group work that focuses on treatment (Vinter 1974), group therapy (Rose 1977), rehabilitation and resocialization (Garvin and Glasser 1974b), personal growth and enhanced ability to cope effectively with the environment (Northen 1969; G. Wilson and Ryland 1949), enhanced social adjustment (H. Trecker 1955); as well as group work where the goal is socialization (McBroom 1976), prevention (Garvin and Glasser 1974a), and those socioeducational groups oriented toward imparting knowledge and skills to prevent role transition problems (Radin 1974b). To cover this range of objectives groups in this Quadrant are labeled treatment/growth client groups.

The composition of these groups can be quite diverse, and may include clients at a mental health center (Mandelbaum 1973), drug-involved adolescents (Citron 1978), battering husbands (Geller 1978), recent widows or widowers (Toth and Toth 1980). Mackey (1980) has identified these groups as growth-oriented, and has included psychotherapy, encounter, and social work groups in this category. We quote from his description of such groups because it is very similar to ours and because it indicates why we view certain social psychological topics as particularly relevant to work with such groups:

> Growth-oriented groups are usually led by professionals from various disciplines who value empathic ways of working with people. Affective as well as cognitive involvement in the group, an introspective atmosphere, interpersonal support, mutuality of goals, and differentiation of group members' needs, all are important ingredients of the modus operandi. Interventions that promote understanding about the meaning of interactions among members are seen as essential sources of learning and change. . . . The question to be addressed is whether certain developmental processes play a part in the life of these groups regardless of their specific objectives." (Mackey 1980:26)

Mackey's description links clearly to the topics reviewed in the next section: group cohesiveness, group composition, norm enforcement, group development, and role playing as a group activity.

The distinction we have made between client groups and facilitator of change groups does not, to our knowledge, completely parallel any prior distinction in the social work literature, yet all the varieties of groups included in our categorization have been discussed, as the above citations indicate, and the distinction overlaps with others in the literature. G. Wilson's (1959) differentiation between task-oriented and growth-oriented groups is similar in part. Growth-oriented groups would all fit into Quadrant D, client treatment/growth groups, but certain task-oriented groups, such as those focused on achieving educational objectives for self-betterment goals, would also be located in Quadrant D. Other task-oriented groups, such as administrative or community planning and coordination groups, would be classified here as facilitator groups, in Quadrant C. Hartford's (1971) delineation of three categories of group use—for effects on participants, for collective problem solving, and for change in social situations or conditions outside the group—also shows certain overlap with the present distinction. Groups designed for their effects on participants are typically client treatment/growth groups and those focused on problem solving and changing social conditions are usually facilitators of change groups. Yet here, too, the mapping is not perfect. For example, if efforts are on learning skills to help care for someone else, we would classify the group in Quadrant C even though the group is affecting participants' behavior. An emphasize on changes in conditions outside the group may characterize certain client groups (Quadrant D), as for example a support group of working mothers one of whose goals is to develop ways to increase their husbands' participation in child care in order to alleviate their own role strain.

We propose the differentiation between facilitator and client groups because it seems a viable and useful way to organize the social psychological literature that relates to social work with groups. It is however, an idealized categorization. Some groups contain elements of both types and the purpose of a group can change over time. A group of battered wives who initially are brought together by a social worker as a growth group with an emphasis on mutual support and enhancement of individual functioning may later engage in social action such as the development of a safe house that could serve them as well as other victims (Glasser et al. 1974; Northen 1955). Mothers of preschool children who join a group focusing on how they can facilitate their children's educational success may also find that improving their personal accomplishments or marital situations become an important goal. Social workers thus need to be aware of the social psychological theory and research relevant to both major types of groups so they can be applied appropriately as needed. We are not suggesting that certain social psychological processes occur only in groups composed of clients whereas others occur only in groups whose members come together to facilitate change in the problems of other individuals. Rather, the division of the social psychological subjects between this and the following section is meant to signify areas of primary rather than sole applicability. Before exploring these topics in detail, however, a brief overview of basic concepts of group dynamics relevant to both major types of groups is necessary and is presented below.

DEFINING PROPERTIES OF A SMALL GROUP

Up to this point we have been using the phrase "small group" as if its meaning were obvious. We could probably all agree that some collections of individuals are small groups—a nuclear family consisting of husband, wife, and small children who all live in a single residence—and others are not—five strangers riding in an elevator together. But in many instances there would not be agreement about whether a particular aggregate of individuals constitutes a group, and consequently one of the basic questions for theories of group dynamics is that of the minimal characteristics of a collectivity that warrant calling it a group (Cartwright and Zander 1968; Shaw 1976).

At least ten different properties of collectivities have been identified as relevant to the definition of a group, but for our purposes related to social work we will identify four key elements in labeling an aggregate of two or more individuals as a small group: 1) they engage in face-to-face interaction; 2) they are few enough in number to notice absences; 3) they are interdependent; and 4) they perceive of themselves as a group. The first two elements in the definition define the collection of individuals as "small" in number and the last two identify them as a unit. A small group, according to this definition, is a system, that is, a collection of interdependent parts with a boundary. Interdependence can be of several varieties; it can involve mutual gratification of the same or different needs, mutual control over rewards and punishments, or a shared common fate, as in team sports. When these four characteristics are all present we propose to consider the individuals as constituting a small group and would expect that the various properties of groups related to their influence on members' attitudes and behaviors would be observed.

This discussion should make it obvious that each of the four elements in our definition of a small group is itself a variable that can assume several values rather than a distinct condition that is clearly present or absent; face-to-face interaction can vary in frequency and duration; size may vary from two to about twenty and the absence of all members may not be equally observed; interdependence can be of several types, discussed above, and cover relatively narrow or broad areas of members' outcomes; and members may be more or less sure about who is in or out of the group. Consequently, the various properties of groups may be more or less evident in different small groups; the more clearly a collectivity reflects these key elements the more clearly should be the impact of group membership on individual behaviors.

Furthermore, one or more of these elements may be absent. Social workers do not, however, limit their professional contacts to small groups that meet all the criteria listed above. They may work with groups that are so large that a member's absence is not noticed. There is no clear numerical limit to this aspect of the definition, but many writers (e.g., Shaw 1976) suggest that more than twenty persons are unlikely to meet this criterion. When treatment "groups" are initially formed the members may neither perceive themselves as a group nor be very interdependent.

Many social workers form or work with groups in which the participants have relatively little choice about joining or leaving, as would be true of groups in prisons, schools, hospitals, and the like; the members may not be forced to remain but the alternatives are often so bad that no real leeway exists. In the terms of Thibaut and Kelley (1959), members' comparison level for alternatives is so low that a minimum amount of reward is needed to keep them in the group. Thus the reinforcements provided by the members, or the interdependence, may be minimal, at least initially. For this reason, it may be more appropriate for social workers to use the term quasi group to define some of their groups, that is, as an aggregate of individuals having some, but not all they key elements of a small group. Eventually a quasi group may turn into a small group, as defined above, but that is not certain. Mayer (1966) identified various types of quasi groups and describes them as potential groups, a term that captures the essence of the meaning.

Another way of describing the same concept is to state that an aggregate has to meet certain criteria in order to be an entity or system, for example, interdependence or common fate; and the extent to which these criteria are met is referred to as the entitativity of the aggregate (D.T. Campbell 1958). Aggregates with low entitativity should be analyzed at a smaller system level, or at the level of the individual; aggregates with high entitativity can typically be described at the level of the system concerned. Aggregates with moderate entitativity probably need to be analyzed at two levels, one lower and the level concerned (Thomas 1967b). Thus, a quasi group can be described as an aggregate with moderate entitativity and both individual personality variables and group dynamics generally need to be considered to understand its functioning.

IMPACTS OF GROUPS UPON INDIVIDUALS

Small groups are highly significant for change agents because they can have great impact on their members, thus an effective way to influence clients or facilitators of change in others is to influence or change one of the small groups to which they belong. Support for the view that groups are powerful change mechanisms is ample in the social psychological literature. As illustrations, two studies will be described in some detail that indicate ways in which interdependence among collectivities can be enhanced and the effects on individuals of group membership increased. In one investigation (Julian, Bishop, and Fielder 1966),it was demonstrated that members of groups in competition with other groups displayed a lower level of member anxiety under stress than did individuals in groups not in competition. In addition, the working relationships among members were more positive, the level of member self-esteem was higher, and the members' satisfaction with the conditions of group life was greater under the group competition situation. There was no difference in the effectiveness of groups that were or were not competing. The experiment involved a three-month training period during which nine combat engineering squads competed among themselves and received group rewards while eighteen other squads were trained using individual rewards only. Questionnaires assessing the dependent variables were administered before and after the training. The authors concluded that by appropriate environmental manipulation, which can be accomplished through administrative channels, it is possible to organize task groups under field conditions that will lead to improved member adjustment and will not interfere with effective performance. In essence, when the experiment began all the combat squads were probably at least quasi groups; they lived, ate, and trained together, probably noticed one another's presence or absence, but had an unknown degree of interdependence. The experimental squads were made more interdependent by the provision of rewards and punishments for the group as a whole based on individual members' performance during regular training and inspection. The group boundaries and the perception of group membership were also emphasized by the intergroup competition. Unfortunately, this experiment did not control separately for these two potential sources of influence upon the enhanced group morale, as might have been done if group rewards and punishments were based on some a priori standards of excellence in some groups and on inter-group competition in some other groups.

The second, more recent study, was a field experiment which examined the effects of cooperative, interethnic contact on social relationships and attitudes in newly desegregated junior and senior high schools (Weigel, Wiser, and Cook 1975). The experimental condition was a teaching method in English classes that emphasized small randomly constituted interdependent work groups composed of white, black, and Chicano students, who discussed materials, worked towards common goals, and received group rewards in competition with other groups in the same class. In the control condition, the same teachers taught English in a "whole class" method that emphasized class discussion and individual goals and rewards. The results indicated that the interdependent grouping produced less cross-ethnic conflict, more cross-ethnic helping behaviors, and more respect and liking for Mexican-American classmates among white students. In this experiment then, small groups were formed by providing tasks that required face-to-face interactions among four to six children over time, creating interdependence through on-going task activities requiring cooperation and the use of group rewards, and fostering group identification through intergroup competition.

Another interesting finding from this study, however, raises some questions about the use of intergroup competition to foster group identity. The students in the experimental groups were more attracted to their group members, as compared to their other classmates, when they perceived their group as successful and competent in their competitions with the other groups. Thus, students in the experimental groups who were not very successful were not particularly attracted to their groups. The authors therefore suggest other strategies for fostering group interdependence and boundary awareness such as adopting reward methods that assure many winners by use of multiple criteria for competitive success—quality of the product, extent to which all members participated, creativity in class presentation styles—or allocating noncompetitive group rewards based on absolute rather than relative standards—five satisfactory grades on group projects, a given percentage reduction in grammatical errors over time in written assignments. Further research would be needed to determine if small groups operating under these procedures would show advantages similar to those involved in the original type of intergroup competition.

Because the small group can have such a powerful effect, it is used extensively by social workers, mainly in three different ways: 1) as a means of attaining change; 2) as a context of change; and 3) as an agent of change (Cartwright 1967). In the first two cases, a group is created or modified for the purpose of changing individual members. Here the formation of the group is an instrumental goal of the social worker, a goal chosen to facilitate the attainment of the terminal goal which is in a different domain (Sundel, Radin, and Churchill 1974); the group is the means and the context of change. Such use of groups to change individuals lies at the heart of traditional social group work.

Groups are also employed by other types of social workers, however, for example, by those who work with administrators or potential community leaders. In this instance, the worker's goal is typically to help establish a viable independent group with specified objectives so that a force will be created that can work for change elsewhere. Efforts to establish block clubs in ghettos would fall into this category. The group in this situation is used as an agent of change. As is evident from the above discussion, social workers in the interpersonal practice area use groups primarily as a means for achieving change in individuals; those in community practice tend to use the development of viable groups as an end in itself, often as a means of bringing about system change. Client groups are established as a means and context for individual change. Facilitator groups are used for all three purposes as means, context, and agents of change.

In both of the two strategies discussed above, the practitioner's goal would be to transform an aggregate of individuals into a quasi group and then into a small group, for that is where the potency lies. In some unusual instances, the worker may encounter a very cohesive small group whose goals and activities are antisocial, such as stealing, or undesirable from the worker's point of view, for example, organizing the neighborhood to harass some black families who moved into a previously all white area. Should this occur, efforts may be directed at transforming the small group into a quasi group, and then back into an aggregate of individuals.

One of the reasons groups are so potent in changing member behavior is that small groups affect members both passively, that is, without regard to the intentions of the members, and actively, that is, with awareness of the members (Thomas 1967b).

PASSIVE INFLUENCES OF GROUPS ON MEMBERS

Through its passive power, a group influences its members by the social facilitation process, by provision of role models, as a comparative reference group for its members as well as nonmembers, and by provision of status outside the group.

Social facilitation. Social facilitation refers to the process by which the performance of an individual is affected by the mere presence of other individuals who are also performing or are simply observing. According to Zajonc (1968), who has done extensive research in this area, the generalization that explains a great many findings is that the presence of others, as spectators, or coactors, increases the general drive state or arousal level and consequently enhances the emission of dominant responses and inhibits the learning of new responses. Zajonc concluded that the mere presence of others increases the individual's general arousal or drive level, although he does agree that in some unique situations, for example, when individuals are under stress, the presence of others may result in a lowered arousal level. Some investigators have suggested that the presence of others is drive-inducing only to the extent that they are perceived as evaluating (Cottrell 1968; Paulus and Murdock 1971). For example, it was found that performance is not enhanced when the other individual present is blindfolded. It also appears that the mere presence of others is motivationally neutral for neonates. Only through social experience does the presence of others acquire drive value. In most situations, however, individuals are activated when others are nearby and the performance of behaviors that are well learned is increased.

Role models. This phenomenon was discussed previously under the topic of social influence (chapter 6) and will not be elaborated upon here except to indicate that this can be a particularly important reason for using a group as the context for change in individual members. Group composition is critical to planned effective use of this passive means of influence.

Comparative reference group. According to the social comparison theory (Festinger 1954a), when there is ambiguity people will use other members of a group to form an evaluation of themselves and of the physical world. Festinger proposed that people have a need to remove uncertainty and this motivates them to join groups and to use other group members as a point of reference for evaluating their own attitudes, beliefs, and behaviors. Groups of which an individual is not a member can also serve as comparative reference groups; this often occurs when the person aspires to membership in that group (Thomas 1967b). In the latter case the passive nature of the group's influence is obvious.

The passive aspect of a group serving comparison functions is also seen in the classic Asch (1951) experiments where subjects judged the length of lines after hearing other subjects (who were confederates of the experimenter) give clearly erroneous judgments. One of the surprising findings of that experiment was that some people used the judgment of others in assessing the physical world even when there was no ambiguity; another was that the opinions of strangers could have this effect. Asch found that one-third of his sample gave obviously inaccurate judgments about the length of a line on at least half of the trials merely to conform with the unanimous judgments being made by the other subjects, without any overt pressure by the confederates. Three-quarters of the subjects yielded to the unanimous judgment of others on at least one trial. The reason for yielding to the judgments of others, even strangers, in this situation has been attributed to the cognitive conflict that arises when people find that they see the environment differently from others. Should the individuals believe their own perceptions, or should they trust the views expressed by others? According to Cartwright and Zander (1968), although individuals respond differently to this conflict, the demand for uniformity of opinion generated by such a situation seems to be very strong. However, this passive influence of a group need not be detrimental. Milgrim (1965) showed that subjects in an experiment who were ordered to shock a "victim" refused to do so more often when there were at least two other subjects present who refused to participate in the study. Various explanations have been offered for the finding that at least one dissenter breaks the power of a group (or in the caseof the Milgrim study, a powerful experimenter), to elicit compliance from an individual without obvious effort or even desire. Whatever the reason, it does seem clear that when individuals are uncertain about how to perceive or interpret an ambiguous situation, the unanimity by others present concerning the correctness of one interpretation exerts great influence. No additional pressure is needed.

Status or prestige. Simply by membership in given groups an individual may acquire or lose prestige outside that group (Cartwright and Zander 1968). Without any particular action by other group members knowledge of a person's position in a group may affect the ways nongroup members behave; lack of group membership may be similarly important.

ACTIVE INFLUENCES OF GROUPS ON MEMBERS

Because groups can control valued resources and be a source of needed information they can also actively influence members.

Rewards and punishment. A group may control many valued resources for its members including concrete resources, such as access to services, opportunities for financial gain, and interpersonal resources, such as approval or a sense of belongingness. Contingent allocation of resources as rewards or punishments may be used for several reasons. 1. The group has a goal and wishes to move toward that goal. Behaviors that facilitate this will be rewarded; those that do not will be punished. 2. The group is serving a social comparison function for its members. Deviant behavior will unsettle self-judgments of other members and will thus be punished. Conformity reaffirms self-judgments of members and will be rewarded. 3. The group, per se, is highly attractive to its members, either because the members are attractive or the activities are attractive. Any behavior which is deviant and threatens the existence of the group will be punished. Conformity strengthens the group and will be rewarded.

Information. The same reasons that lead to groups sanctioning their members may produce persuasive attempts based on information rather than on resource allocation. Groups can actively change members via cognitive processes (L.H. Levy 1977), by 1) providing rationales for certain actions; 2) providing normative information; 3) providing instrumental information; 4) providing consensual information; 5) expanding the range of alternative perceptions about a given issue; and 6) enhancing discrimination among stimuli and events.

INTERNAL AND EXTERNAL FUNCTIONS OF GROUPS

To conclude this overview of group dynamics, it should be noted that all systems, including small groups, must perform two functions to survive. One, they must deal with the outside world, or the world external to the system. Another way of expressing this concept is to say that systems must achieve their external goals. This function has been called the instrumental function of a system (T. Parsons 1955). It is true that some treatment and growth groups, such as T-groups, appear to have no explicit external group goals, however, even these groups must maintain a place to meet under conditions that are tolerable. Thus, even groups of persons meeting to bring about change in themselves must deal with nongroup world to some extent.

The second essential function of systems is that of maintaining themselves, that is, of having sufficient harmony to prevent the dissolution of the systems. This requirement has been called the maintenance function or the expressive function of a system (T. Parsons

1955). The focus of this function is on the world inside of the system. The tendency of system to perpetuate themselves is not always perceived as an asset by those on the outside, for it appears that once systems function well, they will rarely self-destruct. The transformation of the National Polio Foundation into the Association Against Birth Defects is an example. In spite of the occasional excesses in the expressive function which may exist, it is certain that no system or group can achieve any goal if the members leave.

There is a tendency for groups to swing back and forth between attempts to complete the task, and attempts to maintain the group and satisfy the needs of its members. The swings in activity have been called pendulumlike (Hare 1976), as members become more and more absorbed in the task and neglect individual members' needs, and then in turn lose sight of the task as they turn their attention to group solidarity. Bales (1953) captured the essence of the dilemma in labeling this phenomenon as the equilibrium problem in small groups.

GROUP VARIABLES AND SOCIAL WORK PRACTICE

Small groups can be described in terms of several dimensions: type of leadership, degree of cohesiveness, composition, structures of the group (leadership, peer, communication, sociometric, normative, etc.), and processes of the group (decision making, problem solving, group development, norm enforcement, etc.). Altering any of these characteristics significantly affects the group and often has a major impact on the members. It is this essential that social workers understand these variables, how they influence the group, and how a practitioner can modify them. The topics that are particularly relevant to work with groups composed of facilitators of change are presented in the next two chapters. Chapter 9 covers problem-solving and decision-making functions, and group performance, and chapter 10 deals with leadership and other group structures. The remaining topics will be discussed in section IV with reference to work with clients and treatment/growth groups—group composition, group cohesiveness, norms and their enforcement, the process of group development, and role playing as a group activity.

CHAPTER NINE

GROUP DECISION MAKING AND PERFORMANCE

Problem solving is one of the most important processes in groups that have as their main concern planning an activity, completing a task, or enhancing the knowledge and skills of members so that they can work more effectively with others. (Note: A process is a change in a definite manner over time.) Although decision making and problem solving are not synonymous, they are often used interchangeably. Group problem solving is only one mode of decision making, in which the process emphasizes rational choices leading to a decision. Group decisions can and often are made impulsively or on the basis of some overwhelming emotion. In some groups it is assumed that decisions are made only after a problem-solving process has taken place, but not all groups function this way, particularly those whose members are immature physically or mentally. A social worker's major goal for a group may well be to help members learn how best to approach problems before coming to a group decision. Thus, research findings will be reviewed in this chapter that identify the pitfalls to effective group decision making as well as the conditions that foster successful problem solving. In addition, data that shed light on the issue of when decisions are best made in groups and when they are best made individually will be discussed. Another important concern of practitioners working with groups of facilitators is the ability of the members to carry out the group's decisions and the tasks for which it was formed. Hence, presentation of theory and research on group performance, including the conditions that facilitate and impede effective performance, will conclude this chapter.

GROUP PROBLEM SOLVING

Extensive research on problem solving has shown that given a population of normal adults who have some desire to solve a problem, one can expect a certain sequence to take place if the following four conditions are met: 1) the group does not have clear, complete information about the facts; 2) it does not know how members feel about the situation; 3) it does not know the solution to the problem; and 4) there is interest in maintaining the group because future joint action is contemplated (Bales and Strodtbeck 1968). When these conditions are met the problem to be solved is called "full-fledged." Full-fledged problems can be seen at planning meetings for a family agency, agency staffings of problematic clients, and parent groups deciding how to help members deal with sexually active daughters in their early teens. When one of the conditions listed above is missing, the problem is called "truncated," as, for example, in a meeting held after the situation was throughly discussed at lunch.

In the problem-solving process, the sequence that takes place when groups attempt to solve full-fledged problems is as follows (Bales and Strodtbeck 1968): 1) *orientation* stage or deciding what is known about the situation; 2) *evaluation* stage or deciding what is felt about the situation; and 3) *control* stage or deciding what can be done about the situation. Concurrent with the last phase, the control phase, one finds a peak of both negative and positive affect. The positive affect reaches its zenith at the very end of the meeting, after the negative affect has attained its high point. It is the joke-telling, release-of-tension feeling when everyone knows the problem is solved and the session is essentially over.

It should be noted that when the statement is made that the first phase is the orientation phase it means that if all the acts of a meeting were counted and divided into thirds, the peak of the orientation acts would occur in the first phase. There are not necessarily more orientation acts than any other type in that phase. Similarly, the peak of the evaluation acts would occur in the second phase, and the peak of the control, negative and positive acts would occur in the third phase. This description of the problem-solving sequence was proposed to apply only when the group members are relatively normal, relatively adult, lack serious status struggles, are from out culture, and have no subcultural or previously established norms which would circumvent the process (Bales and Strodtbeck 1968). Groups functioning under strong emotional arousal do not appear to follow the same sequence (Smart and Vertinsky 1977).

The specific observed behaviors for each of the categories used by Bales and Strodtbeck are 1. *Orientation*: Gives/asks orientation or information, clarifies. 2. *Evaluation*: Gives/asks opinion or evaluation, expresses feeling. 3. *Control*: Gives/asks suggestion, direction or possible ways of action. 4. *Positive Reactions*: Shows solidarity (raises others' status, rewards), shows tension release (laughs, jokes), agrees (understands, concurs, complies). 5. *Negative Reactions*: Shows antagonism (deflates others, defends self), shows tension (asks for help, withdraws), disagrees (formality, passive rejection of others). The first three categories pertain to task accomplishment. The last two are in the expressive or socioemotional area.

This analysis of the phases of problem solving is useful for practitioners working with groups for several reasons. First, if the problem appears to be full-fledged and the group does not go through these phases, one can assume that some other factor is affecting the group. For example, if negative reactions peak at the very end, there is more hostility among members than can be attributed to the problem under discussion, or perhaps, some members never really understood the facts or expressed their feelings about the issues. Second, if a worker or group attempts to take short cuts and move on to solutions before all the facts are known or all the feelings are expressed, the problem at hand may not be solved. Finally, if the problem is full-fledged and the group appears to have moved through the orientation and evaluation phases but has difficulty moving on to the control phase, perhaps not all members felt free to express their views or there are "hidden agendas" in the room.

It has been shown by Psathas (1960) that treatment groups follow the same pattern of orientation, evaluation, and control but not in a single meeting. Rather the pattern emerges when one analyzes the member and therapist interactions over a period of months, which is understandable for the problems confronting treatment groups cannot be solved in one session. The implication of the Psathas study is that in treatment groups, just as in task-oriented groups, the worker should suspect that extraneous problems are present which must be addressed when the sequence of orientation, evaluation, and control is not followed.

There are various ways members can facilitate or hinder problem solving in the group. Benne and Sheats (1961) have delineated the functions or roles that are relevant to group growth and accomplishment and have grouped them in two categories; group task roles and group maintenance roles. These two categories resemble the task areas and expressive areas referred to by Bales and Strodtbeck (1968). The task functions or roles include: 1) information seeking or asking for clarification of suggestions or for facts pertinent to the problem being discussed; 2) initiating or suggesting and proposing new ideas or a changed way of regarding the group problem; 3) opinion seeking or seeking information not primarily on the facts but for a clarification of values relevant to what the group is discussing; 4) information giving or offering facts or generalizations which are authoritative or pertinent to the group's problem; 5) opinion giving or stating beliefs pertinent to the suggestions made; 6) coordinating or showing the relationships among various ideas and trying to pull ideas and suggestions together, orienting or defining the position of the group; and 7) energizing or prodding the group to action or decision or attempting to arouse the group to greater or better activity. Likert (1961) pointed out that the group task function and roles of Benne and Sheats all deal with the intellectual aspects of the group's work. In contrast are the maintenance functions and tasks which are concerned with the emotional life of the group. These functions and roles deal with the group's warmth and supportiveness, its capacity to handle intellectual problems without bias and emotion, and its capacity to function as a mature group.

Among these group maintenance functions and roles of Benne and Sheats are: 1) encouraging or praising, agreeing with the contributions of others, or accepting the views and suggestions of others; 2)harmonizing or mediating differences between other members, or attempting to reconcile disagreements and relieve tensions; 3) compromising or operating from within a conflict in which a person's ideas are involved, yielding status, or admitting error to maintain group harmony; 4) gatekeeping or attempting to include all participants in a discussion or to keep communication channels open; 5) standard setting or expressing standards for the group or applying standards in evaluating the group's processes; 6) observing or keeping records of the group's processes and feeding such data with interpretations into the group's evaluations of its own processes; and 7) following or going along with the group, more or less passively accepting the ideas of others.

Processes that disrupt problem solving are also delineated by Benne and Sheats, who refer to these as individual roles rather than group roles. Another illustration of the dominance of individual concerns is reflected in the notion of social traps, that is, situations in which individual group members persist in some behavior that meets their immediate individual needs but that over time uses up the group's resources, thereby damaging the group as a whole and ultimately each member (Brechner 1977). Laboratory groups were less likely to get trapped in this poor problem-solving strategy if they could communicate freely about their individual choices; under those conditions when members' individually oriented behavior began to threaten long-term negative consequences one individual who recognized this could call it to others' attention and elicit a shift in attention to long-range and group consequences. Such activities are sometimes seen in groups where members are nonvoluntary or have hidden agendas requiring them to sabotage the problem-solving process. Newcomb (1978) emphasized the differences in group interactions when membership is voluntary and when it is coerced, and stressed the need for more research in the area. One major difference may be the pervasiveness of disruptive processes in nonvoluntary groups. Certain staff conferences may have this quality, as when teachers feel forced to confer with the social worker and school psychologist about dealing with the difficulties of a handicapped child who has been mainstreamed into the classroom.

Some of the disruptive processes are blocking or being negativistic and stubbornly resistant or opposing without reason; recognition-seeking or trying to call attention to oneself through boasting, reporting on personal achievement, or acting in unusual ways; dominating or trying to assert authority by manipulating the group or interrupting the contributions of others or giving directions authoritatively; help-seeking or attempting to arouse sympathy from other group members whether through expressions of insecurity, confusion, or self-deprecation; and aggressing or deflating the status of others, attacking the group or the problem it is working on, joking aggressively, or trying to take credit for the contributions of others.

In some groups one person fulfills most of the task functions, and another most of the maintenance functions. When this occurs the individuals are described as carrying out the roles of task and socioemotional leaders. It is possible, however, and often very desirable, for many group members to perform these functions. Such sharing of the leadership functions results in greater participation in the discussion and consequently greater group cohesiveness, as well as in greater internalization of the solutions to the problem that are reached. If one person engages in most of the obstructive processes, he or she is filling the role of obstructor but it is also possible, and very likely, for many group members to engage in such behaviors from time to time. An important part of the social worker's job is to be observant about both facilitative and obstructive processes, and to be skillful in knowing how and when to encourage or discourage such behaviors by some or all of the group members. Should the practitioners observe that no one is filling a necessary role, it would be wise for them, unobtrusively, to start filling that role themselves, or to consider adding another member to the group who will. One study investigated the results of "planting" individuals in groups to play out roles that were needed because no one was enacting them (A. P. Goldstein et al. 1967); it was found that other members viewed these individuals as having been helpful persons when the postmeeting reactions were assessed.

The "filling the gap" strategy is based on an interactional rather than a structural role analysis (see chapter 2), and requires that social workers be flexible enough to assume different roles in different groups, or even in the same group as conditions change. For example, if no member initiates suggestions for activities that will move the group toward its goal, the worker may want to take on this function temporarily. Similarly, if no one is harmonizing or encouraging and tensions begin to build in the group, the worker may want to take on these functions until some other member of the group begins to model the workers' behavior. It is often helpful to discuss with group members the nature of problem solving and the functions and roles essential to the process. Then if it becomes evident that some critical functions are missing, the worker can point this out to the members; in established groups, this may be sufficient to motivate one of the members to fill in the gap. In new or less mature groups, it may be necessary for the worker to go further and to encourage one or more of the members to take on a missing role before the group can solve the problem at hand.

The important issue underlying the entire discussion of functions that facilitate problem solving is that these behaviors need not be performed by one individual, such as a group leader or practitioner. These functions can and should be shared among all of the members of a group. The practitioner should make this point clear to the group of facilitators of change and do everything possible to foster members' taking on leadership roles.

GROUP DECISION MAKING

A number of theorists and researchers have looked at the process by which groups make decisions and have concluded that they are not always wise (Hall 1971; Janis 1971a; Shaw 1976; Thibaut and Kelley 1959). Each in turn suggested strategies, focused upon different aspects of the process by which the decisions were made, that would improve the accuracy or wisdom of these decisions.

IMPEDIMENTS TO EFFECTIVE GROUP DECISION MAKING

Based on analysis and observation of decision making in naturally occurring groups, two important types of ineffective decision making have been described: groupthink and decisions based on simple decision rules.

Groupthink. Janis (1971a, 1971b, 1972; Janis and Mann 1977) coined the term "groupthink" to describe the process leading to defective decisions by government leaders who were supported by their advisors, including the dysfunctional process that took place among President Kennedy's foreign-policy advisers, ending in the decision to invade the Bay of Pigs. According to Janis, groupthink arises when the members of decision-making groups become motivated to avoid being too harsh on their colleagues' ideas. A norm develops: all members should be amiable and do nothing to spoil the cozy "we-feeling" atmosphere (Janis 1971a). Critical evaluation and rationality take second place in groupthink, and members censor themselves lest some disruption occur in the cohesiveness of the group. This phenomenon is likely to occur in groups that are both cohesive and prestigious, or to use Janis' terms, have a spirit of positive self-regard. Directive leadership and high stress are also present (Janis and Mann 1977). Self-censorship leads to an illusion of unanimity—the false assumption that members who remain silent are in total agreement with what is being said. The discussion is limited to a few alternatives, and facts or opinions in opposition to the preferred policy are never iterated. Janis (1972) concluded that the result of the in-group pressure to maintain the group's esprit de corps was a deterioration of reality testing and mental efficiency. The eight specific symptoms of groupthink listed by Janis and Mann (1977) are: 1) illusion of invulnerability; 2) collective rationalization; 3) belief in the inherent morality of the group; 4) stereotypes of out-groups; 5) direct pressure on dissenters; 6) self-censorship; 7) illusion of unanimity; and 8) self-appointed mindguards.

To guard against groupthink and a hidden agenda of maintaining friendly relations at all costs, Janis (1971b; Janis and Mann 1977) suggested that a number of steps be taken. First, the group should be divided into subgroups and each subgroup should arrive at its own decision. Second, an additional meeting should be arranged in a relaxed atmosphere to air any doubts about the solution reached. Third, the role of devil's advocate should be assigned to someone at each meeting so that at least one individual will feel free to disagree without fear of losing friends or being excluded from the group. The leader should be impartial and an outsider should be brought in to evaluate the solution that the group decided upon. Finally, all the warning signals from rivals should be surveyed and alternative scenarios of their intentions constructed.

On the surface, it may appear that groupthink is applicable largely to residents of Camelot, but the phenomenon is far more pervasive. For example, a subgroup of staff members of a social agency that has developed into a highly cohesive advisory group that meets with the agency director to plan policy could be a candidate for groupthink. Treatment groups could also have this problem. For example, adolescents who have been admitted to a high-status group are likely to be reluctant to do anything to disrupt the group or its cohesiveness. Similarly, a cohesive group of ex-drug addicts or ex-mental patients may regard themselves so highly that they are reluctant to say anything that may suggest strong disagreement with the views being expressed.

Simple decision rules. J. Hall (1971) is another researcher who concluded that groups that are reluctant to hear conflicting opinions are ineffective. His criticism extended beyond that of the mere attempt to maintain harmonious relations, however. Hall's research also suggested that attempts to resolve differences by simple, quick decision-making techniques, such as majority rule or averaging opinions, can be damaging. Far more effective, in his view, are decisions based on consensus, or the acceptance of a solution by all members on the basis of logic and feasibility, although the solution reached may not be identical with any single member's views. This means that a single person can block a group if that individual thinks it is necessary. Hall conducted several studies to determine the characteristics of effective problem-solving groups and concluded that well-established cohesive groups are more effective than ad hoc groups with tenuous cohesion, because the former are freer to express conflicts. Well-established cohesive groups often came up with a solution that was unique and creative, and unlike the specific solution of any individual member. Based on these observations, Hall delineated a set of procedures that captured the essential elements of effective problem solving in cohesive groups. Basically the training focused on five sets of instructions, presented here in abbreviated form. 1. Present your position as logically as possible and listen to other members' reactions. Consider these views carefully before pressing your point. 2. Do not assume that someone must win and someone must lose in a stalemate. Look for the next-most-acceptable alternative for all. 3. Yield only to positions that have objective and logically sound foundations. 4. Avoid conflict-reducing techniques such as majority vote, coin-flips, and bargaining. 5. Seek out differences of opinions and try to involve everyone in the decision process. A wide variety of groups—college students, management executives, neuropsychiatric patients who had been hospitalized for periods from several months to several years—were trained in these techniques. Diverse groups were chosen to assess the generality of the findings. Hall matched these groups with similar ones in which subjects were not trained, and gave all groups problems with solutions that could be objectively determined as correct or incorrect. In this study, trained groups did significantly better than untrained groups. Furthermore, many trained groups even did better than their best individual member. (Hall refers to the situation in which a group out-performs its own best member as "synergy.") The groups that improved the most after training and consistently scored the best tried to involve every member. They actively sought out points of disagreement; the most ineffective groups used simple decision techniques such as majority rule and seemed more committed to reaching a decision than to committing themselves to the decisions made. Hall, like Janis, concluded that conflict effectively managed is a necessary precondition for effective problem solving and creativity; there is nothing instrinsic to the group process that makes groups inherently inept.

It is interesting to compare Hall's assessment of cohesive groups as problem solvers with that of Janis. Hall found cohesive groups were effective because they were free to disagree openly with one another. Hall did not explicitly make this statement but it was evident that his cohesive groups had no norm of maintaining harmony. Janis' groups were not only cohesive but thought very highly of themselves. There may have been a fear that the members would lose status if group solidarity were threatened. It appears that cohesiveness in groups does not alone predict effectiveness of decision-making processes. One must also first know how fearful the members are of the group's disintegrating and the norms which ensue. Once this fear is present, the group resembles Hall's ad hoc groups whose cohesion was "tenuous and temporary."

The implication of Hall's research for social workers is that groups, whether newly formed or established, can be trained to become effective problem solvers. The practitioner may not wish to follow the exact training procedures used by Hall, but the important point to be made is that the usual strategies employed for resolving differences in feelings or desires among group members, that is compromise, bargaining, and the like, do not apply in efforts to solve problems with objective right and wrong solutions. Here creativity in proposing solutions and logic in evaluating them are critical. Efforts to pacify offended members' feelings by accepting their solutions will not lead to problem-solving effectiveness. Thus, the worker should seek to help a group delineate whether the issue at hand is one that has a correct solution, or whether there are many possible solutions and other factors such as interpersonal relationships should take precedence in the decision-making process. Situations in which a facilitator of change group could be seeking to find the correct solution to a group problem might include that of a social planning group's assessment of who controls the key resources needed to develop a new service, or that of how to determine the critical decision maker in a complex regulatory agency.

In avoiding quick decision rules, whether in problems with clearly correct solutions or more complex problems such as jury decisions, it is also important for the social worker to recognize that research evidence suggests that reaching a consensus takes longer and is more demanding than is the reaching of majority decisions (Zander 1979). Unanimous decisions are, however, more likely to elicit feelings of confidence in the correctness of the decision.

FACILITATING EFFECTIVE DECISION MAKING IN GROUPS

A number of other researchers have developed and tested specific techniques designed to enhance group decision making, or have investigated the effects of certain group variables on effective decision-making. (See L.R. Hoffman 1979 for a recent review.) They include brainstorming, group composition, and group discussion.

Brainstorming. This strategy for producing new, creative solutions in groups has been studied extensively. The procedures are specified as follows: ideas are expressed without regard to quality, no idea may be evaluated until all ideas have been expressed, and the elaboration of one person's ideas by another is strongly encouraged (Shaw 1976). In spite of the popularity and fame of brainstorming, the research findings on the effectiveness of this procedure are inconsistent. Shaw (1976) suggests that the inconsistency may be due to the fact that in some studies the group members knew each other very well and in others they were strangers. Since there is some evidence that cohesive groups and groups with prior training in brainstorming did better than groups without these characteristics, it is possible that group characteristics are critical variables in the process. Perhaps, Shaw concludes, future studies should be directed at the effectiveness of brainstorming in different types of groups, rather than focus on a comparison of individual versus group productivity of new ideas.

Thibaut and Kelley (1959) explain the inconsistent results in studies of brainstorming in another way. They suggest that the success of brainstorming, at least in part, depends on the willingness of a cohesive group to permit its members to be nonconforming in certain areas while conforming in others. The very expression of unusual ideas or unusual solutions to problems, such as new uses for a familiar object, requires an acceptance of nonuniform behavior among group members. If the group will take advantage of the ideas of all members without any restraint, it is possible for groups, especially cohesive groups, to be highly effective in brainstorming. The message for social work practitioners is evident. If the group of facilitators is to develop creative ideas, there must be tolerance in the group for unusual ideas that have not been tried and tested. Such a tolerance requires hearing the ideas without criticism and encouraging other members to expand and modify the ideas that have been offered. Possibly the worker may suggest specific periods of brainstorming when the rules described above apply. At other times, members may prefer greater caution and criticism in considering alternative solutions to problems. Examples of topics that might benefit from a brainstorming session are techniques for improving attendance at meetings, and inexpensive or cost-free reinforcements that could be offered to persons being cared for.

Although the strategies suggested by Janis, by Hall, and by the brainstorming technique appear superficially to have little in common, they do share one characteristic, that of initially eliciting a wide range of suggestions. Janis warns of premature foreclosure and limiting consideration to a few alternatives. Hall stresses the search for differences of opinions. Brainstorming is based on uncritical acceptance of all ideas. The inference that can be made is that decisions are more likely to be effective when a large number of alternatives are considered at the beginning. The thrust of all three decision-making approaches is that initial diversity can be achieved by following a set of behavioral rules.

Group composition. A different approach to eliciting a variety of initial suggestions is to start with group members who are heterogeneous. At least two studies by the same authors (L.R. Hoffman and Maier 1961; 1966) arrived at that conclusion when comparing the solutions to problems of homogeneous and heterogeneous groups. Although there are difficulties in attaining interpersonal attraction among members who differ widely, it appears that such groups do produce a greater proportion of high-quality solutions to problems than do groups composed of persons very much alike.

Group discussion. All of the authors cited thus far have described what they consider to be types of group discussions that optimize a problem-solving approach to group decision making. Thibaut and Kelley (1959) focus on the importance of the group discussion per se in achieving acceptance of the goal to be reached. Although these authors discuss acceptance of goals, we believe their comments are applicable to the acceptance of solutions to problems. Thibaut and Kelley enumerate three major advantages of group discussion as follows: it can provide clarity about the solution or the goal, it can provide assurance to the members that the group has sufficient consensus and power to achieve the goal, and it can assure members that they will be rewarded for their participation in the group's effort to achieve its goal. Thus, even if the solution appears to be crystal-clear to the leader or a few members, it is essential that the group discuss the matter if all members are needed to act upon the solution in some way. Thibaut and Kelley observe that for consensus about a solution to be reached, a large number of group members must accept the solution and all members must believe they will attain desirable outcomes when the goal is reached. As with process of identification and internalization discussed earlier, acceptance of a solution means that each member is ready to help with the task of enacting that solution without surveillance or sanctions.

There are some risks to fostering group discussion, however. If there are individuals who are not voluntary members of the group, they may use the discussion as an opportunity to resist and obstruct any consensus about the decision (Thibaut and Kelley 1959). Fouriezos, Hutt, and Guetzkow (1950) studied "self-oriented" behavior in decision-making groups and described it as showing no regard for the attainment of the solution to the group's problem. Groups showing a high incidence of self-oriented behavior expressed less satisfaction with the group's decisions and met for longer times but completed fewer agenda items. According to Thibaut and Kelley, nonvoluntary group members are more likely than voluntary members to exhibit self-oriented behavior and thereby impede the reaching of consensus. It is likely that specific self-oriented behaviors would closely resemble the individual roles in groups described by Benne and Sheates (1961) and reviewed earlier in the chapter. All of the above strongly suggest to social workers that they use caution in fostering group discussions to arrive at consensus about decisions to be made if group membership is nonvoluntary. It is important in such situations to consider the motivations of individual members as well as group factors. This caveat was referred to in the discussion of entitativity. It might be preferable to wait until nonvoluntary members become attracted to the group through their activities, the attractiveness of other members, and/or the recognition that the group can be instrumental to their achieving desired outcomes. Inasmuch as it is not always necessary for all members to accept the solution for the group to carry out the action (Thibaut and Kelley 1959)—a large majority will often suffice—discussions may be fruitful if there are a few nonvoluntary members, provided most of the members are freely participating in the group.

POLARIZATION OF GROUP ATTITUDES AND BEHAVIORS AFTER GROUP DISCUSSION

One group decision-making phenomenon that has been extensively researched by social psychologists because of its intriguing nature was originally described as the risky shift. The risky shift, as its name implies, refers to the tendency of groups after group discussion to arrive at decisions that involve more risk-taking than is found by averaging the individual members' decisions arrived at alone prior to the group discussion. In truth, not all groups have demonstrated the risky shift; on the contrary, some have demonstrated a conservative shift. Most of the early research on the topic involved use of the choice dilemma questionnaire developed by Wallach, Kogan, and Bem (1962). An example of the twelve dilemmas presented in the questionnaire is "An electrical engineer may stick with his present job at a modest but adequate salary, or may take a new job offering considerably more money but no long-term security." The respondents indicate their preference between two courses of action that vary in riskiness and in the degree of reward achieved if the chosen course is successful. For each dilemma, the respondents also indicate the lowest probability of success that they would demand before recommending the potentially more rewarding alternative. Probabilities of success are listed as 1, 3, 5, 7, and 9 chances out of 10 with a category of 10 to be used if the respondent would never recommend the risky alternative. The subjects in the early studies using the choice dilemma questionnaire were asked to complete the questionnaire individually, then as a group after having arrived at consensus following a discussion, and then again individually after the group decision process. Both the group decision and the averaged individual decisions after group discussion were typically found to be riskier than the initial averaged individual decisions.

The explanations offered for the phenomenon of the risky shift include leadership, or the fact that riskier individuals will be more influential and emerge as leaders, diffusion of responsibility, or the fact that no one individual feels personally responsible for decisions reached by the group, familiarization, or the fact that discussing the issue increases its familiarity and familiarity fosters riskiness, and risk as a value (proposed by Brown, 1965), or the fact that where riskiness is seen as a value, individuals who tend to see themselves as risky and will select a riskier choice if the group discussion reveals that others are riskier than they are (Wrightsman and Brigham 1973).

Empirically, the best-supported explanation of the risky shift is that risk is a value in our culture (Helmreich, Bakeman, and Scherwitz 1973). Wrightsman and Brigham (1973) point out that groups of individuals who feel they are more cautious than their peers do not shift toward riskiness. Similarly, when the costs become very great, for example when a child is hurt, caution becomes a value rather than risk and a shift toward caution is observed. G.S. Sanders and Baron (1977) also support the risk as value explanation but propose it is the social comparison process (Festinger 1954a) that is at work. According to this theory, people fail to adopt extreme opinions which they value for fear of being labeled deviant. Once they discover that others hold similar views, they can comfortably move to that position themselves.

Recently, a different hypothesis has been offered to explain the shift to riskiness (Burnstein and Vinokur 1975, 1977; Vinokur and Burnstein 1974, 1978). This position holds that group shifts toward risk only occur when the arguments for riskiness tend to be superior, and other group members can be convinced to alter their views. Analysis of actual discussion content supported this hypothesis. The nature of the arguments made were the critical variables affecting group decisions. As research continued in this area a number of findings emerged which suggested that group discussion sometimes moved the group toward more conservative decisions and that even on the choice dilemma questionnaire shifts toward more cautious decisions occurred for certain items even though the average effect across all items was in the risky direction. This led to a reconceptualization of the phenomenon and a relabeling of it as "group polarization" (Moscovici and Zavalloni 1969). Group polarization is defined as the strengthening of a dominant tendency in a group after group discussion; when the dominant initial tendency in a group is toward risk, discussion leads to a risky shift;

when the dominant initial tendency is caution, the postdiscussion responses of group members are even more cautious. In two important review articles (Lamm and Myers 1978; Myers and Lamm 1976) the generality of this phenomenon was established in laboratory groups and much evidence was also cited indicating its occurrence in a number of significant real-world situations as well. Furthermore, polarization is not limited to risk or caution. Group discussion can polarize opinions and behaviors that are prosocial—e.g. the amount of time and money donated to charity, or antisocial—e.g. administration of punishment. It can polarize bargaining demands, simulated jury decisions, and many other group decisions. These reviewers also conclude that the bulk of the evidence suggests that the strengthening of the initial dominant tendency after group discussion is largely determined by the information exchanged: "Arguments which emerge . . . predominantly favor the preferred alternative. Since it is unlikely that any given person will have considered all these arguments . . . some . . . are likely to be persuasive. . . . Group influence resides in the substance of what other people have to say, not merely in exposure to their position" (Lamm and Myers 1978:169). But they also point out that there is good evidence that information received in a group discussion is different and has different impact from simply having individuals exchange written statements of their individual positions. Reasons are that active discussion may elicit more attention, new ideas often appear in discussion as one member's remarks stimulate thoughts and statements from another, the open expression of ideas elicit an enhanced commitment to that idea by the speaker, and to support a individual's desires for appropriate self-distinctiveness, opinions expressed publicly are often slightly more extremely or forcefully stated than similar ideas expressed by other group members (this is the basis for social comparison induced polarization).

These conclusions have a number of implications for social work practitioners. When group members have a dominant tendency on a key issue, i.e., when most members support a particular choice, group discussion can be an effective tool for enhancing commitment to that choice based on group polarization. For example if the choice involves aspirations or demands concerning an upcoming negotiation with another group, intragroup discussion can lead to a tougher negotiation stance. Depending on the situation, then, the practitioner may wish to foster group discussion among like-minded individuals, avoid such discussion, seek to eliminate the dominant opinion tendency prior to group discussion by inviting participants with differing opinions, or seek to create a dominant tendency by modifying group composition. Illustrations of situations in which each of these strategies might be employed can easily be given. Parents of severely handicapped children seeking to obtain support for maintaining their children at home rather than in institutions would probably be benefited by group discussion. In contrast, a social worker in an agency for male juvenile offenders might be concerned about group discussions concerning evidence of manliness—these may lead to greater risk-taking behavior if the group members highly value risk taking as a personal characteristic. Groups composed of teenaged males are often likely to hold these norms, so it is reasonable to assume that they would be more likely to demonstrate a shift toward riskiness after a group decision than would groups composed of individuals with different norms, elderly widows, for example. In the former case group discussion might be avoided or the group composition modified to prevent enhancement of illegal activities. In the latter case, some members of the Grey Panthers might be introduced to the group to prevent enhancement of cautious attitudes that can limit the lives of elderly widows. In helping to compose planning committees within an agency or community, then, the initial attitudes of the members would be a very important consideration. It is hard to predict the likely decision of a committee with no dominant tendency prior to group discussion. Under situations of strong intergroup conflict, such as during school desegregation in some communities, the proliferation of groups composed of like-minded individuals is likely to polarize further those groups' opinions and to add to community conflict.

It is interesting to speculate about the possible connection between groupthink, as described originally by Janis (1971a; 1971b) and by Janis and Mann (1977), and the group polarization phenomenon. Although Janis does not describe the poor decisions resulting from groupthink as a shift toward riskiness, the groups he studied did in fact do just that, e.g., decided to invade the Bay of Pigs, decided to escalate the war in Vietnam, decided to cross the forty-ninth parallel in Korea. Among the symptoms of groupthink and defective decision making listed by Janis and Mann are "illusion of invulnerability" and "failure to examine risks of preferred choice." Finally, among the procedures Janis and Mann recommend to counteract the conditions that lead to groupthink is, "when a rival organization is involved, [to] survey all warning signals from rivals and construct alternative scenarios of their intentions." Thus, it is possible that groupthink is generally more likely to result in a decision that is too risky than in one that is too conservative. But this has not been tested and the apparent relationship may be a function of the particular groups Janis (1971a) originally studied. One wonders if a study of business organizations might not reveal "groupthink" leading to bad conservative decisions. Such groups could show high cohesiveness, insulation of the group, illusion of invulnerability, belief in the inherent morality of the group, a spirit of positive self-regard, and have a directive leader. They could also devalue risk taking (Janis 1971a). Perhaps the decision of American automobile manufacturers to stick to their tried and true large car models rather than risk consumer rejection of fuel-efficient smaller cars was an instance of groupthink resulting in what appeared to be a conservative decision.

GROUP VS. INDIVIDUAL DECISION MAKING

The above discussion highlighted the fact that group decision making is not always wise. One may well ask why anyone should try to have groups arrive at decisions at all. The answer is twofold: 1) groups have the potential to be far more effective problem solvers than individuals, given certain circumstances, and 2) many individuals often are needed to carry out a decision and group decision making can enhance the execution of such decisions. Groups have been shown to be more effective on tasks in which divergent solutions or a variety of information is required, that call for a division of labor and cumulative individual contributions, in which questions must be framed or information must be remembered, in which a number of steps must be correctly completed in a definite order, in which individuals can recognize and correct errors, or in which stimulation or interest arousal is needed (Shaw 1976; Thibaut and Kelley 1959; G. Watson and Johnson 1972). Groups are not as effective as individuals when the task to be performed or the solution to be reached requires centralized or qualitative organization of parts (Shaw 1976; Thibaut and Kelley 1959). Thibaut and Kelley pointed out that the right answers tend to win out in groups, probably due to the greater confidence of persons with knowledge, but this may not be true in groups where there are large differences in power not correlated with differences in competency. It even has been suggested by several researchers that the superiority of groups in some circumstances is merely due to the fact that their performance reflects that of the most capable group members; this suggests that if one knew beforehand who these individuals were, it would be more economical to assign them the problems. Shaw (1976) expands upon that point and states that if the effort invested in problem-solving is measured by man-hours required for solution, individuals have been found to be superior. Thus, although groups may be more effective than individuals in reaching decisions requiring logic, groups are not likely to be more efficient. In spite of these negative factors, Thibaut and Kelley concluded that in the long run it may be more economical to have groups solve problems instead of turning to the most expert individual because general participation in developing a means to achieve a goal will heighten the members' understanding of the tasks to be performed, and will enhance their commitment to reaching the group's goal. What appears to be efficient in the short run may be inefficient in the long run.

The above discussion suggests that practitioners working with individuals who can be facilitators of change in others may want to consider carefully the conditions under which the group is the desired decision maker or problem solver, and the conditions under which an individual member with expertise or the practitioners themselves should be asked to solve the problem at hand. As was pointed out in the discussion of strategies for reaching synergy, the critical issue is whether members' motivation to work on group tasks or member interrelationships are of prime importance, or whether there is a simple question that needs to be answered in the least costly manner. An example of the former type of problem where motivation is important would be how to raise funds so that a group of volunteer classroom aides could take a trip to visit some schools or hospitals that are highly effective in working with handicapped individuals. An example of the latter problem would be how to allocate the funds raised so that the least expensive means of public transportation could be selected to get the group to the institutions.

In addition to the specific conditions cited above there is one other condition relevant to social work which appears to benefit from group rather than individual decision making: when a risky decision is to be made and it is undesirable for single individuals to feel guilty about that decision. In addition to the evidence cited in the prior discussion of the risky shift, there are indications that an individual tends not to take responsibility for poor group outcomes evolving from group decisions, in spite of the fact that the individual was part of the majority supporting those decisions (Schlenker and Miller 1977). On the other hand, individuals do associate themselves with positive outcomes arising from group decisions they helped to make, and are more likely to value the group's product (Zander 1979). These result support the suggestion of Heider (1944) that there are self-serving motivational biases that protect self-esteem and that color attributions and perceptions. Although this phenomenon may not be relevant to groups of facilitators of change whose purpose is primarily to improve their own skills in caring for others, it may well be important to those facilitators of change groups consisting of administrators or staff members of one or more agency who must select between undesirable alternatives. Such situations might arise when decisions must be made about placement of delinquent children or youngsters whose parents have been abusing them, or when decisions must be made about services to be cut when a budget is reduced. In all of the above situations, individual guilt and remorse can be reduced or prevented by arranging for groups rather than individuals to make the decisions, providing, as was noted previously, the dominant tendency in the group supports the riskier choice and that choice is seen as desirable by the worker.

GROUP PERFORMANCE

The differential effectiveness of various groups has been explored extensively by social psychologists but no overall explanation has emerged. Rather, some factors that have an impact on group productivity have been determined. One such factor, the nature of the leadership, will be discussed in detail in the next chapter. Other relevant factors that have surfaced are the principle used to dispense rewards, the motivation to achieve of the group, the presence of an evaluator, the match of the personality predisposition of the individual member with the role assigned in the group, and the match of the individual's personality predisposition and the reinforcements available in the group. Before these issues are examined, a general model proposed by Hackman and Morris (1975) for learning why some groups are more effective than others will be described.

A MODEL FOR STUDYING GROUP EFFECTIVENESS

Hackman and Morris (1975) argue that we really do not know why some groups are more effective than others, and that research has generally not supported the use of groups to perform important tasks. The problem is that research has generally concluded that group effectiveness is affected by group interaction and we do not really know how to study group interaction. The model proposed by Hackman and Morris suggests that three summary variables account for most of the variance in group effectiveness: member effort, task performance strategies used, and knowledge and skill of group members. These three variables themselves are affected by three input variables: norms of the group, task design, and group composition. If the norms are altered regarding the selection of task performance strategies, the group's effectiveness can be modified. If the task design is altered, for example by making the work performed visible, member effort can be affected. Finally by altering the group composition, one can alter the knowledge and skill of group members. Hackman and Morris's (1975) summary of this conceptualization, is shown in table 3.3.

In addition to delineating the input factors impinging upon the summary variables, Hackman and Morris also indicate how the interaction process itself could enhance or reduce the three summary variables, task performance strategies, member effort, and members' knowledge and skill. For example, there is a decrement in task performance when there is a norm to use familiar strategies brought to the group instead of to seek the best one to fit the present situation. On the other hand, norms also may foster the development of new functional strategies. Insofar as member effort is concerned, group interactions may create coordination problems thereby decreasing effort, but group interactions may also serve to stimulate members and enhance member effort. Finally, in regard to members' knowledge and skill, interactions may not use the talents of the members, on the other hand they may serve to increase knowledge and skill.

Hackman and Morris' (1975) conceptualization suggests that if research is to shed light on variables influencing group effectiveness, there is a need to focus more carefully on the factors influencing member effort, performance strategies, and member knowledge and skill, rather than on the determination of predictors of effectiveness in groups per se. At this point, the model carries few specific messages for social work practitioners but, implies that to enhance the group's

Table 3.3
The Hackman and Morris (1975) Model of Group Effectiveness Factors

Summary Group Process Variables That Affect Group Performance Effectiveness	*Input Group Interaction Factors Manipulable to Change Group Process and Performance*		
	Norms	*Task Design*	*Group Composition*
Task performance strategies	X	—	—
Effort	—	X	—
Knowledge and skill	—	—	X

productivity, one should think about modification of group norms, task design, and group composition (the inputs), for they in turn influence the summary variables that determine group effectiveness: task performance strategies, effort put forth by members, and member knowledge and skill. Although this is not discussed by Hackman and Morris (1975), it would also appear worthwhile for practitioners to use whatever strategies they can to improve the summary factors and not confine themselves to influencing group interaction mediators. For example, the social worker may increase the efforts of halfhearted members by providing a model of someone who is working hard to achieve the group's goal. Or the worker may increase the members' knowledge about the task at hand without altering the membership by bringing some books, magazines, films, or videotapes to some group sessions. The real test for the worker is to determine which summary variable is creating problems, and then to design some approaches for remedying the situation. For example, it is foolish to bring films and books to a group of facilitators of change who know what needs to be done to increase the independence of those in their care, but do not have the motivation to do so.

ALLOCATIVE PRINCIPLES FOR DISTRIBUTING REWARDS

One group variable affecting member effort not mentioned in the Hackman and Morris (1975) model was discussed and researched by Leventhal and his colleagues (Leventhal 1976a; Leventhal, Michaels, and Sanford 1972). That factor is the rewards provided by the group's leader. Leventhal points out that there are two major principles leaders can apply in allocating rewards: the norm of reciprocity (or equity) and the norm of equality. If the norm of reciprocity is employed, the leader will give rewards to recipients in proportion to the usefulness of their actions. When the norm of equality is applied, the leader will give equal rewards to all members regardless of their activities. There are advantages and disadvantages to each principle. The norm of reciprocity tends to maximize the group's performance and productivity over a long-term period, for the better performances will be rewarded and, as a result, task behaviors of the members will be strengthened. The bond between the high producer and leader will also be strengthened. The relatively few rewards this principle provides to poor performers stimulates them to leave the group. The disadvantage of the norm of reciprocity is that it leads to dissatisfaction among poor performers and perhaps even antagonistic behavior or loss to the group of the poor performers. To avoid this and still employ the norm of reciprocity, the leaders may maintain secrecy about the distribution of rewards, mislead recipients about the basis for reward allocation, or enhance the poor performers' estimates of the value of the rewards they did receive.

The norm of equality results in better interpersonal relationships, particularly if the group is committed to an egalitarian approach. However, productivity may suffer. Leventhal (1976a, 1976b) suggests a compromise between the two approaches which avoids the greatest disadvantages of the equity and equality allocation principles. The compromise involves reducing the differences in reinforcements that would be allocated if rewards were completely contingent upon utility of the members' actions (thereby reducing interpersonal problems associated with equity) but not giving everyone equal rewards (thereby reducing deleterious effects on group productivity linked to equality). One way to implement this approach is to give the good performers almost as much as they deserve and then overreward the poor performers.

Other less common principles leaders can use in dispensing rewards are allocations based on the needs of individual members, on the abilities of individual members, and on the basis of prior agreements. Each of these has advantages and disadvantages, as did the norms of reciprocity and equality. At least two factors affect allocation decisions: the approval given by others to the norm selected, and the specific benefits the leader seeks—different norms give different benefits (Leventhal 1976a). Clearly, if the leader wishes to give top priority to group productivity and effectiveness, the norm of reciprocity will be the predominant approach to dispensing rewards. But if the leader feels that member satisfaction is most important, emphasis will be placed on equality in distributing rewards. Leventhal (1976a) summarized the analysis by stating that the way leaders handle problems of allocation determines their success in facilitating the attainment of group goals and maintaining their position.

From the social work perspective, other issues can be of equal, if not more importance than efficiency. For example, the practitioner may be particularly concerned about maintaining the group's cohesiveness, about enhancing the self-esteem of the members, or about modeling a style of dispensing reinforcements which group members can use in their own families or jobs. The major implication of the Leventhal perspective for social workers is that it is essential to be aware of the norm used in allocating a reward, be that reward an opportunity to select the next problem to be discussed, or to receive a hand-drawn certificate of merit to acknowledge meritorious work. Another important implication is that workers must be aware of the consequences of the allocative principle they employ for the members and for the group's functioning. The Leventhal work also communicates the message that there are several allocative principles that can be employed, and the perceptive practitioner will consider all of them before making a decision about the norm to use with any particular group. Further, the worker should be aware that the analysis of allocation principles and their consequences is applicable in any setting, certainly in a family where sibling rivalry is likely to flourish or in foster homes or institutions where there is likely to be competition for the attention and reinforcements of the caregiver. Finally, not only should practitioners be concerned about their own allocative principles, but also about the allocative principles used by group members as they dispense rewards to those in their care.

A GROUP'S MOTIVATION TO ACHIEVE

Zander (1971; 1974) tackled the issue of member effort from a different perspective than Leventhal's—by focusing on motivations of group members. Zander suggested that just as individuals have motivations to achieve, so too do groups. The effort of any individual in a group reflects not only that individual's achievement motivation in relation to his or her own outcomes but also the motivation that arises in the group concerning the group's performance. Thus groups with high achievement motivation have been found to behave similarly to individuals with strong achievement motivation: they tend to choose more realistic goals and to work harder for them than groups with weak group achievement motivation. As might be expected, the task strategy selected and the effort exerted by groups with strong desires for group success can pay off in increased group productivity. These ideas and findings have two main implications for social workers. First, where group performance and productivity is of concern, the social worker should focus on creating conditions that foster strong group achievement motivation or desire for group success. Second, when the productivity of a particular individual is of concern, the social worker can use a group with strong motivation to achieve as a means of overcoming the problematic individual's lack of personal achievement motivation. The former circumstance is an instance where the group is primarily designed as an agent of change; in the latter circumstance the group is essentially a means or context for individual change.

Zander (1974) suggests a number of ways to nourish group desires for success—including all group members in the process of goal setting rather than having external agents set the group's goals, providing accurate and continual feedback to groups about their performance, and using rewards for group accomplishment. These are all strategies that social workers could employ. He also suggests ways of overcoming the low level of achievement motivation of some individuals. A particularly effective strategy is to place those with low motivation in a central spot in the structure of the highly motivated group—the net result will be behavior typical of high achievers, for example, the goals selected will be moderate and feasible. If practitioners are working with more than one group and have the power to place members into any onc of the groups, as do some social workers in hospitals, schools, and community mental health facilities, this strategy may be useful. Given this choice, it would be desirable to place the new member who appears to have relatively little desire to become actively involved in any group's efforts into the group which appears to generate the most enthusiasm about their activities, providing that this dissimilarity is counterbalanced by other bases for attraction to the group. Zander's work suggests that the reluctant, unmotivated member is likely to be carried along by the hard-working group. In contrast, placing the unmotivated parent in a group with little motivation will only add to the ineffectiveness of the individual and the group.

THE PRESENCE OF AN EVALUATOR

Some groups must acquire new knowledge in order to be effective. There is evidence that learning is enhanced when individuals feel they are going to be evaluated; Henchy and Glass (1968) refer to the phenomenon as evaluation apprehension. Classroom teachers discovered this long ago; if they want students to learn new material quickly, they tell their pupils there will be a test on the topic next week. Social work practitioners are not going to give examinations but it is possible for them to indicate that the members will be compared with the standard established by other groups, and that in order to determine whether the standard was reached, it will be necessary to determine how well the group succeeded in learning the material at hand. Some type of evaluation can thereby be built into the session. Although the study by Henchy and Glass showed that evaluation by an expert was the factor responsible for the enhanced learning, the issue may not be the degree of expertness of the evaluator but the desire to perform well before someone who cares about the results. Thus, the social worker could ask members to test one another to determine how well the new knowledge or skill was learned and the results could then be compared with the standard set by others who resemble the members. Examples of new knowledge and skills that group members may want to master is how to communicate empathy to the persons in their care, how to learn what emotion is being felt by these individuals, and how to teach the persons being cared for to anticipate the consequences of their acts.

THE MATCH BETWEEN MEMBER PERSONALITIES AND GROUP ROLES AND REINFORCEMENTS

The match between personality of the individual member and group conditions is another factor that has been shown to be highly relevant to group effectiveness. The essence of the findings concerning person-group match is that when there is congruence, the productivity and effectiveness of the group is greatly increased. It is more difficult to determine what characteristic of the group member must be considered. Smelser (1961) studied the role demands members encounter in groups and found that if individuals who are very high in dominance are assigned to subordinate positions in work groups, their productivity goes down; however, if those individuals are given dominant positions in groups, their productivity increases. Analogous results were obtained with individuals very low in dominance. Smelser concluded that dyads characterized by congruence of personality and role assignment performed more productively than did those characterized by incongruence. The results certainly apply to small groups as well as to dyads.

D. Watson (1971) performed a similar experiment, but considered the reinforcements available as a result of the group's activities and its power structure. He selected male undergraduates who were high or low in dominance and placed them in a group where they had high or low power in a task-oriented group. The results indicated that all the high-dominance subjects enjoyed the task situation, but the subjects who were both high in dominance and also in a high power position sent the most communications and most task-relevant communications in the group's assigned task. Watson concluded that personality, group structure, and the reinforcements available in the group affect an individual's performance in a group. Performance is best when the personality predisposition to enjoy certain types of reinforcements meshes with the rewards available in the group due to its activities and the individual's position in the group.

The congruence between a group's power structure and the personality of its members has also been shown to affect group productivity in another laboratory study in which male undergraduates worked together to assemble a model building (J.P. Wilson, Aronoff, and Messe 1975). A leader-follower group structure elicited more productivity from individuals with strong safety concerns; an egalitarian structure more from those who emphasized self-esteem.

The importance of matching member's personalities and group structure and process has also been documented in a recent review of studies of psychotherapeutic success (Baker 1979). A number of studies using both actual treatment groups and laboratory analogues suggest that individuals with internal locus of control orientations both prefer and function more effectively within less directive treatment modalities; treatment settings more controlled and directed by the therapist are the preferred mode for clients with external locus of control orientations.

The way in which a social worker can apply these findings depends upon whether the worker is starting with individuals for whom a group will be created or with a type of group for which members are to be selected. If practitioners start with individuals, for example, volunteers to be trained in patient care, then it behooves them to make an assessment of conditions the individuals find reinforcing, e.g., achievement, power, affiliation. Once this is determined, the worker should then create a group that offers opportunity to obtain those rewards and, if at all possible, assign the individuals group positions that do not conflict with their personality predisposition. On the other hand, if a group is already under way and additional members are sought, for example, a planning committee for a new social program, the practitioner would do well to select members whose personality needs would be met by the group's activities. For example, if a potential member desires to be well liked and is seeking companionship, a task-focused planning group that offers few opportunities for socializing would probably be inappropriate. Similarly, an individual with high achievement motivation is likely to be dissatisfied in most cases with a group focused on interpersonal relationships. The issue of whether only individuals who gain gratification from controlling others should be put in positions of leadership will be discussed in greater detail in the section on leadership to follow. At this point it can be said that the findings of Watson and Smelser indicate that such a match is likely to optimize productivity of the group. The worker will have to decide whether that is the major criterion to be considered in assigning members to group positions.

CHAPTER TEN

LEADERSHIP IN GROUPS

Leadership can be defined as the use of power to influence others for the purpose of performing a shared task. It must be differentiated from power, which refers to the potential for influencing others. A powerful person, for example, a strong boy in a gang, may rarely exert his influence but so long as it is believed that he is capable of influencing others when he chooses to, he has power. Unless he uses that power to influence others, however, he is not a leader. This suggests that social workers meeting natural groups for the first time, e.g., friendship groups, work groups, clubs, may not be able to assess correctly who the powerful members are; those individuals may choose not to use their potential for influence on that occasion. In sum, not all powerful people choose to exert leadership, but all leaders must have some source of power.

Practitioners working with groups, especially groups of facilitators of change, need to understand how different leadership roles are likely to affect the group's performance, how leaders develop in groups, and how stable patterns of leadership (as well as communication and liking structures in groups) affect members' satisfaction and performance. Each of these topics is discussed in this chapter, and it concludes by linking research and theory on leadership to that on the sources of social influence in interpersonal relationships, as previously discussed in chapter 6.

THEORIES OF LEADERSHIP

TASK AND SOCIO-EMOTIONAL SPECIALISTS

Extensive research, especially by Bales (1966) and Bales and Slater (1955), has shown that two specialists tend to develop in newly formed groups, each of whom performs one of the two essential functions all systems must perform, the instrumental function and the expressive function. The instrumental task leader will tend to initiate action, keep the members focused on the goal, organize the group, and emphasize the production of a product. The socioemotional leader who meets the expressive needs of the group will tend to be sensitive to the feelings of others, mediate disputes, encourage and support other members, and relieve tension with humor. Based on observational analysis of interactions among group members, Bales and Slater described the process of role differentiation that occurs in groups and results in leadership differentiation along task and socioemotional dimensions (Burke 1967). Any group's attempt to reach a goal through coordinated activity leads to tension and hostility, for when one person engages in the task, another is denied the opportunity; in reaching decisions, some ideas are selected and others rejected. Thus, there must be some departure from equality of participation. When there is inequality, the person who is highly active in the task area is the primary source of change and of tension and is consequently the target of some hostility. It is this individual's action which deprives others the opportunity to act and forces them to adjust their behavior and ideas. Bales presents several possible explanations for this phenomenon. Among them is the likelihood that any person who takes the lead in finding solutions to problems will threaten some values held by other members and provoke some disturbance. Another explanation offered is that it is difficult to make substantial contributions in small groups without talking a great deal. Indeed, much research suggests that the best way to become a leader of a group is to talk more than other members (Zander 1979). Yet this may be resented by others as a threat to their own status and a frustration of their own desire to talk.

Because the person most active in the task area, the task leader, is the principal source of tension, that individual is unlikely to be effective in resolving the tension. Someone else must assume that function. The result is therefore the development of task and socioemotional role differentiation. This tendency is a result of the social processes common to all social systems. It is not the result of gross differences between members or upon any particular task demand. Bales (1966) himself, however, described a set of conditions under which the task leaders would not be disliked, that is when the task leaders received more communications than they sent, or in Bales' terminology, when the task leaders had a high feedback ratio. Further, for task leaders with a high feedback ratio there was no relationship between how much the leaders talked and how much they were disliked by other members. For those with low feedback ratios, however, the more they talked, the more they were disliked. Bales concedes that on rare occasions "a great man" will emerge who will fill both roles, task leader and socioemotional leader. Such individuals are very unusual, however.

Verba (1961) disagreed with Bales' conclusion and suggested three factors that may have led to the repeated research findings that "great men" are rare and that role differentiation takes place with different task and socioemotional leaders arising. According to Verba, these studies are typically conducted on college campuses and the values commonly held by undergraduates make them hostile to instrumental, directive behavior. Other adults may hold different values. In addition, the task in laboratory groups is set by the experimenter rather than by the group members; under these conditions, the members are likely to react negatively to any task actions. Finally, in groups where there are no external sources for legitimating leadership, the emergent leaders must prove themselves to their groups and must make use of every opportunity to validate their positions. They must engage in task-relevant activities almost continuously, and in so doing, they violate the expectations of group members, and tend to alienate other members. This situation creates socioemotional problems, which are relieved by other persons, and a differentiation along task and socioemotional lines is created. On the other hand, legitimate leaders would have time and energy to engage in supportive activities, would thereby create fewer socioemotional problems, and there would be less hostility toward them. Little or no role differentiation would ever emerge.

Burke's (1967) research identified a condition that mediated the development of differential leaders in a university laboratory research investigation. When the undergraduates participating felt the task given to their group was legitimate, there was little differentiation between the task and socioemotional leadership, probably because the task activities of the leader were not resented. When the task was not seen as legitimate, the situation described by Verba as arising in a laboratory developed, and task-relevant acts elicited hostility from other members. Waxler and Mishler's (1970) research on family groups suggests it is the artificial conditions of the laboratory studies that foster the development of two leaders.

Thus it appears that there need not be a separation of leadership roles into one that is focused on the goal and one on the feelings of group members. Rather, specific conditions in the group foster this differentiation; such differentiation is not inherent in the group process. Whether the emergence of a task and a socioemotional leader in groups must occur or merely often occurs need not be a prime concern to practicing social workers. The important points are to be alert to the possibility of two leaders, and when dual leadership does occur, to help develop cooperation between the dual leaders. The group can be destroyed if the two leaders are antagonistic toward one another or attempt to sabotage one another's efforts. If the social worker observes that such rivalry is developing, strategies are needed to establish harmonious relationships between the two leaders. This may be achieved by meeting with them separately and discussing the problem or by asking the two to work on a specific task whose success depends upon their cooperation. If the outcomes are sufficiently gratifying to the two leaders, the antagonism may diminish as they find their goals and interests are identical.

The finding that task leaders with high feedback ratios are not disliked has major implications for social work practice in groups. If the worker observes that an inordinate amount of tension is being generated by task leaders who give far more communications than they receive, the practitioner might discuss the situation with these leaders in private, and/or proceed to reinforce any indication of their talking less in the group and listening more. In addition, the importance of the workers' encouraging more feedback to their own behavior should not be overlooked. Verba's observations about the differential behaviors of leaders who are accepted by group members and leaders who are not also are relevant to social work practice. The warning is clear that if the worker imposes a leader on the group when the group does not view the worker as appropriately possessing that authority, that individual is likely to generate hostility. It is possible that the situation cannot be avoided, for example, if such an appointment is essential for the self-esteem of the imposed leader or if the task requires an individual with specific skills to lead the effort. Resentment might also be expected when a group member takes on a leadership position without legitimate sanction from the group. In those instances, the worker had best be prepared for tension in the group and be ready to enact the role of socioemotional leader until some other group member steps into the position.

THE CONTINGENCY THEORY OF LEADERSHIP

Bales (1966) suggested that there is one ideal type of leader, the "great man", who has the qualities of both an instrumental and expressive leader. R. K. White and Lippitt (1960) also suggested that one type of leader is always best—in their view, the one who is democratic. It has been questioned, however, whether or not there is one type of ideal leader. More recent extensive and sophisticated research by Fiedler (1967; 1978) and others using his model (Chemers and Skrzypek 1972) suggests that there is no ideal leader; rather, the type that is most effective depends upon the match between the characteristics of the situation and of the leader; a leader may be good in one situation and poor in another. When conditions are very good or very bad in a small face-to-face group, a task leader appears to be most effective, with effectiveness defined in terms of the goal attainment of the group. In intermediate situations, however, the socioemotional leader is most effective. Fiedler used three dimensions to assess how good or bad a situation was: 1) the position power of the leader, or the leader's control of resources; 2) the clarity of the task; and 3) the members' liking, respect, support and loyalty for the leader. Presumably in "good" conditions, where leaders have considerable control and influence, internal harmony will prevail without much assistance from the leaders. Hence, leaders in these situations can focus on goal attainment. In "bad" situations, leaders may be unable to establish internal harmony no matter how sensitive and considerate they may be. Thus, such efforts are wasted. It is only when the situation is moderately strained and the leader has only moderate control that the socioemotional approach on the part of the leader is most effective. Since the effectiveness of a group is contingent upon an appropriate match between the leader and the situation, Fiedler's theory is called the contingency model of leader effectiveness (Fiedler 1967).

In over 300 experimental tests of this theory with laboratory and real-world groups, Fiedler and others used a relatively simple technique for determining whether a leader was task-oriented or interpersonally oriented. The method involved administering a bipolar adjective scale to the leaders in which they are asked to describe the one person with whom it was most difficult to work. The score obtained was interpreted as reflecting a motivation toward task versus interpersonal success in groups. If the leaders rated their least preferred coworker (LPC) quite negatively, they were considered to be task-oriented and to have a high motivation to achieve; if they rated their least preferred coworker relatively favorably, they were considered to be primarily interpersonally oriented and to have a high affiliation motivation (Fiedler 1968). In Fiedler's view, these are basic personality predispositions and are not readily altered. It is therefore better to engineer the situation to dovetail with the predisposition of the leader than to try to modify the leader's interaction style in a given situation. Engineering the situation would involve either an external agent, such as a social worker or management consultant, modifying the power of the leader's position, and/or altering the clarity of the task, and/or doing something to change the members liking of the leader, or an external agent training the leader to effect these kinds of situational changes (Fiedler, Chemers, and Mahar 1976).

It is difficult to imagine a social worker attempting to make a group situation worse than it is, but it may be possible to intervene in such a way that an unfavorable situation is made somewhat more favorable when the leader is person-oriented or to make a moderately favorable situation very favorable when the leader is known to be task-oriented. For example, the worker can make efforts to restructure the task so that it is very clear what needs to be done. Committees often start out with relatively unstructured goals and/or unstructured paths to an agreed-upon goal; these ambiguities could be reduced. It may also be possible to increase the power of the leader by giving that person more decisions to make, such as how the reinforcements available are to be distributed to group members, or by encouraging the leader to acquire enhanced expertise. It may be more difficult to increase the members' liking and respect for the leader but by expressing liking and respect themselves, practitioners can model a different attitude toward the leader. Following the modeling with differential approval of members when they indicate a positive feeling toward the leader may help increase the attractiveness of that individual. Because members are more likely to endorse their leader when the group is successful, when members get more rewards than the leader, or when the leader is not permanantly fixed in office (Michener and Lawler 1975), the worker could also attempt to modify these factors. The leader could also be given training in providing positive feedback to members' comments as a way to increase their liking for the leader. If these approaches do not work and a change in leader is not possible, the worker may try to alter the composition of the group by adding members who have similar interests and background as the leader. This strategy may enhance the popularity of the leader.

It is important to emphasize that, under Fiedler's theory and research, changes in the situational control and influence available to leaders must be matched with the leader's personality. For example, relationship-oriented leaders enhance group performance more under conditions of moderate control than conditions of high control. Thus, it would not be wise to seek to enhance the position power, member support, or task clarity for a relationship-oriented leader in a moderately favorable situation. It would, however, be helpful to increase the favorableness of a situation from a moderate to a high control level for a task-oriented leader. Fiedler (1978) describes two task situations of moderate control that are particularly germane to facilitator of change groups. First are situations in which the tasks require free expression of members' opinions, attitudes, and information, such as policy or decision-making committees or organizations in which leaders act as coordinators rather than controllers of group activities. In such situations it is not surprising that the relationship-oriented leader who uses tact, is sensitive to others' ideas, and can act to reconcile members' conflicting views is effective, whereas the task-oriented leader who is enforces structure and control and is less concerned with interpersonal relations is not a very effective group leader. Second are situations in which the leader has position power or control over rewards and punishments and the task goal and plan is clear, but the group is not supportive of the leader, such as certain work groups or agency staff situations which are other instances of moderate control. An agency director may be seen as having legitimate power and the agency goals and procedures may be clear but if the staff do not support and like the director, the leader would have to be quite tactful and sensitive to avoid the group engaging in subtle sabotage. A task-oriented leader would be less likely to attend to the interpersonal problems than a relationship-oriented leader and hence would be less likely to achieve group effectiveness.

If given a choice about groups but not leaders, the worker should try to create or select a group that has characteristics meshing with the leader's predispositions, rather than try to change a group situation already in existence. For example, when composing a group of facilitators of change, if the worker knows that the likely leader is not very tolerant of divergent opinions (a low LPC person), it would be important to create favorable conditions by selecting other members who are similar to that individual in age, ethnicity, or interests and by structuring the task so that it is as unambiguous as possible. An example of an ambiguous task would be learning how to improve the relationships between caregivers and care recipients. An unambiguous task would be learning how to increase the care-recipients' independence in dressing and feeding themselves. On the other hand, the worker may be involved with an on-going group and the question of selecting a new leader or asking a member to serve as leader may arise. In this instance, the worker would do well to assess the three dimensions of the situation incorporated into Fiedler's theory and to assess potential leaders as to their expressive or instrumental tendencies. The worker may not wish to use Fiedler's instrument, but it is not too difficult to create an ambiguous situation and observe whether the potential leader selects a task to work on or prefers to socialize with the others.

THE DEVELOPMENT OF LEADERSHIP

Some investigators have been concerned about how leadership could be elicited and nurtured in individuals who did not move readily into leadership positions. The general conclusion that can be drawn from the findings is that it is possible to create group leaders; they are not necessarily born. This point is particularly relevant to social work practitioners because there are many situations when it is desirable to foster leadership in someone rather than to passively accept the leader who emerges in the group. Leadership development may be necessary to achieve intervention goals. For example, a teacher who recently was reprimanded by the principal may need some self-confidence to function effectively in a training group. There are also occasions when the worker may wish to foster leadership in a particular person for instrumental reasons. An example of this situation is one in which the leader who is emerging is destructive to the group's cohesiveness or wishes to use the group for purposes other than the group goal, perhaps to advance a career. Another member may have the potential for restoring the group's direction but is hesitant to do so, possibly because of intimidation by the dominant participant. Another instance in which the worker might wish to help a member become a leader is when the group appears to be generally apathetic and one individual has the potential to enliven the interactions Finally, to ensure an egalitarian ambiance in a heterogeneous group where there are differences in ethnicity, race, sex, or economic status, the worker might wish to have the leadership position rotated among all members, or at the minimum, be certain that leadership does not remain confined to one subgroup.

EXPERIMENTAL MODIFICATIONS OF LEADERSHIP BEHAVIORS

There are strong indications that merely appointing someone to a central position in the group or to the leader's position will result in that individual's behaving like a leader and the other members' perceiving that person to be the leader. In one of the early studies of leadership creation, Bavelas et al. (1965) showed that by reinforcing a low-status group member with a green light for speaking up and by symbolically punishing other members with a red light for participating, the low-status member was perceived as a valuable member of the group with high leadership ability. In addition, the low-status person enjoyed the experience. Hastorf (1970) performed a similar study using signal lights and then turned them off for a subsequent discussion. It was found that while the feedback signals were used the originally quiet participant became one of the most dominant contributors and others rated him as most influential. Furthermore many of these changes continued after the signal lights ceased. The researcher interpreted the findings as the result of the boost in self-esteem which the quiet man received when he spoke and others listened. Thus, it appeared that positive feedback about effectiveness in communication led to increased self-ratings of leadership ability and effectiveness. Nydegger (1975) replicated the 1965 study of Bavelas and colleagues, and discovered that reinforcing other members for agreeing with the created leader resulted in members giving the created leader high ratings for leadership, whereas symbolically punishing them for agreeing resulted in low ratings. He concluded that leaders function in some way to increase or decrease costs to other members. The link to social work practice is readily made. A good strategy for fostering leadership is to personally reinforce participation by the individual involved, to avoid reinforcing other members for participating, and to reinforce other members for agreeing with the "leader." It is significant that the self-ratings of the created leaders rose in the Bavelas and colleagues' (1965) study, suggesting that it was not merely other members whose attitudes change but the "leaders" attitudes as well.

Waxler and Mishler (1970) found that by merely placing persons low in "ascendence" in a central position and placing persons high in "ascendence" in a peripheral position, as determined by the number of people with whom the individual could communicate, it was possible over time to alter significantly the activity levels of both types of individuals. In the first group task, the personality variable (ascendence) was the most important variable, but by the third task, the activity of the person low in ascendence in a central group position was significantly greater than that of the high ascendence individual in a peripheral position. The conclusion was reached that over a short period of time, the role demand effects predominated over the personal effects in determining behavior in a group. In this case, no manipulation of reinforcements by the experimenter was necessary to create a leader. The role demands were sufficient. Thus, if the practitioner can develop a situation in which the demands upon the individual slated for the position of leader are considerable, differential reinforcement of the behaviors of the members of the group may be unnecessary. The expectations associated with the role are sufficiently powerful to alter the behavior of the "leader" as well as the "followers." It certainly would not hurt to express approval of the new leader's behavior, but the Waxler and Mishler study suggests it may not be necessary so long as the role demands in the group are clear and strongly require certain behaviors of leadership. Examples of clear role demands are expectations that the leader will have an agenda for each meeting, will give out assignments, will review the work that had been performed the previous week, and will summarize what was covered during the session.

Similar to the findings of Bavelas and colleagues (1965), Nydegger (1975), and Waxler and Mishler (1970), were the results of the investigation by Beckhouse et al. (1975). These researchers found that where subjects were "pushed to lead, they led" even when not predisposed that way initially. When subjects were pushed to follow, persons predisposed to lead followed, that is, they increased their socioemotional activity. Beckhouse and colleagues investigated the variable of "the responsive behavior of followers," one of the three factors proposed by Hollander and Julian (1968) as interacting to determine who leads. The other two factors were the personality aspects of the leader relevant to goal attainment, and the situational context. The approach Beckhouse and colleagues used to study follower responsiveness was to take the perspective of altercasting, or determining a reciprocal role partner's behavior by one's own behavior. It was reasoned that the formal position one occupies in a group does not completely determine one's role performance. Rather, role performance is also affected by how group members act to cast the role of others (alters). Leaders are altercast through pressure to meet the role expectations of the followers. Research has shown that leaders tend to meet the role demands of groups regardless of their own personalities. Although established leaders have some flexibility in departing from norms, that is, they have some idiosyncratic credit (Hollander 1958), by and large, leaders follow followers. Beckhouse and colleagues tested the hypothesis that when the stakes are low, the personal predisposition of leaders who do not see themselves as leaders will predominate. Since there is little motivation to participate actively in an uncomfortable situation of role incongruity, the nonleader is likely to be passive or withdraw. However, when stakes are high, it was hypothesized that personality factors would not be important. That is, passivity or withdrawal is less likely when nonleaders have more vested interest in task success. To test the hypotheses, Beckhouse and colleagues used sixty-four subjects, all undergraduate male students. Willingness to accept the leadership role was measured by a self-concept questionnaire. The subjects were dichotomized into those who saw themselves as leaders (e.g., agreed with the statement, "I enjoy trying to work out different approaches to solving problems and getting the group to go along with them") and those who did not. The second variable, the stake factor, was introduced by having the students' respective professors tell them at the beginning of the semester that they had to participate in outside work sessions as part of the course requirements. Half of the subjects were told that their effort in these sessions would be graded and would count for one of the six papers for the course. The other half were simply told that their work was part of their course requirements and no actual grade would be given.

The final variable, the direction of reciprocal altercasting, was a within-subject measure and the hypothesis was that altercasting would affect leadership behaviors regardless of personality. Each subject took part in two work sessions with two different students in each session; all four were confederates of the experiment. The subject was always told by the experimenter that he was to assume the leadership in the group and be responsible for task completion. In one session, the confederates were directed to altercast the subject into a superordinate or leader role. In the other session the confederates altercast the subject into the alternate subordinate role. Thus each subject experienced both forms of behavior on the part of the confederates, with random variation in which type of altercasting was first. The sessions were taperecorded and assessed by two judges who were ignorant of the experimental design.

The results confirmed earlier studies in the area: appointed leaders exhibited behaviors complementary to the pattern of altercasting by their followers. When pressed to lead, the subjects led, asserting greater authority, increasing task activity, and reducing socioemotional activity while increasing their emphasis on the group task. There was no difference between subjects who saw themselves as leaders and those who did not. When confronted with followers who attempted to take over the show, the appointed leaders shifted their behaviors to those related to group cohesion and increased their socioemotional activity while decreasing their overall activity. This caused some discomfort for the natural leaders, who expressed their feelings by acting somewhat nasty. As hypothesized, in the higher stake condition, the subjects "hustled" more, showing greater overall activity level. However, the higher activity did not come from increased directiveness as hypothesized but from more positive socioemotional activity and more questions about the task. In general, stake was not as powerful a variable as predicted.

The most pronounced behavioral adjustment to role incongruity was made by the appointed leaders who did not see themselves as enjoying leadership and who were confronted by passive followers. To adapt to the situation they enormously increased their activity in the task question category, particularly in asking for suggestions and opinions. It was an effort to draw out their followers. The nonleaders in the appointed leader role also increased their task answers but less than did the natural leaders. Thus the nonleaders appeared to be negotiating for a comfortable role in the situation where an authority figure gave them leadership responsibilities but their followers did not treat them as leaders. The findings also reflected the lack of symmetry between natural leaders and natural nonleaders. "Those who often lead find it easier to follow than those who usually follow find it to lead" (Beckhouse et al. 1975:566).

This study was discussed in detail not because it is likely that social work practitioners can make all the group members confederates in pushing one person into leadership behaviors, but rather, because it provides evidence that persons who do not see themselves as leaders can function effectively in that position if forced to do so (or at least male undergraduates can do so). Unfortunately, the study was not replicated with other populations but until negative evidence is offered, it is probably safe for practitioners to assume that unless strong evidence exists to the contrary, virtually all group members have the potential for functioning as leaders in the appropriate situation.

THE APPOINTMENT OF LEADERS

As was implied in the discussion of the study of Beckhouse and colleagues (1975), leadership can be seen as a series of transactions between leaders and followers. Hollander and Julian (1970) also propose that leadership is a form of exchange where the leader fulfills the followers' expectations, helps to achieve group goals, provides a rewarding resource for others and in exchange receives status, esteem, and greater influence. This view is in keeping with Nydegger's (1975) observation that leaders must provide rewards and reduce costs for followers. Hollander and Julian performed several studies to examine the effects of three variables on perceptions of leaders' legitimacy: source of authority, competence, and motivations regarding the task and the needs of the followers. The findings were that the source of authority, that is appointed or elected, made no difference. However, both the competence and motivation of the leader were significantly related to the followers desire to have the leader continue in that role, to be their spokesperson: in sum, to their acceptance of the leader as legitimate. It was also found that groups make more demands on elected leaders than on appointed leaders. The researchers explained this finding by saying that the group feels it has greater control and responsibility in the case of elected leaders. Alternative leaders will be considered for the future if the present one does not facilitate group goals. Thus the elected leader must be successful to get a high rating. But when the leader is appointed, the group felt it was not in control and gave these individuals high ratings if they were either competent or if the group succeeded. Similar results were found in a study that also varied the sex composition of three-person groups who jointly completed a puzzle task (Eskilson and Wiley 1976). Whether the leader was appointed by chance—drawing straws—or by competence—supposedly derived from test scores and special information on the puzzle task—did not affect the group's performance or the members' choice of a future group leader; instead the leader's behavior in the group was the critical variable. The leader's behavior, in turn, was complexly related to the sex of the leader and the other members.

The most salient application of these two sets of findings to social work practice is that in situations when the group perceives the social worker as legitimately conferring authority the worker need not fear to appoint a leader who is competent or is motivated to achieve the group's goal and is considerate of members' feelings. The members will accept this individual as a legitimate leader and be less harsh on this person than on a leader they had voted upon.

Another finding from the Hollander and Julian studies is also relevant. Leaders who had a strong sense of legitimacy, that is, believed they had a strong endorsement from the group to continue as the leader, deviated more from group norms and said less to the group when deviating than leaders who did not feel strongly endorsed. This suggests to workers that they should anticipate that competent leaders will act independently at times and will not always follow the group's norms. Leader compliance cannot be taken for granted. In essence, these effective leaders who have helped their groups to achieve the groups' goals, and who have conformed to the groups' norms as a sign of their motivation to belong to the groups, earn credits which may be drawn upon in deviating from the norms. These credits are labeled "idiosyncrasy credits"; competent and effective leaders acquire such credits and use them to support nonconformity (Hollander and Julian 1970). Rose (1972) described idiosyncrasy credit in somewhat different terms; he referred to it as the "fruits of high status" and delineated the fruits as protection from punishment or loss of status for deviating from the group's norms. Such protection is not usually available to low-status members. On the other hand, it was found that high-status members were punished less for minor deviations from the norms than were middle-status persons, but were punished more for major deviations (Wiggins, Dill, and Schwartz 1968).

All of the above indicates that the occupant of the leader's position does not behave in the same way as do ordinary group members, and is not treated in the same way. Clearly, practitioners must be aware of who is the group's leader and be prepared for differential behavior.

OVERCOMING STATUS EFFECTS ON LEADERSHIP

When discussing status of group members, it must be pointed out that members do not enter groups with equal status. The differential status structure, that is the differential ranks in prestige that members have outside of the group in the larger community, come with them into the group meeting. For example, certain occupations, ethnic groups, races, and educational levels are accorded more prestige than others in our society. The theory of status characteristics and expectation (J. Berger, Cohen, and Zelditch 1966) posits that the power and prestige order in a newly constituted group of high-and low-status members comes to parallel the relative ranking on a status characteristic initially held by members of the group. Berger and colleagues cite a body of empirical research showing that initial differences in social status produce a power and prestige order resembling the initial ranking in new group tasks even when competence at the task has no relationship to the status characteristic. The theory suggests that group members use the knowledge of each other's status to evaluate probable competence when other bases for estimating competence are lacking. Members of some minority ethnic and racial groups are ranked lower in status in the larger American society than others, and the theory indicates that this ranking will continue to obtain in heterogeneous groups.

An in-depth study was conducted to determine what interventions were needed to produce a competence or leadership ranking which bore no relationship to race of member in biracial groups of junior-high-school-aged males (E.G. Cohen and Roper 1972). The conclusion was that both black and white males had to be clearly informed about the greater competence of the blacks on a previous task before as many blacks as whites would be selected as leaders when the group worked on a new task. In addition, when the blacks were informed that the self-confident verbal behavior they displayed on the old task was relevant to the new task, the effect was most pronounced. For white students not made aware of the blacks' abilities on the previous tasks, the ranking of leadership and assignment of competence in the new situation resulted in duplication of the status ranking in the outside world. Cohen and Roper concluded that assigning a high degree of competence to low-status individuals (blacks) on a general performance characteristic will modify the effects of the low status on a new task—that is the expectations for competence would be raised—only when both high- and low-status group members (whites and blacks blacks) are treated. Further, spelling out the relevance between the training and the new task further decreases the probability of high-status, that is white, dominance.

Lockheed and Hall (1976) conducted several studies which indicated that sex is also a status characteristic and that the lower societal status of women has effects similar to those of race on group behavior. In support of the theory of status characteristics are the findings that women show less activity in mixed groups, have less influence, and initiate fewer task-oriented acts but initiate more acts in the socioemotional area. Lockheed and Hall proved there is nothing inherent in women that impels them to behave in this way: in all-female groups, women initiated as many task-related acts as did males in all-male groups.

To overcome the sex-role socialization with which members enter groups, Lockheed and Hall gave some women experience in a task and then put them into mixed-sex groups. The result was an increase in the task-relevant initiations by these women. There was even some carryover into another situation where these women again were more active and initiated more task-related acts. Lockheed and Hall concluded that when expectations for competence are established within a group, they generalize to new tasks, although in a weaker fashion. They suggested a series of steps to lessen male dominance in mixed-sex groups where diffuse status characteristics would structure the power and prestige ordering of a group unless something is done to interfere with the status diffusion process. We enumerate these steps because they may have relevance for any situation in which some members enter a group with a lower status than other members; the suggestions are not limited to differential status due to sex differences.

To overcome status differentials in groups, one could: 1. State that the low-status members have competence in areas relevant to the task. 2. State that the high-status members do not have competence in those areas. 3. Role model influencing behavior for the low-status members. 4. Reinforce competence behaviors by low-status persons. These steps can be accomplished within a particular group. More long-range and extensive interventions would be required to disassociate particular statuses, such as that of females or poor blacks, for example, from attributions of incompetence. It might be appropriate to attack the status differentiation process in grade schools, where children may learn expectations about links between competence and particular statuses.

A specific scenario suggested by Lockheed and Hall (1976) by which women can succeed in becoming competent leaders of mixed-sex groups is for the supervisor (if it is an occupational group) to create opportunities for women to demonstrate their competence before men and to provide opportunities for public recognition of the women's performance. Cohen and Roper would surely endorse this approach. Without doubt, this intervention technique has far wider application and can readily be enacted by social workers involved with groups containing members of differential status in the wider society (e.g., different educational levels, different ages, and different racial groups.) Similarly, the other suggestions described can be implemented to some extent by practitioners who desire to foster leadership, especially task leadership, in a member of low status. The worker can tell the group how skilled the low-status member is in some area the group is concerned about, for example, art, sewing, coping with social agencies, budgeting, or first aid remedies. If necessary, the worker can train the low-status members in relevant areas by modeling and applying differential reinforcements. It is unlikely that the practitioner would wish to denigrate any group member's abilities but this may be unnecessary if the abilities of the low-status member are stressed and the worker reinforces competent behaviors by those persons in the presence of other members. Withholding reinforcement from the high-status members at this point may be sufficient.

Rose (1972) suggests a very similar strategy in discussing low-status youngsters in children's groups. He too suggests reinforcing the performance of low-status children in highly valued behaviors if the activity is in the child's repertoire, and withholding reinforcement from higher status members. However, as Lockheed and Hall (1976) imply, this may be insufficient and it may be necessary to train the low-status person to carry out valued activities, particularly activities which no one else in the group performs. This eliminates the necessity of ignoring a similar performance by a high-status person. Rose offers the following example of employing this technique. "At one meeting the activity was a quiz on wild animals. The therapist tutored Wilbur on this subject several weeks before. Since the group valued intellectual accomplishments they responded by praising Wilbur, who had frequently been called a 'retard' at past meetings" (170). Although this example occurred in a treatment-oriented group, the same principle could easily be used in facilitators of change groups, e.g., a prison guard whose leadership abilities have been ignored by a planning committee could be provided advance information on a forthcoming topic.

If the skill the low-status person possesses or can be trained in is not highly valued by the group, Rose suggests using that skill to earn the group a highly desired reward. Even though the skill is not valued, the reward is. For example, a group that values sports may earn a trip to a baseball game by the efforts to improve his grades of one low-status person who is not sports-oriented. The practitioner working with adults, particularly in socioeducational groups, cannot use the precise methodology described by Rose, but adaptations are possible. For example, if a low-status group member manages to get her children to bed at a reasonable hour this can be used as the basis of a group celebration, for example, a pot-luck dinner. It may take several such strategies to transform that individual into a leader in the group, but the point to be emphasized is that the worker is not confined to sitting back pasively and hoping the group will begin to respect a particular member more than they do. The worker can intervene to alter the reinforcements available to group members, can apply differential reinforcement, can model an attitude of respect, can offer individual instruction to some members, and can even modify the activities of the group so that they focus on the skills and abilities that the low-status person already possesses.

STRUCTURE OF LEADERSHIP AND OTHER GROUP STRUCTURES

Before proceeding to discuss leadership structure of the group, it is important to note that the professional working with a group is not usually considered a member of the group. Although a social worker is physically present in direct service or facilitators of change groups, he or she is not, professionally speaking, a member of the group. Rather, practitioners are usually partially removed from the groups to whom they relate as helpers (G. Wilson 1959). The practitioner may initially function as a leader exercising influence relevant to the attainment of the group's goals; as the group begins to stabilize, however, some members will emerge as natural leaders or the worker may encourage some members to take leadership roles. In either case, it is these individuals that will be discussed below. The worker will be looked upon as an "ex-officio" member of the group. We recognize that in certain staff groups, for example, a social worker may indeed be a group member and not in a special helping role. Since that is not the situation of major concern here this specific circumstance will not be discussed.

Several references have been made previously to group structures, for example, status structures, but no definition of structure has been offered thus far. For our purposes, a structure refers to a pattern of interrelationships at one point in time that can be diagramed. This is similar to Zander's definition: "The structure of a group is composed of its parts (persons, roles, offices, sub-units) and the relationships among these" (1979:446). An alternate definition of group structure is the set of relatively stable attributes of the group in terms of which the group can be analyzed or described (Rose 1972). Other slightly different definitions include the pattern of habitual, organized ways group members interact (D. Watson 1971), and the regularities that develop over time in the kinds of interactions that exist in interpersonal situations (Garvin and Glasser 1974b).

The theme of stable patterns cuts across all these definitions. Among the group structures most relevant to practitioners are the patterns of interpersonal liking or sociometric structures, the patterns in which group members communicate or communication structures, the distribution of leadership functions or the influence (leadership) structure, and the pattern of rules which members accept or the normative structure. Structures can refer to positions in the groups such as the authority structure, to the pattern of liking among individuals such as the sociometric structure, or to the pattern among the norms in the normative structure. (The structure of a norm or set of norms will be described in the following section as part of the overall discussion of norm enforcement.) The difference between a pattern of positions and a pattern of persons can be illustrated with the communication structure. If the pattern or structure can be diagramed by drawing one circle representing the group president, another the group treasurer, and a third the group secretary, the structure is the formal communication structure and refers to positions regardless of individuals occupying those positions. If, on the other hand, one can only describe the pattern in terms of particular individuals, an informal communication structure is being discussed. Here, positions are insufficient to describe the structure. Communication structures can be wheel shaped:  , circular:  , all channel:  , chain: , and so forth. Authority or leadership structures can be hierarchical:  , horizontal:  , or anarchical:  . One could also diagram other interpersonal relationships such as who confides in whom (the confidence structure) or who can affect the outcomes of whom (the power structure). When power is acknowledged as legitimate, it typically becomes associated with a position, not a particular person, and is referred to as authority. Thus one would talk about the authority of a president but the power of his righthand man. It is also possible to rank individual members of a group in various dimensions such as wealth, intelligence, education, best ideas, and prestige, to produce a ranking structure. The fact that a person's out-of-group status can affect the group's functioning has already been discussed.

Although the different structures can be defined independently, they are usually not unrelated. For example, positions in a sociometric structure tend to be related to positions in a power structure. Thibaut and Kelley (1959) have pointed out that persons who are *least* involved in personal relationships have the most power to affect the outcomes for the other persons, for they may leave the relationship at any time. The communication structure is also related to the sociometric structure and power structure. Kelley (1951) referred to communication as substitute locomotion—your words and thoughts go where your feet would like to go. One study of social workers, psychologists, and psychiatrists showed that people in small groups tend to talk to those they perceive as more powerful than themselves and not to those they perceive as less powerful (Hurwitz, Zander, and Hymovitch 1968).

The structures found among positions in a group or among individuals in a group are important to social workers because first, the group's structure affects its output, and second, a person's location in a structure is an important determinant of his or her feelings of self-worth and attraction to the group for any particular location in a social structure offers differential opportunities for gaining certain types of reinforcement. For example, those near the center of the communication structure tend to like their group; those away from the center do not, for the central position offers rewards to those who gain pleasure from influencing others. It has been shown that when the rewards offered by a particular position in a social structure mesh with the personality characteristics of the occupant, the result can be an enhancement of the satisfaction obtained from the group, and a morale booster for that individual (D. Watson 1971). For example, if the coordinator of a group is the kind of person who finds directing others rewarding, the net effect is enjoyment of the situation. If that individual is low on dominance, however, and high on the need for affiliation, the outcome is likely to be quite different. This phenomenon is an illustration of the larger issue of person-role fit which has been explored considerably, by Veroff and Feld (1970) for example, in the social psychological literature. The person-role fit concept focuses on the articulation between the demands of a role and the characteristics of the individual who is performing that role.

It is significant that a child's place in the various structures in a classroom has been found to affect the youngster's achievement in school. In concurrence with Lockheed and Hall (1976), E. G. Cohen (1972) reported that females and black and brown children were less active and participated less in class than did white males. She attributed this finding to their lower status in the larger community. The expectations of both the individual children and of the teachers that these youngsters will be less involved in classroom activities were thereby fulfilled. The result is that the achievement status of the youngsters paralleled their social status. Since teachers demand more of the high achievers and reward them more (Brophy and Good 1970), the achievement differences become accentuated. The achievement status of students even affects teacher expectations of the youngsters in nonacademic areas, so that once again the child with the initial low status is confronted with reduced expectations. Sadly, Cohen (1972) also found that teachers appear to go along with the sociometric status of the students and promote the academic success of popular students to avoid open warfare with a student status system. Cohen summarizes the situation by saying " . . . learning partly depends on the formal and informal structure of the classroom. Depending on the nature of the status systems in the classroom and depending upon the location of the actor in those various status systems, different kinds of teacher-student interaction will take place, and different degrees of learning" (449).

Cohen's warning to teachers is particularly relevant to practitioners working with groups of facilitators of change where the learning of new content is one of the major purposes of the group, as in training paraprofessionals or relatives to care for handicapped patients. Not only must social workers be sensitive to their own expectations about members who occupy a low status in the occupational or educational ranking systems of the country, the workers must also be prepared for reduced expectations about self-performance by these very persons. Such expectations cannot be permitted to remain intact if learning is to be maximized.

There is a direct causal linkage between group structures and group output and a social work practitioner may well focus on modifying group structures rather than individuals within the group, to have an impact on the group's effectiveness. Training one or two individuals to become more assertive in the group may help the group develop a more egalitarian communication structure and thereby enhance its effectiveness as more ideas are contributed to solve the problems. On the other hand, through differential reinforcement, the worker may increase the participation of all members and so make the communication structure more egalitarian. By engaging in both interventions, the worker may achieve the goal of a more egalitarian communication structure even more quickly than by using either strategy alone.

Group structures can be viewed as independent or dependent variables by the workers. Viewing structures as independent variables, one can better understand members' behaviors or feelings by knowing the group's positional, interpersonal, or normative structure. For example, when one member is the worker's link with the group, thus the center of the communication network, the worker can assume that member's attraction to the group is high. Viewing the structure as a dependent variable, the worker may try to modify the group structures by manipulating the variables that affect structures. Garvin and Glasser (1974b) listed four such strategies. 1. Altering the program for the task a group undertakes can establish a particular communication or power structure. For example, an activity might be selected that required a powerful leader to coordinate diverse member tasks. Alternatively, an activity that enables all members to share equally in the power distribution, all to engage in the same activity and to share the fruits of their efforts, such as collecting magazine articles on parenting, can be selected. 2. Using behavior modification techniques or differential reinforcements for the members can encourage or discourage behaviors such as participation in the discussion. The earlier discussion on creating leaders included suggestions for using behavioral techniques to alter the leadership structure. 3. Problem-solving strategies and logical reasoning can be employed when problems in group structure arise. The difficulty can be presented to the members, for example, that some members say virtually nothing at the meetings, and then through the problem-solving process discussed in the previous chapter, the group can try to solve the dilemma. Garvin and Glasser suggested that the group may decide rationally and purposively to employ operant conditioning procedures themselves, for example, to express pleasure when the nonparticipants do make comments, or may design a modification in the group's programs, for example, to assign each member a meeting in which that individual will discuss something that happened with their care recipient that week. 4. The composition of the group can also be changed to modify one or more of the group structures. This again can be group decision, or a decision of the practitioners themselves. Not only will adding or subtracting different personalities strongly affect what occurs in the group, but the addition or subtraction per se alters the size of the group—this has a powerful effect on member participation and satisfaction (Cartwright and Zander 1968). (The topic of group composition will be explored in detail in a later chapter when treatment groups are discussed.) In sum, group structure is one of the important mediating variables between group input and output and it should not be ignored.

LEADERSHIP AND SOCIAL INFLUENCE

Leadership has been defined as the exercise of influence relevant to a groups' goals, thus the concepts of leadership and influence are closely related. The discussion of social influence in chapter 6 is therefore applicable to an understanding of the power base of leaders. The reader is advised to review that chapter, thinking of group leaders as the influencing agents referred to throughout the discussion. The highlights of the discussion on social influence will be reviewed briefly below.

The fit is not perfect but one can translate two of Kelman's (1965) sources of power into the type of leaders described by Bales (1966) and Fiedler (1967). The clearest overlap is among the socioemotional leader (Bales), the leader who gives a high rating to his least preferred coworker (Fiedler), and Kelman's leader whose influence is based on attractiveness. The task leader in Bales' terminology and the leader giving a low rating to his least preferred coworker in Fiedler's work are similar to some extent to Kelman's influencing agent with means control who evokes compliance. There is no direct equivalent in the work of Bales or Fiedler for Kelman's influencing agent with credibility who is followed because the content of his or her ideas are sound and fit into the ideological schema of the person being influenced, although there is some overlap in as much as the task leader in Bales' schema is defined in part as the person in the group with the best ideas. It is possible, and this is highly speculative, that the reason this last type of leader described by Kelman does not emerge in small groups, which Kelman did not study, is that no one person consistently has the soundest ideas that fit into the members' ideological schemas in peer groups. Rather, credibility tends to shift, with the individual whose ideas are judged most sound from moment to moment being viewed as the leader. Such groups do exist and are referred to as colleagial relationships.

Two other researchers who have also written extensively about the basis of power are French and Raven (1968). They enumerate five bases of power, four of which are similar to the concepts utilized in the theories of Bales, Fiedler, and Kelman, that is, control of rewards, control of punishments, referent power or the power to evoke identification, and expert power. The fifth base listed by French and Raven, legitimacy, is not central to the analyses of the other theorists and will not be included in this discussion.

Finally, Thibaut and Kelley (1959) described in slightly different terms three types of social influence that operate to induce conformity to norms. They do not designate different names for the three types of agents of influence but merely refer to them as three "cases." The first case is one in which A controls B's behaviors by applying negative sanctions, thus reducing outcomes for B. This process requires active surveillance by A. Thibaut and Kelley call this influence process one of transforming fate control (A determines B's fate) into behavior control (A determines B's behavior) entirely by the use of negative sanctions. In the second case, tne agent (A) employs only positive sanctions to convert fate control over B into behavior control. Here monitoring is not needed—B can be counted on to present evidence of conformity to A in order to receive rewards. However, if A continues to provide rewards for B's conforming behavior, by the principle of association, ultimately A as a person will acquire reward value to B. B will begin to value what A values and a stable role relationship will develop. In the third case, B is under control from a task and receives rewards and costs from the task itself, for example, by being correct. The agent's

Table 3.4
Summary Comparisons Among Various Conceptions of Leadership

	TYPES OF LEADERSHIP ROLES		
Researcher	*Maintenance-oriented leader*	*Goal-oriented leader*	*Collegial relationships*
Fiedler	High LPC.	Low LPC.	—
Bales	Socioemotional leader	Task leader	—
Kelman	Attractive influencing agent	Influencing agent with means control	Influencing agent with credibility
French and Raven	Referent power	Power to reward and punish	Expert power
Thibaut and Kelley	Agent using positive sanctions who became rewarding himself or herself.	Agent using negative sanctions	Agent who is a credible intermediary

function is then that of an expert or trainer who helps B make appropriate responses to the task. A is influential to the degree that he or she is a credible intermediary. Although Thibaut and Kelley analyze the three processes separately, in their view, all are likely to be used by a group or agent to gain conformity.

Table 3.4 summarizes what has been said thus far. It should be emphasized that the fit is not perfect; only general trends are indicated.

After reviewing the literature on attempts of leaders or influence agents to achieve conformity, Ring and Kelley (1963) concluded that the best strategy might be one that provides punishments for detected instances of concealment, very mild punishments for revealed errors, and strong reward for revealed conforming behavior. When it is not clear that a relevant response has been made, Ring and Kelley recommend a neutral reaction as probably best.

To summarize the relationship between leadership and power, power refers to the potential for influencing others. Leadership refers to the use of power to influence others for the purpose of performing a shared task. Powerful persons may rarely exert their influence but so long as it is believed that they are capable of influencing others when they choose to, they have power. However, unless that power is used to influence others, no leadership is involved. On the other hand, a leader must have some source of power. Thus all leaders have power of some type, but not all powerful people choose to exert leadership.

CONCLUDING COMMENTS ON SECTION III

Although we have confined our attention in this section to group processes, it is important to recognize that the concepts discussed in the preceding section on dyadic interventions with facilitators of change in others are also quite relevant to working with small groups of facilitators of change. The social psychological theory and research on altruism and helping (chapter 7) and on social learning principles (chapter 8) can be useful to practitioners seeking to set up groups composed of facilitators of change or working with on-going groups whose members are concerned with the care of others.

Furthermore, the dimensions of small groups to be discussed in the next set of chapters in terms of their relevance to groups composed of clients—group cohesiveness, group composition, norm enforcement, group development, and role playing as a group activity—are relevant as well. And the group variables explored in this chapter in relation to groups of facilitators of change, that is, problem solving, decision making, group performance, leadership and group structures, are important in groups comprised of persons whose problems are the target of change. All group dimensions are relevant to all types of small groups. But, in the authors' view, some variables are particularly critical in certain types of groups, hence the division.

SECTION FOUR

IMPLEMENTING GROUP INTERVENTION PLANS WITH CLIENTS: QUADRANT D

INTRODUCTION

In this final section on the application of social psychology to the intervention phase of social work practice we focus on those concepts with particular relevance to efforts by practitioners to bring about change or to stabilize desirable behaviors through planned on-going interactions among small groups of individuals designated as clients. By clients we mean individuals whose own problems are the primary target of change. These problems may exist already and their alleviation may be the major concern, or the problem may be a potential one—here the primary focus is on prevention of its occurrence or of its exaccerbation. These goals can be accomplished by changes in the clients' own behaviors or attitudes or by their learning how to effect changes in their social environment. The characteristic that differentiates between groups of clients and groups composed of facilitators of change is the members' prime purposes in participating. If it is to achieve change in their own problems the group is composed of clients. If the members' purpose is primarily to acquire knowledge and skill in order to care for or rear someone else more effectively or to engage in social action to bring about change in larger systems and thereby prevent or alleviate problems, it is a group composed of significant others who are facilitators of change, in our terminology.

It should be noted at the onset that clients need not be deviant, maladjusted, nor disturbed. They may be, but they may also be adequately functioning individuals who wish to enhance their own development. To include both deviant and nondeviant members in the discussion to follow, we will refer to groups composed of clients as treatment/growth groups. M. A. Lieberman (1976), who extensively reviewed the literature in the area, concluded that individuals who go to psychotherapists for "repair" resemble those who go to encounter groups or sensitivity groups for "growth." Most who attend growth groups have been found to have scores comparable to psychiatric clinic populations on symptoms, life stress, and help-seeking motivations. Some current work on consciousness-raising groups suggests similar results. According to Lieberman, "Despite wide ideological differences between psychotherapy, human potential movements, and consciousness-raising groups, individuals enter all those systems with degrees of psychological distress and motivational goals that are indistinguishable" (1976:228). Thus our combining treatment and growth groups in this chapter appears to be justified on empirical as well as conceptual grounds.

To provide the reader with a means of linking the discussion here of treatment/growth groups to other social work literature, a brief review of the major approaches to social group work will be presented before we turn to the social psychological theory and research. The group-dynamic concepts to be discussed later in this chapter are applicable to all approaches to social group work, for the one thing they have in common is worker interaction with a group of individuals whose problems or potential problems are the targets of change. A full analyses of the many varieties that have been developed would be beyond the scope of this book, but a summary will be presented in the context of the classification offered by M. A. Lieberman (1975). Lieberman's orientation is that of a psychologist, not a social worker, but his categorization is relevant to group work by all the helping professions and provides a good backdrop for a discussion of social group work. Lieberman cites three major orientations of group-based healing activities—behavioral, humanistic, and dynamic—and describes their basic characteristics as well as their shortcomings.

Behavioral group methods are based on social learning theory, and focus on specific mechanisms viewed as essential to help individuals change, such as modeling, reinforcement, behavioral rehersal, arousal enhancement, relaxation training, and cognitive restructuring. (For example, see Sundel & Lawrence 1974; A. A. Lazarus 1968; Rose 1977; Wodarski, Feldman, and Flax 1973.) Lieberman suggests that the weakness of this approach is its basic assumption that the leader is in control of the situation and can determine what will be modeled, ignored, etc. It is more likely, however, that power and influence are considerably more diffused in a multiperson relationship, and that unlike in a dyad, no simple assumptions can be made about what will be reinforced, modeled, or vicariously learned. Most social psychologists would agree, Lieberman states, that behavior which becomes reinforced in groups can be explained in terms of group norms. However, recent studies indicate that group norms are not necessarily a function of leader behaviors or desires. Thus there are theoretical and technical problems with a behavioral approach which, in the view of Lieberman, have not yet been addressed in the behavioral literature.

Humanistic or existential approaches to group interventions emphasize the human being as a developing person and the goal is actualization of the latent potential of group members. Examples of groups using this approach are encounter groups, T-groups, and Gestalt groups. The major concepts that have been developed describe the basic conditions of the relationship between the therapist and single client, that is, the dimensions of worker empathy, unconditional acceptance, and genuineness. Lieberman argues that too few concepts have been developed in this approach to take into account the social forces introduced when change induction takes place in a group. The group is used only to provide support, give feedback, and provide a sense of communication. Group forces are not otherwise employed or analyzed.

In psychodynamic approaches to group treatment, the source of human problems is seen as intrapsychic, inner conflicts which individuals have carried with them over a lifetime. Therapy involves mastery of these conflicts. The two major processes involved in therapy are the interpretation of resistance and the analysis of transference. These core ideas have been translated into group therapy in toto from psychoanalytic theory, according to Lieberman, so that the classic set of operations of dynamically oriented group therapists are interpretations of resistance and the analysis of transference. The major contribution of the group is to enable members to understand and observe their own neurotic behavior as it is manifest in the conflicts stimulated by the group. Although there are variations within this approach, e.g., Adlerians and Sullivanians, in Lieberman's view none of these theorists examines the crucial differences between group and dyadic contexts.

It is noteworthy that the literatures of psychology and social work are so disparate that the categorizations offered of orientations to social group work focus on very different dimensions and use a different vocabulary to describe the dimensions perceived as relevant. The classic analysis of types of groups led by social workers was made by Papell and Rothman (1966), who identified three practice models: the Social Goals Model; the Treatment (Remedial or Preventive) Model; and the Reciprocal or Mediating Model.

The Social Goals Model has its origins in the earliest traditions of social group work practice, for example, in settlement house work. The social goals approach sees social change as brought about by responsible members of groups taking action. Democratic group process is considered fundamental and social participation is seen as leading to mental health. The role of the group is to develop a skilled citizenry with the worker serving as a model for responsible citizen efforts at social change. A major portion of its theory base rests on concepts of powerlessness, anomie, and alienation. The type of service offered is largely concerned with socialization. Grace Coyle (1948), one name associated with this approach, believed that for the individual's deepest growth he or she must be socialized, socialized presumably into becoming an active citizen. To the extent that the Social Goals Model seeks to use groups to achieve societal change or change in others, it should not be classified under treatment/growth groups. However, inasmuch as this model is traditionally listed as one of the approaches used by social group workers who focus on individual change, it is placed in this section. The method is neither pure social group work nor pure community organization. Papell and Rothman (1966) classify the Social Goals Model as one of the social group work models but criticize it as being too close to community organization and underemphasizing individual dynamics.

The Remedial Model was developed at the University of Michigan School of Social Work and is closely associated with the names of Robert Vinter (1959, 1965, 1974) Paul Glasser, and Rosemary Sarri (Glasser, Sarri, and Vinter 1974). In this model, the group is conceptualized as both the means and context for the treatment of individuals; the worker's role is directive, planned, and goal-oriented (Churchill 1974). This treatment model is primarily concerned with the remediation of problems of psychological, social, or cultural adjustments through the use of a selected group experience. It links casework to groupwork with its focus on treating dysfunctions. A more recent explication of the model focuses on problem prevention as well as problem alleviation (Glasser and Garvin 1974). In the remediation approach, the worker carries out the role of change agent, the group's purpose is to remedy or prevent social dysfunctioning, the types of activities include the use of direct and indirect means of influence including extragroup means, and the theory base is role theory, ego psychology, and group dynamics. Papell and Rothman (1966) criticize this approach for underemphasizing the use of the group in normal development and as a vehicle for meeting individuals' expressive needs. In addition, the remedial approach assumes that the worker has knowledge and knows how to act on this knowledge, neither of which is always true. Finally, Papell and Rothman believe this method leaves too little provision for the group to be sustained and to contribute to its environment.

The Reciprocal Model is most closely associated with a single theorist, William Schwartz (1959, 1962). The theoretical base for this approach derives from systems theory and field theory. According to Schwartz, one cannot properly speak of "groupwork" because the system in which the method is practiced must be considered first. He states that it is more accurate to speak of a social work method practiced in various systems in which the worker is located, e.g., the family, the small friendship group, the hospital ward, etc. Since goal setting is an intrinsic part of the worker-client relationship, it is meaningless, in the view of supporters of this model, to speak about the worker's goal for the client. There are no specific social or therapeutic goals initially. They evolve out of engagement of worker and client. Individual members are seen as helping one another as well as being helped by the worker. According to Whittaker (1970), workers in this model carry out their function if they focus on the symbiotic interdependence of the client and society, and attempt to mediate between the two. In the Reciprocal Model, the worker is a mediator or resource person who lends a vision to the group and searches out common ground of members' needs. The worker asks the group what it wishes from him or her. The major activity is engaging the group members in the process of interpersonal relations, and the objective is the enhancement of interpersonal relationships. Here the group is conceptualized as a social system including all the members and the worker; each group is an organic whole which can be comprehended only as an entity (Churchill 1974). The practitioner works with the group, not for it or to it. According to Churchill (1974) the reciprocal model is based on existential beliefs and the process is as important as the outcome of the experience. Papell and Rothman (1966) criticize the Reciprocal Model for having no basis for assessing change in individuals since there are no expectations or analyses of individual dynamics. Further, they argue, workers in this model tend to abdicate their authority and are too permissive. Finally, there is a lack of clarity regarding the program for the group other than serving as a mutual-aid system, according to Papell and Rothman.

Theories and models have evolved since the seminal Papell and Rothman article. In the latest issue of the Encyclopedia of Social Work (1977), four articles on social group work appear. One, "The Behavioral Modification Approach," is written by Edwin J. Thomas (1977), and presents particular methods of group interventions based on learning theory for use in the alteration or stabilization of observable client behaviors. The second is, "The Developmental Approach," is written by Emanuel Tropp (1977). It emphasizes the humanistic approach and self-actualization. The third article is entitled "The Interactionist Approach" and is written by William Schwartz (1977). It is clearly the current version of the Reciprocal Model. The fourth is labeled "The Organizational and Environmental Approach" and is written by Paul Glasser and Charles Garvin (1977). It is essentially a current version of the Remedial Model. There is another article, not in the group work section, by Margaret Hartford (1977) on "Socialization Methods in Social Work Practice," which covers part of the area once covered by the Social Goals Model.

In comparing the current approaches to social group work with the classification listed by M. A. Lieberman (1975), it appears that social work and clinical psychology are converging, at least to the extent that both have a behavioral and humanistic model for group treatment. It is apparent that there is no social group work orientation with a purely psychodynamic theory base, although some social work practitioners use group therapy approaches of this type. However, regardless of the professional training of the practitioner, group work involves a group, and therefore the social psychological literature of group dynamics is applicable, particularly concepts of group cohesiveness, group norms, and group development.

CHAPTER ELEVEN

GROUP COHESIVENESS

The concept of group cohesiveness is a relatively simple one yet when it is examined closely, it becomes extremely difficult to describe with precision. In simple terms, group cohesiveness is the degree to which members of a group desire to remain in that group (Cartwright, 1968), the attractiveness of a group for its members (Frank 1957), the resultant of forces pulling individuals to a group (Cartwright and Zander 1968), and those forces which act to keep a person in the group and prevent him or her from leaving (Collins and Raven 1969). These definitions all focus essentially on the total magnetism a group possesses for individual members. More differentiated or complex definitions have also been offered that focus on the sources of the magnetism. Secord and Backman (1964) distinguished between three different internal sources of attraction to the group: 1) The interaction itself among group members may be the source of attraction. This may occur because the needs of the members are complementary, their interests and attitudes are similar, or the organization of the group and the setting in which the interaction takes place are conducive to friendly interaction. 2) Members are attracted to the group because each individual finds the group activities per se inherently rewarding. 3) Members are attracted to the group because it is a means to achieving other ends, or they believe that only through group action can they achieve a desired goal, or believe they can achieve higher status outside of the group because of membership. Frank (1957) describes four sources of group cohesiveness: the member perceives the group as potentially meeting a personal need; the member likes the other members; the member likes the group activities; and the member sees the group as conferring prestige or status.

In contrast, Hagstrom and Selvin (1965) concluded, after conducting an empirical study asking female college students why they selected their current living unit, that there were only two basic factors involved: the members were attractive as individuals, and the goals of the individual were fostered through membership in the group, for example, they provided opportunities for making friends and having dates. One can combine the two factors of the group as a means to an end and the group as a source of status into the second Hagstrom and Selvin factor, but it is clear that the attractiveness of the group's activities per se did not emerge in their study. Perhaps its absence was due to the nature of the groups studied, living units, which engage in many activities. In any event, member attractiveness, referred to by virtually all discussants of the topic as one of the variables fostering cohesiveness, is closely related to the expressive or socioemotional function discussed by T. Parsons, Bales and Shils (1953). The factor of the group as a means to some desired goal is, in essence, Parsons' instrumental function. Thus, the two bases for attraction to groups acknowledged by authorities on group dynamics coincide with Parsons, Bales, and Shils' (1953) two fundamental requirements of all systems, including individual human beings. The conclusion one can reach is that groups are attractive because they meet basic human needs.

Finally, to link group cohesiveness directly with clients, cohesiveness in treatment groups has been described as serving the same function as a positive transference relationship between doctor and patient in dyadic relationships (M. A. Lieberman, 1975). A sense of belongingness motivates members to stay in the group and to work on problems, and the pain associated with therapeutic exploration is eased by the feeling of attraction to the group. Focusing on the expressive factor, Lieberman stated that cohesiveness in therapy groups offers members unconditional acceptance that supports risk taking; he adds that it is the "psychological glue" that permits members to reveal themselves and still maintain self-esteem.

We next turn to the consequences and antecedents of cohesiveness, and note that this term is used in lieu of "cohesion" to emphasize that groups can have varying degrees of attractiveness for members and are not simply cohesive or lacking in cohesion.

CONSEQUENCES OF HIGH GROUP COHESIVENESS

Because of the important consequences of high cohesiveness this group characteristic is very crucial for practitioners leading treatment/growth groups. Among the results of high cohesiveness in groups are the following: 1) The group norms have more influence on members' behaviors, for influence attempts from group members are more readily accepted when desire to maintain the group's approval is high; 2) the group's boundary becomes clearer and less permeable; 3) membership is maintained and attendance is high; members do not drop out; 4) participation in the group is facilitated; communication among group members is more frequent, more revealing, and more satisfying; 5) the members' senses of security and self-esteem are enhanced; 6) members feel freer to express a diversity of behaviors within the group's norms. These consequences of high cohesiveness can be both beneficial and detrimental to the goals of individual members and the group as a whole. The social influence that members in highly cohesive groups have over one another has been studied extensively as leading to both desirable and undesirable outcomes.

Conformity to group norms. The basis for the power of group norms is conceptualized by Thibaut and Kelley (1959) as rooted in the members of highly cohesive groups having a great amount of fate control over one another, that is, ability to reward and punish one another, for members wish to belong to the group and wish the approval of their members. Fate control can readily be converted into behavior control to gain compliance from deviant members who do not accept the goals or norms of the majority The conversion is made when rewards are given only for conforming to the group's norms, and punishments given for nonconformity. Thibaut and Kelley concluded that high cohesiveness in groups can ensure a high degree of desired behavior because of the large amount of fate control available. It has also been pointed out that groups cannot force more compliance than their cohesiveness will withstand (Festinger, Schachter, and Back 1968). If the punishment meted out to deviants exceeds their desire to remain in the group, they will simply leave if they can. The corollary is, the more cohesive the group, the more power to modify members' behavior.

Because cohesive groups have power to enforce norms, the outcomes of high cohesiveness are not always desirable from the point of view of the group worker or the larger system in which the group functions. That is, group norms that are antisocial, antileader, antischool, or antiwork are as effectively enforced as those that are prosocial, proleader, proschool, or prowork. M. A. Lieberman (1975) referred to this phenomenon in criticizing the behavioral model of change-inducing groups. A number of studies have shown that because members are so responsive to group norms, norms can control productivity (Guttentag 1970). When a norm of high productivity is present, high productivity continues even after external pressures from group members have been removed (Berkowitz 1955). However, when the norm is low productivity, group cohesiveness is associated with poor work performance (House 1966). As a result, those working with highly cohesive groups should devote considerable effort to make sure that group norms will not be contrary to the practitioner's purpose for the group.

One empirical study that found the social influence associated with high cohesiveness facilitative of the practitioner's and group's goals involved sixty-five low-income mothers of children in a preschool program (Wittes and Radin 1971). Two parent education groups were developed with the same curriculum and the same social worker leading both groups. But in one group, the lecture-discussion group, more change in childrearing practices occurred than in the activity group, which focused on activities for mothers related to the education of their children. "Strong" members of the discussion group, that is, those who attended at least one-half of the eighteen meetings scheduled during the year, showed a more pronounced trend away from authoritarian childrearing attitudes than did "strong" members of the activity group. In addition, the "strong" members of the discussion group demonstrated more supportive behavior toward their children during the biweekly home visits made by the preschool teachers than did the "strong" members of the activity groups. Since the curriculum and the social worker leading both groups was the same, the conclusion reached was that the nature of the group interaction was responsible for the differences found. "Although the lecture-discussion group began with the leader doing most of the instructing, it soon evolved into a group in which members brought up their own specific concerns and assumed the leadership. They became a cohesive group deeply involved in the discussions. Strong group norms developed for utilization of their new childrearing methods. . . . The cohesion that developed among the members . . . was powerful in enforcing the new norms" (48). On the other hand, in the activity group the social worker continued to act as a teacher and structured the program according to her initial plans. The high cohesiveness that developed in the discussion group required time to develop, however, and those who attended infrequently (the "weak" members) did not share the group's feelings of mutual attraction. As a result, they showed less change than did "weak" members of the activity group.

Terborg, Castore, and DeNinno (1976) also found that high cohesiveness takes time to develop and also that there are both positive and negative effects of the norms that develop in highly cohesive groups. All one hundred thirty-three students enrolled in a course were divided into forty-two groups of four types based on their members' similarity in attitudes and level of ability. One type was composed of students high in ability and similar in attitudes toward current events, another of students high in ability and dissimilar in attitudes, and the other two had students low in ability and either dissimilar in attitude or similar in attitude. The students worked on six projects during a three-month period that would count 25 percent of their final grade in the course. Group performance and cohesiveness were the dependent variables that were measured periodically for all groups. The groups that were attitudinally similar expressed the greatest cohesiveness—they felt they got along very well with the other members and would like to socialize and work with them in the future. But the correlation between cohesiveness and the group's attitudinal similarity did not become significant until the fourth group project. The relationship between cohesiveness and performance—the instructor's grade for each project—was positive and significant for the first task, but significant and negative by the sixth and final group project. The authors interpreted the findings as indicating that all the groups realized by the middle of the semester that they would not get lower than a B for their projects, and they stopped trying or working hard. Clearly the more cohesive groups worked the least by the end of the term. Terborg, Castore, and DeNinno (1976) commented that the results provided additional evidence for equivocality between cohesiveness and performance; the association can be positive or negative. The study also found cohesiveness related to attendance at group meetings. The low ability-low attitude similarity groups with the lowest cohesiveness exhibited the highest absenteeism rates of all the groups.

In the Wittes and Radin (1971) study the norm-enforcement consequences of cohesiveness had positive outcomes; in the Terborg, Castore, and DeNinno (1976) investigation it had mixed results. Friedman and Jacka (1969), however, found only negative consequences. Two groups were established composed of male high-school students and the subjects were asked to negotiate an agreement on an experience each group had undergone which produced different impressions about the length of time a buzzer sounded. The negotiating was done by a single group member who left the group after it had arrived at a consensus about the buzzer's duration. The main findings were that when the group members believed the negotiator was deviating from the group consensus position they downgraded their opinions of him, and when the negotiator received feedback from the group indicating their disapproval of his action, he shifted his negotiating position to the exact group consensus position. The authors interpret this to mean that the solidarity of the group and the loyalty of its negotiator acted against the interests of the group in reaching an agreement that was necessary to the group. They conclude that group cohesiveness works counter to concession and agreement when two groups meet through member-representatives. Although it is doubtful that the tendency of cohesive groups to resist concessions to outside groups will have much relevance for treatment/growth groups, the practitioner should be aware of the phenomenon, especially when working with children's groups in schools or community centers. The group typically meets for only one hour each week but the children will continue to live and work together with nongroup members for the other hours and days of the week. Augmenting tensions among classmates and neighbors will not benefit the children or the adults who are nearby.

The research of Sakurai (1975) helped explicate some of the conditions under which the results of group cohesiveness will be negative, even detrimental. The issue is of great significance to social work practitioners for they may well be exacerbating the problems of group members by fostering cohesiveness unless they understand which variables interact with cohesiveness to produce undesirable outcomes. Sakurai adopted the two-dimensional model of group cohesiveness proposed by Hagstrom and Selvin (1965), focused on interpersonal attraction for members and the instrumental function of the group, although he labeled the latter interdependence, for the instrumental factor suggests that members cannot achieve the goal they desire without the help of other group members. Sakurai's investigation then tested the following hypotheses: 1) When cohesiveness is based on interpersonal attractiveness (the interdependence factor is low and the attractiveness factor is high), there will be little difference in the conformity level regardless of whether conformity is perceived as having promotive or detrimental consequences for the group's welfare; and 2) When cohesiveness is based on the interdependence of members for goal attainment (the interdependence factor is high and attractiveness low) there will be less conformity when it is perceived as having detrimental consequences than when conformity is seen as promotive of the group's welfare.

The theoretical basis for the hypothesis concerning attractiveness is both the balance theory of Newcomb (1953) and the dissonance theory of Festinger (1957). These theories state that if a member likes other group members and these members feel positively toward a specific standard or norm, the member will also feel positively toward the standard, to be in balance or to end dissonance with the other group member's attitudes. Similarly, the member will not endorse the standard if the group rejects it. According to this view the effect of the member's conformity on the group's task performance is irrelevant to the occurence of conformity—conformity pressures are based on the individual's desire to maintain balanced interpersonal relations. When cohesiveness is based on interdependence, however, conformity's occurence is predictable from exchange theory (P. M. Blau 1964; Thibaut and Kelley 1959), according to Sakurai's hypothesis. This theory assumes participants will attempt to minimize costs of obtaining maximal rewards from an interaction. Because in interdependent cohesive groups rewards come from the success of the group as a whole, conformity that reduces group efficacy is costly because the desired end will not be achieved. This is not likely to be offset by the returns from conformity per se, thus detrimental conformity will be less likely than promotive conformity.

The study was a laboratory investigation and involved twenty undergraduates who believed they were members of groups that were high in both interdependence and attractiveness, low in both, or high in one and low in the other. High attractiveness was induced by telling the subjects that the members chose one another; high interdependence was created by telling the subjects that individual rewards would depend on group performance. The students were given a visual problem, false information about what other group members were saying, and were asked to give their own judgments on the problem. The results confirmed the two hypotheses: members of the groups whose cohesiveness was based on interpersonal attraction conformed to the opinions of others regardless of whether those opinions appeared to be correct or incorrect, but members of the groups whose cohesiveness was based on interdependence conformed to the opinions of others only when they appeared to be correct. The author concluded that cohesiveness is not unidimensional and that both inherent attractiveness and instrumental value of a group must be considered in order to describe how cohesiveness combines with other variables to predict behavior. Sakurai goes so far as to suggest that each of these dimensions should be considered attributes of groups and not merely subdimensions of group cohesiveness. This would involve discarding the "familiar and convenient concept of group cohesiveness" but it would have the advantage of fostering the study of groups from a multidimensional perspective.

The author's suggestion is logical but it is unlikely that a concept central to group dynamics for decades will be abandoned. However, Sakurai's investigation warns all researchers that groups cannot be described simply as cohesive; the basis for the cohesiveness must be determined if the consequences of cohesiveness are to be understood. The Friedman and Jacka (1969) study did not explicitly describe the basis for the group's cohesiveness but all members were male high-school students who volunteered to participate in the project after school and whose opinions on the experimental task were similar. There was nothing to suggest that they were interdependent, in the sense of their group membership enabling them to achieve some goals. Thus it is reasonable to conclude that the basis for the group's cohesiveness was member attractiveness. The finding that the negotiator conformed to the group's standard even though the conformity was detrimental to the group's goal of negotiating an agreement would therefore be in agreement with Sakurai's findings and theory.

Expression of feelings. Another consequence of cohesiveness that is highly relevant to social workers pertains to the expression of feelings. Although this is generally desirable in treatment or growth groups, Pepitone and Reichling (1955) as well as Lippitt and White (1958) found that highly cohesive groups express more hostility and express it more directly than do less cohesive groups. Guttentag (1970) interprets these findings as suggesting that once group norms have been internalized, members of highly cohesive groups feel freer to behave in moderately diverse ways, which permits greater freedom of behavior within the boundaries of the group norms. Another way of conveying this concept is to say that cohesiveness in groups permits more dropping of roles; people are freer to be themselves, provided the group's norms are not violated. The net result may be surprising to practitioners unprepared for the phenomenon.

Group boundary enhancement. Guttentag (1970) discusses a characteristic of cohesive groups that may help explain the findings of Friedman and Jacka concerning intergroup negotiations. A growth in cohesiveness necessarily entails a stronger definition of group boundaries, a stronger differentiation between group and nongroup members, and an increase in the comparison level for outcomes associated with the group. Thus associations with other groups are cut off and the comparison level for alternatives to the group are lowered, that is, the gratifications that can be provided by alternatives to the group are diminished. Pettigrew (1969) comments on the same phenomenon in relation to the growth of black cohesiveness and expressed the view that this will lead to a situation of racial isolation. He then cites several negative effects of isolation between groups. It generally leads to diverse value development, to reduced intergroup communication, and to uncorrected perceptual distortions of each other. Pettigrew concludes that the movement toward ethnic cohesiveness that emphasizes the boundary between black and nonblack groups has largely negative effects.

Impact on ethnic group members. On the other hand, the issue of the advantages and disadvantages of high cohesiveness in minority ethnic groups was explored in depth by Guttentag (1970) who concludes that in spite of the negative consequences discussed above in relation to intergroup separation, the beneficial consequences tip the scale. The low-status individual gains a sense of rapport and of "interdependence of fate" (Lewin 1948) with other group members. "Protected by the cohesiveness of their group, low-status people feel freer to express hostility directly, and are therefore less inclined to turn inward to self-hatred. The cohesive group is a better instrument for obtaining the goals of low-status individuals, not only because it has greater power vis-à-vis other groups, but also because of within-group effects on productivity which is in consonance with group norms" (124). Guttentag supports the growth of highly cohesive ethnic groups in spite of the fact that such cohesiveness could impede the upward mobility of individual members because they may hate to leave their ethnic group, and they may be sanctioned by the other members if they express a desire to leave. This phenomenon is the mirror-image of the finding that cohesive groups maintain their members. Upward mobility of individual low-status persons often involves desertion of their low-status peer groups. One way to avoid this dilemma is through the peer group working together to enable the group as a whole to achieve upward mobility; in such efforts the positive consequences of cohesiveness could enhance achievement of this group goal.

The discussion of ethnic cohesiveness is primarily relevant to social workers engaged in community organization. However, Guttentag's views are not irrelevant to practitioners focusing on individual change when their treatment/growth groups are composed largely of low-income or low-status members. Such members' self-confidence, self-esteem, and feelings of worth are very likely to increase if the groups become highly cohesive. Surely this will facilitate both treatment and growth. It is difficult to imagine any situation when the worker's goals for group members would call for a reduction in their self-esteem, except conceivably if the members are drug abusers, or law-breakers who deny they have a problem and maintain that everything is going beautifully in their lives.

Impact on members of treatment/growth groups. Although acknowledging the potential problems that high cohesiveness can create, a number of writers have come out firmly in favor of high group cohesiveness as a facilitator of healthy change in individual members of treatment groups. Whitaker and Lieberman (1964) disagree with group therapists such as Slavson (1947; 1957) who emphasize the destructive force of cohesiveness in groups. Rather, they affirm that cohesiveness fosters treatment goals if the group's standards are appropriate, but admit that cohesiveness can function destructively if, for example, group members establish a restrictive norm that only friendly feelings exist in the group. According to Whitaker and Lieberman, this kind of cohesiveness functions to protect members from confrontation with underlying feelings of hostility, envy, or competitiveness which are regarded as dangerous to the group. At most other times, however, cohesiveness can be facilitative of treatment, as, for example, when mutual acceptance becomes established as a group norm, thereby reducing fears and allowing members to express themselves more freely. As with productivity in task groups, norms of cohesive treatment/growth groups can harm or help recovery and self-actualization.

Jerome Frank (1957) wrote a lengthy, perceptive article on the determinants and effects of cohesiveness in therapy groups in which he concludes that despite the potential problems that can arise in highly cohesive therapy groups they can be controlled and the positive effects are more vital. One of the problematic effects of cohesiveness in treatment groups, he states, is that well-established, cohesive groups attempt to exclude strangers as threats to its cohesiveness. The group resents newcomers. At times members of cohesive groups attempt to freeze out newcomers by techniques such as discussing incidents that happened in earlier sessions or talking about members who are absent. At other times, the members will closely question newcomers about personal matters—this may simultaneously express the urge to assimilate the stranger as rapidly as possible and the urge to drive the newcomer out; the process is analogous to hazing.

Another problematic consequence of high cohesiveness in therapy groups, according to Frank, is that the group attacks and scapegoats members whose behavior tends to disrupt its cohesiveness, for example, members who monopolize the discussion or express a derogatory attitude to the group. However, the attacks are sometimes therapeutically helpful for the victims, for the criticism may lead to modification of the undesired behavior. When this occurs, the victims are promptly rewarded by experiencing a greater sense of acceptance by the group. Their self-respect is thereby restored and the new behavior powerfully reinforced. This entire scenario provides a good example of group pressure on deviants to conform.

While scapegoating and rejecting newcomers may be undesired outcomes of cohesiveness in treatment groups, Frank (1957) sees cohesiveness, for the most part, as highly beneficial in helping members function more adequately.

> A cohesive group with "proper standards" protects and enhances self-esteem of its members, fortifies their ability to consolidate and maintain beneficial changes in behavior or attitudes, helps them to resolve conflicts, and facilitates constructive release of feeling. A cohesive group not only exerts pressure on members to change, but strengthens their ability to maintain the changes it has helped to bring about. Allegiance to a group helps members to hold to their decisions. . . . It has been shown that group discussion leads to more permanent change in behavior than individual persuasion. It seems likely that the more cohesive a group is . . . the stronger this force will be. (60–61)

Frank concedes that the cohesiveness of a group might impede attainment of treatment goals if its standards were such as to strengthen member resistance. However, he argues that this is unlikely—because a therapy group can only develop cohesiveness by incorporating the standards of the therapist, the group is safeguarded against detrimental norms. If members do not accept the therapist's terms, they will leave. The rest remain because they desire to be helped and believe the therapist can provide help. Thus therapists can be confident that despite forces toward resistance, the group will incorporate the standards they consider desirable as cohesiveness develops. The one requirement, according to Frank, is that the therapists make their expectations clear. We would add several other limitations to Frank's assumption that cohesiveness does not occur without acceptance of the therapists' standards. The first is based on the recognition that not all treatment groups are composed of voluntary clients who desire help from the particular professional leading the group; in such groups, for example prisoners or abusive spouses referred for treatment by the court, members could develop cohesiveness without incorporating the practitioner's standards. Even in voluntary groups, however, there are likely to be ambivalent feelings toward the group worker which can lead to rejection of at least some of the worker's standards for the group. As

M. A. Lieberman (1975) pointed out, the development of group norms is not entirely dependent on the leader's behavior. Finally, in growth-oriented groups, such as consciousness-raising women's groups for example, it is possible that the leader's authority is considerably less than Frank assumed and hence the group members may perceive that it is the other members rather than the professional leader who are the prime sources of help.

Among other advantages of cohesiveness cited by Frank (1957) is that it enhances the members' self-esteem because of the respect received from others. Their sense of personal importance also increases because they know they have the power to influence others even when they are absent. Further, in cohesive groups, members can work out their inner conflicts if the group norm is that antagonists must continue communicating no matter how angry they become with one another. By putting pressure on members to continue interacting, the cohesive treatment group can often help members reach a successful resolution of their conflict based on more accurate mutual understanding. Finally, a cohesive treatment group with proper norms guides the release of emotion in its members so that feelings are expressed freely but on condition that the members try to understand their own motivations and accept the responses of other members. This is a powerful aid to the therapeutic change of attitude.

Frank also examines the problem presented by cohesive groups that Janis (1972) described as "groupthink," that is, that the more members are attracted to a group, the more they may be inclined to guard against expression of feeling which might be disruptive. Frank describes the resultant problem as the group's being "too comfortable." He states, however, that the therapist's attitude and the desire of the members to express themselves more freely are usually sufficient to counteract this tendency. Frank also notes that cohesiveness does not necessarily imply pressure toward conformity because the norms of a cohesive group may encourage diversity. Members may agree that they will not allow pressures for conformity to develop in certain areas. Thus freedom of thought may flourish or even be enhanced in highly cohesive groups.

In sum, Frank believes that cohesiveness is relevant to therapy because the more attracted members are to a group the more they are influenced by its standards. If these standards encourage diversity of outlook, nondefensive expression of feeling, honest attempts at self-examination, and maintenance of communication under all conditions, "then the more cohesive the group is, the more likely it is to induce therapeutic changes in its members" (63).

Therein lies the dilemma for practitioners. To achieve change in members of treatment/growth groups, cohesiveness is essential. However it can be damaging rather than beneficial if destructive norms develop. It is clearly up to the worker to see that this does not occur. High cohesiveness is like a powerful surgeon's tool. It must be used, but it must be used with knowledge and care if the outcomes are not to be disastrous.

ANTECEDENTS OF HIGH GROUP COHESIVENESS

Knowledge of the variables that foster cohesiveness is essential to practitioners working with treatment or growth groups. When an assessment of group functioning leads workers to decide that increased cohesiveness would be beneficial in a given situation, they must understand how the group's attractiveness can be enhanced. One need not rely on luck. Conversely, when workers conclude that too much cohesiveness exists, attempts can be made to reduce the group member's attractiveness to one another and to the group as a whole. Again, a knowledge of the variables involved is essential or the practitioners will waste time and effort.

The first four variables that can help increase group cohesiveness are related to the factors defining that condition: attractiveness of the members, attractiveness of the activities, belief that the group will help the individual achieve personal goals, and belief that group membership brings increased prestige and status in the outside world. Other factors are also relevant, and will be discussed below. Enhancement of any of these factors can increase the group's cohesiveness. Frank (1957) suggests a number of ways to accomplish that goal.

Attractiveness. The attractiveness of other members can be increased by the leader's pointing out the similarities in their problems, experiences, or personal characteristics. As has been discussed previously, similarity of relevant attitudes, values, or beliefs lead to attraction and liking (Newcomb 1953; Terborg, Castore, and DeNinno 1976). This is especially relevant to groups where social support is the major group goal (Anderson 1975). The leader can also suggest or encourage out-of-group, fence-mending social activities among certain members. Such interactions can increase intimacy between members and help dispel hostilities which the larger group meetings may have elicited.

Instrumental value. The instrumental value of the group can be enhanced by the worker by keeping salient the ways in which the group as a unit can help members fulfill their own needs and goals. For example, the worker can refer to previous group members who achieved their personal goals through the group. The attractiveness of the group's activities can be enhanced by selecting those that are within the members' competence but sufficiently difficult to be challenging. In addition, the practitioner can be explicit about what is required of each member and how success is to be judged. These clarifications can apply to discussions as well in role playing, behavioral assignments, etc. The practitioner should also be certain to express approval for successful performance and should encourage other members to do the same. A person may gain a real sense of achievement in being told he or she was perceptive in playing a role, or in analyzing the behaviors of another role player.

Prestige. The prestige attached to group membership can enhance cohesiveness in a similar fashion. Here the worker's aim would be to affect members' beliefs about how their prestige and status is affected as a result of participating in the group. When members of a group believe that their group confers prestige in the larger society they frequently display signals—buttons, stickers, emblems—that publicly proclaim group membership and, presumably, the individuals' desire to remain members of the group (Cialdini et al. 1976). While such behavior is unlikely in treatment groups it isn't inconceivable in growth groups, and members of both types of groups no doubt can be expected to make their membership known to significant others when they believe it confers status among their normative reference group, as when persons who are mental health professionals convey to their colleagues that they have had personal experience as members of certain treatment or growth groups. Where appropriate, the practitioner can refer to previous group members whose status was improved, and can emphasize any evidence of increased prestige among the members, for example, being questioned by friends and kin about what occurs in group meetings. Extragroup means of influence, as Vinter (1974) referred to it, can also be used to make members aware that their status has increased and that others perceive the group as valuable. With permission of the members, the worker can talk with significant others in the lives of group members (teachers, parents, sibs, spouses) about how important the group is to members, to the worker, to the sponsoring institution. If there is a waiting list for service this can be brought out, and the arrangements made by the family agency, school, hospital, or court to assist the group in forming and meeting can be described. The successes of previous group members can also fruitfully be mentioned. If the social worker cannot succeed in convincing significant others that group membership is an asset, at least the worker should convey the message that membership is not degrading.

Other factors affecting group cohesiveness, less directly associated with the defining conditions of cohesiveness, can also affect the extent of cohesiveness in groups.

Reward structure. Reward structure can enhance group cohesiveness. In a dramatic experiment at a summer camp, Sherif (1958) showed that the presence of superordinate goals fosters group cohesiveness among subgroups. By superordinate goals, Sherif meant goals that are compelling and highly appealing to two or more groups in conflict, but which cannot be attained by the resources and energies of the groups separately. In effect, they are goals attained only when groups work together. Among the superordinate goals that Sherif developed in the camp was obtaining water to combat a water shortage (created by the experimenter unbeknownst to the campers), and securing a much-desired film which could not be obtained alone by either of the two groups, but could be gotten if they pooled their resources.

Sherif started the summer by creating competition in the camp between two groups of normal, eleven- and twelve-year-old boys, well adjusted to school and neighborhood, and academically successful. He then used a variety of techniques to bring the boys together into one cohesive group. The establishment of superordinate goals was the most successful technique. Totally unsuccessful was the strategy of creating situations where the antagonistic groups engaged in activities together, such as eating, which were pleasant but did not require interdependence. On the contrary, such situations occasioned name-calling and abuse of one another. Disseminating favorable information about the out-group was also totally unsuccessful. There was ample evidence, however, that the introduction of superordinate goals substantially reduced conflict and enhanced cohesiveness. There was a sharp decrease in name-calling and derogation of out-group members, blatant glorification of the in-group diminished, and ratings of the out-group members changed from largely unfavorable to largely favorable. Sherif (1958) summarized his findings by saying that methods popularly suggested for reducing intergroup conflict, such as disseminating information and increasing social contact, become effective only when they become part of interaction processes involving superordinate goals which have "real and compelling value" for all concerned.

Recent research in which black and white soldiers from the sourthern region of the United States were placed in small groups in which they worked on a cooperative task—the operation of a model railroad—supports this conclusion if one recognizes the typically separate social group membership of blacks and whites (Blanchard, Adelman, and Cook 1975). The success or failure of the experimental group's cooperative efforts, but not the racial composition of the group, affected the members' interpersonal liking for one another. These studies strongly suggest that in situations where the effort of all members is needed to obtain a goal which all desire, cohesiveness will be enhanced. Such situations may involve raising funds for a trip that is highly desired, or establishing a reward for the entire group if all members complete their assignments. Such arrangements are common in behavioral programs for youngsters where the group reward, or superordinate goal in Sherif's terms, is a trip to McDonald's for a hamburger. The danger of such reward structures is that the one group member who keeps the entire group from receiving its reinforcement is likely to be badly scapegoated, or worse. It has been reported to the authors that when rewards for a group in the armed services are dependent upon each man's doing his job appropriately, the individual who refuses to comply may find himself unexpectedly falling down a flight of stairs. Zimbardo et al. (1973) vividly demonstrated in the filmstrip "The Prison" that pressure is exerted on the single recalcitrant member who prevents a group from receiving its reward, in spite of the fact that the deviant's stance is justified. Sherif did not discuss any such noncompliers at his camp; this may have been because the campers shared the same goals, that of seeing the film for example. Thus changes in the reward structure of a group designed to enhance cohesiveness are likely to do so when the group serves the same instrumental value to all its members.

Common enemy. The creation or existence of a common enemy typically increases cohesiveness. Guttentag (1970) referred to this effect in describing the variables that contribute to group cohesiveness among low-status individuals. She quoted the work of Sherif and Sherif (1965) to support that statement. According to these researchers, opposition to or restriction of the group's activities by outsiders, such as authority figures or other groups, will increase solidarity within the group. Low-status individuals must also see a possibility that cooperative behavior will reduce the threats, Guttentag stated, although such assurance may not be necessary for others. As Sherif and Sherif (1969) demonstrated in their camp experiment, the mere creation of a highly competitive situation between two groups results in intragroup solidarity, as can the presence of a common enemy. These phenomena are well recognized in everyday life. Both sources of intragroup solidarity probably contribute to the continuation of the Mideast conflict and the solidarity within the various Arab nations and within Israel. A nation pulls together when attacked by another country. This occurred in the United States after the Japanese attack on Pearl Harbor, and when hostages were taken in Iran. It did not occur in the Vietnam war when there was disagreement as to who the real enemy was. Thus, although a recent review of the broad social science literature on the proposed relationship between group cohesiveness and an attack from outside the group concludes that the relationship is well-documented, there are conditions when it does not hold. One condition is that in which the group does not successfully handle the external attack and thereby loses its value as a source of security for the members (Zander 1979).

It is not difficult for practitioners working with children's groups to create external "enemies or competitors" to foster cohesiveness in the group—another group the practitioner or a colleague is leading, for example. It is doubtful whether that technique would work in adult groups. However, if there is a "natural" enemy, for example, the city council which refuses to fund a summer camp program for another year, the worker can use the situation to good advantage to increase the group's solidarity.

Group ventures. Successful group ventures increase cohesiveness in a group whose source of attraction is based solely on the fact that it will help members achieve their individual goals. Instrumental groups such as these have been shown to decline in cohesiveness when the group is confronted with failure (Wolman 1960); thus it is not unreasonable to believe that cohesiveness will increase, when the group succeeds. Other research supports this inference (Cialdini et al. 1976; Worchel, Andreoli, and Folger 1977). When cohesiveness is based on member attractiveness, however, or on both member attractiveness and on instrumental factors, group failure does not elicit a significant diminution of cohesiveness (Anderson 1975; Wolman 1960). The differentiation is similar to that observed by Sakurai (1975) who found that members will conform to norms detrimental to the group's success only when cohesiveness rests primarily on member attractiveness; this will not occur in groups whose cohesiveness is based for the most part on instrumental factors. Clearly goal attainment is the central issue in instrumental groups.

One implication for the practitioner of these findings is that unrealistic goals are damaging in groups established primarily to assist members' attaining their personal goals, for failure will most likely lead to a decline in cohesiveness. The worker would do well to avoid this situation by helping the treatment/growth group set attainable goals for individual change. Further, fostering member attractiveness based both on interpersonal attraction and attainment of individual goals can enable groups to withstand delay in goal achievement, but groups based solely on attainment of individual change may not survive long enough for that change to occur.

Lack of alternatives. The absence of an attractive alternative to the group fosters cohesiveness. Thibaut and Kelley (1959), Guttentag (1970), and Secord and Backman (1964) stress the fact that when few gratifications are available from alternatives to the group (the comparison level for alternatives is low), members find the group more attractive. They will remain in the group even when the satisfactions are below their comparison level or the gratifications they feel are due them based on their past experiences (Thibaut and Kelley 1959). Thus for groups composed of low-status members, the low quality of outcomes available in alternative relations helps contribute to the attractiveness of the current group. Guttentag (1970) points out that as groups become more cohesive, the gratifications available from alternative relationships decline. The relationship between the comparison level for alternatives and cohesiveness is therefore cyclical; an initial low comparison level for alternatives contributes to cohesiveness, and once cohesiveness starts to develop, the comparison level for alternatives will decline below their initial low level.

Practitioners usually have only limited ability to affect the comparison level for alternatives as a means to enhance cohesiveness. The worker cannot eliminate other groups and associations the members may have which they find more appealing than the group the social worker is leading—certainly not outside of total institutions. And the worker cannot disband a natural group of friends who engage in attractive activities at the time the group meeting is held. The worker can, however, schedule group sessions at times when there is no strong competition. It would be foolish, for example, for school social workers to hold meetings when the members would ordinarily be having recess.

Conversely, there is usually little difficulty with attendance at the elementary-school level when the group meets during class time. Teachers have different feelings on the matter, as one would anticipate.

Effort to join. The effort expended to join a group fosters cohesiveness. This phenomenon has been amply demonstrated by cognitive theorists (Aronson and Mills 1968), and was discussed earlier in relation to cognitive dissonance theory. When members have to go through an initiation to join a group, or wait until their turn comes up on the waiting list, it is dissonant for them to dislike the group. They cannot undo the effort they have expended. The only way to reduce the dissonance is to convince themselves that they are attracted to the group they have joined. Self-perception theory (D. J. Bem 1972) would offer another explanation for the same phenomenon. Bem would say that the individuals would see themselves as the kinds of people who like such groups because they put forth effort to join. In either case, as distasteful as waiting lists may be, they do serve the function of fostering cohesiveness in the groups eventually formed. Questionnaires that must be filled out before becoming a group member or tests that must be taken would fill the same function. The worker must be careful not to create too many obstacles to joining or the member may decide to drop the entire idea. An optimal amount of effort should be required, but what that level is for each type of individual may have to be determined by trial and error, at least until some research data are collected on the issue.

Absence of coercion. The absence of coercion in group composition promotes cohesiveness. This is the reverse phenomenon to that concerning expended effort. Forcing members to join groups reduces cohesiveness. In coerced groups, not only do members make no effort to join, they may well make efforts not to join. In that case, cognitive dissonance theory and self-perception theory would suggest the group would have a negative attraction. The members would find it repellent. Reactance theory, previously discussed, would also suggest that when individuals have their choices taken away from them, they will react by preferring the opposite of the coerced choice (J. Brehm 1972). Thus, workers would do well to permit potential group members some degree of choice about joining the group. If treatment is required by external agents, the potential member should have some choice about the type to be received, for example participation in a treatment group or assignment to a different setting—a special class, a special program, a special building—or participation in a second form of treatment. It should be noted, however, that at least one theorist (Frank 1957) believes that nonvoluntary groups can be beneficial. Although he admits that such groups are unlikely to produce genuine changes of attitude or behavior, "not too infrequently, however, patients who come to a group under compulsion undergo change of heart and find it genuinely attractive. . . . An example from daily life is that of a draftee who struggles against being inducted but once in the army wholeheartedly accepts its activities and values" (60). In spite of this argument, if they can be avoided, we do not recommend nonvoluntary groups to social work practitioners.

Sharing. The sharing of decision-making and leadership functions fosters cohesiveness. It has been found that groups in which authority and leadership are centered in a single individual tend to be less cohesive than those in which members share in decision-making and leadership acts. For example, in the study of two orientations to parent education with low-income mothers, cohesiveness flourished in the group where members began making decisions and plans (Wittes and Radin 1971). No such burgeoning of cohesiveness occurred in the group where the leader structured and determined the events of each session. Similar results were obtained with another population; it was found that college students rated their class more favorably when the teacher was group-centered rather than leader-centered (Bovard 1951). Children also reacted more positively to a style of leadership that permitted participation in decision making than to one in which one person held all the power, or one in which no leadership was exerted whatsoever (R. K. White and Lippitt 1968). A field experiment conducted in a large business organization employing female clerical workers similarly found that when decision making was shared among the rank and file, worker satisfaction increased significantly; in another division where decision making was moved to higher levels of management, worker satisfaction decreased (N. Morse and Reimer 1956). Additional analyses of those data by two other researchers (Tannenbaum and Allport 1956), however, indicated that people with different personality predispositions reacted in rather different ways to these two types of social organizations. It is also interesting to note that research with psychiatric patients, some of whom had been diagnosed as psychotic for many years, indicated that they performed more adequately when they functioned without a staff member present, who tended to be cast in an authoritative leader role, and when more than one indigenous leader developed in the group (Lerner and Fairweather 1963). In spite of some contrary findings, Cartwright (1968) concluded that a democratic form of organization that encourages widespread participation in decision making appears to induce more attraction to the group than one in which decisions are centralized. The limits on this assumption have not, however, been well tested (Zander 1979).

The application of these findings to treatment/growth groups will be largely influenced by the theoretical orientation of the practitioner leading the group. The worker who adheres to the remedial model of social group work will use a shared decision-making model more cautiously than will one who follows the social goals approach. However, it does appear that if authority and decision making are to be located in a single person, the worker must be certain that other factors are present to foster group cohesiveness or the members may not be in attendance long enough to benefit from the group experience.

TECHNIQUES FOR ASSESSING GROUP COHESIVENESS

As the above discussion indicates, group cohesiveness is a powerful variable affecting members' behaviors and attitudes. Practitioners may wish to foster its growth or decline, but in no case can social workers ignore its influence. The question is, how can practitioners determine the degree of cohesiveness present in the groups they are leading? Inasmuch as there are at least two, and possibly as many as four aspects to cohesiveness, measuring it is a complex process. There are five major approaches, each one plausibly related to the definition of cohesiveness, and each one producing meaningful relationships between its type of measurement and the properties of groups associated with cohesiveness (Cartwright 1968).

Measurement of interpersonal attraction among members. One approach to measuring interpersonal attraction consists of determining a friendship index, or the ratio of the number of selections made within a group when each member is asked to name his or her best friends, to the number of selections that could possibly have been made. This sociometric strategy was used by Festinger, Schachter, and Back (1968) when they attempted to determine the relationship between cohesiveness and group standards in various housing units. The adult residents were asked to name the persons they saw the most socially. This was an attempt to measure the friendships formed within the group, in this case, within the housing unit. Festinger, Schachter, and Back did find a significant association between the index of in-group friendship, or cohesiveness, and the presence of standards of behavior relevant to the housing unit among the tenants. A very similar approach was used in Fairweather's (1964b) study of four self-led task groups of psychiatric patients on a Veterans Administration ward, which found that the residents' sociometric choices were clustered within their own task group. An example of a related, but not identical, approach is found in a study of a classroom by Bovard (1951). He asked each student to rate other students in the classroom on an 11-point scale of degree of liking. An average rating of liking was then computed for each class, and compared across several rooms.

Measurement of evaluation of group as a whole. This strategy focuses on the group as an entity. Bovard (1951) also used this approach in his study when he asked each student to rate his liking for the class as a whole, and then computed an average rating for each of several rooms. Another researcher (J. M. Jackson 1959) asked staff members of a child welfare agency about the amount of benefit the respondents felt they were receiving from members in the group, and also about their attraction to individuals in the group. The coefficient of correlation was .61, indicating that only about one-third of the variance in the members' positive evaluation of the group as a unit could be accounted for by the members' liking for the other people in the group, and vice versa. It is apparent that the two measurements tend to go together but are not identical (Cartwright 1968).

Measurement of feelings of closeness or identification with a group. This approach was used by Converse and Campbell (1968) in testing the hypothesis that large racial and ethnic groups in this country have distinctive voting patterns. To determine the feeling of identification with the group, the researchers asked questions such as "Would you say you felt pretty close to ______ in general?" (the name of the group was inserted), and "How much interest would you say you have in how ______ as a whole are getting along?"—again the name of the group was inserted. Another investigator (Indik 1965) employed the same approach and asked subjects "How strong a sense of belonging do you feel you have to some people you work with?" Cartwright (1968) concluded that the pattern of results from such studies indicates that measures of identification or belonging tap an important component of group cohesiveness.

Measurement of desire to remain in the group. Schachter used this approach in two studies. One involved female undergraduates and the subjects were asked three questions after participating with a group in an activity (Schachter et al. 1968). "How did you like your team?" "If you were taking part in another experience, how much would you like to work with these same girls?" "How much do you think you would like to see your teammates?" The respondents were given a 5-point scale to use in responding to the first two questions, and a 7-

point scale for the third. This discrepancy makes comparison of responses to the last question with those made to the first two difficult, but the mean ratings given to the first two queries were similar but not identical; thus the girls' evaluation of the group as a whole was similar to their expressed desire to remain in the group.

In the second study, Schachter (1968) used male undergraduates and asked them the following to assess their desire to remain in the club the experimenter had established. "Do you want to remain a member of this group?" "How often do you think the group should meet?" "If enough members decide not to stay so that it seems this group might discontinue, would you like the chance to persuade others to stay?" Again the replies were similar across subjects, but not identical. For example, 98 percent of the most cohesive group wanted to remain, but only 73 percent wanted to induce others to stay in the club. Behavioral measurements of the desire of members to remain in a group have also been used (Libo 1953; Marshall and Heslin 1975). In this approach members were given the opportunity to leave a group in which they have already participated; groups that retained their members were assumed to be more cohesive than groups that lost their members.

Use of a composite index of several measurements. Because there are several aspects of cohesiveness, some researchers prefer to tap more than one aspect and compute an index of cohesiveness. It has generally been found that the various indicators of cohesiveness tend to be positively correlated. Some investigators have not found significant correlations across measures (Cartwright 1968). An example of the more typical finding is the Blanchard, Adelman, and Cook (1975) study of interracial groups of soldiers in which a 21-item questionnaire covering respect, interpersonal liking, desire to work together in the future and to spend off-duty time together showed very high internal consistency. The picture is unclear and in 1968 Cartwright summarized the situation by saying that a "standard, all-purpose procedure for measuring group cohesiveness does not yet exist (p. 95)." Unfortunately, in a review of the literature in 1979 Zander still had to say that the absence of a reliable method for measuring cohesiveness in a natural setting remains a serious problem.

It is interesting that none of the approaches described above specifically asked members to indicate if they felt proud to be a member of this group, or if they wished to continue the activities in which the group had been engaging. These are two components of cohesiveness that have been described in the theoretical literature but have not been applied by researchers assessing cohesiveness in a laboratory or field study. It is also notable that in listing the techniques of measuring cohesiveness, Cartwright (1968) did not refer to any behavioral measures, although some use has been made of such measures. For example, Fairweather (1964b) measured cohesiveness by observing the social interaction among psychiatric ward members during their recreation hour and found a significantly higher proportion of talking to members of the patients' own task group than to nongroup members. In discussing sociograms in which group members are asked to indicate who they would prefer to spend time with, or like the best, Hare (1962) pointed out that none of them assess actual behavior. Sociograms may illustrate group structures, but not what people actually do. The same criticism is applicable to questions asking group members how they feel about the group or other members. Overlooked in such an approach are actual observations of attendance at meetings, number of late arrivals, or patterns of seating during meetings. One of the few studies to use a behavioral measure (Terborg, Castore, and DeNinno 1976) examined the absences from group meetings and compared those figures in groups varying in the characteristics of members. Members who were dissimilar in attitudes and low in ability showed significantly greater rates of absenteeism than two other types of groups. Unfortunately, Terborg and coworkers did not report the correlation between members' absence rates and their composite index of attraction to the group based on answers to three questions about how the subject and the other members got along together, whether the subject would like to socialize with the members in the future or would want to remain in the group on future class projects.

From the above discussion it is evident that workers have a wide choice of measures they can use to assess their group's cohesiveness at any point in time. It may be wisest to use both behavioral and attitudinal assessments to be certain that no important information has been overlooked. If questionnaires are to be used, it is essential that members complete them anonymously lest they merely give socially desirable responses. It may be advantageous to discuss the results with the members, and ask them for suggestions as to what can be done to make the group more attractive to members, assuming that is a goal of the worker and that the cohesiveness is less than desired. If specific questions are asked about member attractiveness, instrumental attractiveness, activity attractiveness, and prestige of the group, the practitioner may be able to pinpoint the difficulty, and apply remedies that are specifically tailored to the problem.

CHAPTER TWELVE

GROUP COMPOSITION

The discussion of group composition will focus on the group variables of size and heterogeneity, and on the individual dimensions of age, race, ethnicity, sex, and personality characteristics. As an introduction, some words of wisdom of Fritz Redl (1951) concerning group composition will be offered, for they are as relevant today as they were over twenty-five years ago when they were written. Redl cites several basic principles of grouping, and among them are: "Don't leave composition of a group to chance; don't develop blind 'germophobia' or fear that if one member is worse than another, he will wreck the group; and be careful of 'shock effect' that may occur if one member is too far from the behavior level of the group" (86–87). Redl says there is no such thing as a homogeneous group, for if members are matched on one criterion, they are not matched on another. The important point, he argues, is to determine which combination of criteria is most important for the job, and then to compose the group according to these primary criteria. However, he warns, secondary criteria must not be ignored. Members can be more divergent on secondary criteria than on primary criteria but if the deviations are too great there may be a disaster. Among the important secondary criteria Redl cites is the developmental phase the members are in, for as these phases differ, there will be a great difference in sex and language, sophistication, program tastes, and adult relationships. It is difficult to imagine a highly cohesive group composed of eight-year-olds and sixteen-year-olds.

Redl's advice as not based on systematically collected empirical data. In fact, he commented that there was no real research on group composition as yet. In the years since Redl's classic article "The Art of Group Composition" was published in 1951, considerable work has been done to transform the 'art' of composition into something more closely resembling a science. There is still a long way to go, but some of the mystery has been removed. A number of investigators have experimented with different types of group compositions, some varying the personality characteristics of members, some the race, some the sex, some the ethnicity, and others the size of the group. The major findings will be reported here, but the reader is warned that there will be a paucity of theory explaining the results obtained.

Despite this lack of conceptualization, the observed relationships between characteristics of group members and group variables (for example, group cohesiveness, conformity to group norms, and achievement of group goals) are of importance to practitioners in a number of ways. The relationships can be useful in deciding how to select members for newly formed treatment/growth groups, in understanding differences in effectiveness of already existent groups, and in modifying the composition of ongoing groups experiencing difficulties in functioning.

GROUP SIZE

One of the most exhaustive reviews of the research literature on group size was conducted by Thomas and Fink (1963), who examined thirty-one empirical studies of small groups (two to twenty members) in which size was related to one or more dependent variables, such as group performance, member satisfaction, and consensus. In spite of the methodological problems in many of the studies, Thomas and Fink drew the following generalizations: 1. Both the quality of performance and group productivity were superior in larger groups under some conditions. Under no conditions were smaller groups generally superior, but measures of speed sometimes favored small groups, 2. Smaller groups appear to inhibit expression of disagreements and dissatisfaction more than larger groups, but do give each individual more opportunity to interact with other members and to display leadership behavior, 3. There is strong evidence that as size increases, there will be decreasing group cohesiveness and increasing development of cliques, division of labor, and the emergence of several leaders, 4. In general, in problem-solving groups there is more member satisfaction with the group discussion in smaller groups. Thomas and Fink (1963) conclude that more research is needed on the intervening variables between group size and the dependent variables, e.g., the effects of size on reward and time constraints. Finally, Thomas and Fink suggest studying resource inputs such as intelligence of the members, and demand inputs such as the demand for attention, so that an understanding can be gained of *why* size affects other variables.

A more recent study (O'Dell, 1968) supports Thomas and Fink's

(1963) conclusion that small groups tend to inhibit expression of disagreements and dissatisfaction. O'Dell formed groups of two, three, four, and five persons from among the male nonpsychiatric patients at a Veterans Administration hospital and asked them to discuss ways of reducing automobile accidents. The discussions were coded using Bales' (1950) interaction categories. Although almost all of the significant findings occurred in comparing dyads with large groups, it was found there was less inhibition as the group size went from two to three to four to five. Further, tension decreased as the group size increased in size from three to five. In general, the findings corroborated those obtained by Bales and Borgotta (1955) and Slater (1958) who studied problem-solving groups ranging in size from two to seven; they found that as the group size increased, there were significant increases in showing release of tension, giving suggestions, and expressing dissatisfaction and disagreement, and a decrease in showing tension, expressing agreement, and asking for opinions.

O'Dell (1968) did not offer a theoretical explanation of the phenomena observed, but Shaw (1976), in reviewing the O'Dell study, suggests that lower tension in larger groups is probably due to the relative anonymity the provide. This permits greater tension release, although large collectivities may be less satisfying to the members. It is difficult to believe that a group of four provides anonymity for any member, but there may be other factors at work permitting the expression of disagreement and hostility. Possibly, the presence of others may diffuse the responsibility so that if several people express displeasure, no single individual need assume the blame for altering the ambience of good feeling. It is also possible that in the larger group as release of tension statements and disagreements are voiced by one or two persons, other members use that behavior as a basis for social comparison and behave similarly. The greater release of tension and expression of disagreement may also be a reflection of different role behavior. In a dyad or triad, the role behaviors the situation demands may be those attached to the position of friend, whereas in a group of four or five, the role behaviors elicited may be that of committee member who can dispassionately agree or disagree with any topic at hand. Clearly more research is needed to elucidate the dynamics at work.

A recent set of studies suggests that individuals may feel more reluctant to enter a group of larger than of smaller size. This was shown in both observational data based on college students' approach behaviors toward an empty bench or a bench occupied by one, two, three, or four persons, and on a paper-and-pencil questionnaire

(Knowles et al. 1976). These findings should alert the practitioner to be particularly sensitive to concerns a new member may feel in entering an on-going group of relatively large size.

In sum, insofar as group size is concerned, the worker may have to balance member satisfaction with freedom to express negative feelings. Pragmatic issues are also involved of course, and the practitioner will have to decide whether it is feasible to serve a group of four when there are people on a waiting list who could easily be served if the group size increased to eight. One factor to bear in mind is that as the group becomes more cohesive, members may feel free to express feelings regardless of the number involved (Guttentag 1970). Thus, some initial disadvantages of the small group may be overcome in time.

HETEROGENEITY VS. HOMOGENEITY IN GROUP COMPOSITION

Other investigators have examined the mix of the membership as a variable, rather than size. The issue is usually discussed in terms of heterogeneity versus homogeneity. One model that is proposed for treating delinquents suggests that a small number of antisocial youngsters could readily be integrated into groups of prosocial children within traditional agencies (Feldman and Caplinger, 1977; Feldman et al. 1972). The authors believe there would be no negative consequences for the agency's regular clients because empirical research by Asch (1956) and Backman, Secord, and Peirce (1966) indicates that a minority of one is likely to conform to the behavioral norms expressed by the majority. Feldman and colleagues (1972) therefore recommend limiting the number of delinquents enrolled in any prosocial group to one or two. This theoretical argument for such integration is supported by a citation of the researchers' and practitioners' reports of various types of deviants successfully incorporated into traditional agency service programs. These include retarded individuals, orthopedically handicapped individuals, and some with "impaired adaptive behaviors." In the experiment of Feldman and colleagues, fourteen antisocial children were each integrated into fourteen groups composed of prosocial children, and preliminary data indicated no staff overload. Moreover, the integrated children's prosocial behaviors apparently increased, and there seemed to be no negative consequences for regular group members.

Feldman and coworkers (1972) did not specify the other characteristics of the group members but the implication was that both prosocial and antisocial children were of approximately the same age, and of the same sex. Thus the groups can be described as having members similar in demographic or descriptive attributes and heterogeneous, to a limited extent, in behavioral attributes. This grouping resembles that espoused by Bertcher and Maple (1974), and found most effective in two related studies by Fairweather (1964b) and D. H. Sanders, MacDonald, and Maynard (1964). The latter experimenters composed four types of groups of eight to fifteen male psychiatric patients in a Veterans Administration hospital. Two groups were homogeneous in level of social activity, with one group having all members above average and the other all below average. Two other groups were heterogeneous in social activity, with one group composed largely (two-thirds) of above-average members, and the second group composed largely (two-thirds) of members below average in social activity level. By social activity Fairweather meant behavior such as talking to others and being chosen by others. The groups were similar in age, length of stay at the hospital, and living situation prior to hospitalization, characteristics that can be referred to as descriptive attributes. The results indicated that the group with the predominance of members having high social activity, but having some low socially active members, was significantly better than any other group in handling both simple and complex group tasks related to the members' current and future living, e.g., ensuring members kept appointments in the hospital or developing a plan for members' employment after hospital discharge. Thus the findings resemble those of Feldman and colleagues (1972) except that the number of "deviants" was not limited to one or two but comprised one-third of the total membership. Fairweather (1964b), in summarizing the results of his and the D. H. Sanders, MacDonald, and Maynard (1964) studies did suggest, however, that having more than two extremely disturbed patients, i.e. those with hallucinations and delusions, in groups of eight to fifteen members was extremely problematic because the group spent too much of its time dealing with these men to the detriment of the other members. He further proposed two important reasons why heterogeneity biased toward adequate functioning is desirable: 1) it facilitates the development of effective leadership, both because not all members vie for leadership and because there are enough effective members for more than one leader to develop, and 2) it enables norms to develop for member performance that are represented in the behaviors of the more adaptive patients.

Bertcher and Maple (1974) developed a system of measuring the differences in behavioral attributes and suggested composing a group of members who have common descriptive attributes but heterogeneous behavioral attributes. They believe that the similarity in descriptive attributes will foster compatibility and interactiveness, whereas the heterogeneous behavioral attributes will increase the chances that members will have something in their behavioral repertoires useful to the group. When all members have similar behavioral attributes as well as similar descriptive attributes, the group typically holds little promise for those who are seeking new answers, and the blind lead the blind, according to Bertcher and Maple. The goal of the practitioner is to compose a group that is balanced, that is, has the optimum mix of critical behavioral attributes. Critical attributes are those relevant to the group purpose and to the group's desired development. Bertcher and Maple (1974) offer no evidence that their suggested method of composing groups is effective, but a review of the literature by A. P. Goldstein, Heller, and Sechrest (1966) led these authors to conclude that a balanced group is more desirable than one which is either heterogeneous or homogeneous. The question is which specific similarities and differences lead to the most compatible and responsive therapy group.

Goldstein, Heller, and Sechrest (1966) strongly recommend that for greatest efficiency and predictive accuracy, information for balancing purposes should be based on observed group interaction and not on interviews or psychological tests. This emphasis on balance in observable behaviors supports the Maple and Bertcher preference for a group which is balanced on behavioral characteristics. Several years later, Goldstein (1971) wrote a book on a therapeutic attraction and stated that as a result of a number of investigations, it now appears clear that the group most successful in inducing conformity contains members who are of the same sex, age, and status. Combining the two books, one can say that Goldstein endorses the suggestion that treatment groups be composed of members who are similar in descriptive attributes and balanced in behavioral characteristics.

Tuckman (1967), in a very sophisticated study, demonstrated that heterogeneity interacts with task structure to influence groups' performance. Thus it appears that one should not consider heterogeneity in isolation from the group's activity. Groups of three navy enlisted men who varied in dominance and abstractness-concreteness worked on two tasks. Those of intermediate heterogeneity displayed less tendency to structure their tasks and therefore outperformed homogeneous groups on tasks that require little structuring, such as abstract problems. On the other hand, groups with very high or very low heterogeneity showed greater tendency to structure tasks. Perhaps, the author suggests, groups of low heterogeneity act to increase differentiation, and groups of high heterogeneity to reduce it. In tasks where division of labor was effective, usually concrete tasks, a high degree of structure was desirable and groups with very high or very low heterogeneity outperformed groups with moderate heterogeneity. Here, intermediate heterogeneity was a disadvantage. Tuckman concludes that if one could identify the amount of structure needed by the task, and the amount of structure likely to develop in the group from the level of heterogeneity, one could predict performance based on the interaction between group composition and nature of the group task.

The implication of Tuckman's study for practitioners is that one cannot assume that any particular degree of heterogeneity in membership is good or bad until one knows the task of the group. Treatment/growth groups would certainly have to be labeled as unstructured, and thus in this case intermediate heterogeneity may be most effective. Perhaps similarity on descriptive attributes and difference on behavioral attributes recommended by Bertcher and Maple (1974) would meet Tuckman's criteria for intermediate heterogeneity. If so, there would be consensus among key writers about the undesirability of having treatment/growth groups matched on both variables or unmatched on both.

SEX AS A VARIABLE

Heterogeneity and size are abstract concepts that do not give information about specific characteristics. There are at least three such specific characteristics that have concerned researchers in the field of group dynamics: sex, race, and personality predisposition. Ruble and Higgens (1976) cite data to show that the mere presence of persons of another sex in a group, without any verbal interchange, could alter self-perceptions. In their own study, undergraduates were asked to give written descriptions of themselves in the presence of two or three others who varied in sex. In the conditions where two or three males and a single female were present, or two or three females with a single male, the responses of the single individual were less sex-stereotyped than when this mixed and asymmetrical condition was not present. Both males and females who were in the minority of one included in their self-descriptions more traits typically associated with the opposite sex than did their peers in other group compositions. For example, females were more likely to describe themselves as competitive and males as introverted when they were the only member of their sex in the group than when they were in a same-sex or balanced-sex group. The authors offer the following speculation concerning their findings. Previous research by S. L. Bem (1975) showed that men and women are, to various degrees, androgynous. To the extent that individuals regard androgyny as a desirable goal, they should include more opposite-sex stereotypic traits in their self-descriptions when sex-role awareness is heightened as it is in groups composed of a lone member of one sex and all other members of another. On the other hand, if individuals regard androgyny as undesirable, such a situation should result in more stereotypic traits appearing in their self-descriptions. Because the subjects of this study were college students, a group relatively opposed to stereotypic sex norms, the enhanced use of opposite-sex stereotypes in the highly salient minority condition might be expected.

Indirect support for this explanation, based on the effects of sex composition of a group on sex-role awareness and the acceptance of androgynous values, was offered by Ruble and Higgins (1976), who cited two unpublished studies relevant to their argument. Clear sex composition effects were found for fifth-graders, but not for kindergarten children. In kindergarten, there was some enhancement of sex-typed toy activity for the boys and girls in the minority. In the fifth grade, however, girls' feminine responding was found to decrease and their masculine responding to increase when their sex-role awareness was heightened through the sex composition of groups, i.e., when girls were in the minority. Many of the females spontaneously mentioned their desire to be tomboys. Thus, in general, self-descriptions and the sex-typed responses of both children and adults appear to be affected by the sex composition of their group, but whether the direction of the effect is toward or away from stereotypes varies with age. Females of all ages above kindergarten exhibited increased cross-sex responding in unbalanced mixed groups, particularly when they were in the minority. Males in the minority shifted from predominantly sex-typed responding as children to cross-sex responding as adults. This is in keeping with the theory that there is a developmental trend toward androgyny in which individuals, especially males, are more willing to represent themselves as possessing traits associated with the opposite sex. When gender and/or sex-role awareness is heightened, children above kindergarten age represent themselves as what they value most, masculine, and college students represent themselves in terms of what they value, a relatively androgynous self.

Maguire (1973) offered a slightly different explanation, proposing a selective social perception model in which people concentrate on the distinctive aspects of the relationship between self and the social context, or on what is different about themselves and their environment. In support of this model, he reported that sixth-grade children in a classroom where their sex was in the minority were more likely spontaneously to mention their sex when asked to tell about themselves than when they were the majority sex in the classroom.

Both the Maguire and the Ruble and Higgins explanations are founded on the observation that sex becomes more salient when there is an unbalanced group with more of one sex than another. This information can be used in a number of ways by social work practitioners. If one does not wish to heighten the members' awareness of their sexual identity, for example, in a mixed-sex group of adolescents trying to cope more effectively with the death of a loved one, it would be inadvisable to compose a group in which either males or females strongly predominate. On the other hand, if the worker wishes to heighten the members' consciousness of their sex, for example, in a group of ill-groomed retarded adults who are being socialized to function in the outside world after years of institutionalization, an unbalanced sex group might be very efficacious.

RACE AS A VARIABLE

The Maguire (1973) hypothesis about selective social perception in which people concentrate on distinctive aspects of the relationship between themselves and the situation is highly relevant to biracial groups. Selective social perception may be one of the factors accounting for the phenomenon of "racial saturation point" initially discussed by Moreno (1934) and more recently by L. E. Davis (1977). This term refers to "the largest number of outsiders which a particular group will allow to exist within its boundaries." (L. E. Davis 1977:17) According to Moreno's conception, there is no prejudice against a minority until that particular minority group's saturation point is reached. Prior to that point sympathy may prevail, but once the saturation point is reached, the group is likely to experience hostility or a cleavage in which one group moves away from the other. Although Davis questions that no prejudice exists among the majority group members below the saturation point, he recognizes that passage of the saturation point may have profound effects on the expression of prejudice. In an intriguing study Davis sought to determine whether black and white college males exhibited preferences for different ratios of blacks and white in groups in which they would be a member and whether these preferences would be related to the type of activity of the group or its size. He found that there were indeed differences when the subjects were asked to select either five or ten individuals from a list of fifty men described in terms of age, interests, college major, personality, and race: black subjects selected significantly more black members for the groups than did white members and their selection ratio varied both with the size and nature of the group; the choices of the white subjects did not so vary. In particular, black subjects chose a higher proportion of blacks as members of smaller groups (an average of 55.6 percent of the five-member groups) than of the larger groups (an average of 48.2 percent of the ten-member groups) and of the more intimate groups (those that would be on first name basis, with varied topics of conversation) as compared with more formal groups (those that would work on an objective task with minimum conversation). White subjects chose an average of approximately 35 percent black members for both the five-person and ten-person groups. Davis speculated that this lack of variability and relatively low level of cross-race choices among whites reflected a lower racial saturation point for whites, and suggested this was due, at least in part, to the relatively low amount of interracial contact experiences by whites. This meant that the presence of a black member in a group to which a white student would belong would be quite a novel experience and lead to arousal and a low racial saturation point. In Maguire's theory, the "saturation" point may be reached when the racial group in the majority suddenly becomes aware of their distinctive aspects compared to the racial group in the minority.

It is possible that the results of the Davis study would have been different had he used a noncollege population, nevertheless, the implication for the practitioner is that a racial composition which may be comfortable for the members of one race may not be comfortable for another. It appears that members of minority groups may be particularly concerned about the group's composition in small informal groups, feeling more comfortable when more members of their own group are present. Yet members of the majority group would not have similar preferences. Therefore, when considering the number of black and white persons to include in a group, the worker must keep the degree of intimacy of the group in mind. As the Davis study demonstrated, "How many?" is closely related to "How close?"—at least for minority group members.

But the worker may have had as one of the goals of the group the desire to improve race relations, or to phrase it differently, increase the saturation point of one racial group for another. If that is the case, the initial discomfort of majority members to a sizable proportion of minority members may not be a problem; it may even be advantageous. A number of studies have shown that attitudes toward another race can be improved under certain group contact conditions. These will be discussed in detail below.

The literature on the subject of contact between members of different ethnic groups was reviewed recently (Amir 1976). Based on studies of interracial and interethnic contact in the United States and many other countries it was concluded that when the following conditions are met the outcome of the contact is likely to be a reduction of intergroup prejudice: 1) the members of the groups in contact with one another are of equal status, or the contact is with a higher status member of the minority group; 2) the contact situation is one that involves intergroup cooperation, interdependent activities, superordinate goals, or separate goals that can be achieved only by intergroup cooperation; 3) intimate rather than casual contact occurs; 4) the relevant "authority" or the social climate favors and promotes intergroup contact; and 5) the contact occurs under conditions of pleasure such as at camps, concerts, or trips, or conditions of successful accomplishment. Amir also concluded that contact can lead to more negative attitudes under certain conditions: 1) the minority group's members are of lower status; 2) there are mutually exclusive goals or competitive goals leading to zero-sum relationships (i.e., as one group wins, the other loses); 3) the institutional norms are opposed to contact between such groups; 4) the cultures of the groups contain aspects that are objectionable to the other group; and 5) contact is made under conditions of failure, anxiety, or distress. It is noteworthy that conditions that foster positive interracial attitudes closely resemble those that foster cohesiveness. This is not surprising, since one of the characteristics of highly cohesive groups is member attractiveness.

A number of studies have been conducted in recent years to determine some conditions under which attitudes toward members of other racial groups improve; all of them used whites and blacks as subjects. S. W. Cook (1972) asked white coeds to meet with a black woman of the same age for two hours a day for one month and found substantial changes in attitude among the white students. The investigation supported the view that when there is prolonged contact between two individuals who are equal in status, racial attitudes will change. Foley

(1976) replicated and extended Cook's findings among male inmates of a maximum security state prison and also found positive changes in racial attitudes and behavior. Again the power of prolonged contact between individuals of equal status to change racial attitudes and behaviors was demonstrated.

Two studies conducted in a natural setting with children arrived at similar conclusions. In one (Eaton and Clore 1975), data on imitation of adult behavior were collected at week-long summer camp sessions involving prolonged and intimate contact between black and white children, eight to twelve years of age. There were one hundred twelve youngsters in the study, approximately half boys and half girls, all of equal status. On two occasions the campers observed the behavior of unfamiliar black and white adult models responding to the commands of an "Indian Chief." In three separate camp sessions, the proportion of responses of racially different models imitated was significantly higher on the fifth day than on the first day. It was concluded that interracial contact effects were not limited to changed attitudes toward fellow campers of a different race, but generalized to unfamiliar adults in the same setting.

Another study conducted at the same camp examined the effects of the interracial experience on the attitudes and behavior of the youngsters toward one another (Clore, Bray, Itkin and Murphy, 1978). There were one hundred ninety-six children involved, ranging in age from eight to twelve. All were referred by school social workers, were economically deprived, and were from similar backgrounds. Each camp session was one week long, and there were five sessions involved in the investigation; one-half of the campers, staff, and administrators were black and one-half white; one-half were male and one-half female. There were six youngsters and two counselors in each tent, almost always one counselor of each race. Five dependent variables were used, some in the form of questionnaires and some in the form of games or activities, e.g., the youngster was given a camera with a load of film, told to photograph whomever he or she pleased, and the percentage of people photographed of the opposite race was used as the dependent variable. It was found that the male youngsters, both black and white, had significantly more positive attitudes initially toward the other race than did the females. It was thus not surprising that fewer significant changes were found for males than females. For example, there was an increase in cross-race choices in three games for females but not for males. In general, the camp was equally effective for black and white children, with blacks and whites changing at the same rate.

After testing several alternative interpretations of the change in interracial attitudes and behaviors from the beginning to the end of the camp sessions the authors concluded that the only reasonable interpretation was that prolonged, intimate contact between members of equal status of two races accounted for the results obtained. This, however, is only the necessary condition for change, not an explanation of why the change occurred. It may be that children of both races were members of social comparison groups for each of the campers, and, under those conditions, the dissimilarity in skin color was overshadowed by the similarity in attitudes and behaviors. Or possibly, other characteristics became salient, e.g., skill at sports, and in turn, skin color became less relevant as a predictor of behavior. In any case, the practitioner can infer from this study and the previous one by Eaton and Clore (1975), that regardless of other goals that may be achieved, the worked who combines black and white youngsters in a group under conditions of equal status and prolonged pleasurable contact among members and an authority figure supportive of intergroup contact is likely to enhance the positive attitudes the members feel toward the opposite race. Whether the positive feeling will generalize to other situations and settings remains to be investigated.

The explanation offered by Clore and coworkers for the initially more positive interracial attitudes of boys than girls also is significant for practitioners. They suggested that eight to twelve-year-old black and white boys valued physical prowess and both groups possessed talent in the area. For preadolescent girls, however, the shared concern was physical appearance, but the ideal tended to emphasize characteristics of their own race. Hence the greater similarity in "culture" of males than females, and consequently, the more positive attitudes across race. This view suggests that it may be easier to integrate white and black prepubertal boys in groups, but the need may be greater to integrate black and white prepubertal females. A number of studies of school desegregation also support this inference (see Amir 1976).

Thus far, racial differences in groups have been discussed in terms of the relationship among members. Another factor needs to be considered, however—that of the relationship between the worker and the members when there are racial differences. It has been found that individuals are likely to provide experimenters with more socially desirable replies when there is a racial difference between subject and experimenter (L. E. Davis 1977). Davis suggested a similar relationship may hold between group member and worker such that more honest and open answers may be given when the worker and member are of the same race, probably because of the greater comfort experienced, and therefore recommended that, if at all possible, biracial groups be headed by two leaders, one black and one white.

A related finding was obtained in a study of workers in three large industrial plants in the Midwest. Parker (1976) assessed the attitudes of subordinates toward their supervisors, some of whom were white and some black. The workers were also of both races. It was found that white subordinates of white supervisors in predominantly black groups saw their supervisors more favorably than did white subordinates of white supervisors in predominantly white groups. This again illustrates that the minority members in mixed groups are more aware of the characteristic that determines their minority status than are those in more homogeneous groups. As was discussed previously, the same phenomenon is found in groups that are not balanced by sex (Ruble and Higgins 1976). If one were to use Maguire's (1973) model, one would say that selective perception would make race highly salient to the white workers in the predominantly black group with some white members and a white supervisor, and arouse an awareness of worker-supervisor similarity and attraction. In predominantly white groups, race is not likely to be very salient to the white workers, especially when the supervisor is also white. The net effect is that there may be no special comfort or identity with the supervisor, and hence no particularly favorable ratings.

Parker (1976) concluded from his study that different perceptions may be held when the characteristics of the respondents, race in particular, interact with the characteristics of the situation, the racial composition of the group. For practitioners, this means that they cannot pretend that their own race is irrelevant in biracial groups. Members are clearly aware of it, particularly in unbalanced groups, and especially when the worker is the same race as the minority members of the group.

PERSONALITY AS A VARIABLE

A final factor one must consider in composing groups is that of personality characteristics of the potential members. An investigation of male college students indicated that when the personality predisposition of the member dovetails with the group's activity, and/or with the role the individual is asked to carry out in the group, the morale of the individual increases, as does the individual's participation in the group. Thus the gratifications or rewards a member receives from the group experience depend both on the individual's personality and on the nature of the group. Specifically, D. Watson (1971) found that males high in dominance obtained greater satisfaction from a task-oriented group than did males low in dominance; they also communicated more with other members. Further, dominant members who were given positions of high power in the group gave the most suggestions about accomplishing the tasks at hand and offered more opinions and evaluations. Watson concluded that individuals high in dominance, or desire to lead, responded most vigorously when given the opportunity to be directive. A number of studies have attempted to determine the effects of matching clients' generalized expectation for internal versus external locus of control and the degree of structure of the treatment modality. A recent review of these studies (Baker 1979) concludes that there is some support for the hypothesis that successful treatment outcome is associated with a therapist-structured format for clients with external orientations and higher client input for those with internal orientations. Although these studies were almost entirely concerned with dyadic situations, it would not be surprising if a similar effect were found in group contexts. This would suggest that more highly structured forms of group interventions might be more effective than relatively unstructured client-initiated group formats for clients who assume that their outcomes are generally governed by forces beyond their personal control.

The personality predispositions of potential group members cannot be determined precisely, but educated guesses can be made based on social histories, intake interviews, referral sources, and whenever possible, observations of potential members interacting in groups. Using the best judgment they have, practitioners should similarly make an assessment of the reinforcements that would be likely to gratify each potential member and the reinforcements that will most likely be available in the group. If there is a choice of potential members, the worker should attempt to make the best match possible and select members who would find the group most satisfying. If that choice is not available, the worker should attempt to create a group structure and process that would match the personality predispositions of the members who must be included. If neither alternative exists, an effort should be made to create a position in the group that would provide some reinforcements for the member not likely to find the group structure or mode of activity rewarding, for example, the domineering member of an egalitarian group could be designated the dispenser of earned reinforcements.

CHAPTER THIRTEEN

NORM ENFORCEMENT OR ACTIVE GROUP INFLUENCE

Group structures can be conceived of as photographs taken at one moment of the stable interrelationships within a group. In contrast, group processes are changes in a definite manner over time; they can be conceived of as motion pictures. One group process that is of major significance to social workers is norm enforcement; this can also be called group control over members or active group influence on members. In treatment/growth groups, because the focus is on alleviation or prevention of problems of the group members, the development of group norms that support desired changes in members' behaviors is a major goal. The group thus becomes the means and context for individual change (Sundel, Radin, and Churchill 1974).

We begin this chapter by illustrating, defining, and identifying norms, then deal with the theoretical underpinnings of the process of norm enforcement in small groups, address the issue of the structure of a norm, and conclude with some comments on the importance of the development of norms that support effective problem solving by members of treatment/growth groups.

THE EXISTENCE OF NORMS

Before specifically defining what is meant by norms and techniques that can be used to detect them, several articles that support the assertion that the norm enforcement by the group has the power to bring about change in individual members in institutional settings will be reviewed.

ILLUSTRATIONS OF THE POWER OF NORMS

Basing his methodology on the concept of peer pressure, Vorrath developed a treatment program for delinquents known as Positive Peer Culture (Vorrath and Brendtro 1974). Vorrath believes that delinquency is a peer phenomenon and that delinquents can respond to peer pressure for positive, as well as negative, behaviors. Therefore, placing delinquents in a culture that stresses positive and helping concepts for high status position can bring about a change from antisocial to prosocial behavior. Although there are no systematic data available to prove that recidivism is reduced after a youth has been part of a positive peer pressure program, there are many institutions in the state of Michigan as well as in several other states that use this strategy. The youths are placed in small groups of peers with an adult leader and, to a great extent, the youths' life experiences and privileges for the next year are determined by the decisions of their peers. It is the leader's job to ensure the development of a culture or set of norms which sanction the twelve types of problems enumerated by these programs; problems with low self-image (or have "small" feelings), with being inconsiderate of others, with being inconsiderate of oneself, with authority, with being easily misled, with misleading others, with stealing, with lying, with drinking or taking drugs, with "fronting" (or acting the role of a show off who tries to impress others with his superiority), with becoming easily angered, and with aggravating others.

Evidence of any of these problems is sharply attacked by other members of the group, who themselves are punished as a group if they do not detect such problems in other members. Release is dependent upon acknowledging one's own problems and pointing out the problems in others; therefore the group is designed to become an active agent of change toward prosocial behavior. There are some youths who resist the pressure or are able to pretend they have altered their way of thinking; these are not rehabilitated in this program. There are many, however, who appear to respond genuinely to the treatment. The major difficulty these youngsters face after release is that there is no positive peer culture group in the community to support the new behaviors.

Vorrath and Brendtro (1974) acknowledged that Positive Peer Culture had its roots in a program called Guided Group Interaction, which started in the United States Army correctional institutions during World War II (McCorkle 1949). After the war, McCorkle and Bixby introduced the concept at the Highfields Residential Treatment Center in New Jersey (McCorkle, Elias, and Bixby 1958). Subsequently, in Provo, Utah, the principles developed in the army and at Highfields were adapted to help seriously delinquent boys, on the theory that delinquency is a group phenomenon and therefore group techniques should be used to achieve change (Hill and Gruner 1973). Guided

Group Interaction, unlike Positive Peer Culture, deliberately leaves rules and adult roles unclear, in order to create anxiety. This is believed to increase amenability to treatment. Here too release is dependent upon the evaluations of peers, but the delinquents must discover for themselves how they must behave in order to earn release (Empey and Rabow 1961). As the new boy enters the institution, he is forced to turn to his peers, for no one will tell him how long he has to stay or what he has to do to get out. As he begins to associate with other boys, he discovers that important informal norms do exist; for example, norms dictate that no one in the group can be released until everyone is honest and until every boy helps to solve problems. The group has power to impose punishments, which is less true of Positive Peer Culture approaches. These include extending an incarceration initially imposed by the authorities or refusing to release a boy from the program. Although the group has the potential for inflicting harsh treatment, it can be very supportive when the boy begins to conform to its norms. According to Empey and Rabow, the boys can find encouragement in a program which poses the possibility of relatively short restriction and the avoidance of incarceration. For conformity with the group's norms, the rewards are considerable; for defiance of the norms, the sanctions are equally potent. Unfortunately, there is no well-controlled research testing the long-term consequences of participation in this type of rehabilitation program.

The notion of using peer pressure to bring about changes in youths goes back much further than 1949. In the USSR in the 1930s Makarenko (1953) developed a plan for rehabilitating delinquents and educating children which is still practiced there to a considerable extent today (Bronfenbrenner 1970). Classroom behavior is largely controlled by peers in the same row, in the same classroom, or in the same building, and competition between rows, rooms, and buildings is fostered by adults. Inappropriate behavior by one individual is viewed as a reflection of poor control by his or her peers and consequently the entire group is sanctioned. Makarenko described his views in a book published in 1939 in the USSR, but not translated into English until 1953. Fundamental to Makarenko's system is the isomorphism of the group and the individual. Individuality is merely a reflection of facets of group life that is temporarily allowed to be displayed by various group members. Makarenko adamantly refused to admit that any individual could be more important than the group, and believed that the true task of education is to achieve an isomorphism between the individual and the collective (Radin 1970). Thus, according to Makarenko, the behavior of an individual should be a reflection of the wishes, values, and norms of the group.

A similar assumption about the isomorphism of the group and the individual is held in the People's Republic of China, according to the reports of hundeds of refugees interviewed by M. K. Whyte (1974). These adults described the required participation in small groups designed to teach citizens how to alter their society in a correct manner, and the strong pressures toward uniformity employed to bring about individual acceptance of group goals.

This approach may be contrary to the American idealization of the individual, but one cannot assume that peer norms do not have a strong influence in what occurs in classrooms in the United States. E. G. Cohen (1972), citing several researchers, concluded that when the norms of the students support the valuation of achievement, high peer involvement by a student can foster academic performance, but if they do not support achievement, high peer involvement can lower academic performance. Thus it appears that norms do operate in educational settings in this country but they are not controlled or directed by adults as they are in schools in the USSR and in Positive Peer Culture programs in the USA.

The power of norms that evolve entirely from group members was demonstrated by Foley (1976) within a prison setting. The purpose of the study was to determine the personality and situational factors influencing changes in prejudice. The subjects were eighty-three newly admitted inmates to a maximum security prison for males who were tested initially and then three weeks later after they had been assigned to different parts of the prison. A questionnaire completed by three hundred thirty-nine inmates (one-third of the total institution) provided information about the norms of the three parts of the prison: the two-man cells the eight-man cells, and the dormitories. The results indicated that individuals tended to change racial attitudes to agree with the norms of their living areas. The amount of change was dependent upon the inmates' cognitive complexity, self-esteem, and attitude toward people in general. Further, individuals who were not cognitively complex were the most responsive to the group norms and changed the most. The author concluded that in a situation where the interracial norms are positive, attitudes toward people in general and self-esteem are very highly predictive of change in attitudes, and cognitive complexity contributes to the prediction.

Finally, insofar as norms of growth groups are concerned, a research investigation showed that encounter groups that established norms supportive of the development of empathetic relationships were the most effective in producing outcomes of enhanced empathy among members (Anderson 1975).

DEFINITION OF A NORM

According to Thibaut and Kelley (1959), a norm is a behavioral rule that is accepted to some degree by most members of a group. Norms introduce predictability into interactions and reduce the need for the exercise of personal influence which is costly to the influencer and to the individual being influenced. Thus norms are substitutes for the use of interpersonal power. When there is nonadherence to a norm, a member of the group tries to restore conformity by referring to a supraindividual value rather than to the wishes of a single individual. In essence, norms are a means of controlling behavior without entailing the costs and power losses involved in the use of interpersonal power. Although norms are clearly useful in social interaction, they can persist long after their function has disappeared. Such persistence suggests that a complex cluster of norms exists in most stable relationships.

A slightly different definition of norms was provided by M. A. Lieberman (1975), who described a norm as a shared idea of appropriate behavior in a particular group. Norms not only influence participants but are perceived by each as being accepted by most others in the system. Ordinarily, behavior that violates such ideas of the right way to behave is treated as deviant, and is sanctioned by some means to reduce its occurrence. The system is thereby returned to its prior equilibrium. In most cases, sanctions do not have to be exerted frequently or vigorously. The anticipation of sanctions is often as effective in controlling deviant behavior as is their actual application. Although group members seldom discuss them, norms nevertheless serve as substitutes for interpersonal pressure and are in effect unwritten social contracts that can be invoked when troublesome behavior arises.

It is important to emphasize, as Thibaut and Kelley's definition implies, that not all rules governing behavior in a group are group norms. An externally imposed rule, for example a dress code adopted by a school's administration, is not a group norm unless the members of the group to whom the rule is meant to apply, the students in the school, accept it as a rule of conduct. There is no precise way to indicate what proportion of a group must accept a norm before it is considered a norm of that group, but most social psychologists would agree that at least half the members would be the minimal level (Shaw 1971).

ASSESSING THE PRESENCE OF NORMS

Knowing that norms are powerful is insufficient for practitioners; they must also know how to determine when a group norm exists. Similar behavior by most of the members is not the defining criterion. Parallel behaviors may be due to similar experiences in the physical environment, such as getting caught in a sudden shower, or similar experiences in the larger social environment, such as living through a depression or a world war. In addition, group members may have been very similar initially due to membership in the same ethnic or religious group, or to having been raised in the same geographical area such as the deep south, or an urban inner-city area. The resulting common socialization experiences can produce similarities in behavior that have nothing to do with the current small groups the individuals may have joined. Finally, members may model other high-status persons in the group because they are reinforced for doing so by the model, because they hope to receive the reinforcements the high-status persons receive, or because they are identifying with those individuals. Lippitt and coworkers (1968) observed this phenomenon at two summer camps, one for low-income disturbed boys and one for nondisturbed middle-class boys. In both groups, high-status members were modeled but norms were not involved.

In spite of the complexities in analyzing similarities in behavior, it is possible to determine the norms of a group. M. A. Lieberman (1975) cites some practical techniques, for example observing the members and seeking regularities in their behavior, such as unusual attire, that differ from what we are accustomed to seeing. Lieberman also suggests looking for typical behaviors that are missing. Another technique for learning the norms of the group is to observe whether certain members are the focus of the group's attention, especially if members are ganging up on one individual and trying to get this person to change. If so, that person has probably violated a basic group norm. Lieberman points out that norms are most easily discerned when they are violated by a group member.

Another way to determine a group's norms is to ask the members a simple question: "What behaviors would the group find acceptable and what would they find unacceptable?" An alternate quick way is to ask members how they would feel about specific behaviors, for example, crying, pleading for help. Lieberman and some colleagues used a variation of this technique and asked each group member to imagine he was speaking to a new member who wanted to know, in general, what went on in the group, and whether the group would see a particular behavior, for example, being late repeatedly, as appropriate for most members. When at least two-thirds of the members agreed on a behavior as appropriate or inappropriate, it was considered a norm. Lieberman (1975) concluded that posing simple questions offers a handy approach to finding out where leaders need to concentrate their efforts to create a better therapeutic climate.

INFLUENCES ON NORM ENFORCEMENT

Groups apply pressure to achieve conformity to norms in at least three ways: 1) they reward members who conform; 2) they modify communication to the deviant, increasing it to convince the individual to conform and then offer rewards for doing so (Schacter 1968); 3) they reject or punish the deviant by techniques such as ignoring or name-calling, and finally, if deviance continues, communication ceases and the group expels the deviant from the group. The power and motivation of groups to use these techniques of norm enforcement varies with a number of conditions that are described below.

FACTORS AFFECTING GROUP'S POTENTIAL FOR SENDING AND ENFORCING NORMS

Thibaut and Kelley (1959) cite several factors as contributing to a group's potential for norm sending. First is the issue of good communication among group members. This variable is particularly important when the norms are not all universalistic, that is those that apply in exactly the same manner to all members. Particularistic norms, those that apply to certain subgroups, are complex and require very clear communication if they are to be adhered to. Stating the norm is one of the three aspects of norm sending, according to Thibaut and Kelley; the second is surveillance, and the third, application of sanctions. Without clear communication, a statement of the rule is rather difficult, and without a statement of the norm adequate surveillance and effective sanctioning is difficult.

It should be noted that M. A. Lieberman (1975) disagrees with this view and argues that norms are not made explicit until they are violated. Thibaut and Kelley, however, propose that if there is to be conformity the norm must be stated, the group must be certain individual members know that a specific behavioral rule has been accepted by most members, that a specific norm exists. Perhaps that is the ideal situation: Lieberman may be describing what actually occurs in many groups where explicit communication about what is acceptable behavior rarely occurs.

Another factor affecting the group's potential for norm sending is the visibility of the behavior. If members cannot tell when others are defying the norm, for example if it involves an activity carried out in the privacy of one's home, the likelihood of strong norm sending is small. Similarly, if the specific nonconformist cannot be identified, norm sending is considerably weakened. Such a situation may arise when the norm applies to a proposal in a secret ballot election. Surveillance is impossible in these cases.

Most important of all in norm sending, is in Thibaut and Kelley's (1959) terms, the fate control the group has over the members, that is, the ability of the group to control the outcome or fate of its members, to reward when members conform and punish when they do not. Clearly, in a voluntary group if the members do not find the group attractive, they may not care if they are in the group or out. Under those conditions, members have little power to apply sanctions. However, if the group is attractive, if cohesiveness is high and members want to stay in the group, approval by others can be an effective source of normative pressure. In this situation, the members' ability to apply a sanction of disapproval, or even expulsion, can be a powerful mechanism for enforcing behavior control (Kelley and Volkart 1952). The rule of thumb in voluntary groups is that a group's pressure for conformity to norms cannot exceed the members' desire to remain in the group, or the individual will leave rather than tolerate punishment. The situation is obviously somewhat different in nonvoluntary groups such as the cottages in juvenile detention facilities that use guided group interaction or positive peer culture approaches to treatment. In those groups the fate control that the group exerts over members is, at least in part, based on sanctions unrelated to interpersonal attraction among members. The potency of the group in enforcing behavior control in those situations rests on the reinforcement value of the positive and negative sanctions available to the group, as well as on the adequacy of its communication of the norms and its ability to observe deviance and conformity.

Related to fate control and attractiveness of the group is the presence of desirable alternatives for the members. To the extent that there are other gratifying relationships or sources of satisfaction available for members, the pressure the group can exert to obtain conformity is limited. Another way of expressing that concept is to say that when the CL_{alt} for members is high, pressure to conform is relatively low.

One of the most important factors influencing the group's enforcement of a norm is the importance of the behavior to the group, for example, its relevance to the group's existence or attainment of its goal. In treatment groups, for example, violation of the norm of confidentiality or honesty in expressing feelings by a member would typically be more central to the group and hence elicit greater disapproval toward the deviant member than violation of norms concerning tardiness or seating patterns. Groups seek conformity among members because conformity helps the group to achieve its goals, helps in the maintenance of the group as a group, and helps maintain the group as a basis of comparison when no physical reality exists by which members can evaluate themselves. According to the theory of social comparison discussed earlier (Festinger 1954a), people have a basic need to understand how they stand in comparison to others, to evaluate themselves. Thus maintaining a group that serves as a social comparison group is important to the members.

A particular challenge confronts heterogeneous groups in their efforts to attain their goals. In such groups where members differ on major dimensions, such as sex or social class, they are likely to deviate from some of the group's norms, although they wish to remain members. In these instances the group is likely to exert strong pressures toward conformity in order to facilitate goal attainment (Thibaut and Kelley 1959).

It is noteworthy that conformity with norms is not equally demanded of all group members, although there is not complete agreement about the conditions under which pressures to conform are highest. Thibaut and Kelley (1959) conclude from a review of the literature that heightened conformity is expected of marginally accepted members. Fully accepted members are freer to behave independently. Yet Thibaut and Kelley also suggest that conformity to central norms is especially required of leaders or members who represent the group to the external world, presumably because of the important symbolic value of their conformity. The seeming contradiction may be explained by the findings of Wiggins, Dill, and Schwartz (1968), whose study showed that leaders or high-status persons are given greater freedom in deviating from minor group norms so long as their behavior is not detrimental to the group. When their deviant actions hurt the group, however, the sanctions were greater than when a lower status person engaged in the same behavior.

Another possible explanation of the contradiction can be found in the rationale for "idiosyncrasy credit," a phenomenon described and researched by Hollander (1958). According to this concept, and the longitudinal studies done to test it, group members can earn credits (positive dispositions on the part of members) either by competence or by conformity to the norms. These credits can enable the holder to deviate periodically, possibly because it is understood that he or she has internalized the norm and deviations are not the result of resistance to or ignorance of these behavioral rules. Leaders may therefore be using their previously earned idiosyncrasy credit when they are observed to be nonconforming. Another view of this difference in pressure to conform to norms is offered by Berelson and Steiner (1964) who concluded, after reviewing the literature, that high-status members and low-status members feel freer about nonconforming than do those in the middle. High-status members feel free to innovate and low-status members are apathetic and deviate because they have nothing to lose. Perhaps groups exert greater pressures toward conformity on such marginal members because of their apparent lack of commitment to the group. Thus Thibaut and Kelley's discussion of the strong group pressure on marginal members from the perspective of the group and Berelson and Steiner's discussion of the marginal member's tendency to deviate from the perspective of the marginal man may simply be two sides of the same coin.

DEFIANCE OF GROUP NORMS

Cartwright and Zander (1968) offer the following vivid example of pressures on a member who tried to deviate from a work group:

> First we would talk about her unfairness among ourselves. If that did not reach her, we talked about her where she could overhear us. If she still did not change, one of us would approach her in the lounge and ask her if she was trying to kill our jobs. That usually did the trick. (141)

But, members are not helpless in the face of group pressure to conform; there are techniques which can be used to counteract the onslaught. Thibaut and Kelley (1959) and Cartwright and Zander (1968) discuss several such strategies. Among them are the following: norm defiers can avoid exposure to the statement of the rule or misinterpret what was said; they can avoid surveillance; or they can use their own counterpower to render enforcement useless. Such power exists when a group needs or wants a member badly and that individual has attractive alternative groups available, or when the individual has an external source of power such as wealth, influence with policy makers, or knowledge that is valuable to the group. Potential deviants can also avoid sanctions by conforming minimally, or conforming so strictly that their actions are destructive although they cannot be called deviations. For example, if a norm of the group is to give feedback to members about their behavior during a role play, the feedback may be so extensive and so negative that the overall effect is damaging. If there are several deviants in the group, they can form a subgroup and attempt to bring about change in the norms in an effort to make them more tolerable. Recently it has been observed in a number of laboratory experiments that a deviant can influence the other members' opinions simply by vigorously and consistently behaving in opposition to the group norm (Moscovici and Fauchex 1972). The researchers suggest that such consistent expression of different opinions can disrupt the certainty of the majority, who then deal with the disruption in a number of ways including a shift in their own opinions and the group norm as well as the more commonly described efforts to change the deviant's behavior. The conditions under which a minority position is rejected outright or leads to modification of the majority position remain unclear at present.

FACTORS AFFECTING CONFORMITY TO GROUP NORMS

There are conditions that cause members to conform even when they have the potential for violating the norms. The members may get intrinsic pleasure from the behavior, aside from its connection with the group's accepted rules, or the member may find the group's rewards highly valuable (Thibaut and Kelley 1959). An example of this latter circumstance is the situation which evolves when a member desires status in the group very badly and conformity is required for status. Such a situation may arise when a high ranking professional or business executive joins a treatment or growth group and feels the need to obtain the same status there that is held in the outside world. Status incongruity is uncomfortable and individuals try to avoid this condition if at all possible (D. I. Warren and Easto 1972).

An individual's perception of his or her own competence relative to that of the group has also been shown to influence conformity

(Costanzo, Reitan, and Shaw 1968). Either a low view of one's own competence or a high view of the competence of other members of the group leads to conformity to a group norm; self-confidence in one's own ability and lack of confidence in the ability of other group members leads to resistance to group pressures toward conformity.

One factor responsible for nonconformity is reactance, as described in reactance theory (J. W. Brehm and Mann 1975) and discussed in chapter 6. This theory assumes that individuals believe themselves to have behavioral freedom, for example, the ability to hold a particular position on an open issue. When individuals feel their freedom has been threatened or eliminated, reactance is aroused. Reactance is defined as a motivational state that is directed toward the restoration of whatever freedom has been threatened or eliminated. One way to restore a threatened freedom is to exercise it, that is, to engage in the behavior in question, or not to engage in it if the behavior in question was coerced. The more important that freedom is to the individual, the greater the magnitude of the reactance; the greater the outside pressure to engage in the behavior, the greater is the tendency not to do so. In laboratory experiments when individuals placed high importance on freedom regarding the issue at hand and were also highly attracted to a group, the net effect was resistance to the normative pressures both in private and public. However, a sleeper effect was also present. When the group's pressure to conform was removed, the individual with high value on freedom and high attraction to the group changed and conformed to the norm of the group. The authors concluded that the sleeper effect is latent in all influence attempts that arouse reactance; if an influence attempt arouses reactance and therefore has been ineffective, positive influence can still be brought about by removing the pressure. According to J. W. Brehm and Mann (1975), this phenomenon is illustrated in the patient who does not change during therapy but adopts a more functional style of behavior after the therapeutic relationship is terminated. This suggests that in the short run, at least, applying pressure may be counterindicated in groups where there are members who are known to value their independence. Lewis and Ho (1975) suggest that this may be true of groups that include Native Americans who value their independence and noninterference in the affairs of others so highly that if pressure were to be applied it would not only "shorten the group's existence but cause alienation and withdrawal from future group activities" (Lewis and Ho 1975:382). For Native Americans, according to these authors, the individual and the group are definitely not isomorphic.

THE STRUCTURE OF A NORM

Learning the norms of a group and how they are enforced are the first steps for the practitioner; to more fully understand the impact on members of the process of norm enforcement, the next step is to learn some of the characteristics of those norms. This is a more difficult step. J. M. Jackson (1966) delineates several dimensions of a norm, or the structure of a norm as he refers to it, that may have enormous impact on the members. One such aspect of structure is the restrictiveness of the norm, that is, the range of frequencies of the behaviors that are disapproved. (Jackson considered only norms that involved quantifiable behaviors.) If the group expresses disapproval for most amounts of the behavior, such as speaking during a group meeting, the restrictiveness of that norm is great. Another dimension of structure is the degree of crystallization, or agreement about the norm.

Jackson cites as other structural characteristics of individual norms—the strength of the group's feeling of approval or disapproval, and the approval-disapproval frequency ratio, that is, the possible behaviors that would be approved compared to the possible behaviors that would be disapproved. If the approval-disapproval frequency ratio is low, that is, if a member is more likely to be disapproved for exhibiting various amounts of the behavior than approved, membership in the group can be oppressive. Similarly, if the strength of approval given is low and that of disapproval is high, membership can be aversive.

Although it is difficult to measure precisely the complete structure of a norm, the kinds of observational and questionnaire approaches described above for detecting the presence of a norm can be used to assess the major components of its structure as well. The concept is an important one, for it is not merely a question of whether a group has norms or not; it is equally important to know the impact of those norms on the individual member. If the overall effect is to make the group a place where members are continually receiving disapproval, attendance and group attraction are sure to drop. It is incumbent upon practitioners in those situations to do what they can to alter the norms of the group. It is not merely a question of fostering goal-facilitating norms and discouraging their opposites. The worker must also foster norms that will make the group experience, per se, as gratifying as possible. If this is not attended to, the group may dissolve long before any change is achieved in the members.

NORMS IN TREATMENT/GROWTH GROUPS

Unfortunately, it is not possible for group leaders to create the norms they wish. As M. A. Lieberman (1975) states, all social systems develop their own norms about appropriate behavior, and they are not always what the leader would wish. All leaders can do is use their influence to foster and develop norms that will be conducive to treatment or growth. This involves the social influence process that was discussed previously in chapter 6. The important issue for practitioners to keep in mind is that group norms can be damaging or helpful to achieving desired change. They are particularly helpful if they allow pressure to conform to exist only in limited areas of group life so that freedom of thought can be respected (Whitaker and Lieberman 1964). In essence, one of the most powerful techniques for achieving change in group members is to develop a cohesive group that adopts norms facilitative of growth. But, as with cohesiveness, norms can hinder or foster change in a positive direction. It is up to the practitioner leading the group to understand the power of norms in a cohesive group, to be sensitive to the content of the norm and its structure, and to have skills in influencing the group in the direction of adopting rules of behavior that will help rather than hurt the membership.

CHAPTER FOURTEEN

GROUP DEVELOPMENT

The stages of group development can be defined as definite changes through time in the structures, processes, and norms of a group as the group evolves from an aggregate, to a quasi-group, to a group, and then back to a quasi-group or aggregate again. Thus processes such as norm enforcement are themselves incorporated into a larger process of group development. The development of a group in some ways resembles the development of an individual. Just as there are large stages in individual development, which have been designated by Erickson in terms of trust vs. mistrust, autonomy vs. shame and doubt, etc. (E. Erickson 1963), or by Piaget in terms of sensory-motor stage, pre-operational stage, stage of concrete operations, and formal operations stage (Ginsburg and Opper 1969), or by Freud in terms of the oral, anal, genital, latency, and puberty periods (English and Finch 1957), so too have stages been designated by observers of the life of a group.

An appreciation of the fact that groups do develop and change in regular ways can be of enormous help to the practitioner starting a new group, taking over a group which was previously led by someone else, or entering into a relationship with a natural group. Even more helpful is an understanding of the behavior that characterizes the major stages through which the group passes. These regularities as well as limitations on them will be discussed in the remainder of this chapter.

GROUP DEVELOPMENT PHASES

Different theorists have used different terms to conceptualize the phases of group development, but there is considerable agreement among them, as Whittaker (1970) has shown. Among those who have made major proposals are Garland, Jones and Kolodny (1965), Hare (1976), T. Parsons, Bales, and Shils (1953), Sarri and Galinsky (1974), H. Trecker (1955), and Tuckman (1965). The labels used by Tuckman will be used for this discussion because of their clarity, but one could just have readily chosen the terms of any of the others.

Tuckman (1965) reviewed over fifty articles dealing with phases of group development over time, and concludes that there are four major stages, excluding termination, in a wide variety of groups, including therapy groups, T-groups, natural groups, and laboratory groups. He labeled these stages in very graphic terms, as: 1) forming; 2) storming; 3) norming; and 4) performing. The same general pattern emerges, according to Tuckman, whether one examines changes in interpersonal group relations or group task activities. In the social realm, the four stages of development are reflected in: 1) testing and dependency; 2) intragroup conflict; 3) development of cohesion; and 4) functional role-relatedness. In the task realm, the four stages are: 1) orientation to the task; 2) emotional response to task demands; 3) open exchange of interpretations; and 4) emergence of solutions.

The stages Tuckman delineates in the task area closely resemble those articulated by Bales and Strodtbeck (1968) in their systematic observations of problem-solving groups, namely, orientation, evaluation, and control. Only emotionality is missing, which Bales may not have observed in his focus on laboratory groups. Thus it appears that the phases a group goes through in the process of solving a single problem are analogous to the stages the group passes through in its lifetime. T. Parsons, Bales, and Shils (1953) described Bales and Strodtbeck's problem-solving stages as both a microscopic version of the macrocosm and, simultaneously, as a constituent part of it. That is, problem-solving sessions are one phase of group development, but in this phase, the group goes through the same stages the entire group goes through over a longer period. According to Parsons and colleagues, the problem-solving phases would constitute the state of integration in the group's development; in Tuckman's terms, it would probably be the stage of norming, typified by the development of cohesiveness in the social structure of the group and the open exchange of ideas in the task realm.

The interactions that take place in each of Tuckman's stages can be described more precisely. *Forming* is the stage during which members are involved in getting to know one another, seeking similarity of interests, testing boundaries, identifying the task or goals of the group and the ground rules for task accomplishment. The *storming* stage is one of a struggle for power, polarization, often an overturn of the initial leadership or a challenge to the existing structure; in treatment and growth groups where the group task involves self-exploration this stage of emotional reaction to the task is quite clear. The *norming* stage consists largely of developing commitment to the group as an entity, the evolution of stable norms, and the open expression of feelings and ideas. The final *performing* stage is one when cohesiveness is highest, functional roles have been differentiated and are carried out with the result that the group can effectively move toward its goal as well as effectively respond to stress. Sarri and Galinsky (1974) refer to this as the stage of maturation of the group. Tuckman did not include the period of group disintegration as one of the stages in group development in his original proposal (1965), but did later add *adjourning* to his conceptualization (Tuckman and Jensen 1977) because several observational studies identified such a phase (e.g., Lacoursiere 1974; Spitz and Sadock 1973). Other conceptualizations of group development, especially those designed for group practitioners, have recognized the special aspects of the ending of groups. Sarri and Galinsky (1974) call this the termination phase and Garland, Jones, and Kolodny (1965) label it the separation stage. It is the phase in which the previously formed group norms begin to lose their power to control members' behaviors.

GROUP DEVELOPMENT AND INTERVENTION PLANS

One important implication of group development theory for practitioners is that a storming stage should be anticipated in spite of the good feeling present in the forming phase. Such preparation might involve discouraging a growth group from establishing formal leaders at the first meeting or two, for they will be difficult to displace when, as is likely, the group challenges the existing leadership. The worker should also be prepared to deal with the reactions of individuals in treatment groups, who regardless of any formal position, perform leadership functions during early group sessions and whose influence is likely to be resisted later in the group's development. Such challenges to members' and the practitioners' influence can be discouraging. Thus the practitioner might want to prepare the group for the strong differences of opinion likely to emerge, and exert influence to keep the group from breaking apart during the storming stage. For example, the worker might ask the group to think about accusations of mistrust during the period between meetings and not to arrive at any hasty decisions at the moment of confrontaton.

Recognition that norms take time to develop and require the establishment of trust in members and beliefs in the utility of the group would discourage the practitioner from expecting or fostering high levels of self-disclosure in early meetings, even though this may ultimately be desired. Perhaps the absence of group norms regarding self-disclosure is the reason that M. A. Lieberman, Yalom, and Miles (1973) found that self-disclosure tended to be ineffective or harmful in the encounter groups they studied when it occurred early in the group meetings, but was more beneficial during later phases.

The worker who understands group development will also anticipate a growth toward more effective activity as the group matures, and may plan on playing a more passive role as powerful, highly crystallized norms emerge, that is, norms on which there is high consensus (J. M. Jackson 1966). Further, an understanding of the time needed to reach the stage of norming would keep a worker from suggesting group tasks requiring a high degree of interdependence in its early stages; parallel activities may be best initially.

The worker may also wish to prepare the group for termination when it appears that the peak of effectiveness is passed and the norms either become fewer in number or weaker. Preparing clients for termination will be discussed in more detail in the next part of this book but it is important at this point to state that group members may find separation from the group painful or uncomfortable. The worker who anticipates this feeling of letdown may want to provide some way of maintaining the memory of other members, perhaps suggesting the exchange of pictures, planning a brief reunion at some future date, or helping the members find other groups that will meet their needs.

Whittaker (1970) contrasts the activities of social workers using different models of group work as their groups pass through the developmental stages. For example, in the stage of storming or power struggle, a worker using the Social Goals approach would encourage all members to participate in decision making but essentially must go along with the group's decision about leadership structure and work with those leaders who seem to have the support of the majority. If the worker was successful in laying the groundwork for democratic participation, the leaders chosen will most likely represent the total group, but there is no guarantee that this will occur. Workers in the Remedial Model, on the other hand, would allow a certain amount of member rebellion, but would "act in their capacity of group executive and controller of membership roles to forestall the crystallization of any power takeover by a particular clique or subgroup" (Whittaker 1970:316). A worker using the Reciprocal Model would clarify the power struggle and focus on the function of the group, which is to provide a mutual-aid system. However, any rules for the group must emerge from the group and the necessities of the work, rather than from the personal authority of the helping agent.

Thus, the particular strategy workers use to help the group move smoothly and constructively through the phases may well depend on their orientation to group work. All workers, however, should be sensitive to the stages groups move through, and modify their interventions accordingly.

To determine the stage at which a group is functioning, one key factor should be an examination of the strength of the norms. In a study of residents of two housing units, it was shown that norms began to predict and control behavior only after the group had reached some degree of maturity (Festinger, Schachter, and Back 1968). They were not likely to be very powerful initially. By observing the compliance with the group's norms, the new worker in an established group can make an educated guess as to whether this is a group in its infancy, adolescence, middle age, or old age. Similarly, the presence of a power struggle or of well-meshed differentiated group roles provides clues as to where the group has been and where it is likely to go.

FACTORS INFLUENCING THE PHASES OF GROUP DEVELOPMENT

Most theories of group development have evolved from work with particular types of groups. The Bales and Strodtbeck (1968) studies were done with small groups of college men who worked together on a single task. In the literature reviewed by Tuckman (1965), studies of therapy and T-groups predominated. The Garland, Jones, and Kolodny (1965) model of development in social work groups was rooted in the groups seen at a children's agency. It is not surprising then that a number of the unresolved issues regarding group development concern the conditions that limit the observation of typical phases (Tuckman 1965). Variations in setting may affect the time a group spends in any phase. Treatment and growth groups might be expected to evolve norms about intimate self-disclosure more slowly than would task groups. The length of time a group expects to meet together would be likely to affect the speed with which the norming phase is reached. While much work remains to be done on these issues, a few empirical studies do shed some light.

A study conducted to test empirically Tuckman's stages of group development discovered that groups that undergo a considerable change in membership and in task go through Tuckman's first four stages twice (Runkel et al., 1971), The groups of students went from larger groups to smaller groups to select a task, pursue a research investigation, and then present the work in written form. The authors concluded that the fit of the observed groups' activities to Tuckman's (1965) stages was very good but there was a double cycle, which was not surprising since there was a radical change in structure with two different tasks to be completed and with somewhat different members. Psathas (1960) established that in two psychoanalytically oriented treatment groups the three main phases of group movement described by Bales and Strodtbeck did occur. But the sequence of orientation, evaluation, and control was found only when the entire period of the treatment groups' meetings were considered, not during a single group meeting. This was viewed by Psathas as a reflection of the fact that such groups are not confronted by a single problem in a given meeting, but with multiple problems that take several meetings to resolve. Further, he suggests, some treatment groups do not involve pressure for reaching a group decision and may therefore show less variability in control acts—giving and asking for directions or suggestions.

Hill and Gruner (1973) similarly performed an empirical test of Bales and Strodtbeck's (1968) theory of group development, using records of Guided Group Interaction meetings of the Provo, Utah project. There were sharp differences between groups starting with 100 percent naive members (closed groups) and groups that were generated from closed groups and contained members at various stages of knowledge of group procedures. Under the conditions in which members all started at one point and continued meeting for a long time, the theory of group development approximated the behavior pattern in the group. When the conditions did not approach the ideal postulated for the theory, the effects were masked, distorted, or absent. Hill and Gruner concluded that group development theories should be considered theories that depend on pure states, not often obtained in the real world.

Hill and Gruner's (1973) conclusions may be rather severe, but their study and that of Runkel and colleagues (1971) suggest that one should not look too closely for the stages delineated by the theorists unless conditions are ideal, that is, unless dealing with a small group of individuals who join a group at the same time and remain with it until the group terminates, with no new members added. However, it is valuable in working with a group to think about the stages and to attempt to ascertain whether the typical sequence of stages is being followed, and if not, why not. This procedure alone should sensitize practitioners to the fact that the group may be changing as it ages and that modifications in plans are called for. In addition, if the group appears to be fixated at one stage, that of storming for example, there may be unusual problems present which the worker should try to address immediately.

CHAPTER FIFTEEN

ROLE PLAYING AS A GROUP ACTIVITY

Before discussing research and theory on role playing in groups, a general overview of group activities is in order, for role playing is merely one of many possible activities a worker may select when planning a program. Other possibilities are music, dancing, games, trips, athletic events, art endeavors, discussions, and simulations. Program planning is a tool for social workers, for the activities engaged in have important meaning and consequences for group members; both the participants and group processes are influenced by the worker's choices. For example, in a discussion of the "it" role in children's games, Gump and Sutton-Smith (1955) pointed out that high-power "it" roles, as contrasted to low-power ones, lead to less failure for "it," to fewer negative reactions of the group toward "it," to more positive self-feelings for "it," and to more positive feelings about the situation by "it." Further, unskilled players could be helped to have less negative experiences if they were placed in high-power, rather than low-power "it" roles. Thus, in Vinter's (1974) terminology, choosing activities the group will undertake is an indirect method of influencing groups and their members, and should be used to achieve desired objectives. Activities can be described in terms of the following dimensions: prescriptiveness, control by the worker, movement required, competence required, interactiveness possible, and rewards available (Vinter 1974). Though one cannot be sure how members will behave in any given activity, differences in dimensions should be noted and activities chosen with reference to the particular behaviors practitioners wish to induce in group members. Role playing can be described as an activity that has moderate prescriptiveness and control by the worker, requires movement and the ability to verbalize, results in considerable interactiveness among members participating in the role playing, and is generally rewarding to the actors "on stage."

In addition to the dimensions cited by Vinter, Whittaker (1974) added some group dimensions that must be considered in selecting a group activity: group cohesiveness, the group composition, and the group mood. The more heterogeneous the composition, the more difficult it is to find an activity that all members can participate in and enjoy. If cohesiveness is low, Whittaker suggested parallel activities rather than those requiring much interaction and independence. A similar suggestion was discussed earlier in relation to the types of activities appropriate for newly constituted groups that have not yet reached the stage of norming, in which cohesiveness is relatively high.

Role playing would appear to make few demands in terms of the dimensions delineated by Whittaker. Only moderate interdependence is involved, for although role enactment requires appropriate location of other positions in the role set and complementarity of role expectations, role players can write their own scripts. A heterogeneous group can be accommodated by distributing roles according to the characteristics and needs of the group members. Role playing may be particularly useful in groups with low-income members, for these individuals are thought to prefer activities that involve behavior rather than those that rely entirely on verbalization (Gordon 1968; Reissman 1962). Group mood may be problematic but it has often been found that the use of warmup exercises readily prepares the group for role playing. At least this has been shown where children are concerned (Chesler and Fox 1966), and most likely is true for adults as well if a simulation is employed, such as that used in "Hidden Agendas" described by Pfeiffer and Jones (1973). In "Hidden Agendas," role instructions and role briefing sheets are distributed to the players who are supposed to be members of a fact-finding governing board, but who in reality have hidden agendas described in each individual's briefing. The players conduct the role play sitting in a circle and the other members sit in an outer ring and observe. The purpose of the exercise is to determine how hidden agendas affect the group, but as the exercise involves a role play that is removed from their own lives, the members become immersed in role playing in a nonthreatening fashion.

It has been pointed out that group activities including role playing inherently involve action, and action provides an opportunity to practice group participation, to experiment with new roles in a small group situation, and to try out newly acquired peer relating skills (Whittaker 1974). In addition, group activities are of value to the worker as they can be used as diagnostic tools to assess individual group members, group structures, and the decision-making process. The use of role playing as a group activity can also be designed to recreate, in a supportive environment, problem situations that group members have encountered in the past, with the goals of gaining insights into causes of problems and new ways of coping with similar problems in the future (Schopler and Galinsky 1974). In addition, role playing can and has been used to achieve a variety of other goals in dyadic and group treatment situations: to aid participants in learning new roles (Sarbin and Allen 1968), to help overcome the defensive avoidance that can prevent individuals from recognizing the destructive consequences of their current behavior (Janis and Mann 1965; Mann 1967; Mann and Janis 1968; Toomey 1972), or to enhance awareness of the potential consequences of alternative life decisions (Janis and Mann 1977).

RESEARCH ON THE EFFECTIVENESS OF ROLE PLAYING

Role playing does appear to bring about change. Clore and Jeffery (1972), in an experiment with seventy-six undergraduate male and female students, explored the effects of emotional role playing on attitudes and behavior toward the disabled. Th role playing consisted of traveling around the campus in a wheelchair for one hour. The design involved three treatment groups: role players, vicarious role players who walked twenty feet behind a role player in the wheelchair, and controls who just walked about the campus. Both the direct and vicarious role playing led to a more positive response to a specific disabled individual immediately after the experience and to volunteering to take a handicapped student on a tour one month after the experiment. In addition, both direct and vicarious role players displayed more positive attitudes toward the handicapped four months later on a disguised attitude measure ostensibly having no connection to the original experiment: the students were asked to indicate how student funds should be spent and were more likely to choose one alternative that would benefit handicapped students. The explanations offered for these findings will be discussed in the next section.

D. W. Johnson (1971b) conducted a series of experiments in role reversal with children and found that this facilitated social perspective taking, that is, taking the emotional role of another. In addition, when role reversal was used in conflict situations, it was found to induce cooperative behavior between participants. From a theoretical perspective, M. L. Hoffman (1975) arrived at a similar conclusion. In his view, training in role taking or exposure to information regarding the life conditions of others should be especially effective in producing helping behavior when the role playing directs the individual's attention to feelings, and when the individuals are initially empathetic. Working with delinquent boys eleven to thirteen years of age, Chandler (1973) demonstrated that training in role taking plus intensive role playing, which included developing roles and scripts for a videofilm project and studying the videotape of the role plays, resulted in a significantly fewer number of delinquent acts in the experimental group than in the control group and placebo group combined. The control group had no intervention, and the placebo group made videofilms, as did the experimental group, but had no training in role taking or opportunities to examine videotapes of themselves to see how others see them. Once again, the explanation offered by the authors for the findings will be discussed later.

A behavioral perspective to treating delinquents through role playing was taken by Rose and Sundel (1974), in their efforts to reduce the delinquency of a group of male and female offenders eight to sixteen years of age in Detroit. The youngsters presented a wide range of problems, such as truancy, running away, petty larceny, assault, and destruction of property, and over the course of three years from 1965 to 1968 several hundred clients were treated. Behavioral rehearsal was one of Rose and Sundel's treatment techniques, and they described it as a process in which clients produce behaviors in the treatment setting that are desirable for them to perform in real-life situations. The desired behaviors consist either of an entirely new sequence of performances or of behavior that has been rarely displayed in the problematic situation. Behavioral rehearsal was frequently preceded by a model's demonstration, sometimes involving prestigious models of the same race and background as the members, such as popular disc jockeys who were invited as guests to the group meetings (A. Schwartz and Goldiamond 1975). The behavioral rehearsals involved such themes as applying for a job or interacting with the police. At other times, rather than use a model, the workers gave precise descriptions of how the client should act in a given situation. The client then rehearsed the appropriate behavior in the presence of another individual who played the reciprocal role, for example, that of an employer. Behavioral rehearsal was used in combination with other treatment procedures, such as giving clients the assignment to perform the rehearsed behavior outside the treatment situation with monitoring procedures built in.

Rose and Sundel (1974) did not report any data concerning the results of behavioral rehearsal per se, but A. A. Lazarus (1966) compared behavioral rehearsal with nondirective therapy and advice giving, and found that behavioral rehearsal was the most effective means of resolving interpersonal problems. A. P. Goldstein, Heller, and Sechrest (1966) also emphasized the importance of the clients' practicing desired behaviors during therapy sessions for these behaviors to be performed outside the treatment situation. This is similar to George Kelly's (1955) fixed role therapy, which includes the development of individualized role sketches based on assessment of patient problems. Role enactment within the treatment setting and outside is then used as an instrumental means to achieve specified behavioral changes. Rose (1974b) found promising results in a behavioral program for parents that included rehearsal of such behaviors as limit setting and establishing new reward procedures for children. Flowers (1975) described in detail how role playing is used in assertiveness training and reported that the technique had been successful in both homogeneous and heterogeneous groups, and had been used with inpatients, outpatients delinquents, normal participants, therapeutic clients and students. Role playing has also been used to develop appropriate behavior in delinquents, to teach job interviewing skills, to help control aggressive behavior, and to change the social behavior of males who had little experience with dating. (Flowers 1975).

A series of studies by Janis and his colleagues (Janis and Mann 1965; Mann 1967; Mann and Janis 1968; Toomey 1972) has demonstrated the effectiveness of emotional role playing in helping individuals overcome self-destructive habits such as cigarette smoking and excessive alcohol consumption. In the prototypic situation in this approach the counselor creates a scenario that includes vivid exposure to the negative consequences of the behavior. For example, the smoker plays a patient who has just been told by a physician that he or she has lung cancer. In a later scene the doctor arranges for the hospitalization for surgery for the patient-role player. Such fear-arousing role plays have had both short- an long-term effects on smoking behavior and drinking.

Unlike behavioral rehearsal, this use of emotional role playing is not designed to provide practice for desirable behaviors, but rather to require the role players to confront information about their current behavior that has been defensively avoided. Janis and Mann (1977) have suggested another variation on role playing, which they term outcome psychodrama, that can be useful in counseling situations. This procedure was devised to overcome resistances that interfere with adequate consideration of all information relevant to choosing among alternatives for important life decisions, for example in the decision whether to obtain a divorce or to change jobs.

In outcome psychodrama the individual role plays the outcomes of alternative choices. Rather than enact a complementary role that identifies a scenario of consequences, the counselor or other group member plays a complementary role that encourages the clients to project themselves into the future in a vivid fashion. For example, a client trying to decide about a divorce is asked to imagine himself or herself talking to the counselor a year after a decision was made either to get a divorce or to make a genuine effort to keep the marriage going. The counselor and client engage in both role plays with the counselor's major role-playing task being facilitation of the client's projection of the self into the future and improvisation of a retrospective account of what has happened as a consequence of the choice of one or another of the major alternative decisions being considered. The counselor employs various techniques, such as using the present rather than the conditional tense, to help the client get into the role. Although as yet no controlled field tests have been done, Janis and Mann report that in twelve of fifteen clients with whom the technique was used new emotional information about the clients' feelings about the likely consequences of various choices became evident during the future outcome role plays. The complementary role need not be enacted by the professional, nor need it be a professional helping role. A heart-to-heart talk with a close friend some time after a significant life choice has been made would be another appropriate setting for outcome psychodrama. This technique, according to Janis and Mann, not only is a means to uncover information about one's feelings, it can also be used to prepare for possible negative consequences that are uncovered, such as the anticipated loneliness after a divorce or the loss of prestige stemming from a job change.

Sarbin's (1964) early literature review concluded that role playing is effective in achieving attitude and behavior change. More recently, Flowers (1975) arrived at a similar conclusion. In short, it appears that role playing is one of the few techniques used successfully by a wide range of practitioners. The question remains, why does it work? At this point the agreement ceases.

EXPLANATIONS OF THE EFFECTIVENESS OF ROLE PLAYING

Flowers (1975) suggests that it is not role playing per se that is producing the changes. Rather, he views it as providing the situation in which other change-inducing phenomena can be implemented, for example, reinforcement by others, self-reinforcement, direct instruction, modeling, feedback, and most important of all to Flowers, self-evaluation and self-observation. Other explanatory concepts that have also been proposed include dissonance theory, empathy, decentration, attribution theory, learning theory, information retrieval, and the simultaneity of several events.

A brief recapitulation of the basic tenets of dissonance theory, discussed in chapter 5, should make its potential linkage to role playing clear. According to that theory, cognitive dissonance is aroused when an individual behaves in ways that are discrepant with his or her own attitudes and beliefs—providing that the actor assumes personal responsibility for the actions, has some commitment to the behavior, and believes unwanted or adverse consequences have or will be felt by the actor or someone else as a result of the actor's behavior. Dissonance arousal is further enhanced when the actions require effort and when the actor has positive self-regard. Attitude change occurs under these conditions because the unpleasant state of cognitive dissonance can be reduced by a change in one of the inconsistent elements. Once having engaged in a behavior, especially in public, the behavior, and hence cognitions about it, cannot be undone. Thus other cognitions are more likely to change. Applying this explanation to the role playing situation, one can argue that most if not all such situations involve dissonance arousal—in the shy teenager by behavioral rehearsal of assertive behavior, in the smoker by playing the role of a smoker going to the hospital for cancer surgery, in the student who has not given much thought to the problems of handicapped people by experiencing the inconveniences of being confined to a wheelchair. To test the dissonance explanation of the efficacy of role playing Zimbardo and Ebbesen (1970) varied the effort involved in role plays in which undergraduates gave speeches advocating positions with which they didn't agree, and found, as predicted, greater attitude and behavior change when greater effort was involved than when only minimal effort was required. Other similar studies have also been conducted with comparable results (Aronson 1961; Zimbardo 1965). Zimbardo (1965) also showed that the cause of attitude change in role playing resides more in the individual's effort than in an intellectual weighing of pro and con arguments. Clore and Jeffery (1972) suggested that dissonance reduction may possibly explain the change in attitude toward the disabled by the role player in the wheelchair, but does not explain the similar amount of attitude change of the vicarious role player who walked twenty feet behind the wheelchair. The authors agree that if one were to say that the vicarious role players felt the same anxiety as the role player in the chair, and were embarrassed to walk slowly behind the chair, one could interpret the findings of attitude change in both actual and vicarious role players in terms of dissonance theory. But, it is clear, they find that argument difficult to accept.

Clore and Jeffery (1972) prefer to explain the change in terms of empathy. They suggest that playing the role of someone else fosters decentering, or taking the viewpoint of someone else. The net result is an increase in tolerance for the position of others, a more socially mature viewpoint. According to Clore and Jeffery (1972), the empathy explanation involves making the role player aware of a new perspective and inducing the belief that the role player knows how the other individual feels. As the vicarious and true role players were almost identical in empathy scores, the processes at work, Clore and Jeffery believe, are similar to those proposed by Bandura (1969) to account for observational learning. Like the behavior in modeling and vicarious learning, responses induced by role playing are coded and stored to be retrieved when similar situations arise.

Chandler (1973) and D. W. Johnson (1971b, 1975) both focus on decentering in their explanations of their respective findings. D. W. Johnson (1971b) suggests that role reversing leads to taking the emotional perspective of another, that is, recognizing the feelings and motives for feelings of another. Chandler proposes that delinquency is at least partially due to deficient role-taking skills; thus the delinquent is unable to take the perspective of another. The result is a high level of egocentric thinking, or thinking entirely from one's own viewpoint, and ultimately antisocial behavior. Training in role taking reduces the level of egocentricity and subsequently the level of delinquent behavior. In support of this view he cites data from his study that showed the delinquent youths were significantly lower in role-taking skills initially than were the nondelinquents. At the end of the study, boys in the experimental group had increased their role taking skills significantly more than the placebo and control groups combined. Eighteen months later, there were significantly fewer delinquent acts by experimental youths than by the combination of placebo and control groups. The conclusion is that improved role taking ability leads to greater social perspective taking, and finally to more law-abiding behavior.

Clore (1978) suggests that the mechanism by which role playing might change attitudes is related to attribution theory. As was discussed in chapter 3, an attributional bias has been shown whereby individuals tend to attribute their own behaviors to situational factors, but attribute the behavior of others being observed to dispositional factors, that is factors within themselves, such as ability, interests, personality. Clore proposes that after seeing oneself engage in the same behavior as others in a particular situation, one might have less of a tendency to believe that the behavior is due to the personalities or abilities of individuals in the situation. Further, if the behavior in question is devalued or antisocial, one would be less likely to make negative attributions about the individual after role play. The net effect would be a more positive attitude toward the individual whose role was enacted. He cites Storms' (1973) experimental study in support of this view. The reader may recall the discussion of that study in chapter 3; it showed how a change in visual perspectives revised attributions about situational and dispositional causes of behavior. When subjects saw a videotaped conversation of themselves from the point of view of the individual they were conversing with, their perspectives were switched and they were more likely to explain their own behavior on the basis of traits than on situational factors. In addition, observers who saw a tape of the conversation from the viewpoint of the subjects, that is, facing the conversational partner, offered a situational attribution to the subjects' behavior, as had the subjects initially. Clore concluded that changing attributions of a positively evaluated action from a person's character to the situation should reduce attraction. Conversely, changing the explanation of a negative act from the person's character to the situation should increase attraction. Thus, through role playing, one's attitudes toward others may change significantly. Such perspective switching could be valuable in a wide variety of problematic situations, such as marital or parent-child, dealt with in treatment and growth groups.

Another explanation of the effectiveness of role playing is based on learning theory. This interpretation underlies the use of rehearsal by practitioners who are behaviorally oriented. The assumption is that when members of the group enact some behavior they will exhibit in the real world, they receive reinforcement from the other members and the group's leader as their role playing comes closer to what is considered appropriate. Thus their behavior is shaped through role playing. The use of models and direct instruction by the worker to facilitate the learning of appropriate roles is also based on learning theory. An additional element enhancing the learning is the lack of anxiety associated with role playing. Flowers (1975) suggests that group members work up a hierarchy of situations of increasing difficulty so they may role play situations of increasing difficulty, that is increasing in anxiety provocation, as they become ready for more difficult tasks. The goal is for the member to learn to play the most provocative role without becoming anxious. A. P. Goldstein's (1973) structured learning therapy, which combines role playing with modeling, behavioral rehearsal and social reinforcement, illustrates the usefulness of this view.

Corsini (1966), who wrote a book on the use of role playing in psychotherapy, offers his explanation of why role playing is effective. According to Corsini it is the "simultaneity" of cognitive, emotional, and behavioral elements that makes role playing a potent learning method. Role playing involves acting, thinking, and feeling simultaneously. That is the source of its power to achieve change. In addition, Corsini describes role playing as a close representation of real life; it has veridicality. This is a "natural" method for learning and unlearning various reactions to complex life problems. Spontaneity is another factor that makes role playing effective, in Corsini's view. It is rapid, unforced, natural, self-generated behavior in a new situation. Thus the role player learns while reacting, while doing. It is not merely conditional training. The role player does not just learn new behaviors. Rather, the behavior change is accompanied by emotional and intellectual changes. Both the emotional role playing and the outcome psychodrama techniques recommended by Janis and Mann (1977) seem to fit Corsini's description quite closely, as does those experimenters' suggestion that the techniques are devices for affective arousal under conditions that enable clients to take full account of challenging information about themselves. But Corsini's views of why role playing is effective seem less appropriate for behavioral rehearsal techniques (e.g. A. A. Lazarus 1966), where there is little spontaneity.

Corsini's emphasis on the naturalness of role playing serves to remind us that role playing can be viewed from the perspective of role theory as an analogous process to any actual role episode in a system of role relationships (discussed in chapter 2). Taking on a position involves receiving role demands from others, developing one's own conception of the role, and enacting the role, which in turn affects role demands from role partners as well as one's own self-views. According to Sarbin and Allen (1968), the effect of role enactment on self-cognitions is linked to cognitive dissonance, to the selective scanning of information and the improvisation of arguments, and to social reinforcement. Those authors' description of role learning from a dramaturgic model (E. Goffman 1959; Messinger, Sampson, and Towne

1962) is also relevant to understanding role playing as a technique for planned change. They identify parallels between what a professional actor needs to learn a dramatic role and how an individual learns a new social role. The actor needs information about verbal and non-verbal behavior required (the script provides some of this), the opportunity to rehearse or practice the behaviors in relation to actors playing conplementary roles, a coach who models, corrects, reinforces, and directly instructs, and quite a bit of knowledge about the parts of other roles. The therapeutic use of role playing probably also requires these same elements.

In sum, role playing is a powerful tool for achieving change in clients. Whether it "works" because it provides a setting for other techniques, allows the role player to view the world from another's vantage point, enhances one's ability to feel what another is feeling, increases the player's understanding of what makes others behave as they do, enhances the reduction of the defensive avoidance of threatening information, or permits multidimensional learning in an anxiety-free setting, is not of critical importance. Probably all the factors are sometimes relevant. What is significant is that role playing can be engaged in by clients of almost all ages, social classes, ethnic backgrounds, and types of problem. Members can be primed to become role players by a variety of techniques that are simple and nonthreatening. Even those who observe the role players gain something from the experience.

A number of books have described in detail the different types of role playing that can be undertaken. The reader is encouraged to explore the book by Corsini (1966), the chapter by Flowers (1975), the book by Chesler and Fox (1966), the writing on behavioral techniques in groups by Rose (1977), and the volumes by Pfeiffer and Jones (1973) on warming-up exercises for role playing.

CONCLUDING COMMENTS ON SECTION IV

In conclusion we would like to return to a very brief consideration of work with groups composed of facilitators of change in others in order to recognize the relevance of the major topics discussed in this section to such groups. Group norms and cohesiveness can develop in such groups and can facilitate or hinder the achievement of the group's goals. The group's composition will affect not only the processes of cohesiveness and norm development and enforcement, but also the talents available to the group to achieve its instrumental goals. For sustained groups such as local community action groups, the worker's knowledge of the phases of group development can be useful in facilitating the group's problem solving efforts and the encouragement of the most effective leadership (Burghardt 1979). Thus the concepts discussed in relation to treatment/growth groups can also be useful to workers dealing with social change groups or groups concerned with the caretaking of other individuals whose problems are the target of change.

PART FOUR

ENDING SOCIAL RELATIONSHIPS

INTRODUCTION

Termination, the last stage in the intervention process, has a connotation of sadness and finality. It has been suggested that this sorrowful association may account for its neglect in the professional literature (Fox, Nelson, and Bolman 1969; C. Johnson 1974). Termination is said to arouse feelings of separation, loss, death, and abandonment in therapists (Kauff 1977). It is noteworthy that more positive and joyful names are given to comparable transitions in other contexts. One talks of graduation or commencement when a course of study has been completed, and of being launched on a new career, of promotions or retirements in the occupational sphere. In the medical field there are recoveries, recuperations, and rehabilitations. None of these terms carries the aura of depression that envelops "termination." Perhaps if the final phase of a help-giving process were conceived of as the commencement of a new stage rather than an ending of a past phase there would be more in books and journals about the dynamics occurring when a social work relationship ends. In accordance with labeling theory, changing the name may change perceptions of the phenomenon and subsequent thoughts about it as well. For example, with a more positive label, the intervention phase of termination-graduation-promotion-commencement would perhaps elicit attention to more forward-looking concerns: how changes in clients' feelings, beliefs, and behaviors that have occurred during the course of the interactions can be maintained after the relationship ends; how changes can be generalized to other social situations, places and times; how and what new relationships might be formed that would facilitate maintenance and generalization of change; when renewal of the relationship might be appropriate. Similar issues arise when conceptualizing the final phase of a social worker's relationship with a significant other who has acted as a facilitator of change in another person's problems (Kadushin 1977). For want of another commonly used term, however, we will maintain the label "termination," but will try to be cognizant of its limitations.

The topics to be discussed in this introduction to Part Four start with a brief overview of the theoretical social work literature on planned termination. Following it reports of successful planned terminations and termination rituals are reviewed and a discussion of research on client-initiated unplanned terminations is presented. In Chapter 16, on client-initiated unplanned terminations four social psychological concepts and theories—comparison level for alternatives, exchange theory, group cohesiveness, and role theory—are reintroduced. Chapter 17 reviews social psychological concepts applicable to planned termination procedures, including two new topics—psychological inoculation and concepts on ritualistic behavior—and aspects of two social psychological theories reviewed previously—role theory and attribution theory.

OVERVIEW OF THE THEORETICAL SOCIAL WORK LITERATURE ON PLANNED TERMINATION

Before reviewing the social psychological concepts applicable to termination, a brief summary will be offered of how this stage in dyadic or group interventions is perceived by theorists of different persuasions. There appears to be unanimity that termination is an integral part of the planned change effort (Kadushin 1977; Pincus and Minahan 1973; L. Rapoport 1970; Yalom 1970). There is also agreement that the client, client systems, or facilitors of change in others must be prepared long in advance for the end of the intervention. For example, Pincus and Minahan (1973) suggest that workers be clear from the very beginning about the termination date and engage the client systems in periodic reviews of progress and evaluations so they will be used to the process. Further, several weeks before the termination, the client system should be reminded of this eventuality and references made to the coming event more frequently from then on. Fox, Nelson, and Bolman (1969) present vivid examples of the distress to clients that can occur where this principle is not followed and workers inform them that immediate termination is required by the practitioner's departure from the social agency.

The issue of termination is of major importance in task-centered practice among whose key elements are planned brevity, specificity of treatment goals, and the use of contracts or agreements that are negotiated with clients (Hepworth 1979; Reid and Epstein 1977). In this model, termination is dealt with in the first interview so that it is seen as part of the structure of service and does not have a negative quality (Hari 1977). Clients are told in advance about the number of interviews that will be offered, usually eight to twelve sessions, within a period of two to four months. Other short-term approaches that incorporate a discussion of termination into the initial contact or the contract are time-limited behavioral approaches (Sundel and Lawrence 1974) and crisis intervention strategies (Parad and Parad 1968; L. Rapoport 1970).

The functional approach to casework (e.g. Robinson 1962; Smalley 1970) also gives endings an important place within the overall conception that the social worker's conscious use of time phases in the intervention process can enhance effectiveness. Although they acknowledge that endings are linked to fears and sadness, these theorists also note that endings can be welcomed, linked to feelings of accomplishment, and associated with desires to try new powers and skills. All of these typically negative and positive qualities of endings should be exploited by the skilled social worker, according to the functional view. Further, when situational constraints, such as the termination of a convalescent leave from a hospital for a mental patient, do not provide a natural ending point, it is proposed that one should be established at the beginning of the relationship based on the time usually needed for relieving a problem situation. Recognition of the ending time at the beginning can have several positive consequences: reduction of threats to client freedom aroused by seeking help, provision of an incentive to use the contacts productively, and development of the recognition that the inevitable endings in many social relationships can be handled in a positive manner.

Predetermined duration is just one reason for terminating planned changed efforts. Some practitioners suggest that the clients be the sole determiners of when the treatment program will end (Reid and Shyne 1969) or consultation ends (Meyers, Parsons, and Martin 1979). Others propose that workers make that decision, at least on some occasions. For example, Sarri and Galinski (1974) offer several reasons why social workers might terminate group interventions, including the achievement of goals for individuals, and the worker's decision that the group lacks minimal integration and a satisfactory level of cohesiveness cannot be achieved. This orientation to group work clearly gives the practitioner the power to decide when intervention will cease without the necessary agreement of the members of the client system. Several authors with a different orientation are quite explicit about both parties being involved in the decision (Croxton 1974; Fischer 1978; Kadushin 1977; Seabury 1976, 1979). According to Seabury, both client and worker should evaluate the outcome of their attempts to achieve the agreed-upon goal and then reach a mutual decision as to whether to continue with new actions, renegotiate a new contract, or terminate the process. Kadushin (1977) makes similar recommendations about terminating consultation to another professional (or facilitator of change in another person's problems in our terminology). Whether this collaborative approach can be used with very young children or mentally impaired clients is questionable, but it is evident that Fischer, Croxton, Kadushin, and Seabury believe the decision about termination should be made by both parties to the contract when at all possible.

Although there can be diverse reasons for terminating an intervention, some having nothing to do with the client's welfare, as when the worker is leaving the agency (Garvin and Seabury 1979; Moss and Moss 1967), there is general consensus about the components of the termination phase when the termination is jointly planned. For example, Fischer (1978) delineates three: 1. Worker and client (or facilitator of change in others) together assess and evaluate whether the objectives have been achieved. 2. If the terminal goal was achieved, steps are then taken to stabilize the positive changes and generalize the changes from the site of the interventions to the natural environment. 3. The termination process is begun and followup is planned.

Fischer urges that the termination not be abrupt. Rather, the frequency and duration of contacts should be gradually reduced. In addition, the clients should be assured of the workers' continued availability if future problems emerge, at which time a "booster session" may be needed. Hartman (1979) emphasizes that it is particularly important to convey the continued availability of help when terminating work with adoptive parents at the point when the legal adoption procedures are finalized. Both H.H. Perlman (1970) in describing the problem-solving approach, and L. Rapoport (1970), with reference to crisis intervention, make clear that the outcome of intervention is not assumed to be a permanent alleviation of all future difficulties. Fischer (1978) also suggests that at this point the client and significant others be taught the procedures employed for dealing with the resolved problems as well as some of the underlying principles so that the client will be equipped to deal with future problems. The recommendation to involve significant others in the termination phase is unusual in the social work literature and will be discussed in detail at a later point, in chapter 16.

Similar to the above termination procedure is that used in task-centered practice. For example, the goals of the final interview are described as follows: 1) to review and assess what was accomplished; 2) to plan directions for client's continuing work on the problem if this is needed; and 3) to help the client see that the problem-solving process he or she has learned can be applied generally to problems of living (Reid 1978). If it is necessary to refer the client elsewhere, the worker should use systematic linkage methods. These include giving the client detailed information about what to expect from the resource and visiting the resource with the client if possible. Other theorists similarly stress the following as essential to the termination process: evaluating the progress that has been made with the client system or facilitator of change in others, tapering off the relationship with the worker, making efforts to stabilize and generalize the change effort, and facilitating the client system's use of support groups in the community (Garland, Jones, and Kolodny 1965; Garvin and Seabury 1979; C. Johnson 1974; Kadushin 1977; Northen 1969; Rodin and Janis 1979; Sarri and Galinsky 1974; Schopler and Galinsky 1974).

In addition to the above largely instrumental activities, it is generally agreed that the worker should give the client an opportunity to express his or her feelings of loss (Garvin and Seabury 1979) or ambivalence about termination (Garland, Jones, and Kolodny 1965; Northen 1969), as well as their pride and satisfaction at having achieved a desired goal or personal growth (Shapiro 1980). It has already been noted that workers themselves may experience a sense of loss with the termination of an intervention (Rotman and Goldburgh 1976) and ambivalence about the endings. In addition, guilt and feelings of inadequacy or anxiety can occur when a worker's plan to leave an agency precipitates termination (Moss and Moss 1967). Northen (1969) and C. Johnson (1974) suggest that workers express their own ambivalence or sadness about terminating so as to make it possible for clients to recognize and evaluate their own feelings. There are allusions to the fact that workers' reluctance to end relationships with clients may at times impede the successful conclusion of planned change efforts (Hari 1977; C. Johnson 1974; Kauff 1977; L. Rapoport 1970; Rotman and Goldburgh 1976). No theoretical or pragmatic solution to this potential problem is elucidated in the literature but the implication is that workers need to be aware of their own feelings and the possible consequences of these emotions for the intervention process.

In sum, four general issues seem to surface in one way or another in nearly all discussions of what social workers should consider in the process of terminating planned interventions with clients or facilitators of change in others' problems. There should be 1) solicitation of joint evaluations by practitioners and clients (or facilitators of change) of what has been and has not been accomplished; 2) recognition of the need to deal with the positive and negative feelings aroused in clients (or facilitators of change) and social workers by the ending of the intervention relationship; 3) attention to maintaining the gains achieved and generalizing them to other situations and problems; and 4) identification of the possibility that contact could be reestablished without the implications of failure of the present efforts or of the parties involved.

REPORTS OF SUCCESSFUL PLANNED TERMINATIONS AND TERMINATION RITUALS

Numerous examples are provided by practitioners in the social work and other mental health literature of successful terminations of planned intervention through creative application of the principles discussed above (Panzer, Weisner, and Dickson 1978; Wayne and Avery 1979; Weiss 1975). It is significant that these illustrations almost uniformly refer to group interventions. It is unusual for a published report to describe a termination procedure in a dyadic relationship, even more rare when the client is an adult. In contrast, the literature is rich with illustrations of terminations in group contexts. The following discussion will focus primarily on reports of termination rituals rather than the entire ending procedures for rituals are relevant to one of the social psychological concepts to be described in chapter 17 and represent an area about which there is little consensus among social work theorists. Some writers (Northen 1969; Pincus and Minahan 1973) refer to final rituals briefly; others do not discuss the topic at all.

Two of the rare descriptions of termination in a dyadic relationship concern children. In one, developmentally disabled youngsters were served by graduate students in special education, who functioned essentially like Big Brothers, under the supervision of social workers (Panzer, Weisner, and Dickson 1978). Only part of the planned ritual was handled on a one-to-one basis: photographs were exchanged. The remainder of the ending ceremony was on a group basis; a joint farewell party was arranged for all the children and their graduate-student workers. It appeared difficult to have the functional equivalent of a party, or "supercohesive final program" to use the terms of Garland Jones, and Kolodny (1965), when only two persons were involved. Interestingly, the same ritual of exchanging photographs was described by Fox, Nelson, and Bolman (1969) in a planned casework termination with a twelve-year-old girl referred to a psychiatric clinic because of various physical and psychological symptoms. In this instance, however, the client rather than the social worker initiated the photo exchange by arriving at the next-to-last scheduled session with a camera.

The termination procedures used in an extended group program for mothers who were neglecting or abusing their children and had difficulty in forming relationships also included a final party; a potluck luncheon (Wayne and Avery 1979). The event was compared by the authors to rituals signaling transitions and endings. Another component of the termination process was a series of meetings in which craft activities rather than the usual insight-oriented discussions were conducted. These endeavors served the dual purpose of fostering feelings of mastery and of encouraging movement away from other members. The women began relating more toward the material than toward one another. C. Johnson (1974) refers to such terminal activities as "parallel play" or parallel activity and highlights its important role in reducing groups cohesiveness. Wayne and Avery summarized their discussion of the termination process by describing the phase as a time of transition between being in treatment and being an independent, contributing adult no longer in treatment.

A very different group intervention, one utilizing lectures and small group discussions for individuals with difficulties in managing the emotional and social challenges of marital separation, similarly ended in a ritual gala event (Weiss 1975). In the eighth and final esssion, a party was held which gave the participants and staff a chance to talk with one another before the seminar series ended. As recommended in the theoretical literature, the author/lecturer reminded the group members in the sixth meeting that the meeting after the next was the last, and in the seventh meeting, the participants evaluated their experiences in their discussion groups. In the final meeting, before the party, the leader reviewed what had and had not been accomplished and attempted to evaluate the "seminars for the separated." It was felt by the discussion leaders and the author that the participants were now able to start the revised life they wished to live. To reduce the loss of the group's support a reunion was held about six weeks after the last seminar, and an open invitation extended to participants to keep in touch with the group leaders.

RESEARCH ON UNPLANNED TERMINATION

The published reports of successful practice and planned terminations give little hint of the large percentage of interventions that never reach this stage because the clients or facilitators of change in others simply stop coming for service. Various terms are used to describe this eventuality. It is sometimes called unplanned termination (Fischer 1978); others refer to these cases as premature terminations or premature withdrawals from service (McGrogan 1976), early terminations (Koran and Costell 1973), discharges against medical advice (when hospitalization is involved—Miles et al. 1976), or more simply, dropping out (Baekeland and Lundwall 1975). These terms all describe the situation from the professional's perspective when clients or facilitors of change unilaterally decide not to continue in the helping relationship. It is estimated that approximately one-third of those who come for a first interview at social agencies or community mental health centers fail to return for recommended further service (H.H. Perlman 1968; Sue 1977). A recent comprehensive review of studies in psychiatric clinics showed that 10 to 57 percent of the patients never returned after the first visit (Baekelund and Lundwall 1975). When only lower-class or minority clients were considered, the discontinuation rate climbed to one-half (Overall and Aronson 1963; Sue 1977; Sue, McKinney, and Allen 1976). Indeed, one persistent finding in a wide variety of studies is that clients from lower socioeconomic statuses were more likely to be dropouts (Baekelund and Lundwall 1975; Lake and Levinger 1960; Levinger 1960; Maluccio 1979; Sue 1977). Minority status seemed to have an effect over and above that related to such indicators of socioeconomic status as education and income, as Sue (1977) has shown in a three-year study of client records of the community mental health centers in the Seattle, Washington area. Black, Chicano, Asian American and Native American clients were significantly more likely not to return after one interview and if they did return they had fewer further contacts than did white clients. Further, multivariate analysis techniques that controlled for all other predictors of discontinuance—education, income, type of intake worker, type of treatment (individual, group, etc.), diagnoses and treatment goal—showed that the ethnicity of the client was the strongest predictor of premature termination.

DISCREPANCIES BETWEEN CLIENT AND WORKER ATTITUDES, BELIEFS, AND BEHAVIORS

A fairly large body of literature has accumulated over the past two decades concerning predictors of continuance and discontinuance related to clients, workers, and the nature of the services. In spite of the diverse research strategies used, there is surprising agreement about the defining characteristics of clients who terminate contact. They are described in various reviews of the literature as holding perspectives on the nature of the help desired and likely to be received that are discrepant from what they actually experience or what practioners see as valuable (Baekelund and Lundwall 1975; Briar 1966; Fischer 1978; A.P. Goldstein 1962; Levinger 1960; Shyne 1957). This agreement in the literature is, unfortunately, based on only a few well-controlled studies where clients' desires and expectations about treatment goals and process obtained prior to contact were compared to their perceptions after some contact (D. Hornstein and Houston 1976; Overall and Aronson 1963; E.R.G. Rapoport 1976) or to the expectations or preferences of the practioner they later saw (Heine and Trosman, 1960; Lake and Levinger 1960). Often incongruity was only inferred—from an association between client expectations or preferences prior to service initiation and client continuance or discontinuance. These inferences were based on the nature of the specific client perceptions and the researchers' knowledge of the service delivery system. For example, Chavez (1976) studied the treatment expectations of 759 Mexican Americans prior to their initial treatment sessions at an outpatient community mental center and then contrasted those of continuers and discontinuers. Continuers expected a therapeutic milieu involving *consejos* (sharing and receiving through discussion), believed that *los nervios* was a psychological, not physical, phenomenon, expected to be verbally active themselves, and expected the therapist to be a sorter of feelings and problems. The one-third of the clients who came for *direccion* were the most likely to discontinue after the initial session. The author concluded that the continuers were more likely to utilize the services offered because their views of the appropriate roles of self and practioner coincided with those of the professionals at the center, but the professionals' views were not assessed.

Other studies were based on retrospective interviews with clients who had terminated treatment in planned or unplanned ways. This was the method used by Mayer and Timms (1969) in their classic study of British working-class clients who had been seen at a family service agency in London and in a more recent study of family service clients in the inner-city area of a moderate sized American city (Maluccio 1979). Both studies concluded that the clients who broke off contact were more likely to view the type of help received as not what they expected—those who continued contact to a planned termination were more satisfied with the worker and the outcome of the service.

No more than a very brief statement will be made at this point about the specific areas of incongruity that have been proposed to occur between clients who discontinue treatment and the practioners and agencies they encounter. These clients tend to expect a therapist to be active, supportive, and/or medically oriented. Premature terminations are more likely to occur when clients see their difficulties as stemming from factors external to themselves and would like social workers to tell them what to do, or to deal directly with the problem in some way. Discontinuance is more likely when clients do not expect to verbalize at length, to explore their own past, to have to change, or to be highly active participants in the treatment process. All these preferences for how help might be received, expectations about what will occur in the helping encounter, and beliefs about the nature of the clients' problems are likely to cause trouble, because many mental health workers expect just the opposite. Even when clients know what to expect from professionals they may still prefer other modes of gaining help (Dreman 1977).The resulting discrepancies can lead to severe role problems, to lack of mutual attraction, and to low levels of cohesiveness in the dyad or small group, and client-initiated termination without joint efforts to evaluate, resolve unfinished issues, or plan future steps can often occur.

Discrepant expectations can also arise in relationships between practioners and facilitators of change even when they are professionals, as Kadushin (1977) has indicated in his review of studies of consultation. In particular, mental health consultants' efforts to redefine their consulting relationship with teachers as one between equalitarian peers has been shown to be counter to the consultee's expectations that the consultant brings particular expertise to the relationship.

SOCIAL CLASS AS RELATED TO DISCREPANCIES BETWEEN CLIENTS AND WORKERS

In some cases, disparities may be related to the social class, race or ethnicity (Aronson and Overall 1966; Lake and Levinger 1960). Data from two surveys of representative national samples of American adults done roughly twenty years apart, in 1957 and 1976, showed persistent differences in orientations to using professional resources (mental health workers, social service agencies, family doctors, clergy etc.) for help with personal problems as a function of educational level (Kulka, Veroff, and Douvan 1979). Men and women with higher educational levels, especially those with at least some college education, were more likely to have a favorable orientation to using professional resources, as seen in their greater likelihood to have used such help in the past and their greater willingness to describe past personal problems that could have benefited from seeking such help. In contrast, respondents with less education had a less favorable orientation to using professional resources for past problems and were significantly more likely to say that they could handle all future personal problems by themselves without professional assistance; this latter attitude was as pronounced among the least educated adults, those with only a grad-school education, in 1976 as in 1957, while this self-help view was appreciably less in 1976 than in 1957 for the college educated respondents. Thus it seems that clients with varying educational backgrounds are likely to attach quite different meanings to seeking professional help.

Social class even seems to override ethnic differences in some instances. For example, the predominantly low income Mexican-American, Anglo-American, and black-American patients at a psychiatric outpatient clinic in East Los Angeles had essentially similar expectations about therapist behavior prior to their first psychotherapy session (Acosta 1979).

Yet the social class differences in continuance do not seem to be entirely accounted for by social class variations in preferences and expectations concerning treatment. For example, client preference for advice-giving by the practioner seems to be common among middle-class clients, as well as among lower-class and working-class ones (Dreman 1977; Ewalt and Kutz 1976; Maluccio 1979). It is also important to recognize variations in expectations about the client and helper roles among lower-class clients (Overall and Aronson 1963; E.R.G. Rapoport 1976) and within nonwhite racial and ethnic groups (Chavez 1976). These within-group variations have also been shown to predict continuation/discontinuation. Higher discontinuance among lower-class and minority clients may be related to the fact that they receive different kinds of services than middle-class and white clients, and the same service may be differentially effective for various types of clients (Sue, 1977). As Sue (1977) has indicated, we know more about the problems in adequately serving minority clients (and lower socioeconomic status groups generally) than about the conditions needed for truly responsive services.

Various efforts have been directed at reducing discrepancies between client beliefs, preferences, and expectations about professional help and the service they receive. These will be discussed in chapter 16 on the application of role theory to the reduction of unplanned terminations.

PRACTIONER ATTITUDES AND BEHAVIORS

Practioners' attitudes toward the recipient of help are also extremely relevant to discontinuance, according to Baekelund and Lundwall's (1975) extensive review of research on dropouts from medical and psychiatric treatment; dislike of the client, ethnocentrism, and a lack of interest in the client's problem all are predictive of dropping out. Fischer (1978) suggests that the workers' attractiveness to clients and their ability to develop a positive relationship based on displaying empathy, warmth, and genuineness can affect discontinuance—he suggests training practioners in these core conditions. He cites as consistent with this view Beck and Jones' (1973) important study of family service agency clients, which found that a negative relationship between worker and client was the best predictor of discontinuance. Also consistent is Levinger's (1960) conclusion, based on early research in this area, that ease of communication between client and helper in the first interview affects continuance, and Maluccio's (1979) report that lack of openness between clients and family service workers and client dissatisfaction with the worker are associated with discontinuance.

This relationship also seems to hold in various ethnic groups, as shown in a study of patients at an outpatient clinic in East Los Angeles who left therapy without notifying the therapist (Acosta 1980). The Mexican-American, Anglo-American, and black-American patients cited their own negative attitude toward the therapist as one of the most important reasons for their premature termination. Responses in this category included statements that the therapist did not understand me, wasn't skillful, or wasn't interested in me. The three ethnic groups did not differ significantly in the frequency with which they cited these reasons.

Differences in social class and ethnicity between the client and the worker may also influence these worker attitudes and behaviors. This issue was discussed in chapter 1 in relation to interpersonal attraction and only one further type of evidence will be noted here, relevant to practioners' beliefs about the likely benefit of treatment to clients of differing backgrounds. In a provocative study, Friedman and Berg (1978) presented a case history of a fourteen-year old boy to second year graduate social work students. Some students received a case history that identified the boy's family as lower class and others as middle class. The students' own social class origins influenced their judgments, with the lower-class client being given a better prognosis by social work students whose own origins were lower class than by those with middle-class backgrounds. Possibly the middle-class workers' beliefs that lower-class clients are not likely to benefit from social work intervention are communicated to these clients and this affects their continuance in treatment, although this particular linkage has not been tested.

SOCIAL INFLUENCES

Although there has been inadequate attention given to the influence of significant others, such as family members, on client continuance, what evidence there is suggests that this may be an important variable. Maluccio (1979) found that discontinuers were more often pressured to go for help by someone else than were continuers. Referral source was also important to the premature withdrawal of elderly clients at a rural community mental health center (Parkhurst 1977). The relationship to significant other was a key factor for the voluntary patients in psychiatric hospitals who discharged themselves against medical advise (Miles et al. 1976).

Socially isolated clients were more likely to drop out of treatment, as were those with weak occupational or residential ties (Baekeland and Lundwall 1975). Although the reasons for the linkage between continuance and social ties may be complex, the findings indicate the need to attend to clients' social networks in both treatment and termination planning.

PRIOR DISCONTINUANCE

Given that prior discontinuance is predictive of dropping out of later treatment, that most discontinuers do not believe their problems were relieved by their limited contact prior to termination (e.g. Beck and Jones 1973), and that patients with serious problems such as psychosis, alcoholism, and heroin addiction who drop out have been found to be in worse condition at followup than those who stayed in treatment, Baekelund and Lundwall (1975) recommend that the practioner find out if prior dropout has occurred. If so, they suggest the importance of exploring the reasons for it straight away in order to avoid their reoccurrence and to prevent stored up resentments that could result in repetition of discontinuance. The various other factors discussed above shown to predict discontinuance can provide the practioner a framework for identifying these reasons and attempting to prevent their reappearance.

Several social psychological concepts are applicable to the problem and suggest techniques for reducing the prevalence of unplanned client discontinuation. These theories will be discussed in chapter 16. Subsequently, in chapter 17, social psychological concepts relevant to planned termination will be reviewed.

CHAPTER SIXTEEN

UNPLANNED TERMINATION

One concept highly applicable to discontinuance is interpersonal attraction in initial contacts. Since this construct was discussed in chapter 1, the discussion will not be repeated here. It is evident that the higher the client's attraction to the worker, the less likelihood there is of early termination. Instead, to be analyzed below are social psychological concepts with implications for discontinuances after sufficient attraction was present to result in the client's returning one or more times. The four relevant concepts and theories are: comparison level for alternatives, exchange theory, group cohesiveness, and role theory. All four have been reviewed in previous chapters but with a different focus. The perspective to be taken at this point is their relevance to discontinuance in dyads or small groups consisting of workers and clients whose problems may be targets of change or significant others in the lives of potential clients who can be facilitators of change.

COMPARISON LEVEL FOR ALTERNATIVES

Comparison level for alternatives, or CL_{alt} as it is symbolized, refers to the average gratification that a person can obtain from the best available alternative to the present relationship. Thibaut and Kelley (1959), who developed the concept, indicated that whether or not two people voluntarily interact depends on how the outcomes for each person compare with those available in alternative relationships. Unless each individual receives outcomes better than those that can be obtained in his or her CL_{alt} the interaction will cease. If the CL_{alt} represents the average outcome of the best alternative, it should represent a standard or approximately the least that a person will "settle for" in the present relationship. Thus as gratifications approach those available elsewhere, the individual will find it increasingly tempting to disrupt the present relationship.

It is possible to discuss the social worker's comparison level for alternatives, more typically in relation to remaining in the present job rather than with a specific client. However, as the focus of this section of the chapter is on the early termination of clients or facilitators of change the theoretical analysis will be applied to the client's and facilitators' outcomes and decisions, not the practitioner's. Two implications of the CL_{alt} concept are applicable to discontinuance. One is the need for workers to remember there are alternative help-givers voluntary clients and facilitators of change may consult, although these options may never be articulated. The potential substitutes may be other mental health professionals, friends, relatives, or neighbors. There are also experts whose advice is sought, although their formal training is not in the field of counseling. Foremost among them are doctors and clergymen; nearly three-quarters of the respondents in a 1957 national survey who sought some kind of professional help for their personal problems did so from clergymen or doctors, as did 60 percent of a comparable sample surveyed in 1976 (Kulka, Veroff, and Douvan 1979). Mexican Americans frequently consult with *curanderos*, or folk healers, for the solution to many psychological and emotional difficulties (Acosta 1977). Native Americans sometimes seek out medicine men for diagnosis of illness or relief (W. Morgan 1977) and some hospitals have hired them as consultants (*Detroit Free Press* 1979). In the black community one can visit numerous folk healers, for example "root workers" (Spector 1979). Chinese Americans use traditional intermediaries in the Chinese community who provide mental health care (Chin 1976). The important point is that voluntary clients have options, and when the benefits derived from the relationship with the practitioner drop below those obtainable from other helpers, it is likely that the client will break off the relationship even if from the workers' perspective termination is not appropriate. One of the findings, discussed previously in chapter 1, from the Mayer and Timms (1970) study of clients' reactions to an initial interview in London family welfare agencies illustrates this point. Those clients who did not have informal confidants with whom they had shared their problems prior to the agency contact were pleased to have a social worker available to talk with and this was sufficient attraction for them to remain in the social work relationship. In contrast, those clients who had received solace and comfort in prior conversations with friends and relatives were dissatisfied unless the initial agency interview produced a sense of effective problem-solving. Viewed from the perspective of Thibaut and Kelley's concept of comparison levels for alternatives, the former group of clients would be characterized as having had a lower CL_{alt} than the latter group.

Exactly the same issue is relevant to facilitators of change. A teacher may cease consulting a school social worker about problematic children if the benefits of this consultation drop below those perceived possible in informal talks with other teachers or special education personnel. A community organizer may find attendance at neighborhood action committee meetings decreases when the members are invited to participate in the local political organization.

It is also possible for the client to decide to leave and to consult no one else. According to Thibaut and Kelley (1959), the state of being alone is another alternative whose outcomes are considered in evaluating relationships. Perhaps the repeated findings that individuals with weak social, residential, and occupational ties have high discontinuance rates (Baekeland and Lundwall 1975), reflects in part a higher CL_{alt} for aloneness than for interpersonal closeness. Put another way, for some individuals both professional and informal social relationships may provide fewer gratifications or greater frustrations than the solitary state.

The second implication of comparison level for alternatives is that the workers should try to enhance the value of the present relationship as well as make the benefits salient. Thibaut and Kelley (1959) describe this strategy as "building up the value of the product," for example, through "propaganda" or creation of proper conditions for maximal appreciation of rewards obtained. One such approach available to practitioners is the documentation, either verbal or graphical, of the problematic condition of the client at the start of service and at present. For example, if a mother sought help because her child's temper tantrums or defiant behaviors were unbearable, comparing the frequency and severity of such behavior before the start of treatment and after several weeks of service can be very persuasive. Adolescents can be asked to monitor the frequency of their own undesired behaviors, such as watching TV instead of completing school assignments, and examine the reduction, however slight, from the beginning of the intervention to the present. Reports of significant others can be obtained and shared with clients. If there are indications of improvement, the information should be discussed rather than put aside for future sessions on assessment of gains made. If there are observable improvements in the client's dress or grooming, the workers would do well to comment about this fact and not assume it is self-evident. All of the above can be described as parts of the on-going evaluation of progress toward goal attainment with spotlights on achievements. If there appears to be little progress, the worker could indicate that more time may be required to see evidence of improvement or that unexpected obstacles appeared. To avoid this eventuality, initial short-term goals and objectives should be established that will result in early evidence of movement in the desired direction. At the very minimum, any progress that is observed should be noted by the worker and positive comments made about the achievement, with the credit given to the client. When working with facilitators of change, very similar methods could be used to document the benefits to the recipients of service, for example, parents of handicapped children or cottage staff personnel in charge of delinquent adolescents. The strategy of highlighting evidence of progress is also important for community organizers. Rothman (1974) has pointed out that because many low-income persons have a low sense of efficacy, to maintain participation in voluntary associations such organizations should set some intermediate goals that can be readily attained. In terms of our current discussion such efforts would enhance the value of membership in the voluntary association and help keep it above the CL_{alt}. More will be said about this topic in the section on attribution theory.

On a more personal level, the worker should express pleasure in seeing the client or facilitator of change and make every effort not to miss or be late for appointments or meetings. The latter admonishment may be irrelevant to practitioners in social work settings but it is highly relevant to those in host settings such as schools and hospitals. There are always innumerable contacts with staff personnel which must be made. To conduct these sessions at the expense of the client may be costly, however, if it disrupts the atmosphere of positive regard toward the client which is surely one condition "for the maximal appreciation of the rewards obtained," as recommended by Thibaut and Kelley (1959).

Two additional variables capable of enhancing the benefits clients or facilitators of change obtain from social work relationships have been described by A. Rosen (1972). The first, labeled "stimulus response congruence," refers to the extent to which a response by a participant in interaction provides feedback to the other participant that the message sent was received accurately. According to Rosen, there is evidence that as the stimulus response congruence exhibited by therapists in clinical relationships increases, there is greater likelihood that patients will experience favorable outcomes. Rosen suggested that congruent responses to one's communications are generalized or secondary reinforcers, associated with the provision of primary reinforcement of food, warmth, and the like in early childhood. Since adults who do not interpret the child's communications correctly will not provide the desired primary reinforcer, incongruent responses can be considered secondary aversive stimuli. The implication for practitioners is that attentive listening to both the words used by clients and facilitators of change, and the meaning behind the words, is critical. The term used to describe a similar worker characteristic is empathy, as defined by Truax and Carkhuff (1967) and discussed in prior chapters.

The second variable cited by A. Rosen (1972) as affecting client outcomes is the "content relevance" of a response, or the extent to which the content of an interactive response is perceived by participants as relevant to their definitions of the situation. Rosen implies that clarification of role expectations in an initial interview session is just a first step; the therapist's responses throughout the treatment process must continue to reflect an awareness of client's expectations. Irrelevant or discrepant responses by the worker are potential sources of dissatisfaction and possible discontinuance. Lennard and Bernstein's (1960) study of psychoanalytically oriented psychotherapy groups made a similar point about the importance of a continuing symmetry in client-practitioner expectations. They conclude that when overt discrepancies between patients and therapists became too great, especially with regard to the length of further time required for treatment, the patient disrupted the social system by terminating. Kadushin (1977) recognizes a comparable issue in sustaining consultative relationships.

If workers are to avoid such irrelevant responses, it may be wise to restate the role expectations of both members of the dyadic relationship frequently, particularly if there are any changes since the initial contracting session. For example, if the worker will no longer be readily available for phone calls after a crisis has passed, this fact should be clearly stated. Similarly, if standards for reinforcing a client's behavior have risen as the client improved, the client should be so informed. There may also have been shifts in the clients' or facilitators' of change expectations for workers over a period of time. This information too must be made manifest or practitioners may fail to meet the new standards without awareness of the deficiency. Frequent reviews of the contract to be certain the terms are still appropriate is another way to avoid content irrelevance. Such reviews have the additional advantage of allowing clients and facilitators of change to alter their expectations as greater understanding of the intervention process is acquired.

In sum, by increasing the stimulus-response congruence and the content relevance of their replies, practitioners can enhance the gratifications clients and facilitators of change obtain from the social work relationship and thereby increase the likelihood of exceeding the benefits available from attractive alternative interactions. Unplanned terminations may thereby be reduced.

It should be noted that individuals may be below their comparison level (CL) and still be above their CL_{alt}. The concept of comparison level, previously discussed in chapter 4 as relevant to assessing client concerns and frustrations, refers to the neutral point on a scale of satisfaction-dissatisfaction whose values reflect past salient gratifications and frustrations. A relationship that is below one participant's comparison level and yet above his or her CL_{alt} indicates the receipt of less gratification than past experience has led that person to believe is possible, but no current alternatives available that are more rewarding than the present relationship. Such a condition has been described as one in which the client is not attracted to the other member of the dyad but is still dependent upon this individual, a condition clearly not conducive to improved functioning or goal attainment (A. Rosen 1972). In this situation, the voluntary client or caregiver who seeks help is, in reality, an involuntary recipient of social work service. The implication for the practitioner is that the clients' and facilitators' comparison levels, discussed in chapter 4, must be considered along with their comparison levels for alternatives lest the continuers be perceived as satisfied when they are merely dependent, perhaps trapped, individuals who cannot leave because their alternatives are even worse.

EXCHANGE THEORY

Social exchange theory (Crosbie 1972; Homans 1961) is based on the concept that members of a dyad view any activity as a potential source of rewards and costs. Rewards are those components of an activity individuals perceive as beneficial to themselves; costs are those components that individuals perceive as detrimental. Individuals evaluate each activity from the repertoire of activities available to them at any given time in terms of the net difference between rewards and costs, or profits. An individual's motivation to engage in any activity is a function of the relative profits that person expects to gain from the activity. It is assumed individuals will pursue those activities which will yield the greatest expected profit. Decisions to engage in interactions with other particular individuals will depend on perceptions of the profits likely to accrue from that interaction compared to profits available from other relationships. As an interaction develops, the expected rewards and costs may become actualized, but over time achieved rewards and costs may differ from those initially anticipated for two reasons. As an individual's supply of rewards from the partner increases, the value of all additional rewards from that partner decreases. Further, as the individual's supply of his or her own rewards decreases, the value placed upon each additional expenditure increases costs. Both processes lead to a diminished profit from the interpersonal exchange, and when it falls below the expected profit from the next highest valued interpersonal exchange activity available, the individual will terminate interaction with this particular partner. Thus the theory assumes that the rewards available in an interpersonal exchange satisfy needs that can be satiated, hence continuing receipt of rewards of the same type have less value, and that rewards are in limited supply, hence continuing to dispense rewards of the same type increases the value of the remaining supply. It also clearly assumes that people are rational and will function in their own best interests.

Exchange theory is closely related to the concept of comparison level for alternatives discussed earlier, but it has some unique aspects that are relevant to termination, particularly the notion of costs to a member of a dyad, and the relationship of costs to the rewards received. Often, too little emphasis is placed on the costs of being a client who is the recipient of treatment or a facilitator of change who helps alleviate someone else's problems. For clients or facilitators of change who pay money for services received, there is obviously a financial expense, but even if no payment is made, there may be costs in the form of injury to one's pride and self-respect. In an insightful analysis of the social work relationship as a form of gift exchange, Kerson (1978) points out that in gift exchange as a social process, there is an obligation to repay. If gifts are not repaid, higher status ensues for the parties who fulfilled their duties, and lower status for those who did not. The imbalance of status is heightened further when the gift cannot be repaid in kind. This situation clearly applies to clients and many facilitators of change. Bertha Reynolds aptly described the situation over a quarter-century ago: "It hurts to be helped when one is not in a position to repay" (1957).

Thus, it is costly to the client when a financial payment is made and costly when no financial payment is made. A sliding scale may reduce the problem but it does not eliminate it. There is also a cost to clients or facilitators of change in terms of time spent with the worker, and traveling to and from the worker's office. Less often do practitioners spend time, money, and effort traveling to the client's home, though consultation with professional facilitators of change in others does more often occur in the consultee's office. This approach should be tried more often. Whether they work outside the home or at home caring for a family, clients often experience role overload, with time in short supply. Spouses of alcoholics or ex-mental patients, teachers with a mainstreamed handicapped child in their classroom, teenage mothers who are trying to complete their high-school education—all are examples of individuals whose time costs may be very high when they seek assistance as facilitators of change in others. There may be some clients, such as widows or the elderly, with fewer role overload problems but these individuals often have limited budgets and experience difficulty in using buses or subways and in driving. The problems become particularly acute during the snows of winter and the heat of summer. Arranging and paying for baby sitters is another burden carried by many who choose to be clients or to learn better parenting skills.

Nonmaterial costs also accrue to someone who is attempting to change or to learn new skills. When one's equilibrium is disturbed, there is discomfort until a new equilibrium is reached. If there is a prolonged period of disequilibrium, the client may find the treatment process increasingly unpleasant and the facilitator of change in others may experience stress while acquiring new modes of interaction with others. In small groups there is an additional period of stress, the storming phase described earlier, when the norms and leadership are tested. We discussed the potential psychic costs to clients of receiving help in chapter 7, and will only touch on them again here. Being the recipient of help can decrease one's self-regard and signify failure, especially when the help is given in a manner that implies you are the source of your own difficulties rather than that external events or other persons are at least partially responsible. Receiving help can also threaten one's autonomy and decisional freedom. Having to ask for help appears to be more difficult, i.e., costly, than having someone reach out and offer help. To the extent that these costs of receiving help can be lessened, the exchange will remain "profitable" to the client and the likelihood of premature termination will be reduced.

If the rewards received, such as reinforcement from the practitioner, improved environmental conditions, or improved social functioning in oneself or significant others, do not counterbalance the many costs of carrying out the client or facilitator role, the individual is likely to disengage from the relationship. Workers can reduce such costs in several ways. They can acknowledge and express approval of the efforts clients and facilitators of change in others make to continue the intervention. On a more tangible level, practitioners can provide some type of childcare service when help recipients have small children and few resources. In addition, transportation should be offered to those who need it. A comfortable setting for the interview, with coffee or small snacks for children, can also cut the costs a bit. The setting in which the interview is held should be located in an area close to the homes or workplaces of the people being served when there are transportation difficulties. This is particularly important for low-income and minority clients or facilitators of change who may feel some measure of distrust or reluctance to enter the white, middle-class professional's arena. Inconveniences and irritations which are small in themselves may accumulate and eventually outweigh the benefits of engaging in a social work relationship.

Basically, of course, the major efforts of practitioners should be directed at increasing the rewards to the clients or facilitators of change in others by the achievement of the goals set for the relationship. When the major goals are not quickly attainable, however, the techniques for increasing rewards discussed in the previous section, in relation to increasing the value of the current relationship in comparison to alternative ones are particularly important. They are also important when the costs have been cut to a minimum, but are still high.

GROUP COHESIVENESS

Cohesiveness can be described as the total field of forces that act on members to remain in the group (Festinger, Schacter, and Back 1968). It was previously discussed in relation to interventions with small groups of more than two individuals but a worker-client or worker-facilitator of change dyad can be conceived of as special cases of all small groups. The analysis to follow adapts the Levinger and Moles (1979) conceptualization of the marital couple as a two-person group whose continuance or dissolution in divorce or separation can be considered in terms of its cohesiveness to the relationship between practitioner and recipient of social work services.

Just as cohesiveness is one of the dimensions by which a small group or marriage can be described, so too can it be used in reference to a social work dyad. As with a larger group, inducement to remain in the group includes the attractiveness of the group itself and the strengths of restraints against leaving it. Inducements to leave a group include the attractiveness of alternate relationships and the restraints against breaking up the existing relationships (Levinger 1965). A pair's cohesiveness depends upon the net sum of the attractions to the group and the barriers around the most salient outside attractions. Thus there are at least two independent variables that affect the cohesiveness of the marital and social work dyad: 1) the attractiveness of the dyad, that is, the perceived rewards and perceived costs weighted by each one's probability of occurring; and 2) the barriers or restraining forces around the relationship that keep the pair together, such as a marriage or treatment contract, a court referral for marital counseling as part of a divorce proceedings involving children or for treatment of an abusing parent who wants to retain custody of the abused child, or a supervisor's arranging for a case consultation before further action is taken. (Levinger and Moles also discuss a third variable, attractiveness of alternatives, but this issue was reviewed in prior sections of the chapter and will not be repeated.) Combining the two factors, attractiveness and barriers, and dichotomizing the barriers as weak or strong and the attractions as highly positive or low, one can delineate four patterns of cohesiveness in social work or marital dyads. These four patterns are: *Weak Barriers and High Positive Attraction*. Many premarital couples and uncommitted lovers illustrate this pattern according to Levinger and Moles. In social work dyads this occurs when the client or facilitator of change is enthusiastic about the social worker but has made no commitment about continuing for any length of time, e.g., an abused child testing treatment offered by a warm clinician. *Weak Barriers and Low Attraction*. Marital pairs who are seeking a divorce fall into this category. When there is little attraction and no commitment to continue or external constraints to do so, the client or facilitator of change is certain to discontinue unless something is done to change one of the variables, e.g. the chief medical resident reluctantly agreeing to meet with a hospital social worker to discuss the impact on healthy family members of prolonged hospitalization of a family member and finding the consultation is offered by a female worker whom he finds abrasive. *Strong Barriers and High Positive Attraction*. Stable marriages with mutual attraction and commitment are of this type. Similarly, when the recipients of social work services feel this way, they are likely to continue until planned termination since there is a commitment to remain in the form of a contract or other binding forces and enthusiasm for the relationship, e.g. a woman receiving assertiveness training from a sympathetic practitioner for a fixed number of sessions. *Strong Barriers and Low Attraction.* Levinger and Moles (1979) referred to this category as an "empty shell" marriage with apathetic members of the dyad who are forced to remain together because of external restraints. It is comparable to the dyads discussed by A. Rosen (1972) in which clients are below their comparison level but above their comparison level for alternatives. In social work terms, an "empty shell" relationship may describe one with an involuntary client such as a youth on probation who has no positive feeling toward the worker, or an involuntary participant in staff training such as occurs when organizations change goals. These recipients of service are locked into an unpleasant relationship.

Clearly the variables of attraction and commitment must be attended to if the client or facilitator of change in others is to remain until planned termination is reached. The Levinger and Moles (1979) analysis of each of these dimensions is highly relevant for the social work relationship if some modifications are made. According to these theorists, there are three types of rewards that increase attractiveness: material, symbolic, and affectional. For many social work dyads, the word "instrumental" would be more appropriate than "material," although for public welfare clients who seek increased public assistance payment, adequate shelter, or clothes for a child about to start school, material rewards clearly can provide the basis for attraction and continuance in the relationship. Instrumental rewards would include those directly related to the intervention goals, such as improved social functioning, enhanced feelings of well-being, or improved receipt of social support for clients, and enhanced skills at parenting or teaching for facilitators of change in others. Symbolic rewards would encompass the status in some social groups attached to being in treatment or a participant in staff development activities. Affectional rewards would involve approval and social reinforcement coming to the client from the worker or from a spouse, or coming to the facilitator of change in others from the worker or from the significant other whom the facilitator of change is seeking to help. Levinger and Moles listed three analogous types of costs that serve as barriers to terminating the dyad: material, symbolic, and affectional. Material barriers could include the loss of methadone to an addict or money to a participant in a job-training program with a counseling component. Instrumental costs encompass discomfort caused by the clients' problems, or fear of the discomfort that might be created by future problems in preventive-oriented growth groups. For facilitators of change in others, there are comparable instrumental costs, such as those experienced by ward attendants who are trying to improve their skills at patient care in order to cope more adequately with depressed patients. Symbolic costs could include guilt aroused in clients or facilitators of change in others by breaking the commitment or contract, and pressure by significant others to continue the intervention. Affectional costs would pertain to the loss of the worker's respect, approval, and reinforcement.

The above analysis can readily be transformed into practice principles that appear likely to prevent early termination in the midst of the intervention process. The stronger the barriers against discontinuing, the more likely the client or facilitator of change is to remain in the relationship. The barrier may be a firm and clear contract, renegotiated as conditions change. When a client and practitioner reach agreement about intervention goals, procedures and likely number of contacts, each makes a commitment to the relationship that can act as a psychological barrier to its dissolution or as the binding of an individual to a behavioral act (Kiesler 1971). This is one of the functions of contracting, according to numerous social work theorists (e.g. Fischer 1978; Kravetz and Rose 1973; Maluccio and Marlow 1974; Stein, Gambrill, and Wiltse 1974). Based largely on research related to dissonance theory, the following consequences of commitment to an action have been proposed: the act is less changeable, beliefs about the act are resistant to change, and prior attitudes and beliefs inconsistent with the action are likely to change to make them congruent with the action. These effects are dependent upon the degree of commitment, which in turn is affected by such things as the explicitness of the act, the importance of the act for the individual, and the degree of volition or free choice perceived by the actor in making the commitment. All of the above suggests that when clients or facilitators of change freely negotiate a written contract with a practitioner to work on matters of concern to them, strong barriers are erected to the unplanned termination of the relationship.

Barriers to termination may also take the form of strong support from significant others for the continuance of the relationship. This entails involving significant others in the intervention process as early as possible. For example, spouses and/or family members of clients, particularly in ethnic groups such as Mexican Americans, where there is a modified extended family form (Sena-Rivera 1979), should be encouraged to establish readily attainable goals in the initial stages of the intervention process. In addition, it is desirable to perform a concrete service for the client or facilitator of change whenever possible.

An example of a readily obtainable goal for teachers seeking guidance in controlling an unruly class is that of helping them establish two simple rules of behavior for the class that have clear consequences if violated; this procedure often stops disorder. A service which might be performed for a client is that of phoning the department of social services and setting up an appointment for the individual to determine her eligibility for Aid to Families and Dependent Children.

Insofar as symbolic rewards are concerned, the worker can attempt to raise the clients' status by providing an attractive, clean office in which to hold the interviews, with photographs reflective of respect for individuals the clients or facilitators of change in others regard highly, for example, Martin Luther King or Cesar Chavez. Similarly, pictures of families of the same ethnic or racial background as many of the clients or of the aged in facilities for the elderly, express respect for clients and their loved ones. Public statements of support from admired religious and community leaders can be sought, publicized, and displayed in the office and waiting room. Listening attentively when the clients or facilitators of change in others are speaking, addressing them with an appropriate title, and dressing in a way they consider respectful are also essential. This may mean putting aside jeans and sport shirts in the office if the community served perceives this attire as appropriate only for working around the house or relaxing with friends. It is important, however, not to impose middle-class standards of dress or address on other groups. Rather, by consulting with indigenous leaders, practitioners can determine the actions and words communicating respect in each local community.

Affectional rewards have been discussed previously and will not be repeated except to note that in Levinger and Moles' paradigm, these rewards should be sufficiently strong so that the thought of losing them will be a barrier to dissolving the relationship before the goals set for it are achieved.

Although our application of Levinger and Moles' analysis of marital stability and dissolution has focused on dyadic interventions, it should be apparent to the reader that analogous issues could be raised about group interventions There has been very little research on discontinuance in social worker-led treatment/growth groups, and even less in groups composed of facilitators of change in others. Yet there is reason to expect that clients or facilitators of change in others' problems are likely to leave such groups when their attraction to other group members and to the practitioner/leader is low and the barriers to termination of the group ties are weak. The techniques for increasing group cohesiveness previously discussed in chapter 11 are pertinent here, as are the techniques described above for strengthening barriers around dyadic social work relationships.

An exploratory study was conducted by Levinger and Moles (1979) to determine if spouses themselves considered their marriage in terms of attractions and barriers. Fifteen married couples who felt the relationship was successful were asked about the influences that tended to keep the marriage together or to disrupt it. It was found that many of their responses could be coded under types of attractions and some under types or barriers, although those exact words were not used. The authors concluded that the expressions of spouses about their marriage could indeed be translated into the conceptual framework they employed. There is a need for a comparable study to determine if clients who are currently in treatment describe the social work dyad or their treatment/growth group in a similar fashion, and if facilitators of change in others do likewise. If they do, a longitudinal investigation of these recipients of social work services would reveal whether there are differences in perceptions of attractions and barriers between those who remained with the planned intervention effort and those who dissolved the relationship. The finding could hold powerful implications for practice, especially with high risk-clients.

ROLE THEORY

The conclusions of various research reviews that discontinuance was predicted by disparities between clients' and workers' attitudes, beliefs and behaviors can be conceptualized in the role theory terms previously discussed in chapter 2 as a means of assessing client problems (see table 2.1). Viewed this way, the findings suggest several sources of intersender role problems that may be common among clients (or facilitators of change in others) who drop out and, consequently, several means for reducing role problems: 1) the clients' role conception for their own position as client may conflict with the role demands that are received from the practitioners, for example regarding the maintenance of areas of privacy versus wide-ranging self-disclosure; 2) the clients' personal attributes may be incompatible with the role demands from the practitioner, for example, poor verbal skills versus a talking, self-reflexive mode of interchange; 3) the clients' role performance may conflict with the role demands from the practitioner, for example, attacking other group memgers for their opinions versus allowing all group members to express their opinions without reprisal;

4) the practitioners' role conceptions for their own position may conflict with the role demands they receive from the clients, for example, nonevaluative help versus advice giving; 5) the practitioners' personal attributes may be incompatible with the role demands from the client, for example, an English-speaking practitioner versus a client whose primary language is Spanish; and 6) the practitioners' role performance may conflict with the clients' role demands, for example, neutrality in clients' dispute with a profit-minded landlord versus advocacy on behalf of the clients.

Client discontinuance can be seen as a unilateral effort to reduce the role strain, for the act of dropping out is essentially leaving the client position which is the source of the problem. Behaviors often viewed as signs of uncooperativeness may also reflect client efforts to reduce role strain, especially when leaving the position is impossible or very costly. Limiting communication, resisting demands, evading observation through missed appointments—are all common unilateral means of reducing role strain; none of them, however, removes the source of the role problem. Practitioners also use unilateral means to reduce role strain created by role demands of clients or facilitators of change which they perceive themselves as unable to meet or as unreasonable. Practitioners' efforts, although aimed at alleviating the source of the problems, are nevertheless rarely bilateral in nature. For example, workers have focused primarily on changing the clients' role conceptions, personal attributes, or role performance to be more in conformance with the practitioners' role demands. The early efforts at developing role induction interviews or vicarious therapy pretraining all centered on changing clients' ideas about what clients should do, providing skill training, or presenting role models of "good" clients (Hoehn-Saric et al., 1964; Orne and Wender 1968; Truax 1963). Face-to-face or filmed role induction interviews have continued to be used in these ways to prepare clients for both group (Bednar 1974; Curran 1976; Jacobs, Trick, and Withersty 1976; Krueger 1972; Yalom et al., 1967) and dyadic treatment (Benjamin 1976; Childress and Gilles 1977; A. P. Goldstein, Heller, and Sechrest 1966; Heitler 1973; Kirk 1977; Long 1968; Zarchan 1977). While there is some evidence of positive effects on continuance and attendance (e.g. Benjamin 1976; Hoehn-Saric et al. 1964) and on client behavior during treatment (Bednar 1974; Curran 1976; Heitler 1973; Long 1968; Truax 1963), some research has found no effects (Sloan et al. 1970; Strupp and Bloxom 1973; Yalom et al. 1967; Zarchan 1977).

The mixed results for client role induction procedures is not surprising in view of the above analysis of the numerous sources of intersender role problems. Those procedures focus on only limited facets of the problem. In this truncated perspective, the practitioner's role demands for the client are given, as are the agency's policies.

In contrast, bilateral efforts to resolve role conflicts which are more likely to lead to enduring solutions to role problems (Spiegel 1960) require acknowledgement of the conflict by both members of the reciprocal relationship and a willingness to explore changes in both sets of role demands as well as both sets of role conceptions, role skills, and role performance. Two kinds of procedures designed to reduce client discontinuance fit this model of bilateral efforts to reduce client/worker role problems, those related to contracting, and those relating to role induction procedures for both clients and practitioners.

The function of contracting as a means of enhancing commitment to the relationship and strengthening the barriers against discontinuance have already been discussed. Another explicit function of contracting is to increase role congruency between practitioner and service recipient (e.g., Croxton 1974; Garvin 1969; A. P. Goldstein and Stein 1976; Maluccio and Marlow 1974; Seabury 1976). Making goals and expected behaviors of client (or facilitator of change in others) and practitioner explicit and reaching agreement about them should lead to less strain in the client/worker role system and less unplanned termination. Research directed at testing this assumption (e.g., Hosch 1973; H. H. Perlman 1968; Rhodes 1977; Stein and Gambrill 1977; Stein, Gambrill, and Wiltse 1974) has yielded some positive results, but it is impossible to separate out the role congruency consequences of contracting from those related to increased commitment, greater specificty of goals, or enhanced expectations of successful outcome. Still, the evidence on contracting and the compatibility of the approach with a role theory analysis of client discontinuance is encouraging enough for us to recommend that practitioners seriously consider it as an aid to reducing premature terminations.

It is noteworthy that the interest in contracting by social work theorists is mirrored by similar developments among other helping professions. A group of psychologists and psychiatrists at Harvard have recently been writing about the necessity to view community mental health center patients as customers whose requests for services need to be ascertained at the initial interview in order to negotiate an agreed-upon treatment plan between the clinician and the patient (Eisenthal and Lazare 1976; Lazare et al. 1972; Lazare, Eisenthal, and Wasserman 1975). Essentially this is an effort to elicit the patients' views of their role demands for the therapist at the time they first seek help, so that the treatment can be developed in ways that are more congruent to these demands. Elicitation of requests is seen as the first step in a complicated negotiation between patient and clinician over the kind of treatment to be given. The concept of patient request focuses on the kind of instrumental assistance or preferred intervention desired from the clinician on the patient's behalf. To determine the feasibility of getting such requests and to get an idea of their nature, hundreds of patients at an acute psychiatric walk-in service at a general hospital were asked questions such as "How do you hope the clinic can be of help to you today?" Most patients (65 percent) had specific requests, and the variations in the requests (i.e. in their role demands) required differential role behaviors by the clinicians. For example, ventilation requests implied practitioner role behaviors of respectful listening with little feedback, confession requests assumed verbal feedback that put the patients' deeds and thoughts into a less punitive perspective, succorance requests suggested verbal and concrete feedback that focused on giving. The request approach assumes that all voluntary clients wish to have some type of help and that the practitioners' function is to assess the type of help the client desires and try to meet it, rather than try to change the patient's requests to conform to the model of psychotherapy preferred by the clinician. It does not, however, abrogate the clinician's power to judge whether it is ethically possible to meet the request as stated, try to negotiate another request if it is not, refer the client elsewhere where such requests can be met, or decline help if a client request compatible with the practitioner's skills and professional judgment cannot be mutually agreed upon.

Although these authors have not spelled out in detail how the patient and clinician are to negotiate a treatment plan that meets client requests and clinicians' own role conceptions and role skills, they clearly view the elicitation of client requests as the first step in such a negotiation. Hence we view it as similar to contracting. A. P. Goldstein and Stein (1976) explicitly acknowledge the similarity between their concept of negotiated "prescription" building and contracting. These authors argue that to increase the utility of treatment it is important to tailor the procedures to the particular patient and therapist. To arrive at a "prescription" for a particular patient-therapist pair they urge full and extended exchange of preferences and options between the two, as well as education of therapists in a variety of procedures and in knowledge about outcome research that identifies the links between specific procedures and specific types of patients.

Role induction procedures focused on both the client and practitioner are designed to facilitate the achievement of agreed-upon role demands and conceptions for both the client and practitioner positions in the role system. For example, at one community mental health center in the Los Angeles area one hundred twenty low-income patients (blacks, Mexican Americans and Anglos) received role training in the form of a narrated slide show about patient role behaviors (Acosta et al. 1980). The techniques displayed and discussed included trying not to hide one's feelings in order for the therapist to know how to help, being open and honest even if it means disagreeing with the therapist, telling the therapist if you don't plan to come for the next appointment, being assertive about one's own therapy, that is expressing one's desires about its length, the therapist, etc. At the same clinic the psychiatric residents participated in a seminar on issues in treatment of minorities and low-income patients and discussed such things as: the sociocultural characteristics of poor, working-class, and minority patients, the relation of income to stress; how to tailor treatment to the needs and problems of the poor, therapists' prejudices toward poor, unsophisticated clients, etc. The seminar's goal was to make the clinicians more sensitive to the needs of these patients and aware of the possible variations in their own role behaviors that might be required. A self-instructional handbook is being prepared for the psychiatric residents' use. To test the effectiveness of these training techniques, control groups of patients and psychiatric residents did not receive them. Comparisons are to be made of the therapy benefits and behaviors of the patients and therapists. Though these results are not yet available, we would expect the procedures to help reduce client discontinuance.

Another approach to resolving role conflict, other than the two previously discussed, i.e., unilateral change by the client and bilateral changes by client and practitioner, is that of unilateral change by the worker. Such efforts to change practitioner role behavior to meet client demands have been described in a family guidance clinic with Cuban immigrant clients (Szapocznik, Scopetta, and King 1978). In that setting, for example, since the clients often viewed the therapist as holding an authoritative position, the therapists were more willing to take initiative and responsibility during early contacts. These approaches are in keeping with Fischer's (1978) recommendation that in addition to, or perhaps even as a substitute for, client role induction procedures, there should be elicitation of client expectations for the caseworker, such as to give advice, and attempts by the worker to meet these expectations, especially during early stages of intervention. The power of this unilateral approach to reduce client discontinuance has not as yet been established.

The contracting and joint role induction procedures described so far do not take into consideration other important inputs to the system, i.e., the social influences on the practitioner's own role conception and role demands for the clients and the comparable influences on the clients. Suffice it to say that when these social influences contribute to role problems they must be attended to; agency policy and colleagues' opinions affect practitioners and may require modifications to achieve role congruence between client and worker. So, too, if the views of spouses, friends, and coworkers of what it means to be a client are salient these may need to be dealt with during contracting between client and worker. Essentially then we are suggesting that role problems linked to client discontinuance can be analyzed in comparable ways to those used in assessing any problematic role system and this may require adjustments anywhere in the system of role relationships.

CHAPTER SEVENTEEN

PLANNED TERMINATION

Thus far the discussion on termination has focused upon theories relevant to endings unplanned by the worker. However, social psychological concepts are also applicable to the second type of termination, that which is planned, expected, and desired by both the practitioner and the client or facilitator of change in others. In this case, the goal is not just to avert an ending of the relationship that is premature from the worker's point of view, but to foster the stabilization of the gains made and facilitate their generalization into new settings. Two concepts that have not been presented previously are highly relevant to these objectives. One concerns psychological inoculation and the other ritualistic behavior. In addition, aspects of two theories that were reviewed in prior chapters, role theory and attribution theory, will be discussed as they apply to achieving stability and generalization of new desired behaviors.

PSYCHOLOGICAL INOCULATION

The term psychological inoculation is used here as a general label encompassing all of the cognitive modification approaches which involve preparing individuals in advance for potentially disruptive experiences to come by having them anticipate or experience non-extreme stress, temptation, or distraction in contexts where coping efforts can be tried out and reinforced. Included are Janis and Mann's (1977) concept of emotional inoculation, Meichenbaum's (1975) stress inoculation skill training, the various self-instructional programs described by Pressley (1979), the self-management methods of Kanfer (1975), and Ellis and Harper's (1978) "rational emotive therapy." To clarify the discussion to follow, a more precise definition will be offered. Psychological inoculation is the process of providing information to individuals concerning experiences they are likely to encounter in the future that may present difficulties either in the form of pain, anxiety, temptation to perform undesirable behaviors, or other negative consequences. Through this experience, the individuals are expected to become familiar with the stimuli to which they will be exposed and to develop strategies for coping with the anticipated situation. One of the common coping techniques is verbalizing to oneself about how one should behave. The psychological inoculation procedure may include opportunities to practice coping strategies in realistically problematic situations. The underlying principle in psychological inoculation, as in physical inoculation, is that a person's resistance is enhanced by exposure to a stimulus which is strong enough to arouse defenses without being so powerful as to overcome them (Meichenbaum 1975).

THEORY AND RESEARCH RELEVANT TO PSYCHOLOGICAL INOCULATION

The term emotional inoculation was used by Janis and Mann (1977) to describe an intervention in which an individual is exposed to preparatory information about specific losses, stress, or setbacks that may follow after a decision, the means by which these negative consequences can be overcome, and the environmental conditions that can be used to reduce these setbacks. The purpose of this procedure is to reduce postevent and postdecision distress by increasing self-confidence and by fostering the development of specific beliefs that have a reassuring effect during and after the stressful events. This type of inoculation can be used with individuals or groups. Janis and Mann discussed a number of studies where counselors, primarily in health and career settings, introduced preparatory information making overlooked risks salient before decisions were implemented. The results showed that the decision maker was then less vulnerable to postdecision regret if that risk subsequently materialized.

Three steps are described as essential to successful emotional inoculation: calling the client's attention to information about impending losses and risks, encouraging the client to work out ways of self-reassurance when stress is encountered, and supplementing the client's spontaneous efforts to arrive at effective reassuring beliefs by providing new information about how to handle stressors or mitigate their effects. To accomplish the first step of preventing the client from overlooking potential negative consequences, Janis and Mann suggest that counselors could present their own views on these matters, cite evidence from other authorities, or ask clients to participate in role plays designed to elicit potential setbacks. The second step of facilitating self-assurances can include reminders of successful past actions that had overcome setbacks and other efforts to bolster self-confidence. In illustrating how to carry out the last step in their emotional inoculation procedure Janis and Mann cite a variety of cognitive and behavioral coping devices that have been used. In the former category are such things as having surgery patients mentally rehearse how they will reassure themselves about postsurgery pain through telling themselves that the pain will ease in a short while, or helping clients considering a reconciliation in a troubled marriage develop plausible explanations that do not involve threats to self-esteem for instances of rejection by their spouses. Examples of information relevant to coping behaviors that have been suggested include knowledge of how to turn over with the least pain after abdominal surgery or concerning the availability of the marriage counselor for emergency sessions after divorce.

The findings from a number of different types of investigations by their own group and other investigators (Janis 1971c; Meichenbaum 1975; Meichenbaum, Turk, and Burstein 1975) combined to convince these authors that emotional inoculation procedures would be effective for any decision requiring one to undergo short-term losses before attaining the long-term gains that constitute the main positive incentive for adopting the course of action. Further, a number of laboratory studies indicated that a person is less likely to display strong emotional reactions or extreme changes in attitude when confronted with a disagreeable experience if previously exposed to a preparatory communication that predicted the unpleasant event (Epstein and Clarke 1970; R. S. Lazarus and Alfert 1964; Staub and Kellett 1972). The dampening effect of forethought about an unfavorable consequence is believed to stem from the fact that the anticipated event is not a surprise when it materializes and the person is prepared to cope with it. The "work" of worrying appears to result in high stress tolerance (Meichenbaum 1975). When persons expect some kind of loss or pain, they develop reassuring concepts, for example, "I will gradually feel better," that enable them to tolerate somewhat better unexpected forms of loss, such as periods of social isolation during postoperative convalescence. This same principle may apply to other areas, such as approval and disapproval from significant others, self-approval or disapproval, and gains and losses accruing to significant others (Janis and Mann 1977).

The implications of the emotional inoculation theory for practitioners in the termination phase are evident. If clients or facilitators of change in others are to maintain their new behaviors in the context of their family, school, job, etc. without the support of the social workers, they must be prepared to cope with the challenges and problems that will arise. For example, if a male adolescent was participating in a group at a correctional setting following the principles of Positive Peer Culture (Vorrath and Brendtro 1974), he must be ready to face former friends and acquaintances outside of the institution who are not familiar with the important code words that were developed, such as "check yourself" and "small feelings." Further, those outside peers will not provide approval when he acknowledges his own misdeeds, as was the case with former group members. The adolescent may even be ridiculed for the very behaviors that were praised in the Positive Peer Group. The worker involved in such a program, or one similar, must delineate for the youngster whose treatment program is coming to an end the unfavorable things that are likely to occur so the client can prepare himself to handle these hurdles. It may even be necessary for the worker to help the youth develop specific coping strategies to meet these rebuffs. A teacher who has been learning how to help an adolescent develop better study skills so he can complete his school assignments would need to be aware of these same issues when ending that facilitative relationship, for this youngster too may be exposed to ridicule from friends for engaging in these new school-related behaviors.

Janis and Mann (1977) did not provide detailed procedures that counselors might use to implement the three main steps in emotional inoculation, although many illustrations are given of their use with surgery patients and persons making marital and career choices. Others, however, have been more specific and developed a set of procedures focused on "cognitive modification" strategies (Meichenbaum 1975), which improve the abilities of the participants to feel less stress and anxiety in those unfortunate circumstances. The aspect of psychological inoculation that would prepare one to act upon the environment to reduce anticipated stress is not pursued by Meichenbaum's approach. Meichenbaum (1975) used the term "cognitive modification" to describe interventions focused directly on altering the individual's cognitive state to reduce stress. This global label can be applied to a number of different approaches employed to change the "internal environment" (Pressley 1979) rather than the external environment, and thereby prevent or diminish anticipated painful experiences or deviant behaviors. Meichenbaum delineated three basic types of stress-reducing cognitive interventions. The first was increasing the individual's sense of control over the aversive stimulus. Presumably individuals will see potentially aversive stimuli as less threatening if they perceive themselves as having some measure of control in the situation, for example, if they have the opportunity to decide when they want to rest. The control obtained reduces the sense of "learned helplessness" developing from unpredictability and lack of control. (The importance of enhancing clients' feelings of competence was discussed earlier, in chapter 8.)

The second strategy is cognitive relabeling, particularly regarding attributions as to the cause of a problem or unpleasant state. By changing the attributions individuals make of the origin of aroused states, one can change the emotion felt (Schacter 1966). (The possibility of modifying a client's attributions was also reviewed previously, in chapters 3 and 5.) The third strategy involves providing information about the nature of the stimulus, for example, telling a mother who is distrubed about the aggressive behavior toward a peer of her four-year-old son that such activity is normative for children of that age. In this way, the stress experienced by the mother can be reduced (R. S. Lazarus et al. 1965). Meichenbaum (1975) referred to this technique as altering emotional appraisals.

Meichenbaum (1975) described his work as a translation of the above modifications of cognitive states into self-statements the client could rehearse. However his approach is sufficiently unique to warrant labeling it a fourth strategy for reducing anxiety through cognitive modification. The name Meichenbaum selected for his program was "stress inoculation skill training." This approach combines the techniques of cognitive relabeling with training in relaxation and self-instructional coping skills. In addition, the trainees are provided the opportunity to test these new skills under actual stress conditions, that is, while awaiting a shock to be administered within the next three minutes, to defuse their dread of losing control. Meichenbaum used this program in a number of studies and found it to be particularly effective in reducing fear and also in generalizing the stress tolerance to new phobic areas. Rather than being desensitized to a single object, his trainees had developed an altered cognitive set applicable to many fearful situations. Traditional desensitization procedures were as effective as stress inoculation skill training in reducing the anxiety caused by a specific phobia, such as fear of snakes, but not in enabling the phobic individuals to cope with new diverse fears.

The cognitive relabeling aspect of the training involved informing the trainees in detail about the physiological changes they would be experiencing during situations arousing anxiety and providing labels that focused on these specific physiological reactions, e.g., my heart is beating very fast, I can tell the adrenalin is flowing, rather than the fear, e.g., I am scared. Training in self-instructional coping skills involved helping the trainees to develop a script for themselves which they could repeat when confronted by stress. There were four types of self-statements to match the four phases of a stress reaction: stage of preparing for a stressor (e.g., "I can develop a plan to deal with it"); stage of confronting a stressor (e.g., "Relax, I'm in control. Take a slow deep breath"); stage of coping with feeling of being overwhelmed (e.g., "It will be over shortly," "Just try to think of something else"); and stage of reinforcing self-statements (e.g., "I did it!" "It worked"). In addition to the three basic steps of discussing the nature of emotion and stress reactions, rehearsing coping skills, and testing these skills under actual stress conditions, stress inoculation training involved a variety of therapeutic techniques such as didactic teaching, modeling, reinforcement and discussion. Meichenbaum (1975) stated that at this point in our knowledge, it is best to use a multifaceted approach to translating "learned helplessness" into "learned resourcefulness."

It was suggested by Meichenbaum (1977) that stress inoculation skill training could be used as a preventive intervention technique, especially with high-risk groups, and need not be confined to use with already anxious individuals. According to this theorist-clinician, given the increasing demand for people to deal with stress, the possibility of using stress inoculation for prophylactic purposes is most exciting. The notion of providing individuals with a prospective defense against anxiety is analogous to medical inoculation against biological disease. In addition, stress inoculation may enhance the individual's self-concept, for it was found that clients in stress inoculation groups frequently reported spontaneously that they had successfully applied their new coping skills in other stressful situations, including final exams and dental visits.

Various other types of self-instructional programs designed to establish self-control in children, particularly those who are impulsive or likely to engage in behaviors that create problems in school, were reviewed by Pressley (1979). For example, six- to eight-year-old boys who were presumed to manifest a good deal of impulsive behavior were trained to use verbal self-instructional procedures to solve intellectual and social problems (Camp et al. 1977). Preschoolaged children who were instructed to use temptation-inhibiting verbalizations, such as "No, I'm not going to look at Mr. Clown Box," worked longer and more consistently on a task than did control subjects instructed to make irrelevant verbalizations when annoyed by a Clown Box, or given no verbalization instructions (Mischel and Patterson 1976).

Another example of a self-instructional procedure was referred to as "guided participation" by Mahoney and Thoresen (1974). In this methodology, impulsive children are taught to use self-verbalizations to control their behavior. First they see such self-verbalization modeled and then they are required to execute the response themselves with guidance given during an instruction period, for example, warning themselves to work slowly when working on tasks requiring close examination. Pressley (1979) also reviewed a number of studies, many by Meichenbaum, in which children were provided with a strategy of self-verbalization to control their behavior and instructed when to use the self-instruction. In addition, the children were typically given the opportunity to use the self-verbalization immediately following the training. These studies showed that cognitive strategies could be used by children to affect their self-control, for example, in classrooms, but the studies did not show that the children could spontaneously use the strategies in new situations. According to Pressley, more needs to be done to see if children can be trained to generalize self-control techniques where they had not been previously employed. There appears to be little doubt, however, that self-verbalization can be taught to children for self-control if the situation can be specified during the training period. Pressley (1979) did not refer to the techniques as "inoculation," but they are closely related to Meichenbaum's skill training program to prepare anxious individuals to withstand stress. In the educational and child development literature Pressley reviewed, the difficult situations to be coped with were often referred to as temptations or distractions rather than anxiety, and the goal of the training programs was to inoculate relatively impulsive children against becoming disruptive in the face of seductive stimuli, rather than fearful when confronted with stress, but the underlying principles are very similar. Thus they have been discussed together and conceptualized as varieties of psychological inoculation procedures. For similar reasons, Kanfer's (1975) interest in training individuals in self-management skills also can be viewed as related to psychological inoculation. Kanfer argues that it is necessary to enable people to temporarily free themselves from the immediate control of their environment when the environment is not supportive of desirable behaviors, for example, when the relevant behaviors receive conflicting evaluations from parents and peers. Other behaviors cannot be brought under environmental controls because the relevant behaviors are not ordinarily public, for example self-evaluations or fantasies. In both cases Kanfer suggests three phases of training in self-management: self-monitoring, self-evalution, and self-reinforcement. Kanfer viewed self-control as a special case of self-management where the behavior is conflictual because it has both positive and negative consequences to the individual.

Finally, certain aspects of "rational emotive therapy," as described by Ellis and Harper (1978), can be conceptualized as a type of psychological inoculation. According to these authors, some individuals tell themselves various "crazy" things which have a negative influence on their behavior and self-esteem. If these persons can be taught to modify their internal dialogue to rational coping statements, much of the difficulty would be eradicated. For example, in an application of Ellis and Harper's theory to performance anxiety, Nagel (1980) suggested that musicians who experience this problem should be taught to change their self-statements before a performance from "I must play perfectly, I must not have a memory slip," to "It would be nice if I play well but if I don't, it is frustrating but not the end of the world." According to Nagel, by lowering the self-inflicted pressure, the chances for a successful performance are enhanced.

APPLICATION OF PSYCHOLOGICAL INOCULATION CONCEPTS

The psychological inoculation concept is readily applicable to social work. The various techniques included in this concept, i.e., emotional inoculation, stress inoculation, self-instruction, and self-management, are proposed as a basic intervention strategy by their proponents. We, however, are suggesting that the techniques can be particularly relevant to the termination phase of a variety of intervention approaches, including psychodynamic ones, because they deal with one of the important issues of planned termination—how to maintain and generalize new learning that has occurred in a helping relationship when that relationship is ending. Ideally, when a successful intervention and planned termination has taken place, former clients should be able to maintain the newly acquired behaviors in the formerly problematic situations which were the target of the change efforts. Similarly, facilitators of change should be able to continued to perform the activities or provide the support needed by other persons on whose behalf their assistance has been enlisted. In addition, it is desirable that both be able to generalize the new behaviors to quite different contexts and interactions when appropriate. The findings on psychological inoculation suggest that the service provider can facilitate successful termination by following the procedures below in work with clients or facilitators of change during the final stages of an intervention.

1. Describe in specific detail the problematic situations that may be encountered after termination of regular contact with the worker.

For example, if the client had difficulties controlling the expression of aggressive feelings, the worker might delineate several interactions at length which might be highly provocative, such as being ridiculed by hostile peers for failing to defend family members. The client would also be asked to give the worker concrete instances likely to occur and the worker and client could build upon those examples. A similar approach would apply to parents who had been participating in a training program to assist them in helping their children to stop expressing anger through highly aggressive behaviors. The group of facilitators of change might be asked at one of these last sessions to anticipate situations in which a peer might encourage their child to show that he was tough by retaliating physically to any verbal taunt. Workers would then ask facilitators of change to think of similar provocations that children might face.

2. Help formulate coping strategies. Working with the clients' preferences, the worker could help the clients develop a script of phrases that are likely to induce self-control or rational coping. The four stages of stress reaction delineated by Meichenbaum should be kept in mind: preparing for a stressor, confronting a stressor, coping with feelings of being overwhelmed, and congratulating oneself for having come through. Alternatively, for clients whose natural environment does not provide reinforcement for newly learned and desirable behaviors, a useful strategy would be to help them develop behaviors that specifically recruit reinforcements from others, for example, by seeking out individuals outside their own family who approve of their actions (Kanfer 1975). Working with facilitators of change in others as in the prior step, the practitioner could outline the ways in which the parents could teach the children to respond to peer pressure in other ways than by complying with role demands for a fight, for example, by suggesting alternatives to responding to the taunt or of ways to turn the taunter into a friend and thereby bring gratification instead of bruises.
3. Model the use of the strategy in a simulated situation, or provide tapes of others employing the strategy when faced with the potentially problematic situation. Clients or facilitators of change could also observe role plays in which their peers cope with the kinds of problems they could encounter.
4. Rehearse the strategy and provide reinforcement as appropriate. If at all possible, the worker should help clients arrange to encounter real situations likely to stimulate problematic behavior before termination, so as to give them the opportunity to practice the coping strategy and to have the worker reward its successful use.

> Examples of such "dress rehearsals" might be asking the shy clients to go to a public dance or singles bar and remain for two hours regardless of how unpleasant the experience may be. Workers involved with groups of handicapped clients learning basic social and occupational skills might ask the group members to select jobs they would like to have and make applications in person for the position. Rewards would then be given for reports of successful dress rehearsals as well as observations of effective rehearsals in the worker's office prior to this event.

As the literature suggests that children have difficulties generalizing self-instructional strategies to new situations, it will be necessary in working with youngsters to obtain from significant others as many examples as possible of problematic situations the clients are likely to encounter. For example, in attempts to help groups of children adjust to life with severely retarded siblings, consultations with their mothers about times and places most embarrassing for the youngsters will enable practitioners to discuss in detail numerous situations, rather than merely one or two, likely to be stressful.

The psychological inoculation procedures described can also be helpful to community organizers. For example, workers focused on helping low-income men and women assert their rights with powerful community leaders, landlords, or agency executives may well wish to use the steps recommended to dispel fears of confronting new officials once the organizer ceases working with the group. In sum, acquainting clients and facilitators of change in others with details of problematic situations likely to occur after termination, helping them to develop self-instructional coping strategies, rehearsing, modeling and reinforcing these strategies, and then testing them in genuinely difficult situations are procedures applicable to both interpersonal practice and community organization, to individuals and groups, to the aged and the young, and to those whose own problems are targets of change as well as facilitators of change in others problems.

RITUALS

A ritual is any set form or ceremony. Although not directly related to social work practice, death rituals are not totally unrelated to termination, as was suggested earlier in the introduction to Part Four. Thus, the brief review of the functions of rituals to be presented will include references to both death rituals and life event rituals. The utility of rituals for planned termination will then be explored.

THE FUNCTIONS OF RITUALS

A number of authors have discussed the function of rituals held when someone dies. According to Kluckhohn (1962) these ceremonies have promoted the adjustment of individuals and the integration and survival of societies. T. Parsons (1951) suggests that rituals in the case of bereavement serve to organize the reaction system in a positive manner and to put a check on disruptive tendencies. A funeral is a symbolic assertion that a person is important to the immediate relatives and to the entire group. Funeral rituals may also be one of the conformity-producing elements of a society, for individuals seek to be remembered positively (Vernon 1970). This view is supported by Gouldner and Gouldner (1963), who indicate that funeral rituals "motivate men to perform their roles well during their lifetime. It may be said of a person who violated the values of the society that no one came to his funeral, and no man wants that said about him. The respect shown to the dead man is thus important to the society of the living" (486). Funerals can also have functions in maintaining group solidarity. It has been suggested that the large number of ethnic groups in the United States helps explain the many elaborate funeral ceremonies taking place; these rituals serve to reaffirm the importance of the ethnic group (Vernon 1970). Fulton (1973) emphasizes the gift-giving nature of death rites. By the exchange of gifts, human beings declare their love for their fellows. Christmas, weddings, and funerals are characterized not only by the exchange of gifts but also by the setting aside of old quarrels. Halloween traditionally allows children to express their hostility toward adults in a socially sanctioned way; Mardi Gras allows adults to express feelings not typically sanctioned.

Rituals may then serve the function of permitting a controlled expression of anger and also provide a means of reducing guilt or anxiety; both functions facilitate harmonious interaction of group members and reaffirm the importance of the group. Vernon (1970) summarizes the value of rituals by stating that they are sociologically functional and psychologically therapeutic.

Elaborating on the therapeutic nature of funeral rituals, Pine (1974) indicates that they provide a mechanism to help people accept a loss by receiving empathy in a socially acceptable manner. In addition, funeral activities provide an opportunity for people to reconstruct reality for themselves and for social groups of which they are a part. The social reconstruction of reality is important. Of the few families who did not experience the social gathering of the funeral ritual, most later reported having difficulty with friends who seemed unwilling or afraid to communicate with them regarding the death (Pine 1974).

On a more general level, it has been pointed out that both primitive and modern cultures provide many examples of rites of passage which allow individuals to let go of one stage of development and social organization, and attach themselves to a more advanced stage of behavior, responsibility, and understanding (Reed 1974). Confirmations, bar mitzvahs, graduations, retirement, and farewell parties all illustrate such rites of passage.

Also important are rituals of status reversal (Turner 1969). These rites involve a switching of roles, for example, some fun days at high schools are rituals of this type—some students become the principal and teachers for a day and the teachers and principal are the students. Turner suggests that in looking back on that day students and teachers may share memories of this ritual and this facilitates perceiving one another as unique individuals and not merely as occupants of specific positions. Such status reversal rituals may be particularly useful when some of the individuals will be leaving their current roles for the ritual helps the formation of future relationships on different terms; the ritual is thus a way to move from one world to another, helpful to all concerned.

APPLICATION OF THE CONCEPT OF RITUALS TO PLANNED TERMINATION

This discussion will focus on the psychological functions rituals can fulfill in planned terminations. The sociological functions of rituals are generally not as relevant to the termination of social work interventions unless the worker and client(s), or facilitator(s) of change are perceived as a group whose existence should be maintained. Such situations may arise when practitioners plan to maintain contact with the client system, perhaps in a different role. For example, if a community organizer expects to work with other individuals in the neighborhood and hopes to use the present group members as supports for such endeavors, it may be important to reaffirm the solidarity of the worker-client system in spite of termination of the current relationship. A worker in a host setting such as a school or a correctional institution may wish to highlight the continued bond between practitioner and student or inmate, although the intensive nature of their relationship may end. In this way, the worker is available if some future problems arise and can facilitate the former client's involvement in productive activities although their face-to-face contacts are minimal. After the end of a consultation relationship with the ward staff who developed an innovative way of working with their patients, the worker may wish to maintain an identity with the staff to facilitate future work in that setting. Clearly, in some situations termination rituals are important for sociological reasons, for the survival of a continued identity, regardless of any benefits that may accrue to an individual's psychological well-being.

More typically, termination rituals in social work practice are important because they facilitate a smooth transition to the ex-client state (Wayne and Avery 1979), help clients let go of one stage of development and attach themselves to a new one (Reed 1974), or serve as a reality reminder (Pincus and Minahan 1973). As was indicated in the introduction to Part Four, little attention has been paid to this function in dyadic relationships or in the triadic case of family treatment, as contrasted with group work contexts. Part of the problem may be that the social work tradition against accepting gifts from clients (Kerson 1978) aborted the development of norms involving the exchange of any mementos at termination except photographs. Although pictures may be meaningful for children and youths, they are often inappropriate for adults.

Perhaps the notion of an ending ritual that requires the client to give something to the worker is unrealistic but there may be exceptions to this statement. A worker could ask a client to sign a book that is kept as part of the worker's professional files with a few comments; initials can be used instead of names if the client prefers anonymity. The completion of a questionnaire or form used to assess the views of the clients or facilitators of change about the service received can serve ritualistic functions as well as important evaluative ones. In turn, under certain conditions the worker can give the client or facilitator of change in others a document indicating that the program was successfully completed. Such certificates were distributed at the completion of parent education program to members who attended a specified number of sessions (Radin and Wittes 1974). The recipients, low-income mothers of preschoolers, expressed great pride in the documents, which resembled diplomas. Certainly any intervention program which has an educational component, as is the case in many preventive intervention efforts and staff development approaches, can effectively employ some of the gratifying traditional rituals of high-school or college graduation.

It is possible for practitioners to distribute certificates of accomplishment at termination without receiving anything in return from the clients, even a statement in a notebook, but as Kerson (1978) pointed out, denying clients an opportunity to return practitioners' gifts of treatment denies clients an opportunity to maintain their status in the relationship. Even clients who are paying for the service they receive may wish to provide a small exchange gift for nonmaterial gifts, such as counseling, are difficult to measure and return in equal quantity (Kerson 1978). If given a choice of a small gift, workers might express preference for something made personally by clients.

As samples from the literature cited earlier indicated, a common termination ritual in social work groups involves eating together. The setting may be a fast-food restaurant or a wine and cheese party at the office, but food is invariably present. Sharing food is often associated with close family feelings, thus the strong emotions elicited at a final joint meal helps make the occasion memorable. Although it is virtually never reported in casework relationships, a termination ritual involving food could be developed. One possibility when adults are involved is for the worker to bring a bottle of wine and cheese to the last session. This is something that can readily be shared by two people sitting in an office. If wine is inappropriate for the client, the worker might bring a cake and serve tea from an elegant tea service. Coffee is rather informal and commonplace in an office and might not be effective for a termination ceremony. Ice cream and cake might be thoroughly enjoyed by some adults as well as most children. The important point is to have the client experience an unusual event involving sharing food with the worker. In this way there will be a clear demarcation between the time the client is receiving service, before the food is served, and the time the individual is no longer occupying the client position, after the food is gone. Such rites of passage may well help clients see themselves in a new position vis-à-vis the worker, that of friend rather than help recipient, and facilitate their forming new role-relationships elsewhere. As there are no norms for such rituals at present, the worker might alert the client to the coming event to enhance its importance, and encourage colleagues on the staff to share in the ritual-development process.

The report concerning the program for recently separated individuals provided a clue to another possible termination ritual. Weiss (1975) indicated that the wine and cheese party at the end of the last meeting gave the group members and staff conducting the sessions a chance to talk to one another for the last time. There was an implication, not articulated, that in doing so they no longer were in the positions of seminar participant and seminar leader in these interactions but were in positions of greater equality of role obligations.

The shift from a helping relationship to a social one, from one based on the expertise of the worker to that of peer status has also been acknowledged in family treatment by Haley (1976). In the case illustrations he provides evidence of this. To one young boy he says in the final interview, "From now on we are just going to be friends."

Perhaps a termination ritual appropriate for individuals, couples, or families in treatment would be an event that clearly indicates that the old role behaviors are no longer appropriate. One way to indicate this transition is to meet in a different room where no desk or box of tissues is present. Such a change of scenery might also be accompanied by the final sharing of wine or ice cream and cake. The worker might delve into topics on this occasion not discussed previously, such as anecdotes about family members, summer vacations, and movies, plays, or books enjoyed. Conversation of this nature, rather than "interview" talk, may also help clients realize that they are leaving one position and entering a new one with new role demands. No extended recommendations are offered here for termination rituals when clients are served in groups because these ceremonies occur so frequently. However, it is suggested that group members be given something tangible to keep as a memento of the role transition that occurred. Certificates and group photographs serve this purpose very well. In the latter case, signatures and personal comments of all members, including the worker, might usefully appear on the back of the pictures as a reminder of the positive feelings toward the group and the goals achieved. This mutual expression of affection can help the members accept the loss of the group as expressions of sympathy at funeral rites comfort the bereaved and help them accept the loss of loved ones (Pine 1974).

In concluding the discussion of termination rituals, the comments of Atchley (1975) on turning points in life are pertinent. He defines turning points as changes in situations that alter the individual's usual strategy for coping with day-to-day life. They are points at which the individual ceases to be one thing and becomes something else. To the extent that the content and prerequisites of future positions can be known, it is possible to prepare in advance for change. Concrete cultural prescriptions, such as rites of passag or rituals, make for predictable anticipation and smoother transitions but unfortunately few turning points involve changes in position that are so clear-cut, in Atchley's view. Surely the termination of social work intervention is often a turning point for the client or facilitator of change, and it is one turning point which can readily be given a ritual to make the change proceed more smoothly. There is no reason for the profession not to develop some appropriate rites for the occasion and to employ research strategies to assess the differential impact of various ending ceremonies compared to no ritual at all.

ROLE THEORY

Role theory was discussed in depth in chapter 2 and briefly in the previous chapter, but one component not explored thus far is highly relevant to termination and procedures designed to ensure the stabilization of gains made during the intervention. That component is the anticipatory socialization of reciprocal role partners. To review some major aspects of role theory relevant to to this point very briefly, recall that each position in a social structure has a set of role expectations linked to it. Each occupant of a position receives role expectations and has a reciprocal partner holding a complementary position subject to complementary role expectations. For every role receiver there is a role sender communicating expectations. Thus one cannot speak of husbands without wives, children without parents, teachers without students, or leaders without followers, even if some positions are currently unoccupied. Anticipatory socialization is the process of learning the rights, obligations, resources, and outlook of a position one will occupy in the future (Atchley 1975), or the process of learning the norms of a role before being in a social situation where it is appropriate to actually behave in the role (Burr 1972). The importance of undergoing anticipatory socialization is repeatedly stressed. For example, it has been described as serving a personal and societal function by preparing individuals for specific and expected behaviors related to social roles (Gerber 1974). According to other authors (Albrecht and Gift 1975), adults may have resources but they will be confused about how to mobilize the resources and lack a clear definition of what is expected for them in their positions if their anticipatory socialization has been inadequate. Burr (1972) hypothesizes that the amount of anticipatory socialization an individual has undergone positively influences the ease of transition into new roles. He supports this proposition by describing a number of empirical studies performed on launching into marriage and parenthood, which indicated that the more prior experience with aspects of the new position to be filled the easier the transition into the new role requirements. For example, it was found that the severity of the crisis when parenthood occurs is less when one of the members of the couple had taken a course in preparation for marriage (Dyer 1963).

The importance of an individual's preparing for new role demands is often emphasized, but rarely explicated is the importance of preparing individuals to be responsive reciprocal role partners, sensitive to changes in the behaviors of their role counterparts, and ready to change accordingly. There are many examples in the literature of problems that develop when one member of a role relationship fails to change as the partner changes. For example, a study of methods for enhancing the leadership behavior of black youngsters working in pairs with white youngsters demonstrated that merely training the black children to be more assertive did not result in changed leadership patterns unless the white children were also given a training program stressing the competency of the black youngsters (E. G. Cohen and Roper 1972). It is difficult to be a leader when your partner refuses to follow.

Another example of the need to provide anticipatory socialization for reciprocal role partners, not just single role players, emerges from the literature on grief and bereavement. Gerber (1974) emphasizes the value of anticipatory bereavement for the person experiencing a loss. The author then pointed out that initial plans cannot be made independently during the anticipatory bereavement period; others must be involved, for example, to arrange for the care of the children or relocation. This is a critical stage in planning for the bereavement period. How significant others respond to the initiatives of the person who will be bereaved determines how difficult the period after death will be for the survivor. If the significant others indicate that preparations are premature, an uncertain period after death occurs is likely. This analysis suggests that preparing people for the widow or widower role solves only part of the problem; family life education programs must also socialize participants for the role of close relative of the bereaved or soon-to-be bereaved.

Thomas' (1967a) analysis of problems in role synchronization highlights another instance when anticipatory socialization of role partners would be beneficial. Four types of role asynchronies involving a disabled individual were described. In all cases, the behaviors of the disabled and those with whom they interacted did not mesh. The asynchrony relevant to termination in social work practice is "imposed handicap." This occurs when the disabled individual behaves validly, that is, realistically, but others behave toward the disabled persons as if they were more handicapped than they actually are. The phenomenon has been described as altercasting by some role theorists (Beckhouse et al. 1975). According to Thomas (1967a), an enduring imposition of a handicap may result in a fictitious handicap—the individual may display more handicapped behavior than the disability actually warrants. One basic condition giving rise to role synchronization problems is ambiguity about the rules of behavior, as is often the case for the disabled. When such role ambiguity exists, there are more opportunities for alternative ways of interacting with the role player or for role optionality. As a result, those who interact with the handicapped may behave so as to imply more or less of a handicap than actually exists.

The Thomas conceptualization of role asychrony, as well as the other role complementarity problems discussed, holds clear implications for termination procedures in social work. Preparing one role player for a new script without involving the other important members of the cast may be as ineffective as rehearsing a play with one of the leading actors absent—one could go through the motions but it would be very hard to predict that the opening night performance would be successful. Thus, if a practitioner has been working with a single family member concerning some problematic behavior, for example, depressed feelings, and the other family members are unprepared to respond to this individual in a new fashion, for example, by being supportive of even limited efforts to engage in social activities, the former client may readily slip back to a more withdrawn pattern of behavior. Similarly, school social workers' attempts to help adolescents improve their attendance patterns will most likely fail in the long run if the students' teachers continue to regard them and respond to them as truants in spite of improved performance. Not only role theory, but labeling theory as well predicts a relapse into the former pattern—labeling youngsters as delinquent creates a self-fulfilling prophecy. In role terminology, when role senders continually communicate expectations of delinquent or truant behavior and do not reward and acknowledge evidences of altered behaviors, the role receiver is likely to begin meeting those role demands. Thus a meshing in reciprocal role partners will result, but in a dysfunctional pattern. As a fictitious handicap can be developed when significant others impose a disability (Thomas 1967a), so too can "fictitious delinquency" or "fictitious learning problems" be developed. The latter phenomenon is not unknown in schools with middle-class teachers and low-income minority children (Rist 1970).

To avoid problems of fictitious dysfunctional behavior, the worker engaging in the termination phase would do well to involve as many family members as possible. Thus if the clients are an elderly parent and his middle-aged daughter residing in the same home, the termination procedure should include the daughter's children as well. The new interaction pattern between the seventy-year-old and the forty-year-old will not be maintained unless the fifteen-year-old in the family alters her behavior accordingly. Similarly, focusing a child management program on mothers and ignoring fathers creates problems, as the following quote indicates.

> Although the mothers' new child-rearing practices were successful in achieving desired behavior from their children, they were often a source of friction with their husbands, who felt their wives were "too soft" on the children when they gave explanation with their requests. These fathers did not believe in reinforcing a child for his good behavior because it "should be happening anyhow." Rather, they believed in punishing bad behavior. (Wittes and Radin 1971:47)

Not reported in the published Wittes and Radin article was the fact that the mothers felt unable to convince their husbands that their new approach to childrearing was wise; they asked the worker to talk with the men in the belief that she had more status than they. Although the results of the study were positive in terms of altering mothers attitudes and subsequently their children's cognitive functioning (Wittes and Radin 1971; Radin 1972b), the outcomes may have been even more impressive had a planned effort been made from the start to involve husbands in the project, at least to some extent. From a social learning perspective, had the fathers reinforced, not punished, mothers for the use of praise instead of aversive stimuli, the new maternal child-management system might have been established earlier and more firmly. In addition, the youngsters might have responded sooner to consistent messages.

It is not suggested that significant others become clients in the entire intervention program, although this may be desirable in some cases. Rather, the importance is stressed of having at least one or two contacts with influential people in the client's life prior to termination. Naturally this would require the consent of the client; they should not object in most cases if the purpose is explained. No confidences need be violated, but the significant others should be aware of the new behaviors and goals, for example, changed career aspirations, whose stabilization and generalization to new situations are desired, and of the ways in which their own behavior can enhance or hinder these changes. Social learning theorists would refer to these significant others as natural mediators of reinforcement in the environment. If a new behavior is to be maintained, it cannot depend entirely upon past reinforcements from change agents. The approval of these natural mediators is important, for the rewards that will eventually be forthcoming from the more functional behavioral patterns may not be evident immediately. Fischer (1978) suggested teaching significant others along with clients effective intervention principles and practices so that future problems could be prevented or treated. Such instruction has the additional advantage of providing clients with reciprocal role partners who are likely to understand and reinforce their efforts at self-help. In situations in which significant role partners cannot be involved directly in planned termination efforts, whether because of their unavailability, their unwillingness to participate, or the unwillingness of the client system to permit their direct involvement, attention should still be given to indirect ways of gaining their support in the maintenance of changes achieved during the intervention. As part of psychological inoculation efforts with clients, potential negative reactions of role partners should be specifically explored and strategies developed to help the clients deal with such reactions on their own—through persuasion, reinforcing their significant others for behaviors that complement their own goals, or seeking out other role partners who might be more supportive. Delinquent girls, for example, have been taught how to call the staff's attention to their own work when self-evaluations were positive so as to elicit external reinforcements (Stokes and Baer 1977). In this way the girls were better able to maintain gains they had made previously.

There is another alternative in certain circumstances where it is impossible to involve complementary role partners in the termination process, and that is to use system interventions. For example, when the role partners are coworkers or supervisors, preventive programs in the employment settings involving many members of a role set, not merely those who occupy one position, would be beneficial. "Retreats" or in-services training sessions for entire school faculties or departments are no longer unusual. The approach should be encouraged in other occupational spheres, particularly where social policy, e.g., affirmative action for the handicapped, minorities, and women, is bringing about major changes. Role problems for such individuals who are newly hired may be considerably reduced if prophylactic programs are instituted ahead of time informing the other employees of the competence of the individuals to be hired. The work of E. G. Cohen and Roper (1972) and Lockheed and Hall (1976) concerning the need to inform white children of the competence of their black partners and men about the competence of female associates pointed to the difficulties those discriminated against may have in establishing themselves if their future role partners do not undergo some form of anticipatory socialization.

ATTRIBUTION THEORY

Attribution theory pertains to the causes that people attribute to behaviors they observe in others as well as themselves (see chapter 3). The origins are believed to be either internal to the individual (dispositional), or external (situational). The causal attributions may strongly influence expectations held for future behavior by the observed individual. The relevance of attribution theory for termination of treatment was highlighted by Rodin and Janis (1979). Although they linked the theory of attribution to medical treatment, much of what they said is equally relevant to psychological interventions.

When clients believe that the changes in their behavior are due to the efforts of practitioners, situational attributions are being made; the clients do not see the changes as originating within themselves. The net effect is that they will not expect the behavior to continue when contacts with the workers are ended. On the other hand, if dispositional attributions are made and clients see themselves as the origins of the improvement, they are more likely to anticipate the improvement will remain after termination of the contact with the professional. It is therefore critical that individuals terminating helping relationships hold dispositional rather than situational attributions about their responsibility for their new behaviors. Rodin and Janis (1979) offer several suggestions to medical personnel to foster internal attributions in the termination phase which are readily applicable to social work practice. If the client begins to improve and tries to attribute the improvement evidenced to the worker, the practitioner should highlight the client's role in the change. It is also essential for workers to maintain their attractiveness to clients or facilitators of change in the termination phase, for this permits their influence to be based on referent power, rather than the power to reward or punish. When workers are perceived as likable, benevolent, and admirable, they have referent power and those they influence are likely to maintain their feelings of control because compliance is not based on visible reinforcements or punishments in the environment. Thus, those influenced will perceive themselves to be acting on the basis of internal self-motivation factors. Such a belief is beneficial in two ways: it will foster dispositional attributions about changes in behavior, and it will increase commitment to the change. Both variables foster stabilization of change post-termination. To ensure the attractiveness of the worker during the termination phase when clients may have adverse reactions to separation, Rodin and Janis suggest that the professional give reassurances of continued positive regard of the client. In addition, the professional should give reminders that continue to foster self-attributions of the changes which took place. These reminders can take the form of a review of the efforts the clients or facilitators of change made and the results that followed. The obstacles that they overcame to achieve their goals should also be enumerated. The final thought to leave with the recipients of service in the last face-to-face meeting is that they themselves were responsible for the success of the intervention. As gratifying as it may be for the practitioner to receive expressions of appreciation about the good work performed, the clients or facilitators of change need to be reminded that it was they who were responsible for the change. Haley (1976) stresses these points in his exposition of a problem-solving strategy for family therapy and gives a concrete example of a case involving a phobic child and his parents. The family rather than the therapist is given credit for changes that have occurred—thus they may deal with each other rather than the therapist in resolving future problems. Dispositional attributions at termination are particularly beneficial to those who generally perceive themselves as powerless, for feelings of being responsible for one's own improvement can foster feelings of efficacy in other areas as well, as has been implied on numerous occasions in this volume. A sense of competency is a goal applicable to virtually all recipients of social work services, in all contexts, in all settings.

AFTERWORD WITH QUESTIONS FOR RESEARCH

In concluding this book we find ourselves in a similar position to that of social workers terminating any intervention. We have tried to present social psychological theory and research in a fashion that illuminates their relevance to practice, and hope that the ideas presented will continue to influence our readers long after the last page is turned. As with most social work interventions, the ultimate goal is generalization, that is, use of the new knowledge outside of the setting in which it was first encountered. In this case, we hope the fresh insights will be transferred from the classroom and university to the practice site. Throughout the book we have attempted to illustrate some of the incredibly diverse situations in which practitioners might apply the ideas discussed to facilitate the generalization process. If we have succeeded in this planned change effort, the readers' future professional activities will reflect an awareness of social psychological knowledge in practice areas the authors referred to, and in other areas we never considered. Thus, like all terminations, this one is both an end and a beginning. It is the end of the authors' generation of concepts and possible applications; it is the beginning of the readers' use of the material when practice problems are encountered.

In another way as well, we see this book as the beginning of an ongoing process. If we view the current endeavor from the research utilization and practice development schema of Rothman (1978) or the developmental research and utilization perspective of Thomas (1978a), our review of current social psychological theory and research and suggestions about possible applications to practice are only the first steps in the development of new practice knowledge. We have begun the process of converting generalizations from social psychological research and theory into statements about how changes in one set of variables might affect changes in another set of variables. We have also begun to indicate how these manipulations might be implemented in particular practice situations. As Rothman (1978) has pointed out, these efforts at converting generalizations into action principles necessarily involve cognitive leaps and inferences. Further work is clearly needed, however, in the transformation process, including the further specification of the practice inferences we have drawn from conceptualizations and research findings and their testing under various sets of circumstances.

We hope that readers of this book, both those who are primarily interested in practice and those whose major orientation is research, will participate in these next steps. To facilitate this involvement and to illustrate some of the tasks that remain to be done if social psychology and social work are to be more effectively linked, we conclude by listing a few of the many research questions raised in the preceding chapters. We hope our readers will consider addressing them (or questions the readers raise themselves) as they engage in their professional practice.

PART ONE: BEGINNING SOCIAL RELATIONSHIPS

CHAPTER 1. INTERPERSONAL ATTRACTION

1. What is the relationship between a client's liking for a worker after the initial contact and continuance of the contact between client and worker? Does this relationship vary for different types of clients, e.g., men and women? old and young? Does it differ when the contact is with a social worker and a "significant other" rather than with a client whose own problems are the target of change?

2. What is the relationship between a client's continuance and that client's evaluation of the worker's warmth and competence? Does this relationship differ for clients who have used other professional sources for prior help with their problems? For clients who have used nonprofessional sources, such as family and friends for prior help? For "significant others" seeking help in caring for other persons?

3. Is there a relationship between a client's evaluation of whether progress toward problem resolution was made during the first contact and the client's return for further contact? Does a similar or different relationship hold for evaluations by "significant others"?

4. Is there a linear relationship between similarity and attraction for clients with low self-esteem and indigenous aides? Or is maximum attraction to the worker based on an optimum amount of similarity between clients with very low self-esteem and indigenous aides?

5. Are clients with high self-esteem more attracted to social workers

like themselves than those who are different? Does the same relationship hold when the worker is a peer counselor?

6. Does a worker meeting clients of different race or ethnicity who tries to establish a comembership increase the clients' liking for the worker as compared to a worker who does not identify comembership?

7. Are there certain areas of attitudinal similarity that are more closely linked to liking between client and helper than others? For example, is similarity on instrumental values, such as being hard-working or helpful, more or less important than similarity on terminal values, such as having a life focused on accomplishments or one devoted to friendship and caring for others?

8. Does the proposition that the social worker's liking for the client enhances the client's attraction to the worker apply in cases of child abuse, spouse abuse, or alcoholism?

9. Does teaching social workers strategies for communicating empathy (or taking the perspective of another) increase a client's liking for a worker across racial or ethnic dyads?

10. Is there a relationship between the level of a social worker's empathy or warmth and success with the client? A client's willingness to risk changes? A client's use of the social worker as a role model? The power of the social worker as a reinforcer?

11. Is there a positive relationship between a worker's liking for clients of the same sex and the client's physical attractiveness? Is there such a relationship across race/ethnic dyads?

12. Is there a positive relationship between a client's liking for workers of the same sex and the worker's physical attractiveness? Or between a client's judgment of the worker's ability to be helpful and the worker's physical attractiveness?

13. Is there a relationship between a worker's evaluation of the severity of a client's problem(s) and the physical attractiveness of a same-sex client?

14. Do the findings for questions 12 and 13 hold true when the worker and client differ in sex? Are there ethnic differences in this regard?

15. What variables are associated with the liking of non-YAVIS clients for their social workers?

16. Do different variables influence the interpersonal attraction between a worker and another when the other is a "significant other" and not a client whose own problems are the target of change? Does it matter whether the "significant other" is professionally involved with the individual whose problems are the target of change? a member of the family? a friend or stranger?

PART TWO: UNDERSTANDING SOCIAL FUNCTIONING

CHAPTER 2. FRAMEWORK OF ROLE THEORY

1. Can a client's role conceptions or role demands on a reciprocal role player be changed unilaterally via audio-visual material or reading? Via discussions with others with different role conceptions of that role? Via role playing or simulations?

2. Can a client be taught to generate multiple possible solutions to role problems? To analyze the sources of role problems? Is a client with role problems who learns to generate many solutions to role problems and/or to analyze role problems more able to resolve future role problems than a client who receives equal amounts of attention from a social worker but no role training?

3. Would a "popular, simple" film, videotape, or handbook on the analysis and resolution of role problems help clients on waiting lists who appear to have role problems resolve their own role problems, as compared to a similar group of clients who received other information?

4. Is a client's evaluation of his or her various role performances differentially related to overall self-esteem as a function of the importance the client attaches to various life roles?

5. What is the relationship between a client's overall self-esteem and that client's perception of a role partner's evaluation of the client's performance in major life roles? Are the perceived evaluations of various role partners differentially associated with a client's overall self-esteem depending on the importance attached to the various roles?

6. Do changes in a client's evaluations of his or her performance in central life roles or in his or her perception of the evaluations of important role partners correlate with changes in overall self-esteem during the course of treatment? Are these changes in evaluations of role performance related to achievement of intervention goals in other areas?

CHAPTER 3. THEORIES OF ATTRIBUTION

1. Are clients who attribute their problems to purely situational or purely personal factors more likely to change their perceptions by use of audiovisual means designed to change perspectives? group discussions? or simulations?

2. Would a "popular, simple" handbook of basic attribution theory concepts given to clients on waiting lists whose personal problems appear to be linked to inappropriate attributions alter those attributions compared to a similar group on waiting lists given other material to read?

CHAPTER 4. FRAMES OF REFERENCE FOR SELF-EVALUATION

1. Would success at a series of worker-specified real-life tasks decrease an overall self-perception of incompetence? For example, would success at arranging for economical and effective home or automobile repairs the next two times needed or at planning and preparing meals for children for the next two weeks improve the self-evaluation of a client who feels unable to cope with everyday life after a spouse has died or left home?
2. Would clients with inappropriate social comparison groups or comparison reference groups change their bases of comparison after exposure to instructional films, tapes, or discussion groups composed of members with different social comparison groups?
3. Is it possible to develop a simple way to assess one's social comparison group and give this instrument to a client to complete? Would this facilitate a client's ability to find appropriate comparison groups for different aspects of his or her life?
4. Can Cantril's ladder be reliably used with children? If so, do the aspirations and feelings of relative deprivation of handicapped children change from before to after mainstreaming? Do the aspirations and feelings of relative deprivation of black and white children change from before to after integration? Do the responses of children in all-white, all-black, and integrated schools differ? Do the responses of various ethnic groups, e.g., Chicanos, blacks, Asians, etc., correlate with demographic data regarding a group, such as income, percentage of total population in area, education?
5. Do various types of status inconsistencies correlate with specific types of symptomology, e.g., acting out, introjections, psychosomatic ailments, etc.?
6. In a long-term study, would reduction in status inconsistencies be accompanied by symptom changes? Are there symptom changes in students whose income, education, and occupation status become equal after years of inconsistency?

PART THREE: CHANGING BEHAVIORS AND ATTITUDES

SECTION I. IMPLEMENTING DYADIC INTERACTION PLANS WITH CLIENTS: QUADRANT A

CHAPTER 5. ATTITUDES

1. Does having a client describe and write down all the reasons for engaging in a particular course of action increase the likelihood that the action will be carried out?

2. Can reliable techniques be developed for assessing the relative importance to a client of personal attitudes about a proposed course of action and the attitudes of significant others toward this action? If so, can it be shown that efforts to bolster the component with the lesser weight (if this facilitates goal attainment) increase the likelihood that the action will be carried out?

3. Does encouraging a client to carry out an action that is not fully supported by the client's attitudes lead to changes in the client's relevant attitudes after the behavior actually occurs? If so, does emphasizing the client's choice in deciding to actually engage in the action enhance the attitudinal change?

4. Does concluding each contact between a social worker and client by asking whether the client wishes to return for further contact (and thus, to accept personal responsibility for the decision) enhance the likelihood of return? Given such an acceptance of personal responsibility, does a behavioral commitment to return by having the client select and write down the time and date of the next appointment further increase the likelihood of return?

5. Will providing a vivid, concrete experience, e.g., via a videotape or narrative of someone who behaved in a desirable way, affect a client's inaccurate self-perceptions more than a statistical description of how typical individuals react to that situation? If so, does the similarity between the client and person in the film in terms of sex, age, ethnicity, etc., affect the potency of the example?

CHAPTER 6. SOCIAL INFLUENCE

1. Would a content analysis of client-worker interchanges reveal evidence of greater client reactance when the worker's language includes the use of strong suggestions about a course of action to pursue in keeping with the worker's views as compared with interchanges where the worker's language is more tentative, or devoid of compliance requests? If so, do these effects vary for different categories of clients? For example, are adolescents more likely to exhibit reactance under these circumstances than younger children? Are incarcerated juvenile delinquents more sensitive to the language of the worker than delinquents in programs that divert them from the penal system?

2. Is it possible to develop reliable instruments to assess whether or not a client perceives the worker as a person with whom to identify? If so, is it possible to increase a client's identification with a worker through the worker's use of rewards?

3. Is it possible to develop reliable instruments to assess whether or

not a client perceives the worker as someone with expertise? If so, is it possible to enhance a client's view of the worker's expertise by external means, such as by displaying diplomas or certification documents on the wall, or by providing written statements from prior clients attesting to the worker's effectiveness?

4. If the assessment instruments described in questions 2 and 3 are developed, can it be determined whether a client is more influenced by a worker perceived as having expertise or by a worker with whom the client is likely to identify?

5. Does a worker with means control over a client perceive that individual as having less ability and motivation to achieve than does a worker in the same context without means control?

6. Can a worker with power over a client perceive evidences of ingratiation tactics during interviews as well as a noninvolved worker observing a videotape or reading a transcription of the sessions? If not, can workers be trained to be more sensitive to such tactics?

7. Does a worker with power respond more favorably to a client who uses ingratiation tactics than to a client who does not? Are some workers likely to respond more favorably to these tactics than others? If so, are there certain characteristics that are descriptive of such workers, e.g., sex, age, education, experience?

SECTION II. IMPLEMENTING DYADIC INTERACTIONS WITH SIGNIFICANT OTHERS: QUADRANT B

CHAPTER 7. ALTRUISM AND HELPING

1. What are the conditions under which highlighting the needs of a client enhances the likelihood of a significant other agreeing to offer help?

2. Are there some types of client needs that are more likely to elicit assistance from another professional, e.g., high dependence and low ability? Are these the same as those client needs likely to elicit help from a relative or friend? e.g., is the norm of reciprocity more salient here?

3. Are school personnel more likely to give special help to a child with difficulties when they attribute the causes of the problem to forces external to the child than when they attribute the causes to the child's own behavior? If so, would a more effective strategy in eliciting teachers' help be to try and change their attributions or to try and make the norm of responsibility more salient?

4. Would a worker be more successful in recruiting individuals to

act as tutors or regular visitors to a juvenile facility if vivid descriptions and pictures of the specific individuals and the reasons they need help are provided than if recruitment efforts are more focused on the total group of individuals and the various reasons why they need help?

5. Does the enlistment of one of the more popular children in the class as a special helper for an unpopular handicapped child increase the incidence of offers of help from other classmates to a mainstreamed handicapped child? If so, do these offers persist even when the model loses interest in serving as helper?

CHAPTER 8. SOCIAL LEARNING THEORY

1. Are there certain categories of clients for whom observational learning would be more effective than self-regulation to reduce predictable distress? For example, is observational learning preferable for preschoolers? for grade schoolers? Are certain cognitive abilities needed for use of self-regulation techniques? At what level of mental retardation or mental impairment associated with senility are such techniques feasible to use? Are self-regulation and observational approaches to new social learning equally effective for severely depressed, for paranoid, for schizophrenic patients?

2. Can reliable techniques be developed to assess a client's perceived threats to free choice? If so, can these instruments be used to assess whether certain frequencies, durations, or intensities of worker reinforcement for desired client behaviors significantly reduce a client's feelings of free choice? Can these instruments be used to determine how much reinforcement is sufficient to encourage clients to undertake potentially unpleasant actions, without threatening their belief in the self-determination of their behaviors?

3. If a relative of a patient who has to engage in unpleasant treatments at home is encouraged to have the patient choose the time and place for treatment, does the patient participate more regularly or exhibit less distress during the treatment than if the caregiver makes these decisions?

4. Would external locus of control orientations of individuals in group homes or halfway houses be altered if the consequences of their possible actions are frequently discussed with them, and then the consequences ensued? If so, would alteration of the locus of control orientation concerning some areas of their life, e.g., their behavior in that setting, affect their expectations concerning outcomes in the larger community?

SECTION III. IMPLEMENTING GROUP INTERVENTION PLANS WITH SIGNIFICANT OTHERS: QUADRANT C

CHAPTER 9. GROUP DECISION MAKING AND PERFORMANCE

1. Does the instruction of members of task-oriented groups in the basic phases of group problem solving (namely orientation, evaluation, and control) facilitate problem solving of these groups? For example, are such groups less likely to undo prior decisions at subsequent meetings than are groups working on similar tasks who have not had such training? Would the same results be obtained with groups composed of adults from different subcultural backgrounds, such as Asian Americans or Puerto Ricans? For groups composed of adolescents or children? For mixed-sex groups as well as all-male or all-female groups?
2. Would observational studies of nonvoluntary task groups reveal greater evidence of individually oriented behaviors that are disruptive to group functioning than studies of voluntary task groups? For example, would such differences appear between staff development workshops in which attendance is required versus those in which it is voluntary?
3. Can written guidelines based on Hall's analysis of the components of effective group decision making be developed and tested with ongoing groups such as educational planning groups for handicapped children in schools or hospital discharge staff committees? Do groups trained in this way arrive at decisions that are more likely to be carried out by all members? Do such meetings take more time to reach a decision than comparable meetings conducted by untrained members?
4. Do groups with high cohesiveness generate more new ideas via brainstorming techniques than do less cohesive groups? Is brainstorming a more effective technique when used after groups have met together several times than when used during an initial group meeting?
5. Is the confidence that individuals indicate in stating their opinions in a group associated with the likelihood that the group will accept the opinion as its own? If so, can training self-effacing members in ways of presenting their ideas forcefully and confidently affect their influence upon group decisions?
6. Is a decision arrived at after group discussion more likely to be carried out than the same or a comparable decision arrived at by an individual member and presented to the group for its execution? Does the decision-making authority of the individual affect the likelihood that the group will carry out the decision?

7. Do members of a staff-training or socioeducational group whose performance is rewarded on strict equity principles develop less mutual attraction than those in a group in which rewards are equally distributed regardless of performance? Or where equity and equality principles are combined?

8. Is a group more effective in attaining performance goals when some attention is paid to performance level but where differentials in rewards are kept low than when rewards are directly proportional to performance?

9. Do the above variations in allocation of individual rewards affect the attendance of good and poor performers in different ways?

10. Does the cultural background, sex, or age of group members modify the consequences of distributing rewards according to the principle of equity or the principle of equality?

CHAPTER 10. LEADERSHIP IN GROUPS

1. Can task leaders be trained to elicit high levels of feedback from other group members? If so, do task leaders who successfully increase the other members' feedback to them also increase the other members' liking for them? Do the above results vary with the sex of the target individual or the sex composition of the group?

2. Can the participation and other leadership behaviors of nonprofessional members of agency advisory boards be increased by direct reinforcement of such behaviors by the social worker? By appointing them to recognized leadership positions such as chairmanship of a subcommittee? Under the above circumstances is it also necessary to provide the professional members with information about the expertise of the nonprofessional leaders in order for the latter to be perceived as competent to be selected as leaders by the total group?

3. In groups consisting of relatives of individuals with a particular disability where external status differences in members exist (e.g., of sex, race, education, or occupation) can the duplication of external status hierarchies within the group be reduced by the social worker's reinforcing the contributions of members having externally low statuses? By assigning tasks with greater power to members with lower external status?

3. Does altercasting individuals who do not express interest in leadership roles result in increased leadership behaviors for all types of individuals? For example, is this true for aged, low-income persons? for women? Does the social class, ethnic, or sex composition of the group affect the consequences of such altercasting? For example, do

women who have been altercast into leadership roles in groups composed primarily of men exhibit as much leadership behavior as when the members are mostly women? Does the social class or ethnicity of the members affect the consequences of such altercasting?

SECTION IV. IMPLEMENTING GROUP INTERVENTION PLANS WITH CLIENTS: QUADRANT D

CHAPTER 11. GROUP COHESIVENESS

1. Will a client group with cohesiveness based primarily on instrumental factors be less likely to conform to norms detrimental to the group's goal attainment than a group with cohesiveness based on member attractiveness?
2. Is a group of adult clients with cohesiveness based on member attractiveness more likely to survive a major failure in an important group task than a group with cohesiveness based on interdependence? If the clients are children, does a similar difference hold?
3. Does whether or not a client has been on a waiting list prior to beginning participation in a treatment/growth group affect the client's initial attraction to the group? If so, does this relationship persist after the first meeting? Does the length of time a client on a waiting list affect the answers to the prior questions? Do certain characteristics of a client affect the answers to the prior questions, such as age, level of self-esteem, and prior experience with social workers or social agencies? Do very long waits lead to negative attraction to a treatment/growth group?
4. Do certain kinds of obstacles to joining a group enhance group attraction for certain types of clients? For example, will filling out tests and questionnaires enhance a highly educated client's attraction to a group but not that of a client with lower educational levels?
5. What are the interrelationships among various indices of cohesiveness in treatment/growth groups? For example, will questions assessing members' pride in being in a group correlate significantly with other questionnaire and behavioral measures of cohesiveness? Will questions assessing members' wishes to continue the activities their group is engaged in correlate with other questionnaire and behavioral measures of cohesiveness?
6. Are there certain levels of cohesiveness early in group development that are so low that the social worker's efforts to enhance this characteristic are very likely to be unsuccessful? Under such circumstances would dividing the original treatment/growth group into two

or more new groups increase the social worker's chances of developing sufficient cohesiveness for goal attainment?

7. Do community or other task groups with high levels of cohesiveness exhibit more dysfunctional behavior in negotiating with other groups over attaining a desired goal, or avoiding a negative consequence, than comparable groups with lower cohesiveness? Does the same hold true for professional groups in residential settings or in large institutions?

CHAPTER 12. GROUP COMPOSITION

1. What is the relationship in treatment/growth groups of group size to members' receipt of rewards dispersed (e.g., words of approval)? To members' satisfaction with group discussions?

2. Which assortment of client problems in groups homogeneous in descriptive characteristics is associated with the most client improvement? Different types of family problems? A mix of family, work, and friendship problems? Problems that differ in role setting but that can be ameliorated by the same treatment, such as assertiveness training?

3. What is the relationship between member attractiveness and group size? For example, is the average attractiveness the same in client groups of ten and groups of four?

4. Will whites' saturation point for black members be lower than blacks' saturation point for white members in adult client groups? Will the same amount of discomfort be displayed by black and white group members of an adult treatment group when over one-third of the members are of the other race? For example, will attendance, participation in group discussions, expression of hostility, engagement in individually oriented behaviors, be affected in the same way and to the same extent under these circumstances for black and white members? Would similar results be obtained for biracial groups of children? For male, female, and mixed-sex biracial groups?

5. Can a group of clients with a similar problem achieve sufficient cohesiveness for group maintenance and goal attainment if the members hold opposing views on relevant political or ideological issues? For example, automobile workers coping with reactions to long-term unemployment who have widely differing views on the contribution of labor unions and government regulations to the economic problems in the country? Or, a support group of mature women returning to school who disagree on the issues of abortion and the Equal Rights Amendment?

CHAPTER 13. NORM ENFORCEMENT OR ACTIVE GROUP INFLUENCE

1. Will a client who values independence and is highly attracted to a group conform to group norms if there is group pressure to conform? Will the client leave the group?
2. What measures of a client's attraction to the group are the best predictors of attendance? length of time client remains in the group? tardiness?

CHAPTER 14. GROUP DEVELOPMENT

1. Do treatment or growth-oriented groups established to meet for a fixed number of meetings differ in the phases of group development from groups of similar clients who do not establish a termination point at the outset? Are there variations in the length of time spent in all phases or just in certain phases? For example, is the forming phase especially affected by a time limit?
2. How much change in membership can a client group undergo without significant shifts in the phase of group development? Does the size of the group have an affect on this? The length of time the group has been meeting before the new member(s) is/are introduced? The cohesiveness of the group prior to the change in membership? Do the prior relationships hold for other types of groups, such as committees?

CHAPTER 15. ROLE PLAYING AS A GROUP ACTIVITY

1. Does the use of role-reversal role plays in client groups affect the members' empathy toward their role partners? Does it affect their causal attributions of their partners behaviors? Do these shifts occur for all role problems, e.g., marital problems? interracial problems in work groups? for all clients, i.e., for members of both sexes? all ages and all racial and ethnic populations?
2. In groups including two or more members of a role set, are the results more powerful if role plays involve members of the same role set or members of different role sets? For example, in groups composed of middle-aged adults and their aged parents, or parents and their adolescent children, is there greater attitude change if members of the same or different families participate in the role-reversal role playing?
3. Is there a point of diminishing returns in which further role playing in a client group leads to less attitude change rather than more?
4. Would follow-up studies of clients in group treatment who participated in outcome psychodrama, role playing the possible conse-

quences of important decisions they were contemplating, find more satisfaction with the decisions ultimately reached than clients in other forms of group treatment? For example, would this be true of a client confronting career choices? With a client experiencing marital problems? With a pregnant teenager considering whether to terminate her pregnancy or to have her baby?

5. If a group composed of individuals who must alter their diets for health reasons engages in "emotional role playing" stressing the negative consequences of ignoring the dietary restrictions, will the members show more adherence to their diets six months after the group terminates than will members of a comparable group using other treatment approaches?

PART FOUR: ENDING SOCIAL RELATIONSHIPS

CHAPTER 16. UNPLANNED TERMINATIONS

1. Is a client who has alternative possible help sources within his or her family more likely to discontinue treatment than one whose alternatives involve other professionals? Than one with no other alternative?

2. Is a client who receives regular information about his or her progress less likely to discontinue treatment than one who does not? Does it matter whether the progress information is based on the client's own self-monitoring of behavioral changes or on data provided by the social worker?

3. Can the reasons that a client gives for remaining in or ending dyadic or group treatments be coded into the types of attractions and barriers described by Levinger and Moles (1979)? Do facilitators of change in the problems of others describe their relationships with social workers in similar terms? Can continuation to a jointly planned termination be predicted from a client's description during initial contact of sources of attraction to the relationship and barriers to its dissolution?

CHAPTER 17. PLANNED TERMINATIONS

1. Would follow-up studies of clients who were exposed to psychological inoculation as part of planned termination show greater maintenance of gains achieved during the social work intervention than would studies of those who were not? If so, is this maintenance influ-

enced by the nature of the initial problems? By the post-termination stresses encountered?

2. Do similar findings to those previously described occur when psychological inoculation procedures are used in terminating contacts with "significant others" whose interactions with the social worker have been focused on other persons' problems? Does it matter whether the significant others are in professional, family, friend, coworker, or stranger role relationships with the individuals whose problems are the target of change?

3. Would follow-up studies find that those clients who participated in rituals during their final contacts with a social worker report greater satisfaction with what was accomplished during the intervention? Would they report fewer difficulties in maintaining the new or revised behaviors and attitudes that were the outcome of the planned change efforts?

4. Are certain termination rituals more likely to be linked to post-termination satisfaction and persistence of desired outcomes? For example, are eating rituals more potent than those involving the exchange of photos? Are specific type of rituals more effective for individuals with certain characteristics, e.g., those with given educational or ethnic backgrounds? those who are facilitators of change in the problems of others?

5. Would follow-up studies show that the involvement of significant others in the termination process has measurable effects on the adequacy of clients' post-termination functioning?

6. Would follow-up studies show that clients who attributed their improved functioning at termination primarily to their own efforts had fewer post-termination problems in social functioning than did clients who attributed their goal attainment primarily to their social workers?

7. Would follow-up studies show that workers who attributed their clients' goal attainment primarily to the clients' own behaviors were more effective practitioners than those who attributed client change primarily to the workers' skills and abilities?

REFERENCES

Aboud, Frances E. 1976. Self-evaluation information seeking strategies for interethnic social comparisons. *Journal of Cross-Cultural Psychology* 7:289–300.

Abrahams, R. B. 1972. Mutual help for the widowed. *Social Work* 17(5):54–61.

Abrahamson, L. Y., M. E. P. Seligman, and J. D. Teasdale. 1978. Learned helplessness in humans: Critique and reformulation. *Journal of Abnormal Psychology* 87:49–74.

Acosta, F. X. 1977. Ethnic variables in psychotherapy: The Mexican American. In J. L. Martinez, Jr., ed., *Chicano Psychology*, pp. 215–231. New York: Academic Press.

Acosta, F. X. 1979. Pretherapy expectations and definitions of mental illness among minority and low-income patients. *Hispanic Journal of Behavioral Science* 4:403-10.

Acosta, F. X. 1980. Self-described reasons for premature termination of psychotherapy by Mexican Americans, black Americans, and Anglo-American patients. *Psychological Reports* 47:435-43.

Acosta, F. X., L. A., Evans, J., Yamamoto, and S. A. Wilcox. 1980. Helping minority and low-income psychotherapy patients "Tell It Like It is." *Journal of Biocommunication* 7(3):13-19.

Adams, J. 1963. Toward an understanding of inequity. *Journal of Abnormal and Social Psychology* 67:422–36.

Adams, J. S. and S. Freeman. 1976. Equity theory revisited: Comments and annotated bibliography. In L. Berkowitz, ed., *Advances in Experimental Social Psychology* 9:43-90. New York: Academic Press.

Aderman, D. and L. Berkowitz. 1970. Observation set, empathy, and helping. *Journal of Personality and Social Psychology* 14:141–48.

Aderman, D., S. S. Brehm, and L. B. Katz. 1974. Empathic observation of an innocent victim: The just world revisited. *Journal of Personality and Social Psychology*, 29:342–47.

Adorno, T. W., E. Frenkel-Brunswik, D. J. Levinson, and R. N. Sanford. 1950. *The Authoritarian Personality*. New York: Harper.

Aguilar, Ignacio. 1972. Initial contacts with Mexican-American families. *Social Work* 17(3):66-70.

Aiello, J. R. and S. E. Jones. 1971. Field study of the proxemic behavior of young school children in three subcultural groups. *Journal of Personality and Social Psychology* 19:351–56.

Ajzen, I. 1971. Attitudinal vs. normative messages: An investigation of the differential effects of persuasive communications on behavior. *Sociometry* 34:263–80.

Ajzen, I. and M. Fishbein. 1970. The prediction of behavior from attitudinal and normative variables. *Journal of Experimental Social Psychology* 6:466–87.

Ajzen, I. and M. Fishbein. 1972. Attitudes and normative beliefs as factors influencing behavioral intentions. *Journal of Personality and Social Psychology* 21:1–9.

Ajzen, I. and M. Fishbein. 1973. Attitudinal and normative variables as predictors of specific behaviors. *Journal of Personality and Social Psychology* 27:41–57.

Ajzen, I. and M. Fishbein. 1977. Attitude-behavior relations: A theoretical analysis and review of empirical research. *Psychological Bulletin* 84:888–918.

Albrecht, G. L. and H. C. Gift. 1975. Adult socialization: Ambiguity and adult life crises. In N. Datan and L. H. Ginsberg, eds., *Life-Span Developmental Psychology*, pp. 237–51. New York: Academic Press.

Aldous, Joan. 1974. The making of family roles and family change. *The Family Coordinator* (July), 23:231–35.

Amir, Y. 1976. The role of intergroup contact in change of prejudice and ethnic relations. In Phyllis A. Katz, ed., *Toward the Elimination of Racism*, pp. 245-308. New York: Pergamon Press.

Anderson, A. B. 1975. Combined effects of interpersonal attraction and goal path clarity on the cohesiveness of task oriented groups. *Journal of Personality and Social Psychology* 31:68–75.

Anderson, C. C. and A. D. J. Cote. 1966. Belief dissonance as a source of disaffection between ethnic groups. *Journal of Personality and Social Psychology* 4:447–53.

Anderson, J. D. 1975. Human relations training and group work. *Social Work* 20:195–99.

Argyle, M. 1975. *Bodily Communication*. London: Methuen.

Argyle, M., F. Alkema, and R. Gilmore. 1972. The communication of friendly and hostile attitudes by verbal and non-verbal signals. *European Journal of Social Psychology* 1:385–402.

Argyris, Chris. 1975. Dangers in applying results from experimantal social psychology. *American Psychologist* (April), 30(4):469–85.

Arkin, R. M. and S. Duval. 1975. Focus of attention and causal attributions of actors and observers. *Journal of Experimental Social Psychology* 1:156–71.

Aronson, E. 1961. The effect of effort on the attractiveness of rewarded and unrewarded stimuli. *Journal of Abnormal and Social Psychology* 63:375–80.

Aronson, E. 1973. Dissonance theory: Progress and problems. In L.S. Wrightsman and J.C. Brigham, eds., *Contemporary Issues in Social Psychology*, pp. 310–23. 2d ed. Monterey, Calif.: Brooks-Cole.

Aronson, E. and J. Mills. 1968. The effects of severity of initiation on liking for a group. In Dorwin Cartwright and A. Zander, eds., *Group Dynamics*, pp. 119–24. 3d ed. New York: Harper & Row.

Aronson, E., J. A. Turner, and J. M. Carlsmith. 1963. Communicator credibility and communication discrepancy as determinants of opinion change. *Journal of Abnormal and Social Psychology* 67:31–36.
Aronson, H. and B. Overall. 1966. Treatment expectations of patients in two social classes. *Social Work* 11(1):35–42.
Asch, S. 1951. Effects of group pressure upon the modification and distortion of judgments. In H. Guetzkow, ed., *Groups, Leadership, and Men*, pp. 177–90. Pittsburgh: Carnegie Press.
Asch, S. E. 1956. Studies of independence and conformity: I. A Minority of one against a unanimous majority. *Psychological Monographs* 70 (9, whole no. 416).
Atchley, R. C. 1975. The life course, age grading, and age-linked demands for decision making. In N. Datan and L. H. Ginsberg, eds., *Life-Span Developmental Psychology*, pp. 261–78. New York: Academic Press.
Atherton, C., S. Mitchell, and E. Schein. 1971. Locating points for intervention. *Social Casework* 52:131–42.
Bachman, Jerald G. and Patrick M. O'Malley. 1977. Self-esteem in young men: A longitudinal analysis of the impact of educational and occupational attainment. *Journal of Personality and Social Psychology* 35:365–80.
Backman, C. W., P. F. Secord, and J. R. Peirce. Resistance to change in the self-concept as a function of perceived consensus among significant others. In C. W. Backman and P. F. Secord, eds., *Problems in Social Psychology*, pp. 462–467. New York: McGraw-Hill.
Baekeland, F. and L. Lundwall. 1975. Dropping out of treatment: A critical review. *Psychological Bulletin* 82:738–83.
Baer, D. M., R. F. Peterson, and J. A. Sherman. 1967. The development of generalized imitation in young children. *Journal of Experimental Analysis of Behavior* 10:405–16.
Baer, D. M. and J. A. Sherman. 1964. Reinforcement control of generalized imitation in young children. *Journal of Experimental Child Psychology* 1:37–49.
Baker, E. K. 1979. The relationship between locus of control and psychotherapy: A review of the literature. *Psychotherapy: Theory, Research and Practice* 16:351–62.
Bales, Robert F. 1950. *Interaction Process Analysis: A Method for the Study of Small Groups*. Cambridge, Mass.: Addison-Wesley.
Bales, R. F. 1953. The equilibrium problem in small groups. In T. Parsons, R. F. Bales, and E. A. Shils, eds., *Working Papers in the Theory of Action*, pp. 111–61. Glencoe, Ill.: Free Press.
Bales, Robert F. 1966. Task roles and social roles in problem-solving groups. In Bruce Biddle and E. J. Thomas, eds., *Role Theory: Concepts and Research*, pp. 254–63. New York: Wiley.
Bales, R. F. 1970. *Personality and Interpersonal Behavior*. New York: Holt, Rinehart and Winston.
Bales, R. F. and E. F. Borgatta. 1955. Size of group as a factor in the interaction

profile. In A. P. Hare, E. F. Borgatta, and R. F. Bales, eds., *Small Groups: Studies in Social Interaction*, pp. 396–413. New York: Knopf.

Bales, R. F. and P. E. Slater. 1955. Role differentiation in small, decision-making groups. In T. Parsons and R. F. Bales, eds., *Family Socialization and Interaction Process*, pp. 307–52. New York: Free Press.

Bales, R. F. and F. L. Strodtbeck. 1968. Phases in group problem-solving. In Dorwin Cartwright and A. Zander, eds., *Group Dynamics: Research and Theory*, pp. 389–98. 3d ed. New York: Harper & Row.

Balgopal, P. R. 1971. Sensitivity training: A study in theory and its applicability to social work education. Ph. D. dissertation, School of Social Work, Tulane University.

Bandler, R. J., G. R. Madaras, and D. J. Bem. 1968. Self-observation as a source of pain perception. *Journal of Personality and Social Psychology* 9:205–9.

Bandura, A. 1967. The role of modeling processes in personality development. In W. W. Hartup and N. L. Smothergell, eds., *The Young Child: Review of Research*, pp. 42–58. Washington, D.C.: National Association for the Education of Young Children.

Bandura, A. 1969. *Principles of Behavior Modification*. New York: Holt, Rinehart and Winston.

Bandura, Albert. 1977. *Social Learning Theory*. Englewood Cliffs, N.J.: Prentice-Hall.

Bandura, A., ed. 1971. *Psychological Modeling: Conflicting Theories*. Chicago: Aldine-Atherton.

Bandura, A., N. E. Adams, and J. Beyer. 1977. Cognitive processes mediating behavioral change. *Journal of Personality and Social Psychology* 35:125–39.

Bandura, A., J. E. Grusec, and F. L. Monleve. 1967. Some social determinants of self-monitoring reinforcement systems. *Journal of Personality and Social Psychology* 5:449–55.

Bandura, A., R. W. Jeffery, and E. Gajdos. 1975. Generalizing change through participant modeling with self-directed mastery. *Behavior Research and Therapy* 13:141–52.

Bandura, A., D. H. Lipsher, and P. E. Miller. 1960. Psychotherapists' approach-avoidance reactions to patients' expressions of hostility. *Journal of Consulting Psychology* 24:1–8.

Bandura, A. and B. Perloff. 1967. Relative efficacy of self-monitored and externally imposed reinforcement systems. *Journal of Personality and Social Psychology* 7:111–16.

Bandura, A. and R. H. Walters. 1963. *Social Learning and Personality Development*. New York: Holt, Rinehart and Winston.

Banikotes, P. G., J. M. Russell, and J. H. Linden. 1972. Interpersonal attraction in simulated and real interactions. *Journal of Personality and Social Psychology* 23:1–17.

Barocas, R. and F. L. Vance. 1974. Physical appearance and personal adjustment counseling. *Journal of Counseling Psychology* 21:96–100.

Baron, R. A., D. Byrne, and W. Griffith. 1974. *Social Psychology*. Boston: Allyn & Bacon.
Baron, R. M. and R. L. Gantz. 1972. Effects of locus of control and type of feedback on the task performance of lower class black children. *Journal of Personality and Social Psychology* 21:124–30.
Bar-Tal, Daniel. 1976. *Prosocial Behavior: Theory and Research*. Washington, D.C.: Hemisphere.
Batson, C. D. 1975. Attribution as a mediator of bias in helping. *Journal of Personality and Social Psychology* 32:455–66.
Batson, C. D., J. S. Coke, M. L. Jasnoski, and M. Hanson. 1978. Buying kindness: Effect of an extrinsic incentive for helping on perceived altruism. *Personality and Social Bulletin* 4:86–91.
Bauer, E. A. 1973. Personal space: A study of blacks and whites. *Sociometry* 36:402–8.
Bavelas, A., A. H. Hastorf, A. E. Gross, and W. R. Kite. 1965. Experiments in the alteration of group structure. *Journal of Experimental Social Psychology* 1:55–70.
Baxter, J. C. 1970. Interpersonal spacing in natural settings. *Sociometry* 33:444–56.
Beach, A. L. 1969. Overcoming underachievement. In J. D. Krumboltz and C. E. Thoresen, eds., *Behavioral Counseling: Cases and Techniques*, pp. 241–48. New York: Holt, Rinehart and Winston.
Beck, D. F. and M. A. Jones. 1973. *Progress on Family Problems*. New York: Family Service Association of America.
Becker, W. 1971. *Parents Are Teachers: A Child Management Program*. Champaign, Ill.: Research Press.
Beckett, J. O. 1976. Working wives: A racial comparison. *Social Work* 21:463–71.
Beckhouse, L., J. Tanur, J. Weiler, and E. Weinstein. 1975. . . . And some men have leadership thrust upon them. *Journal of Personality and Social Psychology* 31:557–66.
Bednar, R. L. 1974. Empirical guidelines for group therapy: Pretraining, cohesion, and modeling. *Journal of Applied Behavioral Science* 10:149–65.
Bem, D. J. 1967. Self-perception: An alternative interpretation of cognitive dissonance phenomena. *Psychological Review* 74:183–200.
Bem, D. J. 1970. *Beliefs, Attitudes, and Human Affairs*. Belmont, Calif.: Brooks-Cole.
Bem, D. J. 1972. Self-perception theory. In Leonard Berkowitz, ed., *Advances in Experimental Social Psychology*, 6:1–62, New York: Academic Press.
Bem, S. L. 1975. Sex role adaptability: One consequence of psychological androgyny. *Journal of Personality and Social Psychology* 31:634–43.
Benjamin, B. A. 1976. Effects of role induction training on counseling process and client expectations in a pre-trial diversion program. *Dissertation Abstracts International* 37(5):2626–27.
Benne, K. and P. Sheats. 1961. Functional roles of group members. In L. P.

Bradford, ed., *Group Development*, pp. 51–59. Washington, D.C.: National Education Association.

Benoit-Smullyan, E. 1944. Status, status-types, and status-interrelations. *American Sociological Review* 9:151–61.

Berelson, B. and G. A. Steiner. 1964. *Human Behavior*. New York: Harcourt Brace Jovanovich.

Berger, J., B. P. Cohen, and M. Zelditch, Jr. 1966. Status characteristics and expectation states. In J. Berger, M. Zelditch, Jr., and B. Anderson, eds., *Sociological Theories in Progress*, pp. 29–46. Boston: Houghton-Mifflin.

Berger, S. M. and W. M. Lambert. 1968. Stimulus-response theory in contemporary social psychology. In G. Lindzey and E. Aronson, eds., *Handbook of Social Psychology*, 1:81–178. Reading, Mass.: Addison-Wesley.

Bergin, A. 1962. The effect of dissonant persuasive communications upon changes in self-referring attitudes. *Journal of Personality* 30:423–38.

Bergin, A. E. 1966. Some implications of psychotherapy research for therapeutic practice. *Journal of Abnormal Psychology* 71:235–46.

Berkowitz, L. 1955. Group standards, cohesiveness, and productivity. *Human Relations* 7:509–19.

Berkowitz, L. 1970. The self, selfishness, and altruism. In J. Macaulay and L. Berkowitz, eds., *Altruism and Helping Behavior*, pp. 143–53. New York: Academic Press.

Berkowitz, L. 1972. Social norms, feelings, and other factors affecting helping behavior. In L. Berkowitz, ed., *Advances in Experimental Social Psychology*, 6:63–108. New York: Academic Press.

Berkowitz, L. and L. R. Daniels. 1963. Responsibility and dependency. *Journal of Abnormal and Social Psychology* 66:429-36.

Berkowitz, L. and L. Daniels. 1964. Affecting the salience of the social responsibility norm: Effects of past help on the response to dependency relationships. *Journal of Abnormal and Social Psychology* 68:275–81.

Berscheid, E. and E. H. Walster. 1969. *Interpersonal Attraction*. Reading, Mass.: Addison-Wesley.

Berscheid, E. and E. Walster. 1974. Physical attractiveness. In L. Berkowitz, ed., *Advances in Experimental Social Psychology*, 7:159–215. New York: Academic Press.

Bertcher, H. J. and F. Maple. 1974. Elements and issues in group composition. In P. Glasser, R. Sarri, and R. Vinter, eds., *Individual Change through Small Groups*, pp. 166–208. New York: Free Press.

Best, D. L., J. E. Williams, J. M. Cloud, S. W. Davis, L. S. Robertson, John R. Edwards, H. Giles, and J. Fowles. 1977. Development of sex-trait stereotypes among young children in the United States, England, and Ireland. *Child Development* 48:1375–84.

Biddle, Bruce J. 1979. *Role Theory: Expectations, Identities, and Behaviors*. New York: Academic Press.

Billingsley, Andrew. 1968. *Black Families in White America*. Englewood Cliffs, N.J.: Prentice-Hall.

Birns, B. 1976. The emergence and socialization of sex differences in the earliest years. *Merrill-Palmer Quarterly* 22:230–54.

Blanchard, F. A., L. Adelman, and S. W. Cook. 1975. Effect of group success and failure upon interpersonal attraction in cooperating interracial groups. *Journal of Personality and Social Psychology* 31:1020–30.

Blau, P. M. 1964. *Exchange and Power in Social Life*. New York: Wiley.

Blau, Z. S. 1978. *Aging, Social Class, and Ethnicity: A Comparative Study of Anglo, Black, and Mexican-American Texans*. Ann Arbor, Mich.: School of Social Work, University of Michigan.

Bott, E. 1971. *Family and Social Network: Norms and External Relationships in Ordinary Urban Families*. 2d ed. London: Tavistock.

Bovard, E. 1951. Group structure and perception. *Journal of Abnormal and Social Psychology* 46:389–405.

Bradley, G. W. 1978. Self-serving biases in the attribution process: A re-examination of the fact or fiction question. *Journal of Personality and Social Psychology* 36:56–71.

Brechner, K. C. 1977. An experimental analysis of social traps. *Journal of Experimental Social Psychology* 13:552–64.

Brehm, J. W. 1966. *A Theory of Psychological Reactance*. New York: Academic Press.

Brehm, J. W. 1972. *Responses to Loss of Freedom: A Theory of Psychological Reactance*. Morristown, N.J.: General Learning Press.

Brehm, J. W. and A. R. Cohen. 1959. Reevaluation of choice alternatives as a function of their number and qualitative similarity. *Journal of Abnormal and Social Psychology* 58:373–78.

Brehm, J. W. and A. R. Cohen. 1962. *Explorations in Cognitive Dissonance*. New York: Wiley.

Brehm, J. W. and M. Mann. 1975. Effect of importance of freedom and attraction to group members on influence produced by group pressure. *Journal of Personality and Social Psychology* 31:816–24.

Brehm, J. W. and J. Sensing. 1966. Social influence as a function of attempted and implied usurption of choice. *Journal of Personality and Social Psychology* 4:703–7.

Brehm, Sharon S. 1976. *The Application of Social Psychology to Clinical Practice*. New York: Wiley.

Briar, S. 1966. Family services. In H. S. Maas, ed., *Five Fields of Social Service: Reviews of Research*, pp. 9–50. New York: National Association of Social Workers.

Brickman, P. and A. E. Holland. 1979. *Helping on a hotline: A study of parental stress service*. Unpublished manuscript. Northwestern University.

Brief, A. P. and R. J. Aldag. 1976. Correlates of role indices. *Journal of Applied Psychology* 61:468–72.

Brim, O. G., Jr. and S. Wheeler. 1966. *Socialization after Childhood: Two Essays*. New York: Wiley.

Brink, J. H. 1977. Effect of interpersonal communication on attraction. *Journal of Personality and Social Psychology* 35:783–90.
Brock, T. E. 1965. Communicator-recipient similarity and decision change. *Journal of Personality and Social Psychology* 1:650–54.
Brock, T. C. and A. H. Buss. 1962. Dissonance, aggression, and evaluation of pain. *Journal of Abnormal and Social Psychology* 65:192–202.
Broll, Lorraine, Allan E. Grosse, and Irving Piliavin. 1974. Effects of offered and requested help on help seeking and reactions to being helped. *Journal of Applied Social Psychology* 4:244–58.
Bronfenbrenner, U. 1970. *Two Worlds of Children: U.S. and U.S.S.R.* New York: Russell Sage.
Bronfenbrenner, U., J. Harding, and M. Gallwey. 1958. The measurement of skill in social perception. In D. C. McClelland, ed., *Talent and Society*, pp. 29–111. New York: Van Nostrand.
Bronson, M. 1977. Women and psychotherapy: Sex roles and clinical bias. *Smith College Studies in Social Work* 48(1):45–47.
Brophy, J. E. and T. L. Good. 1970. Teachers' communication of differential expectations for children's classroom performance. *Journal of Educational Psychology* 61:365–74.
Broverman, I. K., S. R. Vogel, D. M. Broverman, F. E. Clarkson, and P. S. Rosenkrantz. 1972. Sex-role stereotypes: A current appraisal. *Journal of Social Issues* 28(1):59–78.
Brown, Roger. 1965. *Social Psychology*. New York: Free Press.
Bryan, J. H. and M. A. Test. 1967. Models and helping: Naturalistic studies in aiding behavior. *Journal of Personality and Social Psychology* 6:400–7.
Buckley, N. K. and M. W. Hill. 1970. *Modifying Classroom Behavior: A Manual of Procedures for Classroom Teachers*. Champaign, Ill.: Research Press.
Bugenthal, D. E., J. W. Kaswan, and L. R. Love. 1970. Perception of contradictory meanings conveyed by verbal and nonverbal channels. *Journal of Personality and Social Psychology* 16:647–55.
Burghardt, S. 1979. The tactical use of group structure and process in community organization. In Fred M. Cox, J. L. Erlich, J. Rothman, and J. Tropman, eds., *Strategies of Community Organization: A Book of Readings*, pp. 113–29. 3d ed. Itasca, Ill.: Peacock.
Burke, P. J. 1967. The development of task and socio-emotional role differentiation. *Sociometry* 30:379–92.
Burnstein, E., E. Stotland, and A. Zander. 1961. Similarity to a model and self-evaluation. *Journal of Abnormal and Social Psychology* 62:257–64.
Burnstein, E. and A. Vinokur. 1975. What a person thinks upon learning he has chosen differently from others: Nice evidence for the persuasive-arguments explanation of choice shifts. *Journal of Experimental Social Psychology* 11:412–26.
Burnstein, E. and A. Vinokur. 1977. Persuasive argumentation and social comparison as determinants of attitude polarization. *Journal of Experimental Social Psychology* 13:315–32.

Burr, Wesley R. 1972. Role transitions: A reformulation of theory. *Journal of Marriage and the Family* 34:407–16.

Buss, A. H. and N. W. Portnoy. 1967. Pain tolerance and group identification. *Journal of Personality and Social Psychology* 6:106–8.

Byrne, D. 1971. *The Attraction Paradigm*. Academic Press.

Byrne, D. and C. R. Ervin. 1969. Attraction toward a Negro stranger as a function or prejudice, attitude similarity, and the stranger's evaluation of the subject. *Human Relations* 22:397–404.

Byrne, D., C. R. Ervin, and J. Lamberth. 1970. Continuity between the experimental study of attraction and real-life computer dating. *Journal of Personality and Social Psychology*. 16:157–65.

Byrne, D. and W. Griffitt. 1966. A developmental investigation of the law of attraction. *Journal of Personality and Social Psychology* 4:699–702.

Byrne, D., W. Griffitt, W. Hudgens, and K. Reeves. 1969. Attitude similarity-dissimilarity and attraction: Generality beyond the college sophomore. *Journal of Social Psychology*. 79:155–61.

Byrne, D. and D. Nelson. 1965. Attraction as a linear function of proportion of positive reinforcements. *Journal of Personality and Social Psychology* 1:659–63.

Byrne, D. and T. J. Wong. 1962. Racial prejudice, interpersonal attraction, and assumed dissimilarity of attitudes. *Journal of Abnormal and Social Psychology* 65:246–53.

Camp, B. W., G. E. Bloom, F. Hebert, and W. J. van Doorninck. 1977. "Think aloud": A program for developing self-control in young aggressive boys. *Journal of Abnormal Child Psychology* 5:157–69.

Campbell, Angus, Philip E. Converse, and Willard L. Rodgers. 1976. *The Quality of American Life: Perceptions, Evaluations, and Satisfactions*. New York: Russell Sage.

Campbell, D. T. 1958. Common fate, similarity, and other indices of the status of aggregates of persons as social entities. *Behavioral Science* 3:14–25.

Cann, A., S. J. Sherman, and R. Elkes. 1975. Effects of initial request size and timing of a second request on compliance. The foot-in-the-door and the door in the face. *Journal of Personality and Social Psychology* 32:774–82.

Cantril, H. 1965. *The Pattern of Human Concerns*. New Brunswick, N.J.: Rutgers University Press.

Caplan, R. D. 1972. Organizational stress and individual strain: A social-psychological study of risk factors in coronary heart disease among administrators, engineers, and scientists. Ph. D. dissertation, University of Michigan, 1971. *Dissertation Abstracts International* 32:6706B–07B (University Microfilms no. 72–14822).

Caplan, R. D., E. A. R. Robinson, J. P. R. French, Jr., J. R. Caldwell, and M. Shinn. 1976. *Adhering to Medical Regimes: Pilot Experiments in Patient Education and Social Supports*. Ann Arbor, Mich.: Institute for Social Research.

Carkhuff, R. R. 1971. *The Development of Human Resources: Education, Psychology and Social Change*. New York: Holt, Rinehart and Winston.

Carkhuff, R. and R. Pierce. 1967. The differential effects of therapist race and social class upon patients' depth of self-exploration in the initial clinical interview. *Journal of Consulting Psychology* 31:632–34.

Carlsmith, J. M. and A. E. Gross. 1969. Some effects of guilt on compliance. *Journal of Personality and Social Psychology* 11:232–39.

Carlson, E. R. 1956. Attitude change through modification of attitude structure. *Journal of Abnormal and Social Psychology* 52:256–61.

Carson, R. C. 1969. *Interaction Concepts of Personality*. Chicago: Aldine.

Cartwright, D. 1967. Achieving change in people: Some applications of group dynamics theory. In E. P. Hollander and R. G. Hunt, eds., *Current Perspectives in Social Psychology*, pp. 520–29. 2d ed. New York: Oxford University Press.

Cartwright, D. 1968. The nature of group cohesiveness. In D. Cartwright and A. Zander, eds., *Group Dynamics*, pp. 91–109. New York: Harper & Row.

Cartwright, D., and A. Zander, eds. 1968. *Group Dynamics*. 3d ed. New York: Harper & Row.

Carver, C. S. and M. F. Scheier. 1978. Self-focusing effects of dispositional self-consciousness, mirror presence, and audience presence. *Journal of Personality and Social Psychology* 36:324–32.

Cavan, Ruth S. 1962. Self and role in adjustment during old age. In Arnold M. Rose, ed., *Human Behavior and Social Processes*, pp. 526–36. Boston: Houghton-Mifflin.

Chandler, M. J. 1973. Egocentrism and antisocial behavior: The assessment and training of social perspective-taking skills. *Developmental Psychology* 9:326–32.

Chavez, N. 1976. Mexican Americans' expectations of treatment, role of self and of therapists. Effects on utilization of mental health services. Ph. D. dissertation, University of Denver, 1975. *Dissertation Abstracts International* 36(7):4760A.

Chemers, M. M. and G. J. Skrzypek. 1972. Experimental test of the contingency model of leadership effectiveness. *Journal of Personality and Social Psychology* 24:172–77.

Chescheir, M. W. 1979. Social role discrepancies as clues to practice. *Social Work* 24:89–94.

Chesler, M. and R. Fox. 1966. *Role-Playing Methods in the Classroom*. Chicago: Science Research Associates.

Childress, R. and J. S. Gillis. 1977. A study of pre-therapy role induction as an influence process. *Journal of Clinical Psychology* 33:540–44.

Chin, R. 1976. Montreal Chinese: Studies of personal and cultural identity. An unpublished report on the Chinese Canadian Community in Montreal. (Available from Robert Chin, Department of Psychology, Boston University, Boston, Mass., 02215.)

Churchill, S. R. 1974. A comparison of two models of social group work: The treatment model and the reciprocal model. In P. Glasser, R. Sarri, and R. Vinter, eds., *Individual Change through Small Groups*, pp 266–76. New York: Free Press.

Cialdini, R. B., R. Borden, A. Thorne, M. Walker, and S. Freeman. 1976. Basking in reflected glory: Three (football) field studies. *Journal of Personality and Social Psychology* 34:366–75.

Citron, P. 1978. Group work with alcoholic, polydrug-involved adolescents with deviant behavior syndrome. *Social Work With Groups* 1:39–52.

Clark, M. S., C. G. Gotay, and J. Mills. 1974. Acceptance of help as a function of similarity of the potential helper and opportunity to repay. *Journal of Applied Social Psychology* 4:224–29.

Clary, E. G., A. Tesser and L. L. Downing. 1978. Influence of a salient schema on thought-induced cognitive change. *Personality and Social Psychology Bulletin* 4:39–43.

Clifford, M. M. and E. Walster. 1972. The effect of sex on college admission, work evaluation, and job interviews. *Journal of Experimental Education* 41(2):1–5.

Clore, G. 1978. Role playing and attraction: Working notes on the current state of the problem. Unpublished paper.

Clore, G. L., R. M. Bray, S. M. Itkin, and P. Murphy. 1978. Interracial attitudes and behavior at a summer camp. *Journal of Personality and Social Psychology* 36:107–16.

Clore, G. L. and D. Byrne. 1974. A reinforcement-affect model of attraction. In T. L. Huston, ed., *Foundations of Interpersonal Attraction*, pp. 143–70. New York: Academic Press.

Clore, G. L. and K. M. Jeffery. 1972. Emotional role playing, attitude change, and attraction toward a disabled person. *Journal of Personality and Social Psychology* 23:105–11.

Coates, D. and C. B. Wortman. 1980. Depression maintenance and interpersonal control. In Andrew Baum, J. Singer, and Y. Epstein, eds., *Advances in Environmental Psychology* 2:149–82. Hillsdale, N.J.: Erlbaum.

Cobb, S. 1974. Physiologic changes in men whose jobs were abolished. *Journal of Psychosomatic Research* 18:245–58.

Cobb, S. 1976. Social support as a moderator of life stress. *Psychosomatic Medicine* 38:300–14.

Cohen, A. R. 1962a. An experiment on small rewards for discrepant compliance and attitude change. In J. W. Brehm and A. R. Cohen, eds., *Explorations in Cognitive Dissonance*, pp. 73–78. New York: Wiley.

Cohen, A. R. 1962b. A study of discrepant information in betrothal. In J. W. Brehm and A. R. Cohen, eds., *Explorations in Cognitive Dissonance*, pp. 78–81. New York: Wiley.

Cohen, E. G. 1972. Sociology and the classroom: Setting the conditions for teacher-student interaction. *Review of Educational Research* 42:441–52.

Cohen, E. G. and S. R. Roper. 1972. Modification of interracial interaction. *American Sociological Review* 37:643–57.

Cohen, E. H. 1977. Control of exposure and monitoring in treating children's fear of darkness. Ph. D. dissertation, State University of New York at Buffalo.

Cohler, B. J., H. U. Grunebaum, J. L. Weiss, D. H. Gallant, and V. Abernathy. 1974. Social relations, stress, and psychiatric hospitalization among mothers of young children. *Social Psychiatry* 9:7–12.

Collins, B. E. and M. F. Hoyt. 1972. Personal responsibility for the consequences: An integration and extension of the "forced compliance" literature. *Journal of Experimental Social Psychology* 8:558–92.

Collins, B. E. and B. H. Raven. 1969. Group structure: Attraction, coalitions, communication, and power. In G. Lindzey and E. Aronson, eds., *Handbook of Social Psychology* 4:102-204. Reading, Mass.; Addison-Wesley.

Compton, B. R. and B. Galaway. 1975. *Social Work Processes*. Homewood, Ill.: Dorsey.

Conroy, W. J., E. S. Katkin, and W. L. Barnette. 1973. Modification of smoking behavior by Rokeach's self-confrontation technique. Paper presented at the annual meeting of the Southeastern Psychological Association, New Orleans, April.

Converse, P. and A. Campbell. 1968. Political standards in secondary groups. In D. Cartwright and A. Zander, eds., *Group Dynamics* pp. 199–211. 3d ed. New York: Harper & Row.

Cook, S. W. 1972. Motives in a conceptual analysis of attitude-related behavior. In J. Brigham and T. Weissbach, eds., *Racial Attitudes in America: Analyses and Findings of Social Psychology*. New York: Harper & Row.

Cook, T. D. and B. R. Flay. 1978. The persistence of experimentally induced attitude change. In L. Berkowitz, ed., *Advances in Experimental Social Psychology*, 11:1–59. New York: Academic Press.

Cooper, J. 1974. Population control and the psychology of forced compliance. *Journal of Social Issues* 30(4):265–77.

Cooper, J. and S. Worchel. 1970. Role of undesired consequences in arousing cognitive dissonance. *Journal of Personality and Social Psychology* 16:199–206.

Corah, N. L. and J. Boffa. 1970. Perceived control, self-observation, and response to aversive stimulation. *Journal of Personality and Social Psychology* 16:1–4.

Corsini, R. 1966. *Role Playing in Psychotherapy*. Chicago: Aldine.

Coser, Rose L. and Gerald Rokoff. 1973. Women in the occupational world: Social disruption and conflict. In Peter Rose, ed., *The Study of Society*, pp. 446–63. 3d ed. New York: Random House.

Costanzo, P. R., H. T. Reitan, and M. F. Shaw. 1968. Conformity as a function of experimentally induced minority and majority competence. *Psychonomic Science* 10:329–30.

Cottrell, N. B. 1968. Performance in the presence of other human beings: Mere presence, audience, and affiliation effects. In E. C. Simmel, R. H. Hoppe, and G. A. Milton, eds., *Social Facilitation and Imitative Behavior*, pp. 91–110. Boston: Allyn & Bacon.

Cowan, G., and R. Inskeep. 1978. Commitments to help among the diabled-disadvantaged. *Personality and Social Psychology Bulletin* 4:92–96.
Cox, F. M., J. L. Erlich, J. Rothman, and J. E. Tropman. 1979. *Strategies of Community Organization: A Book of Readings*. 3d ed. Itasca, Ill: Peacock.
Coyle, Grace L. 1948. *Group Work with American Youth*. New York: Harper & Row.
Coyle, Grace. 1958. *Social Science in the Professional Education of Social Workers*. New York: Council on Social Work Education.
Coyle, Grace and Margaret Hartford. 1958. *Social Processes in the Community and the Group*. New York: Council on Social Work Education.
Crosbie, P. V. 1972. Social exchange and power compliance: A test of Homan's propositions. *Sociometry*, 35:203–22.
Croxton, T. A. 1974. The therapeutic contract in social treatment. In P. Glasser, R. Sarri, and R. Vinter, eds., *Individual Change through Small Groups*, pp. 169–85. New York: Free Press.
Curran, Thomas F. 1976. Anxiety reduction as a preliminary to group treatment. *Psychotherapy: Theory, Research and Practice* 13:354–60.
Danet, B. and M. Gurevitch. 1977. Presentation of self in appeals to bureaucracy: An empirical study of role specificity. *American Journal of Sociology* 77:1165–88.
Daniels, Louise R. and Leonard Berkowitz. 1963. Liking and response to dependency relationships. *Human Relations* 16:141–48.
Dansereau, F., J. Cashman, and G. Graen. 1973. Instrumentality theory and equity theory as complimentary approaches in predicting the relationship of leadership and turnover among managers. *Organizational Behavior and Human Performance* 10:184–200.
Darley, S. A. 1976. Big time careers for the little woman: A dual role dilemma. *Journal of Social Issues* 32(3):85–98.
Darley, S. A. and J. Cooper. 1972. Cognitive consequences of forced noncompliance. *Journal of Personality and Social Psychology* 24:321–26.
Davidson, J. and S. Kiesler. 1964. Cognitive behavior before and after decisions. In L. Festinger, ed., *Conflict, Decision, and Dissonance*. Stanford, Calif.: Stanford University Press.
Davis, D. L. 1979. Cultural differences in the development of three ethnic groups: Blacks, Chicanos, and Native Americans. Paper presented at the American Orthopsychiatric Association's Annual Meeting, Washington, D.C., April.
Davis, J. A. 1959. A formal interpretation of the theory of relative deprivation. *Sociometry* 22:280–96.
Davis, J. A. 1966. The campus as a frog pond: An application of the theory of relative deprivation. *American Journal of Sociology* 72:17–31.
Davis, Kingsley. 1966. Status and related concepts. In B. Biddle and E. J. Thomas, eds., *Role Theory*, pp. 67–74. New York: Wiley.
Davis, K. E. and E. E. Jones. 1960. Changes in interpersonal perception as

a means of reducing cognitive dissonance. *Journal of Abnormal and Social Psychology* 61:402–10.

Davis, Larry. 1977. The influence of race upon group composition: A measure of social distance. Ph. D. dissertation, University of Michigan.

Davitz, J. R. 1964. *The Communication of Emotional Meaning*. New York: McGraw-Hill.

DeFriese, G. H. and W. S. Ford. 1969. Verbal attitudes, overt acts, and the influence of social constraint in interracial behavior. *Social Problems* 16:493–505.

Dermer, M. and D. L. Thiel. 1975. When beauty may fail. *Journal of Personality and Social Psychology* 31:1168–76.

Detroit Free Press. 1979. Canada's Dr. medicine man. Sept. 4, pp. 1A, 5A.

Deutsch, F. 1974. Observational and sociometric measures of peer popularity and their relationship to egocentric communication. *Developmental Psychology* 10:745–47.

Deutsch, M. 1962. Cooperation and trust: some theoretical notes. In M. R. Jones, ed., *Nebraska Symposium on Motivation*, pp. 275–320. Lincoln: University of Nebraska Press.

Deutsch, Morton and Harvey A. Hornstein. 1975. *Applying Social Psychology: Implications for Research, Practice, and Training*. Hillsdale, N.J.: Erlbaum.

Deutsch, M., and R. M. Krauss. 1965. *Theories in Social Psychology*. New York: Basic Books.

Dion, K. 1972. Physical attractiveness and evaluation of children's transgressions. *Journal of Personality and Social Psychology* 24:207–13.

Dion, K., E. Berscheid, and E. Walster. 1972. What is beautiful is good. *Journal of Personality and Social Psychology* 24:285–90.

Di Vesta, F. J. and P. Bossart. 1958. The effects of sets induced by labeling on the modification of attitude. *Journal of Personality* 26:379–87.

Dobrof, R. and E. Litwak. 1977. Maintenance of family ties of long-term care patients. Washington, D.C.: National Institute of Mental Health, U.S. Department of Health, Education and Welfare.

Drabman, R. S., R. Spitalnik, and K. D. O'Leary. 1973. Teaching self-control to disruptive children. *Journal of Abnormal Psychology* 82:10–16.

Dreman, S. B. 1977. Expectations and preferences of clients for a university student counseling service. *Journal of Counseling Psychology* 24:459–62.

Duck, S. W. and C. Spencer. 1972. Personal constructs and friendship formation. *Journal of Personality and Social Psychology* 23:40–45.

Duke, M. P. and S. D. Nowicki, Jr. 1972. A new measure and social learning model for interpersonal distance. *Journal of Experimental Research in Personality* 6:119–32.

Duncan, S. 1969. Nonverbal communication. *Psychological Bulletin* 72:118–27.

Durkheim, E. 1951. *Suicide*. New York: Free Press.

Dutton, D. G. and V. L. Lennox. 1974. Effect of prior "token" compliance on subsequent interracial behavior. *Journal of Personality and Social Psychology* 29:65–71.

Duval, S. and R. A. Wicklund. 1973. Effects of objective self-awareness on attribution of causality. *Journal of Experimental Social Psychology* 9:17–31.
Dweck, C. S. 1975. The role of expectations and attributions in the alleviation of learned helplessness. *Journal of Personality and Social Psychology* 31:674–85.
Dweck, C. S. and N. D. Reppucci. 1973. Learned helplessness and reinforcement responsibility in children. *Journal of Personality and Social Psychology* 25:109–16.
Dyer, E. D. 1963. Parenthood as crisis: A re-study. *Marriage and Family Living* 25:196–201.
Eagly, A. H. and S. Himmelfarb. 1978. Attitudes and opinions. *Annual Review of Psychology* 29:517–54.
Easton, F. 1978. The school social worker as an internal consultant for renewal in public schools. *Social Work with Groups* 1:161–72.
Eaton, W. O. and G. L. Clore. 1975. Interracial imitation at a summer camp. *Journal of Personality and Social Psychology* 32:1099–1105.
Ehrlich, Danuta, I. Guttman, P. Schonbach, and J. Mills. 1957. Postdecision exposure to relevant information. *Journal of Abnormal and Social Psychology* 54:98–102.
Ehrlich, H. J. and N. Van Tubergen. 1971. Exploring the structure and salience of stereotypes. *Journal of Social Psychology* 83:113–27.
Eisenthal, S. and A. Lazare. 1976. Specificity of patients' requests in the initial interview. *Psychological Reports* 38:739–48.
Elder, Glen H. 1969. Appearance and education in marriage mobility. *American Sociological Review* 34:519–33.
Ellis, A. and R. A. Harper. 1978. *A New Guide to Rational Living*. North Hollywood, Calif.: Wilshire Book Co.
Empey, L. T., and J. Rabow. 1961. The Provo experiment in delinquency. *American Sociological Review* 26:679–95.
Encyclopedia of Social Work. 1977. 17th Issue. New York: National Association of Social Workers.
English, O. S. and S. M. Finch. 1957. *Introduction to Psychiatry*. New York: Norton.
Epstein, A. and N. Radin. 1975. Motivational components related to father behavior and cognitive functioning. *Child Development* 46:831–39.
Epstein, S. and S. Clarke. 1970. Heart rate and skin conductance during experimentally induced anxiety: Effects of anticipated intensity of noxious stimulation and experience. *Journal of Experimental Psychology* 84:105–12.
Erickson, E. H. 1963. *Childhood and Society*. 2d ed. New York: Norton.
Erickson, F. 1973. Inter-ethnic relations in urban institutional settings. Final Technical Report, December 30, Harvard Graduate School of Education. Washington, D.C.: National Institute of Mental Health, projects MH18230, MH21460.
Erickson, F. 1975. Gatekeeping and the melting pot: Interaction in counseling encounters. *Harvard Educational Review*, 45:44–70.

Erickson, L. G. W. and J. A. Cramer. 1976. Smoking behavior development and modification: An empirical application of three social psychological theories. *Journal of Applied Social Psychology* 6:369–86.

Eskilson, A. and M. Wiley. 1976. Sex composition and leadership in small groups. *Sociometry* 39(3):183–94.

Evans, G. W. and R. B. Howard. 1973. Personal space. *Psychological Bulletin*, 80:334–44.

Ewalt, P. L. and J. Kutz. 1976. An examination of advice giving as a therapeutic intervention. *Smith College Studies in Social Work* 47:3–19.

Ewens, W. L. and H. J. Ehrlich. 1972. Reference-other support and ethnic attitudes as predictors of intergroup behavior. *Sociological Quarterly* 13:348–60.

Exline, R. V. 1971. Visual interaction: The glances of power and preference. *Nebraska Symposium on Motivation*, 19:163–206. Lincoln: University of Nebraska Press.

Fairweather, George W., ed. 1964a. *Social Psychology in Treating Mental Illness*. New York: Wiley.

Fairweather, G. W. 1964b. The task groups: Leadership, communication system, rewards, cohesivenss, norms, and composition. In George W. Fairweather, ed., *Social Psychology in Treating Mental Illness*, pp. 171–95. New York: Wiley.

Feagin, J. R. 1972. America's welfare stereotypes. *Social Science Quarterly* 52:921–33.

Feld, S., D. Ruhland, and M. Gold. 1979. Development changes in achievement motivation. *Merrill-Palmer Quarterly* 25:43–60.

Feldman, R. A. and T. E. Caplinger. 1977. Social work experience and client behavior change: A multivariate analysis of process and outcome. *Journal of Social Service Research* 1:5–33.

Feldman, R. A., J. S. Wodarski, N. Flax, and M. Goodman. 1972. Treating delinquents in traditional agencies. *Social Work* 17(5):71–78.

Felipe, N. J. and R. Sommer. 1966. Invasions of personal space. *Social Problems* 14:206–14.

Fellner, C. H. and J. R. Marshall. 1970. Kidney donors. In J. Macaulay and L. Berkowitz, eds., *Altruism and Helping Behavior*, pp. 269–81. New York: Academic Press.

Fendrich, J. M. 1967. Perceived reference group support: racial attitudes and overt behavior. *American Sociological Review* 32:960–70.

Festinger, L. 1954a. A theory of social comparison processes. *Human Relations* 7:117–40.

Festinger, L. 1954b. Motivations leading to social behavior. In D. Levine, ed., *Nebraska Symposium on Motivation*, pp. 191–223. Lincoln: University of Nebraska Press.

Festinger, Leon. 1957. *A Theory of Cognitive Dissonance*. New York: Harper & Row.

Festinger, L. 1964. *Conflict, Decision, and Dissonance*. Stanford, Calif.: Stanford University Press.

Festinger, L. and J. Carlsmith. 1959. Cognitive consequences of forced compliance. *Journal of Abnormal and Social Psychology* 58:202–10.

Festinger, L., S. Schachter, and K. Back. 1968. Operation of group standards. In D. Cartwright and A. Zander, eds., *Group Dynamics*, pp. 152–64. 3d ed. New York: Harper & Row.

Fiedler, F. E. 1967. *A Theory of Leadership Effectiveness*. New York: McGraw-Hill.

Fiedler, F. 1968. The contingency model: A theory of leadership effectiveness. In D. Cartwright and A. Zander, eds., *Group Dynamics*, pp. 362–80. 3d ed. New York: Harper & Row.

Fiedler, F. E. 1978. The contingency model and the dynamics of the leadership process. In L. Berkowitz, ed., *Advances in Experimental Social Psychology*, 11:60–112. New York: Academic Press.

Fiedler, F. E., M. M. Chemers, and L. Mahar. 1976. *Improving Leadership Effectiveness: The Leader Match Concept*. New York: Wiley.

Fiedler, F. E., T. R. Mitchell, and H. C. Triandis. 1971. The culture assimilator: An approach to cross-cultural training. *Journal of Applied Psychology* 55:95–102.

Fischer, Joel 1978. *Effective Casework Practice: An Eclectic Approach*. New York: McGraw-Hill.

Fishbein, M. 1963. An investigation of the relationships between beliefs about an object and the attitude toward that object. *Human Relations* 16:233–39.

Fishbein, M. 1967. A behavior theory approach to the relations between beliefs about an object and the attitude toward the object. In M. Fishbein, ed., *Readings in Attitude Theory and Measurement*, pp. 389–400. New York: Wiley.

Fishbein, M. 1972. Toward an understanding of family planning behaviors. *Journal of Applied Social Psychology* 2:214–27.

Fishbein, M. and I. Ajzen. 1972. Attitudes and opinions. *Annual Review of Psychology* 23:487–554.

Fishbein, M. and I. Ajzen. 1974. Attitudes toward objects as predictors of single and multiple behavior criteria. *Psychological Review* 81:59–74.

Fisher, J. D. and D. Byrne. 1975. Too close for comfort: Sex differences in response to invasions of personal space. *Journal of Personality and Social Psychology* 32:15–21.

Fisher, Jeffrey David and Arie Nadler. 1974. The effect of similarity between donor and recipient on recipient's reactions to aid. *Journal of Applied Social Psychology* 4:230–43.

Flowers, J. V. 1975. Simulation and role playing methods. In F. H. Kanfer and A. P. Goldstein, eds., *Helping People Change: A Textbook of Methods*, pp. 159–94. New York: Pergamon Press.

Foley, L. A. 1976. Personality and situational influences on changes in prejudice: A replication of Cook's Railroad Game in a prison setting. *Journal of Personality and Social Psychology* 34:846–56.

Foster, H. L. 1974. *Ribbin', Jivin', and Playing the Dozens*. Cambridge, Mass.: Badinger.

Fouriezos, N. T., M. L. Hutt, and H. Guetzkow. 1950. Measurement of self-oriented needs in group discussion groups. *Journal of Abnormal and Social Psychology* 45:682–90.

Fox, E. F., M. A. Nelson and W. M. Bolman. 1969. The termination process: A neglected dimension in social work. *Social Work* 14(4):53–63.

Frank, Jerome D. 1957. Some determinants, manifestations, and effects of cohesiveness in therapy groups. *International Journal of Group Psychotherapy* 7:53–63.

Frank, Jerome D. 1961. *Persuasion and Healing*. Baltimore: Johns Hopkins Press. (Rev. ed., 1973: Schocken paperback.)

Frank, Jerome D. 1962. The role of cognitions in illness and health. In H. H. Strupp and L. Luborsky, eds., *Research in Psychotherapy*, pp. 1–12. Washington, D.C.: American Psychological Association.

Freedman, J. L. and S. Fraser. 1966. Compliance without pressure: The foot-in-the-door technique. *Journal of Personality and Social Psychology* 4:195–202.

Freedman, J. L., S. A. Wallington, and E. Bliss. 1967. Compliance without pressure: The effect of guilt. *Journal of Personality and Social Psychology* 7:117–24.

Freedman, R., A. I. Hermalin, and M. C. Change. 1975. Do statements about desired family size predict fertility? The case of Taiwan, 1967–1970. *Demography* 12:407–16.

French, J. R. P. and R. D. Caplan. 1973. Organizational stress and individual strain. In A. J. Marrow, ed., *The Failure of Success*, pp. 30–80. New York: Anacom.

French, J. R. P., Jr., and B. Raven. 1959. The bases of social power. In Dorwin Cartwright, ed., *Studies in Social Power*, pp. 150–67. Ann Arbor, Mich: Institute for Social Research.

French, J. R. P. and B. Raven. 1968. The bases of social power. In D. Cartwright and A. Zander, eds., *Group Dynamics* pp. 259–69. 3d ed. New York: Harper & Row.

French, John R. P., Jr., W. Rodgers, and S. Cobb. 1974. Adjustment as person-environment fit. In George V. Coelho, D. A. Hamburg, and J. E. Adams, eds., *Coping and Adaptation*, pp. 316–33. New York: Basic Books.

Frenkel, O. J. and A. N. Doob. 1976. Post-decision dissonance at the polling booth. *Canadian Journal of Behavioral Science* 8:347–50.

Fried, M. 1978. Psychosocial adaptation in modern societies: Costs and benefits. Chestnut Hill, Mass.: Boston College. Manuscript.

Friedman, F. G. A. and L. Berg. 1978. Graduate students' judgments about clients: The effects of social class. *Journal of Education for Social Work* 14:45–51.

Friedman, M. I. and E. Jacka. 1969. The negative effect of group cohesiveness on intergroup negotiation. *Journal of Social Issues* 25(1):181–94.
Friend, R. M. and J. Gilbert. 1973. Threat and fear of negative evaluation as determinants of locus of social comparison. *Journal of Personality* 41:328–40.
Frieze, I. H. 1979. Perceptions of battered wives. In Irene H. Frieze, D. Bar-Tal, and J. S. Carroll, eds., *New Approaches to Social Problems*, pp. 79–108. San Francisco: Jossey-Bass.
Frieze, Irene H., Daniel Bar-Tal, and John S. Carroll. 1979. *New Approaches to Social Problems*. San Francisco: Jossey-Bass.
Fulton, R. L. 1973. *The Sacred and the Secular: Attitudes of the American Public toward Death*. Milwaukee, Wisc.: Bulfin Printers.
Gaertner, S. L. and J. F. Dovidio. 1977. The subtlety of white racism, arousal, and helping behavior. *Journal of Personality and Social Psychology* 35:691–707.
Galinsky, M. J., A. Rosen, and E. J. Thomas. 1973. Distinctness of bases of social power. *Psychological Reports* 33:727–30.
Gambrill, E. D. 1977. *Behavior Modification*. San Francisco: Jossey-Bass.
Gardner, G. G. 1964. The psychotherapeutic relationship. *Psychological Bulletin* 61:426–37.
Garland, J., H. Jones, and R. Kolodny. 1965. A model for stages of development in social group work. In Saul Bernstein, ed., *Explorations in Group Work*, pp. 12–53. Boston, Mass.: Boston University School of Social Work.
Garrett, J. B. and B. Wallace. 1975. Effect of communicator-communicatee similarity in political affiliation upon petition signing compliance. *Journal of Psychology*, 90:95–98.
Garvin, C. 1969. Complementarity of role expectations in groups: The member-worker contract. *Social Work Practice, 1969*, pp. 127–45. New York: Columbia University Press.
Garvin, C. D., and P. H. Glasser, 1971. Social group work: the preventive and rehabilitative approach. In *Encyclopedia of Social Work*, 2:1263–93. New York: National Association of Social Workers.
Garvin, C. and P. Glasser. 1974a. The bases of social treatment. In P. Glasser, R. Sarri, and R. Vinter, eds., *Individual Change through Small Groups*, pp. 483–507. New York: Free Press.
Garvin, C. D. and P. H. Glasser. 1974b. Social group work: The preventive and rehabilitative approach. In P. Glasser, R. Sarri, and R. Vinter, eds., *Individual Change through Small Groups*, pp. 34–49. New York: Free Press.
Garvin, C., and B. Seabury. 1979. Interpersonal practice in social work. Ann Arbor: University of Michigan. Manuscript
Geller, J. A. 1978. Reaching the battering husband. *Social Work With Groups* 1:27–38.
Gerard, H. B., S. A. Blevans, and T. Malcolm. 1964. Self-evaluation and the evaluation of choice alternatives. *Journal of Personality* 32:395–410.
Gerard, H. B., E. S. Conolley, and R. A. Wilhelmy. 1974. Compliance, justification and cognitive change. In L. Berkowitz, ed., *Advances in Experimental Social Psychology*, 7:217–47. New York: Academic Press.

Gerard, H. B. and G. C. Mathewson. 1966. The effects of severity of initiation on liking for a group: A replication. *Journal of Experimental Social Psychology* 2:278–87.
Gerber, I. 1974. Anticipatory bereavement. In B. Schoenberg, et al., eds., *Anticipatory Grief*, pp. 26–30. New York: Columbia University Press.
Gergen, K. J., P. Ellsworth, C. Maslach, and M. Seipel. 1975. Obligation, donor resources, and reactions to aid in three cultures. *Journal of Personality and Social Psychology* 31:390–400.
Germain, Carel. 1970. Casework and science: A historical encounter. In R. W. Roberts and R. H. Nee, eds., *Theories of Social Casework*, pp. 3–32. Chicago: University of Chicago Press.
Getzels, J. W. and E. G. Guba. 1954. Role, role conflict, and effectiveness. *American Sociological Review* 19:164–75.
Gewirtz, J. 1969. Mechanisms of social learning: Some roles of stimulation and behavior in early human development. In D. A. Goslin, ed., *Handbook of Socialization Theory and Research*, pp. 57–196. Chicago: Rand McNally.
Gewirtz, J. L., and K. G. Stingle. 1968. Learning of generalized imitation as the basis for identification. *Psychological Review* 75:374–97.
Gifford, C. G. 1968. Sensitivity training and social work. *Social Work* 13(2):78–86.
Ginsburg, H., and S. Opper. 1969. *Piaget's Theory of Intellectual Development: An Introduction*. Englewood Cliffs, N.J: Prentice-Hall.
Glass, D. C., D. Canavan, and S. Schiavo. 1968. Achievement motivation, dissonance, and defensiveness. *Journal of Personality* 36:474–92.
Glasser, P. H., B. Carter, R. English, C. D. Garvin, and C. Wolfson. 1974. Group work intervention in the social evironment. In Paul H. Glasser, R. Sarri, and R. Vinter, eds., *Individual Change through Small Groups*, pp. 292–306. New York: Free Press.
Glasser, P. H., and C. D. Garvin. 1977. Social group work: The organizational and environmental approach. In *Encyclopedia of Social Work* 2:1338–50. New York: National Association of Social Workers.
Glasser, Paul H., R. Sarri, and R. Vinter, eds. 1974. *Individual Change through Small Groups*. New York: Free Press.
Goebel, J. B. and S. G. Cole. 1975. Mexican-American and white reactions to stimulus persons of same and different race: Similarity and attraction as a function of prejudice. *Psychological Reports* 36:827–33.
Goffman, Erving. 1959. *The Presentation of Self in Everyday Life*. Garden City, N.Y.: Doubleday.
Goffman, E. 1963. *Stigma: Notes on the Management of Spoiled Identity*. Englewood Cliffs, N.J.: Prentice-Hall.
Goffman, I. W. 1957. Status consistency and preference for change in power distribution. *American Sociological Review* 22:275–81.
Goldberg, G. 1974. Micro-level intervention: A frame of reference and a practice model. *Journal of Education for Social Work* 10:25–29.

Goldberg, G. N., C. A. Kiesler, and B. E. Collins. 1969. Visual behavior and face-to-face distance during interaction. *Sociometry* 32:43–53.
Goldfried, M. R. and M. Merbaum, eds. 1973. *Behavior Change through Self-control.* New York: Holt, Rinehart and Winston.
Goldstein, Arnold P. 1962. *Therapist-Patient Expectancies in Psychotherapy.* New York: Pergamon Press.
Goldstein, Arnold P. 1971. *Psychotherapeutic Attraction.* New York: Pergamon Press.
Goldstein, Arnold P. 1973. *Structured Learning Therapy: Toward a Psychotherapy for the Poor.* New York: Academic Press.
Goldstein, Arnold P., S. Gassner, R. Greenberg, A. Gustin, J. Land, B. Liberman, and D. Streiner. 1967. The use of planted patients in group psychotherapy. *American Journal of Psychotherapy* 21:767–73.
Goldstein, Arnold P., K. Heller, and L. B. Sechrest. 1966. *Psychotherapy and the Psychology of Behavior Change.* New York: Wiley.
Goldstein, Arnold P., R. R. Sprafkin, and N. J. Gershaw. 1976. *Skill Training for Community Living: Applying Structured Learning Theory.* New York: Pergamon Press.
Goldstein, Arnold P., and N. Stein, eds. 1976. *Prescriptive Psychotherapies.* New York: Pergammon Press.
Goldstein, Howard. 1973. *Social Work Practice: A Unitary Approach.* Columbia: University of South Carolina Press.
Gomes-Schwartz, B., S. W. Hadley, and H. H. Strupp. 1978. Individual psychotherapy and behavior therapy. *Annual Review of Psychology* 29:435–71.
Goode, William. 1960. A theory of role strain. *American Sociological Review* 25:483:95.
Gordon, J. E. 1968. Counseling the disadvantaged boy. In W. E. Amos and J. D. Grambs, eds., *Counseling the Disadvantaged Youth,* pp. 119–68. Englewood Cliffs, N.J.: Prentice-Hall.
Gouldner, A. W. 1967. The norm of reciprocity: A preliminary statement. In E. P. Hollander and R. G. Hunt, eds., *Current Perspectives in Social Psychology,* pp. 272–83. New York: Oxford University Press.
Gouldner, A. W. and H. P. Gouldner. 1963. *Modern Sociology.* New York: Harcourt Brace and World.
Grabitz-Gniech, G. 1971. Some restrictive conditions for the occurrence of psychological reactance. *Journal of Personality and Social Psychology* 19:188–96.
Greenstein, T. N. 1976. Behavior change through value self-confrontation: A field experiment. *Journal of Personality and Social Psychology* 34:254–62.
Gross, Alan E. and Julie G. Latané. 1974. Receiving help, reciprocation, and interpersonal attraction. *Journal of Applied Social Psychology* 4(3):210–23.
Gross, A. E., M. J. Schmidt, J. P. Keating, and M. J. Saks. 1974. Persuasion, surveillance, and voting behavior. *Journal of Experimental Social Psychology* 10:451–60.

Gross, A. E., B. S. Wallston, and I. M. Piliavin. 1975. Beneficiary attractiveness and cost as determinants of responses to routine requests for help. *Sociometry* 38: 131–40.

Gross, Neal, Alexander W. McEachern, and Ward S. Mason. 1966. Role conflict and its resolution. In B. Biddle and E. J. Thomas, eds., *Role Theory: Concepts and Research*, pp. 287–96. New York: Wiley.

Grusec, J. E., L. Kuczynski, J. P. Rushton, and Z. M. Simutis. 1978. Modeling, direct instruction, and attribution effects on altruism. *Developmental Psychology* 14:51–57.

Grush, J. E., G. L. Clore, and F. Costin. 1975. Dissimilarity and attraction: When difference makes a difference. *Journal of Personality and Social Psychology* 32:783–89.

Guardo, C. 1969. Personal space in children. *Child Development* 40:143–51.

Gump, P. V. and B. Sutton-Smith. 1955. The "it" role in children's games. *The Group* 17:3–8.

Gurin, G. 1970. An expectancy approach to job-training programs. In V. Allen, ed., *Psychological Factors in Poverty*, pp. 277–99. Chicago: Markham.

Gurin, Patricia, and Edgar G. Epps. 1975. *Black Consciousness, Identity, and Achievement: A Study of Students in Historically Black Colleges*. New York: Wiley.

Gurin, P., G. Gurin, R. C. Lao, and M. Beattie. 1969. Internal-external control in the motivational dynamics of Negro youth. *Journal of Social Issues* 25:29–54.

Gurin, P., G. Gurin, and B. M. Morrison. 1978. Personal and ideological aspects of internal and external control. *Social Psychology* 41:275–96.

Gurwitz, S. B. and L. Panciera. 1975. Attributions of freedom by actors and observers. *Journal of Personality and Social Psychology* 32:531–39.

Guttentag, M. 1970. Group cohesiveness, ethnic organization, and poverty. *Journal of Social Issues* 26(2):105–32.

Haase, Richard F. and Dominic J. DiMattia. 1970. Proxemic behavior: Counselor, administrator, and client preference for seating arrangement in dyadic interaction. *Journal of Counseling Psychology* 17:319–25.

Haavio-Mannila, Elina. 1971. Satisfaction with family, work, leisure and life among men and women. *Human Relations* 24:585–601.

Hackman, J. Richard and Charles G. Morris. 1975. Group tasks, group interaction process, and group performance effectiveness: A review and proposed integration. In L. Berkowitz, ed., *Advances in Experimental Social Psychology*, 8:45–99. New York: Academic Press.

Hagstrom, W. O. and H. Selvin. 1965. Two dimensions of cohesiveness in small groups. *Sociometry* 28:30–43.

Hakmiller, K. L. 1966. Threat as a determinant of downward comparison. *Journal of Experimental Social Psychology* 2:32–39 (suppl. 1).

Haley, Jay. 1976. *Problem-Solving Therapy: New Strategies for Effective Family Therapy*. San Francisco: Jossey-Bass.

Hall, Edward T. 1966. *The Hidden Dimension*. Garden City, N.Y.: Doubleday.

Hall, J. 1971. Decisions, decisions, decisions. *Psychology Today*, 5:51–54.
Hansson, R. O. and F. E. Fiedler. 1973. Perceived similarity, personality, and attraction to large organizations. *Journal of Applied Social Psychology* 3:258–66.
Hare, A. P. 1976. *Handbook of Small Group Research*. 2d ed. New York: Free Press.
Hari, V. 1977. Instituting short-term casework in a "long-term" agency. In W. J. Reid and L. Epstein, eds., *Task-Centered Practice*, pp. 89–99. New York: Columbia University Press.
Harrison, R. V. 1976. Job demands and worker health: Person-environment misfit. *Dissertation Abstracts International* 37(2-B), 1035.
Hartford, Margaret E. 1971. *Groups in Social Work: Application of Small Group Theory and Research to Social Work Practice*. New York: Columbia University Press.
Hartford, M. 1977. Socialization methods in social work practice. In *Encyclopedia of Social Work* 2:1387–93. New York: National Association of Social Work.
Hartman, Ann. 1974. The generic stance and the family agency. *Social Casework* 55:199–208.
Hartman, Ann. 1979. *Finding Families: An Ecological Approach to Family Assessment in Adoption*. Beverly Hills, Calif.: Sage.
Hastorf, A. 1970. The reinforcement of individual action in a group situation. In K. J. Gergen and D. Marlowe, eds., *Personality and Social Behavior*, pp. 105–20. Reading, Mass.: Addison-Wesley.
Heider, F. 1944. Social perception and phenomenal causality. *Psychological Review* 51:358–74.
Heider, F. 1958. *The Psychology of Interpersonal Relations*. New York: Wiley.
Heilman, M. E., J. Slochower, and M. Deutsch. 1976. The effects of victimization on reactions to other victims. *Journal of Applied Social Psychology* 6(3):193–205.
Heine, R. W. and H. Trosman. 1960. Initial expectations of the doctor-patient interaction as a factor in continuing psychotherapy. *Psychiatry* 23:275–78.
Heitler, J. 1973. Preparation of lower-class patients for expressive group psychotherapy. *Journal of Consulting and Clinical Psychology* 41:251–60.
Heller, K., R. A. Myers, and L. V. Kline. 1963. Interviewer behavior as a function of standardized client roles. *Journal of Consulting Psychology* 27:117–22.
Helmreich, R., R. Bakeman, and L. Scherwitz. 1973. The study of small groups. *Annual Review of Psychology* 24:337–54.
Henchy, T. and D. C. Glass. 1968. Evaluation, apprehension and the social facilitation of dominant and subordinate responses. *Journal of Personality and Social Psychology* 10:446–54.
Hepner, A. and N. R. Cauthen. 1975. Effects of subject control and graduated exposure on snake phobias. *Journal of Consulting and Clinical Psychology* 43:297–304.

Hepworth, D. H. 1979. Early removal of resistance in task-centered casework. *Social Work* 24:317–23.

Heraud, Brian J. 1970. *Sociology and Social Work*. Oxford, Pergamon Press.

Hill, W. F. and L. Gruner. 1973. A study of development in open and closed groups. *Small Group Behavior* 4:355–81.

Hoehn-Saric, R., J. D. Frank, S. D. Imber, E. H. Nash, A. R. Stone, and C. C. Battle. 1964. Systematic preparation of patients for psychotherapy: II. Effects on therapy behavior and outcome. *Journal of Psychiatric Research* 2:267–81.

Hoffman, L. R. 1979. *The Group Problem-Solving Process*. New York: Praeger.

Hoffman, L. R. and N. R. F. Maier. 1961. Quality and acceptance of problem solutions by members of homogeneous and heterogeneous groups. *Journal of Abnormal and Social Psychology* 62:401–7.

Hoffman, L. R. and N. R. F. Maier. 1966. An experimental re-examination of the similarity-attraction hypotheses. *Journal of Personality and Social Psychology* 3:145–52.

Hoffman, L. W. 1976. Change in family roles, socialization, and sex differences. Paper presented at the annual meeting of the National Council on Family Relations, New York City, October.

Hoffman, M. L. 1975. Developmental synthesis of affect and cognition and its implications for altruistic motivation. *Developmental Psychology* 11:607–22.

Hollander, E. P. 1958. Conformity, status, and idiosyncrasy credit. *Psychological Review* 65:117–27.

Hollander, E. P. and J. Julian, 1968. Leadership. In E. Borgatta and W. Lambert, eds., *Handbook of Personality Theory and Research*, pp. 89–99. Chicago: Rand McNally.

Hollander, E. P. and J. W. Julian. 1970. Studies in leadership legitimacy, influence, and innovation. In L. Berkowitz, ed., *Advances in Experimental Social Psychology* 5:33–69. New York: Academic Press.

Hollingshead, A. and F. Redlich. 1956. *Social Class and Mental Illness*. New York: Wiley.

Homans, G. C. 1961. *Social Behavior: Its Elementary Forms*. New York: Harcourt, Brace & World. (Rev. ed. 1974)

Homme, L. 1969. *How To Use Contingency Contracting in the Classroom*. Champaign, Ill.: Research Press.

Horai, Joann. 1977. Attributional conflict. *Journal of Social Issues* 33(1):88–100.

Horenstein, D. and B. K. Houston. 1976. The expectation-reality discrepancy and premature termination from psychotherapy. *Journal of Clinical Psychology* 32:373–78.

Hornstein, H. A. 1972. Promotive tension: The basis of prosocial behavior from a Lewinian perspective. *Journal of Social Issues* 28(3):191–218.

Horowitz, I. A. 1971. The effect of group norms on bystander intervention. *Journal of Social Psychology* 83:265–73.

Hosch, D. 1973. Use of the contract approach in public social services. Los

Angeles: Regional Research Institute in Social Welfare, University of Southern California.

Hosford, R. E. and D. L. Sorenson. 1969. Participating in classroom discussions, In J. D. Krumboltz and C. E. Thoresen, eds., *Behavior Counseling: Cases and Techniques*, pp. 202–7. New York: Holt, Rinehart and Winston.

House, W. C. 1966. Effects of group cohesiveness on organization performance. *Personnel Journal* 45:28–33.

Hovland, C. I., I. L. Janis, and H. H. Kelley. 1953. *Communication and Persuasion*. New Haven, Conn.: Yale University Press.

Huber, J. and W. Form. 1973. *Income and Ideology: An Analysis of the American Political Formula*. New York: Free Press.

Hunt, Raymond G. 1967. Role and role conflict. In E. P. Hollander and R. G. Hunt, eds., *Current Perspectives in Social Psychology*, pp. 259–65. 2d ed. New York: Oxford University Press.

Hurwitz, J., A. Zander, and B. Hymovitch. 1968. Some effects of power on the relation among group members. In D. Cartwright and A. Zander, eds., *Group Dynamics*, pp. 291–97. 3d ed. New York: Harper & Row.

Huston, T. L. and G. Levinger. 1978. Interpersonal attraction and relationships. *Annual Review of Psychology* 29:115–56.

Iannotti, R. J. 1975. The effect of role-taking experiences on role-taking altruism, empathy, and aggression. Paper presented at the meeting of the Society for Research in Child Development, Denver, April.

Iglehart, A. P. 1979. *Married Women and Work: 1957 and 1976*. Lexington, Mass.: Lexington Books.

Indik, B. P. 1965. Organization size and member participation: Some empirical tests of alternative explanations. *Human Relations* 18:339–50.

Insko, C. A., R. R. Blake, R. B. Cialdini, and S. A Mulaik. 1970. Attitudes toward birth control and cognitive consistency: Theoretical and practical implications of survey data. *Journal of Personality and Social Psychology* 16:228–37.

Insko, C. A. and J. E. Robinson. 1967. Belief similarity versus race as determinants of reactions to Negroes by southern white adolescents. A further test of Rokeach's theory. *Journal of Personality and Social Psychology* 7:216–21.

Jackson, E. F. 1962. Status inconsistency and symptoms of stress. *American Sociological Review* 27:469–80.

Jackson, J. M. 1959. Reference group processes in a formal organization. *Sociometry* 22:307–27.

Jackson, J. M. 1966. Structural characteristics of norms. In B. J. Biddle and E. J. Thomas, eds., *Role Theory: Concepts and Research*, pp. 113–26. New York: Wiley.

Jacobs, M., O. L. Trick, and D. Withersty. 1976. Pretraining psychiatric inpatients for participation in group psychotherapy. *Psychotherapy: Theory, Research, and Practice* 13:361–67.

James, W. H., A. B. Woodruff, and W. Werner. 1965. Effect of internal and external control upon changes in smoking behavior. *Journal of Consulting Psychology* 29:127–29.

Janis, I. L. 1971a. Groupthink. *Psychology Today* 5:43.

Janis, I. L. 1971b. Groupthink among policy makers. In C. Comstock, S. Nevitt, and associates, eds., *Sanctions for Evil*, pp. 71–89. San Francisco: Jossey Bass.

Janis, I. L. 1971c. *Stress and Frustration*. New York: Harcourt Brace Jovanovich.

Janis, I. L. 1972. *Victims of Groupthink*. Boston: Houghton Mifflin.

Janis, I. L. and D. Hoffman. 1970. Facilitating effects of daily contacts between partners who make a decision to cut down on smoking. *Journal of Personality and Social Psychology* 17:25–35.

Janis, I., and L. Mann. 1965. Effectiveness of emotional role-playing in modifying smoking habits and attitudes. *Journal of Experimental Research in Personality* 1:84–90.

Janis, I. L. and L. Mann. 1977. *Decision-Making: A Psychological Analysis of Conflict, Choice, and Commitment*. Riverside, N.J.: Free Press.

Jecker, J. D., N. Maccoby, and H. S. Breitrose. 1965. Improving accuracy in interpreting non-verbal cues of comprehension. *Psychology in the Schools* 2:239–44.

Jeffrey, D. B. 1974. A comparison of the effects of external control and self-control on the modification and maintenance of weight. *Journal of Abnormal Psychology* 83:404–10.

Jessor, R., S. L. Jessor, and J. Finney. 1973. A social psychology of marijuana use: Longitudinal studies of high school and college youth. *Journal of Personality and Social Psychology* 26:1–15.

Johnson, C. 1974. Planning termination for the group. In P. Glasser, R. Sarri, and R. Vinter, eds., *Individual Change through Small Groups*, pp. 258–65. New York: Free Press.

Johnson, David W. 1971a. Effects of warmth of interaction, accuracy of understanding, and the proposal of compromises on listener's behavior. *Journal of Counseling Psychology* 18:207–16.

Johnson, D. W. 1971b. Role reversal: A summary and review of the research. *International Journal of Group Tensions* 1:318–34.

Johnson, D. W. 1975. Cooperativeness and social perspective taking. *Journal of Personality and Social Psychology* 31:241–44.

Johnson, D. W. and S. Johnson. 1972. The effects of attitude similarity, expectations of goal facilitation, and actual goal facilitation on interpersonal attraction. *Journal of Experimental Social Psychology* 8:197–206.

Johnson, S. and D. W. Johnson. 1972. The effect of other's actions, attitude similarity, and race on attraction toward the other. *Human Relations* 25:121–30.

Johnson, T. W. and G. Graen. 1973. Organizational assimilation and role rejection. *Organizational Behavior and Human Performance* 10:72–87.

Jones, A. and A. A. Seagull. 1977. Dimensions of the relationship between the black client and the white therapist: A theoretical overview. *American Psychologist* 32:850–59.

Jones, Edward E. 1964. *Ingratiation: A Social Psychological Analysis*. New York: Appleton-Century-Crofts.

Jones, E. E. 1979. The rocky road from acts to dispositions. *American Psychologist* 34:107–17.

Jones, E. E. and K. E. Davis. 1965. From acts to dispositions. In L. Berkowitz, ed., *Advances in Experimental Social Psychology*, 2:219–66. New York: Academic Press.

Jones, Edward, E., K. E. Davis, and K. J. Gergen. 1961. Role playing variations and their informational value for person perception. *Journal of Abnormal and Social Psychology* 63:302–10.

Jones, Edward E., Kenneth J. Gergen, Peter Gumpert, and John W. Thibaut. 1965. Some conditions affecting the use of ingratiation to influence performance evaluation. *Journal of Personality and Social Psychology* 1:613–25.

Jones, E. E. and R. E. Nisbett. 1971. *The Actor and the Observer: Divergent Perceptions of the Causes of Behavior*. Morristown, N.J.: General Learning Press.

Jones, R. A. 1970. Volunteering to help: The effects of choice, dependence and anticipated dependence. *Journal of Personality and Social Psychology* 14:121–29.

Jones, Stephen C. and Dennis T. Regan. 1974. Ability evaluation through social comparison. *Journal of Experimental Social Psychology* 10:133–46.

Jones, S. E. 1971. A comparative proxemics analysis of dyadic interaction in selected subcultures of New York City. *Journal of Social Psychology* 84:35–44.

Julian, J. W., D. W. Bishop, and F. E. Fiedler. 1966. Quasi-therapeutic effects of intergroup competition. *Journal of Personality and Social Psychology* 3:321–27.

Kadushin, A. 1959. The knowledge base of social work. In A. J. Kahn, ed., *Issues in American Social Work*, pp. 39–79. New York: Columbia University Press.

Kadushin, Alfred. 1967. *Child Welfare Services*. New York: Macmillan.

Kadushin, Alfred. 1972. *The Social Work Interview*. New York: Columbia University Press.

Kadushin, Alfred. 1977. *Consultation in Social Work*. New York: Columbia University Press.

Kahn, R. L., D. M. Wolfe, R. P. Quinn, and D. J. Snoek. 1964. *Organizational Stress: Studies in Role Conflict and Ambiguity*. New York: Wiley.

Kandel, D. B. 1978. Similarity in real-life adolescent friendship pairs. *Journal of Personality and Social Psychology* 36(3):306–12.

Kanfer, F. H. 1975. Self-management methods. In F. H. Kanfer and A. P. Goldstein, eds., *Helping People Change: A Textbook of Methods*, pp. 309–55. New York: Pergamon Press.

Kanfer, F. H. 1979. Personal control, social control, and altruism: Can society survive the age of individualism? *American Psychologist* 34(3):231–39.
Kanfer, F. H. and J. S. Phillips. 1969. A survey of current behavior therapies and a proposal for classification. In C. M. Franks, ed., *Behavior Therapy: Appraisal and Status*, pp. 445–75. New York: McGraw-Hill.
Kaplan, H. R. and C. Tausky. 1974. The meaning of work among the hard-core unemployed. *Pacific Sociological Review* 17:185–89.
Kaplan-Vinokur, D. 1975. Family planning decision-making: Attitudes, beliefs and behavioral intentions. Ph. D. dissertation, University of Michigan.
Katz, D. 1960. The functional approach to the study of attitudes. *Public Opinion Quarterly* 24:163–204.
Katz, D. and K. W. Braly. 1933. Racial stereotypes of 100 college students. *Journal of Abnormal and Social Psychology* 28:280–90.
Katz, D. and R. L. Kahn. 1966. *The Social Psychology of Organizations*. New York: Wiley.
Katz, D., I. Sarnoff, and C. McClintock. 1956. Ego defense and attitude change. *Human Relations* 9:27–46.
Katz, Daniel and Richard L. Schanck. 1938. *Social Psychology*. New York: Wiley.
Katz, E. 1967. The two-step flow of communication: An up-to-date report on an hypothesis. In E. P. Hollander and R. G. Hunt, eds., *Current Perspectives in Social Psychology*, pp. 513–19. 2d ed. New York: Oxford University Press.
Katz, Elihu and P. F. Lazarsfeld. 1955. *Personal Influence*. Glencoe, Ill.: Free Press.
Katz, I. 1970. Experimental studies of Negro-white relationships. In L. Berkowitz, ed., *Advances in Experimental Social Psychology*, 5:71–117. New York: Academic Press.
Kauff, P. F. 1977. The termination process: Its relationship to the separation-individuation phase of development. *International Journal of Group Psychotherapy* 27:3–18.
Kaufman, D. R. and I. D. Steiner. 1968. Some variables affecting the use of conformity as an ingratiating technique. *Journal of Experimental Social Psychology* 4:400–14.
Keefe, T. 1976. Empathy: The critical skill. *Social Work* 21:10–14.
Kelley, H. H. 1951. Communication in experimentally created hierarchies. *Human Relations* 4:39–56.
Kelley, H. H. 1952. Two functions of reference groups. In G. E. Swanson, T. M. Newcomb, and R. E. Hartley, eds., *Readings in Social Psychology*, pp. 410–14. Rev. ed. New York: Holt, Rinehart and Winston.
Kelley, H. H. 1967. Attribution theory in social psychology. *Nebraska Symposium on Motivation* 15:192–240.
Kelley, H. H. 1971. *Attributions in Social Interactions*. Morristown, N.J.: General Learning Press.
Kelley, H. H. 1972. *Causal Schemata and the Attribution Process*. Morristown, N.J.: General Learning Press.

Kelley, H. H. 1973. The processes of causal attribution. *American Psychologist* 28:107–28.

Kelley, H. H. and E. H. Volkart. 1952. The resistance to change of group anchored attitudes. *American Sociological Review* 17:453–65.

Kelly, G. A. 1955. *The Psychology of Personal Constructs.* New York: Norton.

Kelman, H. C. 1965. Compliance, identification, and internalization: Three processes of attitude change. In H. Proshansky and B. Seidenberg, eds., *Basic Studies in Social Psychology*, pp. 140–48. New York: Holt, Rinehart and Winston.

Kelman, H. C. 1972. The rights of subjects in social research: An analysis in terms of relative power and legitimacy. *American Psychologist* 27:989–1016.

Kemper, T. D. 1968. Reference groups, socialization, and achievement. *American Sociological Review* 33:31–45.

Kerson, T. S. 1978. The social work relationship: A form of gift exchange. *Social Work* 23:326–27.

Kiesler, C. A. 1971. *The Psychology of Commitment: Experiments Linking Behavior to Belief.* New York: Academic Press.

Kiesler, C. A. and L. Corbin. 1965. Commitments, attraction, and conformity. *Journal of Personality and Social Psychology* 2:890–95.

Kiesler, C. A., M. S. Pallak, and D. E. Kanouse. 1968. Interaction of commitment and dissonance. *Journal of Personality and Social Psychology* 8:331–38.

Killian, Lewis M. 1965. The significance of multiple group membership. In H. Proshansky and B. Seidenberg, eds., *Basic Studies in Social Psychology*, pp. 505–10. New York: Holt, Rinehart and Winston.

Kipnis, D. 1972. Does power corrupt? *Journal of Personality and Social Psychology* 24:33–41.

Kipnis, D. and R. Vanderveer. 1971. Ingratiation and the use of power. *Journal of Personality and Social Psychology* 17(3):280–86.

Kirk, D. L. 1977. A self-instructional program for increasing client's readiness for counseling and psychotherapy: Development and field test. *Dissertation Abstracts International* 38(5-B):2371.

Kissel, S. 1965. Stress-reducing properties of social stimuli. *Journal of Personality and Social Psychology* 2:378–84.

Kleck, R. 1968. Physical stigma and nonverbal cues emitted in face-to-face interactions. *Human Relations* 21:19–28.

Kline, F., A. Adrian, and M. Spivak. 1974. Patients' evaluate therapists. *Archives of General Psychiatry* 31:113–16.

Kluckhohn, C. 1962. Conceptions of death among the Southwestern Indians. In C. Kluckhorn, *Collected Essays: Culture and Behavior*, ch. 8. New York: Free Press.

Knowles, E. S., B. Kreuser, S. Haas, M. Hyde, M. and G. B. Schuchart. 1976. Group size and the extension of social space boundaries. *Journal of Personality and Social Psychology* 33:647–54.

Knox, R. and J. Inkster. 1968. Post-decision dissonance at post time. *Journal of Personality and Social Psychology* 8:319–23.

Kogan, Leonard S., ed. 1960. *Social Science Theory and Social Work Research*. New York: National Association of Social Work.

Kohen, J. 1975. Liking and self disclosure in opposite sex dyads. *Psychological Reports* 36:695–98.

Kohlberg, L. 1966. A cognitive-developmental analysis of children's sex-role concepts and attitudes. In E. E. Maccoby, ed., *The Development of Sex Differences*, pp. 82–173. Stanford, Calif: Stanford University Press.

Kohlberg, L. 1969. Stage and sequence: The cognitive-developmental approach to socialization. In D. A. Goslin, ed., *Handbook of Socialization Theory*, pp. 347–480. Chicago: Rand McNally.

Kolach, S. M. 1965. A study of status inconsistency among social work professionals. Ph. D. dissertation, Boston University.

Komarovsky, M. 1973. Some problems in role analysis. *American Sociological Review* 38:649–62.

Konecni, V. J., L. Libuser, H. Morton, and E. B. Ebbesen. 1975. Effects of a violation of personal space on escape and helping responses. *Journal of Experimental Social Psychology* 11:288–99.

Konopka, Gisela. 1954. *Group Work in the Institution: A modern Challenge*. New York: Whiteside.

Kopel, S. and H. Arkowitz. 1975. The role of attribution and self-perception in behavior change: Implications for behavior therapy. *Genetic Psychology Monographs* 92:175–212.

Koran, J. and R. M. Costell. 1973. Early termination from group psychotherapy. *International Journal of Group Psychotherapy* 23:346–59.

Korte, C. and N. Kerr. 1975. Response to altruistic opportunities in urban and nonurban settings. *Journal of Social Psychology* 95:183–84.

Koslin, B. L., J. W. Stoops, and W. D. Loh. 1967. Source characteristics and communication discrepancy as determinants of attitude change and conformity. *Journal of Experimental Social Psychology* 3:230–42.

Kothandapani, V. 1971. Validation of feeling, belief, and intention to act as three components of attitude and their contribution to prediction of contraceptive behavior. *Journal of Personality and Social Psychology* 19:321–33.

Kounin, J., N. Polansky, B. Biddle, H. Coburn, and A. Fenn. 1956. Experimental studies of clients' reactions to initial interviews. *Human Relations* 9:265–92.

Krasner, L. 1958. Studies of the conditioning of verbal behavior. *Psychological Bulletin* 55:148–70.

Krasner, L. 1971. Behavior therapy. *Annual Review of Psychology* 22:483–532.

Kraut, R. E. 1973. Effects of social labelling on giving to charity. *Journal of Experimental Social Psychology* 9:551–62.

Kravetz, D. F. and Sheldon Rose. 1973. *Contracts in Groups: A Workbook*. Dubuque, Iowa: Kendall-Hunt.

Krebs, Dennis L. 1970. Altruism: An examination of the concept and a review of the literature. *Psychological Bulletin* 73(4):258–302.
Krebs, Dennis and Allen A. Adinolfi. 1975. Physical attractiveness, social relations, and personality style. *Journal of Personality and Social Psychology* 31(2):245–53.
Krebs, D. L. and L. G. Wispé. 1974. Rejoinder: On defining altruism. *Journal of Social Issues* 30(2):194–99.
Krueger, W. P. 1972. Maximizing expectancy in psychotherapy: The role induction interview and verbalized expectations in behaviorally oriented group therapy. Ph. D. dissertation, University of Miami.
Krumboltz, J. D. and C. E. Thoresen, eds. 1969. *Behavioral Counseling: Cases and Techniques*. New York: Holt, Rinehart and Winston.
Kulka, R. A., J. Veroff, and E. Douvan. 1979. Social class and the use of professional help for personal problems: 1957 and 1976. *Journal of Health and Social Behavior* 20:2–17.
Kurdek, L. A. 1975. Perceptual, cognitive, and affective perspective-taking and empathy in kindergarten through third-grade children. Paper presented at the meeting of the Society for Research in Child Development, Denver, April.
Kurtz, J. J. and D. G. Kyle. 1977. Life satisfaction and the exercise of responsibility. *Social Work* 22:323–24.
Lacoursiere, R. 1974. A group method to facilitate learning through stages of a psychiatric affiliation. *International Journal of Group Psychotherapy* 24:342–51.
Lake, M. and G. Levinger. 1960. Continuance beyond application interviews at a child guidance clinic. *Social Casework* 41:303–9.
Lamm, H. and D. G. Myers. 1978. Group-induced polarization of attitudes and behaviors. In L. Berkowitz, ed., *Advances in Experimental Social Psychology*, 11:145–97. New York: Academic Press.
Landis, D., H. R. Day, P. L. McGrew, J. A. Thomas, and A. B. Miller. 1976. Can a black "culture-assimilator" increase racial understanding? *Journal of Social Issues* 32(2):169–84.
Landy, D. and E. Aronson. 1968. Liking for an evaluator as a function of his discernment. *Journal of Personality and Social Psychology* 9:133–41.
Langer, E. J. and R. P. Abelson. 1972. The semantics of asking a favor: How to succeed in getting help without really dying. *Journal of Personality and Social Psychology* 24:26–32.
Langer, E. J., I. L. Janis, and J. A. Wolfer. 1975. Reduction of psychological stress in surgical patients. *Journal of Experimental Social Psychology* 11:155–65.
Langer, E. J. and J. Rodin. 1976. The effects of choice and enhanced personal responsibility for the aged: A field experiment in an institutional setting. *Journal of Personality and Social Psychology* 34:191–98.
Langlois, J. H. and A. Chris Downs. 1977. Peer relations as a function of

physical attractiveness: The eye of the beholder or behavioral reality? Paper presented at the meeting of The Society for Research in Child Development, New Orleans, March.

Langlois, J. H. and C. Stephan. 1977. The effects of physical attractiveness and ethnicity on children's behavioral attributions and peer preferences. Paper presented at the meeting of The Society for Research in Child Development, New Orleans, March.

Latané, B., and J. M. Dabbs. 1975. Sex, group size, and helping in three cities. *Sociometry* 38:180–94.

Latané, B., and J. M. Darley. 1970. *The Unresponsive Bystander: Why Doesn't He Help?* New York: Appleton.

Lazare, A., F. Cohen, A. M. Jacobson, M. S. Williams, R. J. Mignone, and S. Zisook. 1972. The walk-in patient as a customer: A key dimension in evaluation and treatment. *American Journal of Orthopsychiatry* 42:872–83.

Lazare, A., S. Eisenthal, and L. Wasserman. 1975. The customer approach to patienthood: Attending to patient requests in a walk-in clinic. *Archives of General Psychiatry* 32:553–58.

Lazarsfeld, P. F., B. Berelson, and H. Gaudet. 1948. *The People's Choice*. 2d ed. New York: Columbia University Press.

Lazarus, A. A. 1966. Behavior rehearsal vs. non-directive therapy vs. advice in affecting behavioral change. *Behavior Research Therapy* 4:209–12.

Lazarus, A. A. 1968. Multi-modal behavior therapy in groups. In G. M. Gazda, ed., *Basic Approaches to Group Psychotherapy and Group Counseling*, pp. 150–74. Springfield, Ill.: Charles C Thomas.

Lazarus, R. S. and E. Alfert. 1964. The short circuiting of threat by experimentally altering cognitive appraisal. *Journal of Abnormal and Social Psychology* 69:195–205.

Lazarus, R. S., E. Opton, M. Nomikos, and N. Rankin. 1965. The short-circuiting of threat. *Journal of Personality* 33:622–35.

Leeds, R. 1963. Altruism and the norm of giving. *Merrill-Palmer Quarterly* 9:229–40.

Lefkowitz, M., R. R. Blake, and J. S. Mouton. 1955. Status factors in pedestrian violation of traffic signals. *Journal of Abnormal and Social Psychology* 51:704–5.

Leichter, H. J. and W. E. Mitchell. 1978. *Kinship and Casework*. New York: Teachers College Press.

Lennard, H. L. and A. Bernstein. 1960. *The Anatomy of Psychotherapy*. New York: Columbia University Press.

Lenski, G. E. 1954. Status crystallization: A non-vertical dimension of social status. *American Sociological Review* 19:405–13.

Lenski, G. E. 1956. Social participation and status crystallization. *American Sociological Review* 21:368–69.

Lenski, G. 1967. Status inconsistency and the vote: A four nation test. *American Sociological Review* 32:298–301.

Leonard, R. 1975. Self-concept and attraction for similar and dissimilar others. *Journal of Personality and Social Psychology* 31:926–29.
Lepper, M. R., D. Greene, and R. E. Nisbett. 1973. Undermining children's intrinsic interest with extrinsic reward: A test of the overjustification hypotheses. *Journal of Personality and Social Psychology* 28:129–37.
Lerner, M. 1970. The desire for justice and reactions to victims. In J. Macaulay and L. Berkowitz, eds., *Altruism and Helping Behavior: Social Psychological Studies of Some Antecedents and Consequences*, pp. 205–29. New York: Academic Press.
Lerner, M. J. 1971. Observer's evaluation of a victim: Justice, guilt, and veridical perception. *Journal of Personality and Social Psychology* 20:127–35.
Lerner, M. J. and D. T. Miller. 1978. Just world research and the attribution process: Looking back and ahead. *Psychological Bulletin* 85:1030–51.
Lerner, M. J., ed. 1975. The justice motive in social behavior. *Journal of Social Issues* 31(5).
Lerner, M. L. and G. W. Fairweather. 1963. The social behavior of chronic schizophrenics in supervised and unsupervised work groups. *Journal of Abnormal and Social Psychology* 67:219–25.
Leventhal, G. S. 1976a. Fairness in social relationships. In John W. Thibaut, J. T. Spence, and R. C. Carson, eds., *Contemporary Topics in Social Psychology*, pp. 211–39. Morristown, N.J.: General Learning Press.
Leventhal, G. S. 1976b. The distribution of rewards and resources in groups and organizations. In Leonard Berkowitz and E. Walster, eds., *Advances in Experimental Social Psychology* 9:91–131. New York: Academic Press.
Leventhal, G. S. and J. T. Bergman. 1969. Self-depriving behavior as a response to unprofitable inequity. *Journal of Experimental Social Psychology* 5:153–71.
Leventhal, G. S., J. W. Michaels, and C. Sanford. 1972. Inequity and interpersonal conflict: Reward allocation and secrecy about reward as methods of preventing conflict. *Journal of Personality and Social Psychology* 23(1):88–102.
Levin, P. F. and A. M. Isen. 1975. Further studies on the effect of feeling good on helping. *Sociometry* 38:141–47.
Levinger, George. 1960. Continuance in casework and other helping relationships: A review of current research. *Social Work* 5(5):40–51.
Levinger, G. 1965. Marital cohesiveness and dissolution: An integrative view. *Journal of Marriage and the Family* 27:19–28.
Levinger, G. and O. C. Moles. 1979. *Divorce and Separation*. New York: Basic Books.
Levinson, D. L. 1959. Role, personality, and social structure in the organizational setting. *Journal of Abnormal and Social Psychology* 58:170–80.
Levy, L. H. 1977. Self-help groups: Types and psychological processes. *Journal of Applied Behavioral Science* 12:310–22.
Levy, R. L. and R. D. Carter. 1976. Compliance with practitioner instigations. *Social Work* 21:188–93.

Lewin, Kurt. 1948. *Resolving Social Conflicts: Selected Papers on Group Dynamics*. New York: Harpers.
Lewis, R. G. and M. K. Ho. 1975. Social work with native Americans. *Social Work* 20:379–82.
Libo, L. 1953. *Measuring Group Cohesiveness*. Ann Arbor, Michigan: Institute for Social Research.
Lieberman, M. A. 1975. Group methods. In F. H. Kanfer and A. P. Goldstein, eds., *Helping People Change: A Textbook of Methods*, pp. 433–85. New York: Pergamon Press.
Lieberman, M. A. 1976. Change induction in small groups. *Annual Review of Psychology* 27:217–50.
Lieberman, M. A., I. D. Yalom, and M. B. Miles. 1973. *Encounter Groups: First Facts*. New York: Basic Books.
Lieberman, S. 1950. The effects of changes in roles on the attitudes of role occupants. *Human Relations* 9:385–403.
Likert, R. 1961. *New Patterns in Management*. New York: McGraw-Hill.
Lincoln, A. and G. Levinger. 1972. Observers' evaluation of the victim and the attacker in an aggressive incident. *Journal of Personality and Social Psychology* 22:202–10.
Linder, D. E., J. Cooper, and E. E. Jones. 1967. Decision freedom as a determinant of the role of incentive magnitude in attitude change. *Journal of Personality and Social Psychology* 6:245–54.
Linton, R. 1936. *The Study of Man*. New York: Appleton-Century.
Lippitt, R., N. Polansky, F. Redl, and S. Rosen. 1968. The dynamics of power. In D. Cartwright and A. Zander, eds., *Group Dynamics*, pp. 236–50. 3d ed. New York: Harper & Row.
Lippitt, R. and R. K. White, 1958. An experimental study of leadership and group life. In E. E. Maccoby, T. M. Newcomb, and E. L. Hartley, eds., *Readings in Social Psychology*, pp. 496–511. 3d ed. New York: Holt, Rhinehart and Winston.
Litwak, E. and H. J. Meyer. 1974. *School, Family, and Neighborhood: Theory and Practice of School-Community Relations*. New York: Columbia University Press.
Lockheed, M. E. and Katherine P. Hall. 1976. Conceptualizing sex as a status characteristic: Applications to leadership training strategies. *Journal of Social Issues*, 32(3):111–24.
Long, T. J. 1968. The effects of pre-training procedures on client behavior during intitial counseling interviews. *Dissertation Abstracts* 29(6-A):1784.
Looft, W. R. 1972. Egocentrism and social interaction across the life span. *Psychological Bulletin* 78:73–92.
Lopata, H. Z. 1971. *Occupation: Housewife*. New York: Oxford University Press.
Lott, A. J. and B. E. Lott. 1961. Group cohesiveness, communication level, and conformity. *Journal of Abnormal and Social Psychology* 62:408–12.

Lott, A. J. and B. E. Lott. 1972. The power of liking: Consequences of interpersonal attitudes derived from a liberalized view of secondary reinforcement. In L. Berkowitz, ed., *Advances in Experimental Social Psychology*, 6:109–48. New York: Academic Press.

Lovaas, O. I. 1966. A program for the establishment of speech in psychotic children. In J. K. Wing, ed., *Early Childhood Autism*, pp. 116–44. Oxford: Pergamon Press.

Lovaas, O. I., R. Koegel, J. Q. Simmons, and J. S. Long. 1973. Some generalizations and follow-up measures on autistic children in behavior therapy. *Journal of Applied Behavior Analysis*, 6:131–66.

Luborsky, L., M. Chandler, A. H. Auerback, J. Cohen, and H. M. Bachrach. 1971. Factors influencing the outcome of psychotherapy: A review of quantitative research. *Psychological Bulletin* 75:145–85.

Lyons, T. 1971. Role clarity, need for clarity, satisfaction, tension, and withdrawal. *Organizational Behavior and Human Performance* 6:99–110.

Maccoby, E. E. and C. N. Jacklin. 1974. *The Psychology of Sex Differences*. Stanford, Calif.: Stanford University Press.

Maccoby, N., A. K. Romney, J. S. Adams, and E. E. Maccoby. 1962. "Critical periods" in seeking and accepting information. In *Paris-Stanford Studies in Communication*, pp. 45–57. Stanford California Institute of Communication Research.

Mackey, R. A. 1980. Developmental process in growth-oriented groups. *Social Work* 25:26–29.

Maguire, W. 1973. Perceptual selectivity and the self-concept. Paper presented at the meeting of The American Psychological Association, Montreal.

Mahoney, M. J. and C. E. Thoresen, eds. 1974. *Self-control: Power to the Person*. Monterey, Calif. Brooks-Cole.

Makarenko, A. 1953. *Learning To Live: Flags on the Battlements*. Moscow: Foreign Language Publishing House.

Maluccio, A. N. 1979. *Learning from Clients: Interpersonal Helping as Viewed by Clients and Social Workers*. New York: Free Press.

Maluccio, A. N. and W. D. Marlow. 1974. The case for the contract. *Social Work* 19:28–35.

Mandelbaum, A. 1973. Intergenerational groups in a drop-in mental health center. *Social Casework* 54:154–61.

Mann, L. 1967. The effects of emotional role playing on smoking attitudes and behavior. *Journal of Experimental Social Psychology* 3:334–48.

Mann, L. and I. L. Janis. 1968. A follow-up study on the long-term effects on emotional role playing. *Journal of Personality and Social Psychology* 8:339–42.

Marshall, J. and R. Heslin. 1975. Boys and girls together: Sexual composition and the effect of density and group size on cohesiveness. *Journal of Personality and Social Psychology* 31:952–61.

Martin, P. J., A. L. Sterne, and M. L. Hunter. 1976. Share and share alike:

Mutuality of expectations and satisfaction with therapy. *Journal of Clinical Psychology* 32:677–83.
Martin, W. 1971. Seduced and abandoned in the new world: The image of women in American fiction. In V. Gornick and B. K. Moran, eds., *Women in Sexist Society*, pp. 226–39. New York: Basic Books.
Martinez, J. L., Jr. 1977. Cross-cultural comparison of Chicanos and Anglos on the semantic differential: Some implications for psychology. In J. L. Martinez, Jr., ed., *Chicano Psychology*, pp. 29–43. New York: Academic Press.
Maslach, C. 1978. The client role in burnout. *Journal of Social Issues* 34(4):111–24.
Mayer, A. C. 1966. The significance of quasi-groups in the study of complex societies. In M. Banton, ed., *The Social Anthropology of Complex Societies*, pp. 97–122. New York: Praeger.
Mayer, J., and N. Timms. 1969. Clash in perspectives between worker and client. *Social Casework* 50:32–40.
Mayer, John E. and Noel Timms. 1970. *The Client Speaks: Working Class Impressions of Casework*. London: Routledge & Kegan Paul.
Mazis, M. B. 1975. Antipollution measures and psychological reactance theory: A field experiment. *Journal of Personality and Social Psychology* 31:654–60.
McArthur, L. A. 1972. The how and what of why: Some determinants and consequences of causal attributions. *Journal of Personality and Social Psychology* 22:171–93.
McBroom, E. 1970. Socialization and social casework. In R. W. Roberts and R. H. Nee, eds., *Theories of Social Casework*, pp. 313–52. Chicago: University of Chicago Press.
McBroom, E. 1976. Socialization and social group work. In R. Roberts and Helen Northen, eds., *Theories of Social Work Practice with Groups*, pp. 268–303. New York: Columbia University Press.
McCorkle, L. 1949. Group therapy in correctional institutions. *Federal Probation* 13(2):34–37.
McCorkle, L., A. Elias, and F. L. Bixby. 1958. *The Highfields Story*. New York: Henry Holt.
McCroskey, J. C. and T. A. McCain. 1974. The measurement of interpersonal attraction. *Speech Monographs* 41:261–66.
McGhee, P. E. and V. C. Crandall. 1968. Beliefs in internal-external control of reinforcements and academic performance. *Child Development* 39:91–102.
McGrogan, D. T. 1976. Premature termination from psychotherapy: A continuing problem. Ann Arbor, Michigan: *Dissertation Abstracts International* (University Microfilms no. 76-24213).
McGuire, W. J. 1969. The nature of attitudes and attitude change. In G. Lindzey and E. Aronson, eds., *Handbook of Social Psychology*, 3:136–314. Reading, Mass.: Addison-Wesley.

Mead, G. H. 1935. *Mind, Self, and Society*. Chicago: University of Chicago Press.
Mehrabian, A. 1972. *Nonverbal Communication*. Chicago: Aldine.
Meichenbaum, D. 1975. A self-instructional approach to stress management: A proposal for stress inoculation training. In C. D. Spielberger and I. G. Sarason, eds., *Stress and Anxiety*, 1:238–63. New York: Wiley.
Meichenbaum, D. 1977. *Cognitive-Behavior Modification*. New York: Plenum.
Meichenbaum, D., D. Turk, and S. Burstein. 1975. The nature of coping with stress. In I. G. Sarason and C. D. Spielberger, eds., *Stress and Anxiety*, vol. 2. New York: Wiley.
Menges, R. J. 1969. Student-instructor cognitive compatibility in the large lecture class. *Journal of Personality* 37:444–59.
Merton, R. K. 1957a. *Social Theory and Social Structure*. Rev. ed. Glencoe, Ill: Free Press.
Merton, Robert K. 1957b. The role set: Problems in sociological theory. *British Journal of Sociology* 8:106–20.
Merton, Robert K. 1966. Anticipatory socialization. In B. J. Biddle and E. J. Thomas, eds., *Role Theory: Concepts and Research*, pp. 347–50. New York: Wiley.
Messe, L. A. 1971. Equity in bilateral bargaining. *Journal of Personality and Social Psychology* 17:287–91.
Messinger, S. L., H. Sampson, and R. D. Towne. 1962. Life as theatre: Some notes on the dramaturgic approach to social reality. *Sociometry* 25:98–110.
Mettee, David R. and John Riskind. 1974. Size of defeat and liking for superior and similar ability competitors. *Journal of Experimental Social Psychology* 10:333–51.
Meyer, C. H. 1970. *Social Work Practice: A Response to the Urban Crises*. New York: Free Press.
Meyer, Henry J. 1966. Social worker-social scientist. In J. Regensbury, ed., *Some Educational Patterns in Doctoral Programs in Schools of Social Work*, pp. 87–106. New York: Council on Social Work Education.
Meyers, Joel, R. D. Parsons, and R. Martin. 1979. *Mental Health Consultation in the Schools*. San Francisco: Jossey-Bass.
Mezei, L. 1971. Perceived social pressure as an explanation of shifts in the relative influence of race and belief on prejudice across social interactions. *Journal of Personality and Social Psychology* 19:69–81.
Michener, H. A. and E. J. Lawler. 1975. Endorsement of formal leaders: An integrative model. *Journal of Personality and Social Psychology* 31:216–23.
Middlebrook, P. N. 1974. *Social Psychology and Modern Life*. New York: Knopf.
Middleman, R. R. and G. Goldberg. 1972. The interactional way of presenting generic social work concepts. *Journal of Education for Social Work* 8:48–57.
Middleman, Ruth R. and Gale Goldberg. 1974. *Social Service Delivery*. New York: Columbia University Press.

Miles, J. E., M. Adlersberg, G. Reith, and J. Cumming. 1976. Discharges against medical advice from voluntary psychiatric units. *Hospital and Community Psychiatry* 27:859–64.
Milgram, S. 1965. Liberating effects of group pressure. *Journal of Personality and Social Psychology* 1:127–34.
Milgram, S. 1973. The experience of living in cities: A psychological analysis. In L. S. Wrightsman and J. C. Brigham, eds., *Contemporary Issues in Social Psychology*, pp. 120–28. 2d ed. Monterey, Calif.: Brooks-Cole.
Miller, D. T. 1977. Altruism and threat to a belief in a just world. *Journal of Experimental Social Psychology* 13:113–24.
Miller, D. T. 1978. What constitutes a self-serving attributional bias? A reply to Bradley. *Journal of Personality and Social Psychology* 36:1221–23.
Miller, R. L., P. Brickman and D. Bolen. 1975. Attribution versus persuasion as a means for modifying behavior. *Journal of Personality and Social Psychology* 31:430–41.
Milnes, John and Harvey Bertcher. 1980. *Communicating Empathy*. San Diego, Calif.: University Associates.
Mirande, A. M. 1968. Reference group theory and adolescent sexual behavior. *Journal of Marriage and Family* 30:572–77.
Mischel, W. and C. J. Patterson. 1976. Substantive and structural elements of effective plans for self-control. *Journal of Personality and Social Psychology* 34:942–50.
Mizio, E. 1972. White worker-minority client. *Social Work* 17(3):82–87.
Monahan, F. 1941. *Women in Crime*. New York: Ives Washburn.
Morales, A. and B. W. Sheafor. 1977. *Social Work*. Boston: Allyn & Bacon.
Moran, G. 1966. Dyadic attraction and orientation consensus. *Journal of Personality and Social Psychology* 4:94–99.
Moreno, J. L. 1934. *Who Shall Survive?* Washington, D.C.: Nervous and Mental Disease Publishing Co.
Morgan, C. J. 1978. Bystander intervention: Experimental test of a formal model. *Journal of Personality and Social Psychology* 36:43–55.
Morgan, W. 1977. Navaho treatment of sickness: Diagnosticians. In D. Landy, ed., *Culture, Disease, and Healing*, pp. 163–69. New York: MacMillan.
Morse, N. and E. Reimer. 1956. The experimental change of a major organizational variable. *Journal of Abnormal and Social Psychology* 52:120–29.
Morse, S. and K. J. Gergen. 1970. Social comparison, self consistency, and the concept of self. *Journal of Personality and Social Psychology* 16:148–56.
Moscovici, S. and C. Fauchex. 1972. Social influence, conformity bias, and the study of active minorities. In Leonard Berkowitz, ed., *Advances in Experimental Social Psychology* 6:149–202. New York: Academic Press.
Moscovici, S. and M. Zavalloni. 1969. The group as a polarizer of attitudes. *Journal of Personality and Social Psychology* 12:125–35.
Moss, S. A. and M. S. Moss. 1967. When a caseworker leaves an agency: The impact on worker and client. *Social Casework* 48:433–37.

Mott, P. E., F. C. Mann, Q. McLoughlin and D. P. Warwick. 1965. *Shift Work: The Social Psychological and Physical Consequences*. Ann Arbor: University of Michigan Press.

Myers, D. G. and H. Lamm. 1976. The group polarization phenomena. *Psychological Bulletin* 83:602–27.

Nadler, A., J. D. Fisher, and S. Streufert. 1975. When helping hurts: Effects of donor-recipient similarity and recipient self-esteem on recipient reaction to aid. Lafayette, Ind.: Purdue University Manuscript.

Nagel, J. 1980. Is there a relationship between locus of control and cognitive self-statements in musicians who suffer from performance anxiety? Manuscript. (Available from author at 1135 Kim St., Ann Arbor, Mich. 48103.)

Newcomb, Theodore M. 1950. *Social Psychology*. New York: Dryden Press.

Newcomb, T. M. 1953. An approach to the study of communicative acts. *Psychological Review* 60:393–404.

Newcomb, Theodore M. 1961. *The Acquaintance Process*. New York: Holt, Rinehart and Winston.

Newcomb, T. M. 1965. Attitude development as a function of reference groups: The Bennington study. In Harold Proshansky and B. Seidenberg, eds., *Basic Studies in Social Psychology*, pp. 215–25. New York: Holt, Rinehart and Winston.

Newcomb, T. M. 1978. Youth in colleges and in corrections: Institutional influences. *American Psychologist* 33(2):114–24.

Nisbett, R. E., G. C. Caputo, P. Legant and J. Marecek. 1973. Behavior as seen by the actor and as seen by the observer. *Journal of Personality and Social Psychology* 27:154–64.

Nisbett, R. E., R. Crandall, E. Borgida and H. Reed. 1976. Popular induction: Information is not necesssarily informative. In J. S. Carroll and J. W. Payne, eds., *Cognition and Social Behavior*, pp. 113–33. New York: Wiley.

Nixon, S. B. 1969. Increasing task-oriented behavior. In J. D. Krumboltz and C. E. Thoresen, eds., *Behavioral Counseling: Cases and Techniques*, pp. 207–10. New York: Holt, Rinehart and Winston.

Nord, Walter R. 1969. Social exchange theory: An integrative approach to social conformity. *Psychological Bulletin* 71:174–208.

Northen, H. 1955. The place of agency structure, philosophy and policy in supporting group programs of social action. In Harleigh Trecker, ed., *Social Group Work: Principles and Practices*, pp. 236–47. New York: Whiteside.

Northen, Helen. 1969. *Social Work with Groups*. New York: Columbia University Press.

Nydegger, R. V. 1975. Leadership in small groups: A rewards-costs analysis. *Small Group Behavior* 6:353–68.

Nye, F. I. 1976. *Role Structure and the Analysis of the Family*. Beverly Hills, Calif.: Sage.

Oberman, E. 1978. Educational model in behavioral training. *Social Work* 23:121–26.

O'Brien, F. O. and N. H. Azrin. 1972. Developing proper mealtime behaviors of the institutionalized retarded. *Journal of Applied Behavior Analysis* 5:389–99.

O'Dell, J. W. 1968. Group size and emotional interaction. *Journal of Personality and Social Psychology* 8:75–78.

Orcutt, J. D. 1975. The impact of student activism on attitudes toward the female sex role. *Social Forces* 54:382–92.

Orne, M. T. and P. H. Wender. 1968. Anticipatory socialization for psychotherapy: Method and rationale. *American Journal of Psychiatry* 124:1202–12.

Overall, B. and H. Aronson. 1963. Expectations of psychotherapy in patients of lower socioeconomic class. *American Journal of Orthopsychiatry* 33:421–30.

Pallak, M. S. and J. F. Heller. 1971. Interactive effects of commitment to future interaction and threat to attitudinal freedom. *Journal of Personality and Social Psychology* 17:325–31.

Panzer, B. M., L. C. Wiesner and W. D. N. Dickson. 1978. Program for developmentally disabled children. *Social Work* 23:406–11.

Papell, C. P. 1972. Sensitivity training: relevance for social work education. *Journal of Education for Social Work* 8(1):42–55.

Papell, C. P. and B. Rothman. 1966. Social group work models: Possession and heritage. *Journal of Education for Social Work* 2(2):66–78.

Parad, H. and L. Parad. 1968. A study of crisis-oriented planned short-term treatment. *Social Casework* 49:346–55.

Parke, R. D. and W. C. Collmer. 1975. Child abuse: An interdisciplinary analysis. In E. M. Hetherington, ed., *Review of Child Development Research* 5:509–90. Chicago: University of Chicago Press.

Parker, S. and R. Kleiner. 1970. Status position, mobility, and ethnic identification of the Negro. In N. J. Smelser and W. T. Smelser, eds., *Personality and Social Systems*, pp. 353–67. 2d ed. New York: Wiley.

Parker, W. S., Jr. 1976. Black-white differences in leader behavior related to subordinates' reactions. *Journal of Applied Psychology* 61:140–47.

Parkhurst, G. B. 1977. Community mental health: An examination of consumer utilization in a non-public transportation community. Ann Arbor, Michigan: *Dissertation Abstracts International* (University Microfilms no. 77-4077).

Parsons, J. E., D. N. Ruble, K. L. Hodges, and A. W. Small. 1976. Cognitive-developmental factors in emerging sex differences in achievement-related expectancies. *Journal of Social Issues* 32(3):47–61.

Parsons, T. 1951. *The Social System*. New York: Free Press.

Parsons, T. 1955. Family structure and the socialization of the child. In T. Parsons and R. F. Bales, eds., *Family, Socialization, and Interaction process*, pp. 35–132. New York: Free Press.

Parsons, T., R. F. Bales and E. A. Shils. 1953. *Working Papers in the Theory of Action*. Glencoe, Ill.: Free Press.

Patchen, M. 1961. A conceptual framework and some empirical data regarding comparisons of social rewards. *Sociometry* 24:136–56.

Patterson, G. R. 1969. Behavioral techniques based upon social learning. In C. M. Franks, ed., *Behavior Therapy: Appraisal and Status*, pp. 341–74. New York: McGraw-Hill.

Patterson, G. R. and E. M. Guillon. 1968. *Living with Children*. Champaign, Ill.: Research Press.

Patterson, G. R., I. Littman and T. R. Brown. 1968. Negative set and social learning. *Journal of Personality and Social Psychology* 8:109–116.

Paulus, P. B. and P. Murdock. 1971. Anticipated evaluation and audience presence in the enhancement of dominant responses. *Journal of Experimental Social Psychology* 7:280–91.

Pearl, Arthur and F. Riessman. 1965. *New Careers for the Poor: The Nonprofessional in Human Service*. New York: Free Press.

Pearlin, L. I. 1975. Status inequality and stress in marriage. *American Sociological Review* 40(3):344–57.

Pearlin, L. I. and M. L. Kohn. 1966. Social class, occupation, and parental values: A cross-national study. *American Sociological Review* 31:466–79.

Penner, L. A. 1971. Interpersonal attraction toward a black person as a function of value importance. *Personality* 2:175–87.

Penner, L. A., M. C. Dertke and C. J. Achenbach. 1973. The "flash" system: A field study of altruism. *Journal of Applied Social Psychology* 3:362–70.

Pepitone, A. and G. Reichling. 1955. Group cohesiveness and the expression of hostility. *Human Relations* 8:327–37.

Perlman, Helen H. 1957. *Social Casework: A Problem-Solving Process*. Chicago: University of Chicago Press.

Perlman, Helen H. 1960. Intake and some role considerations. *Social Casework* 40:171–77.

Perlman, Helen H. 1968. *Persona: Social Role and Personality*. Chicago: University of Chicago Press.

Perlman, Helen H. 1970. The problem-solving model in social casework. In R. W. Roberts and R. H. Nee, eds., *Theories of Social Casework*, pp. 129–79. Chicago: University of Chicago Press.

Perlman, R. and A. Gurin. 1972. *Community Organization and Social Planning*. New York: Wiley.

Perlmutter, L. C. and R. A. Monty. 1977. The importance of perceived control: Fact or fantasy? *American Scientist* 65:759–65.

Perlmutter, Lawrence C. and R. A. Monty. 1979. *Choice and Perceived Control*. Somerset, N.J.: Halsted Press.

Pettigrew, T. F. 1967. Social evaluation theory: Convergences and applications. *Nebraska Symposium on Motivation* 15:241–315.

Pettigrew, T. 1969. Racially separate or together? *Journal of Social Issues* 25(3):43–69.

Pfieffer, J. W. and J. E. Jones. 1973. *A Handbook of Structural Experiences for Human Relations Training*, vol. 4. Iowa City: Iowa University Associates Press.

Piaget, J. and B. Inhelder, 1956. *The Child's Conception of Space*. London: Routledge & Kegan Paul.
Piliavin, I. M. and A. E. Gross. 1977. The effects of separation of services and income maintenance on AFDC recipients. *Social Service Review* 51:389–406.
Piliavin, I. M., J. A. Piliavin, and J. Rodin. 1975. Costs diffusion, and the stigmatized victim. *Journal of Personality and Social Psychology* 32:429–38.
Piliavin, I. M., J. Rodin, and J. A. Piliavin. 1969. Good Samaritanism: An underground phenomenon? *Journal of Personality and Social Psychology* 13:289–99.
Piliavin, J. A. and I. M. Piliavin. 1972. The effect of blood on reactions to the victim. *Journal of Personality and Social Psychology* 23:353–61.
Pincus, A. and A. Minahan. 1973. *Social Work Practice: Model and Method*. Itasca, Ill.: Peacock.
Pine, V. R. 1974. Dying, death, and social behavior. In B. Schoenberg, A. C. Carr, H. H. Kutscher, D. Peretz, and J. K. Goldberg, eds., *Anticipatory Grief*, pp. 31–47. New York: Columbia University Press.
Pliner, P., H. Hart, J. Kohn, and D. Saari. 1974. Compliance without pressure: Some further data on the foot-in-the-door technique. *Journal of Experimental Social Psychology* 10:17–22.
Polansky, Norman and Jacob Kounin. 1956. Clients' reactions to initial interviews. *Human Relations* 9:237–64.
Pomazal, R. J. and J. J. Jaccard. 1976. An informational approach to altruistic behavior. *Journal of Personality and Social Psychology* 33:317–26.
Powell, F. A. and G. R. Miller. 1967. Social approval and disapproval cues in anxiety-arousing communications. *Speech Monographs* 34:152–59.
Preiss, J. J. and H. J. Ehrlich. 1966. *An Examination of Role Theory: The Case of the State Police*. Lincoln: University of Nebraska Press.
Premack, D. 1965. Reinforcement theory. In D. Levine, ed., *Nebraska Symposium on Motivation, 1965*, pp. 123–88. Lincoln: University of Nebraska Press.
Pressley, M. 1979. Increasing children's self-control through cognitive interventions. *Review of Education Research* 49:319–70.
Psathas, G. 1960. Phase movement and equilibrium tendencies in interaction process in psychotherapy groups. *Sociometry* 23:177–94.
Radin, N. 1970. Preschool programs of the USSR. *Child Welfare* 49:29–36.
Radin, N. 1972a. Father-child interaction and the intellectual functioning of four-year old boys. *Developmental Psychology* 6:353–61.
Radin, N. 1972b. Three degrees of maternal involvement in a preschool program: Impact on mothers and children. *Child Development* 43:1355–64.
Radin, N. 1973. Observed paternal behaviors as antecedents of intellectual functioning in young boys. *Developmental Psychology* 8:369–76.
Radin, N. 1974a. Observed maternal behavior with four-year-old boys and girls in lower class families. *Child Development* 45:1126–31.
Radin, N. 1974b. Socioeducation groups. In Paul H. Glasser, R. Sarri, and

R. Vinter, eds., *Individual Change through Small Groups*, pp. 89–101. New York: Free Press.

Radin, N. 1975. A personal perspective on school social work. *Social Casework* 56:605–13.

Radin, N. 1976a. School social work trends and problems. Paper presented at workshop of School Social Workers of Muskegon Area Intermediate School District, Muskegon, Michigan, May 20.

Radin, N. 1976b. The role of the father in cognitive/academic and intellectual development. In M. E. Lamb, ed., *The Role of the Father in Child Development*, pp. 237–76. New York: Wiley.

Radin, N. 1978. Assessing the effectiveness of school social workers. *Social Work* 24:132–37.

Radin, N. and G. Wittes. 1974. Integrating divergent theories in a compensatory preschool program. In P. Glasser, R. Sarri, and R. Vinter, eds., *Individual Change through Small Groups*, pp. 420–30. New York: Free press.

Radloff, R. 1966. Social comparison and ability evaluation. *Journal of Experimental Social Psychology* 2:6–26 (suppl. 1).

Rapoport, E. R. G. 1976. Lower class patient attitudes and expectations related to dropout from psychotherapy. Ph.D. dissertation, Adelphi University. *Dissertation Abstracts International* (University Microfilms no. 76-14040).

Rapoport, L. 1970. Crisis intervention as a mode of treatment. In Robert W. Roberts and Robert H. Nee, eds., *Theories of Social Casework*, pp. 265–321. Chicago: University of Chicago Press.

Rapoport, Rhona and Robert Rapoport. 1969. The dual-career family: A variant family and social change. *Human Relations* 22:3–30.

Raven, B. H. 1965. Social influence and power. In Ivan D. Steiner and M. Fishbein, eds., *Current Studies in Social Psychology*, pp. 371–82. New York: Holt.

Raven, B. H. and A. W. Kruglanski. 1970. Conflict and power. In Paul G. Swingle, ed., *The Structure of Conflict*, pp. 69–109. New York: Academic Press.

Red Horse, J. G. 1980. Family structure and value orientation in American Indians. *Social Casework* 61:462–67.

Redl, F. 1951. The art of group composition. In S. Schulze, ed., *Creative Group Living in a Children's Institution*, pp. 79–96. New York: Association Press.

Reed, A. W. 1974. Anticipatory grief work. In B. Schoenberg, A. C. Carr, H. H. Kutscher, D. Peretz, and J. K. Goldberg, eds., *Anticipatory Grief*, pp. 346–57. New York: Columbia University Press.

Regan, D. I. and J. Totten. 1975. Empathy and attribution: Turning observers into actors. *Journal of Personality and Social Psychology* 32:850–56.

Reid, W. J. 1975. A test of task-centered approach. *Social Work* 20:3–9.

Reid, W. J. 1978. *The Task-Centered System*. New York: Columbia University Press.

Reid, William and Laura Epstein. 1972. *Task-Centered Casework*. New York: Columbia University Press.
Reid, W. J. and L. Epstein. 1977. *Task-Centered Practice*. New York: Columbia University Press.
Reid, W. J. and A. Shyne. 1969. *Brief and Extended Casework*. New York: Columbia University Press.
Reiss, M. and B. R. Schlenker. 1977. Attitude change and responsibility avoidance as modes of dilemma resolution in forced compliance situations. *Journal of Personality and Social Psychology* 35:21–30.
Reiss, S. and L. W. Sushinsky. 1975. Overjustification, competing responses and the acquisition of intrinsic interest. *Journal of Personality and Social Psychology* 31:1116–25.
Reissman, F. 1962. *The Culturally Deprived Child*. New York: Harper & Row.
Reynolds, B. 1957. *Social Work and Social Living*. New York: Citadel Press.
Rhodes, S. L. 1977. Contract negotiation in the initial stage of casework service. *Social Service Review* 51:125–40.
Richmond, Mary. 1922. *What Is Social Casework?* New York: Russell Sage.
Ring, K. and H. H. Kelley. 1963. A comparison of augmentation and reduction as modes of influence. *Journal of Abnormal and Social Psychology* 66:95–102.
Rist, R. C. 1970. Student social class and teacher expectations: The self-fulfilling prophecy in ghetto education. *Harvard Educational Review* 40:411–51.
Roberts, R. W. and R. H. Nee, eds. 1970. *Theories of Social Casework*. Chicago: University of Chicago Press.
Robinson, Virginia P., ed. 1962. *Jessie Taft: Therapist and Social Work Educator*. Philadelphia, Pa.: University of Pennsylvania Press.
Rodin, J. 1978. Cognitive-behavioral strategies for the control of obesity. Paper presented at the conference "Cognitive-Behavior Therapy: Applications and Issues." Los Angeles, September.
Rodin, J., and I. L. Janis. 1979. The social power of health-care practioners as agents of change. *Journal of Social Issues* 35(1):60–81.
Rodin, J. and E. J. Langer. 1977. Long-term effects of a control-relevant intervention with the institutionalized aged. *Journal of Personality and Social Psychology* 35:897–903.
Rodin, J. and E. J. Langer. 1978. Erratum to Rodin and Langer 1977. *Journal of Personality and Social Psychology* 36:462.
Rogers, Carl. 1961. *On Becoming a Person*. Boston: Houghton Mifflin.
Rokeach, M. 1968a. *Beliefs, Attitudes, and Values: A Theory of Organization and Change*. San Francisco: Jossey-Bass.
Rokeach, M. T. 1968b. Organization and change within value-attitude systems. In M. T. Rokeach, ed., *Beliefs, Attitudes, and Values*. San Francisco: Jossey-Bass.
Rokeach, M. 1971. Long-range modification of values, attitudes, and behavior. *American Psychologist* 26:453–459.
Rokeach, M. 1973. *The Nature of Human Values*. New York: Free Press.

Rokeach, M. 1975. Long-term value change initiated by computer feedback. *Journal of Personality and Social Psychology* 32:467–76.

Rokeach, M. and P. Kliejunas. 1972. Behavior as a function of attitude-toward-object and attitude-toward-situation. *Journal of Personality and Social Psychology* 22:194–201.

Rokeach, M. and L. Mezei. 1966. Race and shared belief as factors in social choice. *Science* 151:167–72.

Rokeach, M., P. W. Smith, and R. I. Evans. 1960. Two kinds of prejudice or one? In M. Rokeach, ed., *The Open and Closed Mind*, pp. 132–68. New York: Basic Books.

Rommetveit, R. 1960. *Selectivity, Intuition and Halo Effects in Social Perception*. Oslo: Oslo University Press.

Ronis, D. L., M. H. Baumgardner, M. R. Leippe, J. T. Cacioppo, and A. G. Greenwald. 1977. In search of reliable persuasion effects: I. A computer-controlled procedure for studying persuasion. *Journal of Personality and Social Psychology* 35:548–69.

Rose, Sheldon D. 1972. *Treating Children in Groups*. San Francisco: Jossey-Bass.

Rose, S. D. 1974a. A behavioral approach to the group treatment of parents. In P. Glasser, R. Sarri, and R. Vinter, eds., *Individual Change through Small Groups*, pp. 348–61. New York: Free Press.

Rose, Sheldon D. 1974b. Group training of parents as behavior modifiers. *Social Work* 19:156–62.

Rose, Sheldon. 1977. *Group Therapy: A Behavioral Approach*. Englewood Cliffs, N.J.: Prentice-Hall.

Rose, Sheldon D. and M. Sundel. 1974. The Hartwig Project: A behavioral approach to the treatment of juvenile offenders. In P. Glasser, R. Sarri, and R. Vinter, eds., *Individual Change through Small Groups*, pp. 404–19. New York: Free Press.

Rosen, A. 1972. The treatment relationship: A conceptualization. *Journal of Consulting and Clinical Psychology* 38:329–37.

Rosen, B. and S. S. Komorita. 1971. Attitudes and actions: The effects of behavioral intent and perceived effectiveness of acts. *Journal of Personality and Social Psychology* 39:189–203.

Rosenberg, M. J. 1956. Cognitive structure and attitudinal affect. *Journal of Abnormal and Social Psychology* 53:367–72.

Rosenberg, M. J. 1960. An analysis of affective-cognitive consistency. In C. I. Hovland and M. J. Rosenberg, eds., *Attitude Organization and Change*, pp. 15–64. New Haven, Conn.: Yale University Press.

Rosenfeld, H. M. 1966. Approval-seeking and approval-inducing functions of verbal and non-verbal responses in a dyad. *Journal of Personality and Social Psychology* 4:597–605.

Rosenhan, D. 1969. Some origins of concerns for others. In P. Mussen, J. Langer, and M. Covington, eds., *Trends and Issues in Developmental Psychology*, pp. 134–153. New York: Holt, Rinehart and Winston.

Ross, M. and D. DiTecco. 1975. An attributional analysis of moral judgements. *Journal of Social Issues* 31:91–109.

Rossi, Alice. 1968. Transition to parenthood. *Journal of Marriage and the Family* 30:26–39.

Rothman, J. 1974. *Planning and Organizing for Social Change*. New York: Columbia University Press.

Rothman, Jack. 1978. Conversion and design in the research utilization process. *Journal of Social Service Research* 2:117–32.

Rotman, C. B. and S. J. Goldburgh. 1976. The psychotherapist's feelings about the adolescent patient. *Adolescence* 11:335–39.

Rotter, J. B. 1954. *Social Learning and Clinical Psychology*. Englewood Cliffs, N.J.: Prentice-Hall.

Rotter, J. B. 1966. Generalized expectancies for internal versus external control of reinforcement. *Psychological Monographs: General and Applied* 80:1–28.

Rubin, Zick. 1973. *Liking and Loving: An Invitation to Social Psychology*. New York: Holt, Rinehart and Winston.

Rubin, Z. and A. Peplau. 1973. Belief in a just world and reactions to another's lot: A study of participants in the national draft lottery. *Journal of Social Issues* 4(4):73–93.

Rubin, Z. and L. A. Peplau. 1975. Who believes in a just world? *Journal of Social Issues* 31(3):65–89.

Ruble, D. N. and E. T. Higgins. 1976. Effects of group sex composition on self-presentation and sex-typing. *Journal of Social Issues* 32(3):125–32.

Ruble, Thomas L. 1973. Effects of actor and observer roles on attributions of causality in activations of success and failure. *Journal of Social Psychology* 90:41–44.

Runciman, W. G. 1961. Problem of research on relative deprivation. *European Journal of Sociology* 2:315–23.

Runciman, W. G. 1966. *Relative Deprivation and Social Justice: A Study of Attitudes to Social Inequality in Twentieth Century England*. Berkeley, Calif.: University of California Press.

Runkel, P. J. 1956. Cognitive similarity in facilitating communications. *Sociometry* 19:178–91.

Runkel, P. J., M. Lawrence, S. Oldfield, M. Rider, and C. Clark. 1971. Stages of group development: An empirical test of Tuckman's hypothesis. *Journal of Applied Behavioral Science* 7:180–93.

Rush, G. B. 1967. Status consistency and right-wing extremism. *American Sociological Review* 32:86–92.

Rushton, J. P. 1975. Generosity in children: Immediate and long-term effects of modeling, preaching, and moral judgement. *Journal of Personality and Social Psychology* 31:459–66.

Rutherford, E. and P. Mussen, 1968. Generosity in nursery school boys. *Child Development* 39:755–65.

Ryan, William. 1971. *Blaming the Victim*. New York: Pantheon.

Saks, M. J. 1978. Social psychological contributions to a legislative subcommittee on organ and tissue transplants. *American Psychologist* 33:680–90.
Sakurai, M. M. 1975. Small group cohesiveness and detrimental conformity. *Sociometry* 38:340–47.
Saltzman, C., M. J. Luetgart, C. H. Roth, J. Creaser, and L. Howard. 1976. Formation of a therapeutic relationship: Experiences during the initial phase of psychotherapy as predictors of treatment duration and outcome. *Journal of Consulting and Clinical Psychology* 44:546–55.
Sampson, E. E. 1969. Studies of status congruence. In L. Berkowitz, ed., *Advances in Experimental Social Psychology* 4:225–70. New York: Academic Press.
Sampson, E. E. and C. A. Insko, 1964. Cognitive consistency and performance in the autokinetic situation. *Journal of Abnormal and Social Psychology* 8:184–92.
Samuel, W. 1973. On clarifying some interpretations of social comparison theory. *Journal of Experimental Social Psychology* 9:450–65.
Sanders, D. H., W. S. MacDonald, and H. M. Maynard. 1964. The effect of group composition on task performance and role differentiation. In G. W. Fairweather, ed., *Social Psychology in Treating Mental Illness: An Experimental Approach*, pp. 196–209. New York: Wiley.
Sanders, G. S. and R. S. Baron. 1977. Is social comparison irrelevant in producing choice shifts? *Journal of Experimental Social Psychology* 13:303–14.
Santee, R. 1976. The effect on attraction of attitude similarity as information about reinforcement contingencies. *Sociometry* 39:153–56.
Sapolsky, Allan. 1965. Relationship between patient-doctor compatibility, mutual perception, and outcome of treatment. *Journal of Abnormal Psychology* 70:70–76.
Sarbin, T. R. 1964. Role theoretical interpretation of psychological change. In P. Worchel and D. Byrne, eds., *Personality Change*, pp. 176–219. New York: Wiley.
Sarbin, T. R. and V. L. Allen. 1968. Role theory. In Gardner Lindzey and E. Aronson, eds., *Handbook of Social Psychology* 1:488–567. 2d. ed. New York: Addison-Wesley.
Sarri, R., and M. Galinsky. 1974. A conceptual framework for group development. In Paul Glasser, R. Sarri, and R. Vinter, eds., *Individual Change through Small Groups*, pp. 71–88. New York: Free Press.
Sawyer, J. 1966. The altruism scale: A measure of cooperative, individualistic, and competitive interpersonal orientation. *American Journal of Sociology* 71:407–16.
Schachter, S. 1959. *The Psychology of Affiliation*. Stanford, Calif.: Stanford University Press.
Schachter, S. 1966. The interaction of cognitive and physiological determinants of emotional state. In C. Spielberger, ed., *Anxiety and Behavior*, pp. 193–224. New York: Academic press.
Schachter, S. 1968. Deviation, rejection, and communication. In D. Car-

twright and A. Zander, eds., *Group Dynamics*, pp. 165–81. 3d. ed. New York: Harper & Row.

Schachter, S., N. Ellertson, D. McBride, and D. Gregory. 1968. An experimental study of cohesiveness and productivity. In D. Cartwright and A. Zander, eds., *Group Dynamics*, pp. 192–198. 3d. ed. New York: Harper & Row.

Schellenberg, James A. 1970. *An Introduction to Social Psychology*. New York: Random House.

Scherer, S. E. 1974 Proxemic behavior of primary school children as a function of their socioeconomic class and subculture. *Journal of Personality and Social Psychology* 29:800–5.

Schlenker, B. R. and R. S. Miller, 1977. Egocentrism in groups: Self-serving biases or logical information processing? *Journal of Personality and Social Psychology* 35:755–65.

Schopler, J. H. and M. J. Galinsky. 1974. Goals in social group work practice: Formulation, implementation, and evaluation. In P. Glasser, R. Sarri, and R. Vinter, eds., *Individual Change through Small Groups*, pp. 126–48. New York: Free Press.

Schopler, J. and M. Matthews. 1965. The influence of the perceived locus of partner's dependence on the use of interpersonal power. *Journal of Personality and Social Psychology* 2:609–12.

Schulz, R. 1976. Some life and death consequences of perceived control. In J. S. Carroll and J. W. Payne, eds., *Cognition and Social Behavior*, pp. 135–53. Hillsdale, N.J.: Erlbaum.

Schulz, R. and B. H. Hanusa. 1978. Long-term effects of control and predictability-enhancing interventions: Findings and ethical issues. *Journal of Personality and Social Psychology* 36:1194–1201.

Schutz, W. C. 1957. *The FIRO Scales, Test, and Manual*. Palo Alto, Calif.: Consulting Psychologists Press.

Schwartz, A. and I. Goldiamond. 1975. *Social Casework: A Behavioral Approach*. New York: Columbia University Press.

Schwartz, S. H. 1970a. Elicitation of moral obligation and self-sacrificing behavior: An experimental study of volunteering to be a bone marrow donor. *Journal of Personality and Social Psychology* 15:283–93.

Schwartz, S. H. 1970b. Moral decision making and behavior. In J. R. Macaulay and L. Berkowitz, eds., *Altruism and Helping Behavior*, pp. 127–41. New York: Academic Press.

Schwartz, S. H. 1974. Awareness of interpersonal consequences, responsibility denial and volunteering. *Journal of Personality and Social Psychology* 30:57–63.

Schwartz, S. H. 1977. Normative influences on altruism. In L. Berkowitz, ed., *Advances in Experimental Social Psychology*, 10:222–82. New York: Academic Press.

Schwartz, William. 1959. Group work and the social scene. In Alfred J. Kahn,

ed., *Issues in American Social Work*, pp. 110–37. New York: Columbia University Press.
Schwartz, William. 1962. Toward a strategy of group work practice. *Social Service Review* 36:268–79.
Schwartz, W. 1977. Social group work: The interactionist approach. In *Encyclopedia of Social Work*, 2:1328–37. New York: National Association of Social Workers.
Scott, J. A. 1974. Awareness of informal space: A longitudinal analysis. *Perceptual and Motor Skills* 39:735–38.
Seabury, B. 1971. Arrangement of physical space in social work settings. *Social Work* 16(4):43–49.
Seabury, B. A. 1976. The contract: Uses, abuses, and limitations. *Social Work* 21:16–21.
Seabury, B. A. 1979. Negotiating sound contracts with clients. *Public Welfare* 37:33–38.
Sears, D. O. and J. B. McConalay. 1970. Racial socialization, comparison levels, and the Watts riot. *Journal of Social Issues* 26(1):133–40.
Secord, P. F. and C. W. Backman. 1964. *Social Psychology*. New York: McGraw-Hill.
Seeman, M. 1959. On the meaning of alienation. *American Sociological Review* 24:783–91.
Seeman, M. and J. W. Evans. 1962. Alienation and learning in a hospital setting. *American Sociological Review* 27:772–83.
Segal, S. P. 1978. Attitudes toward the mentally ill: A review. *Social Work* 23:211–17.
Seligman, M. E. P. 1975. *Helplessness*. San Francisco: Freeman.
Sena-Rivera, J. 1979. Extended kinship in the United States: Competing models and the case of La Familia Chicana. *Journal of Marriage and the Family* 41:121–29.
Sewell, W. H. and V. P. Shah. 1968. Social class, parental encouragement, and educational aspirations. *American Journal of Sociology* 73:559–72.
Shapiro, C. H. 1980. Termination: A neglected concept in the social work curriculum. *Journal of Education for Social Work* 16:13–19.
Shaver, K. G. 1975. *An Introduction to Attribution Processes*. Cambridge, Mass.: Winthrop.
Shaw, Marvin E. 1971. *Group Dynamics: The Psychology of Small Group Behavior*. New York: McGraw-Hill.
Shaw, M. 1976. *Group Dynamics*. 2d. ed. New York: McGraw-Hill.
Shaw, Marvin E. and Philip R. Costanzo. 1970. *Theories of Social Psychology*. New York: McGraw-Hill.
Sheras, P. and S. Worchel. 1979. *Clinical Psychology: A Social Psychological Approach*. New York: Van Nostrand.
Sherif, M. 1958. Superordinate goals in the reduction of intergroup conflict. *American Journal of Sociology* 63:349–56.

Sherif, M. and C. Sherif. 1964. *Reference Groups*. New York: Harper & Row.
Sherif, M. and C. Sherif. 1969. *Social Psychology*. New York: Harper & Row.
Sherrod, D. D. and R. Downs. 1974. Environmental determinants of altruism: The effects of stimulus overload and perceived control on helping. *Journal of Experimental Social Psychology* 10:468–79.
Shibutani, Tamostsu. 1967. Reference groups as perspectives. In E. P. Hollander and R. G. Hunt, eds., *Current Perspectives in Social Psychology*, pp. 74–82. 2d ed. New York: Oxford University Press.
Shultz, J. 1975. The search for potential co-membership: An analysis of conversations among strangers. Ph.D. dissertation, Harvard Graduate School of Education.
Shure, M. B. and G. Spivack. 1977. Interpersonal problem solving intervention for mother and child. Paper presented at the Society for Research in Child Development, New Orleans, March.
Shure, M. B. and G. Spivack. 1978. *Problem-Solving Techniques in Childbearing*. San Francisco: Jossey-Bass.
Shyne, A. 1957. What research tells us about short term cases in family agencies. *Social Casework* 38:223–31.
Sicoly, F. and M. Ross. 1977. Facilitation of ego-biased attributions by means of self-serving observer feedback. *Journal of Personality and Social Psychology* 35:734–41.
Siegel, A. E. and S. Siegel. 1965. Reference groups, membership groups. In Harold Proshansky and B. Seidenberg, eds., *Basic Studies in Social Psychology*, pp. 225–230. New York: Holt, Rinehart and Winston.
Sigall, Harold and Nancy Ostrobe. 1975. Beautiful but dangerous: Effects of offender attractiveness and nature of the crime on juridic judgment. *Journal of Personality and Social Psychology* 31:410–14.
Silver, R. and C. B. Wortman. 1980. Coping with undesirable life events. In J. Garber and M. E. P. Seligman, eds., *Human Helplessness: Theory and Applications*, pp. 279–340. New York: Academic Press.
Simons, H. W., N. N. Berkowitz, and R. J. Moyer. 1970. Similarity, credibility, and attitude change: A review and a theory. *Psychological Bulletin* 73:1–15.
Singer, J. E. 1966. Social comparison—progress and issues. *Journal of Experimental Social Psychology* 2:40–48 (suppl. 1).
Singer, J. E. and D. C. Glass. 1975. Some reflections on losing our social psychological purity. In M. Deutsch and H. A. Hornstein, eds., *Applying Social Psychology*, pp. 15–32. Hillsdale, N.J.: Erlbaum.
Siporin, M. 1975. *Introduction to Social Work Practice*. New York: MacMillan.
Sjoberg, G. R., R. A. Brymer, and B. Farris. 1966. Bureaucracy and the lower class. *Sociology and Social Research* 50:325–37.
Slater, P. E. 1958. Contrasting correlates of group size. *Sociometry* 21:129–39.
Slavson, Simon. 1947. *The Practice of Group Therapy*. New York: International Universities Press.
Slavson, Simon. 1957. Are there "group dynamics" in therapy groups? *International Journal of Group Psychotherapy* 7:144–45.

Sloan, R., A. Cristol, M. Pepernick, and F. Staples. 1970. Role preparation and expectancy of improvement in psychotherapy. *Journal of Nervous and Mental Disease* 150:18–26.

Smalley, R. 1970. The functional approach to casework practice. In Robert W. Roberts and Robert H. Nee, eds., *Theories of Social Casework*, pp. 102–5. Chicago: University of Chicago Press.

Smart, C. and I. Vertinsky. Designs for crises decision units. *Administrative Science Quarterly* 22:640–57.

Smelser, W. T. 1961. Dominance as a factor in achievement and perception in cooperative problem solving interactions. *Journal of Abnormal and Social Psychology* 62:535–42.

Smith, Audrey D. 1972. Child care arrangements of mothers in the Work Incentive Program. In A. D. Smith and D. Herberg, eds., *Child Care in the Work Incentive Program*. Report submitted to the Office of Research and Development, Manpower Administration, Department of Labor, pp. 1–100. University of Chicago, School of Social Service Administration.

Smith, C. R., L. Williams, and R. H. Willis. 1967. Race, sex, and belief as determinants of friendship acceptance. *Journal of Personality and Social Psychology* 5:127–37.

Smith, J. E. 1969. Encouraging constructive use of time. In J. D. Krumboltz and C. E. Thoresen, eds., *Behavioral Counseling: Cases and Techniques*, pp. 234–41. New York: Holt, Rinehart and Winston.

Smith, J. M. and D. E. P. Smith. 1966. *Child Management: A Program for Parents*. Ann Arbor, Mich.: Ann Arbor Publishers.

Smith, M. B., J. S. Bruner, and R. W. White. 1956. *Opinions and Personality*. New York: Wiley.

Snoek, J. Diedrick. 1966. Role strain in diversified role sets. *American Journal of Sociology* 71:363–72.

Snyder, M. and M. R. Cunningham. 1975. To comply or not to comply: Testing the self-perception explanation of the "foot-in-the-door" phenomenon. *Journal of Personality and Social Psychology* 31:64–67.

Snyder, M. and E. E. Jones. 1974. Attitude attribution when behavior is constrained. *Journal of Experimental Social Psychology* 10:585–600.

Sole, K., J. Marton, and H. A. Hornstein. 1975. Opinion similarity and helping: Three field experiments investigating the bases of promotive tension. *Journal of Experimental Social Psychology* 11:1–13.

Sommer, R. 1967. Small group ecology. *Psychological Bulletin* 67:145–52.

Sommer, R. 1969. *Personal Space: The Behavioral Basis of Design*. Englewood Cliffs, N.J.: Prentice-Hall.

Sotomayor, M. 1971. Mexican-American interaction with social systems. *Social Casework* 52:316–22.

Spector, R. 1979. Ethnicity and health: A study of health care, beliefs, and practices. *The Urban and Social Change Review* 12:34–37.

Spergel, Irving A. 1974. Organizing the local community: The social stability approach. In F. M. Cox, J. L. Erlich, J. Rothman, and J. E. Tropman,

eds., *Strategies of Community Organization*, pp. 269–80. Itasca, Ill.: Peacock.
Spiegel, John P. 1960. The resolution of role conflict within the family. In N. W. Bell and E. F. Vogel, eds., *A Modern Introduction to the Family*, pp. 361–81. Glencoe, Ill.: Free Press.
Spitz, H. and B. Sadock. 1973. Psychiatric training of graduate nursing students. *New York State Journal of Medicine*, June 1, pp. 1334–38.
Spivack, G., J. J. Platt, and M. B. Shure. 1976. *The Problem-Solving Approach to Adjustment*. San Francisco: Jossey-Bass.
Spivack, G. and M. B. Shure. 1974. *Social Adjustment of Young Children: A Cognitive Approach to Solving Real-Life Problems*. San Francisco: Jossey-Bass.
Staats, A. W. 1967. An outline of an integrated learning theory of attitude formation and function. In M. Fishbein, ed., *Readings in Attitude Theory and Measurements*, pp. 373–76. New York: Wiley.
Staub, Ervin. 1971. The use of role-playing and induction in children's learning of helping and sharing behavior. *Child Development* 42:805–15.
Staub, Ervin. 1974. Helping a distressed person: Social, personality, and stimulus determinants. In Leonard Berkowitz, ed., *Advances in Experimental Social Psychology* 7:294–341. New York: Academic Press.
Staub, Ervin and D. Kellett. 1972. Increasing pain tolerance by information about aversive stimuli. *Journal of Personality and Social Psychology* 21:198–208.
Stein, D. D., J. A. Hardyck, and M. B. Smith. 1965. Race and belief: An open and shut case. *Journal of Personality and Social Psychology* 1:281–89.
Stein, T. J. and E. D. Gambrill. 1977. Facilitating decision making in foster care: The Alameda project. *Social Service Review* 51:502–13.
Stein, T. J., E. D. Gambrill, and K. T. Wiltse. 1974. Foster care: The use of contracts. *Public Welfare* 32:20–25.
Steiner, Ivan. 1967. Interpersonal behavior as influenced by accuracy of social perception. In E. P. Hollander and R. G. Hunt, eds., *Current Perspectives in Social Psychology*, pp. 266–71. 2d ed. New York: Oxford University Press.
Stern, E. and S. Keller. 1953. Spontaneous group reference in France. *Public Opinion Quarterly* 17:208–17.
Stires, L. K. and E. E. Jones. 1969. Modesty versus self-enhancement as alternative forms of ingratiation. *Journal of Experimental Social Psychology* 5:172–88.
Stokes, T. F. and D. M. Baer. 1977. An implicit technology of generalization. *Journal of Applied Behavioral Analysis* 10:349–67.
Storms, M. D. 1973. Videotape and attribution process: Reversing actors' and observers' points of view. *Journal of Personality and Social Psychology* 27:165–75.
Storms, M. and R. E. Nisbett. 1970. Insomnia and the attribution process. *Journal of Personality and Social Psychology* 16:319–28.
Stotland, Ezra. 1969. Exploratory investigations of empathy. In Leonard Ber-

kowitz, ed., *Advances in Experimental Social Psychology*, 4:271–314. New York: Academic Press.
Stouffer, S. A., E. A. Suchmann, L. C. DeVinney, S. A. Star, and R. M. Williams. 1949. *The American Soldier*. Vol. 1. Princeton, N.J.: Princeton University Press.
Strean, Herbert S. 1967. Role theory, role models, and casework: Review of literature and practice applications. *Social Work* 12(2):77–87.
Strupp, H. H. 1973. *Psychotherapy: Clinical, Research, and Theoretical Issues*. New York: Jason Aronson.
Strupp, H. and A. Bloxom. 1975. Preparing lower class patients for group psychotherapy. *Journal of Consulting and Clinical Psychology* 41:373–84.
Stuart, R. B. 1972. The role of social work education in innovative human services. In F. W. Clark, D. R. Evans, and L. A. Hamerlynck, eds., *Implementing Behavioral Programs for Schools and Clinics*, pp. 3–39. Champaign, Ill.: Research Press.
Sue, S. 1977. Community mental health services to minority groups: Some optimism, some pessimism. *American Psychologist* 32:616–24.
Sue, S., H. L. McKinney, and D. V. Allen. 1976. Predictors of the duration of therapy for clients in the community mental health system. *Community Mental Health Journal* 12(4):365–75.
Suedfield, P., S. Bochner, and C. Matas. 1971. Petitioner's attire and petition signing by demonstrators: A field experiment. *Journal of Applied Social Psychology* 1:278–83.
Sugarman, Barry. 1968. Social norms in teenage boys' peer groups: A study of their implications for achievement and conduct in four London schools. *Human Relations* 21:41–57.
Sundel, M. and H. Lawrence. 1974. Behavioral group treatment with adults in a family service agency. In P. Glasser, R. Sarri, and R. Vinter, eds., *Individual Change through Small Groups*, pp. 325–47. New York: Free Press.
Sundel, M., N. Radin, and S. Churchill. 1974. Diagnosis in group work. In P. Glassner, R. Sarri, and R. Vinter, eds., *Individual Change through Small Groups*, pp. 105–25. New York: Free Press.
Sussman, M. B. 1974. The isolated nuclear family: Fact or fiction? In M. B. Sussman, ed., *Sourcebook in Marriage and the Family*, pp. 25–30. Boston: Houghton Mifflin.
Sykes, G. M. and D. Matza. 1957. Techniques of neutralization: A theory of delinquency. *American Sociological Review* 22:664–70.
Symonds, M. 1975. Victims of violence: Psychological effects and after-effects. *American Journal of Psychoanalysis* 35:19–26.
Szapocznik, J., M. A. Scopetta, and O. E. King. 1978. Theory and practice in matching treatment to the special characteristics and problems of Cuban immigrants. *Journal of Community Psychology* 6:112–22.
Tajfel, H. 1970. Experiments in intergroup discrimination. *Scientific American* 223:96–102.

Tannenbaum, A. S. and F. H. Allport. 1956. Personality structure and group structure: An interpretative study of the relationship through an event-structure hypothesis. *Journal of Abnormal and Social Psychology* 53:272–80.

Taylor, D., I. Altman, and R. Sorrentino. 1969. Interpersonal exchange as a function of rewards and costs and situational factors. *Journal of Experimental Social Psychology* 5:324–39.

Taylor, S. E. 1979. Hospital patient behavior: Reactance, helplessness, or control? *Journal of Social Issues* 35(1):156–84.

Tedeschi, J. T., T. V. Bonoma, and B. R. Schlenker. 1972. Influence, decision, and compliance. In J. T. Tedeschi, ed., *The Social Influence Processes*, pp. 346–418. Chicago: Aldine-Atherton.

Telling it like it is. 1979. *Innovations* 6:3–7.

Telly, C. S., W. L. French, and W. G. Scott. 1971. The relationship of inequity to turnover among hourly workers. *Administrative Science Quarterly* 16:164–72.

Terborg, J. R., C. Castore, and J. A. DeNinno. 1976. A longitudinal field investigation of the impact of group composition on group performance and cohesion. *Journal of Personality and Social Psychology* 34:782–90.

Tesser, A. 1978. Self-generated attitude change. In L. Berkowitz, ed., *Advances in Experimental Social Psychology* 11:290–338. New York: Academic Press.

Tessler, Richard C. 1975. Clients' reactions to initial interviews: Determinants of relationship-centered and problem-centered satisfaction. *Journal of Counseling Psychology* 22:187–91.

Tessler, R. C. and S. H. Schwartz. 1972. Help-seeking, self-esteem, and achievement motivation: An attributional analysis. *Journal of Personality and Social Psychology* 21:318–26.

Thibaut, J. W. and H. H. Kelley. 1959. *The Social Psychology of Groups*. New York: Wiley.

Thomas, E. J. 1967a. Problem of disability from the perspective of role theory. In E. J. Thomas, ed., *Behavioral Science for Social Workers*, pp. 59–77. New York: Free Press.

Thomas, E. J. 1967b. Themes in small group theory. In Edwin J. Thomas, ed., *Behavioral Science for Social Workers*, pp. 89–104. New York: Free Press.

Thomas, Edwin J. 1967c. Types of contributions behavioral science makes to social work. In E. J. Thomas, ed., *Behavioral Science for Social Workers*, pp. 3–13. New York: Free Press.

Thomas, E. J. 1977. Social casework and social group work: The behavioral modification approach. In *Encyclopedia of Social Work* 2:1309–21. New York: National Association of Social Workers.

Thomas, Edwin J. 1978a. Beyond knowledge utilization in generating human service technology. Paper presented at the National Conference on the Future of Social Work Research, San Antonio, Texas, October

Thomas, Edwin J. 1978b. Generating innovations in social work: The paradigm of developmental research. *Journal of Social Service Research* 2:95–117.

Thomas, Edwin J. 1978c. Mousetraps, developmental research, and social work education. *Social Service Review* 52:468–83.

Thomas, Edwin J., ed. 1967. *The Sociobehavioral Approach and Applications to Social Work*. New York: Council on Social Work Education.

Thomas, E. J. and B. J. Biddle. 1966. The nature and history of role theory. In B. J. Biddle and E. J. Thomas, eds., *Role Theory: Concepts and Research*, pp. 3–19. New York: Wiley.

Thomas, E. J. and R. D. Carter. 1971. Investigative modification with a multiproblem family. *Social Casework* 52:444–55.

Thomas, E. J. and C. F. Fink. 1963. Effects of group size. *Psychological Bulletin* 60:371–84.

Thornton, A. and D. Freedman. 1978. Changes in sex-role attitudes of women: 1962–1977, evidence from a 15 year panel study. Paper presented at the Conference on Changing Family, Changing Workplace. Ann Arbor, Michigan, November 6.

Timms, Noel. 1964. *Social Casework: Principles and Practice*. London: Routledge & Kegan Paul.

Titmuss, R. 1971. *The Gift Relationship: From Human Blood to Social Policy*. New York: Pantheon.

Toomey, M. 1972. Conflict theory approach to decision making applied to alcoholics. *Journal of Personality and Social Psychology* 24:199–206.

Toth, A. and S. Toth. 1980. Group work with widows. *Social Work* 25:63–65.

Trecker, Audrey R. 1954. *Committee Common Sense*. New York: Whiteside.

Trecker, Harleigh B. 1955. *Social Group Work: Principles and Practices*. New York: Association Press.

Triandis, H. C. 1959. Cognitive similarity and interpersonal communication in industry. *Journal of Applied Psycholgoy* 43:321–26.

Triandis, H. C. 1971. *Attitude and Attitude Change*. New York: Wiley.

Tropman, John, H. Johnson, and E. J. Tropman. 1979. *The Essentials of Committee Management*. Chicago: Nelson-Hall.

Tropp, E. 1977. Social group work: The developmental approach. In *Encyclopedia of Social Work* 2:1321–7. New York: National Association of Social Workers.

Truax, C. B. 1963. Effective ingredients in psychotherapy. *Journal of Counseling Psychology* 10:256–63.

Truax, C. B. and R. R. Carkhuff. 1967. *Toward Effective Counseling and Psychotherapy*. Chicago: Aldine.

Truax, C. B. and K. M. Mitchell. 1971. Research on certain therapist interpersonal skills in relation to process and outcome. In A. E. Bergin and S. L. Garfield, eds., *Handbook of Psychotherapy and Behavior Change*, pp. 299–344. New York: Wiley.

Tuckman, B. W. 1965. Developmental sequences in small groups. *Psychological Bulletin* 63:384–99.

Tuckman, B. W. 1967. Group composition and group performance of struc-

tured and unstructured tasks. *Journal of Experimental Social Psychology* 3:25–40.
Tuckman, B. W. and M. A. C. Jensen. 1977. Stages of small-group development revisited. *Group and Organizational Studies* 2:419–27.
Turner, R. H. 1962. Role taking: Process versus conformity. In Arnold M. Rose, ed., *Human Behavior and Social Process*, pp. 20–40. Boston: Houghton Mifflin.
Turner, Victor W. 1969. *The Ritual Process: Structure and Anti-structure*. Ithaca, N.Y.: Cornell University Press.
Ullman, L. P. 1968. Making use of modeling in the therapeutic interview. In D. R. Rich and C. M. Franks, eds., *Advances in Behavior Therapy*, pp. 175–82. New York: Academic Press.
Uranowitz, S. 1975. Helping and self-attribution: A field experiment. *Journal of Personality and Social Psycholgoy* 31:852–54.
Varela, J. A. 1978. Attitude change. In H. L. Pick, H. W. Leibowitz, J. E. Singer, A. Steinschneider, and H. W. Stevenson, eds., *Psychology: From Research to Practice*, pp. 121–44. New York: Plenum Press.
Verba, S. 1961. *Small Groups and Political Behavior*. Princeton, N.J.: Princeton University Press.
Vernon, G. 1970. *Sociology of Death*. New York: Ronald Press.
Veroff, J. 1969. Social comparison and the development of achievement motivation. In Charles P. Smith, ed., *Achievement-Related Motives in Children*. pp. 46–101. New York: Russell Sage. 1969.
Veroff, J., and S. Feld. 1970. *Marriage and Work in America*. New York: Van Nostrand Reinhold.
Veroff, J. and H. Melnick. 1977. Personal, situational, and interpersonal attributions of causes of critical life problems. Paper presented at the meeting of the American Psychological Association, San Francisco, August.
Vinokur, A. and E. Burnstein. 1974. The effects of partially shared persuasive arguments on group induced shifts: A group problem-solving approach. *Journal of Personality and Social Psychology* 29:305–15.
Vinokur, A. and E. Burnstein. 1978. Novel argumentation and attitude change: The case of polarization following discussion. *European Journal of Social Psychology* 8:335–48.
Vinter, R. D. 1959. Group work: Perspectives and prospects. In *Social Work with Groups*, pp. 128–48. New York: National Association of Social Workers.
Vinter, Robert. 1960. Small group theory and research: Implications for group work practice theory and research. In Leonard Kogan, ed., *Social Science Theory and Social Work Research*, pp. 123–34. New York: National Association of Social Workers.
Vinter, R. D. 1965. Social group work. In Harry L. Lurie, ed., *Encyclopedia of Social Work*, pp. 715–24. New York: National Association of Social Workers.
Vinter, R. D. 1974. The essential components of social group work practice.

In Paul Glasser, R. Sarri, and R. Vinter, eds., *Individual Change Through Small Groups*, pp. 9–33. New York: Free Press.
Vorrath, H. H. and L. K. Brendtro. 1974. *Positive Peer Culture*. Chicago: Aldine.
Wagner, C. and L. Wheeler. 1969. Model, need, and cost effects in helping behavior. *Journal of Personality and Social Psychology* 12:111–16.
Waite, R. 1968. The Negro patient and clinical theory. *Journal of Consulting and Clinical Psychology* 32:427–33.
Walker, K. 1970. Time used by husbands in household work. *Family Economics Review* June pp. 8–11.
Wallach, M. A., N. Kogan, and D. J. Bem. 1962. Group influence on individual risk taking. *Journal of Abnormal and Social Psychology* 65:75–86.
Walsh, Edward J. 1975. *Dirty Work, Race, and Self-Esteem*. Ann Arbor, Michigan: Institute of Labor and Industrial Relations.
Walster, E., E. Aronson, and D. Abraham. 1966. On increasing the persuasiveness of a low prestige communicator. *Journal of Experimental Psychology* 2:325–42.
Walster, E., E. Berscheid, and G. W. Walster. 1976. New directions in equity research. In L. Berkowitz, ed., *Advances in Experimental Social Psychology* 9:1–42. New York: Academic Press.
Walster, E., G. W. Walster, and J. Traupmann. 1978. Equity and premarital sex. *Journal of Personality and Social Psychology* 36:82–92.
Warren, D. I. 1970. Status inconsistency theory and flying saucer sightings. *Science* 170:599–603.
Warren, D. I. and P. C. Easto. 1972. White stratification theory and black reality: A neglected problem of American sociology. Paper presented at the annual meeting of the American Sociological Association, New Orleans, August.
Warren, R. L. 1979. Application of social science knowledge to community organization. In F. M. Cox, J. L. Erlich, J. Rothman, and J. Tropman, eds., *Strategies of Community Organization*. pp. 85–94. 3d ed. Itasca, Ill.: Peacock.
Watson, D. 1971. Reinforcement theory of personality and social system: Dominance and position in a group power structure. *Journal of Personality and Social Psychology* 20:180–85.
Watson, D. M. and T. D. Graves. 1966. Quantitative research in proxemic behavior. *American Anthropologist* 68:971–85.
Watson, G. and D. Johnson. 1972. *Social Psychology: Issues and Insights*. New York: Lippincott.
Wax, R. and R. K. Thomas. 1971. *American Indians and White People*. Toppenish, Wash.: Center for the Study of Migrant Education. Reprint No. 42, Indian Education.
Waxler, N. E. and E. G. Mishler. 1970. Experimental studies of families. In L. Berkowitz, ed., *Advances in Experimental Social Psychology* 5:249–303. New York: Academic Press.

Wayne, J. and N. Avery. 1979. Activities for group termination. *Social Work* 44:58–62.
Wegner, D. M. and K. Finstuen. 1977. Observers' focus of attention in the simulation of self-perception. *Journal of Personality and Social Psychology* 35:56–62.
Wegner, D. M. and D. Schaefer. 1978. The concentration of responsibility: An objective self-awareness analysis of group size effects in helping situations. *Journal of Personality and Social Psychology* 36:147–55.
Weigel, R. H. and L. S. Newman. 1976. Increasing attitude-behavior correspondence by broadening the scope of the behavioral measure. *Journal of Personality and Social Psychology* 33:793–802.
Weigel, R. H., P. L. Wiser, and S. W. Cook. 1975. The impact of cooperative learning experiences on cross-ethnic relations and attitudes. *Journal of Social Issues* 31(1):219–44.
Weiner, Bernard, ed. 1974. *Achievement Motivation and Attribution Theory*. Morristown, N.J.: General Learning Press.
Weiner, B., I. Frieze, A. Kukla, L. Reed, S. Rest, and R. M. Rosenbaum. 1971. *Perceiving the Causes of Success and Failure*. Morristown, N.J.: General Learning Press.
Weiner, B. and A. Kukla. 1970. An attributional analysis of achievement motivation. *Journal of Personality and Social Psychology* 15:1–20.
Weiner, B. and A. Kun. 1976. The development of causal attributions and the growth of achievement and social motivation. In S. Feldman and D. Bush, eds., *Cognitive Development and Social Development*. Hillsdale, N.J.: Erlbaum.
Weiner, H. 1965. Real and imagined cost effects on human fixed-internal responding. *Psychological Reports* 17:659–62.
Weiss, R. S. 1975. *Marital Separation: Coping with the End of a Marriage and the Transition To Being Single Again*. New York: Basic Books.
Weldon, D., D. C. Carlston, A. K. Rissman, L. Slobodin, and H. C. Triandis. 1975. A laboratory test of effects of culture assimilator training. *Journal of Personality and Social Psychology* 32:300–10.
Werner, P. D., S. E. Middlestadt-Carter, and T. J. Crawford. 1975. Having a third child: Predicting behavioral intentions. *Journal of Marriage and the Family* 37:348–58.
West, Stephen G., Clayde Whitney, and Robert Schnedler. 1975. Helping a motorist in distress: The effects of sex, race, and neighborhood. *Journal of Personality and Social Psychology* 31:691–98.
Wheeler, Stanton. 1966. The structure of formally organized socialization settings. In O. G. Brim and S. Wheeler, eds., *Socialization after Childhood: Two Essays*, pp. 53–116. New York: Wiley.
Whitaker, D. and M. Lieberman. 1964. *Psychotherapy through the Group Process*. New York: Atherton.
White, R. K. and R. Lippitt. 1960. *Autocracy and Democracy*. New York: Harper.

White, R. and R. Lippitt. 1968. Leader behavior and member reaction in three "social climates." In D. Cartwright and A. Zander, eds., *Group Dynamics*, pp. 318–35. 3d ed. New York: Harper & Row.
White, R. W. 1959. Motivation reconsidered: The concept of competence. *Psychological Review* 66:297–333.
Whittaker, J. K. 1970. Models of group development: Implications for social group work practice. *Social Service Review* 44:308–20.
Whittaker, J. K. 1974. Program activities: Their selection and use in a therapeutic milieu. In P. Glasser, R. Sarri, and R. Vinter, eds., *Individual Change Through Small Groups*, pp. 244–57. New York: Free Press.
Whittaker, J. K. 1975. *Social Treatment*. Chicago: Aldine.
Whyte, Martin K. 1974. *Small Groups and Political Rituals in China*. Berkeley, Calif.: University of California Press.
Whyte, William F. 1948. *Human Relations in the Restaurant Industry*. New York: McGraw-Hill.
Wicklund, R. A. and J. W. Brehm. 1976. *Perspectives on Cognitive Dissonance*. Hillsdale, N.J.: Erlbaum.
Wicklund, R. A., V. Slattum, and E. Solomon. 1970. Effects of implied pressure toward commitment on ratings of choice alternatives. *Journal of Experimental Social Psychology* 6:449–57.
Wiggins, J. A., F. Dill, and R. D. Schwartz. 1968. On "status-liability." In D. Cartwright and A. Zander, eds., *Group Dynamics*, pp. 538–46. 3d ed. New York: Harper & Row.
Wilke, J. and J. T. Lanzetta. 1970. The obligation to help: The effects of prior help on subsequent helping behaviors. *Journal of Experimental Social Psychology* 6:488–93.
William, C. Hay and Charles H. Mindel. 1973. Extended kinship relations in black and white families. *Journal of Marriage and the Family* 35:51–57.
Willis, F. 1966. Initial speaking distance as a function of the speaker's relationship. *Psychonomic Science* 5:221–22.
Willmott, Peter. 1971. Family, work and leisure conflicts among male employees. *Human Relations* 24:575–84.
Wilson, G. 1959. The social worker's role in group situations. In Marjorie Murphy, ed., *The Social Group Work Method in Social Work Education*, pp. 129–68. New York: Council on Social Work Education.
Wilson, Gertrude and Gladys Ryland. 1949. *Social Group Work Practice*. Boston: Houghton Mifflin.
Wilson, J. P., J. Aronoff, and L. A. Messe. 1975. Social structure, member motivation, and group productivity. *Journal of Personality and Social Psychology* 32:1094–98.
Wispé, L. G. and H. B. Freshley. 1971. Race, sex, and sympathetic helping behavior: The broken bag caper. *Journal of Personality and Social Psychology* 17:59–64.
Wittes, G., and N. Radin. 1969. *Helping Your Child To Learn: The Nurturance Approach*. San Rafael, Calif.: Dimensions Publishing.

Wittes, G. and N. Radin. 1971. Two approaches to group work with parents in a compensatory preschool program. *Social Work* 6(1):42–50.
Wodarski, J. S., R. A. Feldman, and N. Flax. 1973. Social learning theory and group work practice with anti-social children. *Clinical Social Work Journal* 1:78–94.
Wolman, B. B. 1960. Impact of failure on group cohesiveness. *Journal of Social Psychology* 51:404–18.
Wolpe, J. 1969. *The Practice of Behavior Therapy*. New York: Pergamon.
Worchel, S. 1974. The effect of three types of arbitrary thwarting on the instigation to aggression. *Journal of Personality* 42:300–18.
Worchel, S., V. A. Andreoli, and R. Folger. 1977. Intergroup cooperation and intergroup attraction: The effect of previous interaction and outcome of combined effort. *Journal of Experimental Social Psychology* 13:131–40.
Working definition of social work practice. 1958. *Social Work* 3(2):5–9.
Wrightsman, L. S. and L. C. Brigham. 1973. *Contemporary Issues in Social Psychology*. 2d ed. Monterey, Calif.: Brooks-Cole.
Yalom, I. D. 1970. *The Theory and Practice of Group Psychotherapy*. New York: Basic Books.
Yalom, I. D., P. Houts, G. Newell, and K. Rand. 1967. Preparation of patients for group therapy: A controlled study. *Archives of General Psychiatry* 17:416–27.
Yarrow, M. R., P. M. Scott, and C. Z. Waxler. 1973. Learning concern for others. *Developmental Psychology* 8:240–60.
Yinger, M. 1965. *Toward a Field Theory of Behavior*. New York: McGraw-Hill.
Zajonc, R. B. 1968. Social facilitation. In D. Cartwright and A. Zander, eds., *Group Dynamics*, pp. 63–73. 3d ed. New York: Harper & Row.
Zajonc, R. B. and J. C. Marin. 1967. Cooperation, competition and interpersonal attitudes in small groups. *Psychonomic Science* 7:271–72.
Zander, Alvin. 1971. *Motives and Goals in Groups*. New York: Academic Press.
Zander, A. F. Team spirit vs. the individual achiever. *Psychology Today* 8:67–68.
Zander, A. 1979. The psychology of group processes. *Annual Review of Psychology*, 30:417–451.
Zanna, M. P., G. R. Goethals, and I. Hill. 1975. Evaluating a sex-related ability: Social comparison with similar others and standard setting. *Journal of Experimental Social Psychology* 11:86–93.
Zanna, M. P. and S. J. Pack. 1975. On the self-fulfilling nature of apparent sex differences in behavior. *Journal of Experimental Social Psychology* 11:583–91.
Zarchan, D. 1977. Effects of social class and role-induction on dropout, expectations, and attraction in outpatient psychotherapy. Ph.D. dissertation, Boston University Graduate School. *Dissertation Abstracts International*, 1977, 38(4-B), 1914 (University Microfilms no. 77-21626).
Zimbardo, P. G. 1965. The effect of effort and improvisation in self-persuasion

produced by role playing. *Journal of Experimental and Social Psychology* 1:103–20.

Zimbardo, Philip G. 1975. Transforming experimental research into advocacy for social change. In M. A. Deutsch and H. A. Hornstein, eds., *Applying Social Psychology: Implications for Research, Practice, and Training*, pp. 33–66. Hillsdale, N.J.: Erlbaum.

Zimbardo, P. 1977. *Shyness: What It Is, What To Do About It*. New York: Addison-Wesley.

Zimbardo, P. G., and E. B. Ebbesen. 1970. Experimental modification of the relationship between effort, attitude, and behavior. *Journal of Personality and Social Psychology* 16:207–13.

Zimbardo, P. G., C. Haney, W. C. Banks, and D. Jaffe. 1973. The psychology of imprisonment: Privation, power, and pathology—script for a film strip. Unpublished, Stanford University.

Zuckerman, M. 1975. Belief in a just world and altruistic behavior. *Journal of Personality and Social Psychology* 31:972–76.

AUTHOR INDEX

SUBJECT INDEX

Bei Fragen zur Produktsicherheit wenden Sie sich bitte an:
If you have any questions regarding product safety,
please contact:

Walter de Gruyter GmbH
Genthiner Straße 13
10785 Berlin
productsafety@degruyterbrill.com